THE CORRESPONDENCE OF HENRY CROMWELL 1655–1659

THE CORRESPONDENCE OF HENRY CROMWELL 1655–1659

FROM THE BRITISH LIBRARY LANSDOWNE MANUSCRIPTS

edited by
PETER GAUNT

CAMDEN FIFTH SERIES
Volume 31

CAMBRIDGE
UNIVERSITY PRESS

FOR THE ROYAL HISTORICAL SOCIETY
University College London, Gower Street, London WC1 6BT
2007

Published by the Press Syndicate of the University of Cambridge
The Edinburgh Building, Cambridge CB2 8RU, United Kingdom
32 Avenue of the Americas, New York, NY 10013-2473, USA
477 Williamstown Road, Port Melbourne, VIC 3207, Australia
Ruiz de Alarcón 13, 28014 Madrid, Spain
Dock House, The Waterfront, Cape Town 8001, South Africa

First published 2007

A catalogue record for this book is available from the British Library

ISBN 9780 521 896047 hardback

SUBSCRIPTIONS. The serial publications of the Royal Historical Society, *Royal Historical Society Transactions* (ISSN 0080–4401) and Camden Fifth Series (ISSN 0960–1163) volumes, may be purchased together on annual subscription. The 2007 subscription price, which includes print and electronic access (but not VAT), is £91 (US $147 in the USA, Canada, and Mexico) and includes Camden Fifth Series, volumes 30 and 31 (published in July and December) and Transactions Sixth Series, volume 17 (published in December). Japanese prices are available from Kinokuniya Company Ltd, P.O. Box 55, Chitose, Tokyo 156, Japan. EU subscribers (outside the UK) who are not registered for VAT should add VAT at their country's rate. VAT registered subscribers should provide their VAT registration number. Prices include delivery by air.

Subscription orders, which must be accompanied by payment, may be sent to a bookseller, subscription agent or direct to the publisher: Cambridge University Press, The Edinburgh Building, Shaftesbury Road, Cambridge CB2 8RU, UK; or in the USA, Canada, and Mexico: Cambridge University Press, Journals Fulfillment Department, 100 Brook Hill Drive, West Nyack, New York, 10994–2133, USA.

SINGLE VOLUMES AND BACK VOLUMES. A list of Royal Historical Society volumes available from Cambridge University Press may be obtained from the Humanities Marketing Department at the address above.

Printed and bound in the United Kingdom at the University Press, Cambridge

CONTENTS

ACKNOWLEDGEMENTS

This volume has been many years in preparation and accordingly numerous debts of gratitude have been incurred along the way. Three such debts should be warmly and gratefully acknowledged at the outset, for without them this project could not have proceeded. Firstly, the Henry Cromwell correspondence transcribed and annotated here is contained in three volumes of the Lansdowne Collection held by the Department of Manuscripts of the British Library and I am most grateful to the British Library in general, and to the Head of Administration of Western Manuscripts in particular, for granting permission for this material to be published. The correspondence formed the basis of a Master of Letters thesis by Clyve Jones, awarded by the University of Lancaster in 1969 and comprising in large part an annotated transcript of the majority of the letters. Having decided not to prepare a scholarly edition for publication himself, Dr Jones strongly supported my own proposal to work on the material afresh and to prepare an edition for publication. Thus, secondly, I am enormously grateful to Dr Jones not only for his approval and endorsement of my taking on this project – without it, I could not and would not have taken the idea any further, as he had undertaken detailed work on the manuscript well ahead of me – but also for his unfailing help and encouragement throughout its lengthy gestation. Thirdly, I am enormously grateful to a trio of senior academics for the encouragement, help, and support that they offered at the outset, as I framed a formal publication proposal and embarked upon the work: to the late Professor Austin Woolrych, who had himself worked on the correspondence and had supervised Dr Jones's Masters thesis; to Professor Ivan Roots, who supervised my own doctoral thesis on Protectoral central government and who has remained a valued friend and mentor ever since; and to Professor Blair Worden, who was the pre-1700 literary director for the Royal Historical Society at the time that my proposal was submitted and accepted and as serious work began.

In the years since, a large number of institutions and individuals have offered further invaluable help and assistance, including the staffs of the British Library, the Institute of Historical Research, the Public Record Office/the National Archives, the National Library of Wales, the John Rylands Library, Manchester Central Library, the libraries of the universities of Swansea, Chester, Liverpool, and Manchester, the Cromwell Museum, and Huntingdon Record Office. I am most grateful to the University of Chester for granting me two periods of research leave in recent years, which have been devoted, in part, to furthering this project, and to all my colleagues in the Department of History and Archaeology at Chester for their support and encouragement, especially Professor Graeme White and John Doran, who assisted in the translation of the Latin phrases that pepper the correspondence, and Dr Keith McLay, who is also currently working on the transcription and annotation of an early modern source and with whom I have exchanged ideas on the minutiae of the process. As well as the periods of institutional research leave, in 2003–2004 I was awarded a further four months' leave to complete the principal research and writing, provided and funded by the Arts and Humanities Research Council (AHRC) under the AHRC Research Leave Scheme. I am most grateful to the AHRC for supporting the project in this way and warmly acknowledge the role of the AHRC in facilitating its progress and completion. I am most grateful to the History of Parliament Trust, and particularly to Dr Stephen Roberts, section editor for 1640–1660, for letting me see a small number of MPs' biographies ahead of publication; wherever I have drawn upon that, as yet unpublished, material, a footnote records, acknowledges, and gives full reference to it. I am indebted, too, to Dr Patrick Little, who has in recent years also been working on this collection from both an Irish and an English perspective and who has very kindly shared his thoughts on points of detail and of dating of several letters, and to Dr Ian Archer, currently the pre-1700 literary director for the Royal Historical Society, who has helped enormously in the final stages of this large, lengthy, and complex project.

ABBREVIATIONS

Abbott	W.C. Abbott (ed.), *The Writings and Speeches of Oliver Cromwell*, 4 vols (Cambridge, MA, 1937–1947)
Burton	J.T. Rutt (ed.), *The Diary of Thomas Burton, Esquire*, 4 vols (London, 1828)
Clarke Papers	C.H. Firth (ed.), *The Clarke Papers*, 4 vols (London, 1891–1901)
CSPI	R.P. Mahaffy (ed.), *Calendar of the State Papers Relating to Ireland: of the reign of Charles I, 3, 1647–60 and addenda 1625–60* (London, 1903)
Dunlop	R. Dunlop (ed.), *Ireland under the Commonwealth*, 2 vols but with continuous pagination (Manchester, 1913)
ODNB	H.C.G. Matthew and B. Harrison (eds), *Oxford Dictionary of National Biography*, 60 vols (Oxford, 2004)
TSP	T. Birch (ed.), *A Collection of the State Papers of John Thurloe, Esquire*, 7 vols (London, 1742)

The fate of books is like that of many trees, to bring forth nothing but leaves, being not read by many and veiwed by few

John and Elizabeth Gauden to Henry Cromwell, 24 May 1658

INTRODUCTION

The Henry Cromwell correspondence

This edition of the Henry Cromwell correspondence is drawn from the collection of letters and a small number of associated papers now found in the British Library Lansdowne Manuscripts, volumes 821–823. With the exception of a stray letter of the mid-eighteenth century – which has no connection with Henry Cromwell or, indeed, with the rest of this collection, but which is now bound at the end of the third volume – the collection comprises 536 items dated or datable to the mid- and later 1650s, and linked to Henry Cromwell, younger son of Lord Protector Oliver Cromwell, and to his government of Ireland. The overwhelming majority of these items are original in-letters, sent to Henry Cromwell during his period as chief administrator of Ireland, between summer 1655 and spring 1659, and addressed to him in Dublin or elsewhere in Ireland. The collection also contains a clutch of draft out-letters, mostly by Henry Cromwell and intended for Lord Broghill, together with a small number of letters addressed to other recipients in Ireland and a handful of miscellaneous items (including a trio of army addresses and the key to a code) that found their way into the hands of Henry Cromwell (or his secretary).

As it stands, the material in these three volumes clearly does not represent all the correspondence and other semi-official or non-official letters and papers sent to or received and retained by Henry Cromwell during his period in Ireland. Many letters in this collection criticize the shortcomings of the postal service between London and Dublin and refer to other letters sent to or from Henry Cromwell that had gone astray, that had failed to reach their intended recipients, and that are not found here.[1] Similarly, many letters in this collection make reference to other letters and papers originally enclosed and sent with them, but which are not found within the collection and are apparently no longer extant.[2] In a handful of cases, the writer requested Henry Cromwell to destroy the letter after reading it – 'I pray you burne it',

[1] See, for example, nos 8, 12, 53, 71, 125, and 270.

[2] See nos 9, 19, 26, 28, 39, 41, 96, 151, 174, 176, 187, 213, 214, 269, 282, 304, 309, 313, 329, 367, 377, 396, 404, 423, 432, 443, 465, 480, 486, 493, and 506.

wrote one[3] – and, although in these cases the injunction was clearly ignored and the letters have survived, it is possible that other, more sensitive material was withheld and destroyed.

The uneven chronological coverage found in these volumes also suggests that the collection is incomplete. For example, the collection contains just fifteen items spanning the months September 1656 to January 1657 inclusive and, apart from a single letter and enclosure of 25 November, there is nothing extant from 28 October 1656 to 3 January 1657, a gap of nearly ten weeks. Again, the collection contains no letters between 8 January and 22 February 1658, a gap of over six weeks. Accordingly, and in stark contrast to the generally very full and informative coverage of parliamentary developments during the spring and summer of 1657 and during Richard Cromwell's parliament of 1659, we have disappointingly little here about the opening months of the first session of the second Protectorate parliament or about its brief and divisive second session. It is most unlikely that Henry Cromwell did not, in fact, receive letters recounting parliamentary and other developments over these periods; instead, these ominous gaps again suggest that the surviving collection is incomplete.

Furthermore, a batch of broadly similar papers, comprising over forty original in-letters addressed to Henry Cromwell in Ireland, seems to have become detached from the main collection quite early in its subsequent history and, although these letters do survive, they are now held separately by the British Library, at Additional Manuscripts 43724. This detached batch of letters was known to and used by Thomas Birch when he compiled his *A Collection of the State Papers of John Thurloe, Esquire*, published in 1742, and was noted by Birch as being at that time in the possession of the first Earl of Shelburne. They then passed from Shelburne to his descendants, the Marquesses of Lansdowne, and the majority of these letters were presented to the British Museum by the 6th Marquess in the mid-1930s. A note relaying the descent of these papers, now included both in Additional Manuscripts 43724 and in the main catalogue of the collection, throws light on the likely descent of the bulk of the Henry Cromwell papers now found in the Lansdowne Collection.

The early history of the documents now at Lansdowne Manuscripts volumes 821–823 was probably identical to that of the letters now at Additional Manuscripts 43724, not least shown by the fact that many letters in both collections carry contemporary endorsements in a single hand and a consistent style. All these papers were almost certainly originally collected, held, and retained by the philosopher, physician,

[3] No. 15.

and administrator Sir William Petty. In September 1652, Petty was appointed physician to the English army in Ireland and he quickly enhanced his position and expanded his role there: in December 1654 he obtained a commission from the English parliament to undertake a major resurvey of confiscated land in Ireland. He gained further favour, high office, and extensive Irish land under Henry Cromwell's administration from the autumn of 1655 onwards, becoming not only a clerk to the Irish council but also a friend and confidant of Henry Cromwell and, it appears, his personal secretary.[4] In mid-June 1659, with the Protectorate collapsing and his own time in, and government of, Ireland about to come to an end, Henry Cromwell sent Petty 'as one whom I can best trust' on a highly sensitive mission to England to consult with his 'Dear Brother' – his brother-in-law Charles Fleetwood, who had been instrumental in ending the effective government of Richard Cromwell and, with it, the whole Protectorate – then describing Petty as 'one, that hath been faithfull and affectionate unto me, and, I may say, unto yourselfe also'.[5] Petty's close links to Henry Cromwell continued well after the Restoration: in 1663, Henry granted him a power of attorney[6] and after Henry's death Petty wrote to his widow to praise 'His dear friend who is now with God'.[7]

Thus it is all but certain that both this collection and the related papers now at Additional Manuscripts 43724 were held by Sir William Petty as Henry Cromwell's secretary, were retained by him both after the fall of the Protectoral regime in Ireland and after Henry Cromwell's death, and were then passed down through the Petty family for several generations. After Sir William Petty's death in December 1687, and in consideration of his services to the state, in December 1688 his widow, Elizabeth, was given a barony for life as Baroness Shelburne, while his eldest surviving son and heir, Charles, was created Baron Shelburne of County Wexford in the Irish peerage. Charles died childless in April 1696 but three years later his younger brother – that is, Sir William Petty's youngest son, Henry – was himself created Baron Shelburne, and in 1719 his title was raised to that of Earl of Shelburne. In preparing his 1742 edition of Thurloe's state papers, Thomas Birch consulted and used the batch of forty or so letters to Henry Cromwell that were then in the possession of Henry, first Earl of Shelburne, though Birch was either unaware of, or decided not to draw upon, the much bigger collection of Henry Cromwell correspondence that was presumably also then in the Earl's hands.

4 T. Barnard, 'Petty, Sir William', in *ODNB*.
5 *TSP*, VII, pp. 684–685.
6 British Library, Additional Manuscript 72850, fo. 116.
7 Quoted by R.W. Ramsey in *Henry Cromwell* (London, 1933), p. 372.

Henry, first Earl of Shelburne died without a surviving son in 1751, whereupon his estates and considerable fortune – and presumably also the Henry Cromwell material – passed to a son of his sister, Anne, and her husband Thomas Fitz-Maurice, first Earl of Kerry. This son, John Fitz-Maurice, immediately adopted the surname Petty and was raised to the Irish peerage; he was created Earl of Shelburne in 1753 and was raised to the British peerage as Lord Wycombe in 1760. Upon his death in the following year, his eldest son, William, succeeded to his Irish and British titles and in 1784, a year after resigning as Prime Minister, William was created first Marquess of Lansdowne, in Somerset. It was to his son and heir, John Henry, second Marquess of Lansdowne, that many of Sir William Petty's papers descended, and it was from him in 1807 that the British Museum obtained the Henry Cromwell material now held by the British Library and arranged at Lansdowne Manuscripts 821–823.[8]

The contents of this collection have been organized in several different ways over the years, including at one stage alphabetically by the surname of the writer. Thus the letters now bear a variety of folio numbers entered in ink as well as pencil, and a few of the letters (those which came first under each letter of the alphabet when arranged thus) also carry that letter of the alphabet at the top. The current arrangement within three bound volumes dates from the most recent full reorganization of the collection, undertaken early in the twentieth century, when an attempt was made to put the letters in a strict chronological order, with undated letters placed towards the end of the third volume. Since then, however, errors have become apparent, either because dates were misread or because the original or endorsed dates have been shown to be wrong, and the volumes now contain occasional modern paper slips noting where some of these letters have been misplaced. Moreover, some of the undated letters placed at the end of the collection can, in fact, be accurately and reliably dated through their contents. For this new edition, the correspondence has been placed in chronological order, including those letters which, though undated, can reliably be assigned by their contents to a particular month; a dozen letters that cannot reliably be given a fairly narrow date range have been arranged by alphabetical order of the writer's surname towards the end of this edition.[9]

The collection is generally in a good and clean condition, with evidence of modern conservation to some letters. Occasionally, the paper has been damaged, with some loss of text – sheets have become

[8] G.E. Cokayne (ed.), *The Complete Peerage of England, Scotland and Ireland*, 8 vols (London, 1887–1898), 'Lansdowne', 'Shelburne', and 'Wycombe'.

[9] Nos 521–532.

worn or torn and paper has been lost around the edges, and a few letters contain small holes, often where the wax used to seal the letter had seeped through and the main page was damaged with a small area of paper carrying text being torn away on opening. Some letters retain their original wax seal, though in many cases this is now absent. All the letters were written in English, with a peppering of Latin phrases, but around twenty letters were in part entered in code or cipher. In some cases, this code has been partly or wholly deciphered in a contemporary hand, apparently by the recipient, on the original letter, though in many cases the letters carry no signs of decoding. As no keys to any of the codes employed in this collection appear to survive – the draft code contained in the collection and noted as the final item in this edition is not the key to any of the codes actually used here – modern historians are reduced to making educated guesses in attempting to decipher these sections of the letters.

For the most part, the texts of the letters are clear and legible and, with the exception of the draft letters (principally those from Henry Cromwell to Lord Broghill), they contain remarkably few amendments and alterations. A small number of letters do create some problems of legibility and interpretation, either because they appear to have been written very quickly and carelessly, with characters and words poorly formed, because they were quite heavily amended, or because over the centuries they have become foxed: indeed, one letter is now so badly foxed that its legibility is seriously compromised.[10] Some letters comprise either a single folio or several folios, but the majority are made up of two folios, with the main text of the letter on the recto of the first folio, sometimes carried over onto the verso of that folio, while the verso of the second folio carries the address and any endorsements, frequently including a record of the writer's name and the letter's date, together in some cases with a short note of the main business of the letter. These endorsements appear to be contemporary but they rarely add anything to the information carried in the letters themselves; accordingly, in this edition the information in the endorsement is noted (generally in a footnote) only where it corrects or amplifies the text of the letter.

A collection of correspondence compiled over almost four years inevitably contains a wide variety of material, covers a range of topics, and is of variable quality and importance, with some quite minor items, such as the letters of recommendation that were frequently addressed to Henry Cromwell in Ireland. However, the bulk of this collection is important and valuable, and the information it reveals can be grouped under two principal but overlapping headings: Irish and

[10] No. 456.

English. Letters relating to Irish topics, whether written from Ireland itself or from England, deal with the government and administration of the province; finance; military and security matters; the problems of the English army stationed there; the attempts to find suitable people to fill secular and religious offices in Ireland; the claims, counter-claims, and disputes arising from the Irish land settlement; and a range of more personal issues. The much more extensive, and in some ways more important, English correspondence is dominated by the accounts of Henry Cromwell's friends, agents, and semi-professional reporters relating, interpreting, and analysing political and, to a lesser extent, military developments in London, again supplemented by rather more personal and private letters, illuminating the thoughts and actions of individual politicians and revealing something of the inner workings of central government. There are, in addition, some letters concerned primarily with the personal affairs of the Cromwell family, of Henry Cromwell himself, and of his in-laws, the Russell family. Overall, the collection throws new light both on the difficulties of running Ireland during the Protectorate and on the sometimes fraught relationship between the central government in London and the provincial or devolved government in Dublin, while the letters dominated by English news provide a view of the Protectoral regime over the period 1655–1659 that can be matched by few other single collections, published or unpublished. They give a clear and quite detailed picture of the governments of Oliver and Richard Cromwell as Protectors and shed new light on particular issues, including parliamentary business and management, the kingship controversy of 1657, and the collapse of the Protectorate in the spring of 1659, as well as on the wider questions of the power of, and relationship between, the Protector, his Protectoral Council, and the parliaments of the period, especially the first session of the second Protectorate parliament of 1656–1658 and Richard Cromwell's parliament of the opening months of 1659.

This collection of the Henry Cromwell correspondence has been well known for many years and has been drawn upon by a range of historians. For example, it was used in the early and mid-twentieth century by C.H. Firth and G. Davies in their narratives of the years 1656–1660;[11] by Firth, Davies, and others in more detailed articles on specific issues, such as the kingship controversy, the fall of Richard Cromwell, and the role of the army;[12] and by R.W. Ramsey during

[11] C.H. Firth, *The Last Years of the Protectorate, 1656–58*, 2 vols (London, 1909); G. Davies, *The Restoration of Charles II, 1658–60* (San Marino, CA, 1955).

[12] C.H. Firth, 'Cromwell and the crown', *English Historical Review*, 17 (1901), pp. 429–442 and 18 (1902), pp. 52–80; G. Davies, 'The army and the downfall of Richard Cromwell',

the 1930s in his rather simplistic biographical studies of both Henry and Richard Cromwell.[13] In the process, some of the letters in the collection were transcribed and reproduced in whole or in part, especially by Firth in the second part of his two-part article on 'Cromwell and the crown', by Ramsey in his biographies of Henry and Richard Cromwell, and by R.C.H. Catterall in his study of Richard Cromwell's fall. More recently, Clyve Jones has reprinted the two letters by Oliver Cromwell found within the collection[14] and Toby Barnard has published the majority of the badly foxed letter giving a detailed account of the 1659 election in Cork and Youghal.[15] Both Barnard and Patrick Little have made extensive use of the collection in their work on Ireland in the 1650s, especially Barnard in his monograph on Cromwellian Ireland and Little in his biographical study of Lord Broghill, both of which contain many short quotations from letters within this collection.[16] Most of the letters, however, have never appeared in print, and Firth's strong recommendation in the preface to his first volume of *The Last Years of the Protectorate* – that the Henry Cromwell correspondence, 'primarily valuable for the history of Irish administration, but [. . .with] much information of importance about political events in England', 'should be printed by one of the societies for publishing historical documents'[17] – has hitherto remained unfulfilled.

In bringing to fruition Firth's recommendation, this new edition has drawn and built upon the pioneering work of Clyve Jones, who during the 1960s undertook extensive research on the collection and who in 1969 was awarded a Master of Letters degree by the University of Lancaster for his thesis, 'The correspondence of Henry Cromwell, 1655–1659, and other papers, from the British Museum Lansdowne Mss. 821–823'. This thesis, which comprised an annotated edition of the correspondence and included full transcripts of the great majority of the letters, remains unpublished. Although Dr Jones initially planned to prepare a scholarly edition for publication, his research, writing, and editing took him in a slightly different direction and to

Huntington Library Bulletin, 7 (1935), pp. 131–167; R.C.H. Catterall, 'Two letters of Richard Cromwell, 1659', *American Historical Review*, 8 (1902–1903), pp. 86–89.

[13] R.W. Ramsey, *Henry Cromwell* (London, 1933); R.W. Ramsey, *Richard Cromwell, Protector of England* (London, 1935). Some of the letters have also been used in J.A. Butler, *A Biography of Richard Cromwell, 1626–1712, The Second Protector* (Lampeter, 1994).

[14] C. Jones, 'Two unpublished letters of Oliver Cromwell', *Bulletin of the Institute of Historical Research*, 46 (1973), pp. 216–218.

[15] T. Barnard, 'Lord Broghill, Vincent Gookin and the Cork elections of 1659', *English Historical Review*, 88 (1973), pp. 352–365.

[16] T. Barnard, *Cromwellian Ireland*, paperback edition with new foreword (Oxford, 2000); P. Little, *Lord Broghill and the Cromwellian Union with Ireland and Scotland* (Woodbridge, 2004).

[17] Firth, *Last Years*, I, ix, xi.

a slightly later period of English and British history, and he firmly abandoned plans to pursue publication. The present editor took up the project with the knowledge, approval, and warm endorsement of Dr Jones, who has continued to provide invaluable support throughout its lengthy gestation.

The letters and papers in this collection give superb insights into the administration of Cromwellian Ireland between 1655 and 1659, into the central government of Lord Protectors Oliver and Richard Cromwell from 1655 until the collapse of the Protectorate, and into the relationship between Henry Cromwell's Irish administration and his father's, and then his brother's, London-based Protectoral government. However, as a clearly incomplete set of in-letters, they also present a slanted and imperfect image, of necessity rather one-sided, and they need to be read alongside other surviving material in order to provide a fuller and more rounded picture. For example, this collection gives us tantalizing insights into Henry Cromwell, via the many replies to his letters from his regular, mainly London-based, correspondents; via the responses to his own requests and instructions, praise, and rebukes; and via the often detailed and revealing reports of his reputation in England, of his friends' standing with the Protector and other senior political and military figures in London, and of the way in which his handling of Ireland and his Irish policies were being viewed across the Irish Sea. But Henry Cromwell's own voice is heard here only occasionally or indirectly through the reportage of others, and he speaks to us directly only through a dozen or so drafts of his letters to Broghill; here Henry tends to be hovering in the wings rather than taking centre stage. To supplement and flesh out the image of Henry Cromwell in Ireland, and of so many other issues raised in these letters, the collection should be read alongside other important sources, most notably the letters and papers of the Secretary of State, John Thurloe, and the associated material that Thomas Birch gathered and reproduced in his *Collection of the State Papers of John Thurloe, Esquire*. This huge, seven-volume collection contains many more in-letters to Henry Cromwell in Ireland, notably the regular correspondence maintained by Thurloe himself, as well as scores of letters written by Henry Cromwell during his period in Ireland, addressed to Thurloe, to his predecessor in Ireland, Charles Fleetwood, to his father and brother as Protectors, and to other London-based politicians and agents. In many cases, this material provides the other side of the correspondence featured in this collection and it is here that we find letters from Henry Cromwell and others that either triggered or responded to the letters now in the Lansdowne Collection. Birch's volumes also contain official and semi-official material related to Henry Cromwell's government of

Ireland – reports to and from the Irish council, financial accounts, and so forth – which is all the more valuable as so much of the official documentation relating to the government of Ireland during the 1650s perished when the Four Courts building housing the Public Record Office of Ireland was largely destroyed by fire in June 1922. However, generous selections of this material feature in two published collections produced before 1922, namely the relevant volume of the *Calendar of State Papers, Ireland* and R. Dunlop's *Ireland under the Commonwealth.*[18] This material can be supplemented by some extant batches of official central and local governmental records of Ireland in the 1650s, now found in central and provincial repositories in Ireland. Together, this range of surviving personal, private, semi-official, and official material provides the context for, and enables a fuller understanding and interpretation of, this collection of the Henry Cromwell correspondence.

Henry Cromwell and his governance of Ireland

The arrival of twenty-seven-year-old Henry Cromwell in Ireland in the summer of 1655, not only as commander of the English army there but also as chief administrator of that country, represented something of a gamble and certainly proved a turning point both in the handling of Ireland by the English regimes of the 1650s and in the policies imposed there by the English government in Dublin. This collection effectively opens in mid-summer 1655, by which time Henry Cromwell's appointment had been confirmed and he was preparing to relocate his family from London and Cambridgeshire to Dublin. It closes in the spring of 1659, with the collapse of the Protectoral regimes in London and Dublin, and with Henry Cromwell's time in Ireland rapidly drawing to a close. Thus the collection very neatly spans the four-year period that Henry Cromwell spent in Ireland – he landed near Dublin on 9 July 1655 and took ship from Ireland, never to return, on 27 June 1659. Although he maintained a keen and informed interest in political and personal developments in London, threatened several times in 1656–1657 to resign his offices in Ireland and return to the mainland, and by 1658 was hankering for permission to pay a brief or extended visit to England – all issues referred to or reflected in letters in this collection – in fact, Henry Cromwell remained in Ireland throughout these four years and never once left its shores.

[18] R.P. Mahaffy (ed.), *Calendar of the State Papers Relating to Ireland: of the reign of Charles I, 3, 1647–60 and addenda 1625–60* (London, 1903); R. Dunlop (ed.), *Ireland under the Commonwealth*, 2 vols but with continuous pagination (Manchester, 1913).

Henry Cromwell was born in January 1628, the fifth of nine children and the fourth of five sons of Oliver Cromwell, at that time a minor landowner in and around Huntingdon, soon to represent the town in the third parliament of Charles I, but shortly thereafter to sell up and leave Huntingdon under a cloud.[19] We know almost nothing about Henry's childhood and adolescence, although it is likely that he was brought up in the family home in Huntingdon until 1631, in St Ives from 1631 until 1636, and then in Ely from 1636, and that, like his elder brothers, he spent some time away from home attending Felsted school in Essex. There is no evidence that he ever entered university; instead, by his late teens he was serving as a junior officer in the parliamentary army. He was almost certainly in Thomas Harrison's New Model Army horse regiment that campaigned in northern England in 1648 and he presumably saw action with his regiment at the battle of Preston of August 1648. Later the following year, he was promoted to colonel and given command of a newly created horse regiment sent to Ireland to reinforce the English campaign of reconquest there, led by Oliver Cromwell. Henry crossed from Pembrokeshire to Youghal in February 1650 and then campaigned with other forces and commanders, including the prominent Irish Protestant leader Lord Broghill, in Munster. He remained in Ireland on active military service after his father's return to the mainland in the summer of 1650 and campaigned under his father's successors, initially Henry Ireton until his death at Limerick in November 1651 (Henry Cromwell was reportedly present at the siege of Limerick and was with Ireton when he died) and then Charles Fleetwood. Ireton and Fleetwood were also both allied to him by marriage, successively marrying his sister Bridget Cromwell.

Henry Cromwell appears to have returned to England sometime late in 1652 or early in 1653, for on 10 May 1653, at Kensington, he married Elizabeth Russell, eldest daughter of Francis Russell of Chippenham in Cambridgeshire, a friend and former military comrade of Oliver Cromwell, who had campaigned with him in East Anglia during the civil war of 1642–1646. Henry spent much of the next two years with his wife and in-laws at Chippenham and his first child, a daughter Elizabeth, was born there in September 1654. Around the same time as his marriage, in the spring of 1653, he was named one of six representatives of Ireland in the Nominated Assembly and he played an active role in that body. Assigned lodgings nearby in Whitehall, in November he was elected to the Assembly's short-lived Council of State and was then assiduous in attending

[19] The best concise biography of Henry Cromwell, drawn on here, is P. Gaunt, 'Cromwell, Henry', in *ODNB*.

Council meetings, being identified by a contemporary commentator as one of the moderate members of the Assembly, 'for the Godly Learned Ministry and Universities', though he had no recorded role in the Assembly's sudden resignation in December. The change of regime and his father's elevation to head of state as Lord Protector on 16 December 1653 did not formally alter his position and he did not immediately gain any new military or political offices in the Protectorate. However, in practice, as the younger son – by the 1650s, three of Oliver Cromwell's sons had died and only Henry and his elder brother Richard remained – of the new, albeit non-hereditary, head of state, Henry's role did change.

From early 1654, Henry accompanied his father on some state occasions, commentators and the weekly newspapers began reporting his actions, and in the summer of 1654 he was returned as MP for the University of Cambridge to the first Protectorate parliament. Again, he seems to have been quite active in that body, regularly nominated to committees and serving as teller in three formal divisions. More importantly, in the spring of 1654 he was employed by his father on a mission back to Ireland to investigate the political and religious allegiances of the English army there, and of the military and administrative officials then running Irish affairs. Travelling via North Wales, he spent a little under three weeks in Ireland in March 1654, meeting Fleetwood and other military commanders (including Edmund Ludlow), a selection of Dublin civic dignitaries, and various legal officers. He offered a forthright summary of his findings to Secretary Thurloe, reporting that the army and most of its officers were loyal to the new Protectoral regime, but picking out Ludlow for stinging criticism and his fellow-commissioner John Jones for more tempered criticism for respectively very active and overt and more subdued and semi-covert opposition to the Protectorate. He felt that, on the grounds of its inactivity, inefficiency, and a self-interest bordering on corruption, the Irish administration should be overhauled; and he reported that its head, Fleetwood, was 'too deeply ingaged in a partial affection to the persons of the anabaptists, to answer your end; though I doe believe it rather to proceed from tendernes then love to their principles'. He concluded that Fleetwood would welcome an opportunity to hand over command and leave Ireland, at least for a time, as 'his desire [was] rather to returne, than to continue' there, and he suggested that the Protector's brother-in-law and senior army officer John Desborough be sent to Ireland both to replace Ludlow and to serve as 'deputie' for the recalled Fleetwood.[20]

[20] *TSP*, II, p. 149.

Indeed, over the following months Protector and Council did review and reshape the English government of Ireland. By 1654, the twin policies of active military reconquest and the brutal dispossession and transplantation of Irish Catholics were in essence as complete as they would be, and the English handling of Ireland could shift from naked military control to a degree of more regular civil and civilian style of management, albeit one still supported by a large and continuing military presence. Accordingly, punitive policies might give way to greater moderation, to a more relaxed and constructive handling, if not of the Irish Catholics, at least of the Protestant population, and to a reconstruction of political, administrative, judicial, and religious forms in Ireland, moving them away from the overtly militaristic and improvisational lines of the war years and towards something more traditional, stable, and durable, which might win broader support in Ireland and thus strengthen the Protectoral regime there.

Such goals may have figured in the reorganization of the Irish administration instituted by the Protector and his Protectoral Council in August 1654, which ended the power of a group of parliamentary commissioners. These were a mixture of English military figures and civilian politicians, originally appointed by the Rump in 1650, though the composition of the group had changed in the interim. Only Ludlow, who had resigned earlier in 1654, had had experience of Ireland prior to his appointment, by dint of his military service there. In their place, Protector and Council established an Irish council, whose instructions ranged more widely than those re-issued to the parliamentary commissioners in August 1652,[21] including, for example, new provisions for settling taxation and fiscal affairs in Ireland, and for managing and letting Irish land still held by the state. Like their predecessors the parliamentary commissioners, the six founder-members of the Irish council had few existing links with Ireland – only Miles Corbet, the sole parliamentary commissioner to transfer to the new council, had substantial Irish experience, though a second councillor, Robert Goodwin, had had business dealings with Ireland. More importantly, however, only two of the new councillors, Matthew Tomlinson and Robert Hammond, had had significant army careers and could be considered military figures. Corbet and Goodwin were politicians and had been quite prominent in the Long Parliament; the other two new councillors, Richard Pepys and William Steele, had legal rather than military or political backgrounds. Moreover, Hammond was dead by the end of 1654 and, after a long delay, he was effectively replaced in 1656 by William Bury, a politician and financial expert, further weakening the military representation on the Irish

[21] Dunlop, pp. 263–268 and 437–443.

council and giving that body an even stronger civilian complexion. Thus the establishment of the new Irish council, its instructions and powers, and its membership might all be taken as signs that, in the summer of 1654, Protector and Protectoral Council were looking to change the way in which Ireland was handled and administered.

However, at the same time, in August 1654, Protector and Council, far from recalling Charles Fleetwood from Ireland as recommended by Henry Cromwell, instead confirmed, continued, and enhanced his role as head of the Irish administration. Fleetwood had risen to prominence in the early and mid-1640s as a military figure, as colonel of a cavalry regiment in the Eastern Association Army and then the New Model Army, as an MP from 1646, and in the army politics of spring and summer 1647. He took a curiously low-key role in developments over the next few years – he seems to have played little or no part in the second civil war, took no role in the regicide, and was not part of the Cromwellian campaign in Ireland in 1649–1650 – but he returned to the fore in Cromwell's Scottish campaign of 1650–1651 as lieutenant-general of the horse, prominent at the battles of Dunbar and Worcester. In July 1652, he was appointed by the Rump and commissioned by Oliver Cromwell as commander-in-chief of the English army in Ireland, replacing the dead Ireton, and he crossed to Ireland in September. Over the following two years he was the effective head of the English administration in Ireland, exercising not only military command but also, in co-ordination with the parliamentary commissioners, administrative and political leadership.[22]

Fleetwood's record in Ireland in 1652–1654 reflected both his military pedigree and his endorsement of the generally hostile policies towards the majority Irish population that were adopted by the Rump. Accordingly, he supported and attempted to execute the policy of mass transplantation of Irish Catholic landowners and to redistribute confiscated Irish land to the state's mainly English civilian and military creditors. He supported, or at least acquiesced in the face of, complaints emanating from the English army in Ireland on a range of topics, including military grievances such as arrears of pay and the tardiness of allocating soldiers Irish land. Moreover, despite Oliver Cromwell's warning to him in 1652 to 'take heed also of your natural inclination to compliance',[23] he adopted a very lax and acquiescent approach to signs of broader military discontent and to growing religious and political unrest within the army. He did little to counter either religious radicalism and the spread of fervent Baptism

[22] The best concise biography of Charles Fleetwood, drawn on here, is T. Barnard, 'Fleetwood, Charles', in *ODNB*.

[23] Abbott, II, p. 602.

within the army or the growth of military disaffection in the wake of the political and constitutional changes in England during 1653, so that, by 1654, there was evidence that a number of senior field officers, garrison commanders, and military governors in Ireland were distancing themselves from the new Protectoral regime, using radical religion to reinforce and partly to disguise their republican disaffection. Fleetwood's passive and 'delphic'[24] handling of these issues, his inaction in the face of spreading and potentially subversive and disruptive opinion within the English army in Ireland, caused alarm both in Ireland and in London. It was almost certainly concern over Fleetwood's handling of these issues that led the new Protector to dispatch his younger son to Ireland in March 1654 and Henry Cromwell's resulting report pulled few punches in its assessment of Fleetwood's shortcomings. In the light of Fleetwood's military background and his mixed record in Ireland, of the potential for the new Protectoral regime to change its approach to and policies for Ireland, and of signs that the appointment of an Irish council with a less military appearance may have been leading in that direction, the confirmation of Fleetwood's Irish command in August 1654 and the decision by the Protector and Protectoral Council to appoint him lord deputy of Ireland for a term of three years to 1 September 1657 seemed to run counter to any such intention and to those other initiatives. The surviving sources do not make clear or explicit why Fleetwood was not merely confirmed in command of Ireland but also appointed lord deputy at this stage. His closeness to Oliver Cromwell – Fleetwood had become his son-in-law in 1652 – as well as the genuine affection in which he was held by many in Ireland, particularly amongst the English army and the radical sects there, may have induced Protector and Protectoral Council to stick by him in the summer of 1654.

However, Fleetwood's continuing command in Ireland, now as lord deputy although in co-ordination with a new Irish council, came into question almost immediately, with a proposal that Henry Cromwell be sent to Ireland to play a senior military and political role there. In August 1654, the Protectoral Council had recommended to the Protector that his younger son be appointed commander of the English army in Ireland and be added to the new Irish council and, later in the autumn, with the Protector apparently hesitating, a clutch of senior 'Irish gentlemen', including Lord Broghill, attended the Council in London to urge and support Henry's appointment. At length, in late December 1654, the Protector appointed his younger son major-general of the army in Ireland and formally added him to the Irish

[24] The word is Barnard's: 'Fleetwood, Charles' in *ODNB*.

council.[25] There then followed another significant delay before Henry crossed to Ireland to take up his new posts in July 1655.

Fleetwood's position within this new arrangement remained unclear for a time and some of his own letters during the first half of 1655 suggest that he then believed he would continue in Ireland, presumably working with Henry Cromwell – whose arrival in Ireland he urged, writing 'he will find welcome here; the sooner he comes the better'[26] – but actively retaining the senior position within the Irish administration. However, by late spring rumours were circulating that Fleetwood was to be recalled to England and that Henry would, in fact, supersede him in Dublin, for on 22 June the Protector wrote an emollient letter to his son-in-law, vigorously denying that he was about to be recalled and Henry Cromwell appointed lord deputy in his stead, though also reporting that if Fleetwood had 'a mind to come over' to London he would be welcomed.[27] In practice, by midsummer the assumption on both sides seems to have been that Henry Cromwell would physically replace his brother-in-law as not only military commander but also chief administrator in and of Ireland, for Henry sought and received assurances in London that he would have power to appoint to 'places and offices' in Ireland, while Fleetwood embarked upon an extensive final tour of inspection around Ireland and began making preparations to return to England with his family.[28] By early August, Fleetwood reported that he had received 'his highnes positive commands to returne into England'[29] and, after a month or so working alongside Henry Cromwell in Dublin, Fleetwood and his family left Ireland, never to return, in early September. Several of the opening letters in this collection relate to the logistics of Henry's journey to Ireland and of Fleetwood's return to England and to London.[30] Equally, some letters of summer 1655, originally addressed to Fleetwood in Dublin, either missed him and were opened by Henry Cromwell or were left by Fleetwood for his brother-in-law's use and so have ended up in this collection.[31]

From Fleetwood's departure in September 1655 until the autumn of 1657, Henry Cromwell's official role and title in Ireland were somewhat ambiguous and his position often rather uncomfortable. Fleetwood remained lord deputy of Ireland until his commission

[25] M.A.E. Green (ed.), *Calendar of State Papers, Domestic, 1654* (London, 1880), pp. 321, 328, 382; Dunlop, pp. 468–469.

[26] *TSP*, III, p. 363.

[27] Abbott, III, p. 756.

[28] *TSP*, III, pp. 440, 558, 566, 632, 690.

[29] *TSP*, III, p. 697.

[30] See items 4, 6, 8, 9, and 10.

[31] See items 2, 4, and 6.

expired in September 1657, though he was now an absentee and spent the period in London, where he was a senior army officer and politician, taking his seat on the Protectoral Council. Henry had command of the English army in Ireland and was, in practice, chief administrator of Ireland, although on paper he was starved of political power and his authority was limited to membership of the Irish council. The position, described by the foremost historian of Cromwellian Ireland as one of the Protector's 'least satisfactory compromises',[32] caused enormous problems. Henry was denied full power to develop and implement his own policies in Ireland, and instead was repeatedly compelled to consult, defer to, and win the support or the sometimes grudging acquiescence of the absentee lord deputy, Fleetwood, who had wide political and military influence within Protectoral central government in London and who was generally deferred to on Irish business within the Protectoral Council.

In light of this, Henry Cromwell's already tense relationship with his brother-in-law quickly deteriorated over the period 1655–1657, for Fleetwood's views on Irish policies were often very different from those of his young brother-in-law, just as Fleetwood maintained good relations with radical military, political, and religious figures who quickly came to oppose Henry's approach in Ireland and whom Henry equally quickly marked down as opponents and enemies. Fleetwood could and often did serve, wittingly or unwittingly, both as a hindrance to Henry's Irish policies and as a rallying point for his critics and opponents on both sides of the Irish Sea. Many letters in this collection attest to the tense and worsening relationship between the two men, which clearly almost reached breaking point at times, as well as to clear political differences; to starkly differing opinions about particular military, political, and religious figures and policies; and to the ways in which friends, allies, and agents of the two men were also drawn into something of a power struggle fought out between Fleetwood in London and Henry Cromwell in Dublin. The latter became deeply suspicious of Fleetwood's actions and many letters both in this collection and in *A Collection of the State Papers of John Thurloe* make, repeat, or respond to allegations that Fleetwood and his cronies in London were deliberately thwarting, delaying, detaining, undermining, or slandering agents sent to London by Henry to promote his Irish policies with the Protector, Protectoral Council, or parliament there. As relations deteriorated, Henry and Fleetwood were kept informed of, or became parties to, bickering, allegations, and counter-allegations; disputes about letters that had allegedly been written and were being circulated; and accusations

[32] Barnard, *Cromwellian Ireland*, p. 20.

concerning groundless and scurrilous rumours being concocted or spread by one side to blacken the other. Even allowing for a degree of exaggeration and for the rather prickly, thin-skinned, and over-sensitive nature of the two main protagonists, things clearly became very fraught and unpleasant at times.

Throughout his four years in Ireland, Henry Cromwell was based in Dublin for most of the year, often residing at Cork House in the city, but also using the state rooms at Dublin Castle and, particularly during the summer months, spending time with his family at Phoenix House on the outskirts of the city. Each year, he left his family at Dublin and undertook a late summer and early autumn tour of inspection around Ireland, visiting key towns, garrisons, and strongholds, and also some of the land and property that he acquired by purchase or allocation during his years in Ireland, including the great Portumna estate in Galway, in which he took a keen interest.

For most of the year, Henry Cromwell governed from Dublin, meeting regularly and working in co-ordination with the Irish council established in August 1654 and inherited from Fleetwood. Surviving conciliar records are very thin and it is now impossible to reconstruct much of the day-to-day operation of the central executive or to paint a full and detailed picture of the relationship between, and relative roles and powers of, Henry Cromwell and the Irish council. Some surviving sources, including some letters in this collection, suggest that, from September 1655 onwards, Henry was the dominant figure in Dublin, actively heading the Irish administration, and supported and empowered by his position as commander of the army in Ireland and by his relationship with Protectoral central government in London in general and with his father in particular. However, there are clear indications both in this collection and in correspondence in *A Collection of the State Papers of John Thurloe* that Henry Cromwell was at times hemmed in by the Irish council, was perhaps no more than *primus inter pares* within that body, and that both the small size of the existing council and the opposition he was encountering within it to some of his policies represented serious limitations to his freedom of action, even before the role of the absentee lord deputy was taken into account. Hence Henry's repeated requests, not that he be given more power – he firmly distanced himself from the occasional requests by others that he be made lord deputy or allocated greater powers – or that the basic structure of the Dublin government be changed, but that additional and supportive councillors should be appointed to enlarge the Irish council and, by implication, to ensure a clear majority for his favoured policies in that body. However, despite repeated assurances that additional councillors were being sought across the Irish Sea, very few changes were made over this period. William Steele, originally appointed in 1654, and William Bury, appointed in 1656 to replace the long-dead Robert Hammond, crossed from England to Dublin in the summer of 1656 to join the Irish council, though the former proved as much a hindrance as a help in advancing Henry's favoured policies.

During his first months in Ireland, Henry Cromwell pushed ahead with a range of policies, some new, others continuing Fleetwood's approach. For example, he largely continued and enforced the tail end of the policy of transplanting Irish Catholics, ensuring, for instance, that they were removed from the important town and stronghold of Galway and other walled towns, although there are also signs that he wished to moderate some elements of the anti-Catholic policies. When, in 1657, parliament introduced a new oath of abjuration, requiring Catholics to deny papal power, transubstantiation, and the validity of the Roman church, Henry Cromwell regretted the move, commenting, 'I wish this extrame course had not been so suddenly taken, comeing like a thunder-clapp uppon them'. Thurloe replied that only fresh parliamentary legislation could change the legal position, though he recommended that 'prudent manadgment of it upon the place will be the best way'.[33] However, Henry generally maintained the existing hostile line towards the majority Irish Catholic population, viewing them as enemies of the Protectoral regime and potential allies of the Spanish, mounting occasional military and police operations against Catholic areas, and lobbying for a more effective naval guard around the Irish coast. His rather callous attitude towards the native Irish Catholics is revealed by one of his first initiatives in Ireland, in the autumn of 1655, when he sought to gather together 'a supply of younge Irish girles' to be sent forcibly to stock the new English possession of Jamaica, defending the scheme on the grounds that 'although we must use force in takeinge them up, yet it beinge so much for their owne goode, and likely to be of soe great advantage to the publique'. He soon proposed that between 1,500 and 2,000 young Irish Catholic boys, aged between twelve and fourteen, be rounded up and sent with them to Jamaica, as 'it may be a meanes to make them English-men, I meane rather, Christianes'. He then struck upon the idea of holding together around 1,500 men out of the 5,000 or so being disbanded from the English army in Ireland – Fleetwood had begun the disbandment just before he left, but much of the detailed work fell to Henry Cromwell as his first task in Ireland – and either encouraging or compelling them to go to Jamaica to help colonize that island.[34] The entire scheme, encompassing both Irish

[33] *TSP*, VI, p. 527, and VII, p. 4.
[34] *TSP*, IV, pp. 23–24, 40, 74, 75, 198.

Catholic girls and boys and disbanded English troops, received some rather guarded and lukewarm support from Secretary Thurloe, but was soon allowed to run into the sand. As with so many of Henry Cromwell's proposals for Ireland, the Protectoral regime in London lacked the will or resources to back them up and to bring them to fruition.

At the outset, Henry Cromwell's mission in Ireland was described by his chaplain, Thomas Harrison, thus:

> to put honour upon the publique worship of God, and life into His people, and a checke upon some irregular spirits, whome I rather desire to serve in love and pitty, then to censure [. . . .] The nation lyes like clay upon the wheele, ready to receive what forme authority shall please to give it.[35]

Within the opening months, Henry Cromwell proposed and lobbied for a range of policies, most of them designed to bring greater stability and prosperity to Ireland, to restore elements of traditional life, and thus, he hoped, to win the active support of the Protestants in Ireland for his father's Protectoral regime. Most of these initiatives needed the support of the Protectoral central government and of the lord deputy in London. The regular correspondence between Henry Cromwell and London, between Dublin and the various agents and missions dispatched to London in order to advance Irish policies (much of it found in this collection), is full of business of this kind. Almost from the outset, Henry was requesting more money from London for Ireland and more good people to be sent across, not just as councillors but also as administrators, judges, and ministers in Ireland; these were to become common refrains throughout his years in Ireland. During the autumn of 1655, Henry also sought approval to dispense some of the native Irish population from transplantation, to establish a new militia in Ireland, to set up a naval victualling office in Dublin, and to create a new mint in Ireland so that the existing poor and debased coinage circulating in Ireland, 'which like a cancer hath eaten out the good', could be replaced.[36] During the opening months of 1656, Henry sent several agents on missions to London, bearing detailed instructions that covered these and a range of other requests and policies to be pursued with the Protector, the Protectoral Council, and the lord deputy.[37]

However, the first major initiative – and battle – upon which Henry Cromwell embarked in Ireland was to break the power of religious radicalism in general, and of 'Anabaptism' in particular,

[35] *TSP*, III, p. 715.
[36] *TSP*, IV, pp. 40, 73–74, 198, 307–308.
[37] Dunlop, pp. 560–561 and 612–613.

within the English army in Ireland. Both Henry Cromwell and the correspondents in this collection tended to use the term 'Anabaptism' rather loosely, to cover not only Baptism itself – a faith which had undoubtedly gained a stronghold within the English army in Ireland and in some English communities under Fleetwood – but also other forms of allegedly subversive religious radicalism allied to it. Henry Cromwell believed that Baptism and its allied faiths served as a cover for, as well as themselves encouraged, both insubordination within the army and political disaffection towards the Protectoral regime. While stressing that he had no particular quarrel with Baptism or any other faith per se, and that he was willing to offer Baptists 'equally liberty both in their spirituall and civill concernments with any others',[38] he was determined to end the favoured position that Baptism had gained during Fleetwood's years in charge and to break the hold that it had acquired amongst garrison commanders, town governors, and senior officers as well as amongst the rank and file. The result was a dour campaign fought out not only in Ireland itself but also within governmental circles in London, as Henry Cromwell sought to break the power of the Baptists and their associates, and as leading military and civilian Baptists and their allies sought in turn to thwart him in Ireland and to agitate against him in London, attempting, with some success, to draw Fleetwood and, through him, the Protector into the fray.

Just as Henry Cromwell noted the undue power of the Baptists in Ireland and their undue influence with Fleetwood during his brief visit of March 1654, so the Baptists marked him down as a potential enemy from that time. Contemporaries recorded that the Baptists did not welcome Henry Cromwell in the spring of 1654, that they absented themselves from the formal proclamation of the Protectoral government in Dublin that coincided with his visit, and that 'their invectives and derisory expressions were many and frequent'.[39] In one of his earliest surviving letters from Ireland upon returning as chief administrator in 1655, Henry Cromwell reported that 'all is verry quiett and peaceable, and men nowe doe begin to thinke it is but reasonable, that their shoulde be ane equallitie helde out to all such as have bin fellowe-labourers together, and continue sober and honest', but at the same time he noted that 'there are some amonge us doe think, that they are not well used, if a good place slippe by them'.[40]

Over the following year or more, Henry Cromwell worked steadily to remove Baptists and their allies from several key military and

[38] *TSP*, IV, p. 433.
[39] *TSP*, II, pp. 162–164.
[40] *TSP*, III, p. 699.

provincial offices and to appoint non-Baptists in their stead, thus whittling down Baptist and radical religious influence in military circles and largely excluding radical Baptists and their allies from any direct position or voice within the central administration in Dublin. Some Baptist ministers lost their official, government salaries and were moved from prominent and influential to more obscure areas and parishes. At the same time, through debate and discussion and by adopting a cautious and equitable line, he sought to win over some of the moderate Baptists and to isolate their more extreme colleagues, whose radical faith shaded into military insubordination and political dissent. In January 1656, he assured Thurloe that the Baptists would continue to have 'Liberty and countenance', but 'to rule me, or to rule with me, I should not approve of [. . .] I doe not thinke that God has given them a spiritt of government; neither is it safe they should have much power in their handes'.[41]

Under steady pressure, and despite counter-attacks and agitation in both Ireland and London (much of which is recounted or alluded to in this collection), Baptism slowly lost its favoured position in Ireland, and its potential role as a front and cover for disaffection was reduced, while prominent Baptists and their allies were progressively isolated, neutered, dismissed, or won over. By the time Henry Cromwell returned to Dublin following his 1656 summer tour of the provinces, he felt that the battle had been won:

> I have since my returne bin more courted by the Anabaptists then formerly. Mr Patient and some others, whoe had not bin with me of a longe time before came to visit me, and expressed much to their satisfaction with my management of things here, and that their people had much liberty as they could desire, and much to the same purpose. What this means I must of a sudden imagine. I shall, as formerly, carry it with all moderation towards them.[42]

The victory was complete when, in the closing weeks of 1656, four of the senior officers of the army in Ireland who had adopted the Baptist faith or were allied to the 'Anabaptist' agitation and who had taken the lead in opposing Henry Cromwell, visited him and insisted on resigning their commissions.[43] Other Baptists either fell silent or began courting and supporting Henry Cromwell on his terms. On 17 December, he wrote triumphantly to Thurloe:

> The Anabaptists and others, whose way and principles were inconsistent with settlement and our interest, do find themselves disabled from doing much harm. My inclination now is, having brought them to good terms, not to crush

[41] *TSP*, IV, p. 433.
[42] *TSP*, I, p. 731.
[43] Henry's long and detailed account of the event is at *TSP*, V, pp. 670–671.

> them quite, lest through despair they attempt things dangerous [. . . .] Besides, it is against my conscience to bear hard upon any, merely upon the account of a different judgment, or to do any thing, that might make them think so.[44]

Although Henry Cromwell's battle with the Baptists and their allies had been won, it had come at a high personal and political price. As this correspondence reveals, his relationship with Fleetwood worsened markedly during 1655–1656; he often felt unsure whether the Protectoral central government, his father included, was really supporting him; he was intensely suspicious of what was going on in London; and he sometimes came close to despair or was put on the defensive by the actions of others. For example, he was perturbed when several of his leading opponents agitated in London for Fleetwood's return to Ireland or gained direct access to his father, and he reacted badly when one of them, John Hewson, received a letter from the Protector, which might be interpreted as giving some support to his position and as failing to endorse Henry's stance. As an ally put it in December 1655, 'They say, it is evident by that from his highnesse, that my lord was sent over to be commanded, not to command; to serve, and not to rule'.[45] Equally, Henry was wrong-footed when his own friends and allies petitioned for his appointment as lord deputy of Ireland in place of Fleetwood, correctly seeing that it would not be supported by the Protector but would in some ways both strengthen Fleetwood's position and further sour his relationship with his brother-in-law.

The battle with the Baptists bit deeper still. Even as he succeeded Fleetwood in the summer of 1655, there were signs of personal unease: Fleetwood noted that his young brother-in-law 'may have sometimes some melancholy thoughts, yet I hope he will find it much better then he may at present expect'; while Henry Cromwell admitted upon Fleetwood's departure that no man 'was more troubled to parte with him then myselfe' and that 'I shall have little comforte to stay behind, further then to answer duty'.[46] By early October he was writing to his father, 'Your highness cannot but be sensible, that by reason of my youthe and inabilitie, that my tryalls and temptations are too greate for me, as well as my employment'.[47] Late in 1655, he admitted that, upon his arrival in the summer, he had on one occasion shown 'too much of my owne spiritt (which through grace I am sencible of as my burden)', and was now making a conscious effort to take 'an even

[44] *TSP*, V, p. 710.
[45] *TSP*, IV, p. 349.
[46] *TSP*, III, pp. 697, 728–729, and IV, pp. 23–24.
[47] *TSP*, IV, p. 74.

hande even to those, that have done me all this evill'.[48] Around the same time he reported that his Baptist opponents were 'starke madd [. . . .] They have not had any provocation from me, neither in word or action. I have with all dilegence watched over my owne spirit'.[49] But his youth and inexperience, and the short temper that he knew he possessed worried others, including his father, whose letters of 1655–1656 sought to reassure and support, but also to guide and warn his son, advising him not to be 'over-jealous, lest your apprehensions of others cause you to offend', nor to be 'too hard' on his opponents.[50] In the opening months of his son's government of Ireland, at the height of the contest with the Baptists, it seems that the Protector also sought confidential reports upon Henry's performance in Ireland. Thus, in a letter to Thurloe of October 1655, Thomas Harrison implied that he was providing confidential reports on Henry Cromwell – 'Sir, I assure you, that my lord never saw a line that I writ to you or to his highnesse. I am not unaquainted with the snares and temptations, whereby my lord hath been formerly indangered, and whereof I suppose his highnes may be still fearfull and jealous'.[51] Similarly, it later emerged that Thomas Cooper had been appointed to Ireland by the Protector at the end of 1655 in part to report back on Henry Cromwell's performance – the following year the Protector 'confessed hee sent colonel Cooper over to spy; that Cooper wrote to his Highness that your lordship's actions were prudent and warrantable, and gave not the least grounds for what had bin suggested against you'.[52]

Had Henry Cromwell been aware of this at the time, it would probably have increased his uncertainty still more. Often unsure of his position, feeling that his father and the London government were not properly supporting him but were listening to his Baptist opponents, and sometimes believing his cause to be lost, on occasion he gave way to despair. In December 1655, with reports circulating that Hewson and his allies had been given a friendly reception by the Protector and claims that Oliver Cromwell was not fully supporting his son's stance, Henry, who was at a low ebb because of a sharp and persistent cold, began wailing about 'howe evilly I am requited for my kindness', how he had 'noethinge to quiett my spiritt, but through grace the integritie of my owne harte in my actions' and about how the Protector could 'doe with me as he please, send me into a Welch cottage, if it be

[48] *TSP*, IV, p. 349.
[49] *TSP*, IV, pp. 254–255.
[50] Abbott, IV, p. 146.
[51] *TSP*, IV, pp. 90–91.
[52] No. 139.

for his service'.[53] In response to this and similar sentiments, both the Protector and Secretary Thurloe sought to smooth ruffled feathers, offering support and reassurance. Thurloe advised him that 'Hard sayinges, yea reproaches, and worse, is the portion of the best men in these uncerteyne and giddy tymes, and you must not thinke to goe shott free'.[54]

Six months later, in the summer of 1656, Henry Cromwell went further and wrote several letters to his father and to Thurloe seeking to resign his offices in Ireland and to retire to the mainland:

> Truly sir, accordinge to the apprehension I have of the present state of thinges, I cannot judge it good either for the publique or myselfe to be longer here. I knowe not howe thinges are managed, but sure I am, my enemyes [. . .] insult; my friends droope, myself thereby rendered contemptible, and altogether uncapable of doeing further service.[55]

Again, letters admonishing – Thurloe cautioned, 'Everybody can keepe his place, when all men applaude hym, speake well of hym; but not to faint in a day of adversity is the matter'[56] – as well as reassuring and promising greater support, some of them to be found in this collection, persuaded Henry Cromwell to stay and continue his work in Ireland, and the crisis passed. However, his own uncertainties persisted for, in December 1656, even at the time of his clear triumph over the Baptists and their allies, he was writing to Thurloe that 'I knowe I am a poore creature, attended with many frailtys and weaknesses, and have need to wait uppon God for renewed strength; and truly my late desires of retirement have proceeded frome the apprehension I have hade of my owne unfittness for soe great and difficult a worke'.[57]

By the opening months of 1656, Henry was becoming aware of the emergence and spread of Quakerism, not among the native population, but principally among some elements of the English army, including garrisons and military governors, especially at Cork and Kinsale and more generally in the province of Munster. He feared that Quakerism could become the new Baptism, a cover for military insubordination and political disaffection, as well as a possible vehicle for social upheaval. As early as 6 February, Henry Cromwell was claiming that 'Our most considerable enemy nowe in our view are the quakers', adding that 'I thinke their principles and practises are not verry consistent with civil government, much lesse with the discipline

[53] *TSP*, IV, pp. 327–328.
[54] *TSP*, IV, p. 373.
[55] *TSP*, V, p. 177.
[56] *TSP*, V, pp. 196–197.
[57] *TSP*, V, pp. 729–730.

of an army' and that 'Their counterfeited simplicitie renders them to me the more dangerous'.[58] Accordingly, he acted quickly and firmly to clamp down on that faith, moving or threatening to dismiss military governors and senior officers, and swiftly cashiering junior officers and rank and file soldiers who were found to have converted to Quakerism. Once the Quaker threat was broken and subsided, and possibly as Henry Cromwell came to view Quakerism as no real threat to his political or military control, he gradually relaxed his approach to the remaining civilian Quakers in Ireland.

Although much of Henry's time was taken up by Irish business in 1655–1656 (getting a grip on his new brief; curbing the Baptists and reining in the 'Anabaptist' elements in the army; dispatching to London and liaising with Sir John Reynolds, Thomas Harrison, Anthony Morgan, and other agents there who were pursuing Irish business with the Protectoral central government; and so forth), he retained a wider interest in the domestic and foreign affairs of the Protectoral regime. Letters in this collection show how he was kept abreast of the establishment and running of the new tier of semi-militarized regional government in England and Wales headed by the major-generals, and of the discussions that resulted in the decision to call the second Protectorate parliament, as well as of the rather mixed fortunes of the amphibious expedition sent to the Caribbean. He was also involved in finding troops from the English army in Ireland to be dispatched as reinforcements to Jamaica, an issue which, as several letters in this collection reveal, turned out to be unexpectedly fraught and protracted. Above all, although parliamentary developments during the opening months of the second Protectorate parliament are poorly charted in this collection, Henry Cromwell received a succession of detailed letters about the events of the latter half of that session. Indeed, this collection serves as one of the principal sources for the parliamentary and wider political and military developments surrounding the introduction, revision, and adoption of the new written constitution in general and the kingship question in particular during the period of February to June 1657.

Henry Cromwell's own responses to these developments emerge, albeit sometimes rather cloudily, via the drafts of letters that he wrote or intended to write to Broghill over this period, which are found in this collection,[59] though we have to turn to other sources for fuller and clearer indications of Henry's stance. Although one report claimed that, in December 1654, in his only recorded speech in the first Protectorate parliament, Henry Cromwell had supported a proposal

[58] TSP, IV, p. 508.

[59] Nos 209, 210, 233, 234, 244, 245, and 246.

that his father become king,[60] a series of detailed letters that he wrote to his father and to Thurloe between early March and early June 1657, and which survive in other collections, indicate that, by this stage, he was adopting a far more cautious line towards kingship. He both appreciated the work of the parliamentary majority in bringing forward the new constitutional proposals, many of which he praised as excellent and improvements upon the existing constitution, and at the same time condemned those army officers and others who were agitating against kingship. Nonetheless, he clearly had some reservations about the new title and argued that the supporters of the constitution were making a serious error in focusing so much upon the title and the kingship issue, and in trying to tie all the constitutional proposals to this point. He cautioned that 'to contend over earnestly for a name' ('titles and names are of little moment', he advised his father on 22 April) might imperil the entire edifice and 'for my owne parte, I cannot apprehend the necessity of it'; he wrote further, 'I could never be yet convinced, that all those excellent proposalls of the parliament are soe inseparably affix'd to the name of king, that all should stand or fall together'. In early June, once news of the Protector's firm and final refusal of the crown had reached Dublin, Henry Cromwell seemed not greatly perturbed, writing that as 'providence hath disposed matters thus, lett us be contented, and thankfull to God', commenting that 'I like graduall proceedings best, and this the better, because it seemes such' and concluding that, if for the moment the government had to continue to rest on the old written constitution, he would be content 'that the finishing our settlement bee also deferred till a competint tryall hath beene made of the present way'.[61] Thus, for Henry Cromwell, his father's rejection of the crown in the spring of 1657 was not the hammer blow that it appears to have been for some of the other correspondents in this collection.

A trio of issues more directly relevant to Ireland and Irish business came together to worry and dismay Henry Cromwell during the summer and autumn of 1657, all of them reported or assessed in letters in this collection. The first centred on the reorganization of the military forces in Ireland, an area in which he had already suffered one rebuff. From his opening months in Ireland, he had nurtured plans to establish a militia there and by autumn 1656 he was actively promoting the idea, laying detailed plans and arguing that 'I knowe nothinge of more advantage to the securitie of his highness and the publique interest of this nation, then the effectuall setlinge thereof'.[62]

[60] *Clarke Papers*, III, p. 16.
[61] *TSP*, VI, pp. 93–94, 182–183, 222–223, 330.
[62] *TSP*, V, pp. 493–494.

However, in late October Thurloe reported back that, although the Protector had given the proposal considerable thought and felt that it had some advantages, he believed that it also carried dangers and that on financial and security grounds a militia should not be established, at least for the moment – 'his highnes commaunded [. . .] that you will still have it in your consideration, and beare it in hand, but not to take any finall resolution, or actually to erect it, untill he shall have had a further prospect thereof'.[63] Henry Cromwell was clearly disappointed and continued to press the advantages of a militia force in Ireland, but there was an air of resignation in his comment, 'I doe somewhat wonder this business finds any hesitation [. . .] but I see good and necessarie things fare the worse comeing from my hande'.[64] He tried once more to revive the plan in a letter to his father of March 1657, again stressing the virtues of a militia, but again he received no support or encouragement.[65]

Instead, during the summer and autumn of 1657, a different and unwelcome type of military reorganization was forced upon Henry Cromwell. In an effort to cut costs and curb the military budget, the Protector and Protectoral Council instituted another round of disbandments to reduce the size of the standing army in England and Wales, Scotland, and Ireland. Henry argued strongly and repeatedly that the best way to reduce the army in Ireland was to maintain the existing number of ordinary soldiers but to reorganize the regimental structure and end the regimental organization for garrison troops and thus enable a significant reduction in the number of officers employed. The 'new modell would give opportunitie to weed out so many of those officers, who are either intollerably factious or turbulent, or are manifestly slacke in their duties', so both cutting costs and improving discipline, Henry argued.[66] Moreover, the officers were 'sufficiently tyed by their lands, to attend the defence and preservation of them and themselves', so that even once disbanded they would remain on hand and effectively act as a reserve, whereas ordinary troops once disbanded would probably leave Ireland and could not be recalled in times of danger or emergency.[67] Thus he strongly resisted and resented the plan (which he attributed to Fleetwood and which, despite all his arguments and the promises of consultation that he received, was eventually imposed upon him) to retain the existing regimental structure and with it the establishment and pay of the officers but

[63] *TSP*, V, p. 504.
[64] *TSP*, V, p. 586.
[65] *TSP*, VI, p. 142.
[66] *TSP*, VI, pp. 404–405.
[67] *TSP*, VI, pp. 505–506.

instead to reduce the number of ordinary soldiers per troop, company, and regiment. The arguments dragged on through the autumn and, as late as the first week of December 1657, Henry Cromwell was still resisting the 'absurd and dangerous way' disbandment was being forced upon him, pointing increasingly bitterly to earlier assurances that 'nothing should be done without my concurrence';[68] but at length he had to obey the firm and direct orders received from the Protectoral Council.

The second issue, linked to military reduction, was the weak financial state of the Protectoral regime as a whole and thus the dire financial position into which Henry Cromwell found himself slipping in Ireland. As a cost-cutting measure on the mainland, in the summer of 1657 the subsidy that Ireland received out of the central Protectoral treasury was more than halved from £17,000 to just £7,000 or at best £8,000 per month. Henry despaired, arguing that such a reduction was based on wildly exaggerated estimates of the sums which could be raised in Ireland and that to run the country he needed to receive at least £11,000 per month from England. But his pleas fell on deaf ears, with both Fleetwood and Thurloe assuring him that the deficits accumulating in England precluded any reversal or amelioration of the cuts made to the subsidies sent to Ireland. Despite attempts in Dublin and London to find ways to squeeze more money out of Ireland – investigating whether it was possible to make more from Irish customs, either directly or by farming them out, as well as from rents on Irish land – by the end of the autumn Henry Cromwell was dispatching very gloomy letters to London. He reported that debts were mounting, that the payment of the existing army in Ireland had slipped more than eight months into arrear, and that he must have more cash to pay off the troops who were to be disbanded, the financial position thus adding to his anger at how disbandment was being enforced:

> To speak the truth, I am very much afraid, that I have not been well dealt withall in this business; for besides that I am not thought competent for an affair of this nature, I am put upon an impossibility, viz to disband without money to pay off the arrears.[69]

Thirdly, in the late summer and autumn of 1657, the government of Ireland was again reorganized, involving further divisions, uncertainties, and delays. The power of the Irish council appointed on 17 August 1654 was due to expire in mid-August 1657 and, in fact, the councillors ceased their work slightly ahead of that deadline. The

[68] *TSP*, VI, pp. 648–651, 657–658, 660–662, 665–666.
[69] *TSP*, VI, p. 658.

power of Lord Deputy Fleetwood, who had also been appointed in summer 1654, was due to expire on 1 September 1657. Over the previous two years, Fleetwood had implied several times that he expected to return to Ireland in due course, there had been repeated rumours along those lines, and his supporters and Henry Cromwell's opponents had frequently agitated for his return. As the expiry of his three-year term approached, rumours, speculation, and agitation mounted. In fact, 1 September came and went with no decision taken in London and the Irish administration was left in limbo. Henry Cromwell used 'the leisure of this interregnum' to undertake 'a more nice inspection and visitation of our forces in severall places about the countrey'.[70] However, his attempts to appear nonchalant were undermined not only by his long and detailed letter distancing himself from a petition urging his appointment as lord deputy but also by his fears that the delay had been caused by doubts in London that he was suitable for appointment as head of the Irish administration, leading to renewed offers to stand down – 'If waveing mee would make that settlement more cleare, it were better to take it'.[71]

After several more weeks of drift, uncertainty, and rumour, in mid-November, Henry Cromwell was appointed and commissioned lord deputy of Ireland and authorized to govern Ireland in conjunction with an Irish council, which was named, appointed, and empowered at the same time.[72] The new, five-member council comprised no new members and all but one of the outgoing councillors; for, to his own dismay and Henry Cromwell's puzzlement and anger,[73] Robert Goodwin, one of the councillors who had generally supported Henry within the council, was dropped at this stage. On the one hand, Henry now had enhanced and more assured power to govern Ireland and no longer had to defer to the absentee and often obstructionist Fleetwood, who retained no office in or formal connection with Ireland. On the other hand, he now lacked a clear majority within the Irish council, because on key issues such as his religious reforms he often had only two supporters – Pepys and Bury – with Steele, Corbet, and Tomlinson opposing his policies. Moreover, Fleetwood's influence in political and military circles remained, and, in practice, the Protector and Protectoral Council continued to defer to him on Irish business.

During his year as lord deputy, from autumn 1657 to autumn 1658, Henry Cromwell continued, and in some areas developed or accelerated, the policies he had laid out during his opening two years

[70] *TSP*, VI, pp. 481–482.
[71] *TSP*, VI, pp. 446–447, 481–482.
[72] Dunlop, pp. 672–673.
[73] *TSP*, VI, pp. 599, 647, 648, 650, 661, 683.

in Ireland, most of them focused upon creating more moderate, stable, civilian, and traditional forms at the centre and in the provinces, and upon meeting the needs and aspirations of the 'old Protestants' in Ireland, whatever their former allegiances. Accordingly, in 1657–1658, Henry developed his existing policy of progressively restoring traditional forms of urban and rural administration, with the return of commissions of the peace working alongside the four central courts (so restoring much of the traditional judicial structure in Ireland), and with the issuing of new town charters to restore civilian urban government. There were rather fitful attempts to boost Irish trade and manufacturing, and particular efforts were made to improve some of the key Irish towns, many of them depopulated in the wake of the enforced removal of some or all of their Catholic inhabitants and in a state of physical, social, and economic decline. Many of these efforts focused upon Galway, singled out for state and private resettlement schemes aimed at restoring its commercial and mercantile sector. During a visit in early autumn 1656, Henry Cromwell saw the 'well-built and faire houses [. . .] verry much goeinge to decay for want of inhabitants', while noting the town's potential as a commercial and English colonial base and suggesting that 'if fully planted with English, [it would] have a very great influence for the awing the Irish in this province'.[74] In the end, the English government decided to pass large parts of the town to Gloucester, and later to Liverpool too, to settle the state's debts to those towns; this decision met with a mixed response in Ireland, with accurate predictions that few Gloucester or Liverpool merchants would actually relocate and that the scheme would do little to repopulate or revive the town.

Rather more successful was the awarding of property and trading rights in Wexford to the financier and entrepreneur Martin Noell in part settlement of his debt, for Noell did take an active interest in Wexford's established fisheries and worked to improve them. Elsewhere, the material and financial position of the Protestant church in Ireland was strengthened by the selective amalgamation of poor or thinly populated parishes to increase the salaries of incumbents. Efforts were made to improve education, with plans to establish and finance more primary schools and proposals to set up a second college at Dublin, although in practice few new schools were established over this period and Henry Cromwell's dreams of setting up a new college remained unfulfilled. On the other hand, he did succeed in purchasing and removing to Dublin the library of the late Archbishop Ussher; it later passed to Trinity College, Dublin, of which Henry served as chancellor during this period.

[74] *TSP*, V, p. 494.

Most of these policies of reform are recounted or alluded to in this collection. The correspondence also reveals how, during his year as lord deputy, Henry Cromwell had to struggle with the worsening financial situation in Ireland, exacerbated by the reduction of the English subsidies in the summer of 1657. Hopes that the second session of the second Protectorate parliament would produce a more beneficial financial settlement for Ireland – or at least vote money to pay off some or all of the growing and accumulated debt – were dashed when that session proved short, divisive, and unproductive. In early March 1658, James Standish was therefore dispatched to London by Henry Cromwell with instructions to brief the Protector about the financial situation in Ireland, to stress to him that, despite rigorous economies recently made to the civil and military budgets in Ireland, there was a large accumulated debt and a continuing monthly shortfall, and to seek both a one-off payment of £96,000 to clear the debts and a more generous monthly subsidy from the Protectoral treasury.[75] Although Standish duly lobbied the Protectoral central government in London and was strongly supported by a succession of letters from Henry Cromwell during the spring – increasingly urgent in tone, stressing the dire need for more money in Ireland, and commenting at one stage that 'Hunger will break through stone-walls'[76] – the mission was a failure and Standish returned to Dublin more or less empty-handed, as the growing debts of the Protectoral regime as a whole prevented a more generous provision for Ireland. Instead, by mid-summer Henry Cromwell and Thurloe were both looking to the meeting of another Protectorate parliament as the best and only way to rebuild the finances on both sides of the Irish Sea. However, the serious illness and then death of Oliver Cromwell disrupted plans to summon another parliament for the late summer or autumn of 1658.

The other major policy area that was considered and developed during Henry Cromwell's year as lord deputy was the organization of the Protestant church in Ireland in general and the funding of ministers there in particular. In 1655–1656, in the course of his battle with the Baptists and their allies, Henry was forced into an alliance with a group of Independent ministers, many of them based in and around Dublin and led by Samuel Winter. However, once the power of the radical sects had been broken, he slowly moved away from the Independents and adopted a more conservative religious stance. Thus, although he was initially suspicious of the loyalty of the Ulster Scots, in time he built bridges with them and their church, going out of his

[75] Dunlop, pp. 676–678.
[76] *TSP*, VII, p. 72.

way to conciliate the Presbyterians, allowing them to consolidate their hold over religious life in Ulster, appointing Presbyterians as salaried ministers elsewhere in Ireland (including in and around the capital), and employing a Presbyterian as one of his chaplains. Similarly, he came to support the work of an association of ministers based in and around Cork and led by Edward Worth, many of them former Anglicans and Episcopalians, though incorporating Presbyterians and adopting elements of the Presbyterian church structure. Indeed, he came to see in their regional structure and organization in southern Ireland a possible blue-print for a new national Protestant church throughout Ireland. At the same time, Henry came to see serious flaws in the system of church finance that he had inherited in Ireland: a hybrid scheme in which traditional tithes continued to be collected but with the proceeds going into the Irish treasury, out of which state salaries were paid to those ministers approved or appointed by the government. By 1657–1658 he was critical of this system on a number of grounds – because it was an uneasy mix, 'a mongrel way between salary and tythes' as he put it;[77] because it broke the direct link between congregation and minister at parish level; and because an overhaul of the accounting system in Ireland had revealed that the income from tithes and church lands was falling well short of the costs of the scheme and that ministers' salaries were therefore adding to the growing debts.

In light of this, Henry Cromwell decided to convene a meeting of selected ministers in Dublin in the spring of 1658, to discuss the organization of the church in Ireland and to resolve a rumbling debate about how ministers should be financed, which, he claimed, 'is grown to that scurvy pass' that something had to be done.[78] From 23 April until early May, between twenty and thirty invited ministers met in Dublin to debate the issues and to consider recommendations from Henry Cromwell that had, probably with difficulty and possibly only on Henry's casting vote, been endorsed by the Irish council. The convention strongly supported a proposal to apply throughout Ireland the type of church organization already practised by Worth's association in the south and the Scottish Presbyterians in Ulster, with tighter maintenance of and control over gospel ordinances and ministry, regular ordination, and a fixed, parish-based clergy supported by a return to traditional tithes. Although Worth was immediately dispatched to London to win the Protector's support for this scheme, and despite Henry Cromwell's attempts to claim overwhelming if not unanimous support for the plan,[79] it soon became

[77] *TSP*, VII, pp. 101–102.
[78] *TSP*, VII, pp. 21–22.
[79] *TSP*, VII, pp. 129–130, 145, 161–162.

apparent that the firmer Independents, especially Winter and his allies, were bitterly opposed to large parts of the scheme. Accordingly, as letters in this correspondence reveal, both sides carried the fight to the mainland, lobbying and seeking the support of the different religious factions in England, and attempting to gain access to and thus win over senior Protectoral politicians, especially the Protector himself. In practice, no clear resolution was achieved and little of the new national church structure was accepted, established, and in place in Ireland by the time Henry fell from power. However, during his last year there he did push ahead with changes to the funding of ministers and, during 1658–1659, he restored many direct tithes in Ireland, thus significantly reducing the financial drain of state salaries to ministers.

During the summer of 1658, Henry Cromwell was kept well informed of the declining health of his father – it is noticeable that his provincial tour was shorter than usual and that he was back in the capital much earlier than in previous years – and news of his father's death reached him in Dublin on 10 September, whereupon he immediately had his elder brother Richard proclaimed Protector.[80] He acted quickly to seek and receive declarations of support for the new Protector from the army officers and other officials in Ireland; and Henry offered his own warm support, writing via Thurloe on 11 September and sending a long letter direct to Richard on 18 September.[81]

While thanking his brother for offering to continue and renew his Irish appointment, Henry took the opportunity to wail about past 'burthens' with which he had been loaded since his appointment as lord deputy, including the manner in which Goodwin had been 'put [. . .] disgracefully out of the councill only for being faithfull to me', the necessity of working with a council that acted against him and encouraged others to 'revile and clamour against me', and the 'preposterous and absurd' way in which he had been required to conduct the recent disbandment. While offering to serve the new Protector in any capacity, Henry again sought permission to give up his Irish command, not least, he claimed, because his health was poor and 'I am not able to live always in the fire'. At the very least, he angled for permission to return to the mainland for a time, to confer with his brother in person as well as to enjoy a 'change of air and some recess [. . .] necessary for my health'.[82] As before, Henry's ruffled feathers were smoothed, he remained in office and in Ireland, and, by late September, the new Protector had decided to raise his title to that

80 *TSP*, VII, p. 383.
81 *TSP*, VII, pp. 383 and 400–401.
82 *TSP*, VII, pp. 400–401.

of lord lieutenant, though the formal commission was not received in Dublin until the beginning of November – 'I had great strivings within my breast, before I could prevail with myself to accept and open the commission', Henry wrote to his brother on 3 November.[83] The membership of the Irish council was unchanged, but Henry's standing there declined further when one of his strongest supporters within the council, Richard Pepys, died at the beginning of January 1659.

On several occasions before his appointment as lord lieutenant, Henry Cromwell had sought permission to visit the mainland. In particular, at the beginning of 1658, as the second session of the second Protectorate parliament approached, he clearly hoped that his membership of the new nominated second chamber would require or permit his presence in London for a time, allowing him to speak directly to his father about the needs of Ireland. However, his hopes were dashed and his attempts to mobilize friends to lobby the Protector on his behalf proved fruitless, for his father made clear that he was not 'at all [. . .] disposed' to allow his son to come over 'tho for never so small a time'.[84] However, during the autumn and winter of 1658–1659, after his brother's accession and his own appointment as lord lieutenant, Henry Cromwell pushed much longer and much harder to be permitted to come over. His attempts both to win permission to visit England and to engage friends and allies to promote his case dominated many of Henry's own letters of this period, just as reactions to those requests and reports on whether they were likely to be granted appear in many of the letters sent back to him in Dublin, including several in this collection. In November, Henry was furious when he discovered that his commission as lord lieutenant omitted – Thurloe subsequently claimed by pure mistake and oversight – the usual clause allowing a lord lieutenant to appoint and leave behind a deputy and to visit the mainland whenever he deemed it necessary.[85] During the autumn and winter, Henry sought permission to return, in part on health grounds – apparently perfectly genuine, for his correspondence at this time is littered with references to his illnesses and to his generally poor health. But more than that, he wanted to speak with and offer direct support to his brother, and to be on hand in London to help him quell growing disquiet and opposition in military circles. However, once more his hopes were dashed and his requests were successfully resisted, not only by the group of senior army officers based in and around London who orchestrated military

[83] *TSP*, VII, p. 492.
[84] *TSP*, VI, pp. 788–789.
[85] *TSP*, VII, pp. 492 and 497.

discontent and who eventually overthrew Richard, but also by allies of Henry and of the Protectoral regime who believed that he would be both safer in Ireland and better placed to support his brother from his Irish power base, should a crisis occur.

Thus Henry Cromwell remained in Ireland, watching from afar as his brother's Protectorate parliament met, and as opponents both inside and outside that parliament sought to weaken and undermine the Protectoral regime. He was kept very well informed of developments in London during the opening months of 1659, via the succession of letters that survive in this collection, and which recount in great detail events in parliament and in fair detail the growing discontent and dangers in army circles. Henry Cromwell's own views upon, and response to, these worrying developments are not so clear. While this collection gives insights into his views on the constitutional and kingship proposals of spring 1657, through the drafts of letters intended for Broghill, no such drafts survive from the period of Richard Cromwell's parliament, perhaps in part because Broghill's own political star had waned in the intervening two years and, although a member of the nominated other house, ill-health kept him away until the beginning of March.[86] Unfortunately, on this occasion the letters printed in *A Collection of the State Papers of John Thurloe* do not really fill the gap or fully flesh out the other side of the story, for Henry Cromwell's surviving correspondence to Thurloe and others of this period is infrequent and rather brief and cautious in commenting upon domestic political developments. Perhaps he was deliberately being rather guarded in committing his views to paper, or perhaps ill health really was taking a heavy toll by this stage.

By early May 1659, news had reached Henry Cromwell in Ireland that Richard had been forced to dissolve parliament and that a military coup had effectively curtailed, if not ended, his brother's power. Henry remained in Dublin for several more weeks, playing a waiting game, seeking fuller and clearer news of developments in London, and cautiously exploring his options. In June, one royalist correspondent summed up the position quite fairly, noting that Henry Cromwell was 'proceeding on in his former course, as if his brother were still protector. He is neither so active as he might be, to play his own game, nor so plyable as they would have him here to comply with theires'.[87] Henry dispatched agents to London, as well as a rather bland, noncommittal letter to Fleetwood, promising 'endeavours for the peace of this nation', and a more pointed letter to his brother,

[86] Little, *Lord Broghill*, pp. 167–168.
[87] *TSP*, VII, pp. 686–687.

seeking clear guidance from him as well as from God.[88] At length, once it was clear that there would be no real effort, either from the army in Scotland, or from the fleet, to save his brother's regime, and having received two letters from his brother, the final two datable items in this collection, bewailing his circumstances but failing to give clear directions,[89] Henry too decided to bow to events and to go quietly, rather than attempting to make a stand or to mount physical resistance in Ireland. Accordingly, on 15 June he signed a lengthy resignation letter, addressed to the speaker of the restored Rump, noting that, although he had heard 'nothing expressly' from his brother, he had received firm news that Richard was 'acquiescing' in the change of regime, and indicating that he too would stand aside rather than 'interrupt the peace of these nations'. In any case, he admitted that he had little 'affection' for the new regime and did not wish to continue in circumstances which were 'an indignity to those my neerest relations [. . . and] which inferres the diminution of my late father's honour and meritt', and so was 'ready to yeeld up my charge to any, whom you shall send to receive itt'.[90] After a further letter, confirming that he would obey the Rump's order to return to London and was handing over control to newly appointed parliamentary commissioners,[91] he left Ireland for good on 27 June. He arrived back in London on 2 July, tendered a final report on Ireland to the Rump's council, and then retired with his family to his in-laws' estate at Chippenham. At thirty-one, his political and military careers were over.

Henry Cromwell's record as chief administrator of Ireland was decidedly mixed. He helped shape a more moderate and less militarized approach to Ireland, marked by the return of many traditional forms of civilian rule there, and he reined in both the English army and radical dissent. His regime coincided with a period of order and stability and a modest economic recovery, and he worked with some success to restore elements of the former systems of justice and of urban and local government, and to consolidate the position of the Protestant church in Ireland. On the other hand, he failed to heal the divisions between the various Protestant groups or to establish a broadly supported new Protestant church settlement and, beyond occasional signs of unease and gestures to prominent individual Catholics, he did little to engage with or to ameliorate the position of the majority Catholic population of Ireland. Educational reforms

[88] *TSP*, VII, p. 674.
[89] Nos 519 and 520.
[90] *TSP*, VII, pp. 683–684.
[91] Published in *Mercurius Politicus*, 23–30 June, and quoted in Ramsey, *Henry Cromwell*, pp. 345–346.

stalled and appeals to London for help to improve Irish trade, abolish trade barriers between Ireland and England, protect Irish coasts, or reform Irish coinage largely fell on deaf ears. He was stymied by financial limitations as well as by political opposition or inertia on both sides of the Irish Sea, typified by the failure to appoint additional and supporting councillors and thus to assure him a secure majority in the Irish council. He reversed the imbalances introduced during the governorship of his predecessor and, by showing greater sensitivity to the needs of the Protestants in Ireland, helped to consolidate their hold on power and perhaps to win wider support in Ireland for his own rule and for the Protectoral regime in general. However, when that regime and his control were put to the test in the spring of 1659, he proved unable or unwilling to draw on Irish resources to try to prop up the tottering Protectorate; his own rule in Ireland ended suddenly and with a whimper.

This collection also ends in spring 1659, with a closing handful of items either dated or datable to the first half of May, charting or reflecting upon the collapse of the Protectorate and its immediate aftermath. Overall, the correspondence contains a mass of letters dominated by business that, although never trivial, at least to those concerned in it, might fairly be described as part of the essential routine of administering Ireland at this time: the attempts to find suitable candidates to fill senior political, administrative, and judicial posts in Ireland and to strengthen the Protestant ministry there; the numerous requests and recommendations from or about individuals seeking lesser offices and places in Ireland; the claims and counter-claims arising from the redistribution of land and the allocation of Irish property in lieu of service and arrears; the security of Ireland, including the disposition of troops and the condition of strongholds there; together with letters of courtesy, flattery, and religious exhortation sent to Henry from both sides of the Irish Sea. But, beyond that, the collection provides very rich insights into the government of England and Ireland during the period, the policies and issues pursued by the London and Dublin regimes, and the divisions and factions that at times wracked both, and the sometimes harmonious but often tense interplay between the key personnel and policies that dominated the Protectoral administrations in London and Dublin.

The collection gives a strong impression of Henry Cromwell, albeit often indirectly and through the words and impressions of others: a young man who was decent, honest, and hardworking; who applied himself, learnt quickly, and was able swiftly and usually accurately to weigh up people and siutations; but who was also touchy, thin-skinned, and prey to worries, suspicions, and over-reactions – Firth described Henry's own letters from Ireland as a 'long series of complaints' and felt they showed him to be 'absurdly sensitive to criticism'.[92] We gain an even stronger impression here of Henry's predecessor, brother-in-law, and partner-in-recrimination, Charles Fleetwood, whose letters to Henry are loaded with snide comments and criticisms dressed up as friendly advice, with hurt denials and counter-complaints in the face of Henry's accusations, all blended with oozing protestations of affection and brotherly love, and pious religious exhortation. In some ways, Henry Cromwell and Charles Fleetwood were made for each other.

Although this collection gives some insights into Richard Cromwell both before and after he became Protector (the former from his own slightly wordy and sometimes rather oddly phrased letters to his brother, the latter from the very detailed correspondence on the political and military manoeuvrings during the course of his Protectorate parliament), they pale beside the fascinating images we have here of Oliver Cromwell. There are numerous accounts of meetings with the Protector, particularly in 1655–1657, of discussions with and speeches by him, of Cromwell walking with colleagues around his chamber or glimpsed talking with others in the garden, of Cromwell and his wife sitting up with their ailing daughter, and of the Lord Protector reflecting upon his younger son and his handling of Ireland with such intense affection that he was moved to tears and moved others about him to tears as well. In the opening months of 1657, Henry was both cautioned and reassured by his father-in-law in respect of his relationship with the Protector: 'His Highnes tells me that he heares but seldome from you. I thought good to let you understand so much. He hath, I doe perceive, a love for you, and mentions you with a kind of delight and satisfaction'.[93] Such reassurances sustained Henry Cromwell during his years in Ireland but could do little to reinforce his crumbling power in spring 1659.

After leaving Ireland, Henry Cromwell spent the remainder of his life in quiet retirement in Cambridgeshire. He was not seriously troubled either by the returning republican regime or by the restored Stuarts, though he took care in 1660–1661 to mobilize friends and to write to key figures, including a petition to the king, stressing his loyalty and obedience to Charles II and claiming that, while in Ireland, he had consistently sought to

> study to preserve the peace, plenty and splendour of that kingdom, did encourage a learned ministry, giving not only protection but maintenance to several Bishops there; placed worthy persons in the seats of judicature and

[92] C.H. Firth, 'Cromwell, Henry', in L. Stephen and S. Lee (eds), *Dictionary of National Biography*, 63 vols (Oxford, 1885–1900); Firth, *Last Years*, II, p. 128.
[93] No. 159.

> magistracy, and to his own great prejudice upon all occasions was favourable to your Majesty's professed friends.[94]

Henry was not excepted from the general pardon and, although he lost land in England and Ireland, he was able to retain some property in both countries. In the early 1660s, he acquired Spinney Abbey at Wicken in Cambridgeshire from the Russells, and he spent his final decade there, apparently maintaining a bare conformity with the established church, for a time retaining a chaplain who employed the prayer book 'as little as was possible' but ending his employment when the authorities became interested,[95] and visiting and caring for elderly and dying members of his family, including his mother and a paternal aunt. He drew up his will in 1673, a typically brisk, brief, and business-like document, with little about his faith or the future of his soul or mortal remains, and leaving everything to his 'deare and wel beloved wife' to share out between their surviving children as she saw fit.[96] He died, reportedly of the stone, on 23 March 1674, aged forty-six, and was buried two days later in Wicken church. His widow, who did not remarry and who died in April 1687, lies beside him beneath an inscribed marble slab.

[94] J. Waylen, *The House of Cromwell and the Story of Dunkirk* (London, 1897), pp. 25–26.
[95] M. Storey (ed.), *Two East Anglian Diaries, 1641–1729* (Woodbridge, 1994), pp. 97–103.
[96] National Archives, PROB 11/346, q. 123.

EDITORIAL APPROACH AND TECHNIQUES

This new edition spans the entire Henry Cromwell collection in the three Lansdowne volumes and covers all 536 seventeenth-century items contained within them. The overwhelming majority of the letters are transcribed in full and the entire texts are reproduced here. In a small number of cases the contents are briefly noted; they are not calendared. This applies mainly to minor letters of recommendation, courtesy, or religious exhortation; letters which merely repeat the contents of an earlier letter by that author; some of the more minor letters dealing with disputes over private business affairs or land allocated in Ireland; and the miscellaneous items of non-correspondence. Thus, in this edition, items are either reproduced in full or they are briefly noted; no letter is partly transcribed and partly noted and no letter is calendared. The overwhelming majority of the items, either dated or closely datable, have been arranged in a single chronological sequence, while the few items that cannot be assigned a fairly narrow date range have been placed at the end, followed by the handful of miscellaneous items. Throughout, the aim has been to produce a readable and easily accessible edition of the correspondence, while broadly adhering to the principles and practices recommended in R. F. Hunnisett, *Editing Records for Publication* (London, 1977).

The heading to each item, opening with the item number, is a modern addition. The author's name, both forename (where known) and surname, have been given in a consistent and unabbreviated form. Unless an addressee's name is also given in the heading, the item was addressed to Henry Cromwell. Where the writer's provenance was stated at the head or foot of the letter or in the contemporary endorsement, this has been noted in the heading, generally using modern and consistent spelling of place names, although, if the original spelling was unusual or creates some doubt, it is given in that form in the heading and modern identification is attempted in an appended footnote. In a few cases, especially rather small towns and villages in Ireland, the county name has then been added in squared brackets to help readers identify the location. However, provenances have not been given in the modern headings where none was specified either at the head or foot of the letter or in the endorsement, even if the contents of the letter make it perfectly clear that it was written from, say, London or Dublin. The dates are taken from the letters themselves, again either from the letter head or from the contemporary endorsement. Where it is apparent that those contemporary dates are incorrect, or where incomplete or absent dates can be completed or corrected from the contents of the letter, the additional or amended dates have been entered within square brackets. Dates are generally Old Style, though with the year taken to begin on 1 January; however, in the case of a small number of letters written from the continent, either both Old Style and New Style dates have been entered by the writer or it is now unclear which dating style the writer was adopting. The heading closes by giving the volume and folio number of the letter as currently arranged by the British Library.

Where the contents of a letter have been noted and summarized rather than transcribed, that summary is set in italics, to distinguish it clearly from transcribed material. In the texts of the transcribed letters, the original spelling has been retained; but standard abbreviations, where (though only where) indicated in the original, have been silently expanded, the use of 'u' and 'v' and 'i' and 'j' has been regularized according to modern usage, and the 'con'/'cion' suffix has consistently been amended to the modern 'tion' form. Punctuation and capitalization have been modernized and the use of capitals kept to a minimum. In the case of possessives, an apostrophe has been added, but no new 's' has been inserted where not present in the original. The original paragraph structure has generally been retained, even where out of kilter with modern usage, but occasionally enormously long paragraphs have been silently divided by a new paragraph break to aid the reader. In the main, deleted words and passages, even where still perfectly legible, have been silently omitted; however, where they have significantly changed or apparently garbled the original meaning, they have been noted within angle brackets, thus '< >'; in the small number of draft out-letters written by Henry Cromwell, the deleted material has always been included, again indicated by placing that material within angle brackets. Square brackets have only been employed in the text in conjunction with ellipses, while rounded brackets have been used to show parentheses in the original. Underlinings in the original have also been retained and shown as such, though it is, of course, impossible to be certain whether such markings were made by the writer, the original recipient, or a later reader. Apart from those letters which are summarized, all the text has been transcribed here and an attempt has been made to give a reading for every (undeleted) word, even those that are poorly formed or have been heavily amended: if the reading of a word is uncertain, this has been indicated through an appended footnote. Where the paper has been damaged and some of the original text has apparently been lost, this has been shown as '[. . .]' in the main text, and in most cases an appended footnote indicates the extent of the damage or tries to supply the missing letters, word, or words. Occasional slips of the pen, omissions, and repetitions by the writers have been indicated, and corrections and additions suggested through footnotes.

As well as clarifying textual issues, the footnotes seek to provide sufficient factual context and information to allow clear comprehension of the individuals and issues being discussed. Full and quite detailed information is provided about people, places, and events in or relevant to English and Irish developments over this period; the small number of letters written from abroad, especially by diplomatic agents and others, and passages concerned with foreign developments not directly or immediately relevant to the domestic English and Irish focus of this correspondence, have been annotated more lightly. Where letters in this collection are closely linked to other surviving correspondence or associated papers now found in Abbott, *TSP*, Dunlop, *CSPI*, and the *Clarke Papers*, cross-reference to this material has been made via footnotes. (For full details of these works, see the list of abbreviations on p. ix.)

Many of the footnotes provide biographical information about the writers and about other figures to whom reference is made within the correspondence, and a short biographical sketch will generally be found at an individual's first appearance, although some obscure or minor characters receive no supporting biography. The biographical information contained in the footnotes is drawn in the main from the works listed below. These works are generally not individually acknowledged in the biographical footnotes, although any additional sources drawn upon or referred to are referenced at that point.

W.C. Abbott (ed.), *The Writings and Speeches of Oliver Cromwell*, 4 vols (Cambridge, MA, 1937–1947);

M. Ashley, *Financial and Commercial Policy Under the Cromwellian Protectorate* (Oxford, 1934);

G.E. Aylmer, *The State's Servants* (London, 1973);

T. Barnard, *Cromwellian Ireland,* paperback edition with new foreword (Oxford, 2000);

T. Birch (ed.), *A Collection of the State Papers of John Thurloe, Esquire*, 7 vols (London, 1742);

K.S. Bottigheimer, *English Money and Irish Land* (Oxford, 1971);

D. Brunton and D.H. Pennington (eds), *Members of the Long Parliament* (London, 1954);

B. Capp, *Cromwell's Navy* (Oxford, 1989);

G.E. Cokayne (ed.), *The Complete Baronetcy of England, Scotland and Ireland*, 6 vols (Exeter, 1900–1909);

G.E. Cokayne (ed.), *The Complete Peerage of England, Scotland and Ireland*, 8 vols (London, 1887–1898);

F.D. Dow, *Cromwellian Scotland* (Edinburgh, 1979);

R. Dunlop (ed.), *Ireland under the Commonwealth*, 2 vols but with continuous pagination (Manchester, 1913);

C.H. Firth (ed.), *The Clarke Papers*, 4 vols (London, 1891–1901);

C.H. Firth and G. Davies, *The Regimental History of Cromwell's Army*, 2 vols (Oxford, 1940);

C.H. Firth and R.S. Rait, *Acts and Ordinances of the Interregnum*, 3 vols (London, 1911);

J. Foster (ed.), *Alumni Oxonienses. . .1500–1714*, 4 vols (Oxford, 1891–1892);

M.A.E. Green (ed.), *Calendar of State Papers, Domestic, 1649–1659*, 12 vols (London, 1875–1886);

M.A.E. Green (ed.), *Calendar of the Proceedings of the Committee for Compounding etc, 1643–1660*, 5 vols (London, 1889–1892);

B.D. Henning (ed.), *The House of Commons, 1660–90*, 3 vols (London, 1983);

M.F. Keeler, *The Members of the Long Parliament* (Philadelphia, PA, 1954);

P. Little, 'Irish representation in the Protectorate Parliaments', *Parliamentary History*, 23 (2004), pp. 336–356;

R.P. Mahaffy (ed.), *Calendar of the State Papers relating to Ireland: of the reign of Charles I*, 4 vols (London, 1900–1903);

H.C.G. Matthew and B. Harrison (eds), *Oxford Dictionary of National Biography*, 60 vols (Oxford, 2004);

A.G. Matthews, *Calamy Revised* (Oxford, 1934);

A.G. Matthews, *Walker Revised* (Oxford, 1948);

R.W. Ramsey, *Henry Cromwell* (London, 1933);

J.T. Rutt (ed.), *The Diary of Thomas Burton, Esquire*, 4 vols (London, 1828);

St. J.D. Seymour, *The Puritans in Ireland* (Oxford, 1921);

L. Stephen and S. Lee (eds), *Dictionary of National Biography*, 63 vols (Oxford, 1885–1900);

D. Underdown, *Pride's Purge* (Oxford, 1971);

J. and J.A. Venn (eds), *Alumni Cantabrigienses. . .to 1751*, 4 vols (Cambridge, 1922–1927);

A. H. Woolrych, *Commonwealth to Protectorate* (Oxford, 1982);

A.B. Worden, *The Rump Parliament* (Cambridge, 1974).

THE CORRESPONDENCE OF HENRY CROMWELL 1655–1659

1654

1. From John Gerald, Dublin, 24 April 1654, 821, fos 1–2.

Letter of request, seeking charitable relief and support to help lift the writer and his family out of their sad condition; refers to an earlier unanswered letter to the same purpose of July 1653 and expresses regret at his failure to wait on Henry Cromwell in person during the latter's recent visit to Ireland.[1]

[1] Henry Cromwell was sent by his father on a brief mission to Ireland in March 1654 but was there for less than three weeks.

1655

2. From Arthur Annesley[1] to Charles Fleetwood, London, 8 May 1655, 821, fos 3–4.

May it please your lordship,

Though my personall attendance on your lordship receives a discontinuance by my absence from Ireland, I cannot so much forget the obligation of that noble respect vouchsafed me there and the authority of your lordship's commands as not to waite on your lordship by my letters till a new oportunity admitt me againe the honour of kissing your lordship's hands. And though the impression I am under of your lordship's high civilityes might justifye large acknowledgments, yet beleeving your lordship delights more in obligeing acts then the repetition of them, I forbeare saying more then that I shall retayne a due resentment of my great ingagements to appeare your lordship's servant and am ambitious to receive some commands from your lordship which may witnesse you are pleased so to account of me.

I presume your lordship hath from more knowing hands an account of passages here, yet because in great variety something may be omitted, I shall adventure to acquaint your lordship that though severall at Salisbury and Exceter were condemned for the late action under Sir Joseph Wagstaffe, yet very few of them have beene executed and none of the ringleaders.[2] In the north nothing was done at all, it being judged but a riott, but at the returne of the judges to London justice Newdigate and baron Thorpe were displaced and the first of them practized the next day at the barres in Westminster Hall.[3] At the beginning of the terme the old masters of the chancery were by

[1] Irish-born parliamentarian politician and administrator, excluded from parliament at Pride's Purge, whose political career did not fully resume until the end of the 1650s, but who held minor posts in England and Ireland during the Protectorate and who was returned for Dublin to the third Protectorate parliament. In 1658, Henry Cromwell recommended him for favour as 'a person of eminent parts and abilities [. . .] of sobriety and good affection' to the government (*TSP*, VI, p. 777).

[2] In the aftermath of the royalist rebellion led by John Penruddock, and following trials at Exeter, Chard, and Salisbury, around forty participants were condemned, but in the end only twelve were executed for treason, during the second and third weeks of May.

[3] Judges Richard Newdigate and Francis Thorpe, sent north to try another clutch of royalists at York during April, had questioned whether opposition to the Protectorate could be deemed treason in law and whether the regime's treason ordinance of January 1654 had any legal standing. Although proceedings were abandoned on grounds of insufficient

warrant of the Protector read in court discharged and a lesse number of new ones put in their places. And the commissioners of the great seale, though with much reluctancy and after long opposition, doe now act upon the Protector's new regulation.[4] The last newes from the fleet bound for the Indies is that just five weekes after they loosed from England they arrived at the Barbathoes where they tooke above 20 Dutch vessells trading contrary to the treaty and, takeing in 3,000 fresh men and foure troopes of horse, went on their voyage.[5] The articles of peace with the French seeme all passed but yet the signature is delayed by the Protector, which occasioned their embassador to move for a farewell audience which hath been yet put of, the Spanish embassador being dayly expected, who is at length come very gallantly attended and hath his audience this afternoon. It is said he comes to recapitulate the many civilityes and friendly offices shewed by that crowne to our nation and to expostulate the unkind returnes we have made and to make a quick tryall whither we intend to be upon fairer termes with them.[6] Others are confident that we are at a good correspondence with the Spaniard and that we doe nothing in the Indies but by his permission. This conceipt hath little ground, but a short time will unfold the mistery. Here is newly published a strict proclamation against papists receiveing againe the oath of abjuration.[7] Very few ships are appointed for the summer guard. The army here consent to a reducement and I heare all lieutenant-collonells and lieutenants of horse and foot will be put out of the establishment. I beleeve it will be yet six weekes before the lord Harry or any more judges come thither, though the great seale will be sooner finished.

evidence, Newdigate and Thorpe were summoned before the council on 3 May, questioned and dismissed.

[4] Various officials who opposed and had refused to implement the reforming chancery ordinance of August 1654 were brought into line or removed at the start of the new legal term, especially lords commissioners Bulstrode Whitelocke and Sir Thomas Widdrington, who, following a further month of defiance and not, as suggested here, reluctant compliance, were finally dismissed on 6 June.

[5] The fleet embarked in late December 1654 and arrived off Barbados by the end of January. Much to the dismay of the planters, several Dutch vessels that had been trading with them, in defiance of the 1651 navigation act and of terms confirmed by the Anglo-Dutch treaty of April 1654, were quickly seized. During February and March, 3–4,000 additional troops, predominantly foot though with a few horse, were raised locally and added to the expedition.

[6] The Protectorate was still being courted by both the French and Spanish governments and a new Spanish mission, led by the Marquis of Lede, arrived in London in early May. Not until the autumn was a treaty with France finally concluded and war against Spain formally declared.

[7] A proclamation of the Protector of 24 April called for the rigorous application of existing laws against Catholic priests, Jesuits, and Popish recusants, stressing that suspected recusants take the oath of abjuration – denying Papal supremacy, transubstantiation, purgatory, image worship, and salvation by good works – clearly and without reservation or equivocation.

My leaving Ireland fell so unhappily upon a busy day with your lordship that I could not move your lordship concerning the restraint laid upon Sir Maurice Eustace[8] by colonel Harbert's[9] letter adviseing him in the name of the councell not to goe into Ireland. But when I first mentioned it to your lordship, I found you inclinable to take it of, and truly, my lord, it will no wayes conduce to the good of Ireland that such usefull instruments as he be discouraged or diverted from goeing thither. Therefore I beseech your lordship let it be your owne act of justice to leave him as free as before. My lord, I am very sencible of your many waighty affaires and therefore will conclude this interruption by presentment of my most humble service to my lady, subscribing myselfe, my lord,

Your lordship's most humble servant,
Arthur Annesley

I presented your lordship's letter to the Lord Protector.

3. From William Stane,[10] London, 5 June 1655, 821, fos 5–6.

Letter of request, seeking help in resolving a matter of business involving Sir William Sidley's[11] *reluctance to sell some unspecified property to colonel Sandys*[12] *and Sir John Pettus,*[13] *with Mr Hampden*[14] *and Stane himself acting as intermediaries; requests Henry Cromwell to intervene and speak to Sidley, who was recently at*

[8] Irish politician and judge and a royalist, he was imprisoned in Chester in 1648–1655 but then returned to Ireland and resumed legal practice in Dublin. Although initially viewed with suspicion, by the later 1650s he had won Henry Cromwell's confidence and was involved in various legal and educational matters. In March 1659, Henry supported Eustace's claim to Irish lands and noted that 'I am beholding to this gentleman, and doe owe him a kindnesse' (*TSP*, VII, p. 635).

[9] Thomas Herbert, parliamentarian administrator, served as a military commissioner during the 1640s, and attended Charles I during his captivity in 1647–1649. He served as a parliamentary commissioner in Ireland from 1649 and as secretary to the Irish council from its inception in 1654. He was trusted by Henry Cromwell and knighted by him in 1658.

[10] Stane/Stanes, a distinguished physician, was a parliamentarian administrator and commissary-general of musters in the general staff of the New Model Army.

[11] Sir William Sidley/Sedley had estates in Kent and elsewhere. He married Jane, Dowager Baroness Chandos in autumn 1655 but died the following year.

[12] Robert Saunders, parliamentarian officer, colonel of a foot regiment that served in Ireland in the early 1650s, and later governor of Youghal and Kinsale.

[13] Probably the Sir John Pettus who was a politician and also an active royalist in his native East Anglia and elsewhere during the civil war. He compounded after the war but was arrested and imprisoned by the republican regime in 1650, though he was soon released, perhaps through the intercession of Charles Fleetwood, to whom he was distantly related by marriage. He professed loyalty to the Protectorate.

[14] Probably Richard Hampden, parliamentarian politician – he represented his native Buckinghamshire in the second Protectorate parliament – and second son of John Hampden, the ship-money opponent and parliamentarian hero.

Cromwell's lodgings,[15] *in support of the transaction; and indicates that the intending purchasers were now willing to offer £10,000, well above the £8,200 that the land was really worth.*

4. From Richard Kingdon[16] to Charles Fleetwood, 19 June 1655, 821, fos 7–8.

May it please your excellency,

The particulars I gave your lordship an accoumpt of in my last were on Wednesday morning past the councell and drawne into instructions to this effect: your lordship and the councell are impowered either for a valuable consideration in land or some other way to compound with persons' protests on whose estates there is any incumbrance; where any incumbrance is on an Irish papist's estate the value of the incumbrance is first to bee substracted and the person concerned to receive his land in Connaught according to his qualification in proportion to what remained of his estate after such substraction made; the county of Lowthis to bee deemed in Leinster; noe Protestant delinquent to compound after the 25th of December next, but estates of theirs uncompounded for are lyable to satisfy debts as other forfeited lands in Ireland; that a committee of articles bee impowred to state matter of fact in cases of articles in Ireland and transmitt their judgement to the committee of articles here; that your lordship and the councell may satisfy the arreares of widdowes in Ireland and setle the lands due for such arreare to the use of the commonwealth; that the adventurer and souldier have transferred to them the right the commonwealth hath in any lease made of lands fallen to their lott, and your lordship and counsell to appoint persons as a chancery in the case where instructions for letting have not beene pursued or conditions not observed; the act of oblivion not to extend to estates in Ireland. Your lordship will alsoe receive a letter signifying the councell's desire to know wherein any doubt lyes in the instructions and to receive your sense thereof.[17]

On Friday[18] the lord Henery went hence toward Chester about three of the clock in the afternoone. There accompanyed his lordship the lord Lambert, lord Lawrence, colonel Jones, colonel Sydenham,

[15] At this time Henry Cromwell had lodgings off Whitehall, as well as apartments at the palaces of Whitehall and Hampton Court.

[16] Dublin merchant and administrator, employed by the Irish government on several missions to London during the 1650s, including by Henry Cromwell in spring 1656 (*TSP*, IV, p. 672).

[17] A sound summary of the new, additional instructions passed by Protector and council on 13 June (Dunlop, pp. 518–520).

[18] 15 June.

Sir Gilbert Pickering, lord Strickland, colonel Montague and severall others.[19] These went three mile and there parted. His lordship commanded mee to stay and come with Sir John Temple[20] with the great seale and attend him at Chester this next Saterday, which I am not in a capacity to doe because the great seale will not bee perfected till Saturday. The courts of justice are thus provided with judges: lord cheife justice Peppys and justice Cooke for the common pleas; lord cheife justice Lowther and justice Donnellon for the upper bench; lord cheife barron Corbett and barron Carew for the exchequer; the lords cheife justices and cheife barron to bee commissioners for the great seale and sit in chancery.[21] The £40,000 ordered to bee sent in specie comes in soe slowly that I cannot give any accompt when it's\ like to bee setting forward, though I shall not loose any opportunity to further it whyle I stay. The Spannish ambassador is gone away in displeasure. Our fleet in the Indyes were at Christopher's the 8th of May and tooke in 1,500[22] men. The supplyes for colonel Humphrye's[23] regiment that went with major Sedgewick[24] are gone towards them.

[19] All those named here – John Lambert, Henry Lawrence, Philip Jones, William Sydenham, Sir Gilbert Pickering, Walter Strickland, and Edward Montague – were members of the Protectoral council.

[20] Irish-born parliamentarian judge and politician, excluded from parliament at Pride's Purge, and out of office since the regicide. On indicating that he was willing to resume public office, and with the Protector's strong support (Abbott, III, pp. 722–723), he returned to Ireland in the summer of 1655 and resumed his old office as master of the rolls there.

[21] The list of judges appointed in mid-June is slightly garbled. Richard Pepys and John Cooke were nominated to the upper bench and Sir Gerard Lowther and James Donnellan to common pleas, with Miles Corbet and Edward Carey to the exchequer (Dunlop, pp. 520–521). In fact, Cooke and Carey declined these offices and, much to Henry Cromwell's dismay (*TSP*, IV, pp. 40, 376, 508, 606), Donnellan's appointment was deferred, probably because of his Irish connections, since he was the son of the late Nehemiah Donnellan, archbishop of Tuam.

[22] Second numeral amended and unclear, though it appears to be '5'. This is probably a reference to a foot regiment of around 1,200 men, raised on St Christopher (St Kitts) and adjoining islands, which joined the main expeditionary force on 7–8 April, not May.

[23] John Humphrey, parliamentarian officer, formerly a dragoon commander serving in Scotland in the early 1650s, commanded a foot regiment in the expeditionary force. It was ravaged by ill health upon landing in Barbados in August 1655 and Humphrey himself pestered to be allowed home, eventually being given permission to return to England on health grounds in October 1656.

[24] Robert Sedgwick, merchant and pro-parliamentarian officer in New England in the 1640s and early 1650s. In 1654 he was given command of a naval detachment in America and in the summer of 1655 he led 12 ships and 800 men to reinforce the West Indies expedition. He helped to establish English civil government in Jamaica in 1655–1656; in May 1656 he was appointed commander-in-chief of the army in the West Indies, but he died of natural causes before the month was out.

Adjutant gennerall Allen,[25] controller Tomlins[26] and their wives went yesterday toward Chester. Major Rawlins[27] sets forwards tomorrow. The courts of justice will not bee filled up untill your lordship's sense bee knowne. Doctor Stanes hath beene lately sik. Colonel Rich[28] his wife is dead and soe is Sir William Constable.[29] I crave your lordship's pardon for my troublesome lines and remaine, my lord,

Your excellencye's very faithfull and obliged servant,

Ri Kingdon

I have since the writing hereof received a letter from my lord Henery who was at Northampton last night.[30]

5. From S. Fisher, London, 5 August 1655, 821, fos 9–10.

May it please your lordship,

I suppose it is not unknowne to your lordship that his Highness hath ordered two horses for the greate sadle to be sent your lordship, which are the chesnutt and the spott that come from Oldenbergh,[31] which togeather with the pad that Mr Rey bought wilbe redy to sett forwards on thire jorny as soone as theire sadles and other necessary furniture are made. I was desired by my lord Cleypoole[32] to acquant

[25] William Allen, parliamentarian officer, adjutant-general of the horse in Ireland, had been arrested in England early in 1655 on suspicion of disaffection to the government, but, on promising loyalty to the Protectorate, he was released and allowed to keep his commission. He was one of the leading Baptist officers who opposed Henry Cromwell's religious policy in 1655–1656 and one of four who resigned at the end of 1656.

[26] Edward Tomlins, parliamentarian officer, comptroller of the train in Ireland under Henry Cromwell.

[27] Thomas Rawlins, parliamentarian officer and military administrator in Ireland under Henry Cromwell.

[28] Nathaniel Rich, parliamentarian officer and politician, campaigned in the civil war under the Earl of Manchester and then, in 1645, was given command of a New Model horse regiment. He held aloof from the regicide but supported the republic and was elected to the Rump in February 1649, though he supported its ejection in 1653. However, he quickly became disillusioned with the Protectorate, perhaps because it ran against his radical religious aspirations, was dismissed from the army in 1654 because of his political and religious disaffection, and thereafter was repeatedly arrested, questioned, and imprisoned. He did not return to favour and to military command until spring 1659, after the fall of the Protectorate. His first wife was Elizabeth, daughter of Sir Edmund Hampden and sister of John Hampden, the ship-money hero.

[29] Parliamentarian politician and a regicide, he died on 15 June.

[30] Having travelled through the Midlands to Chester and Holyhead, Henry Cromwell and his retinue were then delayed by bad weather but eventually crossed to Dublin during the second week of July (*TSP*, III, pp. 581, 614, 632).

[31] During 1654, the Protector had acquired several horses from the Duke of Oldenburgh.

[32] John Claypole, the Protector's son-in-law and a Protectoral courtier and politician, was master of the horse.

your lordship with this, as also to derect for theire jorny, and I have advised them to goe safly to West Chester and to receve your lordship's further order from Mr Wally[33] wheather to ship them att Neston or goe to Hollyhed. Mr Kerk hath in his custody a plaine hunting horse which (he saith) is as good as any he knoweth in England of thirty pound price, and it is possible your lordship may send time enough to have him com with the other horses, which if your lordship please to derect to Dr Harrison.[34] I will not presume to trouble your lordship with any apollogie for myselfe, only that I beg the honour of being in your lordship's good opinion and that your lordship would beleeve me to be, my lord,

Your lordship's ever faithfull and most obedient servant,

S Fisher

6. From William Stane to Charles Fleetwood, 28 August 1655, 821, fos 11–12.

My lord,

I received your lordship's of the 22 instant last night. I shall (if the Lord please) bee at Chester the 8 of September if not before.[35] Concerning Wallingford,[36] I gave your lordship formerly an account that her Highnes had taken of Sir Gilbert Pickering[37] and so I hope there will bee provision for all your family. But I tell your lordship truly Mrs Blofeild[38] will bee put to it, especially if you bring more company. I feare your lordship should have remov'd coaches only. I suppose the horse litter will serve some of the children and your sister Duckenfeild's[39] coach will help, and it's not improbable that colonel Zancky[40] will bring his; also there will bee a hackney coach at

[33] Charles Whalley, military commissioner at Chester for Irish affairs.

[34] Thomas Harrison, minister in New England during the 1640s and in London in the early 1650s, became a confidant of Henry Cromwell and accompanied him to Ireland, living in his household, probably acting as a personal chaplain, holding a salaried position at Christ Church, Dublin, and advising the Irish government on religious matters.

[35] Fleetwood and his retinue embarked from Ireland on 6 September.

[36] Wallingford House, near Whitehall, which henceforth served as Fleetwood's London home.

[37] Probably acting in his capacity as the Protector's lord chamberlain.

[38] Presumably the housekeeper at Wallingford House.

[39] Martha, daughter of Sir Miles Fleetwood and thus the sister of Charles Fleetwood, was the wife of Robert Duckenfield, parliamentarian officer and politician, governor of Chester and the Isle of Man in the early 1650s. His principal seat was Duckenfield Hall near Stockport in north-east Cheshire.

[40] Hierome/Jerome Sankey/Zanchy, parliamentarian officer and politician, commanded a New Model horse regiment, which served in Ireland from 1649 onwards, and he held a variety of senior military and administrative posts in Ireland throughout the 1650s; he was

Wrexham much about that tyme and besides I have a reserve in my thoughts. I am so true to your judgement that I bring no body, not so much as Mr Stirrop.[41]

But that is no remedy. The ladyes (and I think my lord Richard,[42] who is now at White Hall), my lord Lambert[43] and colonel Sydny[44] will give your lordship and my lady a meet somwhere. The ladyes would have bin neer Northampton and would have bin going next week, but I tell them your lordship may come by Woodstock and so have put a stop to it till your lordship is come to Chester and so notice may bee given thence or in the way. I have bin twice to seek Mrs Blofeild tooday but missed her. Shee shall have your directions conserning the beds right as shee hath your lettre. Here is no news, all is quiett and more so then it hath bin, only an ill libell written. My lord Lambert and your lordship is mentioned, a pitifull engine.[45] I know you may have thoughts of hurt, but truly God is good to Isreall. Hee hath bin so to your lordship in Ireland and otherwise. My Lord Protector is very kinde to you. I moved his Highnes about Wysset and that said

elected to all three Protectorate parliaments, being returned for Irish constituencies to the first and third. Although Henry Cromwell initially distrusted him, at least in part because of his Baptist sympathies, in 1656 he noted Sankey's apparent compliance while remaining suspicious of him, writing that 'I dare not too much boaste of him at present, least he should leave me in the lurch' and 'I'll trust [him] as farre as I cane see hime' (*TSP*, IV, pp. 376, 407–408, 483–484). Indeed, although for a time Sankey seemed reasonably loyal and won a degree of acceptance and guarded trust, his qualms about the Protectorate came to the surface early in 1659 and led him openly to oppose the regime.

[41] Possibly the Nathaniel Stirrup who in 1656 was appointed a commissioner for discovering concealed property.

[42] Richard Cromwell, eldest son of the Protector and thus Henry Cromwell's elder brother.

[43] John Lambert, senior parliamentarian officer and politician, rose to prominence during the 1640s as a senior officer in northern England, successively holding command of a number of horse and foot regiments. Although he did not campaign in Ireland, in 1650–1651 he strongly supported Oliver Cromwell in Scotland. For a time during the 1650s he was one of the most influential military and civilian politicians, close to Cromwell, an architect of the Protectorate, a Protectoral councillor, and perhaps the second most powerful figure in the Protectoral regime. He was elected to all three Protectorate parliaments.

[44] Perhaps Algernon Sidney, parliamentarian officer and politician, who campaigned in both England and Ireland in the civil wars, but his republican principles led him to hold aloof from the Protectorate. Or perhaps his brother, Philip Sidney, who was an active supporter of the Protectorate and held high office as a Protectoral councillor; but he is invariably referred to at this time by his courtesy title of Lord or Viscount Lisle. It is more likely, therefore, that this is a slightly garbled or strangely abbreviated reference to William Sydenham, parliamentarian officer and politician, who had campaigned in and around his native Dorset in the civil war and was for a time military governor of Weymouth and the Isle of Wight. A Protectoral councillor and elected to both of Oliver Cromwell's Protectorate parliaments, Sydenham was often an ally of Lambert during the 1650s.

[45] *A Short Discovery of His Highness the Lord Protector's Intentions Touching the Anabaptists in the Army*. George Thomason dated his copy 20 August and noted that it had been scattered in the streets at night.

moietie.[46] Hee hath refered it to my lord president[47] who promises his care, and Mr Stirrop and colonel Lloid[48] must follow it. It's of no small moment, some £2,000. I doubt wee shall do no good there as to Metheld,[49] but may do somwhat another way. Wee did before hand provide £2 or 300 for your lordship in case of need. My wife's and my humble and affectionate services to my lady and yourselfe. The children are well. My lord,

Your very[50] servant,

W Stane

I do intend to come on part of my way for Chester toomorrow; I shall take Worcestershire by the way.

7. From John Stone[51] to [Charles Fleetwood or Henry Cromwell],[52] London, 4 September 1655, 821, fo. 13.

Letter of recommendation on behalf of Mr Ogle, nephew of Mr Ogle, MP,[53] *seeking military employment in Ireland.*

8. From Francis Russell,[54] Chippenham, 10 September 1655, 821, fos 14–15.

My lord,

If two of my letters since you went for Ireland have miscarryed I hope you will pardon me and think that others have bin negligent

[46] Fleetwood was seeking discharge of the balance of £1,918 due on several properties in Suffolk and Norfolk, including Wysset le Rose, settled on him by parliament in July 1651.

[47] Henry Lawrence, president of the council.

[48] Probably Griffith Lloyd, parliamentarian officer, captain in Fleetwood's New Model horse regiment, and a trusted colleague.

[49] Possibly Methwold in Norfolk.

[50] Word apparently omitted.

[51] Parliamentarian officer, politician, and administrator, who held a string of mainly financial offices – in the exchequer, wine office, and customs office – during the Protectorate and who was elected to all three Protectorate parliaments.

[52] There is no surviving endorsement or cover sheet, so it is not clear whether this letter was addressed to Fleetwood as the departing lord deputy or to Henry Cromwell as the incoming chief administrator of Ireland.

[53] Henry Ogle, parliamentarian politician, represented the northern counties of England in the Nominated Assembly and Northumberland in the first Protectorate parliament.

[54] Parliamentarian officer and politician, from Chippenham in Cambridgeshire; he was a friend and comrade-in-arms of Oliver Cromwell, campaigning with him in East Anglia and elsewhere during the civil war and succeeding him as governor of Ely. The bond was strengthened in May 1653, when Henry Cromwell married his eldest daughter, Elizabeth. Accordingly, he became a close friend and supporter of Henry Cromwell. He was elected to both of Oliver Cromwell's Protectorate parliaments.

onely. My melancholy I hope, my lord, hath no effects of neglect in it. If I could find that it bore such kind of fruit, I should not love it so well as I doe, nor nourish it in the least, but being tis not my infermity but my choyse, my deare freind and best companion, pray, my lord, accuse it not. I hope you shall never have the least reason to blame it or me for its sake, when I know it counsells and teaches me both to love and honor you. I must confesse by no meanes I can be perswaded to part with it. They wrong it that call it melancholy and think it my enemy, for I am sure tis far better than mirth and jollity, so that I hope wee shall never part; when others have left me, that onely stud by me and gave me sweet counsell and comfort. In it the Lord hath appeared unto me, who loves best to teach in private. My lord, I must returne you thanks for your kind invitation into Ireland. To serve you any where I shall be glad, and so to doe faithfully I have made it my businesse allways. But, my lord, being not perfectly my owne, but at the dispose of my freinds and relations here in England, I cannot say suddenly I must doe this or that without theyre leaves and consents. For my owne part, I care not much where I am, being the Lord of heaven and earth fills all places with His presence, but they who have not fully learned that are tyed to one place more than another, and to them in some measure I am in subjection, and true wisedome will have it so if I serve hir aright. Since I left you at Northampton[55] I have scarce stired from home or scarce received a letter from any. This world parts me and many of my old freinds. The leave wee have taken, it may be, will be long and till that partition wall be downe tis not likely wee shall meet againe. Generall Disborrow[56] was here lately. He made himselfe a kind of stranger both by his lookes and deportment at first, for allthought he came to Chippenham about six at night, yet he offered to be gone presently, askeing me whether his stay would not be inconvenient, but my freedome with him prevailed till the next morning. I spake to him about my eldest sonne,[57] that I had a mind to dispose of in some imployment, but he gave me no answer to it any way. And now, my lord, give me leave to tell you I wonder not at it, nor scarce at any thing of that nature; if it were otherwise I should admire indeed. My love and relations to your lordship will not suffer me to take such a leave of you as I doe of others and unlesse I

[55] Henry Cromwell passed through Northampton on 18 June, en route to Ireland.

[56] John Desborough, parliamentarian officer and politician, commander of a New Model horse regiment, a Protectoral councillor, and newly appointed major-general for south-west England, was distantly allied to Russell, since both had married into the Cromwell family; Desborough's wife was Jane Cromwell, the Protector's sister. He was a co-opted member of the Nominated Assembly and was elected to both of Oliver Cromwell's Protectorate parliaments.

[57] William Russell, aged around twenty when this letter was written.

find your back turned I must be still proffering my love and service to you, as wisedome calls for it and commands me. I can give you free leave to try this world and the men of it. It may be when you have done that throughly, you will find that I am like not many others (thought yet a kind of stranger unto you) but a freind and borne for my day onely wherein it will be most manifest that I am,

Yours in simplicity and sincerity,
Franc Russell

9. From Charles Fleetwood, Birmingham, 18 September 1655, 821, fos 16–17.

Deare brother,

I have heereinclosed sent you a list of the offices for the respective places in the foure courts,[58] which I desire may not come unto publique veiw untill I have acquainted his Highnes with what wee have done, for I confes it doth some what sticke with mee the taking away men's former rights, as also I doubt wee have put in two many into one place, but I shall lett his Highnes know the full of that busines, with the grounds upon which wee did it. Since you spoke to me about my lord Pepes'[59] kinsman I have endevored to bring him within the list. You well know it was read to the councell before I understood anything of his kinsman, and therefore I should desire that you would put him into the gaurd or else to be mustered himselfe and servant in my troope. Or if that be not approved off, to have one of the gaurd to ride with his man in my troope to make way for him. There is one captaine Gardner[60] that came with collonell Sankey out of England now in the gaurd. He desires his continnuance, because one of the gaurd was made a quartermaster in his regiment to make way for him. I have put Mr Loading in two places. You may take which you will for him and dispose of th'other to whom you please. I cannot make way for colonel Blount[61] in the list, and therefore shall desire that a place

[58] After long discussion, and not entirely to Fleetwood's liking (*TSP*, II, p. 733, III, pp. 196, 305), in July 1655 the council decided to revive the traditional central judiciary of Ireland based upon the courts of chancery, upper bench, lower bench, and exchequer.

[59] Richard Pepys, parliamentarian politician and lawyer, baron of the exchequer, chief justice of the upper bench, and member of the Irish council. He proved a loyal and firm supporter of Henry Cromwell in Ireland and was praised by him when he died in January 1659 as 'a good councellor, and a good judge, and indeed a right honest man' (*TSP*, VII, p. 590).

[60] Probably captain Samuel Gardiner, parliamentarian officer, who served in Sankey's New Model horse regiment.

[61] Possibly lieutenant-colonel Robert Blount, parliamentarian officer, who served in a foot regiment in Scotland during the early 1650s and died at Inverness in 1656.

may be made vacant to receave him into the gaurd. I must desire your particuler favour to my cosen Lambert,[62] Mr Browne and three or foure more of the gaurd that came over with mee, togeather with Roe that waited on my wife, that they may be continnued where they are. I must also beseech your respect unto Mr Briscoe.[63] He brings with him one Mr Morsden,[64] a relation of Mr Murcotte,[65] who is said to be a precious good man and fitt for the ministry. If you please to order him £50 for his transportation and £120 he is to have per annum.

Your most affectionate brother and servant,

Charles Fleetwood

10. From Hierome Sankey, Wallingford House, 23 September 1655, 821, fos 18–19.

My lord,

We have beene att length thrugh God's mercy after a troublesome journey brought in safety to this place. My lord,[66] lady and all the litle ones, with our selves, in good health. Their Highnesses excedingly refreshed with the sight of their so neare relations. Most of the counsell, as well as severall of the cheife officers of the army, and many good people else, meeting my lord upon the way with a demonstration of much kindnes and affection. I have not yett had an oppertunity to waite on his Highnes in private, but intend it speedily.

I went this day to the Tower to see generall Venables, who indeed is very sad and much troubled att his unexpected committment.[67] Things

[62] Fleetwood's uncle, Sir Gervace, had married Elizabeth Lambert.

[63] Michael Briscoe, preacher and minister, worked in both his native Ireland and Lancashire during the 1650s. In the summer of 1655 he became a lecturer at Christ Church, Dublin, receiving a government salary.

[64] Gamaliel, Jeremiah, and Josiah Marsden, the three sons of Ralph Marsden, all spent part of the 1650s as preachers and ministers in Ireland. It is not clear which of the three is intended here.

[65] John Murcot, son-in-law of Ralph Marsden, served as an Independent minister on the Wirral in the late 1640s but crossed to Ireland in the early 1650s and then served as a minister in Dublin, Cork, and elsewhere. After a brief visit to England, he returned to Ireland in the autumn of 1655 and died there in December.

[66] Fleetwood.

[67] Robert Venables, parliamentarian officer and politician, commanded a horse regiment in Ireland in 1649–1654. In the summer of 1654, on his return to England, he was elected to the first Protectorate parliament for counties Down, Antrim, and Armagh, but, more importantly, was given the effective joint command, with William Penn, of the naval expedition to the West Indies. Following the rebuff at Hispaniola but the occupation of Jamaica, they both returned to England with much of the fleet in late summer 1655. Upon their arrival, they were questioned by the council in September and imprisoned in the Tower for leaving the West Indies without orders. Both were released by the end of October but lost their commands.

are excedingly ill represented to his Highnes in relation to his conduct and his leaving the army without order, and I feare there hath beene too great a ground for it. I thinke, indeed, tis a sore reproofe both to the instruments that wee ingaged and to those that imployed such a sort of persons. The Lord grant that His dispensations may be of teaching to all.

The Swede goes on very successifully.[68] The poore Protestants in the valleys have, I fear, unworthily putt themselves out of all hopes of releife; have by subjecting their good cause too slavishly to ther enemyes' tearmes.[69] I cam unto nothing concerning Allen[70] because I have had no speech yett with his Highnes. I hope I shall manifest as reall a desire to serve your lordship by a speedy returne as I have upon an honest accompt professed unto your lordship. I have not else to adde, but assume the boldnes of presenting my own and my wife's kinndest respects to my good lady; which being all, committing you to the Lord, I rest,

Your lordship's faythfull servant,

Hie Sankey

11. From Charles Fleetwood, Wallingford House, 25 September 1655, 821, fos 20–21.

Deare brother,

Wee are through the good hand of the Lord brought hither upon Saturday night last,[71] and have great cause to owne the goodnes of the Lord to us in our jorney, He being pleased beyond expectation to enable my deare wife and children to indu[...][72] the jorney. I desire all our praying freinds may remember our condition before the Lord,

[68] The Swedish army was invading Poland and took Warsaw at the end of August.

[69] The massacre in April 1655 of Vaudois or Waldensian Protestants in the Alpine valleys of Piedmont, at the hands of troops of the Catholic duke of Savoy, had deeply affected the Protector and his regime and set back relations with France. After complex diplomacy, a treaty was concluded between the duke and the Vaudois Protestants, though this limited the areas in which the Protestants could continue to hold property. With some reluctance, the Protector accepted that the treaty had closed the issue.

[70] Henry Cromwell was opposing Allen's application to return to Ireland, fearing that his strong republican and Baptist sympathies would foment unrest, especially amongst the English army in Ireland (*TSP*, IV, pp. 55, 108, 190–191). Henry believed that Baptism encouraged military indiscipline and served as a front for political disaffection and disloyalty to the Protectorate, and he was determined both to crack down on army discipline and to curb the powers and privileges that Baptism had acquired under Fleetwood's administration of Ireland.

[71] 22 September.

[72] Paper slightly damaged with some loss of text, though the incomplete word is apparently 'indure'.

and to seeke His face that wee may walke more worthy of such a mercy as wee have receaved. I have bine so much taken up with the cerimonious part that I[73] bine able to mind little of busines since I came, or to acquaint his Highnes with any thing considerable, but I am endevouring and shall doe what I can to send you some money and to dispatch those other affaires which relate to Ireland, but the most difficult part I find wilbe want of money, generall Pen's fleet being come upon them. The miscariages in that busines hath bine a great triall and affliction to his Highnes. I trust the Lord will worke it out in much mercy. I find that the treatie with France sticke upon the account of the Protestants of Piedmont, but I doe thincke there wilbe a sudden conclusion of itt. By reason of our disappointmente in Jamiaca the Spaniards are like to breake with us. He hath had some late successe against the French in Italye.[74] The Swedes continnue victorious in there conquest of Poland.

I find heere that it is not very difficult to gett power for satisfying of the arreares before 49 of such as are now disbanded, if they will accept of the same termes as those who were last disbanded did. I wish you would advise therein and give mee a speedie accompt thereof what may be best done for the publique. Nothing in that shalbe done untill I heare from you. I shall entreate your excuse that I am no more large at present. You shall by the next receave a larger account. With my humble service to my deare sister,[75] I remaine,

Your most affectionate brother and servant,
Charles Fleetwood

I have spoke with captaine Blackwell[76] and he doth advise by all meanes that the army should be paid from the muster in June and not from the third of September. For if it be not from the last payment, wee shalbe in danger of losing that arreare, which he is not hopeles but that wee shall receave it. There are 12[...]o[77] of the Irish foott that are upon there march towards you and wilbe at Chester about the 10th of October and intend to take shipping at Liverpoole. If you find it necessary they should be soner with you, then a passage may

73 Word – perhaps 'have' – apparently omitted.

74 France and Spain were at war in northern Italy.

75 That is, Henry Cromwell (his brother-in-law)'s wife.

76 John Blackwell, parliamentarian officer and politician, was deputy treasurer at war in Ireland and then receiver-general of assessments and treasurer at war; he was probably the John Blackwell returned to the second Protectorate parliament. In this letter, Fleetwood is conveying Blackwell's advice on the financial aspects of paying off part of the English army in Ireland, for, in the summer of 1655, shortly before he left Ireland, Fleetwood set in train procedures to disband up to 5,000 troops there.

77 Paper damaged and a numeral lost – perhaps another zero, since a foot regiment would normally number around 1,200.

probably present at that place. You will doe well to send orders to colonel Sadler[78] to march to Beamorris where you may send two men of warr to convey them over.

12. From William Stane, London, 28 September 1655, 821, fos 22–23.

My lord,

I received this day your lordship's of 18 instant, wherby I perceyve that your lordship hath not received divese[79] letters which I have sent. I am very sensible of your lordship's kindnes and minding mee of that which I rejoyce to doe, and truly it doth much glad mee that the Lord hath putt it into your hart to bee tender of and freindly to those good people in Ireland, which I hope will accrue to your interest every way. I think your lordship knows mee and that I am not led to that severity which perhaps some others are under. But where there is one Father and one Lord Jesus, one faith and one spirit, they are to bee receyved into the same armes of love and kindnes, which doth and will cover many spotts; and your lordship will finde that the more you are led by His spirit and by those ryvers of waters, the more comprehensive you will bee of all those who are of one familye, and you will have the more establishment in your mind in these shaking tymes, and the greate blessing in your other affaires. For if the series of these late alterations bee rememberd, it hath pleased the Lord to do much by the feet of the poore and needy, and such whom the spirit of this world contemnes. I do above any one thing earnestly beg of your lordship, to keep up your retired assemblings and to take in such whom you finde of the most quick and active spirit for God, of all sorts, without distinction, other then what God hath putt. The Lord continue your quiett and mutuall peace and love. I wish wee here did not want it.

My lord deputy hath bin gladly receyved both in the way and in the place, especially by the good people of every kind. Wee have all reason to blesse God for that savourie quick spirit which the Lord hath given him, and which may (because hee is so accessable) ferment and prove usefull here. My Lord Protector did receyve him with much kindnes.

Your lordship heares that general Venables and general Pen are in the Tower. It little consernes mee to look into those matters; their comeing away is by all looked upon strange. But surely in the busines of

[78] Thomas Sadleir/Sadler, parliamentarian officer and politician – he represented Irish constituencies in all three Protectorate parliaments – and colonel of a foot regiment in Ireland, was returning there after several months in England. In January 1655 he had brought over from Ireland a brigade of around 2,600 foot to help counter the expected royalist risings in England.

[79] Apparently a slip for 'diverse'.

Hispaniola the hand of the Lord was evident; three of our own negroes made 600 of our men to run away leaveing theire armes. That was a strange panick feare amongst them; and the quite contrary appeared at Jamaica.

The partie lately imprisoned are not yet released nor that busines put to an end.

My Lord Protector's late fitt was a sore one.[80] Now his Highnes is exceeding well; so is my lord deputy, his lady and family, but my lady Elizabeth very ill.[81] Doth not your lordship forget to write to her Highnes? I rejoyce with you in that part of my lady. The Lord give her health and blesse her fruit.

My poore wife is growne so melencholy that I know not what to say to it, and the worse abundently for my late journey.

My lady Russell[82] sent to mee lately to know how your lordship and my lady doe.

Myne and my wife's affectionate service to my lady and your lordship. I hope your lordship understands colonel Tomlinson[83] and the benefit of conversation with him. My regards to Mr Harris.[84] I am, my lord,

Your lordship's faithfull servant,
W Stane

Indeed, my lord, I have lately receyved the most Christian and savourie lettre from Mr Patience[85] that ever I receyved from any. The

[80] He had been ill since the end of August, suffering from both fits of the stone and malarial-type fevers.

[81] Second daughter of Oliver Cromwell and wife of John Claypole. She suffered a severe illness at this time, possibly linked to pregnancy, and, although she appeared to recover and had another child in 1657, it is possible that her illness of autumn 1655 was the first sign of the disease, probably cancer, that killed her in the summer of 1658.

[82] Katherine, wife of Sir Francis Russell, and thus mother-in-law of Henry Cromwell.

[83] Matthew Tomlinson/Thomlinson, parliamentarian officer and politician, commander of a New Model horse regiment, and from 1654 a member of the Irish council. He was not entirely sympathetic to Henry Cromwell's handling of Ireland, but he retained his position and, indeed, was knighted by Henry Cromwell in the autumn of 1657 'as one, with whom I desire to have a better correspondence, as well upon account of his old kindness for me, as his owne worthiness' (*TSP*, VI, pp. 634–635). He was a co-opted member of the Nominated Assembly but was not elected to either of Oliver Cromwell's Protectorate parliaments, though he became a member of the new, nominated, second parliamentary chamber in the autumn of 1657.

[84] Perhaps Thomas Harrison.

[85] Thomas Patient, Baptist preacher and minister, who was in New England in the 1630s but back in London by 1644 and who established a Baptist church there. Employed by parliament to go to Ireland as part of Oliver Cromwell's expedition in 1649–1650, he initially travelled as an itinerant preacher and army chaplain, but then settled in Waterford and later in Dublin, where he became one of the leading Baptists and for a time chaplain to Fleetwood and the officers there. From 1655 he was again employed as an itinerant preacher

Lord hath filled that man with a great measure of faith and great expresses.[86] I could not but mention it.

13. From Hierome Sankey, Wallingford [House], 2 October [1655], 823, fos 120–121.

My lord,

His Highnes' indisposednes as to health principally (I thinke indeed) occasioned by his laying to heart the losse abroad and dissatisfactions att home makes most things here att a stand. Very many of the dissatisfied people have visited my lord,[87] and tomorrow Simpson, Jessey[88] and 4 more of the cheife of them are to meet my lord privately, who I am to attende upon, and then we shall know what are the things they stand upon. The growing charge of the navyes encurages the distraction. I thinke we have much to eye in this day and may prize the condition of Ireland much, the more when we compare the affaires there with those here. The Lord preserve his Highnes, whose integrity is his support in this day of his tryall. Myne and my wife's dearest respects and humblest service to you and my lady. I committ you to the Lord and rest,

Your lordship's humble servant,
Hie Sankey

Indeed, my lord, I shall mind my obligation.

14. From Charles Fleetwood, London, 5 October [1655], 823, fos 357–358.

My deare brother,

This bearer, our old frind adjutant-generall Allen, will make so slow pase that, by the next post, mine may reach you to give an account of affayres as soone as this. It is his Highnes' pleasure that adjutant-generall Allen showld remaine all or most of the time I am

in Ireland. Although initially suspicious of Henry Cromwell's religious policy, he was one of those moderate Baptists won over by his management of affairs and willing to work with the regime.

[86] Word could alternatively be read as an abbreviated form of 'expressiones'.

[87] Fleetwood.

[88] John Simpson, a Fifth Monarchist, was generally antagonistic towards the Protectoral regime, and was arrested and questioned or imprisoned several times during the Protectorate. Despite his Fifth Monarchist and millenarian leanings in the early 1650s, Henry Jessey, a prominent London Baptist, was more moderate in his stance towards the Protectoral regime, though he criticized some aspects of the regime's religious policies, especially the continuation of the tithe system.

to staye in England and then to return with me,[89] and it being an expensive time with him to bring over his wife hither, it is his Highnes' pleasure he showld receive a hundred pounds towards his charges out of contingent monyes, which I desire you would please to order accordingly. I trust you will finde that satisfaction in him as will be to your content. It is matter of rejoycing to your deare father to heare ther is so right an understanding twixt you and good men, and the more you are enabled to disapoynt some hopes upon that account the greater will be your mercy. His Highnes to heare of this rejoyces him. His interest and his mercy lyes in the saints, and still he is kept, I trust, with a pretious sence therof, and I am not in dispayre but that good men will more and more (through mercy) see wherin lyes their true interest. The Lord keepe you firme ther unto, even to the end, and then I feare you not. His Highnes desired my playnes hearin with you, which my duty and affection will prompt me unto, and when I told him of your carriage in Ireland it did revive him; that will be your mercy, crown and glory. The Lord keepe you and us. I am,

Your most affectionate brother,

Charles Fleetwood

I shall not expect adjutant-generall Allen's return till his wife be up and in a condition to travill and the weather seasonable. During the time of his absence he is to have his pay continued as if presant.[90]

15. From Hierome Sankey, Wallingford House, 9 October 1655, 821, fos 24–25.

May it please your lordship,

Your kind letters I have received, and shall mind your lordship's commands in reference to myselfe. Things here are much att the old passe. I shall not adventure to write much. My lord, I conceive, will go to the councell this weeke.[91] I wish he were oftner att Whitehall for

[89] Suggesting that, at this stage, Fleetwood believed that he would in due course return to Ireland or at least wished to give that impression.

[90] So, although Allen was generally to remain in England while Fleetwood was there (but still receiving his military pay out of the Irish budget), despite Henry Cromwell's strong misigivings (*TSP*, IV, pp. 190–191, 197, 328), he had been given permission to return to Ireland at this stage, ostensibly so that he could rejoin his ailing wife and then bring her back to England once she was fit again; in fact, she did not recover and died in Dublin in December 1655. Thurloe reported that Allen had been given permission to return to Ireland only after expressing 'all manner of satisfaction' and promising 'utmost fidelitie', but a fortnight later he ruefully noted 'I am sorry to heare, that the adjutant general doth deceave some expectations heere, though I confesse he doth not mine' (*TSP*, IV, pp. 107–108, 190–191).

[91] Fleetwood did not, in fact, attend the council until the first week of December.

divers reasons. Exceding many people (I hope honest) and sufficiently dissatisfied come to him, and indeed you know his excellent tempar to deale with them. Wednesday last we mett accordingly, as I gave you a hint, where Simpson, Jessey and severall of the cheifest of all that gange.[92] And after some houres' discourse were spent we parted without making Pressbytes of either side. The subject of our debate will better befitt you ore tenus[93] then in a lettre. All we gained was another private meeting this weeke. The Hispaniola busines pierces deeply, and that other navy under Blake is returned and though we sett a good face of it, yett I assure you twas inexpected.[94] Neither hath any thing bene done to answer so great a charge. His Highnes is much refreshed to heare of the faireness of you to others and theirs likewise to your lordship. Mr Brewster's[95] letter excedingly pleased him. Myne and my wife's humblest service to your lordship and my lady. I committ you to the Lord and rest,

Your lordship's most humble servant,

Hie Sankey

I pray you burne it.

16. From John Winkworth, Ferns Castle,[96] [County Wexford], 17 October 1655, 821, fos 26–27.

May it please your excellencie,

Your message I delivered unto captain Ivory,[97] which was taken as a grate obligation from your lordship. Your disbanded party since

92 Word could alternatively be read as 'gauge'.

93 This Latin phrase could be translated as 'by word of mouth'.

94 Robert Blake, parliamentarian officer and politician – he was returned to every parliament of the period 1640–1656 – had become one of the republic's foremost admirals, giving naval support to Oliver Cromwell's Irish campaign, engaging Prince Rupert's royalist fleet, commanding the naval expeditions that recaptured the Scilly and Channel Isles, and prominent in the Anglo-Dutch War. He commanded a fleet that first swept the Mediterranean for pirates in 1654–1655 and then, in the summer of 1655, was ordered to attack Spanish shipping off the coast of Spain. It returned to the Downs on 6 October.

95 Nathaniel Brewster, a Norfolk minister highly praised by the Protector (Abbott, III, p. 756), crossed to Ireland with or just ahead of Henry Cromwell in the summer of 1655 (*TSP*, III, pp. 503, 660) and took up a salaried position at St Audoen's, Dublin. He became a friend and confidant of Henry Cromwell in Ireland and was sent by him to London in December 1655 to report to Protector and council about affairs in Ireland (*TSP*, IV, pp. 327–328, 348, 373).

96 The medieval castle at Ferns, County Wexford, was held by Irish Catholic forces during the 1640s but was recovered by Oliver Cromwell in 1649.

97 William Ivory, parliamentarian officer, served as a captain in Edmund Ludlow's horse regiment in Ireland, one of the regiments disbanded in the summer of 1655.

the commetting of lieutenant-colonel Scott[98] have been verry wary in letting their discontents come to publique view, but they doe hold often clandestine councils, wherein they endeavor to find out who it was that did discover their discontents to your lordship. In the doing of which they accuse each other, so that in the conclusion I am doubtfull it will appeare they were set on by a person who seemes to represent a parte of honesty and honnour. But whether such actions (if soe) ought to be the practise of such an one I leave to you to judg. Some of the disbanded officers privately (as lieutenant-colonel Candler,[99] etc) talkes more then comes to their shewes and makes a great noise of liberty, which men are not more prone to desire then unapt to beer in the popular sense, which is to do what every man liketh best. But if the divinest liberty be to will what men should, and to doe what they so will, according to religion, reason and law, I hope your lordship envies them not that liberty, it being all (as a man) you desire to enjoy yourselfe. Good men will never desire greater freedoms then good laws allow, whose bonds they count their ornament and protection, others their manacles and oppression. Nor is it just any man should expect the reward and benifit of the law, who dispiseth their rule and direction, loseing justly their safety while they seeke an unreasonable liberty. My lord, in my poore opinion there is nothing that portends more God's displasure against a nation then when Hee suffers the clamours of men to pass all bonderyes of laws and reverance to authority. I am perswaded that that is one of the vanities Soloman speakes of in Ecclesiastes 8: 11.[100] Therefore the ordinary preventive physick in a state against growing maladies is execution and administration of law and justice, and in so doing you will find comfort from Proverbs 10 and the ninth vers,[101] for if you yeeld to any party or faction, contrary to a rule, you will find they will pervert and abuse any act of greatest indulgance and turne it into wantonness. I have no more at presant save only this to add, that my petition to the Lord for your lordship shall be (I hope daily) that you may continually harken unto His commandments and doe them. Then shall your peace be as a river, and your righteousness as

[98] Scott (his forename is not recorded), parliamentarian officer and lieutenant-colonel in Ludlow's regiment, was seen by Henry Cromwell as the ringleader of a group of officers opposing both the disbandment and the Protectoral government, and he had ordered his arrest earlier in October. He referred to Scott as 'the ringlader' of 'endeavours to promote and encourage discontents' and planned to apply 'punishments suiteable of such distempers' (*TSP*, IV, pp. 73–74).

[99] Probably William Candler, parliamentarian officer, a captain in Robert Phaier's foot regiment in Ireland.

[100] 'It is because sentence upon a wicked act is not promptly carried out that men do evil so boldly.'

[101] 'A blameless life makes for security; crooked ways bring a man down.'

the waves of the sea, and your name shall not be cutt off nor destroyed from before Him. Then shall the divell and all his accomplices, who seeke to lay open those wounds againe that were so lately bleeding, and of teareing out the bowels of the commonwealth by embroiling it in new troubles, come to nought. What phrensie it is that possesseth some men is hard to be understood, or what it is they would have. But without doubt no other reason can be imagined of the happy peace and tranquillity which we now enjoy, but that He who stretched out the heavans and laid the foundations of the earth and formeth the spirits of men within them, hath brought that forth, as the accomplishment of His own good will and purpose towards His people. And that you and all in highest authority may make a right use and application of the same is earnestly desired by,

Your excellencie's verry humble and affectionate servant,
J Winckworth

I would intreat your lordship, if you think fit, to let me here this way whether this come safe to your hands. My brother Kingdon will send it safe to me.

17. From Robert Barrow[102] to ?,[103] Carrickfergus, 31 October 1655, 821, fo. 28.

Sir,

Even now I received yours of yesterday's date intimating the receit of orders from Sir John Reynolds.[104] I answer wherunto, be pleased to take notice that I comawnd the forces in theise parts by speciall order from his excellency the lord deputy, by virtue wherof I looke uppon myselfe as concerned to take care of the charge till farther order from his lordship or the lord Henry Cromwell, and therfor apprehend it

[102] Parliamentarian officer, he came to Ireland in 1649 in Robert Venables's foot regiment and in 1650 succeeded Roger Fenwick as commander of his own foot regiment, though that regiment was disbanded in 1653. He retained military office in Ireland until 1656, was one of the leading Baptist officers who opposed Henry Cromwell's religious policy in 1655–1656, and was one of the four who resigned at the end of 1656.

[103] There is no surviving endorsement or cover sheet, so it is not clear to whom this letter was addressed. Clearly, it was not originally addressed to Henry Cromwell, though it was passed to him or otherwise came into his possession.

[104] Parliamentarian officer and politician, originally from Castle Campes in Cambridgeshire. He fought in the English civil war, helped crush a Leveller-inspired mutiny in his own newly created horse regiment in spring 1649, and then campaigned with Cromwell and his successors in Ireland, in the process acquiring land and property there. He strongly supported both the Protectorate and Henry Cromwell's government of Ireland, and was returned for Counties Tipperary and Waterford to both of Oliver Cromwell's Protectorate parliaments. In 1657 he married a daughter of Sir Francis Russell and so became Henry Cromwell's brother-in-law, but he drowned shortly afterwards.

not safe without the same to resigne that trust. Till the receit of which I shall, God willinge, continue my care in that charge as heertofore and when that shalbe sent mee, which I hope will not be denyed (if those in power thinke meet to imploy another) I shall, I hope, freely part therwith to you or who els shalbe appoynted. In the interim give me leave to acknowledge your civilities by your letter manifested to, sir,

Your very affectionate servant,

Robt Barrow

18. From Thomas Brooke,[105] Chippenham, 1 November 1655, 821, fos 29–30.

Letter of thanks for an unspecified favour, and of religious exhortation and guidance.

19. From Philip Carterett,[106] 1 November 1655, 821, fo. 31.

My lord,

Havinge accidentally received the inclosed proclamation from his Highnes, printed heer by the councell's order,[107] and seriously considered it, I have thought it my duty humbly to present it to your excellency, that soe I may receive your excellency's commawnds theron. His Highnes is pleased to comawnd all officers, both[108] civill and military, to take care in their places that his proclamation be putt in due excecution; and I, havinge the honour to be intrusted as advocate-generall to his army in Ireland, should be very unworthey of his favour if I should[109] dilligently obey his soe just, soe much by all good men to be esteemed, comawnds in that declaration expressed,

[105] Perhaps chaplain to Sir Francis Russell at Chippenham, or possibly the more prominent London preacher of that name who was minister at St Margaret's, Fish Hill Street, from 1653 to 1662.

[106] Advocate-general to the army in Ireland as well as judge advocate in the business of transplanting the native Irish, he was involved in various military, financial, and judicial aspects of the Irish administration. He opposed Henry Cromwell's religious policy and was associated with several more prominent opponents of the Protectorate in Ireland (*TSP*, IV, pp. 327–328, 349–350). However, he was employed by Henry Cromwell on a mission to London in the spring of 1656, and then went on to take up an appointment in Jersey (*TSP*, IV, p. 672 and V, p. 45), though he returned to Ireland later in the 1650s.

[107] Proclamation of the Protector, originally issued on 21 September, prohibiting anyone who had assisted the late king from holding any office of public trust until the Protector's pleasure was known.

[108] Word repeated in error.

[109] The pattern of this sentence suggests that the word 'not' was omitted in error at this point, but, since the second half of the letter indicates the author's doubts about enforcing the proclamation, perhaps this sentence was intended as written.

and therfor I take the boldnese to begg your excellency's order in this case. Severall officers in this army have formerly served the king (some of eminent qualitie, others inferior), and yet I am informed that notwithstanding his Highnes his proclamation, they still presume to act in their comawnds, tho as farr as I can heare his Highnes hath not yet signified his pleasure concerning them. Soe that they are, if my information be true, to be reputed contemnors of his Highnes his pleasure, and therfor it lies uppon mee as a duty to prosecute them; but knowinge that I am wholly in my place subordinate to your excellency's pleasure in the excecution therof, I humbly submitt it to your excellency whither I shall proceed to question any such military officers in Ireland who have formerly served the king or otherwise abetted his party and doe presume to act in their imployments befor his Highnes his pleasure be knowne concerning them. Which in discharge of my duty I humbly offer to your excellency and remayne,

Your excellency's most humble servant,

Phi Carterett

20. From Charles Fleetwood, Wallingford House, 5 November 1655, 821, fos 32–33.

Letter of recommendation on behalf of captain Bodham, a godly man from an Independent church in Norfolk and known to Mr Brewster; while in Ireland, Fleetwood had found him temporary employment at Athlone.

21. From William Jephson,[110] Mallow, 19 November 1655, 821, fos 34–35.

My lord,

Did I not thinke it a greater shame that soe good a friend of mine should come to wayte on your lordship without the tender of my most humble respects in a lyne or two, I should blush to thinke your lordship should any more receyve the trouble of this hand, untill I presented my whole selfe to your lordship's service. But I doubt not but the little doctor[111] will give your lordship full satisfaction of the occasions

[110] Parliamentarian officer and politician, of Irish descent on his mother's side, who had fought in both England and Ireland during the 1640s, though his loyalty to parliament had sometimes appeared suspect and he had been excluded from parliament at Pride's Purge. After spending some time in semi-retirement in England, he returned to Ireland in 1653. Fearful that his Irish estates might be sequestrated, he sought to emphasize his loyalty to the Protectoral regime and won partial rehabilitation under Henry Cromwell, sitting in both of Oliver Cromwell's Protectorate parliaments for the towns of Cork and Youghal.

[111] Probably Dr Robert Gorges, who served as a clerk to the Irish council and secretary to Henry Cromwell.

of my stay. My lord, it grieves my heart to see the disadvantadges you are put upon here for want of money, without which certainlye your lordship is the first that ever was put upon without moneye. If your lordship will give mee leave to take the boldnesse to write his Highnesse somthing of mine owne, and others of his and your friends' sense in this particular, I shall doe it very freelye. For really, my lord, I am very sensible of your condition and shall in all thinges, to the best of my capacitye, indeavour to approve myselfe, my lord,

Your most affectionate and humble servant,

Wm Jephson

22. From Thomas Sadleir, Beaumaris, 24 November 1655, 821, fos 36–37.

May it please your excellency,

According to my last, I have sent collonell Axtell's[112] three companies to Hollie Head, all which, or the most part off them, I hope wilbe over beffore this comes to your excellency's hands. I have taken the opertunitie off captain Coleman[113] and a vessel drove in heare by storme, to send over my owne three companies. Captain More will wayght one your excellency for the disposing off them, when it shall please God they land on the other side. Iff it may stand with your excellency's affayres, I humbly begg your favor to them, as to the sending off them to the quarters wher ther concearnments doe lie, off which captain Moore will informe your excellency. In regard wee have noe monies leaft I was unwilling to come my selve till I shiped the last men, which I hope, iff this wind stands, will not bee long after this comes to your excellency's hands. I humbly bege your excellency's order to the treasurer for the payment off the passage off the men, in regard the monies I receive on that account must bee expended for the soldiers' present supply. I rest,

Your excellencie's in all faythffullnesse to serve you,

Tho Sadleir

[112] Daniel Axtell, parliamentarian officer who played a prominent role in both Pride's Purge and the trial and execution of Charles I – he commanded the troops at the trial and so was deemed a regicide. He went to Ireland in 1649 in John Hewson's New Model foot regiment, but in 1650 he was given a foot regiment of his own, disbanded in the summer of 1655. A vigorous and sometimes brutal commander, he was for a time governor of Kilkenny and was returned for Counties Carlow, Wexford, Kildare, and Queen's to the first Protectorate parliament. He was a prominent Baptist, became one of the leading Baptist officers who opposed Henry Cromwell's religious policy in 1655–1656, and was one of the four who resigned at the end of 1656.

[113] Probably Robert Coleman, parliamentarian naval officer, at this time commanding the *Wexford* and operating in the Irish Sea and around the coast of Wales.

23. From Richard Cromwell, Hursley, 27 November 1655, 821, fos 38–39.

Deare brother,

That I doe not oftener write unto you will, notwithstanding my private condition, bare an excuse; for indeed though I much love and honour you, yet writing to my unskilfull hand is very irksome, and could my affections talke some other way, I should not care for appearing in this. I could almost notwithstanding forbidd it when I consider the ardent affections I have for you, there being a beleife in me of community with you, and that forreine distances cannot hinder the opperation of love in good dispositions, nor the many waters betwix England and Ireland squench that beate which admitts of noe winter of snow or froist in that breast where it dwelleth. I can say I have it from bouth sides, it being naturall, but the worth which makes it otherwise then a childish love. And now having entred upon the liste, let me tell you my hearte speaks much more then my expression can declare, and were it[114] love noe more then what can be discovered in its excellency by words, it were a foolish thing, but it is a very great matter and hard to be discoursed. I hope I shall upon all occations mannifest that I have a reall intention, and shall you but reflect youre creddit that I offer not a light and vaine matter, you will make this black paper to shine. The date of this will tell you my being where my patience is exercised[115] and I can boaste of the love of God whoe affords me restraining grace, keeping me within the compasse of my place, and I can just say I am the proportion of a man, my glasse telling me I have my noosse; what God will doe more for me I know not. I am certaine His devine goodnesse hath exceeded my desert. It is not fitting for me to trouble you with these things, but to give your time full liberty for better entertainment. A little divertisment is like a whett to the workman's toole, and give me leave to lett this tell you that there hath been great care in Sir Francis Russell to furnish you with some cattle for feild recreation, most propper for such as are wearyed in the service of their country; and that that worke might not be delayed and the wheeles of it be stopt for want of some spoaks, having a parcell that I had gathered up amongst my freinds, I could not doe lesse (when I came to know what Sir Francis was doeing) then to make some expression of a brother (though poore, it being in doggs, compannions they have been for princes). I ded with very great chearfullnesse lay hold of the oppertunity to present to the kennell

[114] Word amended and possibly deleted.

[115] In 1649, Richard Cromwell married the elder daughter of Richard Maijor, a Hampshire landowner, and settled on his father-in-law's estates at Hursley, south-west of Winchester.

(now I suppose upon there marche to you) eight couple of beaggles, the wholl stock of that kinde I had. Pray take noe notice that there are any from me, for I ought to have made a compleate kennell for you oute of my owne stock of idle kind, fitt for nothinge but to breed doggs. But now I can assure you I have not any but my buck hounds which are abroade; but the pleasure and delight I shall exceedingly content myselfe with, and fearing I shall not leave roome to tender my respects, with my wife's, to your selfe and deare consorte, I shall desire that wee may be knowen to you and how much I am, deare brother,

Your most affectionate brother and servant,

R Cromwell

24. From Hierome Sankey, Wallingford House, 27 November 1655, 821, fos 40–41.

My lord,

I shall not neglect to present your lordship with an accompt of things here during my continuance. I was about 3 daies since with his Highnes, who I perceive is much troubled concerning the petition from Ireland, and asked me of severall things relating therto and concerning severall persons there.[116] I professed to him, as in the Lord's presence, that I did not know nor heare of any offence given by your lordship to the Anababtists, but on the contrary had seene and received severall lettres from them acknowledging your faire and freindly carriage to them. I told him what I was confident they might have, and what I thought they might not have. He sayes this petition confirmes people in their slanderous beleifes of his setting up himselfe and family; and that he had not called for my lord deputy over,[117] but mearly being sollicited

[116] A petition urging the Protector to make Henry Cromwell lord deputy of Ireland in place of Fleetwood, which spread in civil and some military circles in Ireland. It proved an embarrassment to Henry Cromwell, who denied prior knowledge of it and attempted to distance himself from it, because he predicted, correctly, that it would not be supported by the Protector and would merely sour his relationship with Fleetwood and be used against him by his opponents (*TSP*, III, p. 29, and IV, pp. 197, 227, 259–260, 327–328, 348).

[117] Probably strictly true, though the largely unspoken assumption on both sides seems to have been that Fleetwood would return to England in the summer of 1655 and hand over day-to-day control to Henry Cromwell. In a letter to Fleetwood of late June, the Protector had vigorously denied rumours that he would be recalled and Henry Cromwell made lord deputy in his place, but the Protector did write that, if Fleetwood wished to return to England, he would be welcome (Abbott, III, p. 756). In a letter of early August, Fleetwood wrote that he had received from the Protector 'positive commands to returne into England' (*TSP*, III, p. 697), but the phrase is open to various interpretations and in no surviving letter did the Protector lay an absolute injunction upon Fleetwood to leave Ireland.

by Stanes, major Haynes[118] and captain Loyd, who were allwayes insisting upon his debts and pretended his estate did excedingly suffer in his absence, that he was £10 or 11,000 in debt. As to Stanes, he thought he did it designingly; the other two dealt more plainly in it. He beleived Stanes did upon accompt either to gratifie the party he associated with (meaning, as I suppose, Turner[119] and them), or else to reconcile those who were not satisfied with the government to his Highnes therebye. His Highnes sayes he is the unfittest man in the world for that. But notwithstanding their sollicitation till the busines was effected, all the slanders are upon him as though he intended to lay aside my lord deputy.

He told me further that he would call Stane, Haynes and Loyd together and charge it to thir faces, before my lord deputy and some others, what he then alleaged, and was very confident they would not deny it; and that for his part he would be glad if my lord deputy would go back within a month. Well my lord, I know well right it trubles you, but God will owne your sincerity and justifie your love to Him and His. If I were privy to the least whisper of a complaint, I'de acquaint you, for I know you would proffitt therby. Be not angry att my lengthened stay; I did not expect, nor any body else, so long an estrangment of my lord from the counsell. But now that I suppose he is going in and the Irish busines, which we have beene pretty close upon, toward a finishing, you shall see I shall not deserve a chiding; though tis worse than a chiding to be so long a time silent, notwithstanding my severall lettres. My humble service to my good lady. I committ you to God and rest,

Your lordship's most humble servant,

Hie Sankey

[118] Hezekiah Haynes, parliamentarian officer and politician, was major in Fleetwood's New Model horse regiment and campaigned extensively in England and Scotland. Close to Fleetwood, he often effectively commanded the regiment in Fleetwood's absence and, in 1655, was appointed (deputy) major-general for East Anglia, again deputizing for Fleetwood; he represented Essex in the second Protectorate parliament.

[119] Identification uncertain, as several ministers, preachers, and administrators of the 1650s bore this surname.

25. From Charles Fleetwood, Wallingford House, November[120] 1655, 821, fos 42–43.

Letter of recommendation on behalf of Mr Perrin, seeking employment in Ireland to support his large family; reports that Perrin formerly had a place in Ireland but had lost it because of his absence.

26. From Charles Fleetwood, 1 December 1655, 821, fos 44–45.

Since my last I have received yours, but it is so late and the usiall poast night past that I shall not inlarge at present, only presume to send you this inclosed, which I shall earnestly desire you would give me yours and the councell speedy thoughts thearin, they being colonel Hill's[121] proposalls, and are preparing at a committee for the councell's resolution; and I, not desireing any thing should pass without your privaty, doe earnest desire you would speed your oppinion to me upon the same. I am,

Your affectionate brother.

Deare brother,

I canot deny but that I know of the[122] petition you mention long since, and have known so much of unhandsomnes in some about it that I have reason to be satesfied you would have an abhorrency to their actions. But I canot charge my selfe with guilt why some men love me no better, and did they doe what they have done out of a true love and service to your service and your selfe, I might be satisfyed. Our interests are so nearly interwoven, one in another, that they canot stricke at the one but they must hitt the other. Yet this last designe hath, I hope, bine of more use and advantage to me then I could have expected or I am sure they intended; that's my mercy. Deare brother, marke them for untrue frinds who labour to divide us. Thos you call my frinds doe frequently write with great affection and are farre

[120] Paper slightly damaged and date lost.

[121] Arthur Hill, parliamentarian officer and politician with family estates in Ireland, was active in the Irish administration during the 1630s. After some uncertainty, he supported parliament in the 1640s, and during the 1650s he was again active in the political, administrative, and economic affairs of Ireland, being returned for Counties Down, Antrim, and Armagh to the first Protectorate parliament. He was one of a small committee, including councillor Sir Charles Wolseley, that in autumn 1655 presented proposals concerning Ireland – the details of which do not appear to have survived, but which probably related to improving Irish trade and lifting the various duties on trade between England and Ireland – to the Protectoral council, which duly referred them to the Irish council and committee (*CSPI*, p. 818).

[122] Word originally written 'yor' (= your) but then amended to read something closer to 'y^{e}' (= the).

from endevoring to worke by such an indirect engine, but I trust your affections are so intire and you will have such a discerning eye as to discover such deceits. Whatsoever you doe with me, yet be confydent you shall finde me playn hearted, I at least desire it may be so, and faithfull to you on the best account. I hope our affections are so intire that men's subtiltyes canot divert each from other. I am your most affectionate brother.

27. From George Ayscue,[123] Ham Haw, Surrey, 4 December 1655, 821, fos 46–47.

My most honoured and deare lord,

I received your lordship's of November 15th and with it so greate a trouble of spirit that I, who have such passionat affections to your person and so true a zeale to advance your servis and honour, should unhappily be made an instrument to act any thing that your lordship should call an injurie to you, was none of the smalest troubles I have mett with in my life. But truly, my lord, I did not know anything of carying over the petition with me untill wee were ready to saile, when Doctor Loftus[124] brought them aborde to me, at which I was troubled; not at the matter of the petition, but at the slight delivering of them to me. Not, my lord, that I expected out of a selfe vanitie the cerimony of the maior, alldarmen and persons of quality concerned in it to have delivered them to me, but doubting if his Highnes should aske me how I was impowred to present them to him, if I had answred the truth I was fearfull it would lessen the reputation of the petition, especially there being so smalle an number of them readiye. And therfore I desired Doctor Loftus that the maior, aldermen and such gentlemen as weare concerined, and then in towne, would impowre me by there letter to present the petition to his Highnes, and in the meanetime more of the petitions would be ready to be sent over, and that no advantage in the meanetime might be lost I resolved to waite on Mr Secretaire Thurlow[125] as soone as I came to towne and to deliver him

[123] Parliamentarian naval commander, who supported Oliver Cromwell's 1649–1650 expedition to Ireland as admiral of the Irish seas and then campaigned in the Anglo-Dutch War, the West Indies, and the Baltic. Although in semi-retirement from 1654, in 1658 he resumed his naval career as an admiral in Sweden's service, and in 1659 rendezvoused and co-operated with the English fleet in the Sound.

[124] Dudley Loftus, Irish-born politician, judge, administrator, and scholar, held a variety of judicial, financial, and academic positions in Ireland during the Protectorate and was returned to the third Protectorate parliament for Counties Kildare and Wicklow.

[125] John Thurloe, parliamentarian politician and statesman, and a confidant of Oliver Cromwell, served both as secretary to the Protectoral council and effectively as secretary of state during the Protectorate; he was elected to all three Protectorate parliaments and played

those petitions I then had, which accordingly I did before I received your lordship's, leaving the busnesse to his discretion how to manage, which is all that at present is don in it. Here is a report that my lord Fleetwod is to returne for Ireland, but thay see not far that beleeve it, not well undarstanding the true intrist of the present affaires. But it is now time to begg your lordship's pardon for this tedious addresse, to which I doe with all humblenesse subscribe myselfe, my deare lord,

Your lordship's most true and faithfull, humble servant,

George Ayscue

28. From Charles Fleetwood, Wallingford House, 4 December 1655, 821, fos 48–49.

Deare brother,

I have received yours, whereby I understand that you apprehend I have received some misunderstanding concerning you, wherein I must tell you, you are much mistaken. As for the petition, it would argue too much calling into question your judgment if I should say you were guiltie therin. But I confes I doe not thincke his Highnes' interest is preserved[126] by such indirect endevours to divide. And I hope I should have had a hart readie to have laid downe my authoritie at his Highnes' feett, and thereby have given way to what is pretended of desire in relation to yourselfe, without all this stire. And I doe not thincke the petitioners themselves could have immagined his Highnes had so little kindnes for mee, as to have demanded my authoritie which I had from himselfe and the parliament without my consent. But those kind of dividing practises are most unsutable and I am sure most unseasonable at this time, when there is so much labour to bring the common enemy in upon us, from abroad as well as at home; but, deare brother, take heed of giveing way to jelous suggestions. His Highnes can beare me wittnes with what respect and affection I have spoken concerning you, and though men may endevour our misunderstandings each of other, yet I trust it shall not be in there power. I hope I shall not, by any precipitant action of my owne, give any occasion of offence to you, but still manifest that affection which may make it appeare how much I am,

Your most affectionate brother and servant,

Charles Fleetwood

a prominent role in each. He corresponded regularly with Henry Cromwell throughout the latter's time in Ireland and their correspondence, printed by Thomas Birch in *A Collection of the State Papers of John Thurloe, Esquire* (London, 1742), sets the context for and often fleshes out the letters in this collection.

[126] The first three letters of this word have been heavily amended and possibly deleted.

It is very wonderfull how providence hath brought to light some secrett designes tending to disturbance. Have a care of Ulster. Deare brother, colonel Hewson[127] hath write unto me about his brother captain Turner,[128] that he might have captain Brtt's[129] company. I shall not take upon me to dispose of any commands without you. I am sure wee all have reason to love his honest brother. I shall leave it to you to doe what you shall judge of most publique advantage. This inclosed is from his Highnes about Mr Reynolds' busines.[130]

29. From William Malyn,[131] Whitehall, 4 December 1655, 821, fos 50–51.

My lord,

It hath pleased God to afflict the lady Elizabeth Claypole with very great paynes; she was prettie well recovered and at ease about a weeke or 2 since, but her paynes are lately [...]newed[132] upon her. Her Highnesse hath also been ill of late and kept her bed for severall dayes; but praysed be God, her Highness is now in a very good way towards the recovery of her health; and the lady Disbrow hath been also very weake and much troubled with her old greifes, but is now

[127] John Hewson, parliamentarian officer and politician, and a regicide, was colonel of a New Model foot regiment that campaigned in Ireland from 1649, and he served as governor of Dublin in the early 1650s. In 1655, part of his regiment was disbanded and part of it transferred to England, and thenceforth Hewson was based in England and given command of a formed regiment there. A strong supporter of Charles Fleetwood in Ireland, he was out of sympathy with Henry Cromwell's Irish policies, and he was in turn strongly distrusted by Henry Cromwell, who regarded him as a Baptist, an opponent of his government, and a trouble-maker with access in London to Fleetwood and the Protector. He sat for Ireland in the Nominated Assembly and he was elected to both of Oliver Cromwell's Protectorate parliaments, being returned to the first for County Dublin.

[128] Parliamentarian officer (his forename is not recorded), captain of one of the companies in Hewson's foot regiment in Ireland, which were disbanded and paid off over the summer.

[129] Name written thus, apparently in an abbreviated or slightly garbled form. Possibly the captain George Brett who in 1658 was serving in the horse regiment sent to Flanders.

[130] Robert Reynolds, half-brother of Sir John Reynolds, a somewhat lukewarm parliamentarian politician during the 1640s, who held aloof from the regicide but retook his seat in the Rump and held various legal and administrative posts during the 1650s; he was returned to Richard Cromwell's Protectorate parliament. In December 1655, he gained the Protector's strong support for his request to receive forfeited land in County Louth. The Irish council obeyed the Protector's order but felt that, because forfeited land in Louth was earmarked as a reserve to satisfy the claims of the adventurers, the granting of Reynolds's request might create an unfortunate precedent (Dunlop, p. 561).

[131] From humble origins in Essex, Malyn had risen to become Oliver Cromwell's personal secretary by the time of his Scottish campaign of 1650–1651 and retained that position during the Protectorate.

[132] Paper slightly damaged with some loss of text, though the incomplete word is apparently 'renewed'.

better and att more ease. The Lord teach us to understand His mind in these chasticements and sanctify them unto us.

As to newes in reference to the publique: the peace between us and France was proclaymed here on Wednesday last, and on the morrow the French ambassador was feasted att White Hall. The major-generalls, who were sent into the severall counties about setling the militias and raysing of monyes out of the estates of the cavileers, are carrying on that worke apace,[133] which is [. . .]eeding[134] pleasing to all the good partie. This day the judges and severall divines from both universities and other parts of the nation mett att White Hall to advise with his Highness and councill about the propositions tendred unto his Highness by Manasseth Ben Isreael on the behalfe of the nation of the Jewes, who desire in great numbers to come and live within the dominions of this commonwealth. If they may be permitted to trade and to have the free exercise of their religion, they propose to have publique sinagogs for their worship, and some other particulars. But it's supposed they will moderate their demands, having submitted them to the consideration of his Highness and councill. What wilbe the result of this consultation I suppose we shall know in a few dayes. Many good people doe hope that this may be a dawning to the day of the delivarye and restoration of that poore, afflicted people, who through the just judgment of God upon them for their sinns have been soe long in captivity and tossed to and fro; and who knowes but the promises and prophecies concerning them doe draw nigh and doe begin to lay hold of their spirits; and who knowes but that the time, yea, the sett time of their deliverance drawes nigh, seing God doth draw forth the hearts of His people in kindnes towards them.[135] I am, my lord,

Your most humble and obleiged servant,
Will Malyn

[133] The instructions and commissions for the major-generals and their county-based commissioners were issued in October 1655, effectively marking the beginning of this new tier of semi-military regional government in England and Wales.

[134] Paper slightly damaged with some loss of text, though the incomplete word is apparently 'exceeding'.

[135] A commission of councillors, judges, City officials, and divines, convened by the Protector, met during December to hear submissions from Menasseh Ben Israel, an Amsterdam-based Jew, and others, urging that the Jews be formally readmitted and granted commercial and other rights. The very favourable and enlightened views expressed by Malyn may reflect the Protector's opinions, because he was clearly sympathetic to the Jews and, although the weight of opinion prevented their formal readmission, thenceforth the Protector unofficially allowed many Jews to settle in England.

30. From Hierome Sankey, London, 4 December 1655, 821, fos 52–53.

May it please your lordship,

This weeke I receyved your lordship's lettre[136] and your calling. I will not fayle to hast to you. My lord deputy went in to the counsell this day. Yesterday the Protector told me the Irish affaires shuld be considered out of bounds, and I shuld be gone within two or 3 daies. I question not but to gett a dispatch this weeke or the beginning of the next. I am sorry you have had no readier a supply of money, but I hope the accompt I presented last weeke will be in some good measure satisfactory. I am glad with all my heart Blackwood[137] is so discreet and sober. You did yourselfe much right in supressing the petition that was going through the army. His Highnes was excedingly satisfied therewith; and though you did not att all countenance, yett if there had bene more a discountenance of the mayor and aldermen's petition, I thinke it would have done well. We must be true to our principalls, which is equally to countenance and encorage all truly godly; and indeed I never knew that the Anabaptists attayned any such thing or anything like it. His Highnes likes it not, but prefyres they shall be as soone putt into benefices, if they will, as any other. Impartiality is of singular worth, and I am confident the Lord hath spirited you much with a paine of that, which indeed is fitt for this day. I shall take care of the busines committed to me by colonel Herbert. I desire your lordship will not write any more. I hope I shall satisfie you as to my too long stay. I shall hope the product will be some litle advantage to your Irish affaires. If the Lord saw it good, I wish there were not that occasion of truble given to your lordship. I committ you and yours and your affaires to the good hande of the Lord and rest,

Your most humble servant,

Hie Sankey

[136] Perhaps the letter that Henry Cromwell initially sent to Thurloe, asking him to peruse it before forwarding it to Sankey (*TSP*, IV, pp. 254–255).

[137] Christopher Blackwood, minister in Kent and Sussex during the 1630s and in New England in the early 1640s, brought his Baptist faith to Ireland in 1652–1653, initially as minister at Kilkenny. Supported by Daniel Axtell, Blackwood strongly encouraged the spread of Baptism amongst the English army in Ireland, moving to Dublin in 1655 and taking over Thomas Patient's congregation. An active Baptist, in October 1655 described by Thomas Harrison as 'the oracle of the anabaptists in Ireland' (*TSP*, IV, pp. 90–91), he appears to have lost his official, government salary in 1656, though he did not oppose Henry Cromwell's religious policies as strongly as some of his fellow Baptists.

31. From William Stane, London, 4 December 1655, 821, fos 54–55.

My lord,

My lady Elizabeth continues ill, but wee hope mending; her Highnesse is recovred, twas much greife; his Highnesse and the rest well. Here are severall ministers and others meet to debate the reception and liberty of the Jews.

A Spanish ship upon a leek was forced to put in to Tore Bay in the west. It was laden with 30 bays[138] of cloth and 200 seamen provided for their fleet.

I was mistaken in my last; although my lady Russell and her son went down, yet Sir Francis continues in London still.

General Disborrow went down to the west this day to presente his instructions as major generall.[139] His wife's sicknes kept him here till this tyme. The other major-generalls proced in their circuits and have help enough for any part, I heare, and the commissioners hold.

The Lord give in unto you of His presence if in perticular warfares[140] wee are unsafe without it. How can publique employments proced happily without His bare arme, which makes every burden easye?

My affectionate service to my lady. I remaine, my lord,

Your faithfull servant,

W Stane

My services to colonel Tomlinson and all our frinds.

I gave your lordship an account in my last of the late discoverye by takeing of Henshaw,[141] the late king of Scots' agent. It seemes his friends, Charles Stewart and Middleton, sent into Scotland, were conversing and gave encouragement to their freinds there for another day, designeing also against the persons of some in that place.[142]

[138] Possibly a slip for 'bayls', but 'bays' could indicated a number of portions of the ship's hold.

[139] He was major-general of the whole of the south-west region, comprising Cornwall, Devon, Somerset, Dorset, Gloucestershire, and Wiltshire.

[140] Word seems a little strange in this context but is quite clearly written thus.

[141] Thomas Henshaw, spy and conspirator, had been employed by the English republican government in the early 1650s, but by the mid-1650s was supporting the royalist cause on the continent. He had returned to England in the spring of 1654 to support John Gerard's failed plot to assassinate the Protector, but had then managed to escape abroad.

[142] There were persistent rumours of royalist plots at this time, many of them supposedly focused on Scotland, including suggestions that John Middleton, a royalist general, who had been one of the leading lights of the Glencairn rising in Scotland in 1653–1654, but who had slipped away to the continent on the suppression of that revolt in spring 1655, might return to Scotland.

32. From Nathaniel Waterhouse,[143] Whitehall, 4 December 1655, 821, fos 56–57.

May it please your lordshipp,

I received your lordshipp's lettre, wherein you are pleased to say that you thinke you are forgotten of all your frends here. Truely, my lord, I must confess I have been very much too blame, that I have not in all this tyme written unto your lordshipp, but I hope your honor will be pleased to pardon it when you doe truely understand the reason, the which I shall now acquint your honour with, (which is this) wee are now upon some establishment in the family, wherein wee have sett downe a thousand pounds per annum for your lordshipp, the which if his Highness be pleased to pass (as I hop hee will) then I shall proceed to the payment of those bills I have. And then I doubt not but I shall give your lordshipp a very just accompt of my reall affection to serve your honour in whatever I shall bee able, and in the meanewhile shall make bould to subscribe myselfe,

Your lordshipp's most humble servant,

Nat Waterhouse

33. William Stane, London, 10 December 1655, 821, fos 58–59.

My lord,

Just now my lady Elizabeth (wee hope) is fallen into her labour.[144] Truly, if the Lord had not bin so kinde to us, wee do not know what might have bin the issue. Dr Goddard[145] and I have sate up againe each night. I never saw 2 parents so affected (or more) then my Lord Protector and her Highnesse. Truly my lady hath given a sweet testimony in this sicknes if the Lord continue His love further.

All well at Wallingford.

[143] One of two stewards of the Protectoral household, Waterhouse later served as master of the greencloth within the Protectoral household and as an MP in the second and third Protectorate parliaments.

[144] Possibly suggesting that a difficult pregnancy was thus coming towards its natural conclusion, though 'labour' could have other medical meanings, relating to fighting afflictions, and other correspondents who noted Elizabeth Claypole's poor health during the autumn and early winter of 1655 tended to ascribe it to an illness from which she might recover, rather than to complications arising from pregnancy.

[145] Jonathan Goddard, physician, academic, and administrator, had found favour with parliament in general and Oliver Cromwell in particular, accompanying him on his campaigns in Ireland and Scotland in 1649–1651, and was appointed physician in chief to the parliamentarian army, as well as warden of Merton College, Oxford, from 1651. He acquired several academic and administrative positions during the Protectorate, including a professorship at Gresham College in 1655, and served as one of the Protector's physicians.

I have not tyme for news or the enquirie of it. I wish all goe well with you. There are rumors upon those petitions. The Lord guide you; trulye His leadings are best; and surely Hee doth expect from those whom Hee hath brought into power, by signes and wordes, more then ordinary; and a Christian ought to approve themselfs so in every state, publique as well as particular, in all capacities.

I hope your lordship takes care of my lady in that strange land. My service to her ladyship.

No news yet from Jamaica. It's whispered that forreigne states are doeing somwhat.

The major-generalls succeed, and the commissioners in all counties stand and assist.

But I am in great hast. I remaine, my lord,

Your affectionate servant,

W Stane

My lord deputy did not act in the councell till last week.

34. From Charles Fleetwood, Wallingford House, 11 December 1655, 821, fos 60–61.

Deare brother,

The illness of sister Claypoole is so very great that both there Highnesses are under a great triall. You know the dearenes they have unto her and though wee know not how the Lord will deale with her, yet her recoverye is much doubted. This afternoone hath given very great cause of feare. The Lord teach us all by such dispensations our dayes and times are very uncertaine. The Lord knowes when our periods shalbe put, and therefore to improve time whilest it's ours is a great dutie; to worke while tis day least the night overtake us before wee are aware. It is not youth of dayes that can secure us. Happy are those who have Christ in there harte and shalbe found and doing there Master's will.

You must excuse my not inlargeing at this time; both the occasion and my time must pleade for me. The greate success that still it pleaseth God to give the king of Sweeden doth very much alarum forraigne states. I am not without hope but that the Lord may make my Lord Protector an instrument of great good upon this occasion to the whole Protestant interest. He hath, I am perswaded, a very large hart above any for such a worke. The councell, it seemes, lately made an order for part of that money which was intended for Ireland for the use of the navy. But I hope notwithstanding that order, wee shall keepe it for Ireland. Our old freinds the tresurers sticke to us.[146] I hope you will not

[146] Treasurers-at-war, Richard Deane and John Blackwell.

lett honnest captaine Blackwell suffer though a returne be not made in his busines.[147] With my humble service to my sister I remaine,

Your most affectionate brother and servant,

Charles Fleetwood

I must entreate you will take care that captain Shawe[148] may have no prejudice concerning his clayme. His Highness intends him favour. In the meane time I desire your kindnes to him.

My brother Sankey desires you would please to order a man-of-warr to be at Hollyhead about the 28th instant to transport him for Ireland.

Since the writing hearof, my sister Claypoole is fallen into travill and so hir condition very hopefull.[149]

35. From Charles Fleetwood, Wallingford House, 24 December 1655, 821, fos 62–63.

Deare brother,

This worthy good person, colonel Cooper,[150] his Highnes hath commanded me to give him a commission for generall Venables' regiment as also to command in cheife all the forces in Ulster under you, which accordingly I have done. He is to continue both his regiment and pay for them untill there can be some way thought off as an addition to his pay in Ireland, or till he can come to a certaine resolution whether to continnue in Ireland or not. What of

[147] With Oliver Cromwell's support, in 1653 Blackwell had been allocated land in County Dublin and elsewhere (Dunlop, pp. 358–359), but difficulties arose and in 1655 he appealed to the Protector for assistance. Eventually, in May 1657, the second Protectorate parliament passed an act settling upon him land in Counties Dublin and Kildare.

[148] Probably the captain Shaw (his forename not recorded) who arrested Edmund Ludlow at Beaumaris in October 1655 (*TSP*, IV, pp. 87–88), when the latter suddenly left Ireland in defiance of an order from the Protector (Dunlop, p. 538). Shaw reputedly became rich through various offices he held in the Irish administration, especially as receiver of rents for Irish lands set out to soldiers in 1655.

[149] Sentence added at the end of the letter, in the left margin and along the edge of the paper, in a hurried hand.

[150] Thomas Cooper, parliamentarian officer and politician, had commanded a regiment of foot raised in London in 1650–1651, which campaigned in Scotland for much of the 1650s. He was appointed to the Scottish council in the spring of 1655, though that body did not begin work until September 1655. Although he continued in nominal command of his Scottish regiment for some time after his departure, in practice he was superseded in Scotland by Roger Sawrey, and instead, in December 1655, Cooper left Scotland to take over the foot regiment in Ireland formerly commanded by the disgraced Robert Venables. He soon proved himself an able, active, but conciliatory, commander in Ulster and, despite his Baptist faith, loyal to and respected by Henry Cromwell (*TSP*, III, p. 744, and IV, pp. 343, 376, 407–408, 422–423, 433, 551). He was returned for Counties Down, Antrim, and Armagh to the second Protectorate parliament.

kindnes and respect you can show him, I doubt not off. I hope he will prove a person as a healing mercy, which indeed is the great busines wee should mind this day wherein our divisions are like to produce such sad effects, as to lay us naked and bare to a common enemy and there continnuall designes. What there is now on worke by the cavaliere partie colonel Cooper will informe you. His Highness thinckes it convenient you should have more horse in Ulster, which is all at present from,

Your most affectionate brother and humble servant,

Charles Fleetwood

1656

36. From Richard Cromwell, Whitehall, 1 January 1656, 821, fos 64–65.

Deare brother,

Being att Whitehall from whence one sence my coming thither I have troubled you, and this is like to prove another, I professe the only reason why I am not this way more often vissetting you. And peradventure my cautiousnesse may be accounted neglect, but having a clear mark of affection to you, I can by that give my selfe a great deale of quiett. I desire to abandon all thought of unkindnesse and I am certaine it must be high provocation that shall raise such a spiritt in me. As nature hath linked us soe near, soe shall the grace of God tye our affections with cords of true love that cannot be broken. I ought not to robb you of your pretious time, nor should I have gone any further, much lesse troubled you with any new matter, but that I am through the exceeding civility of my countryman, Mr Reynolds,[1] prest in my disposition to answer the obligation of his kindnesse by recommending to your intrested power in the councell of Ireland the consideration of his bussinesse that it may have a speedy dispatch and effectually to answer the expectations which are very much raised even to confidence, for that his Highness hath written on his behalfe. That which is aimed att is that his lands may be sett oute. I need not ofer many arguments, there being a justnesse in it that it should be done and a just disposition in you to see those juste rights speedily and rightly placed; it being a carrecter upon you, hath prouved great reputation; never did private spiritt doe anything that was worthy of living praisse. I desire God to continew such a spiritt to you as may be publique, it being comprehensive you are certaine by its learge cercumference to take in all sorts of people, and soe consequently the people of God; you making noe difference but when the seale is upon a saint and the marke of the beaste upon an enimy to Jesus Christ, yet it preserving property to all sorts and ranks of men. I am ashamed of my tediousnesse to you, and therefore I shall desire your excuse and the presenting my unfeined respects and

[1] Robert Reynolds.

service to my dear sister and your self, I take leave and rest, deare brother,

Your most affectionate brother and servant,
R Cromwell

37. Charles Fleetwood, Wallingford House, 1 January 1656, 821, fos 66–67.

Deare brother,

I am by my sister,[2] the lady Mary Cromwell, desired that you would please to take this gentleman, Mr Robert Turbridge,[3] into your favour, that he may have some convenient fitting imployment in a civill capacitie, he being, as I am informed, a very deserving person. Your kindnes and respect to him is the suit of,

Your most affectionate brother and humble servant,
Charles Fleetwood

38. From Richard Hodden,[4] Kinsale, 4 January 1656, 821, fos 68–69.

My lord,

I entreate leave humbly to offer these few words with the incloased concerning the persons called Quakers, etc.[5] Many of them were prosecuted in the daies of the late bishopps by the name of Puritants (though unblameable in their conversations), and since have faithfully served this comonwealth, even in the worst of times. And the God of glorie therein supported them through evill reporte and good

[2] His sister-in-law.

[3] Perhaps the adventurer of that name of St Martin's in the Fields, Middlesex, who had acted as a trustee for the parliamentarian politician and Protectoral councillor Philip, Viscount Lisle.

[4] Parliamentarian officer, he went to Ireland in 1649 with Hardress Waller's New Model foot regiment, which was partly disbanded in summer 1655, though by that time Hodden was governor of Kinsale. Almost certainly a Quaker himself, he strongly supported the Quakers in Kinsale and was viewed with suspicion by Henry Cromwell. In February 1656 Henry Cromwell reported that Hodden was inclining to Quakerism – he 'is, I feare, goeing that way; he keepes one of them to preach to the souldiers' – while in April he condemned Hodden as untrustworthy and 'a man of atheisticall principles' (*TSP*, IV, pp. 508, 672).

[5] By the winter of 1655–1656 Henry Cromwell was becoming alarmed at the spread of Quakerism amongst the English army in Ireland, and especially amongst towns and garrisons in Munster such as Kinsale, fearful that it might undermine military discipline and – like Baptism – encourage or serve as a front for political opposition to his government and the Protectoral regime (*TSP*, IV, pp. 506, 672, 757). Aware of possible moves against the Quakers, Hodden was writing in defence of Quakerism in general and probably in particular of two prominent Quaker preachers, Edward Burrough and Francis Howgill, who were then touring southern Ireland winning converts.

reporte, and other names of derision, too many here to mention, while bloody minded, evill men and seducers have waxed worse and worse, deceiving and being deceived.

And now, my lord, I beseech you consider that reformation is begun, not finished, and the fowndation and principall parte thereof spirituall, without which all outward formes are but deceipt. As it is written, wee looke for a new heaven and a new earth wherein dwells righteousnes. And it hath bien and is hoped that in this wast lande may be comfortable habitations for religious English men, if thereunto incouraged.

God hath heretofore remembered his servants in their low estate and it will be your joy, strength and happines to owne such in the Lord. And I also beseech you to take notice againe and againe how pollitick and wise in their generation som men are for other ends then your service or the people's soules.

I have nothing to say for such as shall be found fighters against God, denie His holynes, justifie themselves in their abominations, or that commit other misdemeanours or breaches of the peace: God forbid.

These are private lynes to your lordshippe out of a deepe sence of my duetie, and in sinceritie of hearte as in the sight of God, wherein (it's like) few will be soe free and plaine with you, which I the rather am, for that I have (through the tender mercie of God) had full knowledg of divers of the before mentioned persons in England and here. Deare sir, it will never repente you that you incourage vertue and punnishe vice, wherein I beseech the God of heaven to be your guide, in whom I am,

Your excellencie's faithfull and affectionate servant,

Ri Hodden

39. From Charles Fleetwood, London, 8 January 1656, 821, fos 70–71.

Deare brother,

Your freedom I take very kindly as a fruit and effect of your frendshippe, and if you and I showld not retaine our old and hearty affection each to other, whear can we expect it? And therfor give not the least credit to any reports or suggestions which may tend to the contrary, but looke therupon as a serpent to be fledde from. It is the houre of saddnes in that respect that jealousyes takes place even amongst the nearest relations. I confesse to you I did not, nor doe I otherwayes then, looke upon that petition then out of design to devide twixt you and me, and to make our interests at least to be looked upon as contradistinct, which I hope shall never take effect. As for the representations you conceive have bine given me, I see you are mistaken. If you did but know what affection they hath writt with concerning your own person, you would otherwayes believe of them. I confesse clearly to you, whom I have so much reason to love, that I doe feare you may have some too great prejudice against som of them, whom I am deceived if they are not earnest with the Lord in your behalfe. And though I would not write this for a great dell to them, yet if my playnes be a mistake, it will be your mercy now whilst ther is any thing of prejudice in your heart against any one or more. Sathan will be sure to blow that up to the higth and will continually begett and increase jealousyes. And I tell you plainly, I doe feare some may suggest things to your jealousnesing of me, which I know they canot doe nor dare doe it directly, but by consequence; and therfor let us be in this free, one with another, not to suffer so much as a thought by way of reflection or jealousyes each of other. Let others pretend what they will, I doubt not I shall be found your faithfully loving brother.

I have not much at presant to impart unto you of newes. The poore Protestant Switzers are like to engage in a new warre with the Catholick cantons.[6] They have sent for ayde from hence, which we shall be ready to afford as the condition of our affayeres will permitt. Yeasterday we had a meeting with the comittee formerly appoynted for the collection of the Piemonts. They desire you will doe what you can to get in thos collections formerly subscribed. The buysnes is of great importance and what you can to increase the subscriptions and to collect what hath bine subscribed will be very acceptable to his Highnes and councell heare.[7] My Lord Protector hath a great desire to make the peace amongst the Protestants states as large as he can; endeavors will be used accordingly. I presumed embassedors will be suddenly sent. Colonel John Jones[8] is like to goe into Hollande as agent about publicke affayres. Ther was thoughts of his return into Ireland; let me know your opinion therin. If you approve therof it may be don, but without you it shall not. I must desire one word more to you, and that is you would not suffer the way of tyths to goe out of its presant channell, but continue the way of maintenance as of late yeares it hath bine done. His Highnes and councell would be glade it

[6] The uneasy peace in Switzerland was breaking down along sectarian fracture lines.

[7] Eventually around £1,100 was raised by Henry Cromwell in Ireland (Dunlop, pp. 545, 668–669; *TSP*, IV, pp. 483–484).

[8] Parliamentarian officer and politician, and a regicide, he campaigned in his native Wales during the 1640s and served as a parliamentary commissioner for Ireland from 1650 until 1654, when he and his colleagues were superseded by a lord deputy and council appointed by the Protector. Jones had travelled to London in the summer of 1654, shortly before his commission ended, in part to brief the Protector on Irish affairs. He was returned to the second Protectorate parliament.

wer so heare.[9] Ther hath bin some late thoughts of making that worke more easly heare too,[10] as allso in regulating the law. Heare inclosed is the debt ascertained by the comittee of the army. Ther is no way of payment therof but to put it upon compostitions and rebells' lands. Let me know your thoughts therin. Excuse this trouble of,

Your most affectionate brother and servant,

Charles Fleetwood

This inclosed the bishoppe of Armagh[11] desires your favor in its dispatch according to his Highnes' order.

MacNaughton[12] in Scotland hath, it seemes, endeavoured by some of his agents, endeavoured to make disturbances in Ireland by sending some of his instruments thither. The more care you take of the north the better. The common enimy are still at worke; though through mercy be hoped will take litle effect through its timely discovery.

40. William Stane, London, 8 January 1656, 821, fos 72–73.

My lord,

I have little to impart to your lordship, only that I would keep my hand in use, and give your lordship a testimony that I do not forget you and my good lady. Colonel Montague[13] is made generall-at-sea and intends to go in person. If the rest (for the great designes in hand) bee proportionably disposed of, I hope it will prove a great blessing to my Lord Protector and these nations. There will bee some alteration in

[9] Although the tithe system was seen as unsatisfactory and in need of reform, Protector, council, and parliament never found a better and more workable way to fund parish livings, and the tithe system continued in England and Wales throughout the Protectorate. In Ireland, a slightly revised system had been imposed after 1649, with much of the church revenue from tithes and other sources being paid direct to the state, which in turn employed ministers and awarded them government salaries.

[10] Word heavily amended and possibly deleted.

[11] During 1655 James Ussher, archbishop of Armagh and primate of the Protestant Church of Ireland, had been granted by the Protector various leases in Ireland, both for himself and for his son-in-law.

[12] Alexander MacNaughton, Laird of Macnaughton, had been prominent in the Glencairn rising in Scotland in 1653–1654. Although he submitted to the Protectoral government in the spring of 1655, upon the collapse of that rising, he was one of the leading Scottish royalist leaders suspected of renewed plotting in the winter of 1655–1656.

[13] Parliamentarian officer and politician, he campaigned during the civil war until relinquishing his command under the self-denying ordinance. He withdrew from parliament and office in the wake of Pride's Purge and the regicide, but returned to public life in 1653 as a member of the Nominated Assembly. He held a range of senior offices during the Protectorate, sat in both of Oliver Cromwell's Protectorate parliaments, and was a Protectoral councillor. Despite little or no previous experience of naval affairs, he was appointed an admiral by Protector and council in early January 1655, in effect superseding the disgraced William Penn.

the customs, but what is not ascertained, but in his Highnesse' breast, who the persons shall bee. There is some whisper as if that Spaine and France might agree. If it bee possible the convention at Bolonia[14] will bring that and things of like sort to passe. I hope that colonel Zanchey by this is with your lordship. The Lord direct you. I trust you seek Him much and walk humbly before Him. Surely that of a little child is a good subject for His teaching, and I am perswaded in the work in hand all other teaching and wisedome will prove fruitles. It holds good in both warefares. When David went into the sanctuary, there hee learnt understanding, both of his world and that which is to come.

His Highnesse is well, but my Lady Protectoresse cannot bee perfect in health. My lady Elizabeth continues in health. My lady Fleetwood hath a great cold. My lord deputy now follows busines hard; and indeed it is no more then is needfull, the work is great and the hands suiteable to it few. My lord Richard is still in towne. I have not heard lately from Chippnam, but I presume they are well, else Mr Percyvall[15] would give it mee. I am now in Pett France, and my wife also, who is (I blesse the Lord) somwhat better.

Myne and my wife's services to my lady and your lordship. Our respect and service to colonel Zanchye. My service to colonel Tomlinson and all our freinds. My respect to Dr Harrison. I am, my lord,

Your lordship's faithful servant,

W Stane

41. Charles Fleetwood, Wallingford House, 15 January 1656, 821, fos 74–75.

Deare brother,

Haveing receaved this inclosed from my lord Broghill[16] I thought fitt to send it you, though I suppose you may have it alreadie, either from his lordship or Mr Secretary. They are still at worke in Scotland but it's hoped, through the goodnes of the Lord, there designes being much

[14] There were reports of a meeting at Bologna to open the way for full peace negotiations.

[15] John Percival, Irish-born administrator, who sought favour from Henry Cromwell and was later knighted by him, was also known to Sir Francis Russell and may for a time have been employed by Russell.

[16] Roger Boyle, Baron Broghill, Irish-born officer and politician, campaigned against the Catholics in Ireland during the 1640s and supported parliamentarian policies there. In 1649, perhaps in the wake of a meeting with Oliver Cromwell, he was a forceful advocate for the English republic's handling of Ireland, accepting senior command in the parliamentarian reconquest and campaigning extensively under Cromwell and his successors, acquiring substantial Irish estates in the process. He strongly supported the Protector and the Protectoral regime, sat in both of Oliver Cromwell's Protectorate parliaments and was rewarded with a number of offices. From September 1655 until August 1656, he was in Scotland, as president of the Scottish council and, in effect, chief administrator of Scotland.

discovered wilbe prevented. I doubt not of your especiall care of the north. There is a proclamation going out from the councell of Scotland prohibiting any to goe into Ireland without leave.[17] I looke upon it as necessary that you should prevent the like out of Ireland, as also that care may be taken that they keepe no armes. And tis conceaved necessary that a frigott should be ordered upon the coast of Scotland to ply to and againe. I hope you will find colonel Cooper a very active and discreet person to manage the affaires in the north.[18] Through mercy wee are in much quietnes heere, and I trust the generalitie of good people are more inclyned towards satisfaction, though I feare some good men are over hastie. The Lord cleare up His mind to them and us and send a healing spiritt that this precious cause may not suffer through our owne divisions. The saints have a mercy beyond what, I feare, wee have harte to price in his Highnes, whose care and labor for the people of the Lord wilbe rewarded. The worke of the major-generalls in reforming the severall associations and corporations goes on very throughly. Wee are sending two embassadors into Sweethland to endevour a generall peace amongst the Protestants.[19] What ever the issue wilbe, yett I am perswaded the Lord will owne the uprightnes and integritie of hart that is in this action in his Highnes. He hath bine somewhat indisposed this two dayes, but is better then he was. As for forraigne newes, I still refer you to Mr Secretary and must entreate you will excuse this present brevitie from,

Your most affectionate brother and humble servant,

Charles Fleetwood

This weeke's packett is not yett come.

42. From John Reynolds, 19 January 1656, 821, fos 76–77.

May it please your lordships,

I came hither[20] thorough God's blessing by seven this morning, or before eight, and do intend to go no farther than Bewmorris this night,

[17] *TSP*, IV, pp. 342–343.

[18] He had arrived in Ireland earlier in January.

[19] In fact, proposals to send joint ambassadors to Sweden did not materialize at this time.

[20] Probably Holyhead, landing there en route from Ireland to London. Although Henry Cromwell was unwilling to lose him – in September 1655 he had recommended Reynolds for foreign service, but also noted that 'if you take him from hence, you deprive me of my right hande' (*TSP*, IV, pp. 53–54) – Reynolds had received the Protector's permission to make a short visit to England. He left Ireland bearing wide-ranging instructions from Henry Cromwell and the Irish council, who wanted Reynolds to seek from the Protector and Protectoral council the speedy resolution of various Irish affairs, including settling the arrears and pay of the army; encouraging Protestant merchants to move there; and providing for a mint, town charters, and more schools (Dunlop, pp. 560–561).

in regard of my seasicknes, and thence forward with more speede to London.

I have since considered of the letters[21] and do beleive it most unfit that your lordships should be cajoled into power by those under your command, especially since it is to be done by applications to your lordship's owne father. Certainely his Highnes will do as much with information of the contents as by the thing delivered. And I feare there was some supprisall on our part, being so fond of their consent as we gave away our cause. I shall therefore delay presenting the letter untill the returne of the packet and shall than be constrained by virtue of my trust to present the same unto his Highnes. I most humbly kisse your lordship's hands, and beseeching the Lord to preserve and uphold your lordships in all difficultyes, do conclude your lordship's present trouble and remaine,

Your lordship's most obliged and most humble servant,

J Reynolds

43. From Charles Fleetwood, Wallingford House, 22 January 1656, 821, fos 78–79.

Deare brother,

I perceive by yours that colonel Sankey hath sayde somthing concerning my jealousyes of you, and som about you. I know not what he hath sayde but hope he is too worthy a person to speake any thing which may administer matter of suspition twixt us for he knowes my tendernes. But I have sayde so much in my late letter to you of this subject that I hope it will not be in the power of any to divide us (who have so much reason for a onenes both on the account of relation, affection and interest) and I am confydent Jerome will rather mak it his buysnes to heale mistakes then widen them. Deare brother, let's lay aside all jealous thoughts and love one another dearly, and not own them as frinds that suggest any thing to divert a hearty affection, which surely you and I hade each to other as could be expected twixt brothers. If you have any occation to command me you will finde what you may expect from an affectionately loving brother. The Lord teach us both by thes late endeavors to draw a vaile upon one another's affections. I think we had as great endearednes as could be found any

[21] Reynolds was carrying two letters to the Protector: one from the army officers in Ireland, calling for Fleetwood to return to Ireland as lord lieutenant, with Henry Cromwell made lord deputy under him; and a second from Hewson, stressing that Henry Cromwell had had no part in the Irish petition of the previous November, which had requested that the Protector make Henry Cromwell lord deputy in place of Fleetwood (*TSP*, IV, pp. 421–422). Reynolds's reception in London is recorded at *TSP*, IV, pp. 478, 505.

wheare, and I trust the same shall be restored, which I desire may be with advantage.

I am sorry you have not a vessell at Chester; it will make us suspect heare that you are not in that necessity, and it will be the harder to get you any supply within any reasonable time, we being in such sadde straights and necessityes heare that I doe not know which way we can turn to answer our presant necessityes. The fleet sinks deepe. His Highnes hath continnued ill thes tenn dayes, but through mercy is, I hope, recovering; he was this day in the parke. His distemper hath at present somewhat indisposed him as to busines, and then you may easilye beleive how much wee want the maine wheele to carry on our publique affaires. His Highnes is very much inlarged upon this good worke of uniting Protestants, which this worke carrying on by the Protestant Switzers will probably concure with that designe. Certainely the Lord is about some notable and great worke abroad as well as at home. Our affaires heere are through mercy in a quiett posture. I perceave by my lord Broghill that they are still a working in Scotland, and have there expectations heightened from Ireland. Colonel Cooper, I hope, will prove a happy instrument in the north. Wee had this day a great debate about my lord of Arde his case.[22] Wee only concluded with this, that it was not so proper for our determination as for yours, and so have left it to you, which I feare you will find troblesome but it could not welbe prevented. Wee are going on about further instructions as to Ireland upon the proposalls I sent you. Wee shall now, I hope, obtaine a mintt for you in Ireland. Wee have almost concluded with a man this night. There is nothing for the good of Ireland wherein you want power but you may have it, and therefore[23] me know wherein either of publicque or particuler concernment, and you will find mee,

Your most affectionate brother,

Charles Fleetwood

Our affectionate services to your selfe and deare sister. I must entreate you will please so farr to consider this poore petitioner's condition as to continnue her pention to her. I must also desire you will

[22] Hugh, Viscount Montgomery of Arde, an Irish-born Protestant, had supported the royalist cause in Ireland in 1649–1650. Having surrendered to Oliver Cromwell and then retired to the continent, he had been allowed to return to Ireland and eventually, after considerable discussion in London and Dublin, in 1657 he was able to compound for and recover much of his Irish estate. Nevertheless, he was viewed with suspicion by the Protectoral regime and was imprisoned between January and April 1656 (*CSPI*, pp. 580–581).

[23] Word – perhaps 'let' – apparently omitted.

please to cause a speedie returne to be made in the lady Tirconnell's busines.[24]

44. Charles Fleetwood, January[25] 1656, 821, fos 80–81.

Deare brother,

I have received yours wherein I perceave you much troubled with some things relating to colonel Hewson.[26] I cannot tell what you meane thereby. He did not write with reflection upon you to mee at any time; nether doe I thincke he did to his Highnes. I saw one letter which was far from such a thing, that hath expressed much affection and hansomenes concerning you.[27] I cannot thincke he would doe you any ill offices. You have bine otherwise represented by those you suspect then you give creditt unto. I beg of you to take heed of jelousies. I cannot but be plaine with you. I hope you shall not find mee unfaithfull to you upon any account, much les not only in that which may be inconvenient to your owne satisfaction, but also wherein you may be hindred in your publicque worke. It is sathan's designe to foment and encrease divisions. It is much that those you suspect should carry it unhansomly towards you. For this I know, I have receaved severall letters with expressions of much affection. It wilbe your wisdome and mercy to beare with weaknesses and not easilye to give creditt to reports; for reallye tis one of the sadnes of this day that men delight to speake evill one of another and to make it there busines to sow division and make breaches. Doe not thincke you are without a temptation of this sort, even by some who may pretend affection to you, and yett under that disguise prejudice more then by any other way to make

[24] Bridget, widow of Roderick, Earl of Tyrconnel, and wife of Nicholas, Viscount Barnewall, an Irish Catholic, who had supported the royalist cause in Ireland and England in the 1640s and who had been imprisoned in 1654 on suspicion of a royalist plot against the Protector. She was requesting that she and her husband should not suffer sequestration of estates and transportation to Connaught, the common fate of Irish Catholics (*CSPI*, pp. 608–611).

[25] Paper slightly damaged and date lost.

[26] Henry Cromwell viewed Hewson as the English-based agent, and to some extent ringleader, of the group of Baptist officers opposing his rule in Ireland. Henry was alarmed to hear that Hewson had written one or more letters of complaint to the Protector – 'if collonel Hewson must be beleived [...] I must be made a liar, if not worse' – and was exasperated when Hewson and his allies not only tried to smear the petition urging Henry Cromwell's appointment as lord deputy as the work of 'cavaliers and disaffected persons', but also claimed that a letter that they had, in turn, received from the Protector broadly supported their position and complaints (*TSP*, IV, pp. 327–328, 348–349, 349–350, 373).

[27] Perhaps Hewson's letter to the Protector of 16 January 1656, noting that he had now shown the Protector's letter to him to Henry Cromwell, acknowledging that Henry Cromwell had had no part in the petition of November 1655, and also promising 'to doe what I can to heale' (*TSP*, IV, p. 422).

you beleive evill of those who, I hope, intend no evill to you, but waite frequently upon the Lord for you. I confes I cannot thincke that they have unfaithfull harts to you, and indeed for them and the good man for whom I am sure you had a good opinion, and for you now to be suspitious of them and him, makes mee very much to feare that some doe not good offices, but much the contrary. As to what you mention concerning his misrepresentations heere, I know therein as to matter of fact you are mistaken, and therefore hope you are in other things, and if you thincke I may be deceaved in this I shall labor to send you the letter which he sent to his Highnes, that so by your owne veiw you may be convinced. What designe can you imagine for me to have in my desires and endevours to continnue a right understanding betwixt you and others but your good? I am perswaded if you enter into your owne hart you cannot but esteeme me as a deare and faithfull freind, and as I told his Highnes upon discourse of those things, appealing to his Highnes whether I had spoken reflectingly of you, wherein I know he will wittnes for mee, and as I then saide, if I knew anything done amisse by you, it was my dutie rather to tell him then any other thereof. I have a desire to discharge my dutie to you, and what I write at this time I know is for your good, and I desire that you will not passe it over with these thoughts, that what I write is out of prejudice to some particular persons and opinions of others. As for the petition which you are pleased to call inoffensive to you, who might intend no evill thereby, it might be so; but what was in the intention of those who were the contrivers and abettors thereof? I confes I cannot so easilye cleare them, it haveing no other tendancie then to divide; but I may be looked upon as a partie something concerned, and therefore shalbe silent. I hope that whatsoever men shall designe, yet our affections each to other are so much one as well as our interest, that to stricke at the one wil not be looked upon as a respect to the other, and this rightly considered wilbe much the state of the case. Though give me leave to say that a reflection of that kind will, I trust, prove my mercy upon the best account and not my punishment; and though my major's[28] opinion is as though it were inconsistent with our interests for me to returne, yet I hope his politicks much faile him in that petition, and I trust it is not the place of deputie wilbe my errand into Ireland.[29] And if I cannot serve you and the publique in my returne, I hope it is not ambition will invite me thither; but whatsoever I am, and when you have had experience of others, you will find me to bee,

Your most affectionate brother,
Charles Fleetwood

[28] Probably Hezekiah Haynes.

[29] Again hinting that he expected to return to Ireland, perhaps as lord lieutenant rather than lord deputy.

£30,000 is gone towards you. I hope you have appointted a good ship to transport it.

45. From A. Deane, [January 1656], 821, fo. 82.

My noble lord,

My last, I hope, hath arrived att your lordship's hand, and gave an account how affaires then stood, which are yett in the same posture, and nothing new butt the addition of collonell Montague to bee a generall-att-sea. Hee is now gone to Chattam to veiw his ship. Affaires heere looke with a good countenance; and the designe of the major-generals quite extinguisheth the hopes off the malignant party; and I beseach you bee carefull who you trust and confide in. I hope by the next, by some spiritts I have sett a worke, to bee able to wright you word[30] your most clandestine enemyes. I shall wish you all happiness and ever bee, my lord,

The faithfullest of your humble servaunts,

A Deane

My lord, I shall beg the favour that you would bee pleased to give a stopp to any proceedings in the lord Nettervill's[31] estate, either by the adventerour or soldiers, that soe the application hee makes heere in England may bee more effectuall and nott made more difficult by a prepossession in Ireland. Pray, my lord, owne mee in this thing which comes within the compasse of your authority.

46. From Charles Fleetwood, London, 5 February 1656, 821, fos 83–84.

Deare brother,

If my own pen hath not bine the messenger weekly of my affections to you, be pleased to understand and be confydent it was not for want of a due love, but I often write large to you and more then to any other, and somtimes I am forced for want of time to make my servant take in short hand what I have to write, but since you are pleased to have so favorable an acceptation of my scribles I shall not give occation of the like offence, and if in any thing I could demonstrate affection, you have reason and right to expect it. Jerome Sanckey gives me an account of how good an accord ther is like to be amongst you, which,

[30] Word – perhaps 'of' or 'about' – apparently omitted.

[31] John, Viscount Netterville, an Irish-born Catholic and royalist, had been sequestrated, but some of his Irish lands had passed to his wife and, after her death, to their children, thus giving Netterville a continuing interest in his estate in Ireland (*CSPI*, pp. 629–631, 836–838).

if the Lord please to continue amongst you, will be all your mercyes. That is a good word and fitt for us often to minde. Whence comes your contentions or divisions? Com they not from your lusts? And surly did we all consider it arit, we should find too much of that as that which so widens the breach at this day.

We are through mercy in a good, quiet condition, and I hope not so much in the heate of dissatisfaction as formerly. We have still very sadde reproofes from Jameca. Our men dye and sicken very fast that ther numbers are neare halfe in halfe lessened.[32] That keepe to your selfe; also Fortescue is deade,[33] besides severall other feild officers. Ther are still the most saddest, sottish managment of things ther as I think ever was known in any affayre, wherin the Lord's hand appeares exceedingly, even to suffer such a spirit of infatuation that they have acted scarce lik men, suffer their men to starve and in the meantime their provisions lying a rotting. Nay, they hade not so much as built a store house for their provisions till major Sedgwicke cam, who hath in his short time put things in a better and more hopefull posture. The hand of the Lord hath appeared against us; the Lord teach us mor to looke and see what the Lord sayse, and the lesse then we looke at the miscarriage of instruments the better. His Highnes is under trouble about this buysnes yet beares much better then I hade feared he would, and I hope will take the right course in seaking counsell of the Lord in this great affayre, which I trust He will by His presance, and might we but meet the Lord in the way of His judgments, I am perswaded we showld soone finde a blessed and gratious returne, and though we may be at presant under the reproach of our enimyes, yet the Lord who is gratious will pardon and heale and have mercy[34] us his poore ones, who have, I trust, som measure of integrity. I have not received any from you this weeke; you still sende them under Mr Secretorye's cover, and so through buysnes or one thing and another I canot com by them till it be late. I must acquaint you that I belive ther will be a desire of sending 800 or a 1,000 souldyers to the men at Jameca; let me heare suddenly what you can doe therin. I doe think you shall have a return of the men heare in case you sende such a

[32] From over six thousand to around three thousand men.

[33] Richard Fortescue, parliamentarian officer, was given command of a New Model foot regiment in 1645 and campaigned in England in 1645–1646, but lost his military command on siding with parliament against the army in 1647 and was briefly imprisoned in the early 1650s on suspicion of conspiring against the republican regime. The Protector appointed him second-in-command of the West Indies expedition in 1654–1655, and he became effective commander of the land forces there after Venables's departure and the death of major-general James Hearne, but he died in Jamaica in October 1655.

[34] Word – perhaps 'on' or 'to' – apparently omitted.

party from Ireland. My deare brother, I hope I am dearly beloved by you, to whom I am,

Your most affectionate brother.

Our affectionate services to my deare sister.

The poore Protestant Switzers have bine a litle worsted but I hope not considerable. They presse hard for money from hence. I doubt not you will doe what you can in Ireland.

Deare brother, since the former was writt I have received yours which gave me a great reviving with som loving expressions. In that coyn, I hope, I shall pay you with advantage; you are too deare to me to be estranged. I desire we make it our buysnes to love one another more and more. In that I am perswaded we shall please the Lord. I trust this late interposition, so seemingly to be, will be our advantage.

I have lately had a person very considerable out of this citty to desire that some merchants and others might make a bargayn with the state about the howses at Galloway.[35] He is to bring me his proposalls, which I shall hasten away to you, and what your result is that shall be observed.

47. From John Reynolds, 5 February 1656, 821, fos 85–86.

May it please your lordshipp,

I have received the honour of two letters from your lordshipp, wherein I did most gladly reade the effect of my prayers in your lordship's health restored, which mercy I trust the Lord will continue.

The embassy hath beene delivered and will, I doubt not, be successfull in all publique concernements, and I shall endeavour to be happy in that enjoiment; at least thereby diminish and mitigate my private.

I parted even now with the Secretary, who declares greate satisfaction in your lordship's management of affaires and expresses greate affection to your lordshipp, with a greate sense of your Christian and prudent letters, etc.

I have beene with his Highnes and did deliver all my papers from the officers which he reade, except the letter which was so full of parallells to Christ Jesus, as some who saw it affirmed it came neere

[35] The town of Galway had become depopulated because of the enforced removal of the Irish Catholic population in the autumn of 1655 (Dunlop, pp. 546–547, 548–549) and, in consequence, many of its buildings were empty and falling ruinous. Henry Cromwell and others wished to encourage Protestant and mercantile settlement there to revive Galway's fortunes, and several schemes were proposed around this time (Dunlop, pp. 576–577, 620; *TSP*, IV, pp. 483–484, 508, and V, p. 494).

blasphemy.[36] I beseech your lordshipp to take no notice of this, least those who sent over this should be earnest to pursue it. I suppose colonel Clerke's[37] mediation will now be useles.

The instructions, which I received from the councell, have not yet received any answer from his Highnes and the councell heere, but I hope daily for a dispatch. The busines of transporting Irish was referred to the lord deputy and colonel Lambert to represent to his Highnes for his assent, and the commission for setting lands is referred to the committee to prepare instructions. The Lord direct your lordshipp in all your greate affaires. I see little helpe to be expected; no persons heere can be prevailed with who are fit to be councellours. Your lordship's sence of persons would be welcome. His Highnes commanded me to assure your lordshipp of his tender love to you, and that you may be equally precious in the sight of your heavenly Father is the prayer of, my lord,

Your lordship's most humble, faithfull, obliged servaunt,

J Reynolds

48. From Nathaniel Waterhouse, Whitehall, 5 February 1656, 821, fos 87–88.

May it please your lordship,

I am to begge your honor's pardon that I have not aquainted your lordship what I have done as conserninge the payment of those debts you left with me. My lord, I did pay above three hundred pounds of them before I receaved your halfe year's rent, wich was done the[38] 29th of September last. And about 14 dayes since, (and not before) I receaved five hundred pounds of Mr Maidston[39] for that halfe yeare,

[36] The officers' letter to the Protector, which Reynolds had himself signed, suggested that something of Christ's image and spirit could be seen in Fleetwood – 'inasmuch as wee have beheld the lively image of our Lord Jesus Christ in him, and [. . .] have satt under his shaddow with great delight' (*TSP*, IV, p. 421).

[37] John Clarke/Clerke, parliamentarian officer and politician. By the later 1640s he was an officer in Hardress Waller's New Model foot regiment and in 1651, as lieutenant-colonel, he commanded the successful recapture of the Scilly Isles. In 1652 he took command of a new regiment deployed in Ireland, but it was disbanded in summer 1655. Although Clarke was then given nominal command of a regiment in Ireland comprising garrison troops, he spent much of the period in England, sitting in every parliament between 1653 and 1659, representing Ireland in the Nominated Assembly, and Counties Londonderry, Donegal, and Tyrone in the first Protectorate parliament, but mainland seats in the second and third Protectorate parliaments.

[38] Word repeated in error.

[39] John Maidstone, parliamentarian official and politician, worked closely with Waterhouse as steward of the Protectoral household. He was also cofferer of the household and sat in both of Oliver Cromwell's Protectorate parliaments.

allthough it is not as yet confermed by his Highness, but I doubt not but he will be pleased to conferme the allowance to your honor. Since the receaving the £500 before mentioned, I have paid upward of £400, soe as I am out of purse above £200 more then I have yet receaved. And shall, God willinge, as moneyes doe com in, discharge them all with what spead I can. But I doe asure your lordship we are in more strayets of late for moneyes then we have beanne this 4 or 5 yeares. My lord, I am at present confined to my chamber, being not very well, or other wayes I had now sent your honor a partickuler what I have allready payd. But if it please the Lord to give me helth, I shall send it by the next. I besech your honor not to doubt, but that I will doe whatever is in my power and I hope when you shall see howe many of those debts be satisfied, your honor will rest contented, and will see I have not beane neckligent. And soe I humbly take leave and rest,

Your lordship's most humbell servant,

Nat Waterhouse

49. From Charles Fleetwood, [12 February] 1656, 821, fos 256–257.

Deare brother,

The presant time is so short and I in no good condition of wrighting that I must intreat your excuses for my now shortnes. I perceive you are in some wants of more at counsell, which I doe as well presume as heare, but wheare to finde persons sutable is the difficulty. Let me know whom you have a minde unto. It is very hard to get any who are satisfyed and other wayes fitt for such a worke. We finde a want heare of instruments, and the truth is our condition is such that we have few and have very much buysnes, that many things either wholly suffer or are delayed in a great measure through the want of more instruments. Yet I know Ireland's condition to be such, in respect of that defect, that I canot but much desire you wer fully supplyed. As for moneyes, you shall have according to what is allotted allready for Ireland, provided to be sent equall with England and Scotland. We are in great streights for money, and therfor give me leave still to minde you of good husbandry, though I must give you your due, I have not heard anything to the contrary but doe think your care hath bine great therin. We are upon some considerable considerations as to our forrigne transactions. You shall heare more therof. Jamieca buysnes is of great tryall to us, yet I trust we shall see mercy therin. The Lord discover to us the cause of His displeasur. The instructions for the fleet are this day past the counsell.[40] Both the generalls are suddenly

[40] Passed by the Protectoral council on 12 February, thus supplying a date for this undated letter.

to goe. Vice-admyrall Lawson hath dealt unhandsomly in suspending to declare his dissatisfactions till now he was ready to goe forth with his fleet.[41] We hade yeasterday a very pretious day of seaking the Lord, which I trust we shall finde as an oppurtunity which will be returned in great mercye. You have newes from other hands and therfor I may spare you the trouble. Through mercy his Highnes is very well and so are all our relatives. The Lord affect our hearts with the sence of that great mercyes, for certeinly noe people have more cause to owne the mercy of a man's life then at this day we have in his Highnes. I am,

Your most affectionate brother and servant,

Charles Fleetwood

The buysnes twixt Mr Hungerford[42] and my sister Mary is like to com on agayn.

Captain Beake and my cosen Levina are maryed.[43]

I know the councell will passe colonel Hewson's buysnes, having done captain Blackwell's, and therfor I could wish you would pase it in Ireland.[44]

My wife's and own humble services to yourselfe and deare sister. We intreat your kindnes to poore Mrs Shear's 2d sonne.

50. From John Reynolds, London, 12 February 1656, 821, fos 89–90.

May it please your excellency,

I have received the honour of another letter from your lordshipp, which beares date February 6th, wherein your lordshipp referres to a letter from Dr Harrison, which I scarce reade before his Highnes tooke it from me, being desirous to reade it privately. I have taken occasion

[41] John Lawson, parliamentarian naval officer, had campaigned throughout the civil wars as well as in the Anglo-Dutch War. Although appointed early in 1656 to campaign against Spain, he resigned on 11 February, perhaps because he had been passed over by Montague's appointment, perhaps because of his long-standing radical and republican sympathies.

[42] Probably Edward Hungerford, son of a royalist politician and heir to the Farleigh Hungerford estate, one of several unsuccessful suitors for Mary Cromwell's hand during this period.

[43] Richard Beake/Beke, parliamentarian officer and politician, served in Oliver Cromwell's lifeguard and then in Richard Ingoldsby's New Model horse regiment. He married Levina/Levinia Whetstone, daughter of Roger Whetstone and Catherine Cromwell, the Protector's sister, and was returned to the second and third Protectorate parliaments.

[44] The granting of land in Ireland to a long list of parliamentarian officers, including John Hewson and John Blackwell, as settlement of their arrears of salary or as reward for their work in parliament's service, frequently led to complications and gave rise to difficulties and disputes, duly laid before the Irish and Protectoral councils.

to presse for my dispatch in the busines recommended unto me,[45] especially in the determination of the governement, which would quell discontents more than all interposures, of which there is little neede, no provocation being given to occasion them. There is a farther roote of bitternes, not against your lordshipp but your interest, and the interest of his Highnes and the governement and all sober people. There will be a governour appointed to Munster speedily, where much want is and hath beene of sobriety in your officers. I beleive whomsoever your lordshipp recommends will be the person approved by his Highnes, who expresses a greate sense of your condition and rejoices in your lordship's patiant bearing those things which are best remedied by deliberate remedyes. My instructions are going into debate but I have almost obteined my busines without the long way of reports from committees, etc. Colonel Axtel's carriage[46] is il taken, and before this hapned it was desired that his commission as lieutenant-colonel should be suspended. I am most desirous to do my duty to your lordshipp in my returne, but am not satisfyed to leave your lordship's busines (and that of poore Ireland) undone and I would avoide a private undoing also if possible, which I judge more difficult than the other to prevent, for indeede God hath given your lordshipp a large share of affections and prayers. I hope my next will be a clearer manifestation of usefulnes heere, and if your lordshipp will be pleased to performe your promise of affording your good word on my behalfe it will be most seasonable. You know the person and I neede not a cypher or character to describe how I desire to be disposed. If providence had not by an irresistible occurrency diverted my resolutions, no disappointment should have wearied my hope. Dr Harrison is acquainted with the one, and your lordshipp knowes much of the other.

I pray your lordshipp to write letters to your freinds and nerest relations, who do expect letters with some impatientcy. I am, my lord,

Yours until death,

J Reynolds

51. From W. Baret, Londonderry, 18 February 1656, 821, fos 91–92.

May it please your excellencie,

A while since, being att Drumboe castle to draw of the garrison there in pursuance of some orders to thatt purpose, and finding the

[45] His brief included securing from the Protector and Protectoral council further officials to serve in the Irish judiciary and administration, and clarification or enhancement of certain powers that could be exercised by the Irish council.

[46] In criticizing and agitating against Henry Cromwell's handling of Ireland.

said castle little dammified,[47] indeed less than ever I saw anie where soldiers had been garrisond, I could not but take notice of itt and represent itt to your excellencie, thatt if the atturney-generall (whose that castle is)[48] had some cause to complaine the soldiers were not removed, so you may understand he had not much of the spoile they made in itt. May I be trusted? What soever his agent hath asserted to the contrary, the damage is unconsiderable; and that the soldiers were continued beyond the former order unhansomly complained of, the said agent having given consent to itt, which, as I have more fully declared to the major-generall,[49] so I shall not further trouble your lordshipp with itt. Rapho castle,[50] another of our garrisons and verie considerable for quality and situation (being a choyce pile and in the heart of the best Scottish plantation), calls for repayres, which if not speedily afforded, as it will be prejudiciall to his Highness (whose the house is) in the decay and runie of the building for want of timely looking to, so the cost in repairing (if delayed) will (unavoydably) bee much more than whatt now would answer itt. The cittadell[51] next presents it selfe to your lordshipp's consideration, for which (the season of the yeare minding mee of itt) I am once more a suitor that, if it be your lordshipp's pleasure, it should goe on and course may be taken for itt by supplie of moneys. If otherwise, thatt the materialls, as wood, stone and lime, daily wasting and diminished some of them (which all my care cannot prevent) may be sold to pay the debt contracted by them, and the wages of the labourers crying for itt. I take leave and remayne,

Your excellencie's most humble servant,

W Baret

[47] Damnified: injured or damaged.

[48] William Basil, an English-born lawyer with family connections to Ireland, had played a minor role in the parliamentarian administration of Ireland in the later 1640s and in 1649 was appointed attorney-general for Ireland. He had inherited the estate of Drumboe, County Donegal, from an uncle.

[49] Sir Hardress Waller, parliamentarian officer and politician, and a regicide, settled in Ireland in the late 1620s and married an heiress in County Limerick, but he lost his estates in the 1641 rebellion. He campaigned in Ireland in the early 1640s and, from 1645, in England as commander of a New Model foot regiment. He actively supported Pride's Purge and the regicide. He returned to Ireland in 1649, campaigned extensively there under Oliver Cromwell and was in 1650 appointed major-general of the foot in Ireland. He strongly supported the Protectorate and Henry Cromwell's government and was returned for Counties Kerry, Limerick, and Clare to all three Protectorate parliaments.

[50] Probably the fortified bishop's palace at Raphoe, County Donegal, which had withstood a siege in the 1641 rebellion.

[51] Probably at Londonderry.

52. From John Reynolds, London, 19 February 1656, 821, fos 93–94.

May it please your excellency,

I received your lordship's Christian, rationall, kind letter, wherein I reade your lordship's trouble with greater in myselfe. I am exceeding glad that your lordshipp corresponds with the lord deputy, who is somewhat sensible of Axtel's busines, and saide it was an unhappy carriage or passage. I neede not repeate that your interests are united, although I may still feare that there may be some difference in judgement in respect to persons there, and things also, upon which account I am assured your lordshipp hath emploied your patience and tendernes. It will be your lordship's mercy if you have chosen the better part; I meane in respect to the publique, for the private I hope both have chosen it. I have spoken concerning the particulars mentioned in my instructions to his Highnes, and do not doubt of effecting according to your lordship's sense all or most of them. Persons are much wanted. I suppose Sir Robert King[52] would be a good councellour, and colonel Hill,[53] J Lowther,[54] Sir John Temple, as persons wel esteemed. I conceive military men are best emploied in their owne worke with lesse offence and more usefulnes. Mr Francis Bacon[55] is thought upon to be a judge in Ireland. Few able and honest lawyers, or others, who are to be gotten into Ireland. I have moved about the treasury and do understand that a speedy alteration is intended therein. Captain Blackwel is willing to come over into Ireland, there to act, but I would not propose it untill I receive your lordship's pleasure, which I pray signify speedily. And be pleased to write to his Highnes, unto her Highnes, and to your

[52] Irish-born politician and administrator, who lost much of his land in the Irish rebellion and entered the service of the English parliament, acting on various Irish committees during the 1640s. He returned to Ireland in the early 1650s and for the next few years held a variety of administrative, financial, and academic offices there, including commissary-general of the musters. He divided his time between Ireland and England, sitting in the Nominated Assembly and being elected to both of Oliver Cromwell's Protectorate parliaments for Counties Sligo, Leitrim, and Roscommon, but he died in England in the summer of 1657 following a period of ill health.

[53] Arthur Hill. In May 1656, upon his return to Ireland, Thurloe noted that Hill had been 'very usefull to the affaires of Ireland, and hath propounded many very good thinges to the counsell' (*TSP*, IV, p. 773).

[54] Gerard Lowther, an Irish judge who had supported the king in the 1640s but who, like many fellow Irish Protestants, then switched allegiance to parliament and retained office; he was already active in Ireland as chief justice of the court of common pleas.

[55] Parliamentarian barrister and politician, and member of the distinguished legal family of that name, he had supported the parliamentary cause in the 1640s and was returned to the Long Parliament in 1646 as MP for Ipswich, but he was excluded at Pride's Purge and seems not to have retaken his seat thereafter. He represented Ipswich again in all three Protectorate parliaments and was master of requests from 1656 until the end of the Protectorate.

neerest relations, and to Sir Charles Woosele,[56] Mr Secretary and the rest of your lordship's freinds, who may take any occasion to serve your lordshipp in order to your publique.[57]

I should be glad to heare that there were no discontents in Ireland, ill use being made thereof heere by some. Howsoever, it is wel liked that your lordshipp carries it in such manner. I am confident Axtel's affronting your lordshipp will be much for your comfort, and it will be speedily considered how to prevent[58] future. If your lordshipp would be pleased to give a weekly account to my lord Fleetewood, or as often as your occasions require or admit, it would be for your service. His lordshipp hath beene ill these 3 last dayes and was let blood on his right arme this day, and thereby disabled to hold his pen to write to your lordshipp. I shall conclude this your lordship's trouble with my acknowledgements of your lordship's most obligeing and undeserved expressions. I have not any returne to make but of a thankefull, faithfull, devoted heart, which, except the revived affections sacrificed to the person lodged in my secret thought, is entirely yours. And I can say that I more rejoice in the honesty, wisedome and sincerity of your lordship's expressions than in your favours to me, although I price it beyond all favours besides upon publique or private accounts. The Lord prosper, blesse, preserve and guide your lordshipp, and may your lordshipp not faint or be weary of weldoing, being emploied in the worke and in the way of the Lord.

I should be glad to returne to your lordshipp, but I am uncertaine in what weeke it will be. Your lordshipp expressing your good thoughts of me, your faithfull servaunt and poore freind, to her Highnes may possibly hasten my dispatch. This is understood by your lordshipp and therefore I conclude and remaine, my lord,

Your excellencye's most humble, faithfull, obliged, devoted servaunt,

J Reynolds

[56] Sir Charles Wolseley, parliamentarian politician, though his father had been an active royalist in the civil war. His parliamentary career began in 1653 and his prominent role in the Nominated Assembly, springing from political moderation combined with strong support for Independency and religious toleration, led to high office. He became a member of the Protectoral council from its inception and was very active in both domestic and foreign and diplomatic affairs. He was also returned to both of Oliver Cromwell's Protectorate parliaments.

[57] Word(s) possibly omitted. The closing section of this paragraph has been written along the left hand edge of the paper, running at right angles to the main text, apparently ending '[. . .] in order to your publique', and it is possible that the writer forgot to carry over one or more words to the top of the second side.

[58] Word – perhaps 'in' – apparently omitted.

53. From William Rowe,[59] Whitehall, 19 February 1656, 821, fos 95–96.

Reports that some of Henry Cromwell's letters sent to him via Fleetwood had been delayed or mislaid and requests that future letters be sent via Thurloe's packet, as they would then reach him promptly.

54. From Thomas Sandford,[60] Wallingford House, 19 February 1656, 821, fos 97–98.

Letter of courtesy, conveying Fleetwood's apology that, because he had been ill for several days and had that day been let blood, he was unable to hold a pen and write in person, though he hoped to do so by the next post.

55. From William Stane, London, 19 February 1656, 821, fos 99–100.

My lord,

I have bin a stranger to your lordship and myselfe for some tyme, the Lord haveing sent upon mee the afflicton of our last (and only) child's sicknes, which hath continued 3 weekes. Now wee have some hope and yet truly not without danger. However the Lord deale with us, I hope Hee will bee found a God of grace and favour. I must needs say I have found more of His goodnes and sure mercyes under afflictions then the best enjoyments otherwise; but Hee can blesse both, and it is a great witnes of Himselfe when Hee doth soe. This retirement hath taught mee this lesson: that our tyme is short, and that a Christian ought to enjoy all things in the Lord. But withall how short I am of it, and that by reason of the vaile, and for want of beholding the Lord and the things of God, and lookeing upon them so reall, as indeed they are. But on the contrary, I do see how apt I am to realize all present things.

I have not bin at White Hall, till yesterday, for many days. I finde them all well; but not so at Wallingford House. My lady hath bin ill, but now is better, and my lord is takeing physic and somwhat distempered with melancholy mind.

My lady Elizabeth is very well again. My lord Richard and my lord Cleipole in Wiltshire.

I told your lordship of major general Fortescue's death at Jamaica; indeed many offices[61] are dead; I may tell your lordship (which I do

[59] Parliamentarian officer and one time scout-master to Oliver Cromwell; in the spring of 1654 he and Richard Kingdon had been sent from Ireland to England to brief the Protector on Irish affairs. During the Protectorate he served as secretary to the Scottish and Irish committees of the Protectoral council.

[60] Fleetwood's secretary.

[61] Word clearly written thus, but perhaps a slip for 'officers'.

not know any know) neer 100; not above 4,000 souldiers left (many of them sick), and as I remember they were 9,000 at lest left the busines of Hispaniola.[62] Yet is Jamaica probably a good ayre and a fruitfull place; but physitians say great alterations are dangerous. Besides provisions corrupt presently and armyes cary diseases wherever they goe; twas so in Scotland. But sure it's matter of humiliation and seekeing the Lord. I heare Sir Francis Russell went into the country this day. His Highnesse dispenses with Mr Chickley as to decimation.[63] Myne and my wife's humble service to my lady and your lordship. I remaine, my lord,

Your lordship's fathfull servant,
W Stane

56. From John Read,[64] Belturbet, [County Cavan], 25 February 1656, 821, fos 101–102.

My lord,

I have (in obediense to your lordshipp's comands) myself made a stricte inquirie within this preceincte of such persons that were transplanted into Connaught by former orders, and found none returned backe, but only three, whoe had passes, and accordinge to your lordshipp's instructions, made their returne thither. Some fewe of meane quallitie, I am informed, there is, but under the notion of servantes, and soe kept as yett from my knowledge. Butt I shall use my uttmost care in this, as alsoe in all other your lordshipp's comands, humbly remayneinge,

Your lordshipp's ever humble servaunte,
John Read

57. From John Reynolds, London, 26 February 1656, 821, fos 103–104.

May it please your lordshipp,

I may justly be required to give an account of the affaires wherein your lordshipp hath, together with the councell, entrusted me, and I

[62] An exaggeration, since the number involved in the unsuccessful operation against Hispaniola probably totalled around or a little over six thousand.

[63] Thomas Chicheley of Cambridgeshire, politician and administrator, had supported the king in the civil war, been expelled from parliament, and had compounded for his estate after the war. He was one of many who, in 1655–1656, applied to the Protector and council for exemption from the new 10-per-cent tax levied on the wealthier ex-royalists in England and Wales to help fund the system of the major-generals. His appeal for favour may have been helped by his relationship to the Cromwell family, since in 1635 he had married Sir Francis Russell's sister and so was uncle by marriage to Henry Cromwell's wife.

[64] Possibly the major John Read of Henry Cromwell's foot regiment, though there were other army officers and ministers of that name in Ireland during the 1650s.

can prove my diligence by each daye's journall, being attendance at Whitehall. Neither have I intermitted one day or houre wherein any possibility appeared of effecting my busines at the councell, but the lord deputye's ilnes, without whom they resolve no busines relating to Ireland, hath impeded my dispatch. His lordshipp hath not stirred abroade since my last.[65] I was in this evening to receive his Highnes' commands, as I do weekely, and likewise communicate to his Highnes (by his speciall command) my Irish intelligence. His Highnes bad me let your lordshipp know that he hath beene ill more than once and that he is now somewhat better. I can assure your lordshipp his Highnes told me it was time to consider the busines about which I came over and it should be done. The lady Elizabeth still complaines of your forgetfulnes notwithstanding her late sicknes, although I assured her ladyshipp that publiquely and privately your lordshipp did cause frequent prayers to be made for her recovery. Indeede she deserves more your lordshipp's value than ever, having seene much of God in this late visitation, whereby so much more religion shines with her wonted virtue and nobleness, as good men much rejoice, beleiving his Highnes hath comfort in all his children upon the best account.

I have endeavoured and shall endeavour your lordshipp's last commands, viz money, magistrates, ministers, and concerning the first, I hope ere long a supply will be had. Be pleased to send your lordship's sence about captain Blackwel's coming over to manage the treasury; he is verry willing.

There are 2 or 3 ministers ready to come over for Connaught, if your lordshipp approves them, viz Mr Hore,[66] Mr Madford;[67] no judges yet to be found for Ireland. I remaine, my lord,

Your excellencye's most humble and faithfull servaunt,

J Reynolds.

58. From Charles Fleetwood, London, 26 February [1656], 823, fos 353–354.

Deare brother,

The Lord having bine pleased to lay me under some distemper of body, I was silent the last weeke, and since I have lost a deare neace,

[65] Fleetwood was absent from the council between 14 and 28 February.

[66] Perhaps Leonard Hoare, a minister who began his career in New England but returned to England in 1653 and was then rector of Wanstead in Essex until 1662, when he returned again to New England. Despite the news reported here, he does not seem to have taken up a post in Ireland.

[67] Unidentified and not amongst the lists of salaried ministers in Ireland in the 1650s, so again it seems that he did not, in fact, move to Ireland.

daughter of my deare sister Duckingfeilds, which dispensations I have cause to be earnest with the Lord and to begge my praying frinds to be so, that I may understand the voyce of thes reproofes and have a sanctefyed use therof. The Lord knowes what is best for us and hade we hearts to eye Him in all His dispensations we showld se love and faithfullnes in them all. We are poore creatures and are apt to goe a wondering and therfor stand in neade of some reproofes. To turn at them is a duty and will be a mercy. Ther is no life like a close humble walking. The world is too hard for us, therfor showld we by faith more live and waite wheare alone our strength is to support under all tryalls, and to deliver us from all temptations. We are kept by the mighty power of God through faith unto salvation. It's a great word, and that which often showld be upon our hearts to let's se our own nothingnes and His allsufficiency as our only power to be kept by. I am sorry colonel Axtell hath done any thing of late unhandsome towards you. The tendernes you exercise to honest men will be your mercy and I trust the Lord will teach them in humility and love to carry towards you as becometh them. His Highnes hath hade a sore fitt of the stone, but is now recoverd. He is a mercy beyond what we have hearts, I feare, to price. The Lord, I hope, will still lengthen out his dayes longe as an instrument of much more good. We are sending some more shipps; the generalls, I presume, are at seae. The Lord quicken up prayers for a blessing upon that great design, the consequence whearof is very great. Our want is money; our design large, and I doubt more then we are well in a possibility to manage. Ther is no resolution taken up as to that busynes of Jameca, but I presume will suddenly be, and then you shall heare from me concerning men to be sent from you. I shall endeavor as sudden a supply of moneys to be sent as we can gett it. What is promised from hence, I hope, will not be fayled to be sent, though your continuall supplyes by bills will not admitt of any great somme in specie. The companyes shall be reduced heare according to your desires, but till we know what will be done in sending to Jameca I conceeve it is not advisable. It is presumed ther may[68] another reducment in spring. Let me know your thoughts therin. I confesse I think the difference with Spayn makes it doubtfull. I doe not know wheare we shall get men to please you as counsellers. To have men for buysnes and not as shaddowes showld be the thing aymed at. What can you advise hearin? I know many are jealous of my wante of freedom to them. I have reason to be against none who may be fitt for such an imployment, wherin certeinly the good of poore Ireland is much concerned as to the future well settlement therof. I

[68] Word – perhaps 'be' – apparently omitted.

am in no good condition of wrighting and therfor must intreat you will excuse the shortnes of,

Your most affectionate brother and servant,

Charles Fleetwood

The buysnes twixt Mr Hungerford and my sister Mary is now wholly off.

Major-generall Harryson and the 3 other prisoners are lik to be at liberty.[69]

My wife's affectionate salutes to yourselfe, with both to your lady.

59. From John Reynolds, London, 25 March 1656, 821, fos 105–106.

May it please your excellency,

I received your lordship's, wherein I understand your lordship's pleasure concerning my returne. I shall be verry suddenly enabled to effect my busines and to returne also, which I judge better than to come thither without effecting any thing, especially being assured by those who have power to performe, that no point of my publique and private instructions shall be unanswered to my satisfaction and of those who entrusted me. My lord, I can freely affirme that nothing relating to my selfe hath kept me one houre in England or was my prime motive of coming over, but having so faithfull a zeale to the publique and to your lordshipp, I should esteeme it an opportunity not to be recovered if I should not faithfully improve all meanes therein. I hope by the next to give a particular account of all. And having beene by leave and command in the countyes at the assizes of Cambridge and Essex,[70] in the intervall of dispatching colonel Hill's proposalls, I am returned to pursue the busines and service of Ireland, which I have his Highnes' promise shall be intended by the councell. I hope by the next packet to obteine a dispatch and before the next I shall be upon my way into Ireland. I remaine, my lord,

Your excellencye's humble servant,

J Reynolds

I was on Saturday, being the 22nd, at Chippenham. The lady Russell is well and the whole family.

[69] Four republican opponents of the Protectorate – Thomas Harrison, John Carew, Hugh Courtney, and Nathaniel Rich – had been in prison for a year. In fact, only Rich was fully released at this time, for Carew and Courtney remained in gaol, and Harrison was quickly placed under a form of house arrest.

[70] He had recently been added to the commissions of the peace for Cambridgeshire and Essex.

60. From John Thurloe, London, 25 March 1656, 821, fos 107–108.

My lord,

There is nothinge more in the desires and endeavours of your freinds and servants here then to send 2 or 3 councillors into Ireland, in whom your lordship may ripose perfict trust and confidence, as well for their fidelitie and affection towards yourselfe, as abilitie for their worke. How hard it is to finde such persons your lordship may imagine. I doe assure you it hath beene the most part of some dayes' worke to consider of this buissnes, and there is scarce a gentleman in England of our partie but hath beene weighed upon this occasion, but hitherto without fruit. I perceive you are afraid of the returne of John Jones. His Highnes is of an oppinion that he would be of great use to you, and for some reasons that are new to your lordship. He is a suiter to Mrs Whitstone at this tyme, and if that proceeds, he will be under another kinde of obligation then before.[71] But I will not trouble your lordship further upon this account, in respect his Highnes told me he would write hymselfe fully upon this subject. Some other persons are under consideration, but there is soe much uncerteintie about them that I shall not trouble your lordship with their names for the present. I have only sayd thus much that your lordship might see you are not forgott in this perticuler. And to quicken a resolution herein I did comunicate your last to his Highnes, but to none else.

The additional instructions for Ireland are now ready[72] and will be sent unto you very shortly. I sent not the abstract of them as I promised, in respect that I perceive my lord deputye had sent them before to the counsill for their oppinion. The fleet was as farre as Plymouth towards Spayne, but contrary windes have brought it backe to Torbay, where they now ride expectinge a faire winde, and wee account it (as certainly it is) a very great mercy that they have beene preserved in this tempestuous weather, the like whereof hath beene seldome knowne. There was a report that the Spanish plate fleet is come home, but our last letters doe contradict it. Our forreine letters

[71] Jones married the Protector's sister Catherine Cromwell, widow of Roger Whetstone, later in the year. The news caused Henry Cromwell to change his position. Thus, on 12 March 1656 he had vehemently opposed Jones's possible appointment to the Irish council, writing that 'I knowe noe old protestant in Ireland can bee more dangerous and prejudicial to the publique upon that account, then this gentleman', while on 12 April he noted that 'when I writte [. . .] about colonel John Jones, I did not knowe, that he was likely to bee my unkle [. . .] you have silenc't mee as to hime' (*TSP*, IV, pp. 606, 672).

[72] Detailed instructions covering a wide range of business, including the handling and disposal of forfeited lands; the treatment of Scots in Ulster; the revival of the court of admiralty; the export of cloth and horses from Ireland; the establishment of free schools; and the apprenticing of poor children (Dunlop, pp. 578–585).

bringe us noe great newes this weeke, indeed not worth the writinge, nor doe our owne affaires here afford any. I remayne,

Your lordship's humble servant,
Jo Thurloe

The archbishop of Armagh is dead.[73]

61. From Richard Cromwell, Whitehall, 27 March 1656, 821, fos 109–110.

Deare brother,

Though my penn often vissetts you, yet with shame it troubles you, and for that you may well blaime my relation and the great imployment. Starrs the bigger they are the more they are look't upon by those that want them <to> for conduct to there benighted or over clowded conditions and affaires. This gentleman, Mr Osborne, whose petition and personall attendance if by this request of myne they may be admitted as orater to make knowen there bussinesse, will save you a double trouble by reading a coppy of his case in an ill transcript, which to prevent I have not set it downe but rather ground my confidence (that what I desire) you will with a civell ey soe farre countenance as to second the refferrence, that being alsoe seconded to me by my very good freind, I shall not need to force expressions or multiply needlesse words to your ready and ingenuous apprehentions to the helping a just cause in great necessity. I am certaine shall you apprehend it as I doe (the cause of your trouble), there is soe active a righteousnesse in your breast that the person will blesse his happynesse. I have reason to desire that God would blesse you in your waity undertaking, and give you a spirit of right understanding, for hard it is to understand a true professer from a false one; but this may be too serious a subject for mee and therefore I will not only leave offe that for better men and judgments, but alsoe further troubling you at this time. And present my affectionate service[74] yourselfe and deare sister whome the Lord blesse in her howre of great conflict, which I thinck is neare at hand, and that the throwes and shakings may afforde you comfortable fruight and joye that a man child is borne. Give me excuse and it shall indeere, sir,

Your affectionate brother and servant,
R Cromwell

[73] He died on 21 March.
[74] Word – perhaps 'to' – apparently omitted.

62. From John Reynolds, 1 April 1656, 821, fos 111–112.

May it please your lordshipp,

I have not received any notice of a packet this weeke from Ireland, but do hope all is well with your lordshipp and the busines there, the want of money excepted, of which his Highnes and the lord deputy have manifested the prevalency of your letters by using meanes to accomodate your lordshipp with a present summe in specie, which could not be gotten higher than £35,000. It is desired by the treasurers that the money may not be long at the seaside as formerly, but that a ship may be ready to receive the same abord so soone as it shall come to Chester. The time will be about the 21th instant, of which I thought it necessary to give your lordshipp an account.

I have moved about judge Donelan[75] and his commission is promised by the next. Other busines intervening yesterday prevented its dispatch. I have had the lord deputy's full resolution once or twice declared that he will leave the officers to your nomination, and whomsoever you shall propound shall be commissioned, likewise concerning councellours and judges. I do not find a probable meanes of advantaging the publique by the proposall at Galloway. The business of adventure, and that of the London Derry, do fill the citizens' hands, but I shall proceede with it as farre as may be. I have severall times wrote about you to advance two ministers, viz Mr Madford and Mr Hore. The first hath beene lately approved as a godly, able minister. The second is a young man wel knowne to Dr Harrison.

I hope your lordshipp is in some good measure improved in your health and that you take some recreation for the preservation thereof. Some of your neerist relations are inquisitive and very sensible of your condition there.

I beseech your lordshipp to write to my lord Lambert as you promised, and to have a full corrispondency with the lord deputy. Pardon my boldnes. I remaine, my lord,

Your excellencye's most humble and faithfull and obliged servaunt,

J Reynolds

[75] Henry Cromwell had repeatedly urged that Donnellan's long-suspended appointment as a judge in Ireland should be confirmed, writing in January 1655 that he had served parliament loyally throughout the war years, 'hath bin constantly faithfull to the parliament's interest', and 'is of an excellent temper, and godly' (*TSP*, IV, pp. 376, 508, 606).

63. From Thomas Goodwin,[76] 6 April 1656, 821, fos 113–114.

May it please your excellency,

According to your excellencye's commands, and the counsell with you, I have doon what in mee lyeth about the persons you were pleased to write unto mee about as to their call to Ireland.

As for Mr Spillsbury,[77] hee is newly and greatly engaged to a people, a very great people in England, and the engagement hath been carryed on through many turnings and windings of providence, so as hee cannot at present, without breach of many obligations, breake from them.

For Mr Brookes,[78] hee seemed willing (and for his condition, hee also is free), but after all the perswations I could use, and intrist in him, hee ultimately stickes at this, to know to what place hee should bee assigned, having heard of some discouragements, that those who have been sent for over have had themselves returning agayn. I can drive this buisines no further with him than I have doon. When I perswaded Mr Wotton[79] to goe over I then also had treaty with Mr Brookes, who then denyed it, and now agayn upon these grounds I mention. At first I had a more hopefull answer from him, and waited untill hee had spoken unto friends in way of advice; but this is the result of his spiritt. I am sorry I could make no speedyer returne, but I depended on his answer, but much more that my endeavours answer not in the successe to your excellencye's desires, who am, my lord,

Your excellencye's devoted,

Tho Goodwin

[76] Parliamentarian minister, member of the Westminster Assembly, chaplain to several of the republican councils of state, and president of Magdalen College, Oxford. During the 1650s, he frequently preached before the Protector and Protectoral council and effectively served as one of the Protector's chaplains.

[77] John Spillsbury, fellow of Magdalen College, Oxford, and rector of Shetton, Shropshire in the late 1640s, was in 1655–1656 a member of the Worcestershire Association and went on to have links with the Wirksworth classis in Derbyshire and with Bromsgrove in Worcestershire, serving as vicar there from 1657. In March 1654, he had reportedly written 'a sober chiding letter' to the Baptists in Ireland, which had helped to quieten them for a time, Henry Cromwell himself noting that Spillsbury and Henry Kiffen 'have dealt verry homely and plainly with those of that judgment' (*TSP*, II, pp. 149, 164).

[78] The common surname prevents firm identification.

[79] Henry Wootton, fellow of Magdalen College, Oxford, had crossed to Ireland by 1652, for, by the end of the year, he was receiving a government salary as minister at St Audoen's, Dublin. He became prominent in religious affairs in Ireland during the 1650s, holding a fellowship at Trinity College and preaching at Christ Church, Dublin.

64. From William Leigh,[80] Waterford, 14 April 1656, 821, fos 117–118.

May it please your excellency,

It hath pleased God by a spetiall providence to bring to justice one Morrice Hogan, who about September last was supposed to have murthered captain Lions. Hee was apprehended by two English inhabitants of this countye and brought to this place a day before the judges of assize came hither, unto whom I communicated this busines. But it was theire opinions that being theire was noe witnesses to prove hee did personally committ the said murther and being hee denied the fact, and in as much as hee was guilty by marshall law, that wee might rather proceed against him at a court marshall, which accordingly wee have done. Hee did confess hee was with the torys that night captain Lions was murthered, both before and after the murther was committed, and that hee went away with the said torys after the murther was committed and continued with them about 6 months. Wee had strong presumptions to beleeve that hee either committed the said murther or did contrive it by bringing the torys thither. Wee have condemned him to bee hanged and, that it might deterr others, wee intend to hang him in the place where the murther was committed and after to hang him in chains.

I had notice of a small vessell belonging to Dungarvan, which came out of Spaine, which was taken by a Spanish frigot 20 leagues off of the said port. When they had taken the vessell they tooke the master aboard their frigott and put 2 of theire men aboard the Dungarven vessell. It pleased God that night, being last Tuesday night, to bee very tempestuous and darke, by which meanes in the night they gave the Spanish vessell the slip, and are come safe to theire harbour, and brought 2 Spaniards with them. I have sent for the Spaniards hither. I thought it my duty to give your excellency this intimation, that you may understand theire is enemyes upon the coast, and likwise to know what shall bee done with the 2 Spaniards, whom wee shall keepe safe till I heare from you.

I thought it necessary to excuse myseilfe to your lordshipp for not sending an account of the busines of transplantation sooner, before I receaved the comission for transplantation, werein were named colonel Abbott, colonel Lehunt, major Greene[81] and myseilfe; and

[80] Parliamentarian officer, he fought in England in the mid-1640s in Sir Thomas Fairfax's New Model foot regiment and in 1647 went to Ireland in the newly formed foot regiment commanded initially by James Castle and then by Henry Slade. In 1650, he succeeded the late Henry Slade as its colonel and, although that regiment was disbanded in 1653, he retained command in Ireland and served as governor of Waterford until 1660.

[81] All three were parliamentarian officers. Daniel Abbott, an officer in John Okey's New Model dragoon regiment, came to Ireland in 1649 and was given command of a newly

before the receipt of the said comission, I had secured all within this county against whom theire was the least suspition, and all such as formerly through tenderness wee had permitted to stay. As you may perceive by my queries in my last letter, I did intend to have proceed against the said persons, as formerly, by a court marshall. But after the receipt of the comission, having taken a copy of it, I sent the originall away to colonel Abbott and colonel Lehunt, who being then at Cashel attending the assises, none of them came till afterward. Colonel Lehunt going to Wexford, coming through this towne, hee desired the busines might bee deferred till his coming backe againe, which accordingly was done. And then, according to our best understandings, wee proceeded in it and have sent it to your lordshipp. Colonel Lehunt and myseilfe have proceeded in the transplanting the Irish out of this towne, according to your lordshipp's and the counsell's orders, and a late reference to us, of which your lordshipp will receive an account this weeke.

I thought it my duty to acquaint your lordshipp that I intend, God willing, to goe to Limricke next Munday (wee having a quarter sessions heere this weeke). The occasion of my going is that having severall times petitioned your lordshipp and counsell for the possesion of my land, which fell to mee by lott in the county of Limricke, which was denied mee, and having desired captain Hartwell,[82] the receiver of Limricke, to lett mee know to whom the said lands were lett to and for how much, and whether any of it were wast that I might dispose of it, being then upon the place for my best advantage, which was denied mee by the said captain Hartwell without your lordshipp's and the counsell's order to him; and although I did wait upon your lordshipp and counsell at Dublin cheifely for that end and you were pleased to grant mee an order to that effect, which order, I not having opportunitye to carry it myseilfe by reason of my imployment, I sent to Mr Bowman of Limricke with a letter of atturny to take an account of captain Hartwell and to receive what monys should bee due from the

created dragoon regiment, which campaigned extensively in Ireland in the early 1650s. He held several semi-military administrative offices under Henry Cromwell and, in 1656, was elected to the second Protectorate parliament for Counties Tipperary and Waterford. Richard Lehunt campaigned in Fleetwood's horse regiment in the mid-1640s and under Oliver Cromwell in Wales in 1648, and he went with Cromwell to Ireland in 1649 as an officer in his lifeguard. In 1651 he succeeded the late Robert Tothill as commander of a foot regiment in Ireland, disbanded in the summer of 1653. Green's military career is not so clear and well-documented, not least because several officers shared that surname, but he is probably the Eliah Green who, in 1648, was serving in Thomas Horton's New Model horse regiment in Wales and who presumably went to Ireland with that regiment in 1649 under its new commander, Sankey, campaigning with it there throughout the 1650s.

[82] William Hartwell, parliamentarian officer, served as mayor of Limerick in the later 1650s, one of a succession of English army officers to hold that office.

said lands, which notwithstanding hee hath not yet done. His reasons for it I know not, which is the occasion of my going theire. I would not willingly complaine if I might have indifferency, without I desire your lordshipp to pardon this trouble. I remain,

Your excelencye's humble servant,

Wm Leigh

I desire your lordshipp to grant an order for armes for the recruites of this precinct, which recruites are yet with[83] armes, which I minded formerly in a letter to Dr Gorge, which hee returned mee answer to but without an order for armes, it being referred to a comittee of officers to consider of it.

65. From William Pierrepoint,[84] Lincoln's Inn Fields, London, 21 April 1656, 821, fos 119–120.

Letter of thanks and request, seeking favour for his cousin, George Cressy. Cressy was seeking £446 arrears of pay due to his late father, a judge in Ireland,[85] plus nine years' military pay due to him, which had been stopped, in part because he remained in Dublin after the 1643 cessation (though he claimed he was then a prisoner and badly wounded and so had no choice), in part because it was wrongly reported that he had died of the plague.

66. From Hugh Peters,[86] 22 April 1656, 821, fos 121–122.

My deere lord,

You may please by these to understand that I am neither civilly nor naturally dead (as my good hand will you suggeste), but most dangerous it is to bee so spiritually. From my own hand you may have

[83] Apparently a slip for 'without'.

[84] Parliamentarian politician, he was very prominent in the Long Parliament, though he absented himself after Pride's Purge and largely withdrew from political life in the wake of the regicide. He nonetheless remained personally close to Oliver Cromwell and was returned to the first Protectorate parliament and, while not holding senior office, he may have counselled the Protector on important issues.

[85] Hugh Cressy had served as a judge in the king's bench in Ireland from 1633 until the early 1640s.

[86] Radical preacher and divine, he began his career in Essex and London but in the 1630s moved first to the continent and then to New England, before returning to England in the early 1640s. A fervent parliamentarian, he was an army chaplain during the 1640s and strongly supported Pride's Purge and the regicide, before accompanying Oliver Cromwell's expedition to Ireland. He regularly preached before the councils and parliaments of the 1650s and effectively served as one of the Protector's chaplains. Although he remained quite close to the Protector, his influence probably waned during the Protectorate, not least because of increasing health problems.

it that the scandalls sent over to you about my selfe are false and to adde more will doe but little more good. I am still desired by some frends to see Ireland, and if strength increase I trust I shall not fayl so to doe, but have bin long ill and lost very much blood, above 30 ounces: the Lord helpe.

For other things I must bee a suitor that colonel Cooke's[87] arreares, now to bee layd in lands, may have that remembrance in helping on their desires, which will bee very reasonable that are concernd in it. I beseech your lordshipp tender mee herein to preserve children that are fatherles from want. As also my lord deputy gave Mr Dixon his place, which hee long injoyd, and Sir John Temple keeping him out (as hee complayne), a word of your lordshipp would also cure that. And these are all my requests for the present.

And for yourselfe, family, and all yours at your house, my prayers; so these are my counsells ever set as they are, viz:

First. The kingdom of heaven must be sought.

2ly. Mayntayne honnorable thoughts of God in all His dealings.

3. The feare of man, or any sorte of men, brings a snare, and therefore not to be entertaynd; for surely you must never thinke to satisfy all partyes and sorts of men.

4. Dayly intercourse with God answers and takes of most temptations.

5. The least defilement of conscience will cost hot water.

6. And lastly the whole of man is to feare God, etc, Ecclesiastes II.

And for Ireland a laborious, constant, sober ministry, and an industrious hand among all must bee the preservation of Ireland, with a good magistrate to back all. I love and leave and am,

Your lordshipp's servant,

H P

67. From John Desborough, Whitehall, 30 April 1656, 821, fos 125–126.

Letter of request on behalf of his brother,[88] then serving in Scotland, who was petitioning to receive some land in the baronies of Meath in lieu of land originally allocated to him in Ballybritt,[89] where no further land was, in fact, available.

[87] George Cooke, parliamentarian officer, emigrated to New England during the 1630s but returned to England in the mid-1640s and, by 1646, was an officer in Simon Needham's foot regiment. In the winter of 1648–1649 he took command of that regiment and campaigned in Ireland under Oliver Cromwell, who appointed him governor of Wexford. Very active against the Irish in that region, in the spring of 1652 he was ambushed and killed. He left a pregnant widow and two children by a former wife.

[88] Samuel Desborough, parliamentarian politician, then serving as a member of the Scottish council and keeper of the great seal for Scotland; he was returned for Scottish constituencies to all three Protectorate parliaments.

[89] In King's County. His petition of 1655 is in *CSPI*, p. 814.

68. From John Perrott, the Marshalsy, at the Four Courts, Dublin, 1 May 1656, 821, fo. 127.

I, the performer of the Lord for the testimony and true wittness of a good conscience, who sometime have bin a labourer in the gospell of Christ Jesus in some parts of this nation of Ireland, for which and none other cause doe I now suffer bonds such as I have these fiftene days past. Being brought from the cittie of Limericke as an offender in like maner as I was three severall dayes brought at the courte which is called sessions in the same cittie of Limericke, where diverce things were layed to my charge in two severall inditments, but every matter criminall which was theirin inserted being more pretence then in the least measure truth, my inocency appeared in the sight of hundereds before whom my cause was duly examined and largly opened. And lastly my enimies being not able to proseed any other way with mee, this is the issue of the whole worke; my comeing unto Dublin, in which place in like maner I am bold, in the name of the Lord, to hold forth my guiltles cause and to open and lay before thee Henry Cromwell, who art commander-in-cheife of the affaires of Ireland, the ground of my sufferings, and how and in what maner I have bin dealt with by colonel Henry Ingoldesby,[90] governor of the said citty of Limericke.

Upon the first day of the second month, called Aprill, one James Sicklemore and myselfe, being moved of the Lord their unto, wee came unto the said citty of Limericke, where, within halfe of an oure of our comeing unto our loging, colonel Ingoldesby sent an expresse order and command in the mouth of one of his souldiers to bring us before him, in obedience where unto we went, by whom wee were duely examined. In which examination we suddainly saw his end, and that the ground of his strictness and severity with us was neither for licentiousness, lewdness, swearing, lying, drunkeness, or any sin or offence, or breach of the law martiall or civell, but being servants of the true and loving God, and haveing the message of His word in our mouth, who by scorners are reproachfully called Quakers. We suffered what we underwent, both slanders, punches, draggings, imprisonment and banishment, although not at any time being convicted of the breach of any law of the nations. And as by

[90] Parliamentarian officer and politician, who served in his brother Richard's New Model foot regiment in the mid-1640s and then went to Ireland, campaigning there under Oliver Cromwell; the latter gave him the command of a newly formed dragoon regiment in the summer of 1650. He gave strong and allegedly brutal support to Henry Ireton in his operations against Limerick and Clare and was governor of Limerick from 1653 to 1659. He also sat for Counties Kerry, Limerick, and Clare in all three Protectorate parliaments. Prompted by the Irish council (Dunlop, pp. 637–638), itself reflecting Henry Cromwell's attitude (*TSP*, IV, pp. 508, 672, 757), Ingoldsby was taking a very firm line against Quakers in and around Limerick, clamping down on townspeople, itinerant preachers, and converts amongst the English garrison stationed there.

a letter under the said colonel Ingoldesbye's hand, unto us directed, shewes that for nothing but because wee were mett with others, the inhabitance of the towne, at one captain Robert Wilkinson's[91] house. In the feare of the Lord where the misteries of the kingdome of God were opened were we separated from the people (as saith colonel Ingoldesby in his letter), which separation stood in a close prison contrary to the civill government of the three nations, and where not any exceeding the number of three or fower people at once was to come nigh us. And the next day following, with the licence of colonel Ingoldesby, our martiall carried us to the publique meetting place where we heard all that the prest had to say, and he haveing quite ended I, being moved of the Lord, stood up and spoake these few words saying, that it being not contrary to the wholsome lawes of the nations and according to the appostles' doctringe, lett all prophesie one by one, I desiered the liberty of speakeing a few words to the people, to the clearing of my conscience amonge them. Whereupon violent hands was layd upon me and by the rude multitude was thrust out of theire sinagogue and forthwith carried away againe unto prison. And suddainly after a warant was sent unto us with a guard of horse to convay and carry us out of the precinct of Limericke. All which voyolence we suffered, and bore the cruelty done unto us without seeking revenge, but our testimonies did beare against our unjust sufferings.

And about ten dayes after, I haveing occatione of outward business, and being allsoe of the Lord moved their unto, drew me back againe unto the said cittie. As it came to pase one the seventh day neare evening, and the morow following being the first day of the weeke, I went to a meeting againe at captain Wilkinson's house where, as I was speakeing amonge the people mett togeather, I was interupted and, by a guard of souldiers, forced from the true worship of my God, and unto prison was carried wherein close manner I was ordered to be shutt up. For not any, either friend or acquaintance, was tollerated by the governor to come neare me but those who had licence, either by ticket or toaken, from him unto the marshall unto whose custody I was charged. And all this being not cruelty enough, the same first day, at night, a councill was held by sundry called justices of the peace with the cheife ruler and prest, how to send me to Dublin; and haveing not ground enough I was sent for and further examined to catch words from me; and the greatest matter which could be gained was my planness of speech: saying yee and thou, for which cause they would willingly have bound me unto that which they call good behaviour.

[91] Parliamentarian officer, probably serving in Robert Saunders's foot regiment, he was one of the leading Quaker converts amongst the English troops in Limerick, hosting religious gatherings and preaching there.

Soe I said I was a man of noe ill behaviour at all and desiered that the law might be my langwage, which never chargeth any man but in the same langwage of thee and thou! And seeing not any thing would stand, they other wayes determined that I should answere at the sessions what they had to object against mee, where I was indicted with high matters. And as it came to pase, that they saw that not any clause theirin would stand to make me guilty, they indicted me againe, but my inocency appearing unto as many as heare my guiltless cause, as I have said lastly, heare by a gaurd I was sent and as yett know not the cause of my imprisonment.

And all this cruelty doe I suffer under the authority of thy power, whom I thinke hath bin, untill this time, little acquanted with the truth of the matter, and hast only heard one man speake without the answere of the person, who in deepe manor is and hath bin wronged by the unjust, false and slanderous accusations and charges exhibited against me, which not any person in the court where they tryed me would stand before my face as an accuser, which manifestly shewed forth unto all persons the ground of their act of persecuting me, which in the end carried noe better face then of envie, mallice and cruelty, in which wombe the beginning thereof was first conceaved. And where as the same hand is still streached forth, even as Herod's was, to use certain of the church, and the same nature of pretences layd to my charge as was by the persecuting Jewes who slew Jesus, the anoynted Savour, not as He was, the Christ, but as a blasphemer they put Him to death; as likewise in the same manner Paule was called a ring leader of sedition, and the deciples and appostles movers of sediction. And the same is now that ever was and nothing different in the nature, ground roote, fruite and practise, the seeds being but two: the one of the serpent; the other of the woman. And this is even the same generation which put Christ to death and persecuted His deciples, who cry: They are not fitt to live, and cry: Away with them, away with them, who beate, revile, backbitte, scoffe, scorne and make Herod and Pilat freinds in persecuting the righteous seed of God. To shutt up and cast into prison and soe to exercise the lusts of their owne wills upon them without the breach or transgression of any law; turning out of cittyes and townes the free borne in the nation and that have purchased liberty with them that have laboured in the same worke of reducing the nation into peace, and under a civill governmente. And my share of suffering and persecution I have and doe undergoe, as well by beatings, threttenings and cruell markings and scoffings, as by imprisonment and tryalls and hallings before rulers and magistrates. But all being for the Lord's sake and for His ever lasting truthe's sake, I beare with content, it being the yoake of my Lord and Saviour and the takeing up of His crowne of thornes. And seing it is only truly and directly soe and all matters else but pretences and false accusations and slanders heaped up togeather, to continue their cruell hand of persecution upon me, which hath followed me from Limericke unto this citty.

To thee, Henry Cromwell, and to thy councill I lay it (whom God hath sett in high seats of justice and judgment to execute righteousness in your places, without respect of persons; and this account in the dreadfull day of the Lord you shall give of your stewardship unto Him that will take vengance upon the heads of all the unrighteous that have turned equity backward, as well upon the unrighteous preince who setts upon the throwne as the unjust begger that sitts upon the dung hill) to examine and truly try this matter whereof I am accused, without delaying of justice, or slackening your hand in judgment. For as I have declared even soe am I moved of the Lord God of heaven and earth to lay it to your doore, in whose dreadfull name I am bold unto you hearby to publish my wronge. And soe, as you love the everlasting peace and wellfaire of your soules, take heed to yourselves in this matter, wherein I inocently suffer this day in this citty, as I have in sundry townes elce in this land by rude multitudes for the Lord's sake. And this unto you I declare: it's not a matter of light concernement which bore me through the crueltyes which I have under gone; neither in my owne name did I goe forth, or principally about my owne worke, or in any case to eayse sedition, but in the name of the Lord, by comand from His eternall spirit to turne from darkness to the light, and from the nature and ground of tumults and seditions, strife, envies, quarellings, and all manner of lusts of the flesh and deceipts of the heart. This my conscience beares me wittness in the Holy Gost, that for the wittnessing of a good conscience this imprisonment I doe suffer; and for seeking that which is lost in my persecuters, all their cruelty I have undergone to the raising that which lies in the grave, even the puer image of God, that the dead might heare the voyce of the sonn of God and live whose name is Jesus, and He is the light of the world and hath lightened every one that cometh into the world. A measure of which light you have all received, and is God's true wittness, and soe shall stand in the day of the Lord as your justification unto life eternall, or condemnation unto death everlasting. Soe you, the powers of the nation, take heed what you judge and how you judge, and spare not your hand in justice to excecute true judgment upon the offender and transgressor, and to lett the oppressed goe free. Soe unto you all my conscience is cleare, unto whom my guiltless cause is offered and left unto that in your consciences to judge.

I am a lover to your soules and of all just power, and am subject unto every just ordanance of man for conscience sake, but a wittness for God doe stand against all deceipt, envie and hipocricie, and all persecution and violence, and every unjust act, who in the flesh am named of men,

John Perrott

69. From Philip Jones,[92] 5 May 1656, 821, fos 128–129.

Letter of request on behalf of Mr Mansell, who came from an ancient family but whose position as a younger brother rendered him dependent upon employment in Ireland.

70. From Charles Fleetwood, London, 12 May [1656], 823, fos 355–356.

My lord,

My wife and selfe must both of us joyne in one request, that you would please to continue your former kindnes to Mr Beane, old nurse Bradlye's sonne, in his imployment, and that for poore Cromwell's[93] sake, who is now allmost capable to acknowledging a favor. Indead I take Mr Bean to be very honest and trusty. It seemes ther is intended a reducment, which would fall very hard upon him, who hath litle to live upon and in a strange country. Your respects to him is the intreaty of,

Your most affectionate brother and humble servant,

Charles Fleetwood

Both their Highneses are returned from Hampton Court.

71. From Francis Russell, Whitehall, 13 May 1656, 821, fos 130–131.

My lord,

I understand by my brother John that there were letters from your lordship to myselfe and wife out of Ireland, but what are become of them as yet I cannot make out. Tis not impossible but that curyosity of knowing what was within them is the cause that they came not to my hands. Some such thing I am jealyous of, which makes me wary of wrighting. But, my lord, because my love is great for you I shall not

[92] Parliamentarian officer and politician, he rose to prominence in his native South Wales in the 1640s, for a time apparently commanding a foot regiment there, holding the governorships of Tenby, Carmarthen, Swansea, and Cardiff, and amasssing considerable Welsh property. His national political career took off during the 1650s, for he became a confidant of Oliver Cromwell and rose to high office during the Protectorate, serving as the Protector's comptroller of the household and as a Protectoral councillor, and sitting in both of Oliver Cromwell's Protectorate parliaments.

[93] Cromwell Fleetwood, born 1653, son of Charles Fleetwood and his second wife, Bridget, daughter of Oliver Cromwell and widow of Henry Ireton.

forbare sometimes of expressing of it, and I care not though others know it, which may be as curyous to see mine to your lordship as yours to me. Yet, my lord, I must forbare wrighting something of my mind which it may be were not amisse that you knew. Truely, my lord, I am so tyred with the formality and hippocresy of this age that I know not well what to doe, and were it not for my wife and children's sakes I should most certainely goe hide myselfe. I suppose in this world you have and meet with your share of tryalls and trouble, and tis not being out of England that doeth secure you, for twas often in my mind when you left this place that you were but makeing more hast into troubles. I am yet out of all imployment but country ones: to be to great a heretick is as distastfull to some as to be orthodox is to others. My lord, when you are weary of this world doe but send to me, and wee will turne moncks togather, for I professe I doe long for nothing more than a retyrement; the very thought of such a kind of life puts of all my melancholy. Sir John Reynolds will bare us company, I suppose, for he talks to me of such a kind of thing. This I wright in hast, but the next weeke you shall have a large melancholy letter from him that is,

Unfeignedly your lordshipp's true freind and servant,

Franc Russell

72. From Jonathan Goddard, 17 May 1656, 821, fos 132–133.

Letter of recommendation on behalf of the bearer, Clinton Maund,[94] *fellow of an Oxford college, who, despite his comfortable academic and personal circumstances in Oxford, felt drawn to seek public service in Ireland.*

73. From Charles Fleetwood, London, 20 May 1656, 821, fos 134–135.

Deare brother,

I am very glade to understande the willingnes of the men to goe for Jameica. I trust the Lord will make use of them for good ther. I hope you have pitched upon a person, major Moore,[95] very fit for that imployment. If the Lord please to own and be presant in that buysnes I trust we shall, after all tryalls, have cause to own His mercy, and that

[94] Born in Ireland of English parents and educated at Oxford, he became a fellow of Merton College – of which Goddard was warden – in 1649. He did gain employment in Ireland at this time, becoming minister at Antrim and receiving a government salary.

[95] William Moore, parliamentarian officer, had probably served in Ireland since the mid-1640s and may have been the commander of a foot regiment in Ireland that campaigned under Michael Jones in the late 1640s. Entrusted with the new foot regiment to be raised largely from forces serving in Ireland and destined for the West Indies, Moore proved a poor commander, eventually arriving in Jamaica in the spring of 1657 and almost immediately hankering to return home.

the design will prove a happy foundation of light to thos darke parts and make it a rise to a further attempt against that papall interest. I doe not conceive you can have any more to be carryed then 600 men, the shipps being hyred to cary no more then 600. As for their pay, as I told you, they must have a month's advance, cloathes, shooes and stockings, and you must keepe all the vacancyes, both of officers and souldyers, empty till what money you now lay out be by that meanes reimbursed. So they doe in Scotland and so you must; and whear any officers are advanced, and so their pay increased, you must, to answer that, keepe the vacanceyes the longer open. The fraught of shipps must likwise be payde by you upon the same account. The shipps are ready to set sayle for Carrigfergus.[96] Through mercy our deare chilldren and servants are in a hopefull way of recovery. Only poore Biddy Ireton[97] hath still a dangerous, feavorish distemper upon hir. The Lord sanctefy this dispensation to us that we may throughly understand His minde therin. Our major-generalls are most of them com to town and will sodainly meete. What the issue will be I know not, but trust the Lord will please to appeare amongst us. It is a time of streight, and as the Lord instructs and teaches us, so accordingly shall we have a good issue out of all our difficultyes, and the more we make our wisedom to be nothing and expect His appearances as our light and desire His spirit alone to be our councell and wisedome what to doe, the surer and more fixt will our results be. As for newes, I shall not trouble you with any, but referre you to Mr Thurlowe's account; and with our services to your deare lady, I beseach you kisse your deare, sweet, litle ones from us both. I am,

Your most affectionate brother,

Charles Fleetwood

I intreat you will let captain Mutus command a company for Jameica instead of lieutenant Manewering.[98] My lord Lambert formerly writt in his behalfe to me. He is Sir John Thoroughgood's[99] neaphue.

[96] In fact, the ships were severely delayed at Carrickfergus, running up large expenses which alarmed Fleetwood, and the expedition did not set out until early October, only to be forced back by bad weather; some of the ships and men were delayed for several more months.

[97] Bridget Ireton, daughter of Bridget Cromwell and her first husband, Henry Ireton, and thus Fleetwood's stepdaughter.

[98] Parliamentarian officers about whom little is known, though later in the 1650s both probably show up (their forenames not recorded) in newly formed foot regiments sent to campaign in Flanders – Meautys as a captain in lord Alsop's regiment and Mainwaring as lieutenant-colonel in Sir Bryce Cochrane's regiment.

[99] Administrator and pre-war courtier, he supported parliament during the 1640s and held a variety of local offices both in Middlesex and in his native Norfolk; he was also

74. From Edward Whalley,[100] Whitehall, 22 May 1656, 821, fos 136–137.

Letter of courtesy, also offering religious exhortation and guidance and advising Henry Cromwell humbly to follow the Lord.

75. From Robert Phaier,[101] Cork, 26 May 1656, 821, fos 138–139.

May it please your excellencie,

This bearer is the captain which I chose to comaunde the company now bound by your lordship's orders to Amirica. He willingly accepted of the imployment and all the souldiers as willingly received him. His name is Barry Foulkes, and the leutenant is his owne brother, because they may be a comforte to each other in a strange land; his name is Roger Foulkes. Thiere faithfullnesse and vallor is unquestionable and thire conversation as blamlesse, and therfore I present them to your lordship's service. I formorly gave your lordshipp an accoumpt of them, that they are leiutenant-colonel Francis Foulkes'[102] brothers. The ensigne is Michaell Holmes who is now in the north with captain Goodwin's company and is very well knowne in many parts of Amirica, and therfore upon that consideration and the knowledg of other abillities fitt for this imployment I have pitched on him. Captain

elected to the second Protectorate parliament. His late wife, Elizabeth, was the daughter of Thomas Meautys.

[100] Parliamentarian officer and politician and a regicide, Whalley was a first cousin of Oliver Cromwell. In 1643–1644 he fought in Cromwell's horse regiment, and in 1645 was given command of a New Model horse regiment. Having supported the trial and execution of the king, in 1650–1651 Whalley and his regiment campaigned in Scotland under Cromwell, Whalley as commissary-general of the army. He strongly supported the Protector and Protectoral regime, sat in both of Oliver Cromwell's Protectorate parliaments, and in 1655–1656 served as major-general of the north Midlands region, which included his native Nottinghamshire.

[101] Parliamentarian officer, he campaigned for the Protestant cause in his native Ireland (his father had migrated to County Cork from Devon) in the early and mid-1640s, but then came out for parliament and against the king, fought under Fairfax in England in 1648, and was one of the officers at the trial and execution of the king. In 1649 he was given command of a new foot regiment that campaigned in Ireland under Oliver Cromwell and his successors. As governor of Cork in the early and mid-1650s, and then as a commissioner of the peace in County Cork, he was sympathetic to the Quakers – in February 1656 Henry Cromwell believed that he had become a Quaker and was attending their meetings (*TSP*, IV, p. 508) – and other radical religious groups. Around this time there were rumours of a Quaker-inspired mutiny in Phaier's regiment (*TSP*, IV, p. 757).

[102] Parliamentarian officer and politician, he served in Ireland during the 1640s and, although he briefly defected to the king in 1648–1649, he broadly supported the Cromwellian campaign and the parliamentary regimes of the 1650s, acquiring extensive land in Ireland and serving as MP for Cork and Youghal in Richard Cromwell's Protectorate parliament. In part, this note draws upon an unpublished article on Francis Foulke of Campshire House, County Waterford, written by Dr Patrick Little for the 1640–1660 section of the History of Parliament. I am grateful to the History of Parliament Trust for allowing me to see this article in draft.

Goodwin can say more in relation to him. This is all at present, leaveing it to your lordship's consideration, humbly take leave,

Your excellencie's most humble servant,

Rob Phaier

76. From Joshua Hubbard, Barbados, 27 May 1656, 821, fos 140–141.

Letter of courtesy, praising Henry Cromwell's godly work and thanking him for his invitation to minister in Ireland; reports his intention to sail from New England via Barbados and to land at a port convenient for Ireland rather than at London.

77. From John Reynolds, 27 May 1656, 821, fos 142–143.

May it please your lordshipp,

I cannot without more trouble (than is fit to trust to unsafe letters) mention the delay of my expectation of a sober settlement of Ireland. There is little question but there will be something done speedily and, I hope, as your lordshipp or at least your servants heere expect. No meanes hath beene left unattempted to make all good men, yea his Highness, beleive that you discountenance the godly interest and that the carnall, old Protestants is the onely party which adheres to your lordshipp or to whom you do adhere.[103] I trust your lordshipp hath beene acquainted with this formerly, and I know that you have learned to passe thorough good report and bad report. The officers of the army were some of them prevailed upon with this feare, but I do find nothing which may justly disturbe your lordshipp in the discharge of your greate trust and do assure myselfe the Lord's presence will be with you therein. I presume to mind your lordshipp of wrighting to the lord deputy, whereby his lordshipp may be assured of your continued love, which he feares is turned into jealousy; and other things will do themselves if such a correspondency be continued betweene you as is necessary for publique safety and the family, which God hath owned and blessed. I am unwilling to mention my poore endeavours, but if the successe be such as I expect, it may not be unfit that I assume the title of what I in my heart am, my lord,

Your lordship's most faithfull, obliged, humble servaunt,

J Reynolds

[103]John Hewson and his allies had reportedly been spreading rumours against Henry Cromwell along these lines and Hewson had another meeting with the Protector in May 1656, though Thurloe reassured Henry Cromwell that 'Wee are here pretty well used to discourses of that nature, and are not wholly ignorant of men's spirits' (*TSP*, IV, pp. 742–743; V, p. 45). By August 1656, Henry Cromwell had heard that Hewson had become very animated by 'his late transactions in England' and was 'next dore to a mad man' (*TSP*, V, p. 327).

78. From William Stane, London, 27 May 1656, 821, fos 144–145.

My lord,

I have not for a long tyme receyved a lyne. Last week I did not write and in truth have bin ill. But that which most troubles mee is that good people are not more of a peice. I cannot but observe it to bee so with you as well as here, and truly wee do not mend here in that respect. I do not know what more threatens us; sure the Lord will finde out a way to make us agree. I do often think upon the two good bishops in king Edward's days, who were very bitter each to other when the sun shined upon both, but when fire came to judge them, then they were loveing bretheren and were gathered into onenes of spirit.[104]

How much need have wee to watch as to this evill world. It is seene things do us all this mischeife; nothing but the sheild of faith will save us from such fiery darts as the devill casts in everywhere. Every Christian's experience will tell him that when hee beholds the glory of the Lord, though but in a glasse, hee is changed from glory to glory as by that spirit (for that kingdome is like leaven),[105] and from thence the primitive Christians were so rich in grace, so little carefull for the world, so much of one hart; but it is the sadnes of this day that the enemie assaults in the weakest part and wee are found without our sheilds and the spotts of God's people such as if they were not His people; indeed they are scattered strangely.

But that of Ezekiel's bones hath somwhat of comfort.[106] The Lord hath not left Himselfe altogether without witnes, and Hee can returne this captivitye and teach His poore people to consider their owne ways. For truly that is one of the devill's snares; hee puts upon others to blame and reforme them, when that decept and wickednes is so much in every man's own hart, that there is matter of shame and great reason to bee always cryeing unto the Lord.

That of the Swedes routing the Poles is confirmed.[107] No news from our fleet. The major-generalls are in towne, all of them. The results I know not.

I suppose your lordship heares that the narrative of your child's baptism is printed here, which, to deale freely with your lordship,

[104] Hugh Latimer, bishop of Worcester, and Nicholas Ridley, bishop of London, swiftly fell from favour after the death of Edward VI; for their faith both were burnt at the stake by Mary Tudor at Oxford in October 1555.

[105] Leaven: an agent employed for fermenting, changing, or raising.

[106] As part of the biblical account of how God gathered up the Israelites, Ezekiel tells how God restored and brought back to life a plain full of human bones (Ezekiel, chapter 37).

[107] 1656 marked a high point in the Swedish army's campaigns in Poland.

seemes not to bee so resented by good people here and such who are for baptism.[108]

How doth my lady and your son? Your brother Russell (Sir Francis's eldest son) my Lord Protector hath made cornet to his life-guard, which now is made almost a regiment, vizt 160 gentlemen.[109]

All your freinds well; the children at Wallingford recovered, all but Biddye and shee is mending apace.

The Lord gracious and mercifull bee with you and teach you Himselfe. If wee in private capacityes stand in need, sure your lordship, who is so much now upon the stage, need crye unto Him. My affectionate service to my lady. I am, my lord,

Your affectionate servant,

W Stane

79. From John Honner,[110] Dublin, 29 May 1656, 821, fos 146–147.

Letter of request, seeking not only new pikes from the Dublin stores, to replace the old and defective pikes of his infantry company on garrison duty at Inishbofin,[111] *but also firelock muskets so that his men could patrol in boats.*

80. From Daniel Redman,[112] Kilkenny, 31 May 1656, 821, fos 148–149.

May it please your excellency,

Captain Franke's troope, beinge comaunded to stay in England after all the rest of the troopes, was necessitated to make use of above £600 of the other troopes' money, which he is now repayinge, by little and little as pay comes, which has occasioned the contractinge soe great a debt in his present quarters that his troope will not be able to dischardge this great while. I shall, therefore, make it my humble request to your lordshipp that he may continue in this precinct for the winter aproachinge, as also that I may receive your excellencye's

[108] Henry's first son, Oliver, was born on 19 April and baptized by Dr Samuel Winter in Christ Church, Dublin, on 24 April. Detailed accounts of the service appeared in several English newspapers in early May.

[109] During the opening months of 1656, the Protector's mounted lifeguard was expanded from 45 to 160 and reorganized into eight squadrons.

[110] Probably the lieutenant-colonel John Honor, parliamentarian officer, who was appointed in January 1654 as a commissioner for setting out lands in Ulster to disbanded soldiers.

[111] An island off the north-west coast of County Galway.

[112] Parliamentarian officer and politician and a strong supporter of the Protectoral regimes in England and Ireland, he served in Ireland from 1649, becoming major in Oliver Cromwell's horse regiment and later taking command of John Reynolds's horse regiment after Reynolds's death. He was elected for Irish constituencies to all three Protectorate parliaments.

pleasure what other troopes are designed for this precinct, and whether they are already orderred the places where they shall quarter, or that it be left to me to dispose of them. This I humbly desire in regard I knowe not how or where to dispose of my owne troope, which is nowe come upp and was by me designed to quarter in Callan, Knocktopher and Thomastown,[113] and some few in Kilkenny, if not otherwise orderred by your lordshipp. This is all, but to crave pardon for this trouble to your lordshipp, and to subscribe myselfe,

Your excellencye's very humble and faithfull servant,
Dan Redman

81. From William Webb,[114] Dublin, 2 June 1656, 821, fos 150–151.

May it please your excellency,

I have beene latly at Fort Fleetwood, at Bally Moe bridge,[115] and doe finde the worke to bee so forward that it may bee finnished this summer, if the want of money prevent it not. Captain Thomas hath not fully finnished the castle of Termonberry,[116] of which I shall put him in mind shortly. The fortification (at Cam island),[117] being ane earth worke, is in a sade condetion, but I hope shortly that there will bee noe great occation thereof. Severall parts of the fort of Sligo (being ane earthworke) is fallen downe, and the thatch cabbing, that is now the storehouse, is much out of repaire. About tenn pound will repaire the said fort and store, untill such times as some other fortification bee built at the towne of Sligo.

Fort Cromwell att Bellaghey pass,[118] the walls thereof are a building of lyme and stone; within the maine wall there is a rampart of earth in breadth sixteen foot, within that is another wall to keepe up the said rampart. Two of the houses within the said fort are allmost framed. The greatest obstruction now in carrying one the said worke is the great want of moneys. Therefor I humby pray your excellency to bee pleased to give orders suddenly for three or fower hundred pound towards the carrying one the said worke, othere ways the worke men wilbee suddenly gon, not being able live there any longer.

[113] Three towns to the south of Kilkenny, in County Kilkenny.

[114] An engineer in Ireland, who was involved in metal mining in Munster from the mid-1630s; although he was deprived of office in 1649 for suspected disaffection to parliament, during the 1650s he was again employed by the English administration in Ireland.

[115] Ballymoe, in County Galway, lies on the River Suck, which forms the border with County Roscommon.

[116] Termonbarry, close to the River Shannon in County Roscommon.

[117] In County Roscommon.

[118] Bellahy, in County Sligo.

And it would bee hard for to gett worke men againe in those part. I remaine,

Your excellency's most humble servant,

Wm Webb

82. From Charles Fleetwood, Wallingford House, 4 June 1656, 821, fos 152–153.

Letter of recommendation on behalf of the bearer, Mr Gay,[119] *formerly employed by Fleetwood in Ireland as a commissioner for stating the accounts of the army and in other capacities; requests employment for Gay, together with arrears of salary due to him from his period as a commissioner at Athlone.*

83. From Thomas Harrison, London, 10 June 1656, 821, fos 154–155.[120]

May it please your lordship,

On Fryday last after dinner 10. 22. 28. 106d together very privately. Tho severall 39. 40. 31. came to the chamber, none were admitted.

[119] John Gay, one of the clerks of decrees in the newly restored court of chancery and one of several judicial officers who complained around this time that Sir John Temple, himself newly restored as master of the rolls in Ireland, was obstructing their tenure and enjoyment of those offices (*CSPI*, pp. 615–617).

[120] Harrison had been sent by Henry Cromwell to London in the spring of 1656 to represent his and his government's interests there (*TSP*, IV, pp. 742–743). This is the first of seven letters in this collection (letters 83, 89, 92, 94, 101, 120, and 121) by Harrison, all of them from June and July 1656, which are partly in a numbered code. The code is broadly similar to others in use at the time, with each number standing for a complete word or for a person's surname, rather than for an individual letter. The numbers 1–9 were not employed – where they appear in these letters, they simply stand for those numbers themselves. The numbers 10–30 evidently stand for important individuals, such as the Protector, senior army officers and politicians, and others involved in the business of Ireland and of Henry Cromwell in London. The remaining numbers, from 31 up to the 450s (though only selected numbers within that range are employed here) stand for a variety of verbs, nouns, collective nouns, and pronouns, though some of these higher numbers also stand for individuals and thus represent the names of specific people. However, many of the highest numbers, especially those above 400, probably stand for nothing and are rogue numbers included to mislead unofficial attempts to decode the letter; similarly, numbers over 100 preceding and/or following the code for important individuals (10–30) in most cases appear to have no meaning. Alas, unlike some other coded letters in this collection, which carry the decoded words in a contemporary hand above the numbers, these letters have not been partly or wholly decoded here by their recipient; moreover, the key for this code does not survive and it does not seem to have been employed in other extant correspondence by Harrison. Thus, although some of the minor words, especially pronouns, are fairly clear, most of the encoded words cannot be decoded with anything more than intelligent guesswork. Thus the texts of these letters have been reproduced here as in the original, complete with the coded sections, and attempts to decode words, phrases, and whole sentences have been reserved for footnotes.

About an houre after their parting, 11. called 19. 67. 66. his closett, through the roome where 12. and others 39. 40. 31. were together. Before this 29. was willed 66. withdraw, and 13. 25. spake together about 40. settlement 39. 143.. 65. 20. coming 67. 13. told him they had not bene idle, nor neglected the affaire 39. 143. which they were resolved to settle. He desired to have a sight 39. 40. 71s. whilst he read over the extract (which was prepared for his veiw). Somtimes he hummed with indignation at severall passages and sighed deepely when he came 66. 14. 71s,[121] and having read that which was instar omnium,[122] he said, This man here is a good man, as any in the world, I beleive you thinke soe, but that he should so wholly give up himselfe to that party and wrap up himselfe with them is a strange mystery. Well, I see these men must not have what they would etc. He desired to make his owne further observations and collections 72. 40. 71s,[123] and so locked them up in his cabinett, saying he would make no other use of them then for keeping the peace, for which he was so hardly thought and spoken of, and then consented to burne them according 66. 20's[124] desire. 13. then asked what 19. thought 39. 90. 60. Sir Robert King etc, and then had his thoughts 39. 79. 86. 95. etc at large; and in conclusion said they were resolved to adde 3 or 4 and settle a good 35. 67. 143. and to doe somwhat else, that should either prevent and make peevish people quiet, or at least hinder their disquieting and hurting of others, and to that end he had desired 25. 66. 107. 108. 16. who had promised so to doe, and to follow it till it was finished. Although 229. 13. semed sometimes before 103. 66. suspect as if 40. 42.[125] might be too suspicious and fearfull, yet he never exprest any such thing in

[121] 'On Fryday last after dinner the Protector, 22 and 28 talkd together very privately. Tho severall of the council came to the chamber, none were admitted. About an houre after their parting, Lambert called Reynolds in to his closett, through the roome where 12 and others of the council were together. Before this 29 was willed to withdraw, and Fleetwood and 25 spake together about the settlement of Ireland. At Harrison coming in Fleetwood told him they had not bene idle, nor neglected the affaire of Ireland which they were resolved to settle. He desired to have a sight of the letters whilst he read over the extract (which was prepared for his veiw). Somtimes he hummed with indignation at severall passages and sighed deepely when he came to 14's letters,. . .'.

[122] This Latin phrase could be translated as 'an example of all the rest'.

[123] 'from the letters'.

[124] 'to Harrison's'.

[125] 'Fleetwood then asked what Reynolds thought of 90, 60, Sir Robert King etc, and then had his thoughts of 79, 86, 95 etc at large; and in conclusion said they were resolved to adde 3 or 4 and settle a good government in Ireland and to doe somwhat else, that should either prevent and make peevish people quiet, or at least hinder their disquieting and hurting of others, and to that end he had desired 25 to speak with 16 who had promised so to doe, and to follow it till it was finished. Although Fleetwood semed sometimes before 103 to suspect as if the Baptists. . .'.

private, nor the least dislike of any passage, but a very high satisfaction and contentment, promising all possible encouragement etc.

I suppose those jolly humours which somtimes appeared 67. 40. 41. 71s. 66. 102. had their rise from that prudent indulgence, and seming complyance they somtimes mett 108. 72. 11., but 391. 15.[126] and freinds are as safe here as the mercy of a gracious God can make them. I heard first by his Highnesse of your lordship's being ill of a cold, from which I hope you are long ere this delivered. My soule longs earnestly for the reall happinesse of waiting upon your lordship againe, and in order hereunto they want no importune sollicitations in whose hands the businesse here lyes. I humbly begge the presentment of my best service to my most honoured lady, whose prosperity, with your lordship's and the precious little ones, is the subject matter of the dayly prayers putt up by, (my lord),

Your lordship's most obedient f[. . .] in the service of b[. . .][127],

Tho Harrison

84. From John Reynolds, London, 11 June 1656, 821, fos 156–157.

May it please your lordshipp,

I am not a little rejoiced with that good correspondency which I find betweene your lordshipp and the lord deputy and, that one maine point being preserved, I doubt not of a good successe in all your lordship's affaires, and that your lordshipp will prove the greatest blessing to that countrey that it did ever enjoy in a governour.

Since my last I have beene once admitted to a debate of the busines of Ireland, and was charged with the old busines of a petition and such other matters. His Highnes seemed wel satisfyed and did promise that you should receive full encouragement speedily, which if your lordshipp do receive, whereby a sober interest may subsist in Ireland, I shall be verry abundantly contented to quit my station, and if as lawfully called thereunto, as I was first to emploiment, I should rejoice in a settlement heere. But truly, my lord, your lordship's loveing and benigne expressions do so exceedingly overcome all my objections, as unlesse I be detained as one judged unprofitable to the service of highnes,[128] or prejudiciall, I shall waite upon your lordshipp with much

[126] 'I suppose those jolly humours which somtimes appeared in the 41 letters to 102 had their rise from that prudent indulgence, and seming complyance they somtimes mett with from Lambert, but Henry Cromwell. . .'.

[127] Paper damaged, with some loss of text.

[128] It is not entirely clear whether this word is being used as a simple noun, suggesting an elevated or lofty position or office, or as a reference to (his) Highness the Lord Protector.

chearefulnes, without any advantage obteined by my journey more than from your lordship's particular favour.

The lord Lambert hath beene verry ingenuous in the present transaction about Ireland. I should be glad to receive notice of your lordshipp being pleased to write unto him. I am,

Your lordship's most humble and faithfull servaunt,

J Reynolds

I was 4 dayes since at Chippenham where they remembred your lordshipp with much affection and respect.

85. From Richard Cromwell, 14 June 1656, 821, fos 158–159.

Deare brother,

Now the crowds of the congratulations are over for the joye of your welcome sonn, I shall as one truly and sinceerely obleiged give you myne, and with the scripture joye I tender it, desiring that God will make it a blessing to our famuly. I ought to have appologized for my longe stay, but the neare relations of brothers will cutt offe that, espetially betwixt yourselfe and me. Our loves are not to beginn acquaintance. I may be confident my sister quickly forgott her paine for joye, and I doubt not of her delight in being surveyor-generall of the nurcery. It was not only welcome to the parents and neare relations, but all Ireland in there joyes made themselves related to it, a very greate mercy, and is an outward demonstration of God's exceeding love to you, for that the prayers and joyes of soe many hearts should be answered and filled. Ingadgements of an high nature; the choycest outward blessing; the best of temporall blessings; my prayers shall runn for its eternall happynesse, and my requests to God shall be that God will make it an instrument in His quarrell, to defend His churche and people against there enimyes. I rejoyce with you and my sister, soe doeth my wyfe and Hursley freinds. We are dayly expecting the fruight of my wyfe's wombe, and what God pleasses to send will be acceptable.[129] We desire your prayers for us, that with patience we may bare the providences in there occurrencyes, though contrary to our naturall desires, that alsoe our joyes may be moderated. I have suffitiently troubled you and my paper is almost swallowed up, and what roome is left is to testify that,

I am your most affectionate brother and servant,

R Cromwell

[129] Oliver, the only son of Richard Cromwell to survive infancy, was born in July.

My service I desire may be tendered to my sister. My wyfe, father and mother Maijor presents there affectionate services to you and deare consorte.

86. From Richard Cromwell, Hursley, 14 June 1656, 821, fos 160–161.

Deare brother,

I confesse my fault in taking too much of presumption upon me, but were I not sencible of youre pardoning dispossition, I should not adventured[130] soe much priviledge and liberty. The reason of it is for that my affections in the other letter would afforde noe roome to recommend captain Burrell, my former servant, to your favour. He hath soe exprest his affections to me and his reall readinesse to your service that though it be his temper to waite, yet I could not doe lesse in this second oppertunity which providence had put in to my hands but present him, as judging him usefull (because of his steedy principles and cordiall affections) for some imployment. I have discourst with him at learge, boeth of persons and things, by which I dare rende him fitt, if my request may be worthy your taking notice of. Be pleased to excuse this trouble, it being more then the person indends, his fortunes having made him able to waite untell your commands shall order him, which being bestowed upon him will very much ingadge a poore brother whoe is only able to make bare expression of acknowledgments, which shall all wayes be cordially payed by,

Your most affectionate brother and servant,

R Cromwell

87. From John Reynolds, London, 16 June 1656, 821, fos 162–163.

May it please your lordshipp,

I canno[...][131] in any competent measure answer the many obligations which your lordship's goodnes hath bestowed on me, yet I can truly affirme that consciousnes of my duty hath and doth guide me in all things wherein your lordshipp is concerned. I beleive your lordshipp will receive a liking of your moving the forces in Ireland, and an acknowledgement of your industrious and advantageous management of civill affaires. And if it should not come from his Highness, who is the best of men, yet I am sensible you have the best of comforts in a peaceable conscience. I was put to prove it a

[130] Either word omitted – perhaps 'have adventured' – or tense incorrect.

[131] Paper slightly damaged with some loss of text, though the incomplete word is evidently 'cannot'.

mercy that your lordship is there, which being easy to do, it may not be otherwise to write. It is clearely knowne that other Christians besides Anabaptists may live in Ireland, and that ministers may be encouraged, and that others may have countenance and justice. This was formerly beleived otherwise, and theis, without coming to touch upon the former governour, it was fully manifested. And indeede, I have alwayes put much upon times and shall never endeavour the prejudice of the lord deputy, wherein, if I do overcome, it will be my comfort, and I hope your lordshipp is so satisfyed; yea, I know you desire it. I remaine, my lord,

Your most humble and faithfull servaunt,

J Reynolds

88. From John Reynolds, 16 June [1656],[132] 822, fos 94–95.

May it please your lordshipp,

I do exceedingly wonder at this delay occasioned thorough petulancyes of persons contradicting settlement. I did hope to have beene with your lordshipp before this time and to have performed that service which from duty, obligation and affection I ow unto your lordshipp. I do find unexpectedly such persons as professe your principles, yet oppose your governement, and it is much trouble to the cheife ministers heere that you carry on the worke with such a generall opinion. It is expressed to be least you should oppose and injure my lord deputy. I hope your lordshipp hath that reall brotherly love which you were pleased to expresse towards his excellency, and notwithstanding all that love or respect, which I perswade and your lordshipp intends towards him, yet my advice shall alwayes be that your lordshipp do not decline your interest in ministery, magistracy and consistency in things, viz: principles and practises. Herein your father, who is greatest on earth, will abide by your lordshipp, or if it fall out otherwise your heavenly Father will not forsake you, and good men will love you, and your owne conscience be a continuall feast.

Since my last the product of the lord Lambert's and lord deputye's meeting hath beene too farre a leaning to the former prejudiciall counsells, and as I have ground to beleive your poore servaunts have sort[133] somewhat in the debate, but his Highness knowes it and will do according to the judgement of sober men, who generally are for your lordship's encouragement. It is too much trouble to informe your lordshipp of the various intricacyes of persons opposing

[132] Mistakenly endorsed '1657'.

[133] Word could alternatively be read as 'fort'.

a sober settlement in Ireland, wherein selfe designes, emulation, misinformation and prejudice play their parts.

There are whisperings of persons to be put neere you, and that I should be sent into some other emploiment. If my moderation in Ireland was esteemed neutrality, it now will be usefull indeede.

Your lordship's,

J R

89. From Thomas Harrison, London, 17 June 1656, 821, fos 164–165.

May it please your lordship,

Upon Thursday last the declaration 39. 40. 42.[134] came to hand, and was that evening presented by 19. 66. 10.,[135] who read it very attentively and seriously, dwelling upon every expression, and enquiring after the condition of the subscribers, and being told by 20. 11. might now see who had 148d.[136] He held up his hands in admiration, and began 66. 107. 108. 21. about 40. 106.[137] but was taken off by the newes of major-general Worstley's[138] death. 229. 75. had bene with colonel White[139] 65. 40. Tower, to rake up what dirt he could to cast upon poore 420. 20..[140] 21.[141] hopes it doth not sticke though laid on by an extraordinary hand. I have twice since that importuned his Highnes for a dispatch, and this morning spake 66. 22.[142] to hasten. A while agoe 28. 436. was told by 25. 211. that 23. 250. was assured he could not issue 40. 106.

[134] 'of the Baptists'.

[135] 'Reynolds to the Protector'.

[136] '. . .told by Harrison Lambert might now see who had reported'.

[137] '. . .began to speak with Thurloe about the settlement'.

[138] Charles Worsley, parliamentarian officer, fought for parliament in his native Lancashire during the 1640s, and in 1650 was appointed by Oliver Cromwell as lieutenant-colonel of his own newly raised foot regiment, which saw action in Scotland and northern England in the early 1650s and was based in London by 1652–1653, playing an active role in the ejection of the Rump in the spring of 1653. In 1655 he was appointed major-general of north-west England and proved to be exceptionally committed, diligent, and thorough. He died, aged just 33, on 12 June, while attending the meeting of the major-generals in London.

[139] Francis White, parliamentarian officer, was a captain in the New Model foot regiment commanded first by Sir Thomas Fairfax and then by Oliver Cromwell. Prominent in army politics of the later 1640s and a firm opponent of the regicide, he campaigned under Cromwell in Scotland in 1650–1651 and supported his ejection of the Rump in the spring of 1653. He was elected to the second Protectorate parliament in October 1657, and sent to Mardyke to command the fort, but at the end of the year he was drowned while returning to England.

[140] '229, 75 had bene with colonel White at the Tower, to rake up what dirt he could to cast upon poore Harrison.'

[141] 'Thurloe'.

[142] 'to 22'.

to the satisfaction of all parties.[143] He feared 10. 12. 15.[144] would all be discontented but he had nothing but his honesty to trust unto. This day 22. said 66. 21. he was very ready whensoever 13. pleased,[145] and would afford his utmost assistance etc.

For anything that can be discerned by 454. 19.[146] the true cause of all this suspence and delay is a care that the party 425. 39. 40. 41.[147] may not be made desperate on a sodaine, but I am perswaded there is no hesitation nor irresolution at all in the bosome 216. 39. 11.,[148] but all thoughts are made there and will be made legible in the best season. 420. 13. had an account 72. 20. concerning the journy 39. 15.[149] into the north, which had bene 148d[150] as a progresse merely for pompe or pleasure, but the truth being discovered, was very well approved of, and a forwardnes appeared 66. 104. 19. 105.[151] to attend in that service.[152]

I hope the good Lord hath both spared your precious bud and improved the threatning. The eternall God be your refuge upon all alarums, and helpe both your lordship and my lady, and all His with you, to abound in faith and love yet more and more, and to grow up into Him in all things, who is the head, even Jesus who delivered us from the wrath to come, in whome I shall hope (through grace) whilst I live to subscribe myselfe, (my lord),

Your excellencie's most obedient, faithfull, poore servant,
Tho Harrison

90. From George Monck,[153] Edinburgh, 17 June 1656, 821, fos 166–167.

Letter of recommendation on behalf of lieutenant John Verner, who had served him faithfully in Ireland, requesting that Verner either be allowed to buy the land

[143] 'A while agoe 28 was told by 25 211 that 23 250 was assured he could not issue the settlement to the satisfaction of all parties.'

[144] 'the Protector, 12 and Henry Cromwell'.

[145] 'This day 22 said to Thurloe he was very ready whensoever Fleetwood pleased'.

[146] 'Reynolds'.

[147] 'of the Baptists'.

[148] 'of Lambert'.

[149] 'Fleetwood had an account from Harrison concerning the journy of Henry Cromwell'.

[150] 'reported'.

[151] 'to Reynolds'.

[152] In the late summer and early autumn of 1656, as in every year during his time in Ireland, Henry Cromwell left Dublin and embarked upon an extensive tour of inspection around the Irish provinces.

[153] Parliamentarian officer and politician, who had fought briefly for the king during 1644 but was soon captured by parliamentary forces. He was released in 1646 on entering parliament's service and thereafter campaigned loyally and with distinction for the parliamentary cause in Ireland in 1647–1649, in Scotland in 1650–1652, and then as an admiral and joint commander of the republic's navy in the Anglo-Dutch War of 1652–1653. He returned to Scotland in 1654, initially as overall governor, but from 1655 as commander-in-chief of the forces there but sharing power with a council – he himself became a councillor – and civil administration.

he currently held in Ireland or be paid for the building work he had undertaken there.

91. From Charles Fleetwood, 20 June [1656], 821, fos 168–169.

Deare brother,

I am sorry you showld have so much trouble about this Jameica regiment, but I confesse I can neither blame you nor myselfe for mistakes; but it seemes by my lord Lambert that the regiment in Scotland is to consist of 600 men, but they are to rayse no more then 500 in Scotland, and to have a 100 out of Ireland of privat souldyers to compleat that regiment to 600 for colonel Brayn,[154] and the 600 in Ireland are to be under a formed regiment according to former orders; and therfor thus farre lyes the mistake, that besids the regiment you have allready formed, you are to send a 100 private men to compleat colonel Brayn's regiment.[155] My lord Lambert's omission in this must be an excuse to me. You must send thes 100 men with a month's pay as the privat men of the regiment you rayse are to have. I am sorry it showld be thus troublsom, but I think I am not to be blamed, much lesse you can, which I will own, who am,

Your most affectionate brother,

Charles Fleetwood

92. From Thomas Harrison, London, 20 June 1656, 821, fos 170–171.

May it please your lordship,

Your lordship's last gracious, encouraging letter found me in London, where I am likely to remaine till God put it into his Highnesse's heart to give a settlement to the affaire of Ireland and a period to my attendance. I am assured of a good issue, though others 39. 40. 31.[156] decline the businesse all they can. It is a wonder to heare the same things so oft repeated and so much irresolution to be found in the spirits of such persons. I forbeare particulars because I am surprised by the

[154] William Brayne, parliamentarian officer and administrator, was lieutenant-colonel in William Daniel's foot regiment serving in Scotland in the early 1650s; in 1654 he was given command of 1,000 foot sent from Ireland to support Monck in Scotland. He was governor of Inverlochy until 1656. In the summer of 1656 he accepted command of the new foot regiment of 600 men being formed to serve in Jamaica and he campaigned there as both commander-in-chief and governor from his arrival in December 1656 until his death in September 1657.

[155] Thus Henry Cromwell was to supply from Ireland 100 foot to be added to the 500 troops drawn from Scotland and so complete Brayne's new infantry regiment, as well as a separate body of 600 foot drawn from the regiments in Ireland to form the new regiment, under William Moore, to be sent from Ireland to the West Indies.

[156] 'of the council'.

messenger in Sir John Reynolds, his chamber; but I am not moved at all to any discontent, because I am so perfectly secured as to the maine. This morning I was with my lord deputy to desire his hastning the businesse. He called Mr Hewett and willed him to minde him of it when he was with his Highnes. I thinke it my duty not to neglect even such addresses though they finde but slender entertainment. I have a promise of the priviledge of som fredom in discourse with his excellencie the next weeke after Tuesday. I will not be further burthensom to your lordship by multiplying words to little purpose, but with incessant prayers for your lordship's prosperity in soule and body, relations and undertakings, I only repeat that I am, (my lord),

Your excellencie's most faithfull, poore servant,

Tho Harrison

93. From Francis Russell, Chippenham, 23 June 1656, 821, fos 172–173.

My lord,

I have more leisure to wright than your lordship hath, therefore have reason to aske pardon for my backwardnes therein. But, my lord, tis not for want of love that I bare to you, but because I care not for being to impertinent in any thing. Therefore measure me not by my silence least you mistake me. I am, I must confesse, often that which the world call melancholy, yet I think not without some reason considering all things, for I meet with those things which sometimes try me, and it may be you are of the same opinion. God hath appointed me for those tryalls, which to lay upon some others were to heavey a burden. But I cannot complaine that either His love, my owne faith and patience (through His mercy) faile me, and so I am made capable to bare the unkindnesses of men, from whom I could not expect them. Indeed, my lord, your love to me and mine hath a great satisfaction in it to my spirit. Tis so noble a principle that I can wish you no greater a growth in any thing than in it. Thereby you will be greater than your freinds, and overcome all your enemys. He that hath found that pearle needs no other riches to make him considerable or be valued, and allthough it may seeme a fooleish thing to the wise and politick, yet in the end they will know its want and the curse of being without it. Above all things, my lord, nourish love; twill stand you insteed when every thing else shall faile; tis the life of God and the best wisedome of men. I had reall thoughts of viseting you in Ireland this summer, but meeting with some things, which I cannot but tearme unkindnesses (and those from whom I did expect better), I am so wounded for the present in my mind and spirit that to hide myselfe by retyrement is most propper for me, and pleases me best. For any kind of news, my lord, I can send you none, onely through the want of love, iniquity and great jealousys abound among all sorts of men, and the issue is like to prove dangerous, if I understand anything, and the melancholy are of my opinion. My wife is so much taken with hir daughter's last letter, wherein she tells hir such tales of your love and kindnes to hir, that my wife cryed for joy, while I laughed. Will is turned both soldyer and courtyer, which I hope will prove to his advantage every way if the Lord please to give him wisedome. His comeing on the stage of this world is, it may be, a forerunner of my comeing of it. For when he comes of age, which will be next March, if the Lord give him life, I have thoughts of makeing over all my estate to him and to leave him the trouble and busines of this world, which I am weary of more than the men of this world are weary of me. For your father told me lately at our parting that the spirits of some men could not bare me, which I tooke to be somewhat of his one mind likewise, and that which I long suspected. And now, my lord, haveing told you thus much, I shall leave it to you to judge whether or no an absolute retyrement will not best befit and become me. Thus you see, my lord, what we poore hereticks are appointed for, the crosse. Wee must suffer like rogues and among them. But we have through mercy our reward, or else indeed of all creatures we were most miserable; neither Jew nor gentile, cavilere or roundhead of any sect but revile us, and persecuted we are accounted mad at the best, but that we have a devill is our ordenary accusation; but all these things must be. There is a gentleman, my lord, one that is a kindsman to Sir Henry Chichely[157] by marryage. His name is, as I take it, Mereas, an Irishman. I was desireed by Sir Henry to beg your love and favour towards him, and pitty likewise if in any thing he shall apply himselfe to your lordship. I know by his freinds here it will be kindly taken and acknowledged if you shall be pleased to owne him. My lord, I am and have reason so to be,

Your lordship's in all faithfullnes to serve you,

Franc Russell

My wife thankes you for loveing hir daughter so well.

94. From Thomas Harrison, London, 24 June 1656, 821, fos 174–175.

May it please your lordship,

As I am deepely a debtor to the grace of God for the favour I have found in your lordship's eyes, so also to your lordship's charity in

[157] An active royalist during the civil war and knighted by the king in 1645, he was the younger brother of the royalist Thomas Chicheley. Accordingly, he was connected to Francis Russell by marriage and, more distantly, to Henry Cromwell.

so often wishing a period were put to my uncomfortable attendance here. Were his Highnes pleased to permitt me, I should immediately obey your lordship's commands and hasten away. But as I judge it my duty to submit to his Highnesse's pleasure and wisdome, who sees it expedient as yet to detaine me, so doe I sacrifice not only to my affection, but duty also, in waiting to see what God will yet do further for poore Ireland. The last weeke 425. 28. was much 73d. 65. 22's cariage, who being pressed 66. 104.[158] answered with the spirit of a Spanyard. He would not mend his pace etc., nor would he so much as appoint any time wherein 29. 436. might 107. 108. 23. so that 30. 211. concluded there was a designe to withdraw 29. 19. 72. 143.[159] General Desborough shewed much of the same temper, for being pressed by 20. 66. hasten 40. 106.[160] answered, he knew nothing of it, but it should not sticke for him, nor would he undertake to remember any businesse further then he was remembred of it. This shortnes semed strange 66. 21.,[161] who had formerly other manner of reception from him; but yet the trouble arising hence was but small, considering how cordiall and constant 454. 10.[162] remains. I was the last Lord's day with our church and do releive myselfe with such diversions as well as I may; but shall presse all I can this weeke to know his Highnesse's determination. Your lordship's commands, communicated by Dr Gorge, shall be carefully attended. I hope men's ingratitude shall not weaken your lordship's hands in well doing. The only wise God thus contriving and ordering it, the better to reserve requitall to Himselfe. That you and yours (in this perilous juncture, or rather fracture of time) may dayly be preserved and prospered from on high, is the constant prayer of,

Your excellencie's most engaged, poore servant,
Tho Harrison

95. From Gerard Lowther, Dublin, 28 June 1656, 821, fos 176–177.

Letter of courtesy and of thanks for an unspecified favour granted in response to his recent petition.

[158] 'The last weeke 28 was much angered or puzzled at 22's carriage, who being pressed to reply'.

[159] '...wherein 29 might speak with 23 so that 30 concluded there was a designe to withdraw 29 Harrison from Ireland'.

[160] '...by 20 to hasten the settlement'.

[161] 'to Thurloe'.

[162] 'the Protector'.

96. From Robert Southwell,[163] Dublin, 28 June 1656, 821, fos 178–179.

Right honnorable,

May it please your excellency. According to your lordship's comand I have hereinclosed the remembrance given unto your lordship and the councell about repairing the docque at Kinsaile, for the more speedy fitting and setting out of the shipping designed for the guard of that coast, which if your lordship bee pleased to recomend unto some perticuler freinds in England, that may effectually move the right honnorable commissioners of the admiralty in the case, I presume they may give your lordship and the councell some speedy incouragement to sett it forward and to provide for it as they shall judge fitting. Which being done, your lordship will sone finde the good effects of it in the safe guarding of this coast from the enimy, the state's ships being alwaies in a readines to follow and pursue their gennerall instructions, as also to attend your lordship's comands upon every occasion as your intelligence shall require. The officers of the customs in each port heretofore haveing had strict comands from the councell of state to bee exactly carefull in examining all ships comeing from any parts off the sea, and if anything therin might import the service of the state to returne a speedy account thereof, which may now redily bee done by reason of the post setled in all parts of this land. And it was likewise usuall for the state's ships, when they crost those harbours where any custom officers were setled, to send in their long boat and to inquire of them for their intelligence from the sea, and then to proceed accordingly.

My lord, I shall humbly take the bouldnes to acquaint your lordship that I am informed by some of the comanders on this coast that the victualers in England, or some of them, are now labouring to remove the victualling of the state's shipps totally from off this coast and to place it at Milford, which must needs bee very inconvenient and distructive to the service here. That harbour being so far within the channell, and the windes that brings the enimyes' ships on this coast eyther keepes them in, or they are so far to the leeward that they cannot get up to the enimy untill much harme be done. Nor can the intelligence of enimyes being upon the coast come so sone to any other port as to Kinsale, for the reasons aforesaid and in regard of the

[163] Administrator in Ireland, by the 1630s he was customs collector for Kinsale – he retained close links with Kinsale throughout his career – and he sought to defend the town against the Irish Catholics in the wake of the 1641 rebellion. Although he supported Prince Rupert's fleet in the late 1640s, he held a variety of administrative posts in southern Ireland under the parliamentary regimes of the 1650s. He was employed in the business of land surveys and transplantation as well as in maritime and naval affairs, including provisioning naval vessels in and off Kinsale.

frequent coming in of ships from all partes thether. I humbly crave your lordship's pardon for this bouldnes, and remaine,

Your lordship's most humble and most faithfull servant,

Robert Southwell

97. From Edward Wale,[164] Waterford, 28 June 1656, 821, fos 180–181.

Letter of thanks, for Henry Cromwell's assurance that he was not under any suspicion of disaffection, and of request, seeking favour for John Goatly, an apothecary who had served in Ireland under Henry Ireton,[165] and worked first with Dr Waterhouse[166] at the siege of Limerick and later under Dr Dynham at Waterford hospital, before being assigned a regular military salary by Fleetwood; Goatly, his wife, and their three small children were now living in poverty in Waterford and deserved help.

98. From Charles Howard,[167] London, 30 June 1656, 821, fos 182–183.

Letter of request, seeking favour for Robert Mead[168] with respect to his estate near Kinsale.

[164] Chaplain to Fleetwood in Ireland in the early 1650s, subsequently minister in Waterford and paid a government salary. He was a strong supporter of the Protectorate and of Henry Cromwell in Ireland and in 1655–1656 wrote him very supportive and encouraging letters (*TSP*, IV, p. 314; V, p. 66).

[165] Henry Ireton, parliamentarian officer and politician, a regicide, and son-in-law of Oliver Cromwell. He rose rapidly under Oliver Cromwell during the first civil war, was quartermaster-general of the Eastern Association army in 1644 and commissary-general of the New Model Army from 1645, commanding his own horse regiment. He went to Ireland in 1649 as second-in-command of Cromwell's expedition and became overall commander when the latter left Ireland in the spring of 1650. His own Irish campaign concluded with the protracted but ultimately successful siege of Limerick in the summer and autumn of 1651, but he died near Limerick on 26 November 1651.

[166] Joseph Waterhouse, physician to Oliver Cromwell's army in Ireland in 1649–1651, and brother of the Protectoral steward Nathaniel Waterhouse.

[167] Parliamentarian officer and politician during the 1650s, though he had allegedly actively supported the king during the civil war and was subsequently fined by parliament. Despite continuing suspicions, he held a variety of political, administrative, and military offices under the parliamentary regimes of the 1650s, sitting in all three Protectorate parliaments. He was captain of Oliver Cromwell's lifeguards in the early and mid-1650s and colonel of his own foot regiment from the summer of 1656. He was very active in northern England, especially his native Cumberland, and in 1655–1657 he was major-general for the northern counties, in theory as deputy for Lambert. In 1655 he was also named a Scottish councillor.

[168] Possibly the London merchant and adventurer of that name, though he had been assigned lands in County Tipperary.

99. From Charles Fleetwood, London, [June 1656], 821, fos 254–255.

Deare brother,

That which you mention in your last is a thing of necessity to reduce or charge to the revenue allowed us, which will surely be one of the 1st things the counsell when they meet will consider, and concerning which you shall have a speedy account when any thing is don. The counsell's not sitting puts a great stopp to all buysneses. The reason of their not sitting is not fitt for to be communicated by letter.[169] I acknowledg your favor in the reason why I had not the papers about the charge and issues of Ireland sent me. So long as kindnes and love is continued I can passe by all other things, for your true, hearty love I value and desire above all things of complement and cerimony. But I perceive you ar mistaken to think I had the representation from others of it. As one elect to me, I will assure neither others are so ready to give nor myselfe to receive what may occation unkindneses twixt us, but we have so much one interest and reason of cordyallnes that whatsoever is or showld be designed that way we must resolve against, and conclude still with this, that we must dearly love on another. In this you shall not exceed me, and in this let our strife be who shall out goe one another, and if the Lord please to give us this mercy, give me leave to say as it will be a great refreshments each to other, so will our entirnes be a very good concernment to the publicke.

The army is in a good condition of quietnes, and wer our counsell compleate about their buysnes it will much satisfy the publicke, and be a great ease to his Highnes. As for my lady Frances, that buysnes is concluded twixt themselves. My lord Warwicke not answering his Highnes' demands upon his giving £15,000 porcion prevents at presant the consumation, but I doe not see how it can breake off, both partyes being engaged.[170] Sir Edward Mansfeild of Wales is to addresse himselfe this weeke to his Highnes, that he may have leave to make

[169]The council held only ten meetings on eight days during June. The reasons for this are not clear. Although Oliver Cromwell's health was often uncertain between 1656 and 1658, it does not seem to have been particularly poor during June 1656. There is some evidence that Cromwell and his councillors were deeply divided on the best means to solve the regime's growing debts and that the decision eventually taken, to call a parliament, was opposed by some, leading to divisions both within the council and between the Protector and some of his councillors.

[170]Frances, Oliver Cromwell's youngest child, was being courted by Robert Rich, grandson of the Earl of Warwick and son of Lord Rich. It was a difficult courtship, with reservations on both sides, not least because of the Protector's demands for a large financial marriage settlement; many of these issues were set out by Mary Cromwell in a detailed letter to her brother in June 1656 (*TSP*, V, p. 146). Although a settlement was at length agreed and the marriage occurred in November 1657, the bridegroom was then already ailing and he died within fourteen weeks.

known his affection to my lady Mary.[171] I wish he may be worthy of so deserving a lady. My deare wife is not very well at presant. The Lord will give, I trust, that choyce mercy of hir health, which is the greatest blessing I have in this world. With both our humble services to your deare lady, I am,

Your most affectionate brother and humble servant,
Charles Fleetwood

It seemes your commands to colonel Lawrence[172] was not to com to London, which he was very carefull to his howse,[173] but his wife being to be heare I did undertake to excuse his coming hither, wheare I will take care he shall not stay long without your license. Be pleased to spare him in this upon my account, I conceiving it would not be convenient for his wife to come without him. His Highnes hath vacated the order formerly made by the counsell to stopp the presant payment of the £24,000 which belonged to Ireland.

100. From Charles Fleetwood, [June 1656], 821, fos 252–253.

Deare brother,

I much wonder you showld so soone aprehende the busynes about the Jameica regiment, and not be confydent in me that if ther was any such thing you showld have hade the that[174] notice of it, but both by my letters and the counsell's you will understand what is intended as to that part: that the men out of Ireland to be raysed are to goe under a formed regiment and they are to be no more under colonel Brayne's command then all the regiments allready in Jameica are, and therfor it was a great mistake to think that they showld be reduced into colonel Brayne's regiment. His Highnes will, I presume, make a return by the messenger you sent. I am sorry the men have stayde so longe for their shipps. The winds have bine contrary, and the delatorynes of the seamen will, I feare, make you still a sufferer by keeping the men upon

[171] Mary, Oliver Cromwell's penultimate child, was linked with several possible and unsuccessful suitors during the mid-1650s, until, in November 1657, she married Thomas Belasyse, Viscount Fauconberg.

[172] Probably Richard Lawrence, parliamentarian officer, who served under Oliver Cromwell in Ireland as marshal-general of the horse and was given command of a foot regiment there in 1651. He was active in the surveying of forfeited lands and tranplantation, bitterly arguing with several other officials engaged in that business, including William Petty and Vincent Gookin. A strict Independent, he was distrusted by Henry Cromwell as a fanatic and also because of his connection with Hewson, who was Lawrence's father-in-law (*TSP*, IV, pp. 327–328, 433).

[173] Word omitted or phrase garbled.

[174] Superfluous word.

a publicke charge.[175] I have received yours whearby you are pleased to intimate the continuance of your former affection, which I showld most heartily be glade of to receive a certeinty of. But indeade give me leave to be free with you. I have bine very much troubled that I should be looked upon as a person of such jealousy, either upon a publicke or perticuler account, as to have letters to and from me to be opened. I value not what is seen, but certeinly I never deserved so ill from the state as to be under such a suspicion, and indeade this was not sent[176] by information from Ireland nor any have bine ther this longe time, but I cam to the certeinty from the nearest. Deare brother, doe not give credit to such unhandsom suggestions that showld put any upon such practises. This I have longe suspected but never till of late hade so much the certeinty therof as now. I canot deserve so ill, but however you will finde some to be flatterers and me to be,

Your affectionate brother and humble servant,

Charles Fleetwood

101. From Thomas Harrison, London, [June or July 1656], 823, fos 359–360.

May it please your lordship,

I am much affected with your lordship's great love and paines laid out in your last, as in all the rest. God make me worthy (I meane with the worthinesse of congruity) to answer such engagements. I cannot entertaine a thought concerning the inquiry therein mentioned, but that it is made either without the knowledge of 436. 11. 24.[177] prosecuting it, to serve 372. 12. and 103. 39.[178] opposers with a byassing inclination towards whome 211. 19.[179] hath charged him, in his owne thoughts (without any wrong) for a long time, and without which it had bene impossible to have fenced all this while against such full discoveries, and to have winked against so much light; or if it be done by permission or direction 72. 13. 240.[180] it is but to make the way the clearer, and to finde out men's spirits and dispositions to the utmost; for if that were an alleviation, and not rather an augmentation of your lordship's exercise, I may say truly and knowingly 344. 10. 65. 68. is as lonely in this 322. 106. as 391. 17. 67. 143. and what 211. 20.

[175] The ships and men were delayed at Carrickfergus until early October, running up bills of around £10,000.

[176] Word heavily amended and possibly deleted.

[177] 'Lambert and 24'.

[178] Unknown, although 12 may stand for a senior army officer or councillor.

[179] 'Reynolds'.

[180] 'from Fleetwood'.

420.[181] either hopes or thinkes or hath written is not by inference or conjectures, but by plaine, evident, earnest, iterated orall expressions 476. 72. 13's. 438.[182] owne mouth time after time. Dr Owen[183] and others worthy 39. 149.[184] have upon personall knowledge seconded the same 66. 425. 18. 454.[185] All these circuitions[186] are only to demulce[187] 391. 14. 102.[188] etc. If I be deceived tis the plainnes and simplicity of mine owne heart that doth it, and I dare not without evident cause suspect the want thereof in others. 216. 21.[189] fears not what can come 72. 40.[190] north, and though endeavours had bene used abundantly so 66. 148. 17.[191] intended journy thither, it cannot be said that it had obtained, because satisfaction to the contrary was so readily imbraced. My lord deputy was pleased to tell me the last weeke, that his Highnes had hopes the lord cheife baron Steele[192] would be willing to goe over (I thinke) as chancelor; and that the things of settlement were minded and proceeded in as they were able; and this was all could be obtained from his Highness also. I waited this morning severall houres and saw his Highness deepely engaged in the garden with my lord Lambert and Mr Secretary, but could not have any opportunity. I shall attend

[181] 'I may say truly and knowingly the Protector at 68 is as lonely in this settlement as 17 in Ireland and what Harrison…'.

[182] 'from Fleetwood's'.

[183] John Owen, minister, theologian, and academic, served as chaplain to Oliver Cromwell's expeditions to Ireland in 1649–1650 and Scotland in 1650–1651. He was dean of Christ Church, Oxford, from 1651 and vice-chancellor of Oxford University from 1652. He became one of the principal religious advisors to the parliamentary regimes of the 1650s, frequently preaching before parliament and council, serving on a range of religious committees, and advising on or helping to formulate religious policies. He became close to Cromwell and effectively served as one of the Protector's chaplains, but he strongly opposed the offer of the crown in 1657 and urged the Protector to reject it.

[184] 'of note' or 'value'.

[185] 'to 18'.

[186] Circuition: the act of going in a circle, making a circuit, travelling round and about.

[187] To demulce: to soothe or mollify.

[188] Unknown.

[189] 'Thurloe'.

[190] 'from the'.

[191] 'to 17'.

[192] William Steele, parliamentarian politician and judge, supported the parliamentary cause during the 1640s and was appointed by parliament to various legal offices; he took no part in the trial of Charles I, but was prominent in other state trials of the post-war years. He was appointed recorder of London in 1649, a serjeant at law in 1654, and chief baron of the exchequer in 1655. Although appointed to the Irish council in the summer of 1654, he remained in England for some time, sitting in the first Protectorate parliament, before finally crossing to Ireland in the summer of 1656 on his appointment as lord chancellor of Ireland. Henry Cromwell met him in Dublin in October 1656 on returning from his late summer tour of Ireland (*TSP*, I, p. 731). An Independent with Baptist sympathies, his relations with Henry Cromwell were sometimes poor and he opposed Henry Cromwell's more conservative religious policies.

for it dayly. The annexed was given me by Mr Fisher this day, wherein he was married to a widdow of a competent estate; he is very desirous of the continuance of your lordship's favour, though he dare not give your lordship the trouble either of his apologies or of his thainkes. I begge your lordship, Mr Avery (if he call for it) may have the ring I presumed to leave with your lordship. God give your lordship health and chearfullness, and that all our affaires shall have a blessed issue is the unshaken confidence and well-grounded expectation of, (my lord),

Your excellencie's most devoted servant, whilst I have any being,

Tho Harrison

102. From Charles Fleetwood, London, 1 July 1656, 821, fos 184–185.

Deare brother,

I have so litle time to wright, coming late from Hampton Court, that I can only give you this account. That upon Thursday last the oath of secresy was taken off, and therfor now I may give you this account, that the late secret debates hath only this result: to call a parliament the next 17th of September according to the instrument of government. The day of elections in England are to be 17th of August. The day of election for Scotland and Ireland not resolved. It is intended the qualifications shall be exactly kept unto, both for the electors and elected. I neade not tell you the consequence of choosing such persons who are truly faithfull to the cause we have bine and are still engaged in. The Lord dispose of men's spirits to peace, as the issue of this parliament may be; it will make for future peace or division. Ther was many debates befor we cam to this resolution. I trust the Lord hath directed to the best. I beseach you be carefull in Ireland. Ther is very great weight to be expected what the Lord will doe therin. The Lord quicken up the hearts of saints and give a healing spirit. My haste is so great that I must beseach your excuse, with our affectionate humble services to your deare lady. I remaine,

Your most affectionate brother and humble servant,

Charles Fleetwood

103. From John Reynolds, London, 1 July 1656, 821, fos 186–187.

May it please your lordshipp,

I did hope to have beene the bringer of the present newes of a parliament etc, but it hath pleased his Highnes to suspend our dispatch beyond expectation; but I can now assure your lordshipp that there is no delay from any other ground than a desire to please all sober men, in the determination of your busines of Ireland, wherein I must do right to the lord Lambert in testifying his ingenuity in the busines. I suppose his Highnes hath by his owne letters informed your lordshipp with the inside of his intentions and pleasure concerning things and persons. I can, God be praised, acquiesce in the discharge of duty, and may affirme that in all sincerity I have served his Highnes and your lordshipp; neither have I at any time trespassed upon the lord deputy, and although in so thankeles emploiments I may please none of the 3 supreme on earth, yet I hope my duty faithfully discharged to the 3 supreme in heaven will be a comfortable consideration. My lord, I did not understand your lordshipp's meaning about my being chosen councillor[193] upon the same ground as commissary. If it be not from an acceptance of my poore abilityes and faithfulnes, I shall not desire to undertake the one, or to continue in the other. There are at present lord cheife baron Steend,[194] chancellour, and Mr Berry,[195] treasurer, and colonel John Jones.[196] The last is suspended untill your lordshipp shall signify your pleasure; he appeares a person wel affected to you, and is certainely honest and able. As for the souldiery, discipline hath beene so confounded, as it seemes they are all equall. I wish they prove equally deserving in the future. I am certaine they have not bene formerly. My lord, I remaine,

Your excellencie's most faithfull and obliged servaunt,

J Reynolds

104. From Simon Finch,[197] Cork, 5 July 1656, 821, fos 188–189.

May it please your excellency,

My collonel's company and my owne came into this citty yesterday, where wee quarter untill colonel Phaire's men be ready to martch.

[193]Reynolds was not, in fact, added to the Irish council at this stage and never served in that capacity.

[194]Word clearly written thus, as a variant upon or slip for 'Steele'.

[195]William Bury/Berry, parliamentarian politician and administrator, had been prominent in the parliamentary cause in his native Lincolnshire, where he served as treasurer of the county committee. Formally appointed to the Irish council by the Protector on 4 August, he thus brought financial expertise to that body, though suggestions that he would also serve as treasurer in or of Ireland did not come to fruition (*TSP*, V, pp. 196–197, 214, 587, 612, 697, 710). Perhaps more importantly, as a moderate Presbyterian he supported Henry Cromwell's religious policy in Ireland and thus strengthened his hand in dealing with the council.

[196]Although Jones had served in the Irish administration in the early 1650s, and although Henry Cromwell's initial reservations about his possible reappointment had been partly allayed by news that Jones was marrying into the Cromwell family, he was not, in fact, added to the Irish council.

[197]Parliamentarian officer, who fought in both Ireland and England in the later 1640s and early 1650s. He served for a time in Hardress Waller's foot regiment in Ireland but by this stage was lieutenant-colonel of Richard Lawrence's foot regiment.

Their stay is for their ten weeks' pay. Captain Ever's[198] company is martched to Mallow. I came into Corke upon Thursday, and upon my cominge in lieutenant-colonel Wheeler[199] drew of his guards out of the citty, I tellinge him I had noe order for the releiveinge them. He delivered the keies of the gates to the maior's deputy, the maior not beinge in towne, which is very pleasinge to the cittizens. Wee have beene much troubled upon our martch about peeces of eight, which wee received in Dublin, for none will goe here but plate peeces, neither upon the road. I humbly desire your lordship will command my lieutenant to his charge, for my ensigne went from my company as they martched out of Dublin and carryed my companie's pay with him, and never came at us since. Neither can I heare what is become of him, which hath put me to some trouble to gett money for my men. I desire to know whether I shall muster him or not if he comes to the company. This I thought my duty to acquaint your lordship with. Mr maior will give your lordship a full account of a pirat of twelve guns taken upon this coast the last weeke by a Bristow merchant.[200] 27 of the seamen, which are Irish men, are prisoners in the citty gaols. I remaine,

Your lordship's most reall, faithfull servant,

Sy Finch

105. From Charles Fleetwood, London, 8 July 1656, 821, fos 190–191.

Deare brother,

I understand by Dr Harryson that ther is some disquiet upon your spirit.[201] I can cleare myselfe of giving any occation, and certeinly none hath more reason to expect that freedom from you to impart your maladyes unto then myselfe, who have bine and I hope will be as faithfull a frinde to you as any you have. Let men report and say what they please, but in this I must, I believe, wait till God perswades

[198] Probably the captain Ewer who was a nephew both of Secretary Thurloe and of the late colonel Isaac Ewer, the previous commander of what was now Lawrence's foot regiment. In May 1656, Thurloe had recommended him to Henry Cromwell for military employment in Ireland (*TSP*, V, pp. 46–47).

[199] Francis Wheeler, a captain in colonel Ewer's regiment in the late 1640s, but from 1651 lieutenant-colonel of Phaier's foot regiment in Ireland.

[200] At the end of the month, Henry Cromwell sent Thurloe an account of this action, attesting to its veracity and praising the actions of the Bristol merchant vessel and its captain (*TSP*, V, p. 258).

[201] Disheartened by the opposition he was facing in Ireland and by divisions there, and disenchanted by suspicions that some members of the English regime were not giving him full support but rather were working to undermine his position, in late June and early July Henry Cromwell wrote several letters direct to his father and via Thurloe requesting permission to resign his Irish command and retire to England (*TSP*, V, pp. 150, 176, 177, 196–197, 213–214).

your heart to a credit and beleife of the same. I have litle to impart this weeke, neither will my time give liberty much to inlarge. I know not what to say about the stay of the shipps to transport your men for Jameica. Ther is now very positive orders and I hope they are set sayle befor this time. I know the delay therof is very much to your disadvantage in respect of wants of monyes. His Highnes hath now prevayled with the lord cheife baron Steele to goe as chancellor for Ireland. He will about October, I presume, be going. I hope you will finde mercy in his helpe with you. I know not of any other person resolved upon to be sent. Mr Berry, Mr Hopkins[202] and colonel Lilburn[203] have bine under consideration, but I canot say that any of them will be sent. The mistake about the 100 privat men was upon my lord Lambert's account. Ther is one Mr Arnold, whom his Highnes very much values. I beleive you may remember him. His Highnes desires you would get him some imployment, which, if you can, I am perswaded you will[204] him very honest and deserving. I have not much acquaintance with him, but I know his Highnes estemes exceedingly well of him. The Lord keepe you close to Himselfe; arme you against all groundlesse jealousyes. I am,

Your most affectionate brother,

Charles Fleetwood

106. From John Reynolds, London, 8 July 1656, 821, fos 192–193.

May it please your lordship,

The lord deputy professeth greate freindship, and I am assured his lordship is in good earnest. My brother is your lordship's most earnest and humble servaunt.[205]

[202]Perhaps the Edward Hopkins who was an admiralty commissioner and member of the second Protectorate parliament. His appointment to the Irish council had first been considered in the summer of 1654 (*TSP*, II, pp. 492–493) and was considered again at this time (*TSP*, V, pp. 196–197).

[203]Robert Lilburne, parliamentarian officer and politician and a regicide, fought for parliament throughout the civil wars and commanded a New Model horse regiment from 1646. Active in army politics in the late 1640s and at the king's trial, he served under Oliver Cromwell in Scotland in 1650–1651 and from 1652 to 1654 was commander-in-chief of the English forces in Scotland. From 1655 to 1657 he was major-general of Yorkshire and his native County Durham, in theory as deputy for Lambert, and was elected to both of Oliver Cromwell's Protectorate parliaments. His radical and Baptist sympathies and his support for religious separatists may not have made him an ideal councillor in Henry Cromwell's eyes and, like Hopkins, he was not in fact appointed to the Irish council.

[204]Word – perhaps 'find' – apparently omitted.

[205]The opening two sentences have been squeezed into the space originally left between 'May it please your lordship' and 'I am verry much troubled' and were evidently added after part or all of the remainder of the letter had been written.

I am verry much troubled at the receipt of your lordship's letter and do verry much desire to waite upon your lordship. Whence can such resolutions come but from your melancholy. For I do professe, my dearest lord, both his Highness and councell, and all intelligible persons heere, are satisfyed with your lordship's proceedings and are resolved to give all encouragement to your lordship in the future; and I am confident there is no one suggestion touching you credited by any honest man. Whatsoever is now presented to you, although wrote in a remisse or free style, is the observation of severall weekes, and although I have not effected all which I desired, yet whatsoever concernes your lordship is fully answered, and if the parliament did not give some caution to his Highness in respect of your lordship's relation (so neere), resolutions would be made more publique. My lord, I do most earnestly beseech you thinke not of stirring seriously from your station. God now blesseth whatsoever you take in hand, and I have cause to feare the contrary if you quit His cause. And certainely the sober settlement of Ireland is betraied if your lordship comes away now you are past the worst of opposition. And although some persons, on both hands, may be blamed for their zeale, yet no one stone hath come neere your lordship, which none of us who relates to Ireland have missed. And I do professe, without designe or flattery, it hath beene the whole aime of my stay to see that secured, and I know it is. And although I never see Ireland in any publique capacity, yet my hopes shall be that you will abide there and pursue the good worke begun by you, otherwise I shall not thinke of returning, being the remaining marke of envy. I remaine, my lord,

Your excellencye's most faithfull and humble servaunt,

J Reynolds

107. From Elizabeth Butler, Marchioness of Ormond,[206] London, 9 July [1656], 823, fos 322–323.

My lord,

His Highnes and the counsell haveinge grantede an order upon my petistione, referinge it to and impowringe the deputye and counsell

[206]Born into an aristocratic Irish family, in 1629 she married her cousin, James Butler, subsequently the twelfth Earl and the first Marquess and Duke of Ormond, the leading Irish royalist of the 1640s. Like her husband, she then spent several years in exile on the continent. In 1653, the English regime granted her – though not her husband – permission to return to Ireland, living at Dunmore, County Kilkenny, and receiving £2,000 per year from part of her extensive Irish estates. In the spring of 1656 she petitioned the Protector, requesting that further sections of the Ormond estates, deemed forfeit to the state during her husband's lifetime and currently rented out on short leases to tenants who had no interest in preserving or improving the property, should instead be leased to her. That petition was referred to the English council, which in turn, on 8 May, referred it to Henry Cromwell and the Irish council (*CSPI*, pp. 606–607, 829).

of Ireland to proside tharupon as thay shall see cause, I should have bine the presenter of it myselfe unto your lordships, but that for the more speede have sent this berar to attend and know your lordship's and the counsell's pleasure what you and thay shall think fitt to doe upon what is now transmitede unto you. Not beinge in a redenes as yet to solisset it in persone, though I have the intentions of it, as beinge hopefull that your lordships will find nothinge in my desiers, when you shall have considerede them, but what will appiere soe resonabell as may inclyne you to countenanse and befrind mee hearin; that with much thankfullnes doe acknowlege to have found soe oblidginge to mee in my formar consarns as I cannot dout you willbee less to mee in this, when tharby you cannot hindar but on the contrarye further and increase the stat's revinue by permitinge mee to become tenant unto my owne estate duringe my lord's life, I beinge willinge to give as much rent or more for it then anye other will; not out of anye expectatione I have to bee a presant gayner tharby, but to presarve it from a totall wast and ruene, which is otherwise like to happene when noe sartantye of time can bee grantede, wherby to incorage tenants to settell upon it and make improvments. Soe as if I may by your lordship's menes obtayne this favour, it shall with much gratitude bee ownede to you by, my lord,

Your lordship's humbell sarvant,

E Ormonde

My lord, I have one favour more to desier of your lordships, that my sarvis may bee presented unto my lady Cromwell.

108. From Francis Russell, Whitehall, 11 July 1656, 821, fos 194–195.

My lord,

I was not willing to loose the opportunity of this messenger, being I had a desire (before I knew he was for Ireland) to present you with my love and service. Something I have, my lord, to say unto your lordship, but what it will be I know not, being keept here in ignorance by your father, who commanded me to post it up to him, but now I am here I am allmost as ignorant of his will and pleasure as I was before I came to towne. But you know him so well that I neede not advise you to wonder. I am told, my lord, but whether it be true or not I cannot tell, that he intends me for your service in Ireland. Indeed, I could wish he would speake out, and that quickly, for these two things I much long for and desire: to serve your lordship, and to be out of this pittyfull, confused isleland. If any thing can make me to looke back to my owne country with love and desire tis Chippenham, in which place I could allmost beg rather than abound elsewhere, but my Lord God is knocking us all of this world so that wee must looke after[207] those things which are not seene, and is our mercy if well understood. I hope, my lord, to tell you by the next post that I am prepareing for Ireland. If not I shall be troubled, being most willing (now you have tryed many men and freinds) that you should, in these times of hippocresy and dissimulation, have some experience of a mad man and a heretick, that is,

Most soberly and sincerely your lordship,

Franc Russell

There is another young Oliver come into this troublesome world,[208] so that yours is to be called but plaine Noll.

109. From Charles Fleetwood, Wallingford House, 12 July 1656, 821, fos 196–197.

Deare brother,

I have seldome such a freind as this[209] to commend to you. I doubt not but you remember how I valleu him, haveing knowne him long and injoyed sweet fellowship with him. And since I returned into England I find him still full of savour and a very sober, reconsiling person, in respect of all sorts of differences. I wish wee had more of his mind and then it would be better with us; but this I need not say, seeing he is no stranger to you, nor you to his spiritt. I doubt not of your freedome to give a dispatch to his perticular affaire, about which he undertakes this jorney in the behalfe of himselfe and the rest of the commissioners. His long stay would be sad; his wife, who is with child, can ill bare his absence, besides a losse in his trade. I shall desire that the lands you appoint him may be as neere Limbricke as you can, and contiguus and sett out to them with the most advantage. I will not further trouble you, but entreate your favour to him and care of him, for my sake, who am, deare brother,

Your most affectionate brother and humble servant,

Charles Fleetwood

[207] Word amended and poorly formed.

[208] Richard Cromwell's son.

[209] Methuselah Turner, a London linen draper, was chairman of a powerful nine-man committee established by the English council and parliament in 1653 to oversee and administer the allocation of Irish land to adventurers and soldiers. As reward for their work, in September 1654 the Protector and English council directed that Turner and his fellow-commissioners be allocated land in Ireland to the value of £2,621 (Dunlop, pp. 446–447; *CSPI*, pp. 821, 827, 829).

110. From Simon Finch, Cork, 14 July 1656, 821, fos 198–199.

May it please your excellency,

Senc my comeing heere I have endevred to enforme myselfe of the condission of this contry, which is verry peacable at[210] present; and the way to keep them soe, I humbly concive, would be to have 300 foot and 90 horse quarterd here to be redy at sound of trumpitt and beat of drum. The plases convenyent for them is Cork subberbs 120 foot and 35 hors; and in Bandon 100 foot and 30 hors; and at Banty[211] 80 foot and 25 hors. I have offered this to the major-generall and my collonel;[212] and if I have done amiss I humbly desyer your lordship will attrebeut it unto my desyers to keep up his Highnes' intrust and peace of the nation, for the inhabytanc heere are a mix sort of peoples. A great part desyer Charles Stuart apon any termes, I believe; and for the ministers, I have heard they never mention his Highnes nor councle in there prayers, as they doe in Dublin and in other places, nor pray for his Highnes' councle heer. I made bould to aquant Mr maior with it, and Dr Worth.[213] They boeth promysed to speake to Mr Aires[214] to doe it. But for my part I shall carry it civilly to all sorts of people. 4 of my collonel's companys ar come up, and 4[215] of colonel Phaire's march this day. The great incoragment I have recived from your lordship embouldons me to be trublesom to you with these rud lines, which I crave pardon for, and remane, my lord,

Your excellency's most reall, faithfull servant,

Sy Finch

My lord, I humble[216] concive the disperceing all our men into petty garrysons is to preserve the fingers and tooes, and leve the head in danger.

[210] Word repeated in error.

[211] Presumably Bantry in County Cork.

[212] Sir Hardress Waller and Richard Lawrence respectively.

[213] Edward Worth, dean of Cork from 1645, was a firm supporter of the English government of Ireland and of orthodox Protestant doctrine and church discipline, leading him to oppose the spread of Baptism and Quakerism in Ireland. As head of an association of ministers in County Cork, loosely based on a Presbyterian arrangement though with members sympathetic to Episcopalianism, he was out of tune with Fleetwood's relaxed approach to religious radicalism, but he strongly supported the more conservative policies of Henry Cromwell and was, in turn, rewarded with a government salary and a string of religious appointments in the latter half of the 1650s. In 1655 he became minister at Waterford, but he had returned to his Cork power base by 1658.

[214] Joseph Eyres, minister in County Cork, a member of Worth's association, and a strong supporter of his policies.

[215] Figure heavily amended and poorly formed.

[216] Apparently a slip for 'humbly'.

111. From Thomas Harrison, London, 14 July 1656, 821, fos 200–201.

May it please your excellencie,

Matters of concernment I dare not but give by a speedier conveyance. This is only, in all humility, to lett your lordship know that I was acquainted with this gentleman, the bearer hereof, Mr Jenner,[217] in New-England. We came over from thence in the same vessell together, and I do verily beleive him to be one who hath obtained mercy to be faithfull, and who may be usefull to the soules of men, in communicating somwhat of the good knowledge of the Lord unto them. Mr Brewster (I perceive) first drew him to looke towards Ireland, and can give a further account of him; which also may be had (if your lordship shall see cause) from,

Your excellencie's most engaged, devoted, poor servant,

Th Harrison

112. From William Stane, London, 14 July 1656, 821, fos 202–203.

My lord,

I can not omitt such an opportunitye as this good freind is, although by my absence from London I am a stranger and have nothing worthy of your lordship's notice. Captain Lloid, who was sent to the generalls and fleet upon the coasts of Spaine, is returned;[218] and £80,000 the effect of the peace with Portugall.[219] Our agent there hath bin hurt (the attempt was further,[220] but not to danger; twas upon the late embassador's brother's score). It hath bin much disowned by the king of Portugall in his lettre to his Highnesse.[221] The parliament for the

[217] Thomas Jenner, minister in New England from 1635, returned to England around 1650 and, until the mid-1650s, held a parish in Norfolk. During his period in Ireland, from 1656 to 1659, he was at different times minister at Drogheda, Limerick, and Carlow.

[218] Griffith Lloyd had been sent to the fleet, carrying a letter from the Protector of 28 April 1656, full of detailed naval and military intelligence, and leading questions that the admirals were to consider (Abbott, IV, pp. 148–149).

[219] Part of the brief of the English admirals was to intimidate Portugal, threatening to attack her plate fleet or to sever her links with her colony in Brazil, to induce her finally to ratify the Anglo-Portugese treaty of summer 1654, giving English warships and merchants access to Portugese ports and markets, and securing freedom of worship for English Protestant residents.

[220] Word clearly written thus, but perhaps a slip for 'murder'.

[221] Philip Meadows, an administrator and diplomat trusted by Thurloe, was sent by Protector and council to Portugal in February 1656 to secure ratification of the 1654 treaty. His diplomatic efforts were initially unsuccessful and, worse, on 1 May he was attacked by vengeful relatives of the late brother of the Portuguese ambassador to London, who, in the summer of 1654, had been convicted of murder and executed by the Protectoral regime. Luckily, Meadows escaped with a slight gunshot wound to the hand. Although the English admirals urged Meadows to depart immediately and relished an opportunity to

generaltie gives consent and hope of better settlement. The marchants here make sad complaints, so many of their ships being taken by the Dunkirk enemie. My Lord Protector, her Highnesse, and all your familye are in health, so are all at Chippenham. My lord, although it need not I am perswaded, yet I must and can do no lesse then beg your favour and kindnes to my freind Mr Turner, who comes over on purpose for himself and the rest in commission with him. Your lordship knows, and all men can witnes, what paines that committee have taken and how well they have descharged that trust, for which this was their recompence. I know no person in the world for whom I would more beg a kindnes, which is your lordship's favour in the despatch of his busines, and that the land to bee sett out for them may commence as neer Limerick towne as may bee. His wife is in such a condition that I feare shee may suffer much if his absence should bee long, and I am sure his trade also will receive much damage.

Your lordship knows Mr Turner so well that I need say nothing as to that, but give your lordship this assurences: that to my best understanding hee is of a greate temper and sober conversation, and one whom I have found (by much experience, and contrary to report) of a healeing spirit in this divided day.

My humble service to your lordship and my lady. I hope your sweet children are in health. I remaine, my lord,

Your lordship's faithfull servant,

W Stane

The report that the kinge of Spaine hath releived Valencyne in Flanders and defeated the French is not ascerteined.[222] The duke of Brandenburge hath made a legue offensive and defensive with the king of Sweds and is gone in person against the Poles.

113. From Hugh Peters, 15 July 1656, 821, fos 204–205.

My lord,

I must bee somthing to you though you have given mee no worde long; alas, you need not feare where you are so beloved and honord. But I leave you to your liberty. Sir John[223] coming tomorrow to you will say all.

attack Portugese interests and enforce harsher terms, Meadows persisted with diplomacy and a somewhat chastened Portugese crown ratified the treaty on 31 May. The settlement included payment of £50,000 (not £80,000) in compensation for damages caused to English shipping by Portugese-backed royalist privateers.

[222]The report was true.

[223]Reynolds.

The French are beaten sadly; the king of Sweden not so he. These have, it seeme, the world in shaking. To you, I say keepe where God hath placed you with expectation, humility and quietnes. Love the truth and peace; bee open and playne (as you are) in all your worke; turne your hart outward from God and godly men and feare nothing. I think you are in your place and worke. Beleeve mee the world is shaking; God keepe us stedfast. I was at Cambridge commencement where you are deer etc.[224] Let mee have a word, I can be secret. If not, I can and must be still,

Your H P

Your brother hath a son. Salute your lady and all with you, your secretary, as I can write no more yet.

114. From Charles Fleetwood, Wallingford House, 16 July 1656, 821, fos 206–207.

Deare brother,

This is on the behalfe of the bearer, Mr Jenner, who is a freind of Mr Brewster's, well knowne to him. I hope he may be of good use in Ireland; therefore I recommend him to your care to provide for the setleing of him where he may be of best use and fitlye incourag'd. He hath at present left a place of £150 per annum, therefore I suppose less by you there will not be thought convenient for him. Your respects to him is desired by,

Your affectionate brother and servant,

Charles Fleetwood

115. From John Reynolds, London, 16 July [1656],[225] 822, fos 152–153.

May it please your lordshipp,

I shall not neede to trouble your lordshipp farther than to acquaint your lordshipp that I am appointed to waite upon your lordshipp speedily, and shall come by the way of Bristoll or Milford, as I shall find opportunity, partly in respect of my owne occasions, but principally in relation to your lordshipp's abode (as I heare for one month) at Kilkenny.[226] I hope things are wel there as heere, God be praysed, and

[224] Henry Cromwell had links with Cambridge, since he sat as MP for the university in the first Protectorate parliament and was on the board of visitors.

[225] Mistakenly endorsed '1657'.

[226] In late summer, Henry Cromwell usually toured a selection of important towns and garrisons in Ireland and his 1656 itinerary did, indeed, involve an extended visit to Kilkenny in late August and September.

I can affirme of a truth, that there is not the least ground of doubt or discouragement, which is all at present from,

Your most assured and most faithfull, devoted servaunt,

J Reynolds

116. From Charles Fleetwood, London, 17 July 1656, 821, fos 208–209.

Deare brother,

I did so latly wright to you that I shall only present you with our very affectionate salutes, and your deare lady, having nothing of consequence to trouble you with. Captain Loyde is returned from the fleet, who are in a good condition, but no action, nor I feare lik to be, the Spanyard having drawn a great strength of foote along[227] their coasts and their shipps not appearing out of the harbours, which they well fortefyed. The Portugall, for feare of our surprising his Braseill fleet, hath ratifyed the peace with us. Whither the probability of that surprise or this peace is most considerable to us is hard to say, but what the Lord doth is best.

The lord cheife baron, Mr Berry and, I think, Sir Francis Russell, will be with you in September. I presume all thes are according to your desires. I hope we shall get the monthly assessments from hence duly payde you; no more is to be expected. The addition of your counsell will increase your charge, which I suppose you will otherwise contract. My haste you must excuse, who am,

Your most affectionate brother and servant,

Charles Fleetwood

117. From William Lockhart,[228] Chaulny, 10/20 July 1656, 821, fos 210–211.

Letter of courtesy, reporting that he was forwarding an account of the siege of Valenciennes.

[227] Word heavily amended and poorly formed.

[228] Soldier, parliamentarian politician, and diplomat, he fought for the king in the Scottish engager army and was imprisoned after the battle of Preston, but he felt snubbed by the Prince of Wales (the future Charles II) and from 1652 he supported the English parliamentary regimes. He helped negotiate the terms of the Anglo-Scottish union, became a trusted colleague of Oliver Cromwell, and, in 1654, married into the Cromwell family, wedding a widowed niece of the Protector. He sat in both of Oliver Cromwell's Protectorate parliaments, was appointed to the Scottish council in 1655, and, early in 1656, was sent as ambassador to France to work for a firm Anglo-French alliance against Spain on terms favourable to the Protectoral regime.

118. From Charles Fleetwood, London, 20 July [1656], 823, fos 343–344.

Deare brother,

I hope this bearer can whitnesse how farre I have bine from incurring any just censur in doing any thing which might be unhandsome to youreselfe, and therfor I desire all unkindneses may be forgotten twixt us. I have bine a faithfull frinde and servant to you, and doe not give eare to suggestions which may administer matter of jealousyes; but let's be confydent one of another, and if I could finde your freedom to me as of old I showld then be satisfyed. I hope Sir John will be an instrument to beget and increase this good understanding. I shall not neade to aquaint you with any thing heare, but leave you to Sir John's relation. The errand about which he cam was of that nature that I think it could not be expected I showld be active about it, being what concerned myselfe,[229] and I have too much of that which the world calls honour allready. The Lord give me a better heart to improve what He hath allready given me; but I think the subject matter will easily creat a right understanding in any, that I did no more appeare in this buysnes. Ther are great endeavors in the gayning of elections. The Lord's appearance in this must be our only refuge; which that we may finde is the desire of,

Your most affectionate brother,

Charles Fleetwood

119. From Charles Fleetwood, London, 22 July [1656], 823, fos 345–346.

Deare brother,

I have received yours whearby you expresse some trouble of minde. I canot pleade guilty of having a hand therin, but can resort to his Highnes to cleare me wither I have not manifested a true affection and faithfullnes to you; and as I have told him, I held it not fitt if I hade any thing to except against you at any time to declare it to yourselfe and not to possesse a father with prejudices against a son, and therfor be not so unkinde as to harbour such jealousyes as causlessly, I feare, you retaine still; and therin you take prejudice against one, so farr as it is so, against as true a frind as any you have, and the unworthynes of any who labour to suggest the contrary will, I hope, be discovered and slighted by you. I have not time much to wright, and could have more

[229]As part of his mission, Reynolds had carried to the Protector a letter from a group of army officers in Ireland calling for Fleetwood to return to Ireland as lord lieutenant, with Henry Cromwell as lord deputy under him.

satisfaction in wrighting had I more assurance of the return of your old frindshippe. We are now beginning to think of our elections. The Presbyterians are very much labouring. The choyce is yet uncerteine what it will be. The Lord alone can despose of the hearts of the choosers, and when chosen give them quiet, peacefull spirits. This late defeat of the French by the Spanyard hath much hightned the Spanyard. Both armyes lyes neare each other, but I think at presant the French are not so well recruited as to attempt any thing, but must be upon the defensive posture. Somthing will be don heare, but at presant it is under secresy and therfor I cannot be so perticuler as by the next I may. I hope it may be an inlet to further good to the Protestant cause. I intreat you will take care that colonell Clarke may be one chosen for the parliment.[230] He will be very usefull as to Ireland. Excuse my haste, who am,

Your most affectionate brother,

Charles Fleetwood

Our humble services to your deare lady, and kisse your deare and sweet ones from us both.

120. From Thomas Harrison, London, 22 July 1656, 821, fos 212–213.

May it please your excellence,

Your lordship will understand that not long agoe it was moved here that 436. 12.[231] should hasten 66. 143. 66. 107. 108. 15.[232] and so having setled a right understanding and good correspondency, forthwith to returne. Your lordship will easily apprehend why this project proceeded not, as 425. 14.[233] could not much desire it, so I am perswaded 454. 10.[234] could not approve it, but that he is willing to say or doe or offer any thinge that might give content. When this was off, then 438. 28.[235] must goe, though that broke not forth here till the beginning of the last weeke. He comes as a messenger and mediator for peace, fully furnished with instructions 72. 16. 420.[236] and hath depth enough to make compensation for the plainnes and shallowness 39. 476. 19.[237] who perhaps hath misinterpreted the promises made

[230] In fact, John Clarke did not sit for an Irish seat in the second Protectorate parliament and instead sat for Cardiganshire.

[231] Unknown.

[232] 'to Ireland to speak to Henry Cromwell'.

[233] Unknown.

[234] 'the Protector'.

[235] Unknown.

[236] 'of Reynolds'.

[237] 'from 19'.

concerning himselfe, but yet rejoyceth in a perswasion that good things are really meant and intended concerning your lordship.

On Wednesday last, 391. 86.[238] was 3 or 4 hours in private 108. 11.[239] who saith he ratled him soundly and told him he neither had the spirit of prayer nor preaching, though he lately gave a tast of his guift, in a bitter invective at Worcester House[240] upon that conference when 322. 29.[241] was booted and spurd. His journey seemed not to be minded, which put him into heats and high expressions. Mr Peters also was inclinable to that journey, so he might be backe before the parliament begin. On Saturday, in the afternoone 30. 371.[242] went from hence well apaid, and, thought we had great cause to be theinkfull unto God things were so well, 229. 13. told him 211. 11.[243] would do us reason.

Colonel Markham[244] presents his most humble service to your lordship and would, I perceive, much rejoyce in the favour of a line from your lordship's pen. I beleive he hath bene serviceable in most places where he came, and on the last Lord's day in the evening at Hampton Court, whereof I suppose he will give your lordship an account, and if so your lordship will thereby be confirmed in all things, save what may relate 66. 20.[245] returne. Whereof he saith he could observe no syllable of a graunt, though he urged and watched narrowly for it, as that whereby both himself and others will make the estimate of their owne condition. His Highness' goodnesse and wisdome encourageth to hope for it notwithstanding. It would not only be an affliction but a ruine to be cutt of from the priviledge of waiting upon your lordship, and I trust, through the mercy of God, I shall not, while I live, be made uncapable of evidencing that I am, (my lord),

Your excellencie's most devoted, faithfull, poore servant,

Tho Harrison

[238]Unknown.

[239]'with Lambert'.

[240]Worcester House, London, was the base for a number of civil and military financial committees during the 1650s.

[241]Unknown.

[242]Unknown.

[243]'Fleetwood told him Lambert'.

[244]Henry Markham, parliamentarian officer and politician, first appears in military records in the mid-1640s, as an officer in Edward Rossiter's New Model horse regiment. He served in Ireland during the 1650s and held a string of financial and administrative offices there, though in the second Protectorate parliament he sat for a Scottish seat; he sat for Counties Kildare and Wicklow in the third.

[245]'to Harrison's'.

121. From Thomas Harrison, London, 29 July 1656, 821, fos 214–215.

May it please your excellencie,

I am here with that silence and submission which is due to God and my superiours, waiting for the appearance of Mr Morgan,[246] without making any vaine importunities for a dispatch, which I know till then cannot be obtained, whatever it may be after.

Last weeke Mr Barrington,[247] his Highness' auditor, (whose debtour I am for very many civilities) was pleased voluntarily to lett me know that there lately passed somthing touching 40. 106. 39. 143.[248] very agreable to the desires 39. 436. 19.[249] and very good respect expressed 66. 425. 20.,[250] but he might go no further. Peradventure your lordship knowes the particulars, or will do shortly.

Yesterday 454. 117.[251] told me how abundantly his Highness declared his satisfaction unto him and his full beleife of all the true and honest relations that have bene made; and yet for a while things are and must be carried as if it were otherwise. He said 79.[252] (I thought he meant 86.)[253] told 438. 10.[254] that 420. 11.[255] hearkned to lyes, and when a prince did so, all his servants were wicked, whereunto he received a sharpe reply as he well deserved. Some thinke the best expedient for settlement will be to remove those who are judged most active and zealous on both sides, and then try what the rest will doe. There will be a necessity of your lordship's continuance there to protect 40. 476. 44.[256] I say to protect them, for I dare say their provoking spirit and deportment will soone bring them to stand in need thereof. I thinke your lordship cannot imagine what horrid, wicked untruthes are here invented, and vented even at Wallingford House to avile and disgrace a poore creature, who never by thought, word or deed gave

[246] Anthony Morgan, parliamentarian officer and politician, had initially fought for the king in the civil war, but came over to parliament in 1645 and, with Sir Thomas Fairfax's support, became an officer in Ireton's New Model horse regiment. He served in Ireland from 1649 and acquired both land and a string of judicial and administrative offices there, and he represented Irish constituencies in all three Protectorate parliaments. Trusted by Henry Cromwell, in the summer of 1656 he was sent by him to lobby Protector and council on behalf of his Irish policies.

[247] Abraham Barrington, the Protector's auditor and clerk of the board of greencloth in the Protectoral household.

[248] 'the settlement of Ireland'.

[249] 'of Reynolds'.

[250] 'to Harrison'.

[251] Unknown.

[252] Unknown.

[253] Unknown.

[254] 'the Protector'.

[255] 'Lambert'.

[256] 'the Baptists'.

any occasion for such reports. I do not hasten much to undeceive those that suck them in, that their owne errour and breach of rule may in due time the more effectually afflict them. I am greived I can at present no otherwise serve your lordship then by the poore prayers of,

Your excellencie's most devoted, poore servant,
Th Harrison

122. From Charles Fleetwood, London, 1 August 1656, 821, fos 216–217.

Deare brother,

When quartermaster-generall Vernon[257] was in town he complayned of my lordshippe towards him in reducing his pay, when as it was contrary to the establishment sent from England, and no other generall officer was reduced in pay but himselfe, allthough the rest of the generall officers hade the same advantage in their arreares as he had, and yet without any reducment of their pay, which you wer pleased to consider and to continue his former pay; which I desire you will please still to continue to him, it being that which will be allowed heare in the establishment, and therfor I intreat you will cause it to be added ther, I meane the 5s per diem. I am confydent he truly loves you, and your favor will not be to a person ungratefull or unworthy of it, and I confesse it troubles me I should be harder to him then others. I am blamed by some for being too kinde to some, and by the same looked upon as too hard. Integrity will be my best defence. I am,

Your most affectionate brother,
Charles Fleetwood

123. From Thomas Harrison, London, 5 August 1656, 821, fos 218–219.

May it please your excellencie,

I remaine here with my health shaken and my spirit sometimes somwhat shattered and discomposed when I take to heart my

[257] John Vernon, parliamentarian officer, was for a time quartermaster-general of the English army in Ireland. An ally of Allen, Axtell, and Barrow, and thus one of the leaders of the Baptist-inclined opposition within the army to Henry Cromwell and his religious policies, he was suspected by Henry Cromwell of fomenting unrest in Ireland (*TSP*, IV, pp. 376, 402–403, 433). He had spent the first half of 1656 in England and his sudden return to Ireland at this time was viewed with dismay by both Henry and Oliver Cromwell; Henry reported that Vernon 'boasts much to every body of his plaine or rather saucy dealeing with his highness', while Thurloe replied that 'I thinke his highnesse is obliged to doe something therein, that may signifie his dislike towards hym' (*TSP*, V, pp. 278, 303–304, 327). He was one of the four prominent Baptist officers who resigned at the end of 1656.

detention here, which is the triumph of my adversaries and the wonder of my freinds; and I thinke of most of the sober godly about this towne, who are both amazed and sadded to see such power in their hands who have seldome had the grace well to manage it. But I am abundantly refreshed by those sweete and gracious lines your lordship hath bene pleased to bestow upon me by Mr Bradley.[258] I assure your lordship I shall not account my poore life or any of the concernments thereof deare unto me, so I may be enabled in any measure to answer that generous and most obliging sweetnesse soe seasonably and constantly expressed towards such a poore worme as I am. The messenger's mother had the malice to tell my lord deputy that I was married to my maid, and that not before there was neede. Whether will this raging unreasonable fury hurry them? The Lord looke on, if not to require, yet to rebuke it. My freinds of the church (to whome I preached at the Charter-House the last Lord's day) do heare of this malice and enquire when I shall have liberty to refute and remove from it, though they are as desirous of my poore ministry as satisfied in my innocency. If what I feared at first should prove true, that their former disappointment by my means is never to be forgotten or forgiven, and that my attendance upon your lordship (how innocent soever even as to them) should prove prejudiciall to your excellencie, I professe a readinesse rather to quitt whatever is most precious to me and to embrace a ruine as to this world, then to inconvenience your lordship, whose growth without checke or interruption may prove such a comprehensive blessing, such a glorious mercy to these nations. But if through infinite grace these sons of Zeruiah[259] prove not too hard for us no outward mercy can be named in the same day with my being restored to my station and service to your lordship, and to my most noble lady, to whome is presented the unfeigned service of, (my lord),

Your excellencie's poore, faithfull servant,

Tho Harrison

[258] Unidentified, though the letter may imply that he was a messenger, presumably one of the officials carrying state papers between London and Dublin.

[259] Biblical reference to King David's half-sister. Her three sons, Joab, Abishai, and Asahel, held military command in David's army but proved ruthless and unruly; after two of them were involved in a vengeance killing, in response to the death in battle of their third brother, David admitted that they were beyond his control (see, in particular, 2 Samuel, chapters 2 and 3).

Dr Winter[260] hath bene severall times with his Highness, and this day in particular, and gives the same report with others of his Highness' full satisfaction, and will shortly give your e[. . .][261] an account thereof.

124. From Charles Fleetwood, London, 5 August 1656, 823, fos 351–352.

Deare brother,

I have cause to be trouble[262] at the recentment you have against som whom you call my pretended frinds. I think none but truly are your frinds, but are mine, and therfor take heade of too great jealousyes; and would you but please to let me know what they have sayde or don to your offence I showld, I hope, at least quitt myselfe of faithfullnes to you, but I know you are misinformed in many things, and in perticuler that which relates to major Morgan was from a person who hath no relation to Ireland, though to yourselfe he hath, which I only cam to know from his Highnes himselfe, though I canot deny that some practises of his have bine offensive to me and others. As for Dr Harryson, I will say nothing of him, nor of the other at presant, but could I speak with you I would unbosome myselfe to you. I doe not think any man belonging to Ireland made it a desire to have any person removed whom you desired to keepe; but if you knew as much as I doe, which you showld if I could either speake with or wright unto you, that none elce might see or know of, you would then I am confydent think so well of some as you now.[263] I desire to have no personall prejudice of any man, but I am perswaded you are much more mistaken in some persons then you think I am in others. I would not doe any thing for to grive you. I have that affection for you that

[260]Samuel Winter, Independent preacher and minister, moved to Ireland in 1650, serving as chaplain to the parliamentary commissioners in Dublin. A gifted preacher and teacher and, from 1651–1652, provost of Trinity College, Dublin, he was favoured by Fleetwood's regime but became disenchanted by its lack of religious discipline and the spread of Baptism. However, although he remained very active in Ireland throughout the mid- and late 1650s, especially in the Dublin area where he sought to organize an association of ministers, lobbying both Henry Cromwell and his father on occasional visits to England in support of his congregationalist plans for Ireland, Henry Cromwell tended to favour Edward Worth's more conservative proposals and Winter's influence was limited.

[261]Paper damaged with some loss of text, though the incomplete word is probably 'excellency'.

[262]Apparently a slip for 'troubled'.

[263]Sentence may be incomplete, with one or more words omitted in error – perhaps the sentence should end 'you would then I am confydent think so well of some as you do now' or even 'you would then I am confydent not think so well of some as you do now'. Alternatively, the final word could be interpreted as the verb 'know' to give the sentence a grammatical, if somewhat vague, conclusion.

will not suffer me to doe any thing unhandsomly towards you, and therfor pray be more free with me wherin any person whatsoever gives you any trouble; and if I can give you ease I shall rejoyce therin, but to burden you I hope it shall not be beyond what becomes a dear brother. I have writt so often upon this subject that I hope the Lord will give a full satisfaction to your own heart of my integrity, and unites us together in our former union and affection; which that we may minde mutually is the desire of,

Your most affectionate brother,
Charles Fleetwood

I am much troubled at some discourse which is sayde I hade once with you in the Phoenixe gallery,[264] wheare only yourselfe was presant and another, and that ther I showld say that colonel Markham had bine a cavileire and was pulled out by the eares by the parliament forces,[265] which I am confydent was very much misreported for I never heard any such thing that I can remember. I begge you will doe me right therin, and what you know of it send.

125. From Francis Russell, Chippenham, 9 August 1656, 821, fos 220–221.

My lord,

I doe beleeve our letters from Chippenham to Ireland doe sometimes miscarry, for my wife tells me that she hath often written unto hir daughter, but understands by hir last that they come not unto hir, and I doe not find by your lordship's last to me that you have met with all those I sent you, therefore you must not censure us of neglect or want of love. Sir John Reynolds, who is I suppose now with you, can tell you much of what I would you should know if he will open my cabynet to your lordship as well as his owne. He is your faithfull freind and servant, I am confident, and truely tis his honor so to be, haveing undertaken to serve you; but tis hard to find many such, for love and faithfullnes are not the fashions of this world. That you meet with some difficulteys in your imployment I wonder not much at, for my part I never thought it would be otherwise, haveing seene something more of this world and the men of it than your selfe, and you must follow me hard if you think to overtake me. I cannot sometimes but laugh at your tryalls, for which you must pardon me for I am but seldome merry, and yet I am innocent in that kind of

[264]Phoenix House, on the outskirts of Dublin, was used by Fleetwood and by Henry Cromwell after him as an official residence, especially during the summer months.

[265]Surviving sources do not point to any active royalism or royalist military service by Markham in the opening years of the civil war.

mirth, but withall I am both afflicted and troubled with you, being well sensible of your burden. Some discourse I had with your father (when I was in towne last) concerning you. I must not tell you what it was, but this I can asure you, that he loves you and knoweth your frame and temper exceeding well. He is a wise, good man and of great experyence. I have noe news to wright you, liveing at a distance from it, onely this, I find in the country that no man knows what this new parliment will bring forth, but questionlesse, something very remarkeable. I know not what to think or say of it, but a long time they have bin as a kind of dead rotten peeces of governement to me; in short I neither can love or like them, as the condition of these nations stand. My service to Sir John Reynolds, and pray let him know that myselfe and some others of his Cambridgeshire freinds were resolved to have made him a knight for this shire till we heard he was gone for Ireland. I writ to him about it, but my sonne sent me word that he was gone before my letter came. His brother Bocking[266] is parted for Wales, to stand either with or against the master of the horse.[267] Colonell Jones of the counsell[268] seemed loath to have him a Welsh parliment man, but he will try his owne strenght and interest without him, so being a bold Brittan he cares not much for him. My lord, I hope this will come to you, and tell that I am, my lord,

Your lordship' faithfull freind to serve you,

Franc Russell

126. From Thomas Harrison, London, 12 August 1656, 821, fos 222–223.

May it please your excellencie,

Next to the refreshings I receive dayly from the upper springs, are those which your lordship's gracious letters doe every weeke afford me. It is no small comfort unto me that the maine businesse is so well over, as I yet hope it is, and that the cheife exercise now is that of your lordship's charity towards your poor servants. Surely that high generosity which you now evidence and act forth in adhering to a poor instrument will not only declare how worthy you are of faithfull freinds and servants but preserve those so, that are so, and purchase others, and confound those that are otherwise? Yet might I know it to be your lordship's interest I would begge your lordship, at least for the present, to desert me, and to abandon me to that ruine designed for me, unles God helpe his Highness to looke through all the juglings

[266] No-one of this name was returned to the second Protectorate parliament.

[267] John Claypole, returned for both Carmarthenshire and Northamptonshire.

[268] Philip Jones, returned for both Breconshire and Glamorganshire.

and divelish devices of men mad upon their idoll of soveraignty and dominion, whereunto they have sacrificed their soules and consciences and devoted all men to destruction that stand in the way to hinder them.

I am told by a freind that others (besides Anabaptists), even officers of the army, are made to sollicit his Highness against my returne. Colonel Hewson hath attempted to vilifie me to some of our church but hath not prevailed. I have dealt with him according to rule. He seemed satisfied and promised to make me so at his returne by bringing forth the authors of his most malicious, groundlesse slaunders. God hath much supported me by Isiah 51: 7, 8, and 54: 17.[269] I heare my lord Broghill is expected here within a forthnight. If your lordship be pleased to write a line to him and, by enclosing it, honour me with the delivery thereof, it may not prove in vaine.

Mr Osminton[270] last weeke was with me, doubtfull whether to returne or noe, and earnestly inquiring after mine, saying all the ministers of Ireland would make my usage the rule of their expectations, for if Ireland were too hott for one that had such a shelter, what might the rest looke for! As for their hell-bred report, it moves me not unlesse to pitty and stand amazed at their malice and shamelesnesse, no part thereof ever nearer my heart then to murder my father and mother. According as herein I am clear or faulty, so let your lordship account of,

Your excellencie's true servant,
Tho Harrison

I tooke your lordship's advice, as one of Jonathan's arrowes shott to poore David,[271] an excellent expedient to finde out your father's intentions towards me, and through glorious grace doe finde them so full of candour and sweetnes that I shall never s[. . .]iently[272] expresse my thainkfullnes to God and him.

[269] Verses assuring the faithful that they should stand firm against taunts and reproaches and that with God's help such charges would be rebutted.

[270] Thomas Osmington was, in 1654, receiving a government salary as minister at New Ross but he returned to England in 1656 and apparently did not go back to Ireland, since, in the later 1650s, he was minister at Lydd in Kent.

[271] The biblical story of how David, unsure whether Saul intended him good or ill, sought guidance from Saul's son Jonathan; Jonathan was to sound out his father and then convey the answer, good or bad, to the hiding David by firing three arrows either in front of or beyond his hiding place (see 1 Samuel, chapter 20).

[272] Paper damaged with some loss of text, though the incomplete word is probably 'sufficiently'.

127. From Anthony Morgan, London, 12 August 1656, 821, fos 224–225.

May it please your exellency,

I have forborne to troble you with an account of my proceedings in those things the councell were pleased to committ to my care.[273] I have made my daily applications to my lord deputy, and only to him for his furtherance. He sais I came very seasonably for the counsell heer were about to take of £2,000 per month from your allowance from hence, in consideration of the £2,000 raised by your new taxe there. I remain,

Your excellency's most faithfull servant,

Ant Morgan

128. From Nathaniel Partridge,[274] Wallingford House, 12 August 1656, 821, fos 226–227.

My lord,

I have many particuler and personall obligations lying upon me to love and serve your honour, which together with the serious consideration of the generall and publique necessities of your nation favorably[275] sway with and alure my affections unto Ireland (if the Lord will soe farr owne a nothing creature) to the helpeing forward the Lord's worke with you. I was honoured with, and incouraged by, a letter from your lordship, together with the honourable councell, of the 16th April last, inviteing me earnestly over. At which time, and for some monthes after, it pleased the Lord to afflicte my family with the meazles, which prevented my journey over, and since my family recovered I have beene staid by urgent busines to get up some monies oweing me and some other thinges. The which occasions haveing stayed me soe long I thought it good to signifie to your lordship the continued beat[276] of my spirit (notwithstanding the many invitations I have to abide here) to come unto you. And if I may but receive a word from your lordship's hand for my further incouragment I shall looke

[273] Morgan's wide-ranging instructions, dated 22 July and in part repeating the instructions given to Reynolds the previous January, focused upon the financial and economic settlement of Ireland (Dunlop, pp. 612–613).

[274] Minister, formerly of Warwickshire and Oxfordshire, who went to Ireland in the early 1650s as chaplain to the parliamentary army there, was a regular preacher at Dublin in 1654, and was for a time Fleetwood's own chaplain in Ireland. He may have returned to England with Fleetwood in 1655, because it is noticeable that he is addressing this letter from Fleetwood's London house. It is not clear whether he returned to Ireland at this stage.

[275] Word amended and poorly formed.

[276] Word poorly formed and could alternatively be read as 'bent'.

upon it as from the Lord, and soe forthwith (through divine assistance, together with the helpe of your prayers) waite upon the God of Israel for a prosperous journey with all conveniente speed unto you. Now the Lord of His rich mercy fill your lordship with His spirrit and furnish you with every grace suitable to your station and occasions, makeing you such a blessing to the nation that all the daughters of Sion may rise up and call you blessed. Thus craveing your pardon for this boldnes, I commend you and yours to the Lord, and subscribe,

Your lordship's most humble servant,

Nath Partridge

129. From Charles Fleetwood, London, 13 August 1656, 821, fos 228–229.

Deare brother,

I have very litle to wright, nor have received any from you this post. We are so full of buysnes and shall be in preparation for the next parliment that I doubt litle will be don effectually for Ireland befor the parliment. The treasurers say they have so constantly returned you by bills of exchang what is due that they are not behinde hande with you above £1,000[277] but will tak the best care they can for your speedy supplyes. I am sorry you showld have any reviving of your troubles by Vernon's returne. I am sure he hath no grownd from me or any elce so to doe, and indead in anything which may weaken your hands in your worke I hope you showld finde me a faithfull and affectionate brother to you, and thos whom you may most confide in will not, I hope, be more true to you then myselfe. But of this I say still so much, and so litle is I feare beleived, that I shall forbeare further inlarging then to let you know you will finde me,

Your most affectionate brother and servant,

Charles Fleetwood

It pleased Dr Harryson to show me a letter whearby it seemes ther hath bine somthing writt from one in this house, which gave a reflection upon him as to scandall. What I heard by that person I presently showed my dislike of any such discours; and that I am sure will be justifyed that I did my part therin and am not to be blamed. I desire wherin he is injuryed he may be righted, and if otherwayes may be convinced, I hope, I have not bine unchristian to him.

[277] Originally written '10000' but the final zero appears to have been deleted.

130. From Charles Fleetwood, London, 19 August 1656, London, 821, fos 230–231.

Deare brother,

I have received yours with much trouble that still your jealousyes continues of me and looke upon me as a person useing underhand wayes and meanes to give you discontent, which is a thing so contrary, I hope, to my practise that in time you will be convinced therof, and give me leave to say the burden I am made to beare upon such accounts is greater then any I know you beare. I have not added to yours. Doe you take heade by your jealousyes to adde to mine? As for major Morgan and Dr Harryson, I know not wherin you are so personally concerned that everything which relates to them you must be so concerned in. Though as to them, what, I beseach you, is don to offende? Have not you sent major Morgan as a publicke agent? Doe I deteine Dr Harryson? Give me leave to say I deserve not to be challenged upon their accounts. As for one of them, if he hath don evilly ther is more lyes at the stake to suffer then his name, even the gosple. Though I would be loath to say he is in anything guilty, but if any of my family have reproached him I shall not protect them and desire not to reteine jealousyes of him. But as I told him, my exceptions wer I feare he hath not bine so carefull to maintaine love twixt you and myselfe as becam him. As for matter of exception against him, I am neither his accuser nor his judge. If any have scandelised him, let not me be looked upon as a person concerned therin. What I have done I can, I trust, justify, which I presume is much mistaken by you, which makes a censure passe upon me as in your last seemes to be. If his Highnes hath writt anything to you concerning either of them I canot pretend to know what it is, but you are mistaken in your informer of what may relate to this buysnes. I would not willingly greive you but I confesse it hath sadded me to finde your easynes to beleive and harbour hard thoughts of me. I have bine tender of you and deserve not otherwayes from you. Dr Harryson hath had a pretious name and doe not desire to take it from him, and hope he canot but say I have bine regardfull to his reputation. If any who belongs to me hath otherwayes caryed it to him, let them and not me be reproved. I desire to know the Lord's meaning in this and other tryalls what of evill I can be <reproached> convinced,[278] for I showld be glade you will be free in telling me and let not mistakes be of prejudice. I am still fearfull that either thes or som others have bine instruments to foment such jealousyes twixt us. I think it concerns the publicke as well as our perticulers better to

[278] Originally 'reproached' but that word has been deleted and 'convinced' added in its stead, possibly as a slip for 'convicted'.

understand one another. What your thoughts are, yet you will finde me,

Your most affectionate brother,
Charles Fleetwood

131. From Thomas Harrison, London, 19 August 1656, 821, fos 232–233.

May it please your excellencie,

I cannot but repeate my humble and heartie acknowledgment of your lordship's most noble and truly Christian charity in continuing so constantly to afford me the honour and comfort of your love and letters. The good Lord by His gracious spirit make up a rich supply unto your lordship for the defect of creature succours and services. Though nothing in the world can vindicate me and cleare me as to the world but my returne into Ireland, yet I thinke the designe is that even the most opposite should be first so farre satisfied as not to gainsay it, but rather that the motion for it should come from them, that so a face of union may appeare to the world, which is thought a thing very advantageous and desireable. His Highness hath abundantly expressed both to myselfe and to my freinds his satisfaction and resolution to sticke to me and vindicate me, and bids me have patience but a very little little while longer. But if your lordship thought it worth the while to desire it as a kindnes of my lord deputy that he would hasten my dispatch with my little ones before winter come on, I am confident one word of his mouth would effect it, for it is but expected and wishd to come that way, that all may appear as well pleased. My lord deputy told me plainly that he suspected me, and all that were near your lordship, to have a hand in dividing betwixt him and your lordship. I assured him your lordship had a heart full of love and honour for him, and if he were sensible of any decay or distance of affection the best way was to consider when this began and upon what occasions. He presd me to discover what I had observed distastfull in any degree to your lordship. I told him I thought your lordship had to himselfe wittnessed some dislike of some men's imperious demaunding commissions, which yet your lordship was far enough from imputing unto him, any more then their showing his letters in courts, and glorying in their power and privacy with him, etc. I did what I could handsomely to make him sensible that himselfe and those whom he favoured, not your lordship nor your servants, were any whit culpable this way. He seemed passionately desirous of a redintequation[279] of love, wherein I helped on what I could by giving

[279] Redintegration: a restoration or renewal of wholeness.

testimony to your lordship's most assured forwardnes therein to have all things rightly understood, and all mistakes removed. I cannot relate things so fully as in such a case as this were needfull, but I hope your lordship will beleive (however these broken scraps may looke) that I used my utmost care not to lett anything fall to your lordship's disadvantage. The manifestation of your lordship's further pleasure in this or any other [. . .]ervice[280] will be exceding wellcome to,

Your excellencie's poore servant,

Tho Harrison

132. From Anthony Morgan, London, 19 August 1656, 821, fos 234–235.

May it please your excellency,

Last weeke my lord deputy moved the severall articles of my instructions to the councell, and it was committed to the Irish committee, of which my lord Lambert being cheife I waited upon him at Wimbleton[281] on Saturday last,[282] where he was pleased to admit me to the debate of the severall heads, and gave me his opinion thereupon, and promised to get a committee and give a speedy dispatch unto them. Mr Thurlow hath not yet enabled me to give your lordship a good account of the business he undertooke about arrears. I remain,

Your excellency's faithfull, obedient servant,

Ant Morgan

133. From Elizabeth Butler, Marchioness of Ormond, Dublin, 19 August [1656], 823, fos 324–325.

Letter of request, repeating her earlier request[283] *to be allowed to rent some or all of her estates, deemed forfeit to the state during her husband's lifetime, currently left waste or being despoiled of timber and other assets; had already approached Fleetwood on this matter, who understood the disadvantages both to the state and to herself of the current situation.*

[280] Paper slightly damaged with some loss of text, though the incomplete word is probably 'service'.

[281] His principal seat was at Wimbledon, south-west of London.

[282] 16 August.

[283] See no. 107.

134. From Martin Jubb,[284] Belfast, 21 August 1656, 821, fos 236–237.

Letter seeking an answer to his earlier request, that the company with which he served in England be continued to him.

135. From Richard Husband, 1 September 1656, 821, fos 238–239.

Letter giving notice that, once the wind was favourable, he intended to cross to Carrickfergus.

136. From William Webb, Dublin, 1 September 1656, 821, fos 240–241.

Letter of request, seeking a speedy issue of £400 to pay the workmen repairing Fort Cromwell at Bellahy; also noting the shortage of civilian workmen available to repair the fortifications in Connaught and so requesting direction that soldiers might be employed to undertake this work for an additional 6d per day over and above their regular military pay.

137. From Henry Lawrence,[285] Whitehall, 9 October 1656, 821, fos 242–243.

My lorde,

I was unwillinge to loose the opportunity of this very worthy lady, the bearer, to give your lordship thankes for the honour of the letter I lately receav'd from you. I know your lordship to bee to much a person of honour and vertue and reason to carry it hardely to different judgements that ar of peaceible and quiet spiritts as to civill affayers; besides that liberty upon the account of conscience is the greate product of this warre, and is certaynely the greate designe that God hath on foote in the worlde, that men may have liberty to searve Him accordinge to theire understandings. Which, where men ar not in utter darkenes, I take to bee the onely cement of peace. But, my

[284] Possibly the Jubb/Jubbs who in the early 1650s was serving as a captain in Axtell's foot regiment in Ireland.

[285] Parliamentarian politician, he moved to the Netherlands in the 1630s, in part on religious grounds: he inclined towards Independency, though he also appeared to have Baptist sympathies. He returned to England in the mid-1640s and became a member of the Long Parliament, but he did not support the regicide and later criticized the Rump. A friend and ally of Oliver Cromwell, he returned to favour and high office in 1653 and, from the advent of the Protectorate, he served as president and head of the Protectoral council of state and thus was potentially one of the most powerful politicians of the period; he also sat in both of Oliver Cromwell's Protectorate parliaments.

lorde, I neede not say much of this subject to a person of your reason and education and conscience, and your lordship may be assured I shall have no aptnes to receave reports to your prejudice, of one I so much esteeme and honour. Our affayers heere, by the blessinge of God upon us abroade[286] (of which your lordship hath had the account), and the present good temper of the parliament, make our enemyes heere and abroade gnash theire teeth, and gives a fayre advantage of doinge further what is good. I will not trouble your lordship farther; but if chance to sende a daughter into your country, as this lady will tell you it is not impossible, I hope carryinge hersealfe as a good subject shee shall injoy the favour of your lordship's and my ladye's protection. My lorde, I am your lordship's most humble and most faythfull servant,

He Lawrence

138. From Charles Fleetwood, London, 14 October 1656, 821, fos 244–245.

Deare brother,

I cannot but acknowledge your favour to Mr William Franckland[287] in my absence, who came into Ireland much uppon my account, and I did thincke he had bine provided for, but since I understand his place is little worth which I gave him in the uper bench. I shall therefore desire your particular favour to him and care of him. He is qualified with parts and faithfullnes to be publicquely usefull and must beseech you will putt him into some imployment which may give him incouragement to continnue in Ireland. He is a deserving gentleman and one for whom I have a respect, which I hope wilbe argument enough to obtayne your kindnes to him. And shall add no more but that I am,

Your most affectionate brother and humble servant,

Charles Fleetwood

[286] Almost certainly a reference to the recent Protectoral naval victory over a Spanish plate fleet, secured by Vice-admiral Stayner and his squadron off Cadiz during September.

[287] With John Gay, he had been appointed by Fleetwood joint clerk of the restored Irish chancery, but his exercise of, and income from, that office were allegedly being obstructed by Sir John Temple (*CSPI*, pp. 615–617).

139. From Vincent Gookin,[288] Westminster, 21 October 1656, 821, fos 246–247.

My dearest lord,

Wednesday last by colonel Philip Jones I had admission to his Highness. My late coming to his Highness had this advantage, that it did not apeare to be soe much of designe as the solicitous and hasty impudence of your enemyes, who thrust themselves into his Highness' presence as if they brought an alarum with them against some terible mischiefe, which his Highnes should as in consideratively[289] relish as if Whitehall were on fire.

I made the delivery of the ancient Protestants' petition[290] my only errand, which I had drawne out in parchments with the names all engrossed in 6 columnes, the length of which drawe out was about 5 or 6 yards. His Highnes caused Secretary Thurloe to reade it. Philip Jones, Mr Rolt[291] being only present with us when it was read, his Highness was pleased to speake thus, viz

That hee rejoyced in this union of those people there; that hee received their petition with very great satisfaction; that hee would give the petitioners, on all occasions, testimonyes of his tenderness for them; and gave mee order to let the persons concerned know soe much from his Highness; that hee was very glad to heare your lordship was soe acceptable to them as by their petition was alledged; that hee was not perswaded easily to send your lordship over, being sensible of the weight of the trust would be comitted to you and of those passions in you, which hee knew you had from your father; that hee had received some complaints against you, and that hee confessed hee

[288]Parliamentarian politician, with family connections to Ireland, he returned there by 1649 and thereafter consistently supported the parliamentary regimes and Protestant interest in Ireland. In turn, he was rewarded with a string of offices within the English and Irish administrations, including the surveyor generalship of Ireland. However, his questioning both of the policy of enforced transplantation of the native Irish Catholic population and of the influence of the English army in Ireland won him enemies on both sides of the Irish Sea. He was generally supportive of Henry Cromwell's handling of Ireland, was returned for Bandon and Kinsale to all three Protectorate parliaments, and was particularly prominent during the second as an ally of Lord Broghill and as one of a clutch of loyal Cromwellians representing Irish constituencies.

[289]Word originally written 'considerably' but then amended.

[290]The petition, in which Gookin may well have had a hand, strongly supported Henry Cromwell and his policies and urged the Protector and the English regime to bolster Henry Cromwell's stand against a small minority of impetuous wreckers inside and outside the army who were opposing Henry Cromwell in Ireland. Its contents can be gathered from Gookin's detailed letter to the Protector of 22 November (*TSP*, V, pp. 646–649).

[291]Edward Rolt, parliamentarian diplomat and son of Oliver Cromwell's cousin, served in the Protectoral lifeguard and was in 1655–1656 employed by the Protectoral regime on a diplomatic mission to Sweden.

sent colonel Cooper[292] over to spy; that Cooper wrote to his Highness that your lordship's actions were prudent and warrantable, and gave not the least grounds for what had bin suggested against you; that if this petition should be made publique it would be sayd it was his owne contrivance. To all which I answered that his Highness' interest in the petitioners was much greater than I thought his Highness would or could believe from my testimony; that the management of the publique revenue, which called me to Dublin, tooke up soe much of my time that I seldome had the happiness to be with your lordship, much less to be privie to your personall actings. However, I could not but heare that ill offices had bin done you to his Highness, it being made publique by your enemyes on the opinion, as I conceived, of their success, and by your frends as matter of their trouble. But by whome that mischiefe was done I could not say, but desired his Highness to consider and observe wheather any person of or from Ireland did ever say any thing to his Highness to your prejudice, who was not either accidentally by his custome to rule unlimitedly or naturally a man of a proud and haughty spirit (at which his Highnes smiled).[293] That your Lordship did (as became one in your place) dispence your respect and favour to every person in proportion to the trust hee bore in the comonwealth, and if such dispensations had formerly bin unequall or disproportionable it must follow that some must have more, others lesse of your lordship's countenance than formerly, and consequently noe marvaile if the persons disapointed were angry. That the dilligence, caution and prudence which appeared in all your actings, the generall and ample acceptation of them and of your person to all sorts of men there, except those few that will be pleased with nothing done by any that are greater than themselves, and your bearing those barbarous affronts done to your person with that patience and sobriety which would have made persons of far lesse fire in theyr natures than is in yours have transgressed, did plainely evince that the Lord sent you thither and kept you there and would, wee hope, make you a great blessing to that land. That the petition did receive discountenance in some countyes by such who pretend satisfaction to the goverment, and that it was wholy stifeled in one county, namely Typerary. To which his Highness smilingly replyed, hee could easily beleive that. And I continued that I could not only cleare his Highness from knowing any thing of the petition but your

[292]Thomas Cooper, sent to Ireland and given command in Ulster at the end of 1655.

[293]If this is a sly reference to Lord Deputy Fleetwood, and, assuming Gookin was being truthful in his account, he was sticking his neck out in mocking and attacking the Protector's son-in-law in this way.

lordship too, and that your secretary advized mee against it least it might be misinterpreted by enemyes.

While I was replying to this effect his Highness rose from his seate and comanded me to walke with him to and fro in the roome, during which time colonel Jones and the Secretary withdrew. After which his Highness in repeating his satisfaction from my discourse discovered that affection by his teares, which I confess made mee water my plantes too. I desired his Highness to give mee leave to write to him what should at any time occurre to my memory, which I might judge worthy his knowledge. At which instant my lord deputy coming in I parted, and doe intend to draw up a lettre to his Highness wherein, God willing, I shall take freedome to speake plainely, and I hope what will be of use. A copie of which lettre I shall presume to send to your lordship by Mr Ralph King,[294] whose going over is upon these considerations:

1st. Because of colonel Markhame's and my continuance heere, there will want a comittee there to give your lordship an account of anything necessary for your knowledge touching the revenue.

2ly. During our being there other business tooke from us the oportunity to act upon your lordship's and the councel's order touching the fraudulent taking and holding lands from the state, especially in the north, in which affayre noe man can act with soe much advantage as Mr King.

3ly. The examination of the tenants observing the conditions of their 7 yeares' leases is a weighty business and will proove advantagious to his Highness in the encrease of the revenue and discovery of much selfishness in those that most cry it downe, which cannot be done without one of us.

4ly. The absence of us all at once may put an oportunity into the hands of some, who undeservedly love us not, to put into that imployment such who I may modestly say may doe it worse.

5ly. Mr King's interest in the north is very considerable, and doubtlesse some things may fall out wherin hee may be very serviceable to your lordship there.

6ly. The comittee heere may have occasion to use such transcripts from thence, the dispatch of which noe person can better solicite than Mr King.

[294] Parliamentarian politician, who came from a Protestant family in Ulster and was a Londonderry alderman. He held a variety of mainly financial offices in Ireland under the parliamentary regimes of the 1650s – for example, from 1657 he was a commissioner for setting out lands and for granting leases – and he represented Londonderry and Coleraine in all three Protectorate parliaments.

7ly. The affayres of parliament all goe on heere with soe much unanimity that hee may be spared without the least prejudice to affayres heere.

Mr King's going being for these reasons thought necessary, it was judged better and more safe and convenient hee should goe upon the parliament's licence rather than your lordship's, for some reasons hee will give your lordship, which with what is in this lettre humbly offered to your lordship will, I hope, obtaine your lordship's pardon for his going over and the manner of it. By him I shall make bold to send your lordship a character for the more safe and sercet[295] conveyance of your lordship's comands to, my lord,

Your lordship's most faythfull and obedient servant,

Vin Gookin

140. From Nathaniel Fiennes,[296] Whitehall, 28 October 1656, 821, fos 248–249.

My lord,

I am ashamed to confesse, and yet I can not denye it, that I have a good while since receaved two letters from your lordship whereunto I have not yet made any returne. The truthe is that I was in continuall expectation of Mun Temple's[297] returne into Ireland, by whose handes I did thinke to have returned an answer, from whose handes I had first the honour to receave a letter from your lordshipp. Since which time I receaved an other from the handes of colonel Morgane. In bothe which letters your lordshipp was pleased to testifie bothe your greate affection towardes me and your entier confidence in me, which must needes heigthen the desier I have allwayes had to doe your lordshipp some reall service, which when ever it shall be in my power to doe, I hope I shall be founde as forwardes therein as possibly I have been backewardes in ceremonies and complements. For besides that your lordshipp knoweth I am not a man of that stuffe, I have

[295]Word originally written 'seret' and the writer, seeing the error, has added the missing letter, but in the wrong place. Clearly 'secret' was the intended word.

[296]Parliamentarian officer and politician, prominent in parliament from the early 1640s and as an army officer from the outbreak of war until his disgrace following his surrender of Brisol in the summer of 1643. His political career resumed from the mid-1640s, but he was secluded at Pride's Purge and remained out of public life and public office until the Protectorate. He was appointed a Protectoral councillor in 1654 and a commissioner of the great seal in 1655, and he sat in both of Oliver Cromwell's Protectorate parliaments.

[297]Edmund Temple, parliamentarian officer, who fought for the Protestant cause in Ireland in the later 1640s and served as a captain in Henry Cromwell's horse regiment in Ireland during the 1650s.

very litle leasure for such things. And allthoughe my employements lying chiefely in an other way have taken from me the opportunitie of being fully acquainted with the Irish affaires, yet in generall I doe understand that your lordshipp, in the place wherein you are, doe give greate satisfaction to all sober minded men, and to his Highnesse himselfe in particular, which is matter of much rejoicing unto, my lord,

Your lordshipp's moste humble servant,
Nath Fiennes

141. From John Bridges,[298] 25 November 1656, 821, fos 250–251.

May it please your excellency,

By a freind that had lately beene att Wallingford House I was informed of a meeting of 30tie officers, whoe resolved vigorously to opose a settlement in that greate point;[299] but I cannot say the meeting was there. Yet thus much your lordshipp may bee assured of, that there are 5 greate persons that have a private inspection into the demeanours of some your lordshipp hath formerly heard of, whoe have discovered soe much, that it is resolved (if I am not misinformed) that in case a present course bee not taken to cut of the lapps of theire exorbitancyes, it will bee too late; but it's probable this may come to your lordshipp by some better hand. My lord, on Friday morning last[300] goeing into the speaker's chamber, I found major-general Berry[301] very earnestly to contend with another gentleman about the succession. I interpose. Hee leave his prey and assailes mee. I undertake him. After some passages in comes major-general Desborough and parts us by carryeing my antagonist away. But hee turnes back and (sowerly enough) bidds mee reduce my scattered notions into writing,[302] and hee

[298]Parliamentarian politician, a friend of Richard Baxter and with connections to Worcestershire, he seems to have spent part of the mid- and late 1650s in Ireland and acquired a range of financial, educational, and administrative offices there. He sat in both of Oliver Cromwell's Protectorate parliaments and represented Counties Sligo, Leitrim, and Roscommon in the second.

[299]Whether the office of Lord Protector should be elective, as provided for under the existing Protectoral constitution, or hereditary.

[300]21 November.

[301]James Berry, parliamentarian officer, a friend of Richard Baxter and with connections to the West Midlands, fought for parliament from the outbreak of the civil war, initially in Oliver Cromwell's horse regiment. He may have served under Cromwell in Ireland in 1649–1650 and was with him in Scotland from 1650, in the following year becoming commander of a horse regiment then serving in Scotland. He was major-general for Wales and the central Marches from 1655 until 1657 and represented Worcestershire in the second Protectorate parliament.

[302]See no. 142.

would answeare them. I willingly yeelde, and ymediately withdrawe into an inner roome, and having done the businesse, as I was uppon my returne into the howse to deliver it, I mett major-general Desborough in the tobacco roome, offer him the grounds of my dissent, and tell him if hee can give better reasons e contra,[303] I'le submitt. Hee reades them, confesseth they weare not easily answeared, but tolde mee there was greate reason for the thinge, being led to it by providence, and therefore thought they weare to depend uppon God for an yssue. I replyed I might not dispute against the necessity of the thing when done, but that which at one tyme may be convenient, att another tyme may bee mischeivous, and when it shall appeare soe, it is the duty of those in place to take care ne quid detrimenti respublica caperet,[304] or to that effect. Then hee discoursing of the inconveniencies by a sodaine alteration of the constitution from elective into hereditary, I tolde him that might bee avoided and the impendent dainger by a competition uppon his Highness's death prevented, and offered as a present expedient, that his Highness might nominate his immediate successor, and tolde him the greate and only objection of jealousy would bee removed, for doubtles hee would nominate such a one as hee should have noe cause to suspect. Hee replyed hee was very free to that, and soe doe all officers of the army and others I speake with, which are not a fewe. Having done which the general and I went in to the howse, and delivered major-general Berry what I promised. The next morning hee gave mee his answeare, which I have sent your lordshipp under his owne hand, together with my arguments. I have scribled out a reply, but want tyme to transcribe it, being post night. Your lordshipp may perceave by all this that I beleeve the nights are very longe at Corke House.[305] I could heartily wish I had some better divertisements to present your lordshipp with. But nowe I can only take my leave as becomes, my lord,

Your excellency's most humble servant,

J B

I heartily pray there may bee nothing of distast betweene my lord ch[306] and_________.[307]

[303]This Latin phrase could be translated as 'against'.

[304]This Latin phrase could be translated as 'lest any damage should be done to the state'.

[305]The principal residence of the governor of Ireland, and thus of Henry Cromwell, in central Dublin close to the castle.

[306]Probably Lord Chancellor Steele.

[307]Line drawn in original to indicate word(s) deliberately omitted.

142. Draft of John Bridges to Major Generall Berry, [enclosed in no. 141], 823, fos 320–321.

Sir,

You require mee to reduce my scattered notions (as you call them) into writing, which (to obey you) I have hastily done, and shall bee glad to receave your reflections that, if it may bee, our different judgments in this particuler may bee reconciled.

Where every man in the nation hath a like right to the government by the death of the Lord Protector (as by this present constitution hee hath) itt may not reasonably bee doubted, but uppon every chainge there wilbee a competition; especially whilst there is an entire army in each nation, under the conduct of (it may bee) of persons of different interests, besides severall other persons of couradge and high commaund.

2ly. If there arrise a competition, itt's most probable those forces, that are kept on foote for the preservation of the publique peace, will bee divided according to the number of competitors.

3. Theise competitors will not probably agree to cantonize the comonwealth (as Alexander's captaines) but come to blowes.

4. Hee that is worsted, will rather submitt to any that may bee in a condition to releeve him, then his immediate antagonist, as beinge more safe, and more sutable to the common humour of all men.

5. Where will hee finde any more likely to give him releife against his present adversary, or afford him more honourable tearmes, then the heire of the Stuart's lyne?

6. If the heire of that family shall bee admitted uppon such an advantadge as a considerable part of the army, and such other strengths as may bee dependent uppon itt, itt can not well bee imagined (if consideration bee had to what hee may bringe from without, conjoyned with his olde party heere) but hee will render himselfe very formidable.

To theise considerations add but this, that when the bodies of theise nations shall consider that uppon every chainge they shall bee subject to the callamityes of warr, and at the end of every warr bee indaingered to bee attainted as traitors by the conqueror, what can bee the result but that it's better to settle uppon the olde bottome, and better that some particuler men suffer then that the whole bee ruined. And most, even of those men that have beene obnoxious, will bee apt to beleeve that uppon a tymely application they may, uppon reasonable tearmes, purchase theire pardons.

Sir, remember the speaker's chamber (whilst there is a crowde) is inconvenient for such a taske. I hope you will therefore passe by the crudenes and indigestidnes of theise lynes. The reason of my haste being an earnest expectation to receave somethinge of sattisfaction from soe greate a master of reason as you are esteemed by, sir,

Your humble servant,

J Bridges

1657

143. From Robert Evans, Bridewell, 3 January 1657, 821, fos 260–261.

To Henery Cromwell and Hardress Wallar, freinds.

Whereas I cane answer for demanding my pay and a discharg from thee Henery Cromwell in a miutinous and sedissous maner, it is falce, I disowen it, for I came in the feare of God to desire a discharg of thee which thou did promis me. I demanded it not in a miutinous nor sedisous manner, as that of God in thy conscience may wittness and as many peopele whoe were then present may wittness to the contrary, and when I came to thy house to looke for thy promis I was put out of doors by the shoulder. Then I came to thee again and gave thee a paper sheweing the justnes of what I desired of thee and in it demanded my wages not in a miutinous nor sedisous maner as yee falcely accus me and as that of God in all your consciences may wittness to the contrary, and to the light of Christ in all tender consciences who reads that paper I leave it to judg whether thos words be spoken in a miutinous and sedisous maner which are written in that paper.

Also to thee Hardress Wallar and the rest of thy asistence at the court marshall, soe called, from whom I receved an unjust sentence without the breath of any just law, although I desired thee and the rest to make it appier wherin I had transgrased any just law of God but yee did not. Have yee passed sentence upon me becase I could not respect your persons and soe transgras the just law of God whoe is noe respecter of persons? Which of all the holly men of God who judged for God in ages passt is your example to pass a sentence of imprisonment, make slave and banish a serven for demanding his wages when he hath don his master's worke faithfully and hath leave to depart from his service? Doth the scriptures which you say you owen justify you hearin?

Henery Cromwell, I desire thee to cause som care to be taken wherby I may have my cloths and other things of myn which is left with the compainy where I was doing thy service and the comonwelth's. Allsoe I demand a discharg in writtings of thee, being chife in the nation accordeing to man, and my wages alsoe whereby I may paye monys where I owe it as at Athlon, Balymoor[1] and other places, for

[1] Athlone and Ballymore, County Westmeath.

things which I had need of whilst I was in the service, for which things I am free to paye before I be banished out of the land, if I may have my due, and if not upon your accounts I leave it to answer the Lord.

Written by one not knowen to any of you but by the name of Rob Evans, a prisoner for the truth' sake.[2]

144. From Edward D'Oyley,[3] Jamaica, 5 January 1657, 821, fos 262–263.

Letter of thanks for assistance in setting out his Irish lands.

145. From Francis Bolton,[4] Milford Haven, 10 January 1657, 821, fos 264–265.

Letter of apology for exceeding the length of his pass and offering to return to Ireland immediately if required, though also requesting that, in the light of his delayed departure from Ireland, a recent though unspecified alteration in his condition, and the current winter weather and dangerous seas, he be allowed a little more leave before returning.

146. From Charles Fleetwood, Wallingford House, 28 January 1657, 821, fos 268–269.

Letter of recommendation on behalf of the bearer, an unnamed colonel well known to Henry Cromwell, asking that he be favoured in the allocation of Irish lands to meet his English arrears and noting that the bearer was also carrying a letter from the Protector to the Irish council directing that he have a lease of the lands currently in his hands.

[2] The tone of the letter and the repeated and pointed use of the 'thee' form of address suggest that the writer was a Quaker.

[3] Parliamentarian officer, who campaigned in Ireland in the late 1640s and went to the West Indies in 1654–1655 as an officer in Robert Venables's foot regiment. In March 1655 he was appointed commander of a new foot regiment raised in Barbados and, in the autumn of the same year, he succeeded Richard Fortesque as commander-in-chief of the forces in Jamaica. Although for a time he was displaced in favour first of Robert Sedgwick and then of William Brayne, after their deaths he was reappointed overall commander in Jamaica.

[4] Parliamentarian officer, who campaigned in England in the mid-1640s in John Okey's New Model dragoon regiment and was, in 1649, selected to serve in Ireland, in a newly formed dragoon regiment under Daniel Abbott. Later in the 1650s he was serving in Ireland in Henry Pretty's horse regiment. His apprehensions about crossing the Irish Sea proved well-founded, for he was drowned in the summer of 1659 when crossing from Ireland to England.

147. From Richard Lawrence, Cork, 30 January 1657, 821, fos 270–271.

Letter of defence, responding to reports that Southwell and Saunders[5] *had alleged that he had been negligent in transferring provisions from the* Sapphire*; recounts in detail how bad weather had forced him to unload the* Sapphire *in Cork harbour, bringing the bread she was carrying ashore and storing it in a quayside house until another vessel arrived from Kinsale; admits that a small quantity of the bread had become damp and spoiled either while in the* Sapphire *or while being transferred to and from the store, though all possible care was taken. His work in Cork upon the accounts of the new recruits being almost complete, he intended to move on to Kinsale and then return to Dublin.*

148. From John Reynolds, Clonfert, County Galway, 30 January 1657, 823, fos 15–16.

May it please your excellency,

I meeting with this bearer, Mr Eyre, found him verry ambitious to serve your lordship in your affaires at Portumna,[6] in which I beleive verry capable to advantage your lordship's interest there. I shall presume farther to recommend him unto your lordship's favour in the letting of your bishops lands of Clonfert,[7] where he hath expended much money and setled himselfe in it so long as he hath lived in Connaght. I have hea[...][8] that he carried himselfe faithfully and industriously in the service wherein he was emploied and I am assured that your lordship will receive the testimony of Sir Charles Coote[9] and other worthy persons concurrent thereunto.

[5] Robert Southwell and Robert Saunders.

[6] Henry Cromwell acquired by allocation and purchase several estates in Ireland, most importantly the house, park, manor, and lands of Portumna, in County Galway, taken from the Catholic and royalist fifth Earl and first Marquess of Clanricarde and confirmed to him by the second Protectorate parliament. Although he never resided there for any length of time, instead merely visiting it on his customary late-summer tour of Ireland, Henry Cromwell undertook improvements to the estate and the main house, usually referred to as the castle but in reality a grand, rectangular, fortified mansion with corner towers, built in 1618.

[7] Also in County Galway, about twelve miles north-west of Portumna, and the site of an early medieval cathedral.

[8] Paper damaged with some loss of text, though the incomplete word is probably 'heard'.

[9] Parliamentarian officer and politician, of an Irish Protestant family, who opposed Charles I's dealings with the confederate Catholics and came out for parliament in 1644. Appointed parliamentary lord president of Connaught in 1644–1645 (an office he retained throughout the period), in the later 1640s and early 1650s he was prominent in the campaigns to secure Ulster and Connaught, commanding both a horse and a foot regiment. He was a firm supporter of Henry Cromwell and the Protectoral regime in Ireland and he was, in turn, trusted and favoured by Henry Cromwell and received his warm support and recommendation, Henry praising him as one who 'hath soe eminently and successefully

Your lordship's favourable justice to Mr Eyres will oblige him everlastingly to[10] continue your lordship's devoted servaunt, and the farther manifestation of your lordship's acceptance of my humble addresse will engage,

Your lordship's most humble servaunt,

J Reynolds

149. Draft of a letter by Henry Cromwell to Lord Broghill, [January 1657], 823, fo. 336.

Lord Broghill,

I am very glad to understand to <understand> by your lordship's last, that you were so plaine with his Highness, in that matter of greatest concernement,[11] who certainly cannot bee safe unlesse he follow some such advice as your lordship gave him, but must expose these nations and his family to much calamity. I cleerely concurre with your lordship that now is the time of doing somewhat to purpose, the designes of the major generalls beeing now become visibly dangerous, and especially his Highness having so complyant and well affected a parliament to back him therein, and the sober people beeing withall generally big with hopes of seeing that good day of settlement. <And> If the Lord shall encourage him <thereto> to this worke, I dare undertake His interest here will not bee found inconsiderable towards it.

<I have always heretofore esteemed your lordship upon the> <Tis high tyme> Tis high time that his Highness should see the necessity of throwing himselfe upon men of interest and sober principles; for certainly those hee now deeleth with (I meane the major generalls) will one time or other give him the slip, as I have not long since beene bold to intimate to his Highness himselfe.[12]

I have ever heretofore much esteemed your lordship upon the account of your personall vertues, but that demonstration what your lordship has given of your principles also in these late transactions

served the publique, and doth still remayn as intirely faithfull to the present interest' (*TSP*, III, p. 691; V, p. 494). He represented Counties Galway and Mayo in all three Protectorate parliaments.

[10] Word heavily amended and possibly deleted.

[11] Possibly the militia or decimation bill, introduced into the second Protectorate parliament on 25 December 1656 and debated during January 1657, which would have regularized and continued the tax on former royalists introduced by Protector and council in 1655 to fund the new semi-militarized system of regional administration in England and Wales overseen by the major-generals. Its rejection by parliament, with Broghill prominently opposing it, effectively marked the end of that system.

[12] In early February 1657, Thurloe told Henry Cromwell that his recent letter to his father had been well received by him but that the Protector had then burnt it (*TSP*, VI, pp. 38, 53).

<doth endeare> doth infinitely endeare your lordship unto mee, as I hope it likewise will to all good men. It troubld mee but to heare your lordship name retirement, but indeed, my lord, <I> I promise to beare you <r lordship> company in these resolutions, if things shall not in some measure stoope to your lordship's wishes and endeavours, which are not onely the wishes but the studyes of,

Your etc,

although my lord deputy has 2[...][13]

I <am glad> your late letters have awakend you to write so well to purpose. What you wrote of Haynes[14] was considerable. I hope those heates will ripen some wholesom fruite.

I desire you to forbeare a while those high words tell you see those have litle settled, and when you see that des.[15] desperet[16] pray study her. Wee may goe all thither, for if wee gett but to the moon the M G[17] will poursue us thither. In this crisis of affairs be criticall in your enquires. Upon which account I must bee <[...]>[18] endure to spare, although otherwise I could bee impatient of your stay. <I shall take care if you st> And indeed if you stay much longer I fear Platten,[19] your adventured lott will scarse afford you profit[20] but I shall endeavor to keepe you and the rest to the same of advance money as were in at your going from hence. As you see occasion <a word of> mind Portumna.

Doe but ad brimstone to the saltpeatre, etc.

150. From Oliver, Viscount Fitzwilliam,[21] Westminster, 3 February 1657, 821, fos 272–273.

My lord,

I find that your lordship's and the rest of the counsell's answer to the lords comisioners of the great seale's letter, which was directed

[13] Paper damaged with some loss of text.

[14] Major-General Hezekiah Haynes.

[15] Possibly an abbreviated form of Desborough – Major-General John Desborough introduced and strongly supported the militia bill – though the identification is uncertain.

[16] This Latin word could be translated as 'despairs'.

[17] Could be singular or plural, standing for 'major-general' or 'major-generals'.

[18] Word heavily deleted and now illegible.

[19] Possibly Platin, County Westmeath.

[20] Uncertain reading of a poorly formed and amended word. Indeed, the whole final paragraph is written in a rough and loose hand.

[21] An Irish Catholic landowner, who succeeded to the Irish title of second Viscount Fitzwilliam of Merrion in 1650. As an active supporter of the Irish rebellion and the king's cause during the 1640s, he had lost most of his Irish estates, although, by an ordinance of Protector and council of 1654, his wife obtained restoration of some of his Irish property (*CSPI*, pp. 808, 811, 840–841).

to your lordships in a busines wherein I ame concernd, is retarded by alderman Edwards[22] or some others, whoe pretend to faulsefie the report made by Mr attournie-generall Bazil to your lordshipps, as allso the certeficatts of the commissioners for sequestration, whoe have all reported and certefied that the lands in dispute were sequesterd as beinge waste lands and for noe other cause. One Fugill[23] (as I take him) clearke of the commissioners for sequestration, did with the said commissioners atest the same, and now I heare that he certefies that the said lands were sequesterd for the delinquencie of one Plunket. This Fugill with all beforesaid have signd the contrarie under theire hands. Colonel Herbert, clearke to your lordships, hath signd with his hand the order made by your lordships of the councell for restoringe the possession of the said lands to the proprietor, for that they were sequesterd as wast lands. All which the said Fugill, it seemes, endevours to faulsefy, when as indeed the said lands could not, by anny law or rule made in England or Ireland, be sequesterd for the delinquencie of anny person whatsoever but of John Trevor,[24] whoe was the lessee and posessor of the land, and he was noe delinquent as I heare. It is true that the rent might have beene sequesterd if Mr <Plunket> Hulle had beene a delinquent, but not the land. But hee is an English man and was never in Ireland, nor never delinquency was laid to his chardge, as is provd heere in court. Wherefore I humbly crave that your lordships' answer to the lords comissioners' letter may not be delaid, and that the report allreddie made by the attournie-generall, Mr Bazil, to your lordships of this business may be accordingely reported by your lordships to the lords comissioners of the seale heere. In which doinge, and pardoning the presumption I take to give your lordship the trouble of these lines, your lordship will infinitly add to the manny former great obligations which you have beene pleasd to chardge me with. One thinge more I presume to begge of your lordship, that is that I may have the order of preemption made good unto me, which your lordship and the rest of the councell promist me when I was last in Ireland, which was that when the lease of Baggethrath[25] should be expird that I should have it att the same rent before anny other. The lease is expired att Easter next, and I humbly begge that you will lett

[22] Identification not certain, but possibly Jonathan Edwards, an English doctor and preacher who worked in Ireland during the 1650s, was a commissioner for setting out allotments of land in Ardee, County Louth, and was also one of the four masters in the Irish court of chancery.

[23] Again, the identification is uncertain, but possibly Thomas Fughill, a fellow-commissioner with Edwards and others in setting out allotments of land in Ardee.

[24] The common forename and surname prevent firm identification.

[25] Probably Baggetrath/Baggotrath, a manor and castle close to seventeenth-century Dublin, now absorbed within the city itself.

my cousin Annesley[26] rent it from your lordships untill my cominge (which by God's leave wilbe att or soone after Easter) att which tyme your lordships wilbe paid a considerable sume of monny by my wife's trustees for the redemtion of it.[27]

My wife craves leave that shee may heere present hir most humble service to your lordship and your noble lady. And I shall begg leave to stile myselfe, as really I ame, my honored lord,

Your lordship's most humble and most faithfull servant,

Fitzwilliam M

If your lordship shale please to comaund me to bringe you what sort of doggs or haulkes you shall nominat this springe, your lordship shalbe obeid. I humbly crave pardon for the blotts in this letter.

151. From John Hewetson[28] to the Irish Council, Kildare, 6 February 1657, 821, fos 276–277.

May itt please your lordshipps,

In obedience unto your orders to me directed bearing date the 31st of December last,[29] and in refference to your former orders of the 17th of August and fifteenth of September last, to the former sheriffe directed, I have hereinclosed sent unto your lordships the list of such as were proprietors or in armes, according to the best of my owne knowledge or what I could learne att present, and many of them dangerous persons. Which I humbly offer to your lordshipps' grave wisdomes and remayne,

Your honours' most faithfull servant,

Jn Hewetson

[26] Sir Arthur Annesley.

[27] At this time, the trustees of Fitzwilliam's wife, Lady Eleanor Hollis, daughter of the late Earl of Clare, were seeking to recover, for the use of her and her children and in respect of her marriage portion and other interests, not only various loans but also some of the Irish lands held by her late father-in-law, the first Viscount Fitzwilliam, and mortgaged or leased out by him before the rebellion. Some of this property had been leased to people who became Irish rebels and so was now forfeit to the state and leased out to new holders. In the spring of 1657, the Protector and English council supported these claims and referred the matter to Henry Cromwell and the Irish council for favourable settlement (*CSPI*, p. 840).

[28] Son of a minister in Ireland, in November 1656 he was appointed sheriff of Kildare and Carlow.

[29] Requiring sheriffs to return to the Irish council lists of all Irish Catholics who were transplantable but who had not yet been transplanted (Dunlop, p. 648).

152. From Vincent Gookin, Westminster, 10 February 1657, 821, fos 278–279.

Detailed letter of request, on behalf of his brother,[30] *who was pursuing a long-standing claim for payment of his debenture and whose case had been referred by the Protector and English council to Henry Cromwell and the Irish council; sets out the reasons why the suspension of the debenture was unfair and should be lifted and why allowance should now be made to his wearied, persecuted, and indebted brother, who had been pursuing this claim for the past four years.*

153. From Robert Saunders and Robert Southwell to the Irish Council, Kinsale, 16 February 1657, 821, fos 280–281.

Right honnorable,

May it please your lordshipps. Wee have thought it our duty to put your lordships in mynd that the ship Playne Dealing being now ready together with her convoy[31] and that they onely wait for a faire wynd, of which there being not at present any great likelyhood, and the 14th daie of February being past unto which tyme collonell Moore's men with the new recruits were payd off, and as yet no orders for any further pay unto them, wee doubt that the want of it may occasion some trouble amongst them and consequently obstruct the present service unles some speedy course bee taken for their weekely paie during their stay here or sum other way setled for their satisfaction, which wee humbly leave unto your lordships' graver judgment and remayne,

Your lordshipps' most humble servants,

Ro Saunders Robert Southwell

[30] Robert Gookin, parliamentarian officer, whose military record was disputed – it had been claimed he was not a member of the regular, standing army – and is obscure, but who reportedly saw action at Ross and elsewhere in Ireland. For allied claims by Robert Gookin, see *CSPI*, pp. 623–625.

[31] After months of delay, Moore's regiment, bound for the West Indies, had sailed from Carrickfergus in early October 1656, only for the commander and almost half his men to be forced back into Cork by a storm which revealed the inadequacy of their vessel, the *Two Sisters*, described by the Irish council as a 'crazy vessel' (Dunlop, p. 646) and by Henry Cromwell as 'olde and crazie', rotten, and not capable of such a voyage even if refitted (*TSP*, V, pp. 494, 570). She was presumably a sister ship to the even more ill-fated *Two Brothers* (see no. 176). The men spent the winter in 'the great islande nere Corke', running up further costs but 'prevented of running frome their colours, which I am apt to beleive they would attempt, havinge received that discouragement allreadie at sea', Henry Cromwell noted (*TSP*, V, p. 570), while the Irish council looked for an alternative vessel and sought further recruits. By early February, the *Plain Dealing* had been earmarked for the voyage, with either the *Paradox* or the *Basing* to provide an armed convoy (Dunlop, pp. 632, 646, 651). Moore and his men finally sailed in early March.

154. From Sir Charles Wolseley, Whitehall, 18 February 1657, 821, fos 282–283.

My lord,

I received a letter some while since from your lordship concerninge Sir Hardresse Waller, which I shall most punctually obey. It gave me exceedinge much content that your lordship would please to command me in any thinge. I beseech you let me beg your leave to recommend most earnestly the bearer of this, collonell Ridgely,[32] unto you and present him as an object of your lordship's favor. He is a man of much integritye and of as great merritt from the commonwealth by his actings and sufferings for it, I thinke, as most men in this nation. I shall not troble your lordship with any thinge farther about him because he comes recommended by two hands that I know will be most prevalinge with your lordship, by his Highnesse and allsoe by the councell. I shall not venter, my lord, to give you any account of publique affayres heere because I know you receive it from much better hands, but shall conclude this troble to you with this request, that you will reckon me,

Your lordship's most affectionate, most faythfull, humble servant,
Ch Wolseley

155. From Charles Fleetwood, Wallingford House, 19 February 1657, 821, fos 284–285.

Letter of recommendation in support of the bearer, Simon Rudgeley, whose case had come before, and was being supported by, the English council.

156. From Edward Whalley, Whitehall, 19 February 1657, 821, fos 286–287.

My lord,

It is to all your cordiall freinds and servants a very great rejoycing to heare that the Lord hath made you so eminently instrumentall for good to his people in Ireland. I shall pray the Lord would keepe your

[32] Simon Rudgeley, parliamentarian officer, campaigned in his native Staffordshire during the civil war and played a prominent role in the administration of that county during the 1640s, but by the 1650s he was heavily in debt. On 10 February, the Protector had written to Henry Cromwell, recommending Rudgeley to him and directing that he be given an office, military or civil, in Ireland, together with lands upon which he could settle (Abbott, IV, p. 404; *CSPI*, p. 838; D.H. Pennington and I.A. Roots (eds), *The Committee at Stafford, 1643–45* (Manchester, 1957), *passim*).

lordship[33] in a humble frame under so great mercyes and draw you nearer to Himself by them. My lord, I must not forget my continued thankes to your lordshipp for your perculiar favours to myselfe, as also those accumulated upon my sonne,[34] who makes it[35] his ambition to serve your lordshipp, and that he might bee rendred more apt for his Highnes' and your lordshipp's service, he desires to spend some monethes in France, to which purpose his Highnesse hath bin free not onely to give him leave with the continuation of his pay but very much encouraged him to continue a yeare in France. Hee hath likewise obteyned the approbation of the lord deputie Fleetewood. And neither hee nor myselfe can in the least doubt of [. . .][36] lordshipp's concurrence in extending the like favour to him, which that you would be pleased to doe is the earnest and humble request of, my lord,

Your lordship's most faythfull and obliged servant,

Edw Whalley

157. From Charles Fleetwood, Wallingford House, 22 February 1657, 821, fos 288–289.

Letter of recommendation, written at the behest of Lord Commissioner Lisle[37] and on behalf of Lisle's kinsman, Mr Jennings,[38] requesting that Jennings and his servant be employed in the army in Ireland, mustered together either in the guard or in some other troop until vacancies occurred there.

[33] Paper damaged here and after 'great' and 'Himself', though apparently with no loss of text.

[34] Probably his younger son, Richard Whalley, parliamentarian officer, who served in Ireland in the 1650s in Henry Cromwell's horse regiment. In June 1658, the Protector recommended him to Henry Cromwell, noting particularly his linguistic skills and his excellence in Latin, French, and Italian (Abbott, IV, p. 821). In April 1658, Henry Cromwell wrote to Whalley senior, praising his son's education, reporting that 'we want such men for our foreign negotiations' and giving him further leave to stay 'for his further improvement or other benefit' (*TSP*, VII, p. 73).

[35] Word amended/blotted and possibly deleted.

[36] Paper damaged with some loss of text, though the missing word is probably 'your'.

[37] John Lisle, parliamentarian politician and judge, and a regicide, supported the parliamentary cause throughout the 1640s, both as an MP and as an administrator in his native Hampshire and the Isle of Wight, and played a leading role at the king's trial, advising on legal aspects of proceedings. He was a commissioner of the great seal from 1649 and held other offices under the republic, but moved smoothly to support the Protector and Protectorate. He sat in both of Oliver Cromwell's Protectorate parliaments, continued as a commissioner of the great seal, became a commissioner of the exchequer, and presided over major state trials.

[38] William Jennings, whose earlier and subsequent military career appears obscure and unrecorded.

158. From Charles Fleetwood, [24][39] February 1657, 821, fos 274–275.

Deare brother,

I must entreate you will please to excuse my making use of another's penn at this time, which is occasioned by bringing a new modle of goverment into the howse, the perticulars of which I presume you will have from other hands. It desires my Lord Protector to take upon him kingshipp and during life to declare his successor. It also setts up another howse of parliament in the nature of a howse of peeres. These are the two cheife alterations in itt. That when Charles Stewart is in preparation with a considerable army to transport himselfe into England, men's minds should now againe divide about goverment, the which, though never so good in itselfe, will aske time to gaine men's satysfaction, and therefore I doubt twill prove the more unseasonable because some things in itt have bine against our latter engagements and resolutions. The only hopes of honnest men is that the Lord will so manage his Highnes' hart in this busines, who wee know hath bine a man of great prayer and faith, and to whom the Lord hath given much of His councell in darke cases, and I trust will still owne him with a more then ordinary presence of His at this time. It will concerne you to have your forces in a readines, for it is from very good hands that Charles Stewart intends action very suddenly, and though it is pretended that England is the place intended, yet I cannot thincke Ireland to be secure. Your care of which is not doubted by,

Your most affectionate brother and most humble servant,

Charles Fleetwood

159. From Francis Russell, Whitehall, 24 February 1657, 822, fos 234–235.

My lord,

I know not what to present you with but my love, service and respects, for I doe verily beleeve I can send your lordship no news, for sure I am that you have it fully from better hands. Tis about a moneth since I heard from you, allthough I have written twise (as I take it) within a moneth, or neere that time. But I know you are full of busynes, therefore onely expect to heare from you at your leysure. His Highnes tells me that he heares but seldome from you. I thought good to let you understand so much. He hath, I doe perceive, a love

[39] Although Fleetwood clearly dated this letter 4 February, that must be an error as the new consistution was not presented in parliament until 23 February. It may be that this is therefore a slip of the pen – albeit a slightly strange one – for 24 February and that this is one of a clutch of letters of that date describing the events and document of the previous day.

for you, and mentions you with a kind of delight and satisfaction. My appeareing lately against the major-generalls, and being for a change of the governement, hath made that party looke upon me as a kind of courtyer and cavileere. Dick Norton[40] hath bin lately in towne. He would not come into the house, but is returned home as grave, wise and doged as ever. He sayeth that he will keepe Portsmouth safe and lookes upon that as his onely duty. I have thoughts sometimes, but know not well whence[41] they doe arise, that I may see you ere long in England. But what to desire herein I cannot say, but if you like it I can wish for it. Our affaires here to me seeme in a kind of od condition: jealousys on all sides are great, no man knoweth well each other. My love to your wife, and let me be, my lord,

Your lordship's faithfull freind to serve you,

Franc Russell

160. From William Jephson, London, 24 February 1657, 821, fos 290–291.[42]

My deare lord,

I receyved lately the favour of your lordship's letter of the 11th instant, for which, and all the rest, I am only able to returne the gratefull tribute of my thankes. There was yesterday brought into the

[40] Richard Norton, parliamentarian officer and politician, campaigned in southern England during the civil war and was prominent in the parliamentary administration of his native Hampshire and as governor of Southampton and Portsmouth. A friend of Oliver Cromwell, he was elected to the Long Parliament in 1645 and, although political moderation led to his removal at Pride's Purge, he retook his seat in the Rump in 1651. He supported the Protectorate and was elected to all three Protectorate parliaments, but he became increasingly disenchanted by the continuing military tone of the parliamentary regimes and, although not excluded, seems rarely to have sat in the 1656–1658 parliament.

[41] Word heavily amended and could alternatively be read as 'where'.

[42] This is the first of seven letters in this collection (nos 160, 171, 191, 206, 212, 227, and 235) by William Jephson, all of them of the period February to May 1657, which are partly in a numbered code. The code is broadly similar to others in use at the time, with the lower numbers each standing for a letter of the alphabet and the higher numbers standing for prominent individuals, groups, or collective nouns. Although these letters have generally not been decoded here by their recipient and, as with Harrison's code, no key appears to be extant, the smaller numbers (standing for individual letters of the alphabet) can easily be decoded and the identities of many of the individuals and groups denoted by the higher numbers are quite clear. C.H. Firth worked through most of these letters and decoded large parts of them in his article 'Cromwell and the crown', *English Historical Review*, 18 (1903), pp. 52–80. Accordingly, in these letters those parts of the text which can reliably be decoded have been reproduced in that form and only where the meaning is uncertain or unclear has the letter been left in its original coded form and possible or probable meanings indicated in footnotes.

parliament (by Sir Christopher Packe)[43] an humble addresse to his Highnesse desiring him to accept of the kingly office, and to declare his successour, and to constitute another house of parliament, not exceeding 70, nor under 40, and severall other thinges touching the priviledg of parliaments and libertye of the subject. It beeing ghuest what this meant, twas debated till 3 in the afternoone, before it could bee brought to a question for reading of it; but then there was to the vote 144 in the affirmative and but 54[44] in the negative, and yet they held us out untill six at night before it could bee resolv'd to resume it this daye; which was done accordingly, and the whole morning spent in debate upon the businesse in generall, and a motion to bring it into a grand committee (which wee had felt the smart of in the last parliament), but at length resolv'd to bee debated in parts in the house. 402. and 1111.[45] are the fierce sticklers against it. The more then ordinary opposition of the latter upon pretences of religion, which most men think him not much guilty of, I thinke drives on the businesse the faster. Fleetwood and general Desborough speake against it but calmlye. Those I wrote in my last continue firme, 310. and 1306.[46] pretty equally divided. In fine, my lord, in probabilitye of humane reason, wee are in good hopes of a settlement amongst ourselves. But that which gives some disturbance is our jealousye of the Dutch, who have done somthinges towards us, which looke unfriendlye, but they disowne any of those actions upon a publique account. I hope that God, who hath hitherto carryed us thorough soe many difficulties, will still bee our support. His Highnesse hath made mee one promise more, of writing to your lordship for mee concerning the 50 by captain Whaleye.[47] I shall only kisse your lordship's hands, and take leave to subscribe myselfe, my lord,

Your most affectionate and humble servant,

Wm Jephson

[43] Parliamentarian politician and London-based merchant and financier; as a rising figure in metropolitan politics and administration he strongly supported the parliamentary cause during the 1640s and 1650s, and as lord mayor in the mid-1650s he became a prominent supporter of Protector and Protectorate. He was rewarded with a string of mainly financial appointments and in 1656 was sent on a diplomatic mission to Sweden. He was elected to represent the City of London in the second Protectorate parliament and was very active within parliament, not least in presenting this proposal on 23 February 1657, though he claimed to have had no hand in its drafting.

[44] The voting figures have been heavily amended but are quite clear.

[45] Probably 'Sydenham and Lambert'.

[46] Probably 'the army and the officers'.

[47] Possibly Richard Whalley or his elder brother, John Whalley, parliamentarian officer, who was also serving in Henry Cromwell's horse regiment in Ireland.

161. From George Monck, Dalkeith, 24 February 1657, 821, fos 292–293.

May itt please your excellencie,

Having the opportunitie of this bearer, I make bold to acquaint your excellencie with what newes I heare, which is, that Charles Stuart intends this summer (if monies doe nott fayle him) to give us some trouble both in Ireland and Scotland, and I heare the earle of Ormond is to come over into Ireland, and also Inchiqueene,[48] if they can perswade him and Middleton hither; and Mr Secretary Thurloe writes worde to mee that they intend likewise to give them trouble in England, butt itt is nott visible to mee by their preparations which way they are able to doe itt. I have a greate ambition to bee a planter under your excellencie if I could gett butt libertie to bee loose from my command heere, which I hope in a short time I shall have. I have nothing else to trouble your lordshippe withall, butt to lett you know that I am,

Your excellencie's most humble servant,

George Monck

162. From Anthony Morgan, London, 24 February 1657, 821, fos 294–295.

May it please your excellency,

Wee are now at that crisis which was expected. Yesterday a remonstrance was brought in to the house for their consent to be offered in their name to his Highness. It containes these heads, vizt: that his Highness would accept the title, stile, dignity and office of king; that he would appoint and declare his successor; that their might be 2 houses of parliament, one of which (not called lords in the remonstrance) should not exceed 70 nor be under 40 persons; that their should be trienniall parliaments not to be dissolved in 50 dais; that members legally chosen, if excepted against as not qualified, should be tried by a committee of parliament and the councell, and an appeal lye to the house; the qualification of electors and elected are sutable to those in the instrument of government; that none should be of the privy councell but such as should be approved by parliament; commanders of the armys after his Highness's death to be made by consent of parliament; that no disturbance should be given to ministers; liberty to all but in the excercise of popery, prelacy, or disturbance of the civill peace.

[48] James Butler, Marquess of Ormond, and Murrough O'Brien, Earl of Inchiquin, the principal supporters of the king in Ireland during the 1640s.

Sir Christopher Pack offered this paper to the house. The whole debate reflected upon him. In the question whether it should be admitted or not he was well backed, but gave some advantage against himselfe by privatly confessing to one satte by him that he had never read it, who charged him publiquely with it in the house. Sydnam[49] moved a committee might be appointed to find out the contrivers of this remonstrance. Captain Baines[50] moved he might be called to the barr. Many arraigned him, but upon the question whether it should be read or not the house devided; 144 were for it, 54 against it. This day wee contended hard about the manner of considering the paper, and resolved tomorrow morning to read it by parts. Lord Lambert is violently against it. Desborow, Sidnam, lord deputy, Strickland,[51] Pickering[52] and some others of the councell are against it. Lord president Lawrance, Philip Jones, Mountegue,[53] Sir Charles Wolsly, lord Fines,[54] Skippon,[55] Thurlow are highly for it. Sir Richard Onslow[56] is head of the country party for it. Sir William Strickland[57] against it. All the long robe[58] are keenly for it. The Irish all for it but Cooper, Huson

[49] William Sydenham, the Protectoral councillor.

[50] Adam Baynes, parliamentarian officer and politician, was by 1646 serving as an officer in John Lambert's horse regiment and became a protégé, trusted agent, and close colleague of Lambert. As such, he rose (and later fell) as Lambert's power waxed and waned, acquiring property and public offices during the 1650s. He sat for his home town of Leeds, where he maintained a power base, in Oliver Cromwell's two Protectorate parliaments.

[51] Walter Strickland, parliamentarian politician and diplomat, served as parliament's ambassador in the Netherlands from the early 1640s to the early 1650s. He reportedly became close to Cromwell after his return to England in 1651 and was a founder member of the Protectoral council, very active in domestic, foreign, and diplomatic affairs throughout the Protectorate. He sat in both Protectorate parliaments of Oliver Cromwell.

[52] Sir Gilbert Pickering, parliamentarian politician, supported the parliamentary cause during the 1640s both in parliament and as an active administrator in his native Northamptonshire. He became a friend and ally of Oliver Cromwell, was a founder member of the Protectoral council, was very active in domestic, foreign, and diplomatic affairs throughout the Protectorate, became the Protector's lord chamberlain, and sat in both Protectorate parliaments of Oliver Cromwell.

[53] Edward Montague, the Protectoral councillor.

[54] Nathaniel Fiennes, the Protectoral councillor, probably styled 'lord' because he was a commissioner of the great seal.

[55] Philip Skippon, parliamentarian officer and politician, had a long and distinguished military career, fighting on the continent in the pre-war years and then as parliament's principal commander in London during the 1640s and 1650s, including his service as major-general for London in 1655–1657. He was a founder member of the Protectoral council and sat in both Protectorate parliaments of Oliver Cromwell.

[56] Parliamentarian politician who had been prominent in the parliamentary administration of his native Surrey during the 1640s and sat for that county in both Protectorate parliaments of Oliver Cromwell.

[57] Parliamentarian politician, and elder brother of councillor Walter Strickland, he represented his native Yorkshire in both Protectorate parliaments of Oliver Cromwell.

[58] Those MPs who were judges or practising lawyers.

and Sanky.[59] All the Yorkshiremen are against it but Charles Howard.[60] Last night some of the major-generalls were with his Highness; tarried a quarter of an hower in the roome before one word pased from either. At length they began and complained of the parliament. His Highness answered hastily: What would you have me doe? Are not they of your own garbling? Did not you admit whom you pleased and keep out whom you pleased? And now doe you complain to me? Did I meddle with it? And so withdrew without further declaring.

Pray satisfie Gorge that the act about Portum[61] will not be offered to his Highness till severall other acts are ready to offer with it, which may be worth the troble of an interview twixt his Highness and parliament, but that tis safe enough. I thinke tis a great advantage tis so long passing since you are sure what will pass in terminis,[62] because before you can take publique notice of it many orders for setting out lands may purposly pass or be stopped, to make things fitt against the execution, if he means to be guilty of contrivance. Pardon me that I abuse him before your lordship's face; I goe to my country lodging tonight and have not time to doe it to his face.

I remain your lordship's faithfull servant,
A Morgan

163. From John Reynolds, London, 24 February 1657, 821, fos 296–297.

May it please your excellency,

I have delivered your lordship's letters according to direction, and that excellent draught to the lord Whitelocke[63] was with much deserved respect received. We are againe engaged in a long debate which will necessarily postpone our other busines, as well as that of Ireland. I

[59] Irish in the sense of having seen military service in the English army in Ireland. Thomas Cooper represented the Irish constituency of Counties Down, Antrim, and Armagh, but John Hewson and Hierome Sankey represented English constituencies in this parliament, sitting for Guildford and Marlborough respectively.

[60] He sat for Cumberland.

[61] During the winter of 1656–1657, parliament debated a bill that included a provision confirming the Portumna estate to Henry Cromwell (*TSP*, VI, pp. 7–8; *Burton*, I, pp. 223, 259).

[62] This Latin phrase could be translated as 'in the end' or 'finally'.

[63] Bulstrode Whitelocke, parliamentarian politician, lawyer, and diplomat, supported the parliamentary cause during the 1640s, though with some misgivings, and, while he was active in parliament and in negotiations for settlement, he played little part in military affairs and held aloof from the regicide. He served as ambassador to Sweden in 1653–1654 and generally supported the Protectorate, though with reservations, which led to his dismissal as a commissioner of the great seal in 1655, but he retained his role as a treasury commissioner and was consulted by the Protector on key issues. He sat in both Protectorate parliaments of Oliver Cromwell.

suppose your lordshipp will receive it from other hands, and indeede I wish it were so carried as that common fame did not carry abroade our debates in parliament. But the disengenious of some men professing higher principles is such that, although we have the major vote, nothing can be concluded, not so[64] much in 2 dayes' debate as to debate it in the house and not in a grand committeee. I observe wonderfull h l t e f a h a u t n in 4 (and which is more straunge in 3 and 22, and in most 39, except 37) towards 1.[65] I beseech your lordship have good espialls upon the army there, least we be prevented of the good of settlement by disturbances amongst the instruments of peace who manage those of warre. It is hoped that all these heates will end in a calme, but I promise nothing but a constant readines to obey your lordship's commands, and whether I change my stile of addresse or no, yet I will never vary in the substanciall parts of affection and fidelity. The business is so raw at present as it will endure onely gentle handling. The other house or ballance goes heavily on. That of single person is greately approved in the company attending it, being liberty and property regulated and secured. I hope to give your lordship some account of things done as wel as saide. In the meane time I remaine, my lord,

Your excellencye's most humble and faithfull servaunt,

J Reynolds

164. From Henry Ingoldsby, Limerick, 28 February 1657, 821, fos 298–299.

My lord,

Haveinge by the last poast received your commands for the dispose off the £300, which was put into my hands the last summer, accordinge to the first intentions off itt, which was to buy provisions for that division off the feild forces att Kylmallocke[66] and heare abouts, I am enforced to give this account to your lordship in answeare theareunto: that accordinge to your directions, I have gon on in that necessary

[64] Word amended/blotted and possibly deleted.

[65] This curious code or cypher, partly in letters as well as the more usual numbered system, is only very rarely employed by Reynolds in his surviving correspondence of this period and no key appears to be extant. Accordingly, nothing more than unsubstantiated guesses can be offered. The figure 1 may represent the Protector and the other low numerals, including 3 and 4, senior figures in the Protectorate such as Lambert, Fleetwood, or Desborough. 39 appears to represent a group – the major-generals, perhaps – and 37 a single individual within that group who was the only one to adopt a different line towards 1. The letters could represent a single word, apparently a feeling or attitude – positive or negative – taken by 4 towards 1. Beyond that, however, little can be said with any certainty.

[66] Kilmallock, County Limerick.

worke about the greate castle in Lymbr,[67] which thow tis the most considerable fronteere cyttadell in Ireland for Clare and Connaught, being the cheife inlett to both and grand magazeene for thes parts, yett till now itt had not accommodation anuffe within itt for the quarteringe off above three fyles off men for the defence off itt. Neither did itt take in Thomd[68] Bridge, which now by the pullinge downe a slight gatehous and makeinge up a lusty tower in the roome off itt, itt doth soe absolutely command that thear's noe seemeinge possibility for an enemy on that side to prajudice itt, or within much to hurt to itt. The work is but in the midle and not yett finished. I had noe other mony but the provision mony in my hands to doe itt with all, most off which is spent and contracted to bee spent about itt. Therfore I hope your lordship and the councell will take speedy care to supply this place with £300 more for provisions. Uppon which expectation I'le venture to see and cause uppon my score the provisions to bee made by the last off March att furthest, which I suppose is the time intended for itt, beinge confident that I shall not bee left in the lyrch thearein. I must entreate your lordship to take care that this garrison bee supplyed with 2 or 300 barrells off bulletts, theare beinge att present noe plenty off them heere. I shall (God willinge) cause and see that the forces in these parts shall bee in a readinesse and fittnesse to march against the time your lordship shall command them into the feild. Leiutenant-colonel Purefoy[69] shall have speedy notice off your lordship's pleasure to his desiers by, my lord,

Your excellency'se most humble and obleidged servant,

H Ingoldesby

165. From Bulstrode Whitelocke, London, 2 March 1657, 821, fos 300–301.

My lorde,

You are pleased to make so noble and free a returne, expressing your good acceptation of that little piece of service, which I was farre more willing then capable to performe, relating to the buisnes of your

[67] An abbreviated form of Limerick, whose Norman, riverside castle, known as King John's Castle, fell to the Catholic rebels in 1641 and to Ireton in 1651.

[68] An abbreviated form of Thomond. Thomond Bridge, crossing the Shannon in the centre of Limerick, lay adjacent to, but beyond the defensive circuit of, the castle.

[69] William Purefoy, parliamentarian officer and politician, served in Ireland from 1647 in the foot regiment successively commanded by James Castle, Henry Slade, and Edward Leigh; although that regiment was largely disbanded in 1653, Purefoy probably retained links with Ireland, showing up again in active service in 1659 in Robert Barrow's foot regiment there. He sat in both of Oliver Cromwell's Protectorate parliaments, representing Limerick and Kilmallock in the first.

excellence in parliament,[70] that therby my experience is inlarged, that it is much more gratefull to serve one perticular person of honnour then many. I cann only assure your excellence that this act of mine was with unfeigned affection to your service, and butt an earnest of my desires to be commaunded by you.

We are now very buisy in parliament uppon the great point concerning governement, wherin is difference of opinion, as uppon the former great point. I hope it will please the Lorde so to direct us, that our resolutions may be pleasing to Him and for the security of His people. To me, nothing is more satisfactory then a free debate, and I shall hope that the best reason will find best approbation.

My lorde, I have not bin so happy as to have a neerer relation to Ireland, butt my affections to it and to your lordship's commaunds doe sufficiently oblige me to contribute the uttmost of my smalle ability to promote those affaires and bills which doe concerne that countrey. Wherin I shall be very carefull and ready to joine with those worthy gentlemen who serve for Ireland, and who are pleased to doe me the honnour sometimes to conferre with me about those matters.

I feare I may be troublesome to your lordship's more serious affaires. This is only to present my very humble thankes for the favour of your letters, and to take the opportunity to expresse myselfe what I really am, my lorde,

Your excellencye's most faithfull and most humble servant,
B Whitelocke

166. From Nicholas Bernard,[71] Gray's Inn, London, 3 March 1657, 821, fos 302–303.

May it please your lordship,

I have wrott thrise in obedience to your lordship's comands in relation to the lord primat's lybrary,[72] but have not as yet heard of their receipt. I hope there was nothing in either of them any waies

[70] Probably the Portumna bill, which Whitelocke had moved in parliament in late December 1656.

[71] Church of Ireland minister, he was a protégé of James Ussher, ordained by him, serving as his chaplain and through him scooping up a number of positions within the Church of Ireland. He stayed in Ireland after the rebellion, not least to protect Ussher's library in Drogheda. He was imprisoned on a brief trip to London in 1647 but returned to Ireland as minister in Drogheda for 1649–1650. He spent the 1650s in London as preacher at Gray's Inn and also served as one of Oliver Cromwell's chaplains and almoners. Still close to Ussher, he oversaw the archbishop's funeral in the spring of 1656 and the disposal of his possessions, and then worked to protect his late master's reputation.

[72] Henry Cromwell was keen to acquire the celebrated library of the late archbishop of Armagh, perhaps intending it for a second university college that he hoped to establish in Dublin.

displeasing to your lordship. As soone as Sir Tymothy Tyrrell[73] hath concluded with those your lordship hath appointed to treate with them, I shall not faile to see the bookes delivered accordingly, and I observe these other comands received in your lordship's letter to me, and what else shall be comitted to the care of,

Your lordship's most humble and devoted servant,

N Bernard

167. From Charles Fleetwood, London, 3 March 1657, 821, fos 304–305.

Deare brother,

Ther hath bine very litle done this last weeke in the great buysnes, only this day the howse hath past that part that his Highnes doe nominate and declare who shall be his successor. What the Lord will doe with us I canot tell or own. Divisions I much dreade, though I must tell you our common enimy are very active and vigorously dilligent to watch with the 1st oppurtunity to rise, and it is beleived they will suddenly attempt an insurrection if the Lord prevents it not, and that very suddenly. The declaration which they purpose to put forth we have hade a sight of it, which is very short, much upon the usuall theames of liberty to the people and to deliver them from the tyranny, as they are pleased to call it, which they conceive us to be under.[74] This insurrection with that barbarous design against his Highnes' person is yet carying on, but the Lord, I trust, hath in so great and wonderfull mercy discovered a great part of the designes, which through the same gracious presance, we trust, will still be whitnessed against and blasted. The king of Scotts hath a considerable force with him, which if he can lande upon English shoare he hopes to have a great accession of forces from his own party heare, but the Lord who hath owned us still will[75] against all such designes. I know you have an account of all thes things from the Secretary and therefor I shall not further trouble you. Major Owen, having it seemes received his Highnes' comission for Maryborow,[76] hath sollicited me for to have it under the great seale of Ireland. I have consented to a fiat but not to take effect without

[73] The late archbishop's son-in-law, husband of the archbishop's only child.

[74] The plot to assassinate the Protector, led by Miles Sindercombe, had collapsed in January, but further royalist attempts against the regime were feared.

[75] Word apparently omitted.

[76] Henry Owen, parliamentarian officer, serving in Ireland in John Reynolds's horse regiment but currently in London sitting in parliament for Counties Westmeath, Longford, and King's, was governor of Maryborough (now Port Laois), Queen's County.

your consent, ther being nothing which relates to Ireland that I would willingly doe with your dislike. My haste must pleade the excuse of,

Your most affectionate brother,

Charles Fleetwood

168. From Charles Fleetwood, Wallingford House, 3 March 1657, 821, fos 306–307.

Letter of recommendation on behalf of colonel John Fawke,[77] *requesting he be allocated 500 acres in and around Laughlinstowne*[78] *in satisfaction of his arrears.*

169. From Vincent Gookin, Westminster, 3 March 1657, 821, fos 308–309.

My deare lord,

I had the hapiness to receive your lordship's in answer to 3 of mine formerly sent. This is only to give your lordship my humble thankes for that lettre of your lordship, and your advice in it. Tis possible my affection and the strength of my desires after what I would have may make mee judge things tending therto more probable to attaine the wished end than indeed they are, but this I am sure of, that I have not misrelated matter of fact, and my conjectures have soe often hit, that a litle presumption I hope may be the better borne with. My lord Broghill, Sir Charles Woosly and colonel Philip Jones, upon my aquainting them of my sudden departure, were much against it, and told mee that his Highness would be pleased to write to the councell to dispence with mine and colonel Merkham's stay heere for a moneth,[79] and that none might be put in our places till wee came by their direction. I wrote a lettre to that purpose, which the Secretary promised to have signed and sent by this post. And truely, my lord, I

[77] Parliamentarian officer and politician, he campaigned in England during the civil war but, in 1647, went to Ireland as lieutenant-colonel of Anthony Hungerford's newly raised foot regiment. He became governor of his home town of Drogheda but had to surrender it to royalist forces in June 1649. Soon after, he returned to England, where he raised a foot regiment of his own. By 1651 he was back in Ireland as governor of Drogheda; he held a string of civil and military offices in Ireland during the 1650s, was particularly active in the land settlement, and was returned for Counties Meath and Louth to both of Oliver Cromwell's Protectorate parliaments. In part, this note draws upon an unpublished article on John Fowke of Drogheda, County Louth, written by Dr Patrick Little for the 1640–1660 section of the History of Parliament. I am grateful to the History of Parliament Trust for allowing me to see this article in draft.

[78] Loughlinstown, County Dublin.

[79] On 7 January 1657, the Irish council had written to Markham and Gookin, requesting them to seek leave of absence from parliament and to return to Ireland to oversee the letting of state land (Dunlop, pp. 648–649).

humbly conceive that the worke of setting 21 yeare leases cannot be put in execution yet for the preparations to it will take up more than a moneth, and I humbly conceive that one generall order of the councell that all tenants who last yeare tooke lands of the state shall continue in their holdings at the same rents this yeare, except such as complaine of their bargaines, canne be noe losse to the state because the lands were well set last yeare, neither can it be any hindrance to setting the same lands within that yeare for 21 yeares. And for this worke, and setting tythes and excise, Mr King[80] and alderman Hooke,[81] I humbly conceive, will doe it faythfully and effectually.[82] I doubt not but your lordship is fully aquainted with the remonstrance offered the house touching the setlement of the govement in a king and 2 states, and what entertainement the dissatisfied officers of the army had at White Hall. Though I heard it not, I may safely say it was good because it did much good, for the next day they were much quieter and very willing and desirous to be satisfied. The debate of the remonstrance in the house is like to be long, but I hope will receive a good end, most of the good people of the nation and all the rest being for it.

I once more pray your lordship to declare to mee your pleasure wheather I shall hasten over. If soe I will not, God willing, stay heere 3 dayes after I have received your comands. The copie of that lettre to the northerne classis is dayly expected. As soone as I receive it I shall send it to your lordship. One minister had his approbation by the tryers last weeke and will be suddenly in Munster. Hee is a good man. If hee were not my brother I would say more. That which hinders many able men from going into Ireland is the uncertainty of the mayntenance, which our bill for maintenance of ministers will provide against. I am, my lord,

Your lordship's most humble and most obedient servant,

Vin Gookin

[80] Ralph King, alderman of Londonderry, returned for that constituency to the second Protectorate parliament.

[81] Thomas Hooke, merchant and influential alderman of Dublin, who supported the English regimes in Ireland and lent money and supplied provisions to the English army there, and who held various financial and judicial offices in Ireland during the 1650s. In the summer of 1657 he was praised by Henry Cromwell as 'constant to the parlament's interest', 'well affected [. . .] to his highnes's person and governement', 'active in bringing others also to the same persuasion', 'of good repute for godlines and sobrietie, and withal faithfull and industrious' (*TSP*, VI, p. 405).

[82] Eventually, in July 1657, the Irish council commissioned Markham, Gookin, King, and Hooke, as well as Richard Lawrence, to undertake the business (Dunlop, pp. 665–666).

170. From Thomas Herbert, Warb[83] Street, Dublin, 3 March 1657, 821, fos 310–311.

May it please your excellencie,

Itt is not without much anguish of mind that I have been thus long from attending my duty, but am taught to submitt to God's will in all things. I have been lamintably troubled with a difluxion of rheghume[84] and sorenes of throate, which I every day hoped would quallifie. Dr Petty[85] gave mee, from time to time, your lordshipp's leave to attend the cure, and humbly crave one daye's absence or two more, when I trust my payne will be asswaged and that I may comfetably returne to serve your lordshipps as becomes,

Your excellencie's most faithfull and obedient servant,

Tho Herbert

171. From William Jephson, London, 3 March 1657, 821, fos 312–313.

My deare lord,

I gave notice in my last of a remonstrance brought into the parliament to desyre his Highnesse to accept of the title of king etc and divers other particulars, which I doubt not your lordship hath receyv'd from other hands. This hath beene very severely oppos'd, both in the parliament and without doores, by many officers of the armye, who made an addresse of that nature to his Highnesse and receyv'd from him a rounder awnswer then I believe they expected. Many particulars of his Highnesse' speech to them I have written to Munne Temple (which I thought too long to trouble your lordship withall) who will acquaint your lordship with them, if you have them not more exactly from other hands; from honest Downing[86] I had

[83] Probably an abbreviated form of Werburgh Street.

[84] Apparently a variant of 'rheum'.

[85] William Petty, physician, natural philosopher, academic, and administrator, was, by the early 1650s, professor of anatomy at Oxford and vice-principal of Brasenose. He went to Ireland in 1652 as physician to the English army there. In the mid-1650s he was employed in surveying or resurveying the forfeited lands in Ireland, the so-called 'down survey', preparatory to their allotment to English soldiers and investors. A strong supporter of Henry Cromwell, and employed by him as one of his secretaries, he therefore became a target for the more radical opponents of Henry Cromwell, including those – such as Benjamin Worsley – employed under Fleetwood in earlier surveys but displaced, sidelined, and often criticized by Petty.

[86] George Downing, parliamentarian officer, politician, and diplomat, served as chaplain to several parliamentary regiments during the mid- and late 1640s and as scoutmaster-general to the English army in Scotland from 1649. By the mid-1650s he held other, mainly financial offices, and in 1655 was sent on a diplomatic mission to the continent in the wake of the Piedmont massacre. He sat in all three Protectorate parliaments.

them, who was by and heard them. At his house wee had a meeting of most of the officers here of your armye, my lord Howard, colonel Inglesbye[87] and others of this armye, in order to have lett his Highnesse see all his officers were not enemies to this remonstrance; but finding the heate of the others abated, I heare noe more of that. The first part of the first paragraph of the remonstrance (concerning kingship) is for the present layd asyde untill the rules bee agreed upon whereby hee is to governe. This was done by the consent of the Protector (as I have heard from very good hands) for the satisfaction of Fleetwood and 2007,[88] who I thinke will bee now very firme and indeavour to convert their brethren. Whaley, Gof,[89] Butler[90] and divers others begin to come in, and indeed wee had this day but very little opposition in passing a vote to desyre that his Highnesse would bee pleased to nominate and decleare, during his life, who should succeed him in the government of these nations. Lambert hath beene silent, both Saturnsday, yesterday and this day; I suppose hee hath now given up the bucklers.[91] Truly, I hope the time is come when God of his mercye will give us a happy settlement in these nations, that at least amongst ourselves wee may bee free from probabilitye of new warres. I shall add noe more to your

[87] Richard Ingoldsby, parliamentarian officer and politician, a regicide, and a cousin of Oliver Cromwell, supported the parliamentary cause from the outbreak of war, succeeding John Hampden as commander of a foot regiment incorporated into the New Model Army in 1645. He was elected to the Long Parliament in 1647 and supported the regicide. In 1655 he succeeded Howard as commander of a horse regiment then serving in Scotland, but Ingoldsby appears to have remained in England at this period, representing his native Buckinghamshire in both Protectorate parliaments of Oliver Cromwell.

[88] Probably Desborough, though it is curious that, in his previous letter (no. 160), Jephson has used individual encoded letters to spell out his name, rather than using a single, high-number code for him.

[89] William Goffe, parliamentarian officer and politician and a regicide, fought for parliament from the outbreak of the civil war and was, from 1645, an officer in the New Model foot regiment of Edward Harley and then Thomas Pride. Around the time of the regicide, he transferred to the foot regiment commanded by Sir Thomas Fairfax and then by Oliver Cromwell; in 1651, having served as Cromwell's lieutenant-colonel in Scotland, Goffe was promoted to command that regiment. He strongly supported Oliver Cromwell and the Protectorate, sat in both Protectorate parliaments of Oliver Cromwell, and, from 1655 to 1657, served as major-general of central southern England. Although his loyalty was tested by the offer of the crown, which clearly made him uneasy, he remained a firm Cromwellian.

[90] William Butler/Boteler, parliamentarian officer and politician, though prior to his appointment as a major-general in 1655 his military record was surprisingly slight, and he did not gain command of a regiment until much later, in 1659, and then only briefly. As major-general for a group of East Midlands counties, including his native Northamptonshire, his energetic and uncompromising approach won him a few friends but many enemies. He represented Northamptonshire in the second Protectorate parliament, the only parliament in which he sat.

[91] Buckler: a shield or small piece of armour, often carried or worn on the arm, or occasionally a lance or spear.

lordship's trouble, which you constantly receyve, only as a testimony of the obedience of, my lord,

Your lordship's most faythfull and affectionate, humble servant,

Wm Jephson

172. From Anthony Morgan, London, 3 March 1657, 821, fos 314–315.

May it please your excellency,

Last weeke I gave you some account of the remonstrance, which is proposed to the house for them to offer to his Highness. Since, the house kept a day of humiliation.[92] The same day some officers of the army did the like, and having gotten a coppy of the remonstrance, presented it to his Highness with their dissatisfactions to it. Collonell Mills[93] was their mouth. His Highness told them that what they now so much startled at was a thing to which they were formerly reconciled so farr that when they made him dissolve the Long Parliament (for twas done against his judgment) they would have made him king. When he had refused that, they would have had him choose 10 persons to assist him in the government, but because he might be suspected to have too much influence upon them he proposed 140, and those were nominated by themselvs; not an officer of the degree of a captain but named more then he himselfe did.[94] These 140 honest men could not governe; the ministry and propriety were like to be destroyed. Then 7 of them made an instrument of government, brought it to him with the name of king in it, and there was not much counsell or consideration had in the making it, and accordingly it proved an imperfect thing which will neither preserve our religious or civill rights.[95] His opinion was last parliament that it must be mended, but the parliament must not touch it; they must be sent home with no good report of the goverment; it was against his mind.[96] Then you would be mending it yourselvs, when you know I am sworne not to suffer it to be altered but by parliament, and then you might have given me a kick on the breech and turne me going. Then you would have this parliament

[92] On 27 February.

[93] John Mill/Mills, parliamentarian officer, who served in Richard Ingoldsby's foot regiment and succeeded him as its colonel in 1655.

[94] The ejection of the Rump in April 1653 and the establishment of the Nominated Assembly, which opened in July 1653.

[95] The resignation of the Nominated Assembly and the establishment of the Protectorate under a written constitution, the Instrument of Government, in December 1653.

[96] The first Protectorate parliament was abruptly dissolved in January 1655, in large part to kill off its still incomplete Government Bill, a revised constitution designed to replace the Instrument.

called; it was against my judgment, but I could have no quietness till[97] was done; when they were chosen you garbled them, kept out and put in whom you pleased by the instrument, and I am sworne to make good all you doe, right or wrong, and because 120 are excluded I must thinke them malignants or scandalous whether they are so or not.[98] Yet now you complain of those[99] are admitted. I have no designe upon them or you. I never courted you nor never will. I have a sure refuge; if they doe good things I must and will stand by them. They are honest men and have done good things; I know not what you can blame them for unless because they love me too well. You are offended at a house of lords.[100] I tell you that unless you have some such thing as a balance you can not be safe, but either you will grow upon the civill liberties by secluding such as are elected to sitt in parliament (next time for ought I know you may exclud 400); or they will grow upon your liberty in religion. I abhor James Nailer's principle, yet interposed. You see what my lettre signified.[101] This instrument of government will not doe your worke. Choose 6 or 7 out of your number to come and speake with me and[102] will give them further satisfaction, and so good night.

You may easily judge that this hath given occasion to many heady people to consider. I am well asured wee shall have no tumults. Sidnam hath absented himselfe from the house of late, who was most furious. Many others comply and wee goe soberly but slowly on. Wee have postponed the 1st paragraphe about the name of king to be last considered. I have written to Dr Gorge about Sir Timothy Terrell's books. I remain,

Your lordship's most obedient and most faithfull servant,

Ant Morgan

[97] Word – perhaps 'it' – apparently omitted.

[98] In fact, in line with the Instrument, the exclusion of over one hundred MPs deemed hostile to the regime at the start of the second Protectorate parliament had been undertaken by the council.

[99] Word – perhaps 'who' – apparently omitted.

[100] The restoration of a second and unelected parliamentary chamber, as envisaged by the recently proposed constitution.

[101] James Naylor, a former parliamentarian soldier and a very active Quaker preacher and writer, had, in the autumn of 1656, ridden into Bristol with adoring female followers in support, allegedly in blasphemous imitation of Christ's entry into Jerusalem on Palm Sunday, though Naylor vigorously denied this. In December 1656, the second Protectorate parliament tried Naylor, found him guilty, and, although narrowly voting against the death penalty, condemned Naylor to be whipped, pilloried, bored through the tongue, branded, and indefinitely imprisoned, in the process brushing aside the Protector's questioning of parliament's legal or constitutional right to act in this way. While distancing himself from Naylor's actions, Oliver Cromwell was clearly worried that an unrestrained parliament could act in this way and might unleash further religious persecution and so narrow or undermine liberty of conscience.

[102] Word – perhaps 'I' – apparently omitted.

173. From John Reynolds, 3 March 1657, 821, fos 316–317.

May it please your excellency,

I have lesse to write because I have received no commands from your lordshipp for some time, and the publique busines of the new moddell of governement (with some private bills) take up the whole time, and no roome for Ireland in the thoughts of any untill this be dispatched. I shall not write much, but can, I hope, assure your lordshipp of a good settlement by meanes of the unanimity of parliament to adhere to his Highnes, and his Highness' gracious and reciprocall kindnes to them expressed in a speech to the officers, who are united and wel satisfyed. This day the house resolved that the clause of desiring his Highnes to nominate and declare his successour be part of the remonstrance now under debate, and it passed without division or opposition. 39.[103] agreede to the resolve. I went out of the house before the question. I have beene advised not to write many particulars, and I suppose that a copy is sent unto your lordshipp of the whole remonstrance or paper. I shall conclude with an humble suite unto your lordshipp that if major Fox,[104] who hath a peice of my land in his lott, shall apply for a reprizall, that he may[105] have a grant thereof, because I can make my title cleare to what he had before; and having my grant so much short of the first order and intention, I hope this small parcell, which lyes within pistoll shot of Carickhouse, will not be taken from me. Your lordship's favour and justice herein will oblige,

Your excellencye's humble and faithfull servaunt,

J Reynolds

174. From John Bridges, London, 3 March 1657, 823, fos 19–20.

May it please your lordshipp,

By the inclosed, though very rude and crude, your lordshipp will discerne and bee able to make a judgmente not only of the present condition of our affaires but alsoe of the event of the greate businesse that lyes before us. Wee that are uppon the place are of opinion that our worke is more then halfe done, and the rather because the opposite party either lay downe the cudgells or leave the feild, and many (and those not of least consideration) come over to us. That (wee feare) will most stick with us is the ballance, or house of lords as some

[103] Assuming that Reynolds is employing the same code as that used by him in no. 163, 39 is a collective noun, designating a group, perhaps the major-generals.

[104] Perhaps the Joseph Fox serving in Ireland in Anthony Hungerford's foot regiment in the late 1640s, though the identification is uncertain.

[105] The sense of the entire sentence suggests that the word 'not' may have been omitted in error at this point.

call it, of which wee hope to see an yssue within 4 dayes. Wee have had notable contending, both in publique and private, but having spent our powder wee now growe very calme and growe towards a reconcilemente.

The schoolemaster is nowe ready to goe over. If your lordshipp finde him not a person extraordinarly qualifyed for that employmente, never lett mee bee trusted in a business of your nature more. Dr Harrison wilbee able to give your lordshipp some present accompt of his abilities for that worke. I shall ever accompt it my greate honour to bee estemed as, my lord,

Your lordshipp's most humble and most faithfull servant,

Jo Bridges

175. From John Galland,[106] Coleraine, 6 March 1657, 821, fos 318–319.

May it please your exelency,

I have seene an order dated the 17 of February last sined by Doctor Gorge, by order from your exelency, lisensing one Hillman Cary Church and others to shew and implead mee, my leuitenant and ensin, or any of us att the shutts of the said Hillman Cary Church and others, or any of them. But, my lord, I dow not know any reason at all for their said desier, other ways then that I have said to them and others that their is sevrall lands falen to my company by lott in the county of Londonderry, and given to me and them by the commissoners for that purpose, to which lands the said persons dow clam an intrest by virtew of a lease or leases from the earle of Antrim.[107] Yet notwithstanding the said lands are given out to me as befor, which lands I have possessed on that accompt, and dow humbly conseve that the said possion should be in use or any of us till the comonwelth's intrest to the said lands should bee knowen. And therfor humbly intreat that the said order may bee revokd,[108] and if your exelency shall thinck fitt to lisense me I shall with much fredom and redines permit the state's titell to any of the said lands the next teerm, or when your excelency shall give me librty. I humbly intret your exelency to excuse me,

I rest your[109] lordshipp's unworthy servant,

Jo Galland

[106] Parliamentarian officer, serving in Ireland in the foot regiment commanded first by Henry Ireton and then by Fleetwood.

[107] Randal MacDonnell, second Earl and first Marquess of Antrim, was one of the most prominent Irish Catholic royalists of the 1640s. His tentative attempts during the 1650s to build bridges with the English parliamentary regimes in Ireland did not prevent the forfeiture of his extensive estates in Ulster.

[108] Word poorly formed and could alternatively be read as 'resolvd'.

[109] Word repeated in error.

176. From Robert Saunders and Robert Southwell, Kinsale, 6 March 1657, 821, fos 320–321.

Right honnorable,

May it please your excellency. At this instant wee are retourned from on board the Playne Dealing, which wee left under sayle without the harbour. Collonell More being on board with all his men, the wynd being exceeding fayre, and the Basing friggott alongst with him, they left this harbour a little after fowre a clock this afternone, and wee beeseech the Lord to give them a safe and speedy passage. Wee shall not be able by this post to give your lordship and the councell the account our proceedings in this bussines, but by the next, God willing, wee shall. Wee have adventured to pay collonell More for the 14 late recruits, and the six men that lost their cloathes in the Two Brothers,[110] rather then to give any discouragement unto them at their shiping. Wee indeavoured the best wee could get the musters of the men taken, but could not possibly effect it by reason of the great hast in shiping them, but gave a guess very neere the number, yet were forced to depend upon the certificat of collonell More, which wee hereinclosed send your lordship. Two or three were slipt asyde, but others received in their romes. Wee shall make what inquiry wee can after them and get them apprehended if they may bee found. And this much wee humbly beseech your lordship to acquaint the councell with for the present, and so take our leaves to remayne,

Your lordship's most faithfull and humble servants,

Ro Saunders Robert Southwell

177. From Robert Saunders and Robert Southwell, Kinsale, 6 March 1657, 821, fos 322–323.

Right honourable,

May it please your lordshipp. We thought it our duty to give your lordshipps account of fower men of collonell Moore's number at this instant, beinge ten of clock at night, come ashore in a smale boate, which fales out by this occasion. Collonell Moore (when the shipp was saleinge downe with the tyde) sent his marshall on shoare to fetch

[110] After being delayed by want of ships and bad weather at Ayr, the 500 men drawn from Scottish regiments and earmarked for the West Indies (to provide the bulk of a new foot regiment under William Brayne) set sail from Scotland in October 1656. Roughly half the men and a number of officers, including lieutenant-colonel John Bramstone, though not Brayne himself, sailed on the *Two Brothers*, but she was wrecked on the Irish coast in Timoleague Bay near Kinsale with the loss of over 200 lives; there were around 40 survivors. Henry Cromwell relayed the sad news to Thurloe in a letter of 5 November 1656, alleging that the vessel had been 'olde and crazie' (*TSP*, V, pp. 558–559, 570).

out of the towne prizon three men, that lay theire for leaveinge theire colours, one of them haveinge robd a towne's man of some mony, whome he had forgotten untill then. Which the marshall did, and when he had them on board his boate made after the shipp, and rowed as far as the Old Head, but the night cominge on and they beinge out of hopes to fetch them up and in much danger to goe any further, the boatemen turned backe againe. And we have committeed the three men to the marshalcey of this towne untill wee receive your lordshipp's orders concerninge them, as also about theire releife whilest they are heere, both for the marshall and the three prizoners. The marshall's name is Thomas Terrick; the prizoners' names, Phillip Patten, James Robbinson and Gerratt Murren. At theire comminge ashoare we were castinge about what might possibly bee done, and sent for captaine Sherlands, commander of the Kinsale friggot, and would have sent him with them to try, if he might with this night and tomorrowe's saylinge, fetch them up and deliver the men to collonel Moore. But he had not halfe a daye's provission on board him, and withall answered that it was a very greate uncertaintey wheather he might steere the direct cource after them or not, and made it (as we judged it) very unsea<son>able[III] to be done. Then we spoke with the owners of the Playne Dealinge, whoe had a shipp behind and neere ready to goe to Saint Christopher's, and would have had them to take them in and to deliver them to the governor of that island to be kept untill an oportunity served to send them to Jemayca. But this they refused unless we would contract anew for them, and withall we must have sent mayntanance for them there untill they might be sent, soe that we seinge noe way left to send them we have disposed of them as formerly, untill we heere from your lordshipps, alowing the marshall sufficient mayntanance untill then, and to the three prizoners twelve pence a day. Humbly desireinge your lordshipp's directions heerein we take leave, and remayne,

Your lordship's most humble servants,

Ro Saunders Robert Southwell

178. From Richard Cromwell, Whitehall, 7 March 1657, 821, fos 324–325.

Deare brother,

Those things that might be whisperred ought not to be committed to paper, and therefore it is my greate unhappynesse that there should be alwayes such a distance and difficulty of coming to eache other.

[III] Originally written 'unseasonable', but the third syllable has then clearly been deleted.

Though there is a barre to my penn in state affaires, yet I know noe law against brotherly affection, and to testify that is necessary and is a duty I only make now a returne, having lately received one from you, which was full fraughted with kindenesse. And to be wanting at this time would be a double sinn; the single one is too heavy, and the lighter the burthens of unkindenesse are made, the more eassyer and with the more comforte shall I passe through this peevish world. I can say you are some what more happy then others youre relations, for that you are oute of the spatterring dirte which is throwen aboute here; yet with some comforte, it is not soe much this weeke as it was 10 dayes agoe. I know noe newes beinge by reason of some debates in the howse shut oute for a rangler. Only I heare that the howse hath made themselves the commons by voting another howse; they are affraide of tytles; the feather in the cap is allowed to none but such gallants that waites upon ladyes. Robert Riche, my lady Frances' gallant, flyes with his plumes in Whitehall. Dr Owen hath been very angry and went in great haste oute of London. The Irish officers stand to your principles, which is your honour, to send such that are steddy and selfe denyall, preferring the publique good before any private. I know you have better intelligence then I can or dare to expresse, and therefore I shall desire you to be confident of my affections and service, and that you will doe me the favour to present my humble service to my sister. Having nothing more to trouble your more serious thoughts I rest,

Your most affectionate brother and servant,

R Cromwell

179. From John Bridges, London, 10 March 1657, 821, fos 326–327.

May it please your lordshipp,

I shall only presume to give you an accompt of the vote that passed the parliament on Thursday[112] – that his Highness will for the future bee pleased to call parliaments consisting of 2 howses (in such manner and way as shall bee more particulerly afterward agreed and declared in this remonstrance) once in 3 yeares. And since which tyme wee have beene taken upp for the most part in setlinge the people's libertyes, priviledges of parliament and qualifications of the members. The boysterous season is nowe over and there seemes to bee greate hopes of a serenity. Heere was a rumour as if the Anabaptist churches would publish a manifesto expressinge theire dislike of present proceedings, but wee heare little of it att present. My lord of Broghill hath gained to himselfe much honour by his prudent and dexterous deportments in

[112] 5 March.

the house. Since wee are not able to see to the end of this parliament, itt is much desired that the rest of our fellowe members would come and take our places, for many of our Irish members growe weary of theire seates and talke resolutely of theire returne.[113] The weaknes and ymportunity of my poore wife, the greate concernements of my family and my particuler fortunes, doe soe presse uppon mee that I hope your lordshipp will pardon my returne, especially nowe that wee are gotten over greatest difficultyes of the remonstrance. I am in a straight: itt's scarce fitt for mee to come away, yet it's too hard for mee to stay. But where ever I am, I shall esteeme it as a duty to ymprove all occations to manifest myself, my lord,

Your excellencye's most faithfull and most humble servant,

Jo Bridges

180. From Henry Markham, Westminster, 10 March 1657, 821, fos 328–329.

May it please your excellencie,

I did formerly, by other hands, make my humble excuse that I have not yett left this place in order to your further service at Dublin. I have kept my horses five weekes in London still in hopes to have come away, but my wive's weakness hath detayned mee, and indeed yet shee is very weake and her phisitians advise her to try a litle fresh aire before shee undertake a greater jorney, soe as I hope your lordship will pardon mee that I doe not yett attend you. Mr Gookin informes mee that his Highness hath commanded both our stay, and that his Highness will signifie his pleasure to your lordship and the councill. However, I am willing to serve you anywhere, and submitt that to your judgement as you shall appointe. I am, my lord,

Your excellencie's very faithfull and humble servant,

H Markham

181. From Anthony Morgan, London, 10 March 1657, 821, fos 330–331.

May it please your excellency,

I am sorry my wife can comment no better upon my letters. Your lordship made a better guess when you thought my greife melancholly, and if I could give you any reason for it, it were not truly soe.

Nothing hath this week fallen under my observation which I thinke worth your knowledge. All is smooth and faire and looks towards

[113] Although thirty MPs were returned for Irish seats to the second Protectorate parliament, around half a dozen of them – mainly serving officers holding key posts – had been chosen by Henry Cromwell to remain in Ireland on active duty (*TSP*, V, pp. 398–399, 424, 443).

settlement, one party in the house having thrown down the cudgells. I have one earnest sute to your lordship, that you will be pleased to make my reverend good frend, Dr Harison, beleive that I doe not love or honor him the less because I doe not write to him. What I write to others is as if to him, and I hope hee'l abate me the formality. Pray, my lord, excuse this sauciness and thinke the esteem I have of his frendship makes me use my best interest to preserve it. I remain,

Your excellency's most faithfull and most obedient servant,

Ant Morgan

Alderman Tighe[114] is afraid wee shall be boxed out of our farmes where our stocks are in our absence, and, because he could not make me beleive it, desires me to write his fears and address his prayers to your lordship for protection.

182. From Walter Waller,[115] London, 10 March 1657, 821, fos 332–333.

Letter of courtesy, expressing his respect for Henry Cromwell and desire to serve him.

183. From John Reynolds, London, 11 March 1657, 821, fos 334–335.

Letter of recommendation on behalf of Mr Burgh, the husband of the bearer, an unnamed kinswoman of Reynolds, seeking an office and encouragement in Ireland for Burgh, who practised law and who also had Whitelocke's support.

184. From William Moore, aboard the *Plain Dealing*, latitude 1: 48, 11 March 1657, 821, fos 336–337.

May it please your excellency,

It hath pleased the Lord to blesse us with fayre weather since our seting to sea. Since the first day untill this afternoone wee have had the winde westerly, but now wee[116] in hopes that the winde will continew fayre.

[114] Richard Tighe, parliamentarian politician, merchant and alderman of Dublin, and its mayor in 1655–1656. A firm supporter of the parliamentary cause in Ireland, to which he had lent money, and of Henry Cromwell's regime, he represented Dublin town in the second Protectorate parliament. He was excluded at the start of the session, but Henry Cromwell's protests quickly led to a change of heart and Tighe had taken his seat by late September 1656 (*TSP*, V, pp. 477–478).

[115] Parliamentarian politician and son of Sir Hardress Waller; he sat for Limerick and Kilmallock in the second Protectorate parliament.

[116] Word – probably 'are' – apparently omitted.

At my comeing from Kinsale, when we wer reddy to set sayle, I sent our martiall for the 3 prisoners, which had runne from theyr cullers and wer apprehended, with direction to returne in an hower. But upon the master's protestation that if wee stayd soe long for them wee should loose the tyde and probably our passage, wee set sayle and left him beehinde. I humbly beg your excellency's favour towarde him in provideing for him untill he can come to us.

Ther is one sargentt Austen, who the cheurgiane judge unfitt to goe the voyage, who I have returned by captain Hadgesse. He is a stowte soldier and was ever very vigilent, carefull and industriouse in his place. I doe humbly beg your excellency's favour towards him.

Some parte of the bread which was baked in Kinsale, which could not bee put in the bread roome, was stawed in the hauld, and by the commissioners the owners wer to spend the same and to deliver the like quantity of theyr owne bread when they cam to Jamaca. The bread hath bin delivered out to us, and wee finde it allreddy mouldy in the inside. The seamen say that it was of the same sorte which was put into the bread roome, and if soe it will not only bee spoyled beefore our comeing to Jamaca, but it will spoyle the other bread which is sownd and was taken out of the other shipp. I have shewed of the bread to captain Hadgesse who can further informe your excellency thereof.

I did accoumpt it my duty to acquainte your excellency heere with. I shall ever bee a supplycant unto the Lord for your excellency's happynesse and as in duety bounde shall ever remayne, my lord,

Your excellency's most obliged, humble servant,

Wm Moore

185. From George Dillon, 13 March 1657, 821, fos 338–339.

May it please your excellency,

I formerly made bold to acquaint your lordships how my lord Broghill's troope was put by there lands in the county of Limbrick, and since had there lott by order in the county of Kerry and the barrony of Glannarough,[117] which wee are now possest of and have subdevided and disposed of it to our severall uses. Since which tim, I understand that major Ormesby[118] and sum others of the lord Coot's devition are indeavouring to disposess us, which will bee the utter undoeing of the officers and souldiers of the troope, who humbly

[117] Probably Glanarough, an alternative name for the townlands of Glenera in the Bere peninsula, County Kerry.

[118] Robert Ormsby, parliamentarian officer, was major in Sir Charles Coote's horse regiment in Ireland.

desire your lordships would bee pleased to take notis of the injourey dun us. And what rightfull favour may bee dun herein, wee beeseech your lordships to afford it to the troop and to,

Your lordship's most humble servant,

George Dillon

186. From James Berry, Westminster, 14 March 1657, 821, fos 340–341.

Letter of request, on behalf of his good friend Mr Eddowes, who had been treated unjustly in respect of an estate he had bought in Ireland.

187. From Alexander Brayfield[119] to Thomas Herbert, Athlone, 14 March 1657, 821, fos 342–343.

Sir,

I have here inclosed sent you three letters which were sent to me from cornett Thomson, together with the man with whome they were found, who is here in prison. I desire, after you have read them, to sheow them unto my lord and to lett me have his lordship's further pleasure what shall be don with prisoner. Of the letters he will not confess anithing, onely they were given unto him by a poore woman to deliver as directed where he was to goe at his cominge out of Dublin. If I be not in the begininge of Aprill in the barroni of Carberri[120] to sett my land, I shall be a great sufferer. That I may not loose the oppertuniti I humbli intreat the favour that you would gett me leave from my lord. Att present not anythinge further to trouble you with, I remaine, sir,

Yours humbly to serve,

Alex Brafield

As I understand som of those lands that I put in for in barroni of Ballrederri were taken by collonel Barrow. I prai if you can speake with him and perswade him out of it and what chardges he hath beene att for improvements if you thinke good, I will make him satisfaction.

[119] Parliamentarian officer, who went to Ireland in 1649 in Hewson's horse regiment. By the early 1650s, he was lieutenant-colonel of Axtell's foot regiment and, by 1657, was lieutenant-colonel in Henry Cromwell's foot regiment. Henry Cromwell distrusted him, viewing him as a religious radical and an ally of Hewson and his group in stirring up disaffection within the army. Later in 1657 – to the Protector's dismay and ignoring other intercessions on his behalf – Henry had him court martialled and cashiered, condemning him as a 'busie and a turbulent person' and a promoter of 'seditious papers' and for keeping 'correspondence with all others of the like temper' (*TSP*, VI, pp. 505, 526–527, 552, 563–564, 568–569, 599; Abbott, IV, pp. 646–647).

[120] There were several baronies of Carbury (and alternative spellings) in Ireland: in County Kildare, County Sligo, and elsewhere.

188. From Daniel Redman, Kilkenny, 15 March 1657, 821, fos 344–345.

May itt please your excellencie,

Captain Frankes and myselfe weare att Watterford, acordeing to your order, wheare theare mett aboute 100 Quakers and more, besides the parties off them that weare goeing thither, being ten or twelve in a companie, which I ordered our parties off horse and foote that weare aboute thre miles from the towne, on each side the watter, to turne backe againe, which otherwise would, I judge, have increased their number to above 200. There was nott any disturbance att all, onely they mett all in a greate barne wheare justice Cooke,[121] colonel Leigh and severall others spent att least two houres indeavoring to convince them off theire follyes, but too litle purpose. They all dispersed the next day, theire meeteing being onely to take leave off Humphrey Nowtton,[122] theire cheife champion, who was returneing for England; and some reportes there weare that one off theire number was to be sent to Tuarky.[123] Cornett Cooke was very jealous amongst them to defend theire opinions. Our partie off horse and foote weare beateing off boggs and woods and onely suposed to be akcedentally there. I advised colonel Leigh nott to permitt any more such consederable numbers, either off them or any off their adherents, to meete within that cytty. Mr Allen, Mr Vernon[124] and Mr Dayly[125] went to Waterford the day befor this meeteing, but did nott stirr out all that day. Itt was reported both heare and there that my goeing was onely to watch them. They returne by Wexford and soe to Dubline. I have nothing more to troubl your lordshipp with, onely humbly to begg your remembrance of Mr Parrie. I heare Mr Carey is either deade

[121] John Cook/Cooke, parliamentarian lawyer and judge and deemed a regicide, was first connected with Ireland in the 1630s, practising law in Dublin. From the mid-1640s he was employed by the Long Parliament as the state's representative in various legal cases, most notably as chief prosecutor at the trial of Charles I. Later in 1649, he accompanied Oliver Cromwell to Ireland and became an influential and reformist chief justice of Munster. In 1655, he declined a post in the newly restored four courts and, although he continued to sit in Ireland for a time, he returned to England later in 1657.

[122] Humphrey Norton, Quaker missionary, was briefly imprisoned in northern England in 1655. After a period in London, he crossed to Ireland by the summer of 1656 and spent the next few months touring the country, preaching, and seeking converts. In the face of increasing official harassment in Ireland, he returned to England in the spring of 1657 and sailed for New England on 1 June.

[123] Uncertain reading of a poorly formed word.

[124] That is, William Allen and John Vernon, formerly parliamentarian officers, who had resigned from the army towards the end of 1656. In April 1657, Henry Cromwell reported to Thurloe that Allen, Vernon, and their supporters were holding meetings and stirring up trouble in Ireland, though he felt it was still better they were in Ireland than in England at that time (*TSP*, VI, pp. 222–223).

[125] In a letter of December 1656, Henry Cromwell referred to meeting a Mr Doyley, a Baptist, who had been sent from Allen, Vernon, Barrow, and Axtell to arrange the meeting with Henry Cromwell at which they offered their resignations (*TSP*, V, pp. 670–672).

or verry neare dieing. And your lordshipp was pleased to tell me that you would endeavour to helpe Mr Parrie to that imployment, which I begg your lordshipps to remember; and alsoe your pardon for this troubl, remaineing,

Your excillencie's faithfull, humble servant,

Dan Redman

189. From Philip Skippon, Mews, London, 16 March 1657, 821, fos 346–347.

May it please your excellency,

This worthy gentleman, my very loving friend (judge advocate Whalley),[126] being willing at my request to put himselfe to the trouble of bringing a Turkish semiter from mee to be presented unto you, upon noe other accompt but to testify the very great heart affectionate service that I owe unto you; be pleased favourably to accept thereof, though neither the giver nor the guift be worthy of soe much.

Not to flatter but to encourage you, I rejoice, with thankfullnes to the Lord, for what I and other good men heare your excellency labours after, for the publique safety, peace and comfort of honest men; and it is, and shall be through the grace of God, my daily earnest prayer that Hee would please still to stand by you, to be your guide and strength, and good successe is soe reall a worthy way.

I have of late bin very weake by reason of a very sudden and sore visitation my God pleased (though in much mercy) to lay upon mee, that I have not bin abroad about any publique businesse in a moneth's time; and am in noe very good condition at present to indite or write unto your excellency, which I humbly pray you to excuse.[127] And further to accept of the tender of my very humble and hearty service to your right honourable lady; and, if I durst presume, my kind love to Mr Brewster. And soe the Lord God, our heavenly Father, watch over you and yours allwayes, and in all thinges for good, which is the very humble and earnest prayer of,

Your excellencye's most humble and faithfull servant,

Ph Skippon

[126] Henry Whalley, parliamentarian judge and administrator, and the younger brother of the parliamentarian officer and major-general Edward Whalley. During the 1650s, his legal career focused on Scotland, initially as a judge in the Scottish admiralty court and then as judge advocate of the army in Scotland. He was currently in London sitting for a Scottish seat in the second Protectorate parliament. In November 1656 he had petitioned for confirmation of a grant of land in Ireland (*CSPI*, pp. 614–615).

[127] Skippon's attendance at council meetings declined very markedly during the first half of 1657: he was present at just five meetings between January and June inclusive, and was entirely absent from 12 February to 26 May.

190. From Charles Fleetwood, London, 17 March 1657, 821, fos 348–349.

Thes 2 last posts have not com, I suppose by reason of contrary winds. His Highnes hath latly received a letter from lieutenant-generall Brayn of his safe arivall at Jameicah with his men, and his very well liking of that island, and hopes of making good improvement to publicke advantage. Severall planters are gon and going; thos from Meins setled ther; divers allso intending from Barbadoes and this nation, ther being great incouragment to plantations. The Lord may yet smile upon that poore place and give a return to thos prayers and supplications which have bine put up for that design, which I trust hath more in the bowells of it then what the Lord hath by any vissible demonstration as yet borne a whitnes unto. But I am perswaded the Lord hath a designe of great glory against that state, and after all our humblings if we can but by faith live more upon Him, we shall see all our clowdings to make way for the more eminent appearances of Himselfe. The parliament is still going on in the busynes of the settlement. The Lord doth quicken up a spirit of prayer, which is a good pledg of mercy, and will, I hope, prove a strengthening unto his Highnes in what may concern him in this buysnes. The order of councell concerning your armes hath not that effect as it will by reason of the want which is therof in the stores, but I hope that will be shortly supplyed. We are and shall be in wants by reason of the long delay of the monyes intended to be raysed by parliment. The busynes which the howse is now upon takes up so much of time that all other affayres are retarded. One weeke longer will probably give some periodde as to give way for other buysnes, and then I hope what concerns Ireland will have its dispatch. Ther are some endeavors to engage the state of Venice to transport some of the Irish for their service, which I presume will be very wellcom to you, but it is very uncerteine and we have bine so many times disapoynted that I can give credit to nothing till don. The French have no minde to any of them, they being so well affected to the Spanyard and Charles Stuart. I shall not further adde then with our humble services to your deare lady, I am,

Your most affectionate brother.

191. From William Jephson, London, 17 March 1657, 821, fos 350–351.

My deare lord,

Wee have recyv'd noe letters out of Ireland since yesterday was fortnight, which wee much wonder at; for allthough the wind hath hung much easterlye, yett the weather here hath beene soe fayre and calme, as it hath not seemed to us impossible for the post barque to make a passadge. Wee now sit very close, both morning and afternoone, upon the remonstrance, in hope to finish it, eyther this weeke or the beginning of the next; for there is now very little opposition, neyther Lambert, 504. or 403.[128] having appear'd this fortnight; and Desborough, 3005., his brother commissioner of England,[129] and many of the officers of the armye beeing now for it. There came lately (as I am inform'd by 1558., but tis known to very few) to 441. his hands, a letter from 700. to a friend of his in Ireland, highly extolling Lambert, 505., 402. etc of that opinion, and on the contrarye debasing 404., 502., 1557., 2010., and the rest of that judgment as persons not faythfull to the interest of the good people, and giving greate incouradgments to 1224. to hold fast to his principles, and much stuff to that purpose. Hereupon Fleetwood was sent for and 700., and the letter shew'd to them both. Fleetwood was extreamly out of countenance; 700. lept and made greate protestations of better behaviour, but yett flew out in the parliament the next day as much as ever. This makes well for 3013. whom yett 1224. ceases not to maligne.[130] There was latelye a proposition made by some of the chiefe of them to sell 3002.;[131] that is to say that if Fleetwood might bee sent into Ireland, they would all submitt to whatsoever hee would commaund, but I hope the old saying is remembred: The divell was sicke and etc.[132] Wee are now gone through the remonstrance (excepting that of kingship layd by untill last by consent) unto the beginning of the tenth article concerning religion, which, though the difficult point, yett I ghuesse by the beginning of a debate wee had upon it this afternoone, that wee shall get well and quickly thorough it. The blanke in the 7th article (for I take it for graunted your lordship hath a copy sent you), for the summe of the revenue to bee settled, is fil'd up with 13 hundred thousand pounds, whereof one million for maintenance of the navy

[128] Final figure heavily amended. Either 504 or 403 probably stands for Sydenham, another prominent opponent who had largely withdrawn from the fray by this stage.

[129] So 3005 and his unnamed colleague are probably the two commissioners of the great seal, John Lisle and Nathaniel Fiennes.

[130] Alas, most of the encoded protagonists in this section cannot now be identified with any certainty, though the overall drift of the passage is fairly clear – that a colleague of Jephson had recently informed him of an inflammatory letter sent by 700 (who was a sitting MP) to Ireland, praising key members of the anti-kingship/republican group and condemning the supporters of the new constitution as working against the people's interests, whereupon Fleetwood and (his ally or agent?) 700 were sent for (by whom is not clear) and confronted, though promises of better behaviour proved worthless and divisions and personal animosities were continuing.

[131] Unknown.

[132] 'The devil was sick, the devil a saint would be; the devil was well, the devil a saint was he' was an early modern proverb warning that promises and good intentions made in times of adversity might not be kept once the adversity had passed.

and army, and £300,000 for support of the government. With one part of that vote, I confesse, your servant was not well satisfyed, as not liking the parliament should declare soe much as the supposition of the perpetuitye of an army here, though I can not see to the end of its necessarye use. I shall not give your lordship any farther trouble at present, fearing lest I may grow burthensome by my constant tedious letters, but humbly begg pardon for this, and remaine, my lord,

Your most affectionate and humble servant,

Wm Jephson

192. From Benjamin Worsley,[133] London, 17 March 1657, 821, fos 352–353.

May it please your excellency,

Considering I had no expresse leave from your excellency to stay heere so long as I have done, I have the lesse reason to appeare before your lordship with any confidence; and the rather because I am convinced that no reason of my owne ought to be allowed for reason, in this case, as long as I am a person under comand; and this being case (my lord), I shall not presume to produce any excuses to your excellency, or to extenuate my owne blame, but rather to submitt myselfe, with that duty which doth become me, to your lordship's and the councell's pardon.

The things which did indeed, somewhat plausibly, perswade me into this error were, that I apprehended, without some settlement or other were made heere of the interest of the adventurers and souldiors, I should be able to propound very litle settlement to myselfe, or at least very litle understanding in the nature of my service when I returned backe to my duty there. That there would be such a settlement suddenly made, I had not only the incouragement of many, whose indeavours for it I conceived to be sufficiently ingaged by their owne interest, but some inducement further to beleeve it, in regard that I saw severall acts were prepared and actually given into the house in order to it. Beside which (my lord) observing very little union betweene the adventurers and souldiors in this busynesse and not much agreement even among the adventurers themselves, the interest of those who were

[133] Parliamentarian administrator and entrepreneur, he was in Ireland in the early and mid-1640s, working as physician to the army there and scheming to improve saltpetre production. After a spell on the continent he returned first to England, advising the Rump on its commercial policies, and then to Ireland, as secretary to the Irish commissioners and commissioner general for the revenue. In 1653, he became surveyor general for forfeited estates in Ireland but, although he retained that post until 1658, by the mid-1650s he found himself eclipsed by Petty and his survey.

gott into their land being one thing, and the interest of such who were deficient being another, and being imployed, by the councell's order heere, in many meetings with the adventurers, I was somewhat the more prompted to stay to see the yssue of this busynesse. Especially in regard it was the opinion of some that when so many interests should appeare to thwart one another in the house, a right and impartiall information of things would not then be unseasonable. It was also (my lord) not without ground beleeved, that some of those different interests might possibly finde out expedients to accomodate each other, so that the comonwealth's interest were excluded. All which things (my lord) I take the boldnesse to alleadge, not as any sufficient plea for my stay, but rather ingenuusly to lett your excellency see my weakenesse.

This neverthelesse I have really and truly to pleade (my lord), that I have not beene moved to stay heere out of any base or covetuous ends. Upon the truth of which, as also, that I have not at any time beene hasty to grow rich, or (since my first being entertained into publick service) cunningly sought to make advantages to myselfe by my imployment (beyond what was my just due and right), and upon the cleare consciousnesse I have to myselfe that in this no man can reproach me. I am bold, though I cannot any way challenge a merritt to myselfe, humbly to preferre a request to your lordship, and which I hope your excellency will not judge any impudence in me. I had, my lord, about two yeare and halfe since a custodium granted me, by the councell, of the estate of one Gerard Fitz-Gyrald,[134] a rebell in the Queene's county, which estate was wholly waste and without any tennant save a very few cabbins of Irish. The councell being then pleased further to give me an expectation that, in regard the said estate was not land of inheritance but only a forfeyted lease of twenty odd yeares still to come (the right of inheritance being in the earle of Kyldare),[135] they would write in my behalfe to his Highnesse that I might have leave to buy or compound for the said lease with the comonwealth. My lord, I did upon this hope enter upon the land and turne off those Irish that were upon it, and did with a friend putt in a plough and some litle stocke upon it, but have hitherto beene so farre from making any benefitt of it, that what with the deceitfullnesse of some bailiffs that were intrusted, and what with other casualtyes, we are both, my lord, in truth hitherto loosers by it. Fearing therfore, my lord, that this may be canted[136] away from me, to my yet greater

[134] Son of an illegitimate son of the Earl of Kildare, as an active supporter of the Catholic rebellion his estates had been forfeited.

[135] The earldom then rested with George Fitzgerald as sixteenth earl (*CSPI*, pp. 244, 289).

[136] Canted: sold by auction.

dammage, I could not but take the courage to addresse myselfe to your excellency in it, as hoping that by your lordship's intermediation with the councell, I might eyther have leave from their lordships (or be recomended hither) to compound for it at such rates as shall be thought fitt by your excellency and their lordships. Or if this were not sutable to your excellencye's and their lordships' pleasure, yet that at least I might, by your excellency's favor, have an order to continue tennant in it for senven[137] yeares at the rent I now pay. I obleiging myselfe to bestow within that time so much in buylding and other improvement, as your lordship and the councell shall thinke fitt to appoynt me.

My lord, I shall crave your excellency's leave to add that I am the more animated, and indeed constreyned to presse this request to your lordship, because there is hitherto no manner of settlement made for me; and that if your lordship, therefore, should please in this to declyne my humble suyt, I have really very litle, my lord, that I can propound to myselfe in Ireland, having hitherto, as I declared before to your lordship, made no advantages to myselfe during all the time of my service there.

And though I shall presume to wayte heere for your excellency's answer to this, my petition, yet I shall no sooner receive your commands for my returne, but all other things sett aside, I shall forthwith comport myselfe to that duty which doth become, my lord,

Your excellencye's humble servant,

B Worsley

193. From Charles Fleetwood, London, 19 March 1657, 821, fos 354–355.

Letter of recommendation on behalf of the bearer, captain Peter Whitty, relating to lands he claimed in Ireland; Protector and council were supporting his claim.

194. From John Reynolds, London, 19 March 1657, 821, fos 356–357.

May it please your excellency,

I am not yet enabled to present unto your lordshipp a full account of the publique settlement, and therefore Ireland is still in arreare with its 4 bills.[138] The parliament goes on verry unanimously, having past the 9 first articles, and entred this day upon the 10th, which relateth

[137] Apparently a slip for 'seven'.

[138] At least four public bills relating to Ireland – removing wardships and tenures in Ireland, uniting Ireland with England, attainting Irish rebels, and settling Irish adventurers – had been introduced or were pending.

to the religion to be asserted in these nations. The succeeding two will have lesse opposition, whereof the one confirmes the sales and dispositions of lands, and the other disableth cavaleires to beare office and imposeth a fine annuall upon such as will not abjure Charles Stuart. It is now 3 weekes since any letters came from Ireland, and therefore I have the lesse to write unto your lordshipp, but I can assure your lordshipp of some late combinations detected, and seasonably prevented, whereof I suppose your excellency will receive an account by a secret hand, how farre your lordshipp was (excepting one who will alwayes judge himselfe honoured in the meanest share of difficultyes wherein your lordshipp is involved) most aimed at in some late councells. For my owne part, whether I bee continued neere your lordshipp or otherwise disposed, I shall hope not to diminish my true loyalty to his Highnes, and affections to his person redoubled upon your lordshipp. I have proposed your lordship's company to be sent over, and have hastned lieutenant-colonel Floure,[139] and shall hope to follow after. If not, I do rely upon your lordshipp's undeserved freindship, and the gracious favour of his Highnes, that I bee not so commanded as may give occasion to any to conceive that I am removed to gratify any, or that I am as little in the ey of others, as I desire to be in mine owne. This, I suppose, is to be unfolded by your lordship's present and former packet. I, therefore, humbly conclude and remaine, my lord,

Your excellencye's most humble and faithfull servaunt,

J Reynolds

195. From Thomas Rawlins,[140] Belturbet, [County Cavan], 21 March 1657, 821, fos 358–359.

May it please your excellency,

There is parte of the earthworke of the forte of this towne[141] fallen, and more is like to fall if timely care be not taken for the makeing up that already down and repairing that ready to fall. If it be speedily done it will not cost much, which I humbly offer to your excellency's

[139] Henry Flower, parliamentarian officer, first shows up in 1647 in Thomas Rainborowe's New Model foot regiment. He went to Ireland in 1649 in Oliver Cromwell's foot regiment and by 1652 was lieutenant-colonel of Fleetwood's foot regiment.

[140] Parliamentarian officer, who campaigned in England and Scotland from the mid-1640s in the New Model horse regiment commanded by Robert Pye and then by Matthew Tomlinson. Sometime in the early 1650s he moved to Ireland and served both as major in an unidentified horse regiment and as a commissioner for setting out lands in County Kilkenny.

[141] Belturbet, on the River Erne in County Cavan.

consideration, that you may bee pleased to give such order therein as you shall thinke meete, and am,

Your excellency's most obedient and faithfull servante,

T Rawlins

196. From Gualter Frost,[142] Whitehall, 23 March 1657, 821, fos 360–361.

Letter of thanks for Henry Cromwell's favour in appointing his brother John Frost to be deputy clerk of the council in Ireland.

197. From William Webb, Carrickfergus, 23 March 1657, 821, fos 362–363.

May it please your excellency,

This morneing I acquainted captain Richard Down, deputy governor here, that your excellencys have comanded mee to vew and to give orders for the finishing the cittadells of London Derry and Colraine, and the repaireing of the castle of Carrickfargus. I shewed the said captain your excellency's and the councell's warrant (derected unto Mr Samuell Hill, receivor of his Highness' revenue at London-Derry) for 500 pound, to bee by him issued out, for and towards the finishing and repaireing the said garrissons. After the said captain had read the said warrant, before officers hee said unto mee that he would not suffer mee to see, nor to goe in to, the castle of Carickfergus untill hee had your excellency's order to that purpose, which I leave to your excellency's considerration. By his so doeing my labour is lost in comeing hither. I will hasten with all speed unto the other garrisons, where I hope that I shall not find officers that will leape over a block and stumble at a straw. I am,

Your excellency's most humble servant to command,

Wm Webb

198. From John Bridges, 24 March 1657, 821, fos 364–365.

May it please your lordshipp,

I was somewhat confident in the morning, that wee should have laid the topp stone of that greate and noble structure wee have beene soe longe in framinge before this tyme, but wee have not beene able to bringe it to an yssue, notwithstanding wee spent the fore and

[142] Parliamentarian administrator and bureaucrat, throughout the 1650s he served a succession of executive councils, most notably the Protectoral council, in various administrative capacities, including clerk and treasurer of council contingencies.

afternoone uppon the debate of the tytle, which is the first article of the remonstrance, all the rest being finisht on Friday last.[143] The major-generalls and theire party oppose it vehemently, but I doubt not the yssue. Itt is whispered that the lord deputy does ymportunately presse to returne to ________[144]; it will not be assented to, but________[145] is to bee lord lieutenant soe soone as this businesse is finisht. If there bee truth in this I doubt not but your lordshipp will receave it from some better hand, yet I have good reason to beleive it. I feare the rest will not stay the sealing of my letters. My lord,

Your lordshipp's most humble and most faithfull servant,

J Bridges

199. From Charles Fleetwood, London, 24 March 1657, 822, fos 1–2.

Deare brother,

I have bine so late at the howse that I canot wright anything of satisfaction as to any buysnes. The howse hath bine all this day upon that part which concerns kingshippe; a great division ther is about it. Tomorrow will probably determine it and that in the affirmative, which will be a sadde greife to the hearts of good people whose hopes are only in his Highnes. Ther being a designe for which 6,000 men have bine and are to be raysed,[146] of which I presume you have hade some hints from other hands. Thes men's raysing hath occasiond a delay in sending your armes, but I have agayne moved the counsell, and, after this present service is answerd, they have orderd the sending your armes. My haste must pleade the excuse of,

Your most affectionate brother and servant,

Charles Fleetwood

200. From John Reynolds, London, 24 March 1657, 822, fos 3–4.

May it please your excellency,

I received the honour of 2 letters from your lordship's owne hand, of the 4 and 11th instant. In the former your lordshipp was pleased to mention that of your castle[147] which was wholy left to your lordshipp long since; in the latter your lordshipp mentions the quiet frame of Ireland, which causeth his Highness joy and the nation's wonder.

[143] 20 March.

[144] Line drawn in letter where a word – perhaps 'Ireland' – has been deliberately omitted.

[145] Line drawn in letter where a word or words – perhaps 'Henry Cromwell' or possibly 'Fleetwood' (albeit required to continue to act in absentia) – have been deliberately omitted.

[146] For the projected Anglo-French campaign in Flanders.

[147] Portumna.

I could equalise the expressions of the most moderne and auncient flatterers, yet relate the truth of those good reports, which are generally in this nation concerning your lordship's carriage in that land. I am satisfyed many a hearty prayer is put up for you and yours by such as have not the happines of knowing you. This day hath beene spent in a pitcht battell, wherein the postponed clause of the first article, viz: the title and office of king, was debated; nine of a side tooke up morning and afternoone; the names of these worthyes I esteeme too much to insert: the first was lord commissioner Lisle, answered by general Deisborough, replied upon by lords Broghill and Whitelocke. The major-generalls are much averse; onely honest Whaley and Goffe were moderate opposers, almost indifferent; tomorrow will surely end the debate. I conjecture about 60 will dissent and no more.[148] The busines of the mint will be speedily dispatched; the Secretary hath taken it wholy upon himselfe.[149] I hope one or two bills will be the guerdon[150] of your servaunts heere, whose diligence is taken notice of, and also unanimity. Except two persons, all those of Ireland are of one mind. Sir Paule Davis is not yet come in, he hath beene delaied at the councell, but will make his entrance tomorrow.[151] I hope ere long to attend your lordshipp, and if the lord Broghill be in earnest he will visit Ireland this summer, but I beleive his lordshipp will like England for a chaunge, although Scotland be inferiour to Ireland. He hath carried things verry worthily.

Your excellencye's humblest servaunt,

J Reynolds

201. From George Monck, Dalkeith, 25 March 1657, 822, fos 5–6.

May itt please your excellencie,

I received your letter of the 17th of March for which I returne your excellencie most humble thankes; and if your excellencie have att any time any commands to lay uppon mee, if you please to send your letters to the governor of Carickfergus and to direct him to send them to the governor of Ayre – there are posts setled between Ayre and

[148] When the house formally divided, 62 voted against and 123 for.

[149] Henry Cromwell had long been pressing for power to establish a mint in Ireland, in part to make good the shortage of coins in Ireland, in part to begin the process of removing the debased, foreign, and adulterated coinage that circulated there (*TSP*, IV, pp. 307–308, 711–712; VI, pp. 96, 650; Dunlop, pp. 557, 592–594, 657, 665).

[150] Guerdon: a reward or recompense.

[151] Irish politician, from an established Protestant family in Ireland, he was elected to the second Protectorate as MP for Counties Kildare and Wicklow in a by-election but – much to Henry Cromwell's annoyance – was then excluded from parliament by the Protectoral council (*TSP*, VI, p. 71).

this – which letters will come with speede att any time unto mee. I hope by the blessing of God I shall indeavour to keepe all thinges quiett in this country, and I prayse God wee have noe unquiett spiritts as yett amongst us, and I hope that thinges will continue soe. I returne your excellencie and the rest of the councill most humble thankes for your care of my businesse I made bold to recommend to you concerning some lands I came short for my arreares, and if I may bee able to doe your excellencie any service you shall finde noe freind you have in the world more ready to serve you then myselfe. I have one thinge more to trouble your excellencie withall, which is, I understand by a gentleman I imployed to looke after my lands in Ireland, that there is a passage betweene Wexford and my land of Balytramon,[152] and there is a Scotchman hath hired the passage boate though hee gives butt 40s a yeare to the state for itt, and has built a key uppon the land, yett hee does soe exact uppon the tenants that belonge to my land uppon their passage to Wexford that truly I have had some quitt the land, and itt is a great discouragement to any others to take any land of mee. And if your excellencie and the councill please to doe mee that favour as that I may have the grant of the keeping the passage boate there, I should bee very well content to take soe much land short of my arreares as that will come to, being that I may give incouragement to those that may have a desire to plant uppon my land. Which favour, if your excellencie and the councill will please to grant, you will very much oblige,

Your most faithfull freind and servant,

George Monck

202. From Anthony Morgan, London, 30[153] March 1657, 822, fos 7–8.

May it please your excellency,

This day the parliament presented their petition and humble advice to his Highness. He hath taken time to consider of his answer. Captain Franklin[154] tooke his speech verbatim and is transcribing it for your excellency, but Harry Owen will have the honor to send it enclosed to Dr Gorge.

[152] Ballytramon, County Wexford, a small settlement with a castle, across the River Slanes from Wexford and south of Castlebridge.

[153] Apparently an error by Morgan, since the new constitution was presented to the Protector on 31 March.

[154] Possibly the Captain Richard Franklin who served in Ireland during the 1650s in the New Model horse regiment of Henry Ireton and then Fleetwood. Morgan was a fellow-officer in that regiment.

I perceive your lordship dares be just and regulate disorders in your army.

Wee are resolved to prepare all the coches if wee gett seasonable notice to meet them at Tiburne.

Poore Sir Paul Davis is yet in suspence, but I advised him not to complain to your excellency till he is at an issue upon the application you have already made. He thinks he shall be hurt to wound you, but though that may goe farr, yet I think twill be because he hath been hurt already. Qui facit injuriam nunquam condonat.[155] If he be qualified to sitt in parliament they may feare hee'l produce a patent to be clerke of the councell.[156] Wee have agreed for the bookes, and this weeke shall sett hands to worke to catalogue and packe them up in order to be sent for Chester. Wee have undertaken the £2,000 shall be paid before the bookes goe out of town. If the bill be sent, I shall see it be not made use of till performance of conditions. It seemes it is not thought convenient to leave such bookes here to be exchanged for others as you have already there. In this or whatsoever else your lordship shall thinke fitt to use me, I shall to my best power approve myselfe,

Your excellency's most obedient and most faithfull servant,

Ant Morgan

My wife chides me and tells me I am too saucy with your lordship, but I am nere the less fitt to be yours, for you keep groomes and footmen as well as gentlemen.

203. From John Bridges, 31 March 1657, 822, fos 11–12.

May it please your lordshipp,

On Friday night[157] last the parliament finished the greate busines, nowe named the petition of advice, having sate morning and afternoone almost the whole weeke. On Satturday a committee was appointed to acquaint his Highness that they had a businesse of very greate importance to impart to him, and to desire him to appoint a tyme and place for theire attendance. He tolde us that, in respect of our adjournement, it could not bee sooner then Tuesday, and the place appointed itselfe since noe roome in White Hall was capable of our receipt but the Banquetting Howse. Accordingly this day the speaker[158]

[155] This Latin phrase could be translated as 'let nobody condone him who does harm'.

[156] He had been clerk to the Irish privy council in the early 1630s.

[157] 27 March.

[158] Sir Thomas Widdrington, parliamentarian politician and lawyer, was an active and prominent member of the Long Parliament and the Rump, though – like his brother-in-law, Sir Thomas Fairfax – he held aloof from the regicide. He supported the Protectorate and, in 1654, was appointed a treasury commissioner and a commissioner of the great seal. With

(attended by the howse) att eleaven of the clock came thither and, after hee had animadverted uppon the severall heads of that instrument, caused Mr Schobell[159] to reade it; which done, his Highness, having first receaved it, declared the greate sense hee had of the weightines of the subject, and tolde us before hee could give an answeare hee must begg advice from heaven, and deliberate of the severall particulers with himselfe, but withall intimateing itt should not bee longe before wee should heare from him. Most of the major-generalls and that party that most violently opposed it absented themselves, yet I am informed from a good hand, that 6 of them went to his Highness the last night, and tolde him that although whilst it was in debate they opposed it, yet nowe observing a series of providence in it, they weare sattisfyed, and withall that it was his duty to accept it; not withstanding they made use of his non acceptance as a greate argument against it. I should have told your lordshipp that the debate touching the title tooke upp two whole dayes,[160] but uppon the question the affirmatives weare 123 and the negatives 62. I intend to waite for the first opportunity of taking my leave of his Highness the second tyme. I seldome come to him but hee takes occasion to complayne of your backbiters. I beseech you give mee leave to say that your lordshipp's patience and moderation hath wrought wonders, which I doubt not will be a greate encouradgment to your lordshipp to persevere in that way.

My lord, I confesse myselfe of the nomber of those that are least capable of serving you, yet I hope my honest zeale for your lordshipp's service will give mee a right to underwrite myselfe, my lord,

Your excellencye's faithfull and humble servant,

Jo Bridges

204. From Charles Fleetwood, London, 31 March 1657, 822, fos 15–16.

Deare brother,

I have received yours concerning captain Sancky.[161] I hope I neade not speake my readynes to observe any commands of yours, but really

his colleague Whitelocke he lost the commissionership of the great seal in 1655 for refusing to implement fully the chancery ordinance, but he retained office and favour under the Protector and was shortly after appointed chancellor of the county palatine of Durham. He sat for York in the first Protectorate parliament and for his native Northumberland in the second, and was appointed speaker at the start of the session.

[159] Henry Scobell, parliamentarian administrator and bureaucrat, by 1643 was an under clerk to the House of Commons and, having held other administrative posts during the 1640s, in 1649 he became clerk of the commons, a post he retained until 1659; from 1654 he also served as an assistant secretary to the Protectoral council.

[160] 24–25 March.

[161] Identification uncertain. Possibly the Captain Richard Sankey, parliamentarian officer, who served in Fleetwood's New Model horse regiment, though he reportedly left that

thos poore honest men who by your consent wer put into places in the civill judicatoryes have bine so mollested by the former officers and the places proved so unprofitable that I confesse if you aprove therof I am not free to bring in new officers till those of them allready brought in, who are truly deserving persons, are either setled or better provided for. This I presume to offer as my opinion, which if concurrent with yours, I shall offer you of them 3 or 4 names for your aprobation. I would not willingly give you any offence or exception in puting in any offensive to you, in which I hope I shall aprove myselfe carefull to doe nothing justly greivous to you. As for our affayres heare you will, I doubt not, receive a full account that the buysnes of settlement is now befor his Highnes, who, I trust, will be so directed by the Lord as to make it appeare how much it lyes upon his heart the carefull minding of the interest of the saints. It is a great tryall and I hope the measure of strength will be proportionable. Ther is one poore man, Dr Harding,[162] who hath longe bin in the state's service, and it seemes is very poore. He hath a good gift of preaching. I showld wish and intreat he might have maintenance to preach in som places wheare ther is a want. I confesse I have known him allmost from my being a child, and if som subsistance one way or other might be allowed him, I canot think it will otherwise be then a very charitable action. I have heard him somtimes preach very well, and if he would give up himself to preaching I hope he may be an instrument of good. I have not hade a line from him since I cam into England, but I confesse I have a respect for him, hoping in the maine he is one the Lord loves. We are preparing for the expedition for which thes new men are raysed. If the Lord gives His blessing it will prove a choyce mercy. Excuse my hast, who am,

Your most affectionate brother, servant,
Charles Fleetwood

205. From Henry Ingoldsby, Limerick, 31 March 1657, 822, fos 17–18.

My lord,

Heeringe that captain Holmes, a discontented Quaker, has petition'd your lordship and the councell against mee for my actings

regiment in the early 1650s; or possibly the captain Henry Sankey who was employed by parliamentary commanders in Ireland in the early 1650s to negotiate with the native Irish and who, in 1652, was tried for, but acquitted of, the murder of an Irishman.

[162] Possibly the John Harding, pre-war fellow and vice-provost of Trinity College, Dublin, who, by 1653, was a Baptist and who both preached and debated his beliefs in Cork. In 1654–1655, during Fleetwood's governance of Ireland, he was employed on several government committees, including those seeking concealed church lands and setting out procedures for appointing ministers to towns.

towards him and the rest off that fraternity (that once gave to dandgerouse a disturbance to this place), I thought itt my duty for your lordship's satisfaction and my owne vindication to give this ensueinge account off my procedings with those wild, yett subtill and designeinge generation off people.

For the Quakers that are the growth off the towne – vipers bred in our bosomes – they have the liberty quietly to meete amonge themselvs without disturbance, but iff any strandgers crowd in with them and gett crowdes about them, then I thinke myselfe concerned in order to the security off the place to turne the disturbers out off itt, beinge:

1. To answeare the safety off the place with the hazard off my life, which I would not undertake should I not have the liberty to secure the garrison from hudles off discontend spiritts.

2. For those that are strandge Quakers that come from incognita terra,[163] (since I have bin back'd by the councell's authority, which I divulge not) as soone as they come in att one gate I send them out att an other, neaver letting them rest a minute in the garrison after I know off them till they are convayd out off the lybertyse of Lymbr. Some have come late to prevent that course, but I have venturd them in the darke rather then fayle, by which meanes wee are very quiett and are troubled with them very seldome.

3. A proclamation is put out by mee that those inhabitants that entertayne strandge Quakers or Irish papists a night in theire houses with out first acquaynteinge the present governor thearewith shall be turn'd, they and theire familyse, out off the garrison.

4. Those souldiers that weare Quakers, I chasheird them by a court martiall out off the army, not barely for beinge Quakers but for theire disobedience to theire officers, and things off that nature, which has cur'd more then a hundred off that aguish distemper they ware inclinginge to.

5. Those that abus'd the ministers and disturb'd the congregations (before I had notice off them from your councell) I imprison'd for a time, and then sent them from whence they came.

6. A sarjeant, that was chasheird the army about Waterford for abuseinge the cuntry, gave mee such base languadge in a letter, beinge a Quaker, that I was forc'd to beate him into better manners; another fellow I servd soe that brought mee base letters, which has given mee freedome from that trouble ever since.

7ly. On a sabbath day, when I was att sermon, the officer off the guard acquaynteinge mee that att captain Holmese's house theare was a greate number off strandgers and discontented persons togeather, I gave him an order under my hand to goe into the house and see what

[163] This Latin phrase could be translated as 'an unknown land'.

the matter was, and iff that hee found any strandge Quakers theare that hee should secure them on the guard till further orders from mee; but when the officer off the guard came with my order to see the occation off such a meetinge in the garrison, the dore was kept against him, till hee broake itt up with his guard. Phelps, an inhabitant off this towne, kept the dore shutt, and for his offence I clap'd him up in the martiall's for 24 howers or lesse. Leiutenant Waller was amongst that company that resisted the guard, and thow hee pleaded his excuse, yett I thought convenient to suspend him from his imployment for a while to make him sencible off his folly. This is a passadge that fell out 3 monthes agoe, butt beinge assurd that a complaynt is made against mee about itt, I have given this account, as likewise off that off the sarjeant Quaker that I banged for giveinge mee base languadge. The cheife Quakers that wee have inhabitants off this towne are captain Holmes, Mr Phelps and Mr Peirce, that are starke mad att mee that I give not all Quakers, strandgers as well as others, liberty to meete in this garrison, which shall neaver bee suffered whilst I have to doe with itt, since I know them to well to trust them. My thinks iff theire devotion weare soe hott for that which I dare not call a religion, the cuntry att lardge should serve there turne to bee in for the exercise off itt, but noe place will please them but this.

8ly. Perhaps tis chardg'd as a crime against mee for makeing Peirce's wife, a Quaker, (in the absence off her husband) pay 20s for entertayneinge a strandge Quaker in her house a night without giveinge notice, contrary to the proclamation. The money was given to the poore.

My lord, I know not any thinge that I have done that I have not heere acquaynted your lordshipp with. Iff they are faults I have told them you all, but that your lordship has a better judgement then to beeleive them to bee soe is the opinion off, my lord,

Your excellency'se most obleidged, most faythfull, humble servant,
H Ingoldsby

206. From William Jephson, London, 31 March 1657, 822, fos 19–20.

My deare lord,

Though I had the honour the last weeke to receyve two letters from your lordship, yett I was soe unfortunate as to want both matter and time to make any sutable returne. Truely, my lord, as I am unwilling to write anything to your lordship (though I am sure they would bee reall expressions of gratitude) which might looke like complement, soe am I soe unable to expresse how much I thinke myselfe oblidgd to your lordship for all your favours, as I thinke it much better to passe it by in silence, and rather indeavour to expresse it more livelye in my actions. I were unworthy of your lordship's favour (if for nothing else, at least for that) if I did not preferre the kindnesse your lordship hath beene pleas'd to expresse in this businesse of the butleradge, before the thing itselfe, though very considerable. The newes now is of greate importance, but very short. The last weeke hath beene chiefely spent in compleating (that which was at first cald the remonstrance, now) the petition and advice of the parliament to his Highnesse, to assume the name, title, dignitye and office of kinge, etc, which was this day presented by the speaker in the Banqueting House, who introduc't it with a long speech to all the particulars, but spake most copiouslye to that of kingship. His Highnesse made a short replye, that the weyght and length of the businesse did both require time of deliberation, but that hee would take as little as the matter would possibly permitt, but that hee would seeke God for his direction and hop't hee should soe receyve it in an unbiast heart, as that neyther the vaine fancyes of some, nor the lusts of others might divert him from giving an awnswer sutable to the mind of God. The temper of the officers begins to mend in order to that concernment. Lambert, 504.[164] and Desborough still stand out upon the sullen posture. Fleetwood does not mutinye, but lament. Whaley, Butler, Goffe and divers others grown good natur'd, but 1567.[165] as obstinate as could bee imagen'd or wisht. General Mountague caryed the sword before his Highnesse today, hee beeing not there who hath done it most usually.[166] But, my lord, I feare whilst I am about to make up my last weeke's omission I may committ a greater fault by being tedious, I shall therefore only kisse your lordship's hands and remaine, my lord,

Your most humble and affectionate servant,

Wm Jephson

207. From John Reynolds, London, 31 March 1657, 822, fos 21–22.

May it please your excellency,

I am verry much honoured in your lordship's vouchafed correspondency, wherein I am glad to find no more variety; in our times no newes is good newes, and I hope it will still so continue there. The parliament this day attended his Highnes and presented their petition and humble advice in eighteene proposals, which (after a copious speech made by our speaker) was reade publiquely in the

[164] Perhaps 'Sydenham'.

[165] Unknown.

[166] Lambert.

Banquetting House, and than his Highnes was pleased to expresse himselfe with so greate freedome and tender sense of the dealings of God towards these nations as moved many there into teares, and concluded with a promise to take the same into most serious consideration. I do suppose that your lordshipp hath heard of the intended designe in which possibly I may be engaged by his Highnes' orders, but whither I know not, neither can dispute when the highest duty and greatest affection call at once for my submission. I shall most humbly and earnestly beseech your lordshipp, by all your former afforded promises, favours and your lordship's sence of my fidelity to your family, that you be pleased to deale with those in power with his Highnes, that if I be commanded it may bee in a condition and emploiment whereby it may be cleared to all that it is a token of favour and not a willingnes to have me removed from Ireland. On this condition I shall resigne myselfe wholy, and do desire to ly at the feete of the Lord and of his Highnes. I am, my lord,

Your excellencye's most humble and faithfull servant,

J Reynolds

208. From Robert Stapylton, Charing Cross, 31 March 1657, 822, fos 23–24.

Letter of recommendation, taking up an offer which Henry Cromwell had made sometime before while in England, that he would help the unnamed bearer and his wife, who once lived in a high condition but who were now distressed and destitute.

209. Draft of a letter by Henry Cromwell to Lord Broghill, [March 1657], 823, fos 329–330.

But I find that there appeares no new fires but onely new fuell added to the old, which rather smokes then burnes. But for your old Protestants, they are so <tindere drye> hot upon the buisnes, that unless Gorges had happily throwne some water on them <zeale> Dublin had blazed out all into bonefires <at the news of the proposition>.[167] But to bee serious, the sober both of new and old, as I heare, expresse much satisfaction in what has beene done, and <are fearefull> seeme to dread the spirits of some who opposed it. <I wish you wrote> I wish you could <say which> returne mee the like newes from England.

[167] Presumably the proposal for Oliver Cromwell to become king. The phrases used by Henry Cromwell here are similar to those employed by Thurloe in a letter to him of 31 March, where the Secretary notes of 'the persons you mention [. . .] comeinge over', 'I doubt they will finde too much fuel for the fire they will bringe with them' (*TSP*, VI, pp. 156–157).

I have taken (as I hope) sufficient course to keepe things here, so as you shall not need to fear interuptions from home. The resolve you intimated of sinking or swiming in this worke, I like well, and hold it necessary for you know when[168] you have provoked. You will doe well to make his Highness thoroughly sensible of the danger of sleighting this offer; parlaments are not every day so compliant upon these occasions <necessary to gratify those who have deserved well of them>. And I understand that <ther beene> some late passages from his Highness have so wrought upon some of the major-generalls etc, as that it[169] will bee unsafe for his him <Highness> to rely upon their affections, at least not so safe as to cast himselfe upon the better disposed party.

If things proceed, it will follow that both the councill and army in England will need to bee rectified. Upon which consideration I begin to thinke that your stay in England will better answer all the intention that are propounded concerning you then to remove thither.

210. Draft of a letter by Henry Cromwell to Lord Broghill, [March 1657], 823, fos 331–332.

Having been long in my last, and having little new here, I shall bee breife now. I approve your prudence in postponing the first paragraph.[170] I see the opinions of some of the major-generalls are not so unalterable, but that one may see they act as much by humor as judgment or conscience; as it appears in Bery, so easy sliding out of heptarchy[171] into somewhat else; as in Desborough <compliance with> forwardnes in the same. It is much the officers should bee so concerned in directing the goverment, whom it would better become to execute then appoint; but things beeing so, and they having beene so long used to this trade, I am as glad <the old man> the brave old blade did so well instruct his pupill, and I admire their excellent capacityes to understand him so quickly. By all which wee may gather this much is serious, that things which are done upon good ground and resolution doe not find so stubborne opposition as wee are apt to feare. Wherefore I also believe that the worke will grow every day more and more easy. Nor doe I doubt of the exercise of your courage proportionably therein. I am glad his Highness is so fixt upon this

[168]Word poorly formed and could alternatively be read as 'who'.

[169]Phrase 'as that it' appears at the bottom of the first page but is repeated in error at the top of the second.

[170]The decision to postpone consideration of the kingship clause was taken on 2 March.

[171] In a letter to Thurloe of 4 March 1657, Henry Cromwell reported rumours that 'some of the great ones' had been 'talkeing of an heptarchy, and of cantonizing the countrey' (*TSP*, VI, pp. 93–94).

necessary worke, and that hee hath rested upon the effectuall remedy you mention. I hope hee <pitch upon> take the right <persons> sow by the eare. Things are very quiett and likely to bee compliant here with anything which it shall please God to produce.

211. From Edward Feake, Prim,[172] 1 April 1657, 822, fos 25–26.

Letter of thanks, noting that Henry Cromwell and his council had repeatedly confirmed their earlier decision to give him preferency in leasing out 700 acres around Bishappslogh[173] *and had directed the commissioners accordingly, even though their earlier orders to admit him had been wilfully ignored and the commissioners had instead leased the property to Major Redman.*

212. From William Jephson, London, 6 April 1657, 822, fos 27–28.

My deare lord,

Tis noe small trouble for mee that my newes of this last weeke's transactions are likely to bee as litle satifactorye to your lordship as they are to my selfe, and most of those who (in mine opinion) are the most hearty well wishers to his Highnesse's familye and the publike interest of the 3 nations. This griefe is occasion'd amongst us by his Highnesse's demurre (for an absolute nor a parliamentary denyall it cannot bee cal'd, beeing given to a committee and not in full parliament) to the humble petition and advice presented in the Banqueting House upon Tuesday last.[174] The copy of the speech I doubt not but your lordship will have from better hands, therefore I presume not to give your lordship the trouble of it, but have sent it to Munne Temple, who will produce it if you have it not otherwise. Upon the report thereof to the parliament, a vote was past to adhere to the former resolutions, a second addresse to his Highnesse resolv'd upon, and a committee appointed to draw up reasons to inforce their former desyre of a speedy concurrence. Those were this day reported, which were only in generall that the parliament did conceyve (and his Highnesse did acknowledge) that the petition and advice had very well provyded for the settlement of these nations, both in spirituall and civill matters; that twas the advice given him by the representatives of three nations; and that, therefore, there was a greate duty incumbent on him to give his assent. This day a committee was sent to desyre his Highnesse to appoint a time to receyve their addresse, and tomorrow at 3 a

[172] Perhaps an abbreviated form of Primasland, Primaswood, or Primattstowne, all in County Meath.

[173] Bishopslogh, between Bennettsbridge and Tulleherin, County Kilkenny.

[174] Presented on Tuesday 31 March, demurred on Friday 3 April.

clocke is appointed accordinglye;[175] and the house placeth soe much value upon this businesse as that they adjourne and proceed in noe other in the interim. Though his Highnesse excepts against nothing but the title, I doubt there is something more in their view who are soe zealous against this petition. I suspect Lambert may thinke it not for his advantadge that 432.[176] may apointeing[177] and that the army and the officers may looke upon all agreement betwixt the Protector and 439.[178] as daungerous to their interest. In fine, I thinke to many persons anything that lookes like a civil 460.[179] seemes contrary to their interest and principles. Fleetwood did this day professe himselfe to mee to bee a greate enemye to arbitrary government and manifested his unwillingnesse to a totall breach, and perswaded rather to quit the title and accept of the rest. Your lordship cannot imadgine how greate a damp fell upon the spirits of those who were most earnest in promoting this businesse when his Highness demurred to it. I thinke I may without vanitye say I was the chiefe instrument in holding them up to what hath beene since undertaken. What the successe will prove, God knowes. That it may bee such as may tend to the glory of God, the honour of his Highnesse, and the good of these nations, both in their spirituall and temporall concernments, shall bee the constant and earnest prayer of, my lord,

Your lordship's most affectionate and humble servant,

Wm Jephson

213. From John Bridges, London, 7 April 1657, 822, fos 29–30.

May it please your lordshipp,

In my last I gave your lordshipp an accompt of the parliament's addresse to his Highness. On Friday hee directed his letter to the speaker, desireing a committee might attend him, which went to White Hall the same day. I have inclosed sent your excellency a coppy of his speech taken from his mouth and reported to the parliament the next day, which as it gave occasion to the major-generalls and that party to triumph, soe was it a very greate trouble to others and caused many of our best freinds to absent themselves from the <said> howse, as lord

[175] As the committee met the Protector on 7 April to arrange a meeting for 8 April, Jephson may have misdated this letter.

[176] Unknown.

[177] Word in code with a number for each letter and decoded thus by comparison with other correspondence in this collection, but Jephson had apparently garbled the code – possibly 'apointe' was intended.

[178] Perhaps 'parliament'.

[179] Perhaps 'power' or 'settlement' or 'regime'.

Broghill, Sir Charles Wooseley, lord cheife justice[180] and others, which was noe small discouradgement to us that attended. Wee fell uppon the debate whether the parliament should adheere to theire former vote. The debate was earnest, the whole party of dissenters came in and would ravell in to the whole business, but the other stood stoute to make good theire ground. Betweene one and two of the clock it came to a question, whether wee should adheere. The affirmatives weare but 78 and the negatives 65.[181] Yesterday wee fell to it againe, and the absentees perceiving the dainger the whole was put into by theire seduction, came in to our ayde, and after some strugling itt was carryed that the whole howse should attend his Highness with reasons why they could not recede and a committee appointed to drawe them upp, which done the parliament ordered that noe other busines should bee taken nor proceeded uppon till yt weare brought to an yssue. I should have told your lordshipp that the greate argument insisted uppon was howe unreasonable it was (that since his Highness had declared that it was against his conscience to accept of the title) to impose uppon his conscience, and indeede it was taken for graunted by all that hee had soe expressed, but providence haveing soe ordered it that I, having a coppy of the report and carefully observing his Highness' answeare, found it otherwise, and thereuppon sattisfyed the howse to the contrary, which put noe small life into the businesse.

This[182] day the reasons weare brought into the howse by the committee and, the question beinge carryed for an agreemente with the committee, there was another committee appointed immediately to attende his Highness, to lett him knowe that the parliament being desirous to attend him with some businesse of greate importance, and to intreate him to appoint tyme and place for that purpose. Which done they adjourned till two of the clock uppon this consideration, that his Highness might order a meeting this afternoone, but wee found his Highness in his bed chamber under some indisposition, and in that regard the meeting was deferred till tomorrowe 3 of the clock, and

[180] John Glynne, parliamentarian judge and politician, who quickly became prominent in parliament in the early 1640s as a critic of the king's government, though his attempts in the later 1640s to reach a settlement with the king, and his stance against the parliamentarian army, led to a fall from favour and loss of office. He returned to office early in the Protectorate as a prosecutor and judge and, in 1655, was appointed chief justice of the upper bench. He was returned to both of Oliver Cromwell's Protectorate parliaments, representing constituencies in his native north Wales, and, in 1657, was a leading supporter both of the new constitution and of the proposal to revive kingship.

[181] Division of 4 April.

[182] The second paragraph of this letter is written in the same hand as the first, but in a smaller and more compact style, perhaps indicating that Bridges wrote the first paragraph and then attended to other – perhaps parliamentary – matters, before returning to complete the letter.

the place the Banquetting Howse. I have inclosed sent his Highness' speech as alsoe the reasons agreed to bee presented for parliament's adheerence. My lord,

Your excellency's most humble servant,

Jo Bridges

214. From Anthony Morgan, London, [7 April 1657], 822, fos 9–10.

May it please your excellency,

On Friday the articles were signed twixt yourselfe (by your commissioners Sir Theophilus Jones,[183] John Grant and myselfe) on the on part and Sir Timothy Tyrrell on the other part. Your excellency hath at the sealing and signing paid him £500 by the bill you sent to me, and you are to pay £2,000 more 3 months hence. He is to allow £50 towards the charge of making new cataloges and comparing them with the old (that wee may see what is wanting, which he is to make good) and packing and sending them down to Chester. The books are not to be carried out of this town till the £2,000 be paid, so that I conceive tis good to pay it as soon as wee have received the books into our custody, though but one month of the 3 should be elapsed, that they may the sooner arrive at Dublin. I send inclosed in this or Dr Gorge's lettre a copy of the articles, and submitt this and myselfe to your lordship's pleasure, and remaine,

Your excellency's most obedient and most faithfull servant,

Ant Morgan

His Highness hath denied to accept of the government, though he highly approves all but the title king. The house resolved to adhere to their first advice and to doe noe other busines till they had an answer. Therupon wee adjorned as soon as wee mett on Saturday, Munday and this day.[184] Tomorrow the whole house attends his Highnes with a fresh desire he would hearken to the advice of his parliament, and that he would call to mind what duty lay upon him in that case.

[183]Army officer and politician and an Irish Protestant, he broadly supported the royalist cause in Ireland in the early and mid-1640s, but thereafter served the parliamentarians, becoming governor of Dublin under Oliver Cromwell. He commanded a horse regiment in the mopping-up operations of the early 1650s and, although his regiment was disbanded in 1655, he retained military command in Ireland. A loyal Cromwellian and supporter of the Protectorate, he commanded Henry Cromwell's lifeguard and was returned for Irish constituencies to all three Protectorate parliaments. He was a nephew of the late archbishop and thus took an interest in the disposal of Ussher's library.

[184]This report provides a firm date for this otherwise undated letter.

215. From Charles Fleetwood, London, 7 April [1657],[185] 821, fos 115–116.

Deare brother,

I have received yours whearin you are pleased to give me an account of what major Jones hath don[186] in reference to his keeping in the musters, of which I am a stranger, and as to his commission allso, and therfor I hope you think me innocent in the buysnes. I am sorry he showld doe any thing to offende you. I am perswaded he did not doe it willingly, but it may be tooke some incouragment from what others have in reference to their payes, though then reduced, and received lands for their satisfaction, which it is sayde he hath not don, his satisfaction being recovered against him by a tryall at law. He is a good man, though he may be weake in some things. You having given a whitnes against his irregularity, a return of your favor may be the greater obligation. I presume you have a full account of all things in parliment, his Highnes refusing to accept of the kingly goverment. The howse upon consideration hade therof have voted to adheare to their former resolves, and accordingly they attend upon his Highnes tomorrow with the same. His Highnes hath a great tryall, but I trust the Lord will well carry him through it. I am sure thus farre his Highnes hath very much gayned in the opinion and affections of good people. What the issue will be a short time will manifest; in the mean while it concerns all praying freinds to be earnest with the Lord for direction. I doubt not but Sir John Reynolds hath given you an account of his new expedition so farre as he knowes therof, the full of which I think is not known to him, the design being under secrecy. If the Lord prospers it, we may have a nationall mercy therin, which, that we may have hearts affected to seake the Lord for, is the desire of,

Your most affectionate brother and servant,

Charles Fleetwood

[185] Wrongly endorsed '1656'.

[186] On 25 March 1657, Henry Cromwell wrote to his father about 'the present suspention of major Jones', an important issue because 'this business may bee interpreted to concern a whole party'. Jones (his forename is not recorded) had allegedly been listed as a major both for ten months prior to his commission and from after his reduction to captain's rank and his receipt of his full military arrears 'in speciall landes'. He had thus received both unauthorized and unjustified army pay for ten months and later 'whole satisfaction' of arrears, as if completely disbanded 'which otherwise had not belonged unto him'. Henry Cromwell had suspended his salary 'for, besides the manifest injury (I may say cheat) to the state, I see noe reason why soe many worthy persons should be either disbanded wholly or reduced from colonells to privat captaines, whilst this man (whoe never saw any service, nor was ever taken notice of, either for his usefullness in any kind, or for his affection to your highnes or government)' should act thus (*TSP*, VI, p. 142).

I understand my lord Moore's[187] time for paying in his composition is neere elapsed. His bill to inable him to sell lands for the discharging thereof hath bine once read in the howse, and will suddenly be passed, and therefore shall desire the continuuance of your favour to him in getting his time inlarged.

Charles Fleetwood

216. From John Reynolds, London, 7 April 1657, 822, fos 31–32.

May it please your excellency,

I am not able to expresse much certainty in this weeke's intelligence because of the suspence of affaires heere. The parliament hath put of all busines untill his Highnes' pleasure be declared concerning our advice and petition, which will be reinforced with the parliament's finall addresse (as is supposed) tomorrow in the Banketing House. The Lord dispose to a good settlement. I was bold in my last to acquaint your lordshipp with an emploiment of a forraine nature,[188] to which his Highnes hath designed me, but I, wanting your lordshipp's advice and commands, am in some perplexity not being able to decline so sacred authority, nor yet to go on without reluctancy, having few freinds on whom I dare rely except your lordshipp. And indeede if I be not understood as a true lover of your person, family, cause, interest, and not to be adventured but as such, I am verry unhappy having given some testimonyes of all these, but verbum sat.[189] I shall humbly importune your lordshipp's answer to my disturbed lines, and what your lordship's sence is of this busines, and whether you find it agreeable to your lordship's interest and affaires, that I leave your lordshipp. I suppose your lordshipp knowes more of secrets than I do. And I would sooner perish than expose Ireland to a relapse by weakening your lordship's interest and renewed opportunityes to continue the good which the Lord hath wrought by you. I shall

[187]Henry Moore, Viscount Moore of Drogheda, an Irish Protestant royalist, had, after long negotiations, compounded with the English regime in 1653 for almost £7,000. A bill to permit him to sell part of the estate to help meet the fine was given two readings during the first session of the second Protectorate parliament (Dunlop, p. 24; *CSPI*, pp. 543, 668–670; *Burton*, II, p. 170).

[188]The Protector had asked Reynolds to help command the 6,000 parliamentary foot which, in line with the Anglo-French treaty, he had agreed to send to Flanders to support the French campaign there. On 22 April 1657, Henry Cromwell wrote to his father, supporting both Reynolds – 'faithfull and industrious' and of 'good affection' – and this appointment and recommending that it be presented as 'suteable to his merit, and [...] rather a preferment to him than otherwaies, with respect, and in comparison to his present condition here' (*TSP*, VI, pp. 222–223).

[189]This Latin phrase could be translated as 'the word is enough'.

conclude with my hearty desires and prayers for your lordshipp's encrease in favour with God and men, and remaine, my lord,

Your excellencye's most humble and faithfull servant,

J Reynolds

217. From Randal MacDonnell, Marquess of Antrim, Eden, 11 April 1657, 822, fos 33–34.

May it please your lordship,

I am now reduced to such a condition that I can not forbeare to make a complaint to your lordship, and to begge that you will commiserat and releeve me from the continuall persecution of my creditors, who are now so violent that they doe daylie imploye baliffes and soldiars to arreast me. Wherof a considerable number lye daylie in waight by six or seven in a companie to surprise me, which has kept me for a longe time in the nature of a prisoner, that I dare not looke out of dores; and they threaten withall to force the house and carie me to prison, and have disturbed us some nights, which necessitats me to keepe a continuall watch. Wherby I see I must be forever a prisoner, either at home or in a gaole, unlesse your lordship will out of your noblenes and justice finde some certaine meanes to secure my person or to satisfie my debts, which is a grace I heare his Highnes has been pleased to grant to the nobilitie of Scotland; and I presume I may challendge the like as well as others, beinge for ever made uncapable to satisfie them myselfe. And till your lordship has seriouslie considered of this, my humble request, I beseach you to grant a positive order to all soldiers to forbeare to execut anie writts against me by warrants from the civil magistrats, which will be a meanes to give some litle ease from ther perpetuall allarms, and will be a new addition to all your favours, which have tyed my inclination and my dutie to avowe myselfe, my lord,

Your lordship's most obedient, humble servant,

Antrim

218. From Francis Russell, Whitehall, 11 April 1657, 822, fos 35–36.

My lord,

I doe suppose that you will have it from all manner of hands how great a defeat your father hath giveen to the wise and ambitious part of this world. He is at present in a notable, powerfull spirit; tramples this world and the outward majesty of it under his feet. He tells me, and I doe beleeve so much, that he is in great peace and quiet, this worke being over. Many are pleased and very many troubleed with what he hath done, so that there is a new face upon all sorts of people, and likely to be upon all our counsells and actions. Among the news of this world I must needs tell your lordship that your faithfull freind and servant, Sir John Reynolds, is this day gone to Chippenham and myselfe with him. The issue of our journey I shall give you an account of by my next. What this parliment will doe or what will become of them is yet, I think, unknowne, but some change in the governement tis probable they will make before they rise. Here are some jealousys of the Dutch; they and wee are provideing apace, and it may be that will hinder a war. My love to your wife, and if the providence of God brings not you back into England, I hope to see you in Ireland. I must allways be, my lord,

Your lordship's in all love and faithfullnes,

Franc Russell

The treaty with my lord viscount Lisle,[190] about my neece Bodvill,[191] goes on as if it were likely to come to a good issue.

219. From Charles Fleetwood, London, 13 April 1657, 822, fos 39–40.

Letter of recommendation on behalf of the bearer, Mr Course, who had long attended London about legislation related to Ireland, but other parliamentary business had prevented those bills being passed; recommends that, as an able and faithful servant, he be given better employment.

220. From John Bridges, London, 13 April 1657, 822, fos 37–38.

May it please your lordshipp,

I have inclosed sent you a coppy of the petition and advice presented to his Highness by the parliament. The only businesse of the parliament at present is to prevaile with his Highness to accept of the title, for that is the only ingredient whereat hee heesitates. But the parliament is soe fixed uppon it, that they have not thought fitt to proceede in any other busines till his Highness shall give them

[190] Philip Sidney, parliamentarian officer and politician, held the courtesy title of Viscount Lisle as heir to the earldom of Leicester. He campaigned against the Irish Catholic rebels in Ireland in 1642–1643, displaying clear sympathies for the parliamentary cause, and quit Ireland after the cessation, returning there briefly in 1647 as parliament's lord lieutenant. Although not a regicide, he actively supported the Rump and the republic. He strongly supported Oliver Cromwell and the Protectorate and held office during the Protectorate as a member of the Protectoral council, though he did not seek election to the Protectorate parliaments.

[191] Daughter of Russell's sister Anne and her estranged husband, John Bodvill/Bodville/Bodvel, MP for Anglesey in the opening years of the Long Parliament, until he was expelled in 1645 for his war-time royalism.

sattisfaction in that particuler; and to that end, as your lordshipp hath beene formerly advertised, a committee was appointed[192] for a free conference with his Highness to sattisfy him of the reason and necessity of theire demaunds, and they have severall tymes attended his Highness uppon that occasion, laid downe theire reasons, and yesterday his Highness gave answeare to them, which was to this effect:[193] that for his part hee values not one name more then another; that hee had rather have any name from this parliament then any name without it, soe much doth hee value the authority of parliament; but in respect many godly men that have hazarded theire lives in this cause are dissattisfyed with it, and providence haveing with the old family eradicated the old title, hee thinks it his duty to beg of the parliament not to put that uppon those good men which they cannot swallowe, though it may bee theire weakenes. But though men are divided in theire judgments what his Highness will resolve uppon, yet it seemes to mee that since hee allowes an indifferency in the thinge, his greate reason will not permitt him to ballance the resolves of parliament made uppon soe greate a debate and consideration, with the humour of persons without, that can give little of reason besides this, that godly men are dissattisfyed. I beleeve his Highness is jealous there may bee some distemper in the army. The 5th Monarchy men had appointed a rendezvous att Mile End Greene, but the most forwardes, with some considerable quantiti of armes and theire standard, weare surprized before they could gett to horse.[194] Butt that being alsoe in the last pamphlet, I shall not give your excellency the trouble of the relation in this paper. I have sent Dr Gorge the 2 last pamphletts, which give an accompt of our proceedings.

My lord, I am under an obligation and therefore may not give your lordshipp an account of what I knowe, yet in this greate businesse I mai tell your lordshipp my opinion, that notwithstandinge the different judgements and the confidence of our antagonists, I hope his Highness will in a fewe dayes accept of the advice of his parliament. This afternoone wee weare att White Hall to attend his Highness, but by reason of some indisposition uppon him our meeting was put off till tomorrowe. Our antagonists weare in some hope to have surprized us this day in the howse by reason of the absence of a greate part of our freinds, but wee held them upp soe longe till more helpe came. I hope

[192] On 9 April.

[193] The following is a summary of a speech given by the Protector on 13 April (Abbott, IV, pp. 467–474), suggesting that Bridges may have misdated this letter and that it was really written, or at least completed, on 14 April.

[194] The Fifth Monarchist plot, led by Thomas Venner, focused on a planned general rendezvous at Mile End Green on Thursday 9 April, but the ringleaders were intercepted and arrested earlier that day.

it will make us all more cautious hereafter. I present your lordshipp with my humblest servise, and remaine, my lord,

Your excellencye's most humble servant,

Jo Bridges

I have not tyme to correct the scrivener's faults.

221. From Charles Fleetwood, London, 14 April 1657, 822, fos 41–42.

Deare brother,

I have not hade any from you this post, which I presume is occationed by contrary winds. Litle hath past since my last, but the howse adhearing to their former vote of kingshippe, they waited upon his Highnes, who, not giving his consent, occationed the howse to choose a committee to attend his Highnes to urge reasons for his acceptance and to answer objections, and accordingly uppon Satturday last[195] they mett and offered their arguments for it. His Highnes tooke till Monday to answer them, which yeasterday was performed by his Highness with great inlargednes of spirit, a full and signall whitnes beareing to the interest of the people of God, and did acgayn expres his dissatisfaction to this title. Ther are some of us, dissenters, are to have a meeting with som of the cheife of the other opinion, to see how neare we can com to a right understanding one of another in this buysnes, whearin if the Lord please to own us that we can com to a right close, it may be of great mercy to this distracted, divided condition wherin we are. What the issue will be, you shall heare by the next. The Lord give a healing spirit. I neade not tell you what his Highnes' exercise is at this time. Till this buysnes be over nothing else will probably goe on in the howse. Sir John Reynolds will, I think, at last accept the command in this expedition, though I confesse I am not for it, nor was I when at the 1st it was moved. I heare Mr Patricke Carye's[196] widdow is left in a sadde condition. I have bine moved by my lord Broghill to wright, that you would please to let hir have a lease of lands at a small rent. Surly hir condition is sadde and calls for charity. Hir case being so well known to you, who have so much charity to distressed persons, I shall not doubt you will doe what is convenient in such a case. With both our humble services

[195] 11 April.

[196] Probably the Patrick Carey who, in January 1654, was appointed a commissioner for setting out lands at Ardee, County Louth (Dunlop, p. 394) and possibly the Mr Carey (his forename not recorded) recommended by Henry Cromwell in December 1655 for appointment as a clerk in the Irish upper bench (*TSP*, IV, pp. 307–308).

to your deare lady and very affectionate kisses to your sweet litle ones, I remaine,

Your most affectionate brother and humble servant,

Charles Fleetwood

222. From Vincent Gookin, Westminster, 14 April 1657, 822, fos 43–44.

May it please your lordships,

Not long since I presumed to pray your lordship's countenance to my petition,[197] which I apointed Mr Burniston, my agent, to offer to the councell, desiring that the councel would be pleased, in pursuance of his Highness' lettre on that behalfe, to make an abatement of the rent imposed on the lands granted mee by his Highness, more proportionable to the contribution payable thereat, than by the last order of the councell was allowed mee.

By a lettre from my agent, I am informed that before that desire of mine came to your lordship's hands, the councell had received my petition and adheared to their former order, and that your lordship was pleased to advize my agent to petition againe and to vouchsafe him the encouragment of having your lordship's favour therin. My lord, I wish I had words to express my abounding aprehensions of the greatness of your lordship's tenderness and kindness for soe inconsiderable a servant as I am to your lordship. Yet seing my petition hath bin already offered, and a judgment therin given, and that to offer the same againe is against an order of the councell justly as well as expresly forbiding the asking a second time for what hath bin once denyed, I humbly conceive I shall deale imodestly and injuriously with your lordship to desire your lordship againe to apeare for mee in that business; and therefore I have apointed my agent not to offer my petition any more but to receive the councel's order first given therin, and to transmit it to mee, hoping that his Highness, upon the sence of my service for him and expence in that service, will doe that for mee which the councell ought not to doe nor your lordship, without inconvenience apeare in there.

My lord, I never yet sought for any publique employment, nor ever yet refused to act in such place to which my governours called mee. I have sustained great losses for my adhearence to the parliament's cause, and am much lesse in my fortune than when his Highness first invited mee into publique services. And this diminution of my estate hath bin manifestly occasioned by attending those employments in which I could not have refused to act without being disobedient to my

[197] Presumably relating to the Protector's earlier grant of Irish land to Gookin (Abbott, III, p. 341).

masters, in all those state affayres, wherin I have served. My affection for the worke and those who set mee to worke hath extended my poor abillityes to the utmost point of usefulness for the publique they could beare. Had I tooke those advantages others did to indulge those overtures made mee of profit, I might then have doubly done that for myselfe which now I am a suitour to his Highness for. When all my fellow labourers have made good voyages, I have only an empty, weather-beaten ship left mee, and must spend my income in mending her leakes and have not followed a successfull cause, which hath made others fatt, who I may modestly say have not bin soe usefull to the publique. I am soe poore that I am judged by all not to be in travelling case. I shall presume to say to his Highness, that if his Highness grants mee those lands mentioned in my grant, at a suitable rent, it will be a favour, but not without many presidents. All this, my lord, is trueth, and if your lordship shall be pleased to write to his Highness your opinion of mee, and of my desires in this thing, I beleive it will much incline him to shew kindness to mee. If your lordship shall judge it not inconvenient to mention mee thus to his Highness, I humbly beg you will give Mr Burniston leave to attend your lordship for such a lettre, to whom I have written about it.

Sir John Reynolds and major Morgan, besides what your lordship receives from the Secretary, informes your lordship of our greate affayres of settlement, that my narative will be but a repetition with the best and choycest things left out. The great business in expectation is wheather his Highness will gratifie the one party by refusing the title of king or the parliament by accepting it. At the conference with a comittee of the house Saturday[198] hee was pleased to grant that the committee's arguments were strong for the conveniency of the title; that hee would rather take any title from the parliament than keepe a title given him by anybody else; that though good people were dissatisfied with it, their dissatisfaction probably was their infirmity; that hee had soe great an aprehension of the parliament's wisdome etc that their dissatisfaction was nothing, compared to the parliament's advice; that hee did not thinke himselfe in conscience more unfree to that title than any other. Now I conceive the conclusion is soe naturall from those consessions that I cannot beleive his Highness would grant soe much if hee intended to refuse the title. The Lord be his guide, and God in all his difficultyes.

I have bin somewhat distempered of late with melancholy, for which I am in a course of physicke, and have therfore bin somewhat more a stranger to business than at other times; but if your lordship will

[198] Although Gookin is referring to the earlier meeting of Saturday 11 April, he goes on to summarize the Protector's speech of 13 April.

vouchsafe to give mee my taske of worke in any particular affayre, I shall zealously labour to shew your lordship how much I delight in your lordship's service and shall while I am,

Vin Gookin

223. From Anthony Morgan, London, 14 April 1657, 822, fos 45–46.

May it please your excellency,

I received yours of the 1st of April and shall observe your directions about the Conaught land, though the Gloster bill, if it pass as it is now ordered to be engrossed, will engage all the land and houses in Ireland.[199]

There have been 2 conferences with his Highness; this day will be a 3rd, by a committee of parliament. I doubt not but your excellency will have all passages verbatim else I would have sent them; but upon the whole matter I make noe doubt but he will agree to the advice of his parliament, and that the house will adhere to the advice already given.

Sir John Reynolds hath a qualme upon him in the forrein expedition, hopes your excellency will interpose that he may not goe, and looks upon the bare acquainting you with it as a tryall of your regard towards him. He went to my lord deputy, told him he thought it a designe of his to be ridd of him and that therfore he was not willing to goe. Lord deputy told him he knew who had diswaded him. Sir John made no answer; but my lord persued it and told him that Morgan had done it. Sir John assured him that if he thought I had any reason to give against it, he should be the more unwilling because he valued my judgment, but said he did not so much as know my thoughts of it nor had ever spoken with me about it. Thus I escaped a faire scouring, and the retarding the service can not lye at my dore. I have not been at Wallingford House this 3 months till yesterday. My lord used me very kindly, and told me that Sir John Reynolds had been with him and charged him with a designe to send him away, where as

[199] A bill was passing through parliament to confer upon Gloucester land and property in Galway to the value of just over £1,500, recompensing the town for its expenditure and suffering in support of the parliamentary cause during the civil war. While Henry Cromwell and his government wished to encourage new investment and settlers in Galway, some in Ireland viewed this as an unsatisfactory solution, predicting that the corporation of Gloucester would do little to rebuild and repopulate the town. There were also fears that this would open the floodgates to claims from other English towns that had suffered in the civil war, further eating into the urban and rural property available in Ireland to settle the prior claims of adventurers, soldiers, and others (*TSP*, IV, pp. 483–484, 508; V, p. 494; VI, pp. 156–157, 209–210, 261–262, 683; Dunlop, pp. 432, 484, 524, 543, 545, 546–547, 548–550, 576, 647, 661, 662, 666).

(said he) the best is I was the only person against his going, but told me nothing of the passage about myselfe. This plot of the 5th Monarchy men, and such other things as I know my lord must needs see every day amongst his wild party, I hope will undeceive him. He is a good man, and I hope will come to love those who are plain, downright honest without welt or gard, and will not be jealous without cause. The particulars of this last week's occurrences are very remarkable, but so publique that they must come so many wais to your hands that I thinke the best expression of my duty to spare you here. I remain,

Your excellency's most faithfull and most obedient servant,

Ant Morgan

224. From John Reynolds, London, 14 April 1657, 822, fos 47–48.

May it please your excellency,

Since my last wee have beene admitted to two conferences with his Highnes, in so much as some hoped for a settlement; but indeede, we are at present in suspense, that which is offered by some as an expedient not being pleasing to the house, viz, that the present settlement be established without the title of king, which the sense of the parliament doth much oppose and dislike. What the issue will be none can declare. I did hope your excellency would have represented me as a person not to be slightly disposed of but of some use, which I confesse I thinke I am not and therefore cannot presse it, but do with equall regret, as at disgracefull cashierement, exchange my command for the second command of 6,000 foote in forraine service, which is the honorable emploiment now to be conferred upon me; but I have not accepted my commission and do hope it will not be profered. I have offered to go with the title of major-generall of the saide 6,000 under your excellency, or the lord Richard, but I am not willing to serve under another nation, and a forraine,[200] or at best a generall but halfe an Englishman.[201] To this small reputation have the advises of some

[200] France.

[201] It is not entirely clear to whom Reynolds is referring here, though he is clearly stating that he was initially offered the place of second-in-command of the expedition, under someone he viewed as unsatisfactory. This might just be a reference to Thomas Morgan, who eventually accompanied Reynolds to Flanders as Reynolds's second-in-command. Morgan, a very experienced parliamentarian officer, who had seen service in England, Wales, and Scotland and had at different times commanded a foot, horse, and dragoon regiment, was a short, short-tempered, and almost illiterate Welshman, but he was also skilled, brave, respected by his men, and generally popular. Alternatively, Reynolds might here be alluding to William Lockhart, already in France as the Protector's ambassador, who was a Scot, though married into an English family (the Cromwells, since he had married the Protector's niece); in fact, he played no direct role in the ensuing military campaign,

prevailed to bring me. My comfort is that I can defy any imputation but too much fidelity to your lordshipp, which I shall choose to dy asserting, as becomes, my lord,

Your excellencye's humble and faithfull servant,

J Reynolds

Sir Francis and the family at Chippenham are well. Just now captain Russell[202] returned thence, and alighted neere my lodging in Scotland Yard.

The inclosed[203] is the new modell of governement, and it is to be tendred with ours, and this saying, utrum horum mavis accipe.[204]

225. From Edward Whalley, Whitehall, 14 April 1657, 822, fos 49–50.

My lord,

My brother, judge advocate, having acquaynted me by his letter with your lordshipp's hie favour, in not onely owning him as your poor kinsman but vouchsafing him your very great respects, very much obliges me to present you with the returne of my humble thanks. My lord, his debt is mine, which much encreases my owne obligations you have bin pleased to lay upon me, and though noe lesse deserves them, yet none shalbee more gratefull.

The conference betwixt his Highnesse and the committee of parliament, concerning the title of king, still continues. They are to wayte upon his Highnesse this afternoone at 3 of the clocke to give him an answeare to what yesterday he alledged agaynst his assumption of that title. Did not I know you would have a more particuler account given you of all proceedings heer I should be more large. I shall therefore onely add this, that I beleeve yf the parliament continue to adhere to theyr former vote of kingshipp, his Highnes will rather accept of that title then ether revert to the instrument of governement, which is now become very odious, or leave us in confusion, which inevitably we shall runne into yf he refuses. There is onely this bad expedient left us, to dissolve into a commonwealth, which many ayme at, but I hope they[205] expectation wilbe frustrated. My lord, the times are dangerous. I knowe your lordshipp heares more then I can or dare

though he gave active diplomatic support. I am most grateful to Dr Patrick Little for sharing his thoughts on this issue.

[202] Identification uncertain, but perhaps Sir Francis Russell's eldest son, William.

[203] Presumably a handwritten or printed version of the new constitution as it stood at this point.

[204] This Latin phrase could be translated as 'accept which of the two you prefer'.

[205] Apparently a slip for 'theyr'.

write. I shall therefore conclude with the sinceritie of this profession, that I am,

Your excellencie's most cordiall and faythfull servant,
Edw Whalley

226. From Charles Fleetwood, [latter half of April 1657],[206] 821, fos 258–259.

Deare brother,

It having pleased the Lord to vissit my deare Nancy[207] with a very sore distemper, not in the eye of man, I think, likely to recover. What such a tryall is I neade not tell you, when you remember how it was with you when the Lord vissited your sweet Betty.[208] The Lord sanctefy this tryall to us. It is that which hath a voyce in it, which if we have hearts to heare and understand, that will be our mercy. It was a child I did very much love, and if I could finde more weanednes from creature comforts and more fixednes upon that which is durable, the dispensation would not be without an answerable effect. I have not writt any letters this post except to yourselfe, and my presant condition must pleade my excuse that I am no larger, and shall only intreat you would not think of me then as one who did and doe think major Jones, as you represent his action, a great miscareag, and not that I showld excuse such an action. I am sorry he showld give you such an offence. Excuse my haste, who hope my praying freinds will be quickned up to minde our condition, wherin I intreat your incitement, and remaine,

Your most affectionate brother and servant,
Charles Fleetwood

Our humble services to your deare lady.

[206]The letter is undated. However, Fleetwood here elaborates on the case of Major Jones – the unidentified officer whose unjustified financial claims he had mentioned, apparently for the first time, in his letter of 7 April (no. 215). On the other hand, Fleetwood introduces the news of the serious and dangerous illness of his daughter Nancy – it was not mentioned in his letter of 14 April – which he talks about again in his letter of 28 April, reporting then that she had been seriously ill for four or five days (no. 231). Accordingly, this letter can be dated with a fair degree of reliability to the second half of April.

[207]The Fleetwood household at this time was full of children, including his and his wife's children by their first marriages as well as their own children. The child mentioned here may be Anne Fleetwood, Fleetwood's young daughter by his second wife, Bridget Ireton née Cromwell; Anne died during the Protectorate and was for a time interred in Westminster Abbey but her remains were exhumed and removed at the Restoration.

[208]Henry Cromwell's eldest daughter, Elizabeth, born in 1654, who died in July 1659 and was buried at Chippenham.

227. From William Jephson, London, 21 April 1657, 822, fos 51–52.

My lord,

Our transactions here are, as the occurrences from abroad, something extraordinarye. The last weeke hath brought us the newes of the emperour's death,[209] of the Transilvanians' victorye[210] over the Polish generall, of the Portugall's taking the Holland plantation in the East Indies and a squadron of their ships (under the commaund of their admirall Rutter). But of all these thinges, I know your lordship will receyve punctuall relations from more knowing hands, as allsoe of our taking the Spanish gallionne and hir value. As to our affayres at home, wee were this day to wayte upon his Highnesse, who hath now given us all his exceptions (and some additions hee desyr'd might bee made) to the petition and advice. The most considerable were concerning the revenue, that is to say, that a sufficient maintenance for the armye and a competent provision for carying on the Spanish warre might bee by the parliament ascertained, at least for a time. Others there were concerning the election of parliament men, wherein his Highness hinted that hee thought wee had beene too gentle to the Scotch and revolting English of Ireland; another concerning the making good of the ordinances made by the counsell. Many others there were of lesser moment, wherein, I suppose, it will not bee hard to give satisfaction. In conclusion of his Highness' discourse wee made ourselves believe wee had greate reason to percyve that if satisfaction were given in the particulars, the thinges in the petition beeing soe desirable, and settlement a thing of soe absolute necessitye, that hee should hardlye know how to deny it with all its appurtenances. That this was soe generally apprehended by those that desyre it was as visible in their faces as their noses. 502. 1557.[211] etc prinkt up, the army droopt. Affayres seeme well altred since the last. Colonel Inglesbye's regiment of horse came yesterday to towne, which, mee thought, was noe ill signe. God of His mercye direct all for the good of these nations, and protect your lordship in all your undertakinges, which is the constant prayer of, my deare lord,

Your most affectionate, humble servant,

Wm Jephson

228. From Anthony Morgan, London, 21 April 1657, 822, fos 53–54.

May it please your excellency,

Wee have examined the state of the library and find very few books wanting which were in the catalouge. £5 will supply all, in stead

[209] The death of the emperor, Ferdinand III, without an adult male heir opened the possibility of a genuine contest for the throne of the Holy Roman Empire.

[210] Transylvania was acting in alliance with Sweden against Poland.

[211] Unknown.

whereof Sir Timothy Tyrrell hath sent in severall printed books which were not in the cataloge and a chest of manuscripts, so that his dealing being so faire it is my humble opinion that it is not much worth labor to cause Sir Timothy to make good the defect of the cataloge, though the contract oblige him to it. The books are now in our custody. Sir Theophilus Jones keeps one key and Mr Grant another in trust that the books shall not be removed till the mony is payd, so that if the mony were ready tomorrow wee could then send down the books to Chester.

This day the conference with his Highness was continued. He made severall exceptions in writing, but so circumstantiall things that some conclud he will take it and that he hath strengthened our hands, because of that rule, exceptio in non exceptis firmat regulam.[212] I remain, my lord,

Your excellency's most faithfull and obedient servant,

Ant Morgan

229. From John Reynolds, London, 27 April 1657, 822, fos 55–56.

May it please your excellency,

I received the additionall favour of another letter from your lordshipp, and should bee verry ambitious of deserving your lordship's vouchafed kindnes by any undertaking, and could be content to loose myselfe in expressing devotednes to your family; but I must not aspire farther than my present station,[213] and therefore would not willingly remove out of it, thirsting after no greater glory than to be the meanest of your lordship's servaunts and of his Highnes. My former ambition will, I hope, (as in truth it was) be construed affection, which doth not alwayes consider distance, etc.

I have not so much sanguine hope as some of my companions, but do assure your lordshipp our cause is not so given up as that the blades have cause to bee jocund. But I will not be guilty of their errour by anticipation of what may possibly be. The truth is that his Highness hath more satisfyed his owne judgement and conscience than either of us, and hath since beene pleased to accept some poore advice, that we might argue before him the matter in question, which it's hoped will so dispose the minds of all that we shall be satisfyed with his refusall, or they become more willing to submit to his acceptance. The Lord direct, blesse and prosper your lordshipp, which is the prayer of, my lord,

Your excellencye's most humble and faithfull servaunt,

J Reynolds

[212] This Latin phrase could be translated as 'the exception confirms the rule (in cases not excepted)'.

[213] The Protector's commission, appointing him commander-in-chief of the Flanders expeditionary force, was dated 25 April (Abbott, IV, pp. 504–505).

230. From Francis Russell, Whitehall, 27 April 1657, 822, fos 57–58.

My lord,

I doe in this (I think so) desire to take leave of your lordship, for my next is likely to be to the duke of Yorke.[214] Your father beginnes to come out of the cloudes, and it appeares to us that he will take the kingly power upon him. That great noyse which was make[215] about this busynes not long since is allmost over, and I cannot think there will be the least combustion about it. This day I have had some discourse with your father about this great busynes; he is very cheareful and his troubleed thoughts seeme to be over. Sometimes tis thought and sayed that my lord Henry will be sent for into England. I must confesse the very talke and report pleasees me, and I hope twill come to passe with your likeing, otherwise I would not have it so. Your faithfull freind and servant, Sir John Reynolds, is at present in some kind of trouble of mind; your father, I doe beleeve, presses him hard to goe with these new raiseed men into France. What the issue will be I cannot tell, but I rather think Sir John will not goe, unlesse his Highnes lay his absolute commands upon him, and than I suspect shrodely the knight will turne Quaker. Here hath bin some troubles about the busynes of Mr Rich and my lady Frances; they seeme to me yet to continue, and to trouble the minds both of your father and mother more than anything else. I doe not love to make any inquireey about it, so can wright you noe perticulers. My love to your wife, and give me leave to subscribe myselfe, my lord,

Your lordship's in all faithfullnes,

Franc Russell

I was told the other day by colonell Pride[216] that I was for a king because I hopeed that the next would[217] Henry's turne.

[214] Traditionally, the second son of the reigning monarch was created Duke of York.

[215] Apparently a slip for 'made'.

[216] Thomas Pride, parliamentarian officer and politician and a regicide, took up arms against the king from the outbreak of war and by the mid-1640s was lieutenant-colonel in Edward Harley's New Model foot regiment. He was prominent in the army politics of the later 1640s and a firm opponent of parliament's attack on the army, helping first to quell the royalist rising of 1648 and then to purge parliament in early December, a development which usually bears his name. He campaigned under Oliver Cromwell in Scotland in 1650–1651. Despite his radical and republican views, which led to some suspicions and caused him initially to oppose the offer of the crown, he was loyal to the Protectorate. The second Protectorate parliament was the only parliament to which he was elected.

[217] Word – perhaps 'be' – apparently omitted.

231. From Charles Fleetwood, London, 28 April [1657],[218] 821, fos 123–124.

Deare brother,

The Lord's hande is still upon us in the weaknes of our deare Nancy, who hath bin looked upon both by the physitians and others thes foure or five dayes as a dying childe. Our desires to the Lord hath bine that we might have wills to resigne to His will and to be throughly taught by this sore stroake. Ther is, it semes, a litle abatment of one part of hir distemper in the feavor, which gives some reviving, but no more then to incourage still a waiting upon the Lord, who can rayse from the grave; that is hir case. I hope our praying freinds with you are mindfull of us, that the Lord may throughly sanctefy this dispensation to us. Ther is somthing the Lord would have us perticulerly learn if He please to teach us; that will be our mercy. I have not bine abroad thes seven dayes and know litle of anything, being called to this retirment, in which had I better heart I might make that improvment in soule searching, and through the grace of our Lord Jesus gayne spirituall strength against corruption and more communion with Himselfe, which will abundantly recompence my losse. Wherin that the Lord may afforde me His gratious and blessed presence is the desire of,

Your most affectionate brother and humble servant,
Charles Fleetwood

I understand you have sent for collonel Cooper,[219] but it seemes his Highnes hath commanded his stay till this great busynes be fully over. I can give no account therof by reason of my retirment.

232. From Daniel Redman, Dublin, 29 April 1657, 822, fos 59–60.

May itt please your excellencie,

Feareing I shall not have any opertunitie to waite uppon your excellencie to speeke aboute some businesse, and judgeing that my adresse in writeing may be lesse troubl to your lordship att this tyme, made me asume the bouldnesse to aquaint you with an opertunitie that I mett with, which may be off some advauntage to my kinsman, Mr Henary Parrie, iff the consent off Sir John Temple could be prokured, viz, one Mr William Deane, who is one off the clerques in chauncery,

[218] Wrongly endorsed '1656'.

[219] He was in London, serving as MP for Counties Down, Antrim, and Armagh. Worried about the security of Ulster, on 25 March, Henry Cromwell requested the Protector to order Cooper's return to Ireland (*TSP*, VI, p. 143); Cooper himself replied to Henry Cromwell on 21 April, reporting that the Protector had directed him to stay (*TSP*, VI, p. 219).

not getting a livelyhood out off that imployment, has petitioned the lord chauncelor and Sir John Temple to have libertie to sell itt to a person that may be better versed in itt. And myselfe, Mr Charnocke and Mr Baines[220] waited uppon Sir John this day and aquainted hym that your lordshipp would willingly doe Mr Parrie a favour iff an opertunitie weare offred. Sir John was pleased to tell us that he would waite uppon your lordshipp about itt iff he weare so comaunded. I humbly begg your lordshipp would please to apoint either Dockter Gordges or some other to goe to Sir John Temple with your lordship's carakter and recomendation off Mr Parrie, otherwise Sir John intends the favour to one Mr Brewerton. But Mr Deane had rather treate with me aboute itt for Mr Parrie then with any, inregard I shall give hym more then any other person iff Sir John may but be satisfied, whose alone consent we want and can noe way obtaine except your lordshipp be favourably pleased to interpose in his behalfe, which must either be done within a day or two, iff not this night, or elce itt's gone. And being goeing out of towne tomorrow, I humbly begg your lordship's pleasure in this and what other comaunds you have for me, which will be carefully observed by,

Your excellencie's very humble and faithfull servant,
Dan Redman

233. Draft of a letter by Henry Cromwell to Lord Broghill, [April 1657],[221] 823, fo. 335.

I am fuller of expectation then of matter to write, wherefore I shall not trouble you needesly, unless the scene of affaires were on this side. Pray consider that if names and titles onely bee changed, things may easily slide back againe, either where they are, or to a worse condition. Remember that tis not names or words that governe the world, but

[220] Stephen Charnock, an Independent minister, served as an army chaplain in the late 1640s and early 1650s before resuming his studies at Oxford. In 1655 he crossed to Ireland and took up a salaried position as a regular preacher in Dublin and as chaplain to Henry Cromwell. Edward Baines, another Independent minister serving in Ireland, also preached regularly in Dublin.

[221] The dating of this and the following letter is far from certain, but both seem to relate to a period when the Protector's hesitancy and opposition towards the title of king had become apparent but perhaps before his firm and final refusal of the crown had become known. Moreover, in surviving letters, dated 8 and 22 April, Henry Cromwell contrasted the limited importance of the proposed change of title with the real value of some of the political, constitutional, and religious proposals contained within the new constitution (*TSP*, VI, pp. 182–183, 222–223), something which is alluded to here. Accordingly, both letters have been assigned to April 1657. I am most grateful to Dr Patrick Little for sharing his thoughts on the dating of this letter.

things. I wish the constitution of the councill and army may bee tuned to the change, <what> if any bee. I say, I expect from you at present, wherefore pardon this brevity in your etc.

234. Draft of a letter by Henry Cromwell to Lord Broghill, [April 1657], 823, fo. 333.

Having received nothing from you by the last, and observing <the carriage> the unusuall and manifest brashnes of some here (<who> who never approved of mee nor I of them), and with all the clowdines of honeste men, I collect from the whole some grounds to thinke things are not like to be so well as I could wish and as once I hoped. Concerning the title, and the weight of it compared with the other proposalls <that joyned with it> in the parlament's advice, I shall say no more, having deliverd myselfe thereupon at large in my last. <And> For indeed I feare <I> I use to say too much upon the small matter I have to worke upon, beeing, for want of that light which I ought to receive from England, not only putt to guesse and grope at the way of my proceedings, and <rather> also to spin what I write rather out of my owne imaginations, then to deduce any inferences from that particular knowledge of persons and things upon <all> occasions <wherewith I am> which if his Highness thought fitt were necessary for mee. Wherefore whether I shall actually doe his Highness more or lesse service here, I hope I shall have alwayes comfort within myselfe that I have <not wrapt up the one talent <d d> entrusted with me in a napkin but have> done as much as I could out of the small helpe I have received.

235. From William Jephson, London, 5 May 1657, 822, fos 61–62.

My deare lord,

I am very sory to heare the indisposition in your throate still followes you, though I am very glad to receyve the newes of your soe speedy recoverye. Wee are yett gotten but little farther then wee were in our businesse. Wee hopt for a day to have beene appointed for his Highnesse to give his positive answer to the parliament, but hee hath appointed another conference with the committee. I must confesse I am one of those that hope well, for I can not imagine that his Highness would have held the parliament thus long in treaty with a resolution to breake with them at last. Though I find some men very doubtfull that hee may still sticke at the title and offer to accept of all the rest under that which hee now hath. I hope God will prevent that, for I find many men very violentlye bent to leave all to confusion if that bee denyde, and I really am afrayd that if it should soe fall out, the house will bee left soe thynne as that 115.[222] will cary what they please. I am extreame sory to heare your lordship hath, and is likely to receyve, soe much trouble in my businesse, but really, my lord, I find I am both in that and divers other thinges soe pusht at in my absence that without your lordship's support I am like to bee ruin'd, soe that I hope your lordship will pardon mee if necessitye inforce mee somtimes to seeme troublesom. I heare they have now admeasur'd some parcells of my land to give out to the souldiers. All the favour I begg is only that I may not bee condemn'd before I bee heard. I have one humble sute to your lordship, that you would remember mee this yeare for a goshawke, which I have written to colonel Busbridge to take care of if it bee needfull before I come. My lord, I have noe considerable newes to impart this weeke, therefore shall only tender my most humble service to your lordship and your noble lady, and my hearty thankes for the honour you were pleas'd to doe my wife in sending to see her, and begg the favour to bee esteem'd as I shall indeavour in all my actions to approve myselfe, my lord,

Your most affectionate and faythfull, humble servant,

Wm Jephson

236. From John Reynolds, London, 5 May 1657, 822, fos 63–64.

May it please your excellency,

I have beene so exceedingly disturbed by my little perplexityes that I have not so minded the publique this weeke as formerly, but the whole represented by any hand will amount to no more than this, that we yet waite upon God and upon his Highnes to establish governement by a lawfull authority, and that necessity may bee laide aside. Since my last, his Highnes hath againe beene pleased to renew and reiterate his former commands, and although I much urged want of freedome as at other times, and that it might answer his first intention to present those forces being raised and transported and than leave them, yet he hath since altred his resolution, and hath beene lately verry expresse and positive in his commands, which I would obey although I knew my returne would never be, and I judge it to be my duty and do hope to find comfort in this whatsoever the suceese be, which I leave unto the Lord. The parliament do still meete and adjourne; onely a small petition croudes in for an engrosment or reading, but nothing of consequence is admitted untill his Highnes hath returned his answer, which is expected tomorrow. I entreate your lordship to excuse my

[222] Perhaps 'the commonwealthsmen'.

late troubling you, which is now finished by my going into France,[223] and therefore I shall desire to be excused for wrighting weekely unto your lordship. My next must be with the additionall postscript of stylo novo,[224] but I shall hope to have the title of an old servant, and will endeavour to merit (although with greate obstructions to be removed) the title of the faithfullest and not least usefull of your servaunts. Committing your lordshipp to the Almighty' protection, I remaine, my lord,

Your excellencye's most humble and faithfull servaunt,
J Reynolds

My most devoted service to my lady.

237. From G. Gregorye, Rathcoursey, [County Cork], 9 May 1657, 822, fos 65–66.

Letter of request, seeking permission to travel to England to pay his respects to the Protector, and also asking that an estate of 1,000 acres that he had held in County Tipperary for the previous three years and which had not been allocated to the adventurers should now be confirmed to him in lieu of his arrears of £500; once confirmed in possession, he would invest in improving the land and repairing an old ruined castle standing there, on which he had already spent nearly £100; he would much rather settle there than on the remote, dangerous, desolate estate recently allocated to him.

238. From William Jephson, London, 12 May 1657, 822, fos 69–70.

My deare lord,

This can pretend to noe other businesse but to prevent the interruption of my constant respects to your lordship, for really his Highnesse's refusall of the parliament's petition and advise[225] hath soe amaz'd his most reall servants, as I know not what to write or say concerning it; I am sure tis not a discourse fitt for a letter. What resolution will bee taken upon the report of it to the parliament is not yett knowne, for it hath beene differ'd from day to day untill tomorrow. The counsell I find most inclind to is to rayse money for this summer's service and to adjourne the parliament for some monthes. God direct us to something which may preserve these nations from totall ruin. I hope I shall kisse your lordship's hands shortly in Ireland.

[223] He left London on 6 May and sailed from Dover on 18 May.

[224] This Latin phrase could be translated as 'new style', indicating the reformed calendar used on the continent.

[225] On 8 May.

Wheresoever I am, or whatsoever becomes of mee, I shall allwayes indeavour to approve myselfe, my lord,

Your most faythfull and affectionate, humble servant,

Wm Jephson

239. From Charles Fleetwood, London, 12 May 1657, 822, fos 67–68.

Deare brother,

It pleased the Lord upon Fryday last to incline his Highnes' heart to give a positive denyall to the buysnes of kingshippe. The debate about the answer was defferred till this day, but by reason of the speaker's indisposition it is put off till tomorrow. I presume you will heare of a petition from a party of the army; I shall therfor acquaint you how it was.[226] His Highnes having given severall denyalls, they conceived it did becom them to own his Highnes in what he did, and that the howse would please no further to presse him therin. Their intentions, I am confydent, was honest, though the thing was in itselfe very unseasonable, and was, I finde upon examination, a very sudden resolution. When I knew of what they wer about I went and acquainted his Highnes with it, who desired it might be supprest, which accordingly I made all the haste I could, but I cam a quarter of an houre too late, and they being gon to the howse to deliver, I did then hasten thither, wheare I found the debate was wither it showld be reade or not. I moved the howse against the reading of it, and so it was layde aside and nothing was don therin. I confesse I like not armye's interposings, and I think you have don well to keepe off anything in Ireland, and thes honest men who wer engaged in this buysnes I doe beleive did intend well, and had they throughly considerd all circumstances would not have don it, for I am confydent never any army so loved a generall as this poore army doth. The Lord, I trust, will arise and appeare and give us a further clearing what the worke of our day is, which I think all good people showld be very earnest with the Lord to direct us in, for surely none except the Israelites wer ever ledde in such darke paths and wayes as we hitherunto have bine, and yet that to be called a straight way of theirs, and if the Lord make ours so to be at last, what matter of amasing mercy will it be unto

[226]A petition of early May, allegedly initiated by Pride with the acquiescence of Desborough, drafted by John Owen, and signed by over two dozen officers then in and around London, which was presented to parliament by a small deputation of officers, headed by John Mason, lieutenant-colonel of Pride's regiment, early on 8 May, before the Protector made his speech firmly and finally declining the crown. The petition requested that, in the light of the Protector's earlier speeches expressing clear reservations about the offer of the constitution with the title of king in it, parliament should not press the Protector any further.

us. Which, that we may be more ledde in the spirit of faith, and to understand and know, is the desire of,

Your most affectionate brother and humble servant.

My wife's very affectionate salutes to yourselfe and lady, with my humble service to hir.

Their Highnesses are at Hampton Court and will, I think, stay ther this weeke.

240. From Anthony Morgan, London, 12 May 1657, 822, fos 71–72.

May it please your excellency,

That morning his Highness gave his deniall to accept the title, lieutenant-collonel Mason (an Anabaptist) with 3 or 4 more, in the name of some 20 more, offered a petition to the house to desire them not to press his Highness to accept the title of king. The house would not read their petition but were ready to call it a breach of priviledge, but moderation was pressed and the petition layd aside. Tis said his Highness knew nothing of the petition, but when he heard of it was extream angry; cald it a high breach of priviledge and the greatest injury they could have offered to him next cutting his throat; and indeed comming in as it did makes people abroad say he is afraid of his army. This day the report of his Highness's denyall was made to the house. Mr Bodarda[227] moved the house would vindicate their priviledge in respect of the above petition. Mr Goodwin[228] said that wee were concerned to take notice of evill councellors who advised his Highness without dores not to hearken to the advice of his parliament; said it was the quarrell in the beginning with the late king. These things were passed over and the debate about his Highness's answer adjourned till tomorrow morning. Upon a division of the house, on halfe being in the lobby, Sir Thomas Pride exprest much anger against Mr Goodwin and said he should be called to the barr. Harry Owen replied, twere fitter to call you to the barr for killing the beares,[229] for which he was applauded by the crowd about him. Thus your lordship

[227] Griffith Bodurda, parliamentarian politician, was MP for Anglesey in the second Protectorate parliament and for Beaumaris in the third, and held a variety of military and civilian administrative offices in his native north-west Wales and in London.

[228] John Goodwin, MP for East Grinstead, an experienced parliamentarian who sat in all the parliaments elected between 1640 and 1659.

[229] In 1656, as a commissioner for securing the peace of London, Pride had ordered that the bears used in bear-baiting shows and the cocks employed in cock fighting should be destroyed, thus removing an opportunity for disorderly and possibly seditious public gatherings.

sees wee have an Irish champion considerable heer.[230] Lord Fines tells me your lordship is much envied for governing better there then wee can doe heer. In our great business tis resolved by some not to be angry nor recede, but lay the consideration of it aside for a time till wee hope his Highness may have time to be better informed; in the mean time goe on and raise money and doe what other good things wee can, and then if wee can by his Highness's consent adjorne for the sommer.

I am your excellency's most faithfull and most obedient servant,

Ant Morgan

241. From Thomas Rawlins, Belturbet, [County Cavan], 21 May 1657, 822, fos 73–74.

May it please your excellency,

The lady Buttler and Mr Phillpott are come to the towne and affirme that it is your verball order to them to live in the forte. And that wee might not erre either by denying of them that benefitt if it be your excellencie's intentions, or in permitting of them to live there contrary to your order or knowledge, I thought it my duty to give you this accoumpt; and that by what I can learne the buildings and workes of that forte cost the commonwealth no less than five hundred pounds. I have formerly written to your excellency more particularly in this busines, and truely mye intention, both in the former and this, have been only to discharge my duty therein to his Highnes and the commonwealth, and that if they should be damnifyed by their living there, the blame might not ly upon mee. I have heard that some have informed your excellency that what I have written to you about it hath been out of selfe respect. If any have soe don, it hath been without the least ground or reason, for if I had any assureance of continuing heere I should rather desire to live in any other place than that. If it be your excellencye's pleasure that shee shall not live there bee pleased to signify your commaunds therin to,

Your excellencye's most truely faithfull servant,

T Rawlins

242. From Francis Russell, Chippenham, 25 May 1657, 822, fos 75–76.

My lord,

If I doe understand at all my owne temper and complection, I am as much flegmatick as sanguine, and I find it a hard match betweene

[230]Owen was MP for Counties Westmeath, Longford, and King's.

them, yet I am so wise as I care not much which hath the better, for when I am to wise than I am to flegmatick, when to fooleish than I am as much to sanguine; but I am very glad that I know myselfe so well in both my weaknesses. At that time when I writ to your lordship I had pretty good reason to be sanguine, for the little Secretary was so, and he twas that infected so many of us, but I hope I have pretty well recovered that infection, allthough it hath allmost killed divers others. I am glad your lordship is so steadey minded as not to be concerned with any outward glory, for indeed he who is inwardly truely great cares not for shaddows, which are onely the cheifest happynesses of all weake men and minds. And now I could be a little merry with your father and his temper and complection. Suppose I should tell you he often knows not his owne mind, twere but to affirme he is but a man, and like unto many of his freinds and servants who truely love him. William Perepoint and generall Montague will never trust to politicks any more, and the little Secretary tells me that he seeth now that nothing is so considerable in any busynes as simplicity. The truth is your father hath of late made more wise men fooles than ever; he laughs and is merry, but they hang downe theyre heads and are pittyfully out of countenance. All the lawyers are turned Quakers, who before boasted they would make penknifes of the soldyers' swords. My distance from London will not give me leave to make any observations of our present affaires, but withall doubt the army and sectarys are trump and have a notable game in theyre hands, if they can but play it wisely and with modesty, but I feare they are headdy, rash gamesters, which I suppose you well understand. Little Hampden, Sir John Hubbart and Jack Treavor[231] I doubt are very angerey; they had strong dreames of being lords, but now they are awake find themselves but country gentlemen. My lord, I doe beleeve that Ireland is glad of your company, and so would England be to, but whether at[232] yet to wish you there or here I know not. The little Secretary is much in love with you, commends you much to me, but what that meanes I care not to imagine or guesse. My love to your wife; the Lord blesse you both. I am, my lord,

Your lordship's faithfully and in all true love,

Franc Russell

I hope this letter will overtake my last unto your lordship.

[231] Richard Hampden, MP for Buckinghamshire, Sir John Hobart, MP for Norfolk and Hampden's brother-in-law, and probably John Trevor (junior), MP for Flintshire (though his father, Sir John Trevor, also sat in this parliament as MP for Arundel).

[232] Apparently a slip for 'as'.

243. From John Nelson[233] to Robert Gorges, Ross, 26 May 1657, 822, fos 77–78.

Honnourd sir,

Upon the last Lord's day, whilest the minister wass in sermon, the drummer to major Hadden's[234] late companie, by name Robert Whetstone, come in and give publicke disturbance with much bitterness of spiritt and revillings. I have committed him, being a soldier. I desire to know my lord's pleasure concerneing him. Hee is the first Qaker that hath given disturbance heere. It's good to nipp such spirrits in the budd. I am under some distemper and can not inlarg and crave a word from you as to this and the presenting my faithfull service to my lord, with my harty acknowlidgment for his favor in admitting tow files of my men to goe to my lott. Which favor, with those many I have received, I hope hee will not find misplacd. Pardon my trobleing of you and doe that right as to believe mee to be cordially,

Your faithfull, affectionate, humble servant,

John Nelsonn

244. Draft of a letter by Henry Cromwell to Lord Broghill, [May 1657], 823, fo. 328.

My deare lord,

I neither know what to doe or say upon this issue of affaires. Certanly, as you said, the Lord hath yet a further controversy to decide with this poore nation. All honest men here beeing at a stand and a losse both in their private and publiq concernements. I have nothing to support my hopes but that forces,[235] much as his Highness declared his willingnes to comply to severall, and hath not been much pleased since with his diswaders, and had the highest force put upon him that ever was by the 3 grandees,[236] etc. I say, for all these reasons I hope his Highness does but waite a better opportunity to shew his affections to the publiq and his particular freinds. Neither am I a little

[233] Parliamentarian officer, who went to Ireland in 1649 in Robert Phaier's foot regiment and then became lieutenant-colonel of William Reeves's foot regiment there. He was governor of Kilmallock in the early 1650s and of Ross from 1652, in which capacity he became involved, in 1652–1653, in a scheme to transport Irishmen to Spain, allegedly losing at least £2,700 in the business, for which he later sought and – with a letter of support from the Protector of July 1658 bolstering his claim – obtained grants of Irish land in compensation (Abbott, IV, p. 853; *CSPI*, pp. 671, 830, 861).

[234] Richard Hodden, governor of Kinsale.

[235] Word slightly blotted/amended, but it does seem to read thus.

[236] Perhaps Lambert, Fleetwood, and Desborough, who all opposed the offer of the crown.

strengthend in this persuasion that you have yet heart enough not to quitt all, which I desire you and all honest men not to doe, least the predomenant gentlemen obtrude whatsoever they please upon us. My lord, I must and will steere your course, wherefore have a care how you lay it, (besides your owne) for the sake of,

Your etc.

245. Draft of a letter by Henry Cromwell to John Thurloe, [May 1657], 823, fo. 334.

As to the title, I alwayes doubted his Highness' refusall, and therefore was troubled to see the parlament so peremptary therein, fearing lest a stifnes on both sides might produce a breach <betweene> the consequences whereof would be very sad. Wherefor if it bee not too late, I could wish our freinds would consider well of it, whether the matter of a title, either one way or other, ought to bee putt in the ballance with the necessary consequences of such a breach. <For if the parlament rise without providing monyes, his Highness must raise it some other way, which certainly can never bee well taken <of> by these whise advice in parlament hee hath neglected. B> Which, as your lordshipp well observes, would not only ruine his Highness and family, but also leave the liberties and other blessing of this nation, so long contended for, in a very forlorne and remediless condition. I cannot tell what intelligence thes buisy-bodies here have gotten, but they creep abroad like snakes in the warme sun; and indeed this and the drowsines which I find upon the spirits of our better freinds is that which <use> touches mee most, for they are apt to interpret this act of his Highness <rather> prejudiciall unto them; not so much <by refusing> for that his Highness is without the title, as <by thereby> that by refusing it hee seemed preferring <those> that gang before <such> a far better and more solid interest.

246. Draft of a letter by Henry Cromwell to Lord Broghill, [May 1657], 823, fos 337–338.

I am glad in order to <the> dispatch and progresse in other publick buisnes that his Highnes has given his answer,

that it was such as by the parlament's industry and patience may serve at present; and I blesse God that they so truly understood his Highnes' refusal, and were not so distasted at that which might have been gastly resented as an indignity put upon them, but <were> could condisend to patch up the desires of their opposers by putting themselves to the trouble of limitting and circumstantating the present title of protector, so as to make it in some degree consonant to the or titles in office which the law better knowes[237]

and that althought it were not what was propounded by honest men, yett <it that <...>[238] it was as much as the parlament may make equivalent thereunto by declaring the two termes or titles in controversie to signifie but one and the same thing>. <But> Now if this expedient satisfie those who opposed the title king, I shall conclude them sleight persons to contend so much about words, or rather sounds; and if it doe not <satisfie them> I shall <conclude> esteeme of them <juglers to> as pretenders to the contrary of what they mean, and shall <thinke> beleive what you well hinted of them, viz, that there beeing many things in the advice which they <snarled at> disliked equally with that title king, <that those gentlemen> they would have destroyed the whole by pulling downe that one parte, <which they hoped would appeare> supposing it most obnoxious to the men in power. The petition[239] and postscript you sent mee doth very well explaine those dark doings of <theirs> some, who for without the tumultuous forme of a commonwealth will find the way to their ends <would bee> too narrow.

I doubt whether those officers who signed this petition durst attempt such a worke without other props then what appeared, or had not other aimes then what they avow.[240]

I hope the fellow souldiers, whom they so confidently invoke in England and Scotland, will <turne a deafe> give little eare to such seditious alarmums; however, I dare presume those of Ireland doe better understand their duty and interest then to follow them. Here are lately come among us a few, whom I may thinke incendiaries, yett I hope the matter they would enflame is nott <combustible enough> apt to take <such> fire. I am the more pleased with these proceedings because they seeme graduall, and not like those late sudden <flushings, which makes the face of our former projects blush, and certainely> changes, <whereof a small> whose inconveniences a little experience hath detected for having proceeded thus far. I suppose that when men have <had some experience> upon tryall approved of the thing, they will then more easily admitt the same <or see> if necessary, or otherwise bee better content without it <then> then when humor and prejudice onely explodes it.

[237]This block of text – from 'that it was such' to 'which the law better knowes' – which seems to close in a rather garbled way, has been added in the left margin at this point.

[238]Word or words too heavily deleted to be legible.

[239]Probably the army officers' petition presented to parliament on 8 May.

[240]This sentence has been added in the left margin at this point.

I hope his Highness will at length bee convinced of the spiritt which raignes in many at this day, and that the discovery of so many horrid plotts and seditious purposes vouchsafed by the Lord for his information will not prove in vaine. It is cleere many are full of rage and envy against his Highness, who cannot beare that God should exalt him thus eminently above his brethren, and will therefore leave no meanes unattempted to levell him with themselves and the whole nation with confusion. I need say no more, for it seemes to mee all things speeke alowd to this purpose. I have given order to all my well affected officers to have an eye to the <spawnings> progresse of this petition and postscript. I cannot tell what some few may imprudently and usurpingly forge in the name of the rest; but that anything like the army of Ireland should abett it would bee as much the wonder as the greife and trouble of.

I am unwilling to trouble his Highness at this time with matters when I conceive him otherwise taken up. All his freinds need to pray earnestly for him, and <to> strengthen his hands <in the daily difficultyes hee meetes with, I shall (as I have already) doe what's best to checq this petition here and what also I can for the publick and his privacy and to aquaint his Highness that I hope effectually to doe it> that the Lord would mightily at this juncture support his spiritt, and that they would in there severall places as I shall doe in my station; and as for this petition, you may, if you thinke fitt, acquaint his Highness that I shall have a due concerning it <hoping the army her is> [...][241]

I feare lest 103, 104 and 106[242] and their forwardnes have not given rise to the insolent fellowes, and that some <others> of them have not <a finger in the py> done more. I hope his Highness will at length distinguish his true freinds from others, and by degrees wind out power and armes out of the hands of those your lordship mentioned. Pray stand fast, not onely in the howse, but also improve your interest with his Highness to keepe him in mind of those excellent things you hinted; nor lett the humor of our ill-willers grow past cure. Bee not quite discouraged till things grow desperate, for as long as there is life there is hope.

[241] There follow several further words too heavily deleted to be legible. Indeed, this whole paragraph, squeezed in along the side of the page at this point, is heavily amended.

[242] As Henry Cromwell only rarely uses this code in his letters and as no key appears to survive, it is impossible to decode these with certainty, but the most obvious and most plausible explanation is that the numbers stand for Lambert, Fleetwood, and Desborough.

247. From Daniel Redman, Kilkenny, 2 June 1657, 822, fos 79–80.

May it please your excellencie,

Leiutenant Teuch being about a moneth since discharged from prosekuteing the tories with that partie which your lordshipp ordered hym when you weare heare, his business is to petition your lordshipp and the councell for the pay which was ordered hym, he haveing neaver received any thing either for hymselfe or his four horseman but onely ten pounds, which Docktor Gorges paid hym att Kilkenny. I have onely this to trouble your lordship with on his behalfe, that dureing the tyme he was imployed and that any torries remained abroad, he was as acktive and laborious in prosekuteing off them as was possible for any man to be, though his endeavours had nott that successe that both he and others wished. I humbly desire your lordship's assistance that he may have the areares off what was promised hym. There was two off Rian's men that came lately outt off Connaught, and since are turned torries on horse backe in this county, but major Palmer and some off the countrie getting notice off them, in the reare pursued them soe close, both by day and night, that they made them quitt theire horses and tooke one off them, and both theire armes and horses, pistolls and swoords. He that was taken is now in this goaile, and I would wish we had an order to trie hym presently and hang hym out off the way, which I thinke would be off good advauntage to the state. For he tells me that iff he be hanged he will make a hundred more off his country be hanged with hym, but I cannott yett gett out his meaneing (in this businesse). Dermot Rian[243] hymselfe was nott onely the first intelligencer but led that party that prosekuted them untill they weare taken. I humbly begg your lordshipp's assistance that the country may have some small encouragement for this they light uppon though they brought hym in alive, and itt will encourage them to be more aktive. Rian's apeareing in this businesse makes mee to forbeare presseing hym to find out any aditionall securitie as yett, which I feare he cannott well gett. And iff he should be seized prisoner itt's feared by the country that itt will drive out many off his men, but I intend to send for hym and speake with hym speedilie. I humbly

[243]Dermot Ryan, along with Donnogh O'Derrick and others, was held responsible for attacking and murdering a group of Petty's surveyors and, in October 1655, the Irish council had put a price on their heads – £30 for O'Derrick, £20 for Ryan. O'Derrick was taken shortly afterwards but Ryan eluded capture and instead, in January 1657, he surrendered himself to the English regime on terms, offering to answer any accusations of murder which might be laid against him (Dunlop, pp. 542, 649–650). According to this report, he was at this time actively co-operating with the security forces and assisting them in their pursuit of Irish renegades.

begg your lordship's pardon for this trouble, and iff possible leave to goe for Enegland, an[...]aine.[244]

Your excellencie's humble and faithfull servant,

Dan Redman

248. From John Lisle, Chelsea, 5 June 1657, 822, fos 81–82.

May it please your excellency,

The bearer heereof, William Jennings, doth humbly acknowledge your goodnesse and favour towards him. His neere relation to mee made mee a suitor to my lord deputy for his letter to your excellency on his behalfe and now to joyne with this bearer in his petition and most humble thanks for what you have already vouchsafed him. He hath beene in some sea services formerly under generall Blake and was in the late service when some of the Spanish plate fleete was taken. I hope he will alwayes pray for your excellency and soe shall,

Your excellencie's most humble and most obliged servant,

John Lisle

249. From Francis Russell, Whitehall, 7 June 1657, 822, fo. 83.

Deare and honored lord,

I did receive your last letter and hope you have received tow latly from me, for my true love and respects towards your lordship doeth increase dayly. The Lord make me faithfull in it. Your freinds here increase I find dayly. Your enemys, I suppose, know not what to say unto it. Tis true wisedome, I beleeve, and hope, that giveeth you this victory and so good a place in the affections of so many, and thus shall you be blessed if you feare the Lord truely and wait on Him for wisedome, which is pure and powerfull. True humility is the onely greatnes with which if you be but once enlightned you shall not need to feare in all your wayes, but be as bold as a lyon. Therefore feare the Lord onely; be single and simple harted; abhore all craftynes and the crooked devyces of the subtle of hart; tast fully of the good, plaine, old way of honesty and therein fill and delight yourselfe, that your life, wisedome and strenght may be from above, than will God blesse you and yours and this present generation shall praise God for you. Oh my deare lord, love the Lord of all beings with your whole hart, magnifie His name in all your actions, give Him the honor and glory onely for He is good and mercyfull, full of true sweetnes and wisedome. I hope God

[244] Paper damaged with some loss of text, though the incomplete words may be 'and remaine'.

intends you some outward blessing and helpe by your new relation to Sir John Reynolds.[245] If it displeaseth any, theyre harts, I doubt, are not right in true love. Many wonder at this match and are troubleed to guesse what it meaneeth. You know well my temper and fooleish, carelesse wisedome in all things of this nature. If God hath made it wisedome I shall not boast, but be still in thankfullnes and praise His name that He can act for me and mine above all my owne forecastings or thoughtfullnes. Your father loves you truely. God conquers his hart by those good reports which he heares of you, for a wise sonne cannot be but a joy to his father. In love and duty answer him againe that his age may be renewed and strengthened thereby, than will God honer you, and wisedome shall be plaine and easy to you. You shall not need to seeke after hir, but she shall find you out and delight in and with you, makeing you hir companion and familier freind; and what shall part you asunder? You shall than be able to teach the wise, allthough your elders, and instruct the fooleish, for onely wisedome and a constant delight in hir can make you powerfull. Thus, my lord, have I pouered forth my love and those instructions I have learned (by God's grace) from hir. The Lord make us both faithfull to hir, and to manifest hir pleasant doctrines in all our ways. My love to your wife, and that the blesseing of wisedome and rightyous understanding may posses both your soules is the dayly constant prayer of, my lord,

Your faithfull freind and servant in the love that never faileeth and knoweth no end of her service,

Franc Russell

My lord Lambert, I doe beleeve, is inwardly at some distance with Whitehall.

250. From Anthony Morgan, London, 9 June 1657, 822, fos 84–85.

May it please your excellency,

This day the house waited upon his Highness in the Painted Chamber where he passed 39 bills, one of which was for the confirmation of the divisions of land made to the soldiery. Another was that in which Portumna is named. I will advise what is to be done further about it in order to comming to some effect thereupon. His Highness refused to pass the bill for chatechizing in the usuall way, (which is) he would advise upon it.

[245]Probably indicating that a marriage contract had been agreed between Reynolds and Sarah, daughter of Francis Russell. They were married later in the summer.

There was besides many private bills for disposition of land in Ireland. One ugly bill, which was a taxe of £20,000 paiable in 3 months.[246]

Yesterday, by advise of my lord Lambert and others, I moved the house in behalfe of my lord deputy that they would bestow some marks of their favor upon him. Others particularized and propounded £1,500 per annum in Ireland,[247] but contrary to the expectation of all who were privy to the motion, it occasioned a very great debate. Generall Desborow opposed it with vehemence, as he said out of kindness to him. I can not tell whether Bampfeild, Godfrey, Grove[248] and their gang did it upon that account. At last it came to a question, and was carried by one vote[249] that a bill should be brought in to that purpose, but some threaten very much to meet with the bill, so that I suppose it will not be received this sessions least it prove a blemish instead of a favor to my lord. I am sorry I moved it since it occasioned so much stirr, but I thought it reasonable that at parting wee should shew kindness, for I must alwais hope (though I love him well) his commission will never be renewed. I have been extreamly chidden by many for moving it, who say they will not easily forgive me. I am sure I meant honestly. I am, my lord,

Your excellency's most faithfull and most obedient servant,

Ant Morgan

251. From Ruben Eastthorpe,[250] Galway, 11 June 1657, 822, fos 86–87.

Right honorable,

Our Anabaptists in Galway ar now as high as if all Ireland was theirs. Collonell Sadler's lady[251] is dipped for certayne, and they glory therein and ar become most insolent. I suppose neither I nor any minister must live in Galway unlesse he can submit and comply with that party. The governor out of his respecte to his wife is wholly theirs.

[246]An additional levy, over and above the regular monthly assessments, designed to contribute towards the costs of the war against Spain.

[247]The parliamentary diary suggests that Whitelocke and Strickland were the chief supporters of this proposal (*Burton*, II, p. 197).

[248]Thomas Bampfield, MP for Exeter, Lambert Godfrey, MP for Kent, and Thomas Grove, MP for Wiltshire, had all recently expressed opposition to the Protector's veto of the catechizing bill or to the oath required of MPs under the new, written constitution.

[249]The *Commons Journal* records that it was carried by two votes, 45 to 43, in a very thinly attended house (*Journal of the House of Commons: volume 7: 1651–1660* (London, 1802), p. 550).

[250]Minister who held livings in Nottinghamshire and Lincolnshire before the civil war and was preaching in northern England in the early 1650s. He was in Ireland by the mid-1650s, serving as a minister in Galway, and was still there in 1659, by which time he was receiving a government salary.

[251]Wife of Thomas Sadleir, governor of Galway.

I never gave hym or any of that party one passionat word. In two things I only have offended. First, I did refuse to let the Anabaptists to preach in the publique church, at which the collonel was so offended that he reaproched me in high tearmes and threatned to lay down his commission unlesse he might have his desire; secondly, I have baptized some children, which doth so offend hym that he saith if I baptize children in the church he will go out of it, and threatneth to lay down his commission rather then to live under my ministry. The inhabitants of the town do give me all encoragement, but all such as testify their affections to me or my ministry are taken notice of and frouned at, and I do beeleive will be wearied out of the towne. Some ar allready gone, and Mr Clark[252] (our great archbishop) gave sentence that such as were not of his opinion were as bad as Irish Papists. Sir, I know the state doth give much liberty to this faction, but will they give liberty unto them to tread all others under their feet and to get upp their Fiff Monarchy to rule the world, in regard they affirm that they only ar the saints which must judg the earth? Sir, I do beeleive that all the encoragments which the state can give will be little enough to invite honest men to come out of England to plant the empty houses in Gallway, but if the government of the place be given upp to this party, I do beeleive men will as soon chuse to live under the Turks as under the power of these. And by the same favour our Quakers do get ground, and a hundred soldyers and others meet together at a tyme at their assemblies. It is Mrs Sadler's pleasure, and it must be so. And it is a maxime that magistrates have nothing to do with religion (I suppose they mean with their religion), but if any governor or any in the least command become Anabaptists they become most cruel tyrants and will give liberty to none: witnesse John of Leyden, Knipperdoling, Cretinch[253] and the rest of that crew in Germany. Sir, we all long to see you at Gallway. If you uppon strict examination shall fynd that I have not discharged my duty, I will submit to your censure to leave the town. Otherwise I humbly beg your protection, for neither I nor others can sibsist here long if things go on as they now do. Tis pitty that this place, which hath been so eminent, should be given upp to the will of a few mechanick barbers and taylors, and to be destroyed by them. Sir, I forbore to write this fully to yow

[252] Robert Clarke, Baptist minister in Ireland, was a revenue commissioner and a preacher in Connaught in the early 1650s and by 1652 was a minister in Galway, where he was very firm in his promotion of Baptist principles. In 1657–1658 he appeared on an official list of salaried ministers deemed tainted by scandal or insufficiency, and during 1658 he was moved to Offerlane in Queen's County.

[253] Jan Beuckelson van Leyden, Barnhard Knipperdollinck, and Henry and Bernt Krechtinch were leaders of the Anabaptists who briefly gained control of Münster in the Holy Roman Empire in the 1530s.

till now expecting your comming, but I can forbear no longer. My heart bleedeth to consider the confusion hanging over this place. Your presence may yeild seasonable helpe. I hope the state will authorize you to give assistance without noise or klamor. Thus desiring the Lord to make you a happy instrument of much good to this nation, I rest,

Your humble servant,

R Eastthorp

252. From Henry Lawrence, Whitehall, 11 June 1657, 822, fos 88–89.

Letter of recommendation, on behalf of the bearer, Lord Barrymore,[254] *and of religious exhortation.*

253. From Hugh Peters, London, 13 June 1657, 821, fos 266–267.

My lord,

These are to second also the letters of my lord deputy in the behalfe of Mr Dell's[255] kinsman, that hee may gayne some preferment there. Indeed in such things you may doe old frends curtesyes. For other things I am only to write my constant incouragement to your lordshipp in the wayes and things of God, and for the good of that poore nation. I trust yet here wee shall goe beyond the feare of good men and the hope of bad. Your brother, Sir John Reynolds, wee expect back from France,[256] where as yet there is nothing done of note. The king of Sweden prospers, and who can tell but that the Pope is upon a dismall shake at this tyme. Judge Cooke[257] is now with mee and presents his service unto your lordshipp, and so most hartily doth,

Your lordshipp's,

Hu Peters

[254] Richard Barry, second Earl of Barrymore, had, in November 1656, married Lawrence's daughter Martha. In April 1658, Thomas Herbert wrote to Thurloe, urging caution in dealing with Barrymore's claim to land in County Cork (*TSP*, VII, p. 73).

[255] Possibly William Dell, minister, theologian, and educationalist, who was chaplain to Sir Thomas Fairfax and the New Model Army in the mid- and late 1640s and officiated at the marriage of Henry Ireton to Oliver Cromwell's daughter Bridget in 1646. From 1649, he was master of Gonville and Caius, Cambridge, and put forward schemes to expand greatly the number of schools and universities.

[256] Not least in order to prepare for his wedding.

[257] John Cook/Cooke.

254. From John Allin, Arckin Fort,[258] 16 June 1657, 822, fos 90–91.

May itt please your excellencie,

I have sent by the bearer, Lewis Williams, who is imploied by your excellencie to receave and take chardge of the hawkes taken heere, two cast and a halfe of hawkes. Wee usually had heere but one eiry, and this season accidentally there was found another eiry in the iland. For the more secure carryadge of which hawkes and such as came from Boffin, I have sent a boat with him to Gallway and a mann to assist him in the carryadge of them to Dublin. There is nothing of danger as yett apeares in theise parts. In case any such thing happen, itt shalbee comunicated to your excellencie by him whoe remaines,

Your excellencie's faithfull servant to use,

John Allin

255. From Anthony Morgan, London, 16 June 1657, 822, fos 92–93.

May it please your excellency,

I have herwith sent you an act of parliament,[259] attested by the clerke of the parliament. I suppose this the quickest way and it may be as much as need be done. Judge advocate Whaley, I thinke, indends to enrole it in chancery and pass it under the broad seal. If he doe it, you will have the benifitt of it. If he doe it not I thinke you need not put yourselfe to so much unnessessary charge. Your lordship receivs herewith a lettre to the councell. If you judge it of no use pray teare it.

I have received the supplementall bill for Sir Timothy. Wee are packing the books as fast as wee can.

It is yet questionable whether the house will adjorne on Saterday next. I feare wee shall not by that time have dispatched our bills for mony.

The assessment on Ireland for 3 years is £9,000 per mensem. It was moved that the members serving for Ireland might be sent to the Tower for their contest about the proportioning the assesment twixt England and Ireland. There is alsoe an extraordinary taxe of £20,000. This, I suppose, will prevent your issuing orders for the £13,000 per mensem, which otherwise would have soon grown due.[260] I am,

Your lordship's most faithfull and most obedient servant,

Ant Morgan

[258] The principal stronghold on the Aran Isles, County Galway, surrendered to the English parliamentary forces in January 1653 (Dunlop, pp. 311–312).

[259] The act settling the Portumna estate upon Henry Cromwell.

[260] On the assumption that the Irish economy would steadily grow, in 1654 the regular monthly assessments in Ireland had been set at £10,000 per month for 1654–1656, rising

256. From Francis Russell, Whitehall, 16 June 1657, 822, fos 96–97.

Letter of request, on behalf of the bearer, an unnamed old soldier in Ireland related to Mr Pell, that he be given a place in one of Henry Cromwell's horse troops.

257. From Charles Fleetwood, London, 17 June 1657, 822, fos 98–99.

Deare brother,

Wee are now drawing neare to a periodde of our presant sessions, but much feare we shall not be able to give a dispatch to all that is befor us necessary to be don befor our rising. The mony buysnes takes up the full of our time. We have litle of publicke transactions worth your notice. I am sorry to understand ther is any occation for a misunderstanding twixt yourselfe and collonel Hewson. He wrights to me that the letter containing what it did and it being to be sent to myselfe and but from a few, he did conceive it might be don without offence.[261] The Lord teach us all in our severall places to walke with more and more inoffensivenes. Ther are thos who waite for all our haltings, and therfor had neade of often exercising and putting into practise that scripture of being wise as serpents and harmlesse as doves. I neade not tell you the faithfullnes and integrity of that person. Your gentlenes towards him, considering his services and age,[262] I hope will not be evilly returned. I shall endevor the dispatch of what you wright in reference to the affayres of Ireland. When the parliament is up we shall get a perfecting of what the counsell can doe without

to £12,000 per month in 1656, and then going up again to £13,000 per month in 1657. In fact, that proved far too optimistic and, in the course of lengthy debates during June 1657, the second Protectorate parliament first suggested that Irish assessments be set at £10,000 per month and then, after pleas from MPs with interests in Ireland that this figure was still too high – some of them poorly received by the majority of MPs, especially an attempt by several Irish MPs to petition parliament to reduce assessments to just £7,000 per month – Irish assessments were finally set at £9,000 per month.

[261] Hewson's return to Ireland on private business had worried Henry Cromwell from the outset, who feared that he would contact various former colleagues in the army there and foment renewed dissension. His fears were confirmed when Hewson, with Richard Lawrence, promoted a letter from the army in Ireland addressed to Fleetwood, expressing relief and joy at news of the Protector's rejection of the crown. The letter eventually garnered the signatures of fifteen officers serving in Ireland, some of them tricked into signing (or so Henry Cromwell alleged in a letter to the Protector of 5 June), and it was then forwarded by Hewson to Fleetwood via a third party 'in so secret a way that I would not hear of it until it was on shippe boarde', even while Hewson was making 'loving expressions towards me and [. . .] much applauding my management of affaires' (British Library, Additional MS 4157, fo. 182). On 16 June, Thurloe wrote to Henry Cromwell, confirming that he had received the papers about Hewson 'and judge them to be of a very strange nature, as savouringe of an unquiet and devideing spirit' (*TSP*, VI, pp. 352–353).

[262] Hewson's date of birth is not recorded and his age at this time is therefore unknown, though he probably died of natural causes in the early 1660s.

the legislative power. I did desire a perticu[263] of the revenue, which now will be past, I doubt, befor any use can be made therof. The treasurers heare complayn much for want of monyes, and yet bills are charged upon them. I think it would not be amisse if the counsell did wright a letter to his Highnes' counsell heare to presse the necessity of your condition. I have laboured to take off an order they made to suspend the payment of some monyes due for Ireland and to convert it unto another use. I have gott a report from a committee, which will helpe us, but the counsell's not sitting hath hinderd its perfecting.[264] The army heare are all in arreare. I hope we shall suddenly be out of thes difficultyes. I am not unsensible of your condition, and whearin you are concerned you will finde me,

Your most affectionate brother and humble servant,

Charles Fleetwood

I have procured his Highnes' order for installing of rents.

I must intreat you will give leave that Mr Clarke,[265] the apothecary, may passe his accounts to me. He being heare I have concerment in what he is to account, but he is a very faithfull person and being heare canot doe it in Ireland. Captain Briggs desires, and captain Franklin, that their passes may be inlarged for sixe weeks to each of them upon extraordinary occations, as allso Mr Fugill, who it seemes had but for 7 weekes, and one weeke was spent before he cam, and hath no strong body to travell. Excuse this trouble of,

Yours,

CF

As to what you please to wright concerning collonel Saunders, his having a commission for Kinsayle, he hath none, nor his Highnes hath not, that I know of, bine moved therin.[266]

258. From Richard Cromwell, Whitehall, 18 June 1657, 822, fos 100–101.

Deare brother,

Your laste letter I received, which takes notice of one from me to you that pleased you. I know not any thing but affectionate expressions that is worthy the glance of an ey, and for them I dare afferme are more in

[263] Word broken at the end of line, but the writer has forgotten to complete it on the next line. Apparently 'perticular' was intended.

[264] The Protectoral council held just one formal and minuted meeting during the month, on 13 June.

[265] John Clarke served as apothecary general to the army in Ireland and later held the same position with the English army in Flanders.

[266] Though Robert Saunders had become governor of Kinsale by 1659.

my hearte then in my utterance. I will not now launche into that subject, being already in the deepe seas, where I saile in full contemplation withoute either feare of rock or sandes. I finde that your intentions leades towards a more learge information of your sense and thoughts of things, which you promise to my exspectation att the next poste or convenient opportunity. Withoute doubte your experience and distance, with your very good intelligence, knowes how to state matter of fact. We that are soe neare see not soe well as those that are att an advantadgious perspecti;[267] and besides youre owne affaires in the entring into them gave you some sight of persons, whose designe hath been for a long time layed to take roote for the hindring nationall advantadges in settlement, where it might occation difficulty to there getting into the saddle, respecting there owne ambitious mindes and advantadges before religion, peace, or what else that may stand in there way. I dare not be plainer as to particulerrize persons or things, nor need I, you having knowledge of the foxe by his smell. I could fill sheets of observations, and truly were it not to discomposse, knowing your ingenuity cannot but be sencible, I should relate how things are here, and how the publique peace is tumbled and tossed as if it were nothing to breath the veines of one another to a deadly gasping. Physsick is good for the health, but not as meate. But poore nation, what is it we would have? Surely our sicknesses are very greate and our distemper almost incurable. There is noe parte sounde, sick of plenty, madd with liberty; from the head to the foote noe freind, noe soundnesse. Wisdome hath tooken the wings of the morning and hath, I feare, left us. I know your time is pretious, and therefore it is fitt for me first to appologize the hasty scrible of my penn, and then to present myne and my wyfe's affectionate services to yourselfe and deare sister, we boeth praying for your happynesses. And lastly I conclude in this assurance, that I am,

Your most affectionate brother and servant,

R Cromwell

259. From William Pierrepont, 20 June 1657, 822, fos 102–103.

Letter of thanks for the favour bestowed on his cousin Cressy.

260. From Francis Russell, Whitehall, 20 June 1657, 822, fos 104–105.

My deare lord,

I shall onely by this tell your lordship that I received your last, and that I am makeing hast downe into the country where I shall have

[267]Word probably incomplete or curiously abbreviated – apparently 'perspective' was intended.

better leisure and more freedome of thoughts to give an answer to your lordship's than this place will afford me. Besides I am somewhat tyreed in my spirits for want of country ayre and a little retyrement from sitting in the parliment house. This weeke, I hope, will somewhat satisfie my desire and bid me be gone to that place from whence I came, for the parliment is likely to adjourne till towards Michlemas tearme. The news of this place, allthough not considerable for ought that I know, I suppose you will have from better hands. I cannot observe any thing that makes me to think but that all things are likely to goe well. His Highnes seemes to be very soberly cheerefull, a temper that I like very well. God, I think and hope, is purgeing us all by fire and His spirit. I wish we may be vessells fitly prepareed for His use in a true humility of mind, for I cannot distrust the goodnes of God if we can but ly low enough. Tis veryly thought that the match betweene your sister and Mr Rich is upon the point concludeed on. Yesterday Mr William Perepoint and Sir Gilbert Gerard[268] were with his Highnes, I doe beleeve in order to that busynes, and this day my lord of Warwick[269] and the earle of Manchester,[270] a great strangeer at Whitehall. My lord Lisle pretends strong affections still to my neece Bodvell, and I cannot think but that match will be concludeed ere long. This inclosed,[271] my lord, comes from your brother, my lord Richard, who is in good health, onely at present in a course of phisick. My love

[268]Parliamentarian politician, who was close to several of the most prominent parliamentarians of the opening phase of the conflict and was distantly related to Oliver Cromwell. Although he retained minor office during the 1650s, he neither sat in the Protectorate parliaments nor played an active role at this time, perhaps because of his age – he was seventy in 1657.

[269]Robert Rich, second Earl of Warwick, courtier, parliamentarian officer and admiral, politician, and colonialist, supported the parliamentarian cause from the outset and, although he played a minor role commanding land forces, his real value to the war effort was as lord admiral of the parliamentarian fleet. As a political moderate, his influence waned in the later 1640s, he had no part in the regicide, and the abolition of the House of Lords in 1649 deprived him of a platform in national politics. The negotiations for his grandson's marriage brought him closer to the Protector and, although he declined to take a seat in the new Protectoral second chamber, he played a prominent role in the reinauguration ceremony of 26 June 1657.

[270]Edward Montague, second Earl of Manchester, courtier, and parliamentarian officer and politician, supported the parliamentary cause from the outset, commanding the Eastern Association army from 1643 until he lost his command in the spring of 1645. Although he remained active in parliamentary circles during the later 1640s, eventually supporting the army against parliament in 1647, his opposition to the regicide led to loss of influence and this, combined with the abolition of the House of Lords, caused his virtual retirement from public office and public life until the Restoration.

[271] Probably letter no. 258.

to your wife. The Lord blesse you both and all yours. I have reason, my lord, to be,

Your lordshipe's in all that true love can require,

Franc Russell

261. From John Vernon, Waterford, 22 June 1657, 822, fos 106–107.

Letter of request, reminding Henry Cromwell of an earlier promise to allow Vernon to take his family to England, crossing from Kinsale to Barnstaple or Minehead in one of the state's frigates, so protecting them from pirates; thanks Henry Cromwell for past favours and praises his record in Ireland.

262. From John Jones, Chelsea, 23 June 1657, 822, fos 108–109.

Letter of courtesy, sending his own and his wife's good wishes; hearing that there was smallpox within Henry Cromwell's household, he also offered him the use of his own house during the summer.

263. From Edward Montague, Whitehall, 23 June 1657, 822, fos 110–111.

Letter of thanks for the recent letter he had received and of courtesy; also noting that he was about to return to sea.[272]

264. From Anthony Morgan, London, 23 June 1657, 822, fos 112–113.

May it please your excellency,

I have been so close tied to the house least I should loose an oportunity I waite for to pass the bill of attainder (which is engrossed),[273] that I have scarce time left to write least the post should be gonn. I have asked my lord deputy' leave to goe for Ireland; he sais I may when the house rises, but I doe soe much feare he should alter his mind that I can not cheerfully put my affaires in order for my jorny. I humbly begg pardon for this impertinent scrible, and remain,

Your lordshipp's most faithfull and most obedient servant,

Ant Morgan

The house sitts till Thursday.[274]

[272] He left London, en route to rejoin the fleet, in mid-July.
[273] The act of attainder of Irish rebels, passed on 25 June.
[274] In fact, it sat until Friday 26 June.

265. From Charles Fleetwood, London, 23 [June[275] 1657], 823, fos 347–348.

Deare brother,

I understand by Mr Secretory you have sent a perticuler of what the receipts of the revenue in Ireland are, though I could not have it from you; yet I shall see wherin it differs from what was put into committee, necessitated therunto by reason that the committee could not stay for a more perfect account. But I perceive by Mr Secretor[276] this you have sent is not very perfect, which could not well be expected in so short a time. As for the retrenchment of the army's charge, when ther is occasion for it, you shall have timly notice therof; and though it is a thing which of necessity must follow the publicke incomes, being so much lesse then formerly, yet the state of affayres will not give a presant resolution therin; I meane in reference to our enimyes abroade, who though they have not power at presant, yet are continually consulting our disturbances. Through mercy we are in a very good condition of quietnes at home. The howse continues till Thursday, and I beleive canot rise this weeke. Today is brought in a desire to have an oath prepard for his Highnes' parliment and counsell,[277] which I beleive will take up some longer time then was intended; besids we want the perfecting of our money buysnesses. The members are very impatient to be gon, but the publicke will, I hope, have the preference befor their own concernments. We are so much engaged in buysnes fornoone and afternoone that I must intreat your excuse for my shortnes, and to owne me for,

Your most affectionate brother and humble servant,

Charles Fleetwood

266. From John Duckinfield,[278] Carrickfergus, 27 June 1657, 822, fos 114–115.

May it please your excellency,

I thought it my duty to acquaint your excellency that their was one captain Wms[279] (who now belongs to this regiment) that neere

[275] The letter is actually dated 23 July, but the contents make clear that this must be a slip for 23 June.

[276] Apparently a slip for 'Secretory'.

[277] This occurred on 23 June, thus confirming the correct date of the letter.

[278] Parliamentarian officer and politician, who served in Ireland as lieutenant-colonel in the foot regiment commanded first by Robert Venables and then, from the winter of 1655–1656 onwards, by Thomas Cooper. He was, at this stage, acting governor of Carrickfergus, while his colonel was absent in England attending the parliament. Duckinfield himself sat in the third Protectorate parliament for Carrickfergus and Belfast.

[279] Word written thus, apparently as an abbreviated form of 'Williams', but the common surname and lack of a forename preclude firm identification.

uppon twelve monthes since procured a pass for England from your excellency for 3 monthes, and returned not for Ireland till within a monthe, who landing at Dublin, and after some little stay their, tooke his journey towards the noarth to his company, and comes within fifteene miles of his chardges and their stayes till one of his officers (whom he had sent for) came to him and furished him with money; from thence he returned in all hast to Dublin, without asking any leave or comeing up to see his chardge after soe long an absence, and when he intends to returne I know not, he thinking none (heere) worthy an accountt. He yet remaines respited on the rowles for some monthes. I humbly conceave it is much contrary to the commands I received from your excellency for keeping officers with their chardge. Should officers take their liberty at their pleasure, it would be a bad example to others. Had this beene the first time he had practised this course, both by my colonel and myselfe since we were imployed by your excellency, I should not have troubled your excellency theirwith, hopeing freindly advice might have wrought uppon him. But finding him to continue his former custome in neglecting the publique service and his company soe much, made me the more bold humbly to lay this before your excellency, that the captain may for the future better behave himselfe and carry it towards your excellency and the chardge over which he is sett; which with my humble service to your excellency, I remaine,

Your excellency's most humble servant,

John Duckinfield

267. From Henry Whalley, Loughrea, [County Galway], 27 June 1657, 822, fos 116–117.

May it please your excellencie,

By the last I receaved a lettre from Mr Margets,[280] whoe writes that he hath spoake with major Morgan aboute the cerfying[281] your act of parliament[282] into the chancery, and afterwards haveing it exemplyfied under the greate seale, and that the major's opinion is it is an unnessesary charge. My lord, I know they are both in an error in this particular, soe far as it is nesessary upon all occasions to produce your title upon any question in the law or otherwise. It is therefore my humble opinion that sithense Mr Margetts hath failed me, that your

[280] Thomas Margetts, parliamentarian bureaucrat and administrator, clerk to the Irish committee in London in the 1640s, and assistant judge advocate to the army under Whalley in the 1650s.

[281] Apparently a slip for 'certifying'.

[282] About the Portumna estate.

lord intrust some fit person to have it don for your lordship. I profes I am much trobled at this disappointment. My lord, things goe not soe current here with me as I expected, but I hope your excellencie will cleere matters as they arrise. Without your lordship's countenance I shall suffer. Besids I here, but I hope it is but a report, that alderman Smith – I rather beleeve Mr Erasmus Smith,[283] whoe was talked of to be chosen alderman of London – hath an order for greate quanteties of lands aboute Galloway. I hope your lordship will not suffer that since I wrote to your lordship of my want of very much neere 2,000 acres at Athenree.[284] My lord, I and mine stand and fall with your excellencie and we dayly pray for your excellency. Your servant humbly subscribs himselfe,

Your excellencie's most humble and faithfull servant,

Hen Whalley

268. From Bryan Smyth,[285] Londonderry, 29 June 1657, 822, fos 118–119.

May it please your excellency,

I have done my utmost indeavor in forwarding the worke of the cittidall here, and have spent my owne mony and tyme to incorage the worke men to bee speedy; but now at last it is at a stand for want of mony that is passable to cary it on, for though all the care that maybee bee taken to reseave mony from the tresury, yet cannot the poor worke men get bread or meate, for much of it and the market is spoyled alsoe, every man being left by the last proclamation to bee his owne judge what mony hee will reseave. Soe that truely, my lord, the poor wilbee undon if some very tymely remedy doe not enterpose; and for the contrybution it will not bee paid. I thought it my duty this second tyme to present it to your excellencye, who I dout not have bowells of compassion towards the poor. Besids I humbly offer as my poor judgment this Spanish mony might bee all melted downe and turned into English quine, as it is in Scotland. Otherwise the

[283]Merchant and educationalist, who supported the parliamentary cause and was a contractor to the parliamentary armies. He took a keen interest in Ireland and, both as an adventurer and as one of the principal suppliers of the English army there, he acquired extensive property in Ireland; he also bought out many soldiers and other adventurers, thus increasing his stake in Ireland. During 1657, he placed much of his Irish property in the hands of trustees, who were instructed to use the income to set up five new schools in Ireland. Around this time he was elected an alderman of London, but he paid a fine to be excused.

[284]Athenrey, County Galway.

[285]Parliamentarian officer, serving in Ireland during the 1650s in the foot regiment commanded initially by Henry Ireton and then by Fleetwood.

trad and planting of this country wilbee wholy impeded, all sort of Spanish quine being now counterfit and debased. I shall not further troble your excellency having dischargd my duty, save only to desire your lordship in the meane tyme, tell some effectuall corse bee taken, to cause order to bee sent that the tresurer may pay unquestionable mony to the poor workmen, that the worke may goe on. The poor souldiers are put to great losse alsoe by the badnes of the mony. I rest,

Your excellency's faithfull servant,

Bry Smyth

269. From Arthur Annesley, London, 30 June 1657, 822, fos 120–121.

May it please your excellence,

Little of moment occurring since I wrote to your lordship, I directed my last to Doctor Gorge with what was of newes to be presented with my most humble service to your lordship. But Friday last being a remarkable day, as well for his Highnesse' inauguration by the parliament to the protectorship of this commonwealth in pursuance of the government lately settled by the petition and humble advice, as for the many acts then passed,[286] whereof your lordship receives inclosed a list, and the adjournment of the house. I would not omitt giveing your lordship notice thereof though the prints are full thereof and I know your lordship hath the account of particulars from better hands. For so suddain a businesse (for it was not resolved on above three dayes before) it was transacted with much magnificence and order, and had it been at Dublin I assure myselfe none there would have grudged a bonfire to see the Protector receive and owne his office from the civill powers, though there were no bonfires here; and it was observed the lord Lambert and most of the martiall list absented themselves, though I cannot beleeve but they had notice of the solemnity as well as the civill officers.

There is no newes of action yet by the English in France, and the rumors of Callais come to little. I hope to bring the next weeke's newes myselfe to your lordship, and in order to my returne doe beseech your lordship to direct Doctor Gorge that, upon my sending to him, I may have what frigott can be spared to transport me from Blewmorris, Chester or Hollyhead, which shall further ingage me to devote myselfe, my lord,

Your excellencye's most humble servant,

Arthur Annesley

[286] Twenty-three were passed on the final day of the session.

270. From Nicholas Bernard, Gray's Inn, 30 June 1657, 822, fos 122–123.

May it please your lordship,

Since I had the honnor to receive a letter from your lordship concerning the lord primat's lybrary, I have wrott five times to your lordship in relation to it, but have not understood by any of your servants of the receipt of them, and of late suspition hath bene given me of the miscarriage of them. I humbly pray your lordship that I may not lye under any misenterpretation of a neglect of any service you shall comand me, as in this particular I have not bene wanting to my uttmost, and hope there were no passages in my letters, if received, that might displease your lordship. The lybrary is upon its way, and your lordship will find it worthy of that summe. Only there are some manuscripts which the lord primat intended for the presse, which I wish had bene left here for that end, as I humbly desired your lordship would have given order for, which I was mooved unto by diverse learned men here, and I beseech your lordship to take it yet into your consideration. I rest,

Your lordship's most humble servant,

N Bernard

The former letters were sent by the ordinary post; this comes by the packett at Whitehall.

271. From Charles Fleetwood, London, 30 June 1657, 822, fos 124–125.

Deare brother,

I have no good condition of health, having not bine very well thes 2 or 3 dayes, and therfor must intreat you will pardon me that I canot inlarge. The parliment being now up, we shall after a litle time be mor at leisure. At presant the counsell hath not satt[287] that we can doe any thing about monyes, which will be the greatest difficulty we shall meet with. I feare the provission left by the parliment will scarce answer our necessityes. I think it necessary the counsell showld send a letter of desire hither to quicken up the remembrance of you. My part I shall not neglect. We are sending another supply of men into France. The affayres ther are much at a stand, litle action having past. What the Dutch will doe is uncerteine. If the Lord please to give a blessing to our presant settlement, we shall be in a better condition to encounter thos difficultyes from abroade, whear ther are very great endeavors

[287] After 13 June, the Protectoral council did not hold another formal, minuted meeting until 13 July.

to prepare for disturbances heare. But as the Lord hath hitherunto, so I trust still will appear in discovering and preventing thos designs which our old enimyes are now preparing for. But the Lord, who hath owned us, if we may have hearts in faith to wait upon Him, wee shall not feare, and if we may doe nothing to provoake His withdrawing, we neade not care. As to what you mention concerning my former letter relating to the postscript of the officers' petition to the parliment, the postscript was looked upon as a design tending to disturbance, and in the nature of it not to be warranted, and I think very different from collonel Hewson's letter, which could not be intended by me in what I writt. But that buysnes, I hope, is fayrly over, and therfor I desire not to mention a word any more about it, but shall in all things, I hope, laboure to regayn our former dearnes, and let that intirnes be twixt as to give credit to no contrary reports each of other, and then I trust you will have no cause but to esteme me as,

Your most affectionate brother and humble servant.

My lady Claypole hath another brave boye, Oliver his name.[288]

272. From Charles Fleetwood, London, [June 1657], 823, fos 5–6.

Dear brother,

His Highnes, having accepted the goverment with his old title, puts a settlement to that affayre which will give me a liberty to attend the buysnes of Ireland; and therfor shall intreat you will please to let collonel Harbert sende a perticuler of all your former commands and I shall now dilligently attend the same. It hath pleased the Lord to put a period to that good man's dayes, Sir Robert King, which hath occationed many sollicitors for the place.[289] I was endeavord to be preingaged by a person for one befor I was spoken unto for Sir Theophilus Jones, and could not well grant his desires, but I shall not put in any without your consent. Only I shall offer this to your consideration, wither it wer not better to save that charge to the state and only give an addition to Mr Dawson's[290] pay, who you know hath cheifly supplyed that place; but if you think it necessary to be continued, I think you will judg it most necessary to have a through, tryed, honest, carefull man, who may make it his buysnes to inspect that affayre. The person I am somwhat engaged unto I shall afterwards impart to you, but it shall be none whom you

[288]Oliver Claypole, the Protector's grandson, died the following year, probably shortly predeceasing both his mother and his grandfather.

[289]As commissary general of the musters in Ireland.

[290]Thomas Dawson, deputy commissary of the musters.

think not fitt to aprove of. I have that dearnes for you as I hope you shall allwayes finde in me a readynes to comply to your satisfaction. I desire we may still make Jethroe's counsell[291] our practise, which hade thos necessary qualification for imployment: abilityes, fearing the Lord and hating covetuousnes; and surely ther being choyce of such persons qualifyed we may performe a duty in observing the same. The counsell unknown to me hade orderd £14,000 due to Ireland out of delinquents' compositions, which, I understanding, have acquainted the counsell with it, who have referred to a committee, and upon Thursday next the report shall be made. I shall endeavor to doe my part therin, which surly ought to be very tenderly considerd by us not to suffer poore Ireland to run into a condition of want and free quarter, which by orders will quickly be. I must intreat you will give leave to Mr Worsly[292] for a litle longer stay, he having a buysnes of concernment to him, and the truth is I stayd him this weeke. Our humble services to your deare lady.

I am your most affectionate brother and humble servant.

273. From Richard Cromwell, Whitehall, 2 July 1657, 822, fos 128–129.

Deare brother,

Being willing to answer in hast the desire of this bearer, William Evans, one of your lifeguard, I shall excuse my not using my owne hand, nor inlarging more att this time then to recommend to your favour the person of the said Evans. That your lordshipp be pleased, if any opportunity is offered, to consider so farr his services done faithfully these six yeares last past, in the condition he is now in, and (as I am informed) eight more before, sometimes in a better, that he may be favoured with a more advantageous imployment for his better maintenance and of his family. And upon his further informing me of a necessity, laid upon him, to be here in England in February next for to attend a suite of concernment that he hath depending both att the common law and in chancery, I shall also inlarge my desire in this behalfe to your lordshipp that you be pleased to grant him leave for three moneth to beginne with the said next February that he may, in so doing, receive no prejudice in his private affaires or his imployment att that time. This being the occasion of this trouble to you att this

[291] Biblical story of how Jethro advised his son-in-law, Moses, that he could not directly hear and settle everyone's disputes but that he should instead appoint a number of honest, incorruptible, and godly men, instructed in God's laws and statutes, and empower them to hear and resolve all but the most difficult cases (Exodus, chapter 18).

[292] Possibly Benjamin Worsley.

present, I shall onely add my prayers to God for the continuance of His blessings on your person and deare family, resting, deare brother,

Your most affectionate brother and servant,

R Cromwell

274. From Richard Cromwell, Whitehall, 2 July 1657, 822, fos 130–131.

Deare brother,

The bearer hereof, captain Nathaniel Hewett, is the kinsman of Charles Hewett. Hee hath made it his suite to mee to write these unto you in the behalfe of his kinsman, who I perceive by my Lord Protector's serious letter (which with his reference to the councell will lye before you) hath beene a great sufferer. And forasmuch as hee desires noe more than what law and equity gives him, my earnest request is that you will owne him therein, and what favour you shew him shall bee acknowledged by,

Your most affectionate brother and servant,

R Cromwell

275. From Francis Russell, Chippenham, 4 July 1657, 822, fos 132–133.

My deare lord,

I am told that about this time of the yeare you are in your progresse, and I hope in time twill reach as far as Chippenham, for me thinks your father should[293] long as much as your other freinds to see you sometimes in England. We, who know nothing of state affaires, are deviseing you some other imployment for you besides that of Ireland. Sometimes we will have you generall of the English army, than lord admirall, and so to viset us once a yeare and keepe a good correspondency with all your freinds here. Something we have in our heads for you and would not have you buryed in Ireland. You must not laugh at us because we are in good earnest. If I were of your good freind Oliver's counsell, I should set his head a workeing more than the little Secretary, old Rouse[294] or Skipon, for I think they are to grave and wise for this mercuryall, quick age. But the best of it is your father is a notable man, and he

[293]Word repeated in error.

[294]Francis Rous, parliamentarian politician and religious writer, served in the parliaments of the late 1620s and in the Short and Long Parliaments, where he consistently supported the parliamentary cause and was particularly prominent in religious business. By the 1650s, he seems to have supported Independency and he found favour with Oliver Cromwell, sitting as a founder member of the Protectoral council and in both of his Protectoral parliaments. Born in 1580, he was by far the oldest Protectoral councillor and probably the oldest senior politician of the Protectorate.

and all his counsell rides all but upon one horse; I meane, he counsells himselfe. Were it not so, I well know what would become of things. My lord Lambert lookes but sadly. He puts me in minde of a saying of old Solomon's, that there is an appointed time for all things under the sun, to hate as well as to love, to be sad as well as merry. My lord deputy and generall Disbrow beginne to grow in request at Whitehall. Disbrow made a notable speech in the parliment house in answer to one of my lord Lambert's. Twas very like him, blunt and honest. My lord, if your integrety and wisedome continues with you, you will see through all our clouds here, and it may be in time you may by your wisedome helpe to disperse them. My good opinion of you makes me to say anything, but to think much more. I wish you all happynes and true inward peace. My love to your wife. You know I am, my lord,

Your lordship's,

Franc Russell

276. From Henry Whalley, Athenry, [County Galway], 4 July 1657, 822, fos 134–135.

May it please your excellencie,

Haveing this post receaved a lettre from Mr Erasmus Smith that the councill have granted him an order to have the forfeited lands aboute Gallway, I presumed theise lines.

My lord, I am not against his haveing part of those lands, but soe it is, my lord, that the lands at Loughrea and Athenrey fall short of my proportion, and the lands forfeited next adjacent to those at Athenrey are the forfeited lands betweene Athenrey and Gallway, soe as by the act[295] I cannot have any other lands. When I have ended my survey, which I hope wilbe within a few dayes, Mr Smith may have what shal be left. My humble suite to your excellencie is that (if any such order be) it may be rectified. For how shall the commissioners of Laughreah pursue the councill's order in setting me out lands next adjacent, which are onely those neare Galway, if Mr Smith's order be for the same lands, unles they set me out the lands of Balmastoe as next adjasent to Loughreah, which I heare is leased to major Desbrow?[296] My lord, I depend your justice in this matter, and am,

Your excellencie's most humble, faithfull servant,

Hen Whalley

[295] Irish lands had been settled upon him by legislation passed by the second Protectorate parliament.

[296] John Desborough, parliamentarian officer, was major in Daniel Abbott's dragoon regiment in Ireland. He already held property in and adjoining County Galway, including Ballinasloe Castle, roughly midway between Athenry and the southern shore of Lough Ree (*CPSI*, pp. 612, 831; Dunlop, pp. 628–629).

My lord, Mr Smith from London writ to me that he had sold his proportion to auditor-general Roberts.[297]

The rents due at May Day, which I receaved for all the lands and cabins at Laughreah, except the mill without the town, was under £15.

277. From Richard Cromwell, Hampton Court, 6 July 1657, 822, fos 136–137.

Deare brother,

I have of late troubled you with the signing towe letters, recommending the severall persons that were concerned in them. I hope you know the force of importunity and then you are able to give any suit of myne a due and proportionable measure of favour according to the merritts of the persons, which I conceive are better knowen to you then to me. I confesse myselfe guilty of your trouble, which I am alsoe now, att the request of my cosen Smithsby[298] on behalfe of his sonn. I am confident you have a kindenesse for him and his numerous famuly, because you had. And knowing there is noe reason to take offe that kindenesse, as to his continnewed readynesse to serve you in any your commands. And much more for that he is rather lower then higher in relation to the world, he having only as yet the promise of releife and consideration (as much as the present juncture will afforde his Highnesse for his freinds) for his patient waiting and supporte of his drooping spiritts for what is owned or due to him. These and many such like arguments might be used, but I know you know as much of his condition as any other (it being not altered) and therefore I need not make the like appologie for this trouble given you on his request (as for the abovementioned letters) whose request is that you would be pleased to take notice of his sonn and to give him some preferring proffitt that not knowing how the world may be to him or his in there severall fortunes (which is uncertaine to all), this favour of yours to his sonn may in some measure be a helpe and comforte, as God shall inlearge the earth. If you be desarter,[299] I will assure you there is high charity. Excuse me, for I am, deare brother,

Yours most affectionately,

R Cromwell

[297]Edward Roberts, parliamentarian administrator, was auditor general in Ireland and held a variety of other financial offices in Ireland during the 1650s. Despite his Baptist faith, he remained loyal to Henry Cromwell and continued to prosper, acquiring extensive estates in Ireland (*CSPI*, pp. 821–822).

[298]Possibly the George Smithsby, kinsman to the Protector, who was recommended by him to Admiral Penn in December 1654 for employment at sea (Abbott, IV, p. 516).

[299]Uncertain reading of a poorly formed word.

278. From John Trevor,[300] St Martin's Lane, London, 6 July 1657, 822, fos 138–139.

Letter of request, asking that captain Pecke[301] be given a further month's leave before returning to Ireland, to attend to both his own affairs and those of Trevor in London.

279. From Richard Cromwell, Whitehall, 8 July 1657, 822, fos 140–141.

Deare brother,

Youres of the 1st instant came safe to my hands, by which I finde that myne hath a good reception. It must be your goodnesse that can give them soe great an advantadge, not that there is or can be any thinge worthy in my penn. I hope I shall never want a sense of your kindnesse to me. And for giving you trouble, I neither intended it in my preceeding letter or in this. For indeed, there being soe many miscarredges of letters, that it is altogether unsafe for either of us to write anything but what the world may see, nay particulerly oure enimyes, that we are borne in our relations to help one another. You will have the worste of the bargaine, for I may receive advantadge from you, but my condition cannot returne. You will have the honour, it being more honour to give then receive. I thank God I desire to be contented with what condition He shall please to keepe me in. Things are upon the wheele, which moves as slowely as the Egiptian charriots in the Red Sea. But blessed be God we are neither Egiptians, nor enimyes to the Iseralites. Nay, hath not God tooken care for us in giving us deliverances, oute sixe and seven troubles, from the hands of open and private enimys? Indeed, that is our glory that we can boaste in the salvation of God, whoe hath been yesterday, is to-day and will be for ever unto us righteousnesse and peace (temporall and spirrittuall), and to all those that live by faith for and upon Him. My wyfe and selfe present our true and faithfull

[300]Probably John Trevor (junior), parliamentarian politician, son-in-law of John Hampden and thus distantly allied to Oliver Cromwell by marriage, who was elected to the Long Parliament in the mid-1640s but who was excluded at Pride's Purge. His political career really resumed during the Protectorate, sitting for his native Flintshire in all the Protectorate parliaments, and ended as a Restoration politician, diplomat, and, from the late 1660s, junior secretary of state, being knighted in 1668. However, it is at times hard to disentangle his career from that of his father, Sir John Trevor (senior), parliamentarian politician, son-in-law of Sir Edmund Hampden, and thus very distantly allied to Oliver Cromwell by marriage, who sat in the Long Parliament (though he withdrew for a time in the wake of Pride's Purge) and in the second Protectorate parliament, and who was particularly concerned with the affairs of his native north Wales. Knighted in 1619, his political career petered out in the late 1650s and he did not play a significant role in Restoration politics. Father and son died within a few months of each other in the early 1670s.

[301]Possibly the John Peck, parliamentarian officer, who served alongside Henry Cromwell as a fellow-captain in Thomas Harrison's New Model horse regiment in the late 1640s.

respects and services to you and our deare sister, wishinge yee bouth, with your little ones, all happynesse. I rest, deare brother,

Your most affectionate brother and servant,
R Cromwell

My sister Cleypoole, Sunday was sennight, was with easie labor brought to bead off a very lusty boye, whose name is Oliver.

280. From Adam Molyneux, Ballyroan, [Queen's County], 9 July 1657, 822, fos 142–143.

May it please your excelencie,

Accordinge to your lordshipe's commandes I make bould to give this accoumpt of my proceedinges. That this day I have, by God's blessinge, eased the country of the greate trouble it systayned by Hugh Joe Kelly[302] and five other tories in his company, whose heades are fixed upon the forte of Leixe.[303] I have latly given your lordship's secretary to understand of the breakinge of foure gaoles in this province, and one in Munster, all in a weeke's tyme, to the number of fourty prisoners. If sum extraordinary course be not taken with gaolers, my worke and the countrye's burthen are endles. For now I can confidently aferme there is not one torie abraude in Leinster, unles sum of those prisoners prove such. If any of them doe, all care shall be taken for theire suppression that leyes in the power of,

Your lordship's most obedient and faithfull servant to be comanded,
Ad Molyneux

281. From Richard Cromwell, Whitehall, 10 July 1657, 822, fos 144–145.

Deare brother,

Objects of charity being dayly offered to me, who have no other way for their relief then to recommend them by my pen; I hope you will, upon that account, excuse my frequent troubles and this, att present, in the behalfe of these bearers, George and Robert Gradones, father and sonne, who have a neere relation to the cornett of captaine Whalley's troope and an invitation from him to repaire into Ireland for bettering their condition, which (as I am informed of, as well as of their honesty and good affection to the present government) is fallen

[302]Possibly Hugh O'Kelly, Irish rebel in Connaught, who was a signatory to a treaty of summer 1652, under which a large group of native Irish activists in that province made their peace with the English regime.

[303]The original name of the stronghold in Maryborough, now Port Laoise.

of from a good one to need and want. My desire to you for them being that you be pleased, upon further knowledge of their said relation and fittnesse for service, to grant to each of them a trooper's place in the said captaine Whalley's troope or in any other as you shall think fitt. This being to no other intent, I shall adde no more but that I rest, deare brother,

Yours most affectionately,
R Cromwell

282. From Charles Fleetwood, 14 July 1657, 822, fos 146–147.

Deare brother,

I have received yours with the inclosed account of the state of the civill list, which I trust I did not looke so much after, upon a carnall account, as that I still desire all things which concern us both may passe with so much freedom, that as much as may be not to give occation to any to doubt of our true and hearty love, which I hope I shall be carefull to promote. The buysnes of the pay in Ireland will suddenly be setled, I hope befor this letter goes away. The counsell's not sitting hath given an obstruction to many buysneses of moment. This afternoone they are sworn,[304] which I hope will put a speedy issue to such buysneses that are at presant delayed befor us. The Lord give us hearts to answer this great trust, that we may have better hearts to improve our time to performe the worke of our day. We have a short time heare and the faithfull discharge of our duty will be the great buysnes we showld labour after. For the worke that we all are called out unto is not ordinary; I meane the great buysnes of our cause, wherin we all have reason to have a tendernes to our utmost, that so presious a cause may not suffer through our miscarriages. I doubt not you will heare his Highnes' commands to my lord Lambert;[305] such passages of providence are to be teachings to us. Mr Secretary is added one of his Highnes' counsell. I feare the provision of money is so short that ther will be a considerable retrenchment of the charge in Ireland. We must now cutt our coate to our cloath, but I shall endevor to get as much as I can for you. But I wonder that the councell's letter to his Highnes is that £67,000 is only in arreare from England, and yett in the same letter tis said there is 6 monethes and 14 dayes in arreare to the army; but I did interprett the meaning to be of the

[304]This took place on 13 July, perhaps indicating that Fleetwood misdated this letter or that he began it that day but then completed and dated it on the morrow.

[305]The Protector dismissed him from office for his continued opposition to the new constitution, signified by his refusal to take the oath as a Protectoral councillor, and required him to return his military commission.

latter arreare, so that I have prevayled to have that £67,000 to be paid out of the assessments heere and the £20,000 extraordinary sett lately upon Ireland. I must beseech your lordship's pardon that I am forced to make use of another's penn being great hast. I am,

Your most affectionate brother and humble servant,

Charles Fleetwood

283. From William Jephson, London, 14 July 1657, 822, fos 148–149.

Letter of apology, explaining that he had not written lately because he had had no news relating to Henry Cromwell or his service; also reporting that he believed that this would be his last letter to Henry Cromwell, since he expected to be with him in person shortly.[306]

284. From Nathaniel Fiennes, Derby House, London, 16 July 1657, 822, fos 150–151.

Letter apologizing for his long silence in responding to Henry Cromwell's letters and favours, expressing his desire to be of service, and requesting a favour for the unnamed bearer,[307] *his wife's youngest brother, a former Oxford student who desired employment in Ireland and whose father would pay to help secure his future there; Jephson, the writer's cousin, would provide further details.*

285. From Ruben Eastthorpe to Hardress Waller, Galway, 17 July 1657, 822, fos 156–157.

Right honorable,

I am not my owne but Christ's. I am not my owne, but I allso ow my life and all to the commonwealth of which I am a member. My comfort is that in the publique service I was the first minister in England who was sequestred by the late king's own hand and deprived of a good estate and that the remainder was put into the hands of the parliament and there left. I am herby ruined, my family brought low and I cast into much debt. However, I will hold my ferst principles and will willingly engage myselfe to the utmost in the publique service. My hart did burne within me when I considered the misery of Ireland and I thought God had a work to do for me in this place. I forsook all my preferment in England and here I am and am perswaded God hath a

[306]The expectation was unfulfilled, as Jephson was sent on a diplomatic mission to Sweden in the summer of 1657.

[307]The letter's endorsement reveals that this is John Whitehead, who gained a BA and an MA from Oxford in the early 1650s and who was the son of colonel Richard Whitehead and the brother of Frances, Fiennes's second wife.

work for me to do. I hope God will in some measure blesse my labours. I am about a great worke which I will impart to you and humbly beg your advice. If yow approve therof, I beeseech yow to impart it to his excellency, together with the enclosed letter.[308] If I have been over bold, or if you dislike my design, I beeseech you to burn the same and pardon my boldnes. Errors of love may easily obtaine pardon.

Sir, before I came out of England Sir John Reynolds and many members of parliament did entreat me to cast about to get a plantation of rich marchants and tradesmen to inhabit Galway. I have made many attempts in vayn, but I have now at last a faire opportunity to doe publique service, yet I submit to better judgment. The busines is this. I have considered that this place is without inhabitants and few or none ar here but a few inconsiderable, mean persons, unfit to carry on the trade of soe great a porte. I have therfore sounded some wealthy marchants in Holland, men of greate estates able to plant this town and to carry on the trade for the good of this province. They ar allso good Protestants and such as will engage to be faithfull to his Highness and this commonwealth. They will bring their ships, estates and families with them. Their demands ar to have leases of houses for 31 or 40 years at an indifferent rent; 2ly to have liberty of trade as free denisons of this nation, they being subject to all laws and customs as other good people ar. They will give power to a person whom they betrust to act for them and I am chosen to impart this motion to his excellency and the councell, and if it be accepted, and that I may have but a line or two of encoragement to go on, I will be faithfull and not goe a haire bredth from the instructions given me. Though I am most unwoorthy, yet God hath given me some credit amongst these persons that I hope I may be a instrument of some good. Sir, I hope 30, 40 or 60 families, or more or lesse of these persons mixed amongst our English inhabitants, may be useful and safe and such as may repayre the desolate houses and allso bring in greater custome in one yeare then ruinous heaps can yeald rents in many. Sir, when these men ar setled, yow know what use may be made of them. I do hear the inhabitants of Glocester ar to have some houses here but understand that few of them will dwell here and few of them ar fyt to carry on trade. There will be houses enough for them all and all the Hollanders we can get, yet shall not desire any greater number then may stand with the safety of the state. These persons will buy lands in Ireland and some of them bring over ten thousand pounds a man, some more, some lesse. Sir, if the counsel think there is danger in admission of so many as I have spoken of, they may make tryall of twenty, or ten at the first, and so take in more as they please. One of the merchants who is most affectionat in this busines in Rotterdam

[308] Letter no. 286.

and is woorth ten thousand pound; others ar of great estates whose names shall bee speedily made known if they may be accepted of.

But now let me speek as a minister of the gospel. Hath not God broken down the partition wall and made one of all nations, and why should this relation hinder our union with those of the same faith? Sir, I am informed that collonel Markham and other commissioners hath power to let leases. There is another gentleman joyned in trust with me whose bill of exchange in Holland or Rotterdam will passe for £30,000 or forty thousand pounds, and we are desired in our names to take for the merchants above said such houses in Galway and such lands adjacent as the state shall let to the use of the persons above said. And we will faithfully engage that no person shall have admittance or assynment of such houses or leases without a particuler and full approbation of the councel uppon their sufficient enquiry and that the leases made to us in trust shall be voyd in case we do not faithfully perform what is expected from us. It is desired that the councel would reserve some lands near Galway for the advancement of a plantation, for if all be passed away by special orders it will be a great prejudice to the commonwealth. Sir, I beeseech you, as soon as you know the pleasure of his excellency, send me direction what to do before houses be disposed of to others. Thus desiring the Lord to blesse you and your vertuous lady and all your family, with my true respects to my honored freind Mr Wray[309] and his sweet consort, I rest,

Your humble servant,
Ruben Eastthorpe

I hope God will blesse my endeavours to bring in divers of our ignorant Irish to His truth. I am glad of the order made by the councel to send away our Popish preists[310] who much hynder the work and keep pore souls in great fear of the curse with the bell, book and the candle.

286. From Ruben Eastthorpe, 17 July 1657, 822, fos 154–155.

Your excellency hath oft seen how God hath cast down the mighty from their seats and abased the children of pride, and hath made use of despised, weak persons in weighty affairs. Accept therfore, I beeseech you, of the endeavors of your servant, who am bound by many obligations to doe what service I can to the publique; and am much

[309]Identification uncertain, though, in November 1656, Henry Cromwell had recommended for promotion to the governorship of Beaumaris, Captain Wray (his forename not recorded), at that time apparently deputy governor of that town (*TSP*, V, p. 611).

[310]The Irish council's instructions of November 1655 to the lord president of Connaught and the governor of Galway called for the deportation of Catholic priests (Dunlop, pp. 546–547).

encouraged therin by your special favors. Sir, I know not whether this paper may be thought woorthy to be presented to your excellency, or to be burned. However, I beeseech you accept of my honest thoughts. Pore Galway sitteth in the dust and no ey pittieth her; her merchants were princes and great among nations; but now the city, which was ful of people, is solitary and very desolate. Pitty, I beseech you, the ruines, that you may be called the repairer of the breach. Sir, I was desired by Sir John Reynolds and divers members of the parliament to perswade as many merchants of good quality as I could to adventure their estates and persons to make a plantation in Galway. And now I hope God by His providence will enable me to do service in this kynd (if your excellency will encorage me therin). A great marchant in Rotterdam of a vast estate, and divers other merchants in Holland and other provinces in Germany, being Protestants and freinds to the commonwealth of England, I hope will be perswaded to bring over their estates and families and ships to set upp a trade in Galway, desiring: ferst, leases of houses and some land (if it may be) for 30 or 40 years; secondly, to have free liberty to trade as other free denisons of Ireland. If this busines be well managed it may be for the good of this place and of the whole province. I and another gentleman now in Ireland, who is their agent, are betrusted to make these propositions to your excellency, humbly craving your directions, which I shall observe exactly. I have used my best rhetorick to perswade them and to satisfy their scruples, yet have only undertaken to acquaint your excellency with this busines, which is so far ripened that their agent and myself, as trustees, ar authorized to take houses in Galway and leases (which ar to be voyd in case the town be not planted with such honest persons of good estates as you shall approve of). If your excellency approve herof, I humbly beg your derections that I may send an answer into Holland, and other places, to the parties concerned. Sir, I desire to know whether the state will admit of any strangers; 2ly, of what number. Thus blessing the Lord for you, desiring Hym to think uppon you for good and to prosper you in all your great affaires, I humbly rest,

Your excellencye's faithful servant,

Ruben Eastthorp

287. From the Mayor and Aldermen of Gloucester, Gloucester, 24 July 1657, 822, fos 158–159.

May it please your excellency,

The parliament having beene pleased to passe an act[311] for satisfaction of the inhabitants of this city for their losses susteyned

[311] In the summer of 1657, although relating back to the royalist siege of Gloucester fourteen years before, in the summer of 1643.

at the time of the seige by the late king's army out of lands and houses in Ireland, we humbly take leave to recommend our concerments to your lordship, which wilbe more particularly made knowne to you by Doctor Clarges[312] that waites upon your lordship with this letter, whom we have prevailed with to prosecute our desires to your lordship and the councill in Ireland because he hath beene already (out of his love to us) very instrumentall in procuring this act of parliament. And we have much reason to hope for your lordship's favour and assistance to him in this busines because you have often given a testimony, by your kindenes to this place, of your being well pleased with the interest you have in our affections, and we humbly conceive his quality and meritt will not be the least motive to induce your lordship's respect to him on the behalfe of,

Your excellencie's most humble servants,

Luke Nourse, maior	Wm Caple
James Stephens	Jas Clutterbrooke
Antho Edwards	Ed Collett

288. From Philip Jones, Swansea, 25 July 1657, 822, fos 160–161.

Letter of courtesy, apologizing for writing so infrequently and offering his services; and of request, seeking a favour for a poor man, Mr Barcroft,[313] *an honest schoolmaster in Cardiff for the past four or five years and well-respected by sober and godly people, who was moving himself and his family to Ireland and was seeking to settle there.*

289. From Richard Cromwell, 29 July 1657, 822, fos 162–163.

Deare brother,

I shall in this lettre say nothing to you of anie other subject then the recommending the concernements of our very good freind Martin Noell[314] to your especiall kindnes. It hath soe fallen out that hee is

[312] Thomas Clarges, politician, was trained as an apothecary and served in that capacity with the king's army in the civil war, but he came over to the parliamentarian cause during the 1650s, principally as a result of his sister's marriage in 1653 to another royalist-turned-parliamentarian, George Monck. He became Monck's agent in London, and also an agent and messenger for the Scottish and Irish councils, and through Monck's influence he was returned for a Scottish seat to the second Protectorate parliament.

[313] Possibly the Ambrose Barcroft who was listed in 1657 as a schoolmaster in Birr, King's County.

[314] Parliamentarian financier, merchant, and politician, by the late 1640s he held office in the financial and military administration of London and served as MP for his native Stafford in the second Protectorate parliament. However, during the 1650s he really flourished as a businessman with fingers in many pies, including shipping and the transportation of captured Irish, Scottish, and English royalist prisoners to Barbados; trade with the West

mingled in a debt due from the state with captain Arthur,[315] who haveing deserved exceedingly well from the parliamente in all the time of publique tryall, of which many testimonies hath here bin given, obteyned an act of parliamente[316] empowering him to chuse his satisfaction in what part of Ireland hee should desire to purchase. And it seemes Mr Noell and hee, by the advice of some gentlemen of Ireland now heer, have fixed uppon Wexford; and because that town wilbe most convenient as it relates to the trade of fishing, and Mr Noell being the great salt master of England, and haveing contrived bringing people therabout, and to mannage that trade to better encrease, hee would not bee disappoynted of his aimes thereuppon. I find that his Highnes approves very well of it; and I desire you to take the patronage of it, soe that it may bee compassed with the fewer difficultyes or obstructions, and the rather because their affayres are ready for present settlement and action on that place and designe. I pray receive captain Arthur favorably, who will come himself with this lettre, and beleive you doe all the while oblige Mr Noell, and that you also shew a respect and kindnes at the same time to the mediation of,

Your most affectionate brother and servant,

R Cromwell

290. From Martin Noell, London, July 1657, 822, fos 164–165.

It shall not satisfie mee that his Highnes doth mee the grace to approve and recommend an affaire of mine to your lordshipp and the councell, and that my lord, your brother, is pleased to favor mee with his mediation, untill I also have tendered my humblest services unto your lordshipp and acknowledged your continuall countenance and condescentions towards mee at all times, of which I know not how to doubt on this or anie other good occasion, because I still beare about mee the same faithfullnes and regards to your person, and have the honnour to bee owned and lookt uppon as a devoted and perfect servant to all your lordshipp's relations. Among the manie litle dealings I have in the world, I have not found myselfe soe much out at all anie where as in Ireland, untill very lately that my lott hath cast uppon mee

and East Indies and the Levant; the joint running (with Secretary Thurloe) of the postal service; excise farming; and the production of salt. He combined the management of salt works in north-east England with the farming of the salt excise duties.

[315] Probably the Captain Arthur (his forename unrecorded), parliamentarian officer, who campaigned in Dorset during the civil war until captured by the royalists, and who petitioned the second Protectorate parliament seeking compensation for a debt of £2,000 incurred in parliament's service (*Burton*, II, pp. 123–124).

[316] Passed by the second Protectorate parliament in the summer of 1657, entitling him to Irish land to the value of nearly £3,700.

a small seat there, and my election (to which I am empowered by an act of parliament) aimes at a settlemente in Wexford, where I would in the way of my proffesion bee concerned. To which purpose captain Arthur (one of most approved meritt and integrity to the state), with whome I am mingled, will waite uppon your lordshipp with the act of parliamente and manie recommendations in our favour, which wee hope will prevent anie disappoyntments to our bussines and designe. I shall not importune your lordshipp anie further in this, because I dare not distrust your favor in anie thinge that is just and reasonable, when it is to bee conferred uppon, my lord,

Your lordshipp's most humble and faithfull servant,
Martin Noell

291. From Richard Cromwell, 3 August 1657, 822, fos 166–167.

Deare brother,

This bearer, Mr Robert Whitehall,[317] fellow of Merton Colledge in Oxford, having been recommended to me by Doctor Owen, the vicechancelor, Doctor Wilkins,[318] Doctor Goddart and others as a person worthy of favour, and his occasions calling him into Ireland to continue there some considerable time, whereby he is made uncapable of receiving that incouradgment here in England att present, which he might if he should stay; it shall be the first trouble I'le give you upon the account of my new office of chancelor of that university[319] to recommend him to your speciall favour; and to desire that if any place or imployment there should be thought of and seeked for by him, whereof he shall be capable, you will be pleased to assist him with your favour and power for the obtaining of it; wherein you will engage more and more, deare brother,

Your affectionate brother and servant,
R Cromwell

[317] By the end of the year he was working as a schoolmaster in Limerick.

[318] John Wilkins, theologian, philosopher, and academic, was sympathetic to the parliamentarian cause and was based in London during the 1640s, acting as chaplain and preacher, appointed to preach at Gray's Inn from 1645. He was warden of Wadham College from 1648, and from 1652 was a member of a small and powerful university committee advising the chancellor, Oliver Cromwell. In 1656, he married the Protector's youngest sister, Robina, and from the summer of 1657 onwards he became one of the closest Oxford advisors of the new chancellor.

[319] Richard Cromwell succeeded his father as chancellor in July 1657, one of the signs of the increased status and greater public role he was given during the closing year of his father's Protectorate.

292. From Hugh Peters, Whitehall, 14 August 1657, 822, fos 168–169.

Letter of recommendation on behalf of the bearer, Mr Snelling, who had claim to Irish land inherited from his late brother, Major Snelling, and who was seeking employment from Henry Cromwell, perhaps in his troop of horse.

293. From John Reynolds, camp near St Omer, 23 August/1 September 1657, 822, fos 172–173.

May it please your excellency,

I am not more unhappy in any particular of my present emploiment than that I am rendred uncapable of making frequent tenders of my service to your lordshipp, or receiving any commands from your lordshipp, not having in many months the honour of a letter from your lordshipp or any other about you, except by my worthy freind Dr Harrison.

I suppose my letter, giving an account of our notable march from beyond Vervyns into the heart of Flanders, is arrived. Since, we have beseiged and taken St Venant, a considerable passe upon the Lys, where 600 of our English behaved themselves verry stoutely in the approches, and were one greate cause of the governours not daring to abide the utmost hasard, and it was in good time rendred. The enemy being in the trench with a mine fastned to the wall of Ardre, but upon our advance to St Omer they retreated, leaving many behind, who fell into our hands. My lord, it would much please your lordshipp to see 12,000 horse with 8,000 carts and waggons marching over a countrey, and certainely a goodlier sight (except the major-generall in his gallant equipage at the late solemnity in Dublin)[320] cannot be seene. I could delight to divertise your lordshipp with some gaity d'esprit, but indeede we are heere in a poore condition, wanting clothes, foode and money. I hope your lordshipp will be pleased to mind his Highnes for my sake in the behalfe of his French army, and in due time that I may be restored, having warred heere untill 6,000 men are lesse than foure, and without fighting, which is not the fashion of the countrey. Howsoever if I must still fight on, untill my dagger, which was a sword, become an oyster knife, I am content to submit. But your lordshipp is wise thorough God's blessing and honest and will at length do what

[320]Probably a reference to the celebrations held in Dublin on 9 July to mark the formal reinauguration of the Protectorate under the revised parliamentary constitution. Reynolds had probably seen the report of the event, published in *Mercurius Politicus* in its edition of 23–30 July, which described how Sir Hardress Waller, as major-general, had a prominent place in the parade, marching 'in gallant equipage'.

is necessary, I hope. I humbly commit your lordshipp, with my noble lady there, to the Almighty's protection. I remaine, my lord,

Your excellencye's constant, devoted, poor servant,

J Reynolds

294. Draft of a letter by Henry Cromwell to Lord Broghill, [July or August 1657], 822, fos 126–127.

My deare lord,

When your lordshipp did so fright mee with the news of the army's endeavours to force his Highness back into his single capacity of generall, and with that of the knott which was forming against his Highness, which that 103[321] might help to breake hee must not bee disgusted, I told your lordshipp that to save the whole from sinking <I told your lordship that> I would submitt to anything possible; not that the way of lieutenancy and deputy were of my election.[322] I told your lordship withall that 3 things were requisite to make that way possible. As first, that my lord lieutenant should not hearken immedeately to the counsells and appeals from hence, which who can prevent? 2ly, that I may have the dispose of places hapening in my time, but who can assure my time to bee one month? 3ly, <as for bettering> that the councell might bee betterd. If <any> But if some certaine member bee withdrawn it will possibly displeese my <lord deputy> brother Fleetwood, which I would not have done. On the other side, if any bee added wee cannot beare the charge of it. Now what would your lordshipp have mee doe herein? Although I could bee heartily content to act in this manner under my lord lieutenant, and should bee as tender of any honest man that loved him by himselfe; yet since hee will not believe it, and since his Highness is not at leisure to make him understand it, how can I continue in this condition? Inded, my lord, as I then told your lordship, retirement were much better for

[321] Perhaps Fleetwood.

[322] Fleetwood's three-year term as lord deputy of Ireland was due to expire on 1 September 1657, causing renewed speculation about the future government of Ireland and opening the way for renewed sniping between Henry Cromwell's supporters and those of Fleetwood. Indeed, over the summer a petition had circulated in Ireland and been sent to London urging Henry Cromwell's appointment as lord deputy; dismayed and angry, he first tried to suppress it and then distanced himself from it in a long and detailed letter (*TSP*, VI, pp. 446–447); Thurloe reassured him that the issue had done him no harm in London (*TSP*, VI, pp. 455, 493). Nevertheless, in this letter Henry Cromwell seems to be running through the possibility and practicalities of the compromise arrangement, floated in earlier petitions and letters of the winter of 1655–1656, in which he would become lord deputy and continue as governor of and in Ireland, but technically continue to serve under Fleetwood, who would become an absentee lord lieutenant of Ireland. Clearly, Henry Cromwell had serious misgivings about such an arrangement.

mee then to labour so much in vaine as I have and am like to doe. As for him whom you meane (where you say I have employed him and may employ him againe, and one who deales with 104[323]), if hee must bee discountenanced to please 103 – I thinke if 103 knew him and mee, that were not necessary – <yet> but if things <are> bee so <[...]>[324] that 103 must bee wholly <humored> observed, and that hee cannot bee <humored> <so> observed otherwise, I doe not doubt but that person will suffer to bee under a cloud for the publicq good. If not I am mistaken in him. If there bee any other end of that advice I should willingly have more <reason> ground for it then that of his dealing with 104. Against the probability whereof I have many reasons. I should write to your lordship of severall other things, but to speeke the truth I am discomposed and unfitt at this time to adde more then that I am,

If his Highness troubles himselfe to read my lettres, hee cannot but know who of the councill I am weary of[325] – Mr Secretarey doth the same – and surely your lordship also knowes that disease better then the remedy, but let nature wake up.

295. From Richard Lawrence, London, [July or August] 1657, 823, fos 7–8.

May itt please your excelency,

I had longe before this presented that respeckts I owe unto you, had not some unexpeckted discouragements I mett with att my comeinge to London streaghtened mee therein. For I was in hopes when I took my leave of your lordship, that you had received sattisfacktion as to the candidness of my intention, both towards his Highness and yourselfe

[323] Perhaps Desborough or Lambert.

[324] Word deleted very heavily and now illegible.

[325] The Irish council, which had been appointed by the Protector on 17 August 1654 to serve a three-year term and which therefore dissolved itself in mid-August 1657, originally had six members: Richard Pepys, William Steele (who did not cross to Ireland until 1656), Robert Hammond, Miles Corbet, Robert Goodwin, and Matthew Tomlinson. Hammond died in October 1654, shortly after his arrival in Dublin, but William Bury was added to the council in the summer of 1656, restoring the membership to six. Of those, Tomlinson, Corbet, and Steele – who most attracted Henry Cromwell's suspicions and criticism (in June 1658, he wrote a detailed account of Steele's alleged tactless behaviour, dissent, and downright opposition (see *TSP*, VII, pp. 198–199)) – did not always support Henry Cromwell, especially over his religious policy, though in the end all three were reappointed to the new Irish council, empanelled in mid-November when the shape of the new Irish government was finally resolved. Indeed, much to Henry Cromwell's bafflement and anger and his own dismay, the only pre-1657 councillor to be dropped from the new body was the generally loyal Goodwin (*TSP*, VI, pp. 599, 647, 648, 650, 661, 683; VII, pp. 100–101, 145).

in subscribeinge that letter.[326] Butt I since perceave, by some account his Highness had given him of wordes I shouilde speake, itt was not soe. Butt if ever I live to see your face, I hope I shall convince you I had hard measure therein. Butt my lord, your severall yeares' frindeship and kindnesses extended to mee have begotten you a greater interest in my hearte then one, nay mayny, such passadges can eate out. If I had not proffered my duty to you before my benyfitt by you, I shouilde not have run those hazzardes of your displeasure I have done, for I am perswaded you have affecktion to my person, if contrarynesse of principle did not interpose. And hee that knowes your hearte and mine knowes that you are deare to mee. And if I thought the way some takes to serve you did not tende to ruine you and the pretious cause of Christ in your handes, I shouilde rejoyce to run with the formost of them. Butt in the meane while, if I have noe other oportunity to testify the sincerity of my respeckts unto you, I shall doe itt by my earnest prayers to the Lord for you, that you may bee delivered from the danger of your owne natureall temper, your ridged, sowre principles and the flattery of pretended frindes.

I had hope before this to have waited upon your excelency in Irelande. Butt some extreordynary occaisions prevente mee, in consideration whereof his Highnesse was pleased to inlardge my furloe, which my lord deputy[327] promised to give your lordship account of, which with the tender of my effecktionate service to my good lady, I rest,

Your excelencye's sinceer servante,

Ri Lawrence

296. From Jeremy Baines,[328] 1 September 1657, 822, fos 170–171.

Letter of thanks, for Henry Cromwell's favour to him and his eldest son; recounting how his son had developed affection towards a woman of worth related to Henry Cromwell, though the writer had strong misgivings about this, arising from their

[326]The letter of summer 1657 from the army in Ireland to Fleetwood, expressing relief and joy at the news of the Protector's rejection of the crown, which Hewson and Lawrence had promoted. Hence this letter can be no earlier than mid-summer.

[327]Assuming that Lawrence was being strict and accurate in using the title, this letter can therefore be no later than 1 September 1657, because Fleetwood's appointment as lord deputy of Ireland expired on that date.

[328]On 24 June 1657, Henry Cromwell had written to Thurloe recommending for employment (and requesting that he be brought to the Protector's attention), Mr Baynes, a sober, godly minister then working in Ireland, the son of lieutenant-colonel Baynes (*TSP*, VI, pp. 367–368). This letter is probably by the father and largely about the son, probably the minister Edward Baines/Baynes, who was a preacher at St Patrick's and St John's in Dublin in 1656–1658.

very different socio-economic standings, because he had lost heavily in parliament's service, was owed £2,000 by parliament, which he did not expect to recover, and so did not have the means to make a generous settlement upon his son; and noting how he and his wife were content with their current situation and so politely declined the invitation that Henry Cromwell had given him.

297. From Charles Fleetwood, 1 September 1657, 822, fos 174–175.

Deare brother,

The buysnes of the excise and customes, in farming thereof, being now at an issue, the committee not liking of the termes the farmers demanded, we are lik to have a considerable abatment in our revenue, which still will presse upon us the necessity of a reducment, and I doubt I shall not be able to get an addition to beare the civill and millitary lists' charge. I confesse, as I formerly writt, I am not fully satisfyed in the way you propownd for lessening the charge. You know it was formerly attempted, but still upon debate it was not found safe, and I feare in a short time would hazard our garrysons by that mixture, which such a condition would soone bring unto. I thinke the lesse force, well payde and kept strictly to duty without other dependencyes, would be found the more secure and best way.[329] We much incline heare to reduce the foote to 70 in a company, and the horse to 50 in a troope, which would bring the charge within the allowance of 25,000. I shall desire you may be satisfied befor any thing be don heare. We have lately had some successe in France by our English. 600 of them did very good service in the reducing of St Venant. But I feare the French will not performe with us in what was 1st propownded in sending our men. His Highnes hath now sent for a positive resolution, one way or others. They minde their own interests, but litle regard ours, and the designe, I feare, we cheifly intended is litle aymed at or intended by them.[330] We shall suddenly know what they will doe. We have not lately heard from my lord Richard Cromwell, but he is in a very hopefull way of

[329]During the winter and spring of 1656–1657, Henry Cromwell had been urging the establishment in Ireland of a part-time militia, not merely to supplement the regular army in Ireland but also to allow some reduction in the army's size and cost; the regime in London appeared unconvinced and unenthusiastic. By July he was pushing for an alternative scheme of remodelling the army in Ireland, with certain regiments combined and garrison troops non-regimented, thereby retaining the same number of troops but reducing the number of officers and so trimming costs that way. Again, as indicated in this letter, Fleetwood and his colleagues in London were unconvinced and insisted on keeping the existing regimental and unit structure, with the existing number of officers, instead reducing the number of men per unit to trim costs (*TSP*, V, pp. 433, 452–453, 477, 493–494, 504, 586–587; VI, pp. 404–405, 505, 527, 634–635, 647, 649, 657–658, 660–662, 665, 680).

[330]The attempted capture of Dunkirk and Mardyke.

recovery.[331] His lady is gon to him. My cosen Rolt is very sicke of this new distempter. It is as a sickly a time as hath bine known this many a yeare. The Lord teach us to inquire and search into the true cause thereof. Their Highneses and all your relations are through mercy very well, which at this time is double mercy considering how the Lord's hand is stretched out in every country. I know none free. The Lord awaken us with a due sence of His hand and our present mercy is the desire of your most affectionat brother and humble servant.

298. From Richard Cromwell, Pinefield Lodge, New Forest, 9 September 1657, 822, fos 176–177.

Deare brother,

Though I am not at present in a very fitt posture to use my penn (by reason of the breaking my thigh with the fall of my horse), yet the sad complainte of a related ill condition of this bearer, Daniell Machona of Munster in Ireland (whoe is brother to my footeman Florrance), hath made me to give you this trouble to desire youre favourable and charritable countenance to him. He desires he may not be transplanted (according to the order of his Highnesse and councell) for that it will be the utter ruen of him and his famuly, which is now forced to flye unto thee charity of well disposed people for bread to sustaine life untell he can returne, and be continnewed as a tennant to his owne, which priviledge (he saith) he hath compounded for; and, as he informes, hath not forfeited his priviledges by any act either directly or indirectly, which he may lawfully claime upon the artickles with the lord of Musgroves[332] upon his laying downe of armes. That which he saith most troubles him, and the greatest occation of his trouble, is that severall persons comes upon him for things taken

[331] In mid-August, he fell from his horse while out hunting and broke his leg, though it was set and healed well.

[332] Identification unclear. Possibly a reference to Sir Philip Musgrave, royalist officer, who fought for the king in the north of England in 1642–1646 and 1648, and who was then royalist governor of the Isle of Man until its capture late in 1651. In the 1620s, he had succeeded a distant cousin to the barony of Musgrave, and was reported to have been offered but declined a new title from the future Charles II in exile during the 1650s; thus, he might have been referred to as 'Lord Musgrave' in the late 1650s, but he appears to have had no links with Ireland. Possibly, therefore, this is a garbled reference to Donough MacCarthy, Viscount Muskerry, an Irish Catholic landowner with extensive Munster estates, who, after some hesitation, supported the Irish Catholic rebellion and played a very active military and political role in the Confederacy and in support of the royalist cause against the Cromwellian invasion of Ireland. In the summer of 1652, he and his forces surrendered on terms to the English regime and, although in 1653–1654 he was tried and acquitted of being an accessory to murder, later in 1654 it was noted that he was living quietly and abiding by the terms of the articles of surrender, which also covered the men who surrendered with him.

away by him in the time of warre as a souldyer. I know not the course in this case in Ireland, but in Ingland noe courte or jury will allow a sattisfaction of injuryes in the heate of our warres. He tells me that he was charged for his life as a murderer (there being noe salve for those), but he was upon his tryall, and you were pleased to declare him, cleare. I confese his lamantable complaint hath moved me to pitty, that if things doe appeare to yourselfe (or any, by reason of the trouble, that you shall appoint to examine) as he hath related them to me, that then, in the first place, you would be pleased to graunt him the same favour which others hath obtained of his condition and quality. And in the second, that where a just stop may be put to the violent hands of oppressers, whoe takes the advantedges to be strickt upon such as hath acted rudely in a rude time (peradventure according to the commission of his commander). Not that I would countenance disorders of souldyers, whoe are too apt of themselves to take a liberty, but to moderate such feircenesse as will demand impossibilityes of performances, and will make such after reckonings as that the life upon artickles (though such actions, as hath been in generall hinted, were included) not at all gratefull. I must leave the man to your better information, and alsoe my desires concerning him to your conveniency, you knowing best what you are able to doe in these cases. Craving your pardon for this scrible, which my present posture doth in some measure plead, I rest with my service to my sister, deare brother,

Yours most affectionately,

R Cromwell

299. From John Owen, Christ Church College, [Oxford], 9 September 1657, 822, fos 178–179.

My lord,

I received your commands by Mr Wood, in reference unto the statutes of this university to be sent unto you. I shall with the first convenient opportunity endeavour to send or bringe them unto your lordship. I am glad to heare of your indeavour to dispose of that university[333] to the interest of piety and hearminye; and am bold to informe your lordship that our statutes, as those alsoe of the other university, beinge framed to the spirit and good of studdys in former days, will scarsly upon consideration be found to be the best expedients for the promotion of the good ends of godlinese and solid literature,

[333]Either Trinity College, Dublin, of which Henry Cromwell became chancellor in 1655 (very soon after his arrival in Ireland), or possibly the new university college that he hoped to establish in Dublin.

which are in your ayme. I could much rather wish that if the great employments of your lordship's servants in that place will not affoord them leasure to attend such a worke, that you would be pleased to send your commands to some of your freinds and servants in England, men of ability, wisdome and piety, to compose a body of orders and statutes suited to the present light, interest of state, and advantagious discuveryes of literature in the ways and expedients of it, which we do enjoy, that may be submitted to your lordship's judgement. It is not impossible that somethinge not unworthy your owninge might be presented unto you; and that returninge with the advantage of your accept[...] and approbation, it might yet esteeme here also where invetirate prejudic[...] beaten good customes, and in many an affection to an old interest will no[...][334] easily permit the most evidently usefull tendors of alteration to take place. I hope your lordship will pardon this boldnes in him, who prays for you dayly, and is, my lord,

Your most humble and most faithfull servant,

John Owen

300. From William Jephson, Hamburgh, 14 September 1657, 822, fos 180–181.

My deare lord,

Since the many favours I have receyv'd from your lordship have given mee sufficient testimonye of your kindesse, I may from thence assure myselfe that it will not bee unacceptable to your lordship to know into what place of the world providence hath led your faythfull servant,[335] which truly is all the account I can give your lordship at present. On Tuesday last I arriv'd at this towne (which is a very fine scituated place, and a very good countrey round about it), and the next day I wrote a letter to the king of Suede to give his majestye notice of my beeing here, and doe hourly expect his commaunds for my repayre to him. I heare hee is at present at a place cald Wismar, which is about 60 English miles from hence. When I have had the honour to kisse his majestye's hands and to have some discourse with him, I hope I shall bee able to ghuesse what hopes I may have of my returne; then which I desyre nothing more affectionatly that I

[334] Edge of the paper damaged with some loss of text, though the incomplete words are apparently 'acceptance', 'prejudice has'/'prejudices have' and 'not'.

[335] Once the parliamentary session was over, Jephson was sent by the Protector to Sweden, to work both for peace between Sweden and Denmark and for a wider alliance of Protestant powers in northern Europe. His mission lasted a year, and he did not return until August 1658, just a few months before his death.

might have the hapinesse to wayte on your lordship in Ireland, and the friends I have about you, which I can not sett to greate a value upon. This content is now deny'de mee, but I doubt not will in God's due time bee graunted to, my lord,

Your most really affectionate and faythfull, humble servant,

Wm Jephson

301. From Charles Fleetwood, 15 September 1657, 822, fos 182–183.

Deare brother,

I have not heard a long time from you, occationed I presume by your progresse. We are now neare a conclusion of our reducement. I having not heard since the account I gave you of my thoughts about that buysnes, we shall suddenly sende you the result of what is heare resolved upon. We are much streightned in mony, and that which hath bine propounded is that the pay, which is now to be sent, may goe to pay off thos who are to be reduced, and the standing army to forbeare their pay for a month longer, which I say they are not able to doe. Necessity puts us upon such streights, but I shall doe what I can to prevent that extremity upon you. I doe not want affection, desires and endeavors to serve your affayres. I hope we shall obviat this presant difficulty, which is the same as to the other 2 armyes in England and Scotland. Sir John Reynolds is heare arived with some proposalls from marshale Turreine in order to the reducing of Mardik, but we have bine so disapoynted in what we have don allready and the season of the yeare is so farre gon, that I doe think we shall scarce satisfye ourselves in answering the demands. Our affayres in reference to forrign parts are under presant consideration, and have their considerable difficultyes to know what to doe therin, but I trust the Lord will so direct as will be for the best preservation of the good cause we have bine contending for heare, and most answer the advancment of the Protestant cause abroade, which is truly minded by his Highnes. But of thes things you have constant intelligence from other hands. My haste still I must begge you[336] pardon in, we having more then ordinary occations which taks up our time, which otherwise might have given me the liberty of inlarging. Which now I must intreat your excusing him, who is,

Your most affectionate brother and humble servant,

Charles Fleetwood

[336] Apparently a slip for 'your'.

I heare you did refuse the acceptance of Dr Cartrett's comission,[337] which I think was very Christianlik and prudenly don. You will not in the close suffer by such tendernes.

302. From Charles Fleetwood, 22 September 1657, 822, fos 184–185.

Deare brother,

We are at presant com to no certeine resolution about the reducment, but what I formerly acquainted you with will be the proportion allotted for Ireland. That which we incline unto heare is to reduce the foote to 80 in a company (which I think is about your presant number), and the horse to 50 in a troope; the dragoones to the like number. The committee hade thoughts of reducing a regiment of horse and 3 troopes more, so as to leave the whole horse but to consist of 5 regiments, but after some debate it was rather resolved to reduce to 50 in a troope, and 3 troopes. The maner is wholly left to you, which will save me from what some will, it may be, too apt to judg me for to have a design. Some other retrenchments ther will be, but what I now offer will be the most considerable, and therfor though I canot wright authoritativly that it is so, yet probably it will be concluded this way. I offer only you will be heard befor any thing be positivly concluded; but for to save charge I did think it might not be amisse to give you this advertisment that so you might be ordering your affayre, if you think fitt, in such a way as might answer most your presant wants of money, which I feare will grow so fast upon us as to disable us to doe any more then to afforde you £8,000 per mensem from hence, which with the taxe and revenue raysed in Ireland, is the way intended for your subsistance.[338] I hope heare will never want an utmost care and endevor to helpe Ireland what we can, but our occations so much exceede our revenue that we are forced to a frugallity what we can so farre as may stand with safety. My deare wife is much troubled with

[337] Henry Cromwell had upbraided Carterett for his 'gross partiallitie' in supporting the court-martialled and cashiered Alexander Brayfield, and, in consequence, Carterett had offered to resign and to seek civil employment in England. Although tempted to accept the offer, after consulting Thurloe, Henry Cromwell decided to decline his resignation (*TSP*, VI, pp. 527–528, 552, 563–564).

[338] The current plans involved allowing Ireland either £7,000 or £8,000 per month out of the English assessments, which was to be added to the Irish assessments of £9,000 per month and the other revenues raised in Ireland, to make a grand total of either £312,000 (if receiving £7,000 per month from England) or £324,000 (if receiving £8,000 each month from English revenues) per year to cover the full (military and civil) costs of running Ireland. Henry Cromwell raised no objection in principle to the suggestion that he could run Ireland on £324,000 per year, but he argued that the revenues raised in Ireland (other than assessments) were currently running at no more than £70,000 per year and that therefore he needed at least £11,000 per month from England to cover costs (*TSP*, VI, p. 527).

a diffluction of rhume. The Lord, I trust, hath bine pleased in some measure to abate hir distemper, which mercy, that I may have a heart more to improve, is the desire of your most affectionate brother and humble servant.

303. From Nathaniel Fiennes, Covent Garden, 26 September 1657, 822, fos 186–187.

Letter of clarification, stating that in his earlier letter of recommendation for the bearer, his brother-in-law John Whitehead, he had expected Jephson to accompany Whitehead to Ireland and speak in person on his behalf. However, because Jephson had now been sent elsewhere by the Protector, Whitehead was travelling alone, though Sir John Temple had been contacted to speak to Henry Cromwell on Whitehead's behalf.

304. From Charles Fleetwood, 29 September 1657, 822, fos 188–189.

Deare brother,

I beleive you must crave an addition for contingencyes.[339]

I doe finde that the revenue in Ireland is taken heare at a much greater value then, I feare, it will hold out: the rents of lands etc at £50,000 per annum; and the excise and customes at £70,000 per annum.[340] The later is offered heare to be given by som who would be farmers. £23,000 per mensem is intended for the army, and, as befor I told you, was not to be expected above 8,000 per mensem from hence. The perticulers of the whole buysnes of reducement will be sent you by this post if I can get a dispatch therof, and then what shall be wanting in our proposalls, which you may please to offer as amendments, will be taken, and it is much the same that I last weeke did acquaint you with. I know you will heare from other hands our possessing of Mardike. We wer in hopes the French would have attempted Dunkirke, which, by reason of the Spanyards' weaknes in force, was looked upon as very fesible, but they have no minde, we understand, to that attempt, but designe Gravlan, which is more considerable to the French but lesse to us. That place is to be given into our hands if the Lord give successe in the attempt. The French wer to sit down befor it as yeasterday. Our forces have bine of great advantage to the French affayres this

[339]This short sentence has been squeezed in between 'Dear brother' and 'I doe finde that…'.

[340]Making £120,000 per year. With Irish assessments at £9,000 per month and £8,000 per month allowed to Ireland out of English revenues, that would add £17,000 per month or £204,000 per year, thus reaching the grand total of £324,000 per year which the English government thought was needed to run Ireland.

campaine, and if the Lord please to direct for the further carying on of what worke He in His providence shall leade unto, what is allready don may be of much advantage to the good cause we have bine heare engaged in. This French affayre hath taken up so much of our time that the truth is we have had litle leisure to consider our home affayres, and amongst other things the settlement of Ireland, which hath bine discoursed a litle about but no resolution taken therin, which I know must neads distract your affayres, but I hope it will not be longe ere it be brought to a conclusion. With my most humble service to your deare lady, I remain,

Your most affectionate brother and humble servant.

The enclosed is what the committee have thought upon to offer as to Ireland, which is sent unto you to the ende that[341] you have to offer by way of alteration may be speedily sent, and that by the next post, wherin you will have satisfaction. £70,000 per annum is offered, and will be let for the customes and excise in Ireland. I shall be glad of your speedy thoughts therin.

305. From Charles Fleetwood, Wallingford House, 29 September 1657, 822, fos 190–191.

Letter of recommendation on behalf of Mr How,[342] *a godly minister then travelling to Ireland, requesting that he be encouraged and found a place in Ireland which would comfortably provide for him and his family.*

306. From Griffith Bodurda, Inner Court of Wards, Westminster, 1 October 1657, 822, fos 192–193.

Right honourable,

The committee of parliament for improvement of the customes and excise having received proposalls from severall persons for farmeing of both the said dutyes in Ireland for seaven yeares, for which the rent of seaventy thousand pounds per annum was offered, and allthough it was not much doubted by the said committee but the preposers may advance it to one hundred thousand pounds, yet it was judged necessary before any contractt made to signify soe much unto your honour, with desire that you will with all convenyent speede send unto this committee your opinion in writing, whether will bee most for the service of his Highnes and the commonwealth to farme out the

[341] Either a slip for 'what' or a word, apparently 'what', then omitted.

[342] Two ministers of that name are shown as being ministers in Ireland in 1658 – Daniel How and Edward How.

said dutyes or continewe them in the management of commissioners entrusted for that purpose, and to what summe you conceive the customes, as alsoe the imported and native inland excise, may bee raised and improved severally and distinctly every yeare. These beeing the commands of the committee laid upon mee (beeing in the chayre), I could doe noe lesse then in discharge of my trust communicate unto your honour; and therewith take leave to subscribe myselfe,

Your honour's very humble servant,

G Bodurda

307. From Charles Howard, Naward,[343] 2 October 1657, 822, fos 194–195.

Letter of recommendation on behalf of the unnamed bearers, countrymen of Howard's, who had an ordinance of Protector and council and an order under the privy seal for lands in Ireland as compensation for their losses in the late troubles.

308. From John Reynolds, Burbourg in Flanders, 2/12 October 1657, 822, fos 214–215.

May it please your excellency,

I have forborne to trouble your lordshipp with my letters untill I might present unto your lordshipp a probable meanes of waiting on your lordshipp in Ireland. The worke of this campagne being now over, and the designes of the French (and English consequently) being terminated within the narrow limits of securing this place and Mardyke fort, I can see no obstacle to my coming into Ireland for 4 or 5 months in the approching winter; and I am most confident, if your lordshipp be pleased to mention my attending you in your letters to his Highnes, it will be consented unto. Besides your lordshipp's major generall will be desirous of coming to the next parliament.[344] And for my owne part I shall willingly abandon the pleasures of Paris and the French court, to serve your lordshipp in Dublin. I shall hope for your lordship's mediation herein with his Highnes, and will prepare for a grant heere by meanes of the embassadour[345] (who is now heere and desired his service might be presented to your lordshipp in my

[343]Naworth in Cumberland.

[344]In fact, Sir Hardress Waller seems to have remained in Ireland and does not appear to have taken his seat in either the first session or the shortlived second session of the second Protectorate parliament.

[345]Sir William Lockhart.

next letters), and that my master, the cardinall,[346] will deny me no reasonable suite, I have full assurance under the hand and seale of his eminence. I have heere so full a representation of Athlone, my old garrison, that I could not forget Ireland. But my devotions and true affection to your lordship's service is the attractive and sole end of my wrighting, of which I crave your lordship's good acceptance. And recommending your lordshipp, with my honoured lady and all your lordship's, to the Almighty's protection, I take my leave. My lord, I am,

Your excellency's most humble, faithfull and obliged,

J Reynolds

309. From William Hawkins,[347] Blarney, 5 October 1657, 822, fos 196–197.

May it please your eccellency,

It is now more then a yeere since your commands were layd uppon me to offer an expedient for the safe planting of Gallaway. I communicated my thoughts to divers frinds in America from whome I received this inclosed, which I humbly tender to your lordshipp's consideration, beeing assured, that if due encouragements be not wanting, your lordship's desire will be fully satisfied by those, whose principles ar more firme to the present authority then ever the Romans were to Caesar. I humbly pray I may be capable of returning an accompt hereof by December next,

Your lordshipp's most humble servant,

Will Hawkins

310. From the Justices of the Peace for County Monaghan, Monaghan, 6 October 1657, 822, fos 198–199.

May it please your excellency,

Being aboundantly sensible of the late sufferings of the despoyled Protestants of this nation, which beeing presented unto us at our generall sessions of the peace held at Monaghan, together with the enclosed petition to your excellency, wee have thought it our dutty to present unto your excellency the present condition of the Protestants

[346] Jules Mazarin, chief minister of France and effectively its ruler during the minority of Louis XIV.

[347] Parliamentarian administrator, merchant, and adventurer, for a time during the 1640s he was secretary to parliament's Irish committee and from 1648 he was active in Ireland, settling in Cork and becoming commissary general of the victuals in Ireland and, in 1654, a commissioner for the allotment of lands to the adventurers.

in these parts, whoe have great reason to feare a second erruption of the malice of our cruell enemies if not prevented by the providence of God, and your excellencie's care in granting the request of the petitioners, and of,

Your excellencie's most humble and faithfull servants,

R Blayney Ol Hucketill
John Forster Fra Cole

311. Draft of a letter by Henry Cromwell to John Thurloe, 6 October 1657, 822, fos 200–201.

The noise which Mardyke makes in all men's mouthes must, as you say, needs drowne the cry of Ireland. The Lord prosper our forces there. I hope you deale with the French as with men having as many tricks as possible.

I like well enough of the allowance of £324,000 for defraying both the civill and millitary charge, but I say tis impossible to raise 120,000 per annum besides the assessments here. For all the revenues of Ireland, viz, customes, excise, rents of the reserve <lands> counties,[348] bishopps' lands and houses, etc, doe not exceed 70,000. As for the other 50,000, it can never bee had unlesse the quitt rents[349] bee paid by the English acre, for at the Irish[350] it will not bee full 30,000, neither will those rents bee demandable, for ought I know, these <4> 3 or <5> 4 yeares. Wherefore this computation must bee reviewed.

In the next place, I say that 300,000 bee allowed for the military; that the remayning 24,000 will never serve for the civill, for the councill will take up halfe that, neither is there anything allowed for contingencies on the military or concordatums[351] on the civill accompt, without both which there is no living here.

I have received the modell both of the reducement and also the establishment. By both which I find the contrary from what I alwayes thought both cheapest and safest, for therein the reducement is made upon the soldiers, whereas I would have had it on the officers. But supposing those who propounded these things as more able and not lesse affectionat with reference to Ireland then myselfe, I must and will submitt.

[348] Counties Cork, Carlow, Kildare, and Dublin, where land had been reserved for the government's own use and from which state income could be drawn.

[349] The rent paid by tenants in lieu of feudal or manorial service.

[350] 1 Irish acre corresponded to just over 1.6 English acres; hence payments due on land in Ireland were worth far more if calculated by the English acre than by the Irish acre.

[351] Concordatum: a special payment, provision, or grant of money, land, or other property made by the state.

As for my opinion of letting the customes and excise of Ireland to farme at £70,000 per annum, I answer in generall, I wish you had 40,000, provided the exaction of these duties become thereby no more horrible then they are at present. For since wee can make but about 25,000 nett over and above the charges of collecting them,[352] I say there must bee either far greater severity used to raise above double, nay treble including the farmers' gaynes, then now there is, although some thinke there is already too much; or else the farmers have some extraordinary presage of some miraculous increase of trade; or else by the length of the terme of their contract they hope to repaire the losses they expect at first; or else they have some device, by getting good passe from Ireland <to> into England by post cockett,[353] to defraud the customes of <Ireland> England through Ireland; or else they conceive (though amisse) that the customes and excise of Ireland yielding now 70,000 will by their better management yield that sum againe, together with an encouragement to themselves; or else they entend to wind themselves into the state's mony and then leave us in the lurch; or lastly I thinke they doe not understand the busines, and that the admitting of any man to impossible conditions will end in a clamour upon you for releife, and an obstruction and disappointement to your affaires. All this while I cannot but feare I am myselfe mistaken in my conception of this matter.

That is, I think there may bee may some <other> such conditions of desoliation propounded as may acquitt the farmers from paying part of that rent, which with the other heads I desire to heare from you, and <withall> particularly where and by whom <contrareys[354]> matter of equity arising upon this contract shall bee determined.[355]

[352]Although the slow recovery of trade in Ireland during the Protectorate probably led to a gradual increase in the customs receipts, even by 1657–1658 Irish customs were bringing in only around £29,000 per year gross. Hence Henry Cromwell's estimate here that, after deducting administrative costs, Irish customs collected in the old way would yield around £25,000 per year and his great suspicion of this offer from a consortium of customs farmers to handle Irish customs in return for a payment of £70,000 per year to the state. Henry Cromwell supported the principle of customs farming (*TSP*, VI, pp. 538–539), but felt that this offer was unrealistically high and sprang from either naivety or duplicity and would lead at least to a much heavier and unpleasant imposition of Irish customs, if not to outright failure or corruption. Despite his reservations, a contract was concluded on this basis and, through greater rigour and severity, the farmers were able greatly to boost Irish customs income, paying the treasury around £56,000 per year on average for the farm, down to the premature conclusion of their contract in the summer of 1660.

[353]Cockett: a seal belonging to a customs house and more generally an official or privileged document sealed by customs officers.

[354]Uncertain reading of poorly formed word.

[355]This sentence has been added in the margin at this point, with an asterisk to indicate where it was to sit in the main text.

Wherefor I say in the meanetime take this my sense upon my present apprehensions of the thing, and rectify mee by your next where you find mee or the farmers to have mistaken each other, or yourselfe.

The army want their pay for want of an authority to <levy the> apportion the <assessement>.

I have not heard anything of the letres <of> from the committee of parlement as you record.

312. From Charles Fleetwood, 6 October 1657, 822, fos 202–203.

Deare brother,

I have noe more to adde in reference to reducment. I confesse that which I am most dissatisfyed in is as to the trayn and contingencyes, wherin if you please to expresse what parts of the trayn and what garrysons must of necessity be kept, about which the cheife expence of your contingencyes will be taken up, and what you offer upon thos accounts will, I hope, be complyed with heare so farre as we can possibly. The officers of the army wer of opinion as to most of the perticulers. I know some will be suspitious, but I am sure ther is no reason for it, and the whole coming under your inspection will I hpoe[356] preserve me from jealousyes. We have now the care of Mardyke upon us, the French being risen from befor Gravlin through the violence of the waters, which cam down upon them from the drawing up of the sluces. The French have promised to lye 10 dayes neare to Mardike till the lyne be enlarged to hold 2,000 foote and 500 horse, which is necessary, the fort being now very weake and I feare not able to hold out. It is a very considerable place to our affayres, if the Lord please to blesse endeavors in the securing of it. I know you have it from others what is intended in reference to the settlement of Ireland. With our humble service to your deare lady, I am,

Your most affectionate brother and humble servant,

Charles Fleetwood

I am afrayde least the desire of our howsholdstuffe showld inconvenience you, and therfor be pleased to be so brotherly that what we have which may be convenient for your occations, to detaine without price, and have that confydence that what we have ther you may command.[357] Your freedom hearin will be kindnes to your most deare sister and myselfe.

[356] Word garbled – apparently 'hope' is intended.

[357] Apparently, therefore, Fleetwood had left some of his household goods in Dublin in the summer of 1655, when he returned to England, perhaps thinking that he might at some stage return to Ireland and resume residence at Dublin. This letter therefore suggests that, by early October 1657, Fleetwood was aware that a firm and final decision had been taken

313. From Nathaniel Waterhouse, 6 October 1657, 822, fos 204–205.

May it please your excelency,

According to your order, I have hereinclosed sent your lordshipp a just accompt of all such moneys as I have received for your use; and what I have paid, as alsoe what doth remaine at this tyme in my hands. And I am alsoe bould to acquaint your honour that there is the summe of two hundred and fifty pounds due unto your honour the 29th of September last, which I have not as yett received, but I beleeve I may have it in some short tyme. My lord, this is the state of your lordshipp's accompt as it now stands betwixt your lordshipp and mee. All which I humbly submite, and begg your lordshipp's pardon. I make bould to subscribe myselfe,

Your excelency's most humble servant to comand,

Nat Waterhouse

314. From Charles Howard, Naward, 8 October 1657, 822, fos 206–207.

My lord,

I formerly made bold to trouble your lordship in the behalfe of one Meade,[358] whose sonne has relation to a neer frend of myne, concerning an estate he has in Ireland, in which he suffers much through the severity of some, who has gotten some interest in itt. Hee has no other reffuge to flye to but your lordshipp's. I earnestly beg your lordship's favour to him in his demands, as your lordship shall find them reasonable and just. And this shall add to the many favours I reiceived, and further obleidge, my lord,

Your most faithfull servant,

Howard

315. From William Webb, Galway, 9 October 1657, 822, fos 208–209.

May it please your excellency,

At the cittadle of Gallway there is great want of a gatehouse and porculles of iron, also a salley port and iron greatte for it, and two other iron greatts for the water cours, and severall other things of less moment, which should be done with all speed. Therefore I humbly pray your excellency to give orders that a warrant may bee drawne

not to reappoint him to Ireland and, with no prospect of ever returning to Dublin, he was now planning to move his remaining belongings back to England, while letting Henry Cromwell keep what he wanted in Dublin.

[358]Identification uncertain, since several adventurers bore this surname.

up for collonel Sadler to receive sixty pounds, and to bee by him disburshd for the aforesaid use. All at present from,

Your excellency's most humble servant,

Wm Webb

316. From John Reynolds, Calais, 9/19 October 1657, 822, fos 226–227.

May it please your excellency,

I was bold to write my mind in a letter from Burbourg 4 dayes since, which I hope will come safe. Howsoever, I shall renew the same request that your lordshipp be pleased to write unto his Highnes for my waiting on your lordshipp in Ireland this winter. And I am the more desirous of his Highnes' sence therein, because I shall thereby discover whether any do desire to render this emploiment an honourable banishment. And if that (which your lordshipp may please to write) faile, I shall make use of my interest heere to obteine leave, the cardinal having already consented to my absence for 2 months, conditionally I attend the king at Paris. Things heere are in a verry hopefull way, so farre as our designes tend, being terminated within the limits of keeping Mardyke fort, whither I am going least your lordshipp should not speake prophetically, which is the redoubt before Dunkirke mentioned in your lordship's, and there are my quarters, indeede insteade of Chippenham, Dublin or Campes Castle. It is now 14 dayes since I left my dearest, and London, at which time Sir Francis with my lady returned home. Concerning the passages of providence towards me in that affaire, I acknowledge them to be full of mercy, and that none can be more happy in a loveing and faithfull wife than I acknowledge myselfe to be in my dearest Sarah, who is at length come and gone for the present. My lord, I am exceedingly sensible of hard measure towards your excellency, and really if it continues I shall at once abandon all publique emploiments. If the sonnes be smitten what may the servaunts expect? My lord, I am,

Your excellencye's most obliged, faithfull and humble servaunt,

J Reynolds

I have wrote 3 letters to the lord Broghill, but heare not of their reception.

317. From Charles Fleetwood, Wallingford House, 10 October 1657, 822, fos 210–211.

Letter of recommendation on behalf of the bearer, Sir Joseph Douglas,[359] *who desired to settle in Ireland and had some business there.*

[359] A Scottish royalist, knighted by the king in 1633 at the same time that William Douglas, Earl of Angus, was created first Marquess of Douglas, and probably therefore a kinsman

318. From Daniel Thomas, Fort Fleetwood, alias the Bridge of Ballymoe, County Galway, 11 October 1657, 822, fos 212–213.

May it please your excellency,

When I did part with your excellency, I did aquainte you that my slaters, that was covering of collonel Richard Coote's[360] house, would by that tyme I should come downe would bee done and come away thence, which I have found soe, and are heere with mee at Belamoe. Soe that, accordinge unto my promise unto your honour, doe present both their and my owne services, whome are reddy to goe unto the quarry neere unto Portomna, or that neere Killalow,[361] where I am informed by all the workemen that well knowe them, that those at Killalow are farr better then the other neere Portomna. But I will goe with them and search them both, and folow youre honour's orders soe soone as I doe or shall understand your pleasure therein, and prevent with expedition the future danger of the house; and that youre excellency bee pleased to order that soe soone as that the slatte bee reddy, then the ferry boates may bringe them home. I will, soe soone as may bee, cause soe many to bee layd neere the chimneys as shall prevent future danger, untill the season bee to compleate the whole.

My lord, alsoe, I have some English sayers of timber at Balamoe, whoe will have within a fortnight's tyme ended theire worke with mee. Sayers, especially English, both in Dublin and all the nation over, are very rare and scarce to bee hadd, that if I showld part with them now this winter, both them and the slaters, I should not have them agayne. Nor could I gett others, they are soe hard to bee hadd. Therefore, if that I might bee soe worthy to know certainly wheather the bridge of Portomna wilbe built or not, (if built) whether of timber or stone it matter not, yett I could imploy them preparinge for it untill a contract bee made. Which a good preparation must bee had this winter in preparing of stones, raizinge and hewinge, fallinge and squaringe of timber, and drawinge them by land, and especially by water whilst water is, and layd by water in a reddynes against the water bee gon, that they may bee laied in water. Soe that if this winter be lost, which for carriadge is better then the sumer, then the summer next wilbe wholy lost in preparinge, and not soe good; and the summer after

of Douglas. He served as an agent and emissary of the Scottish royalist leaders during the later 1640s.

[360] Parliamentarian officer, and younger brother of Sir Charles and Chidley Coote, he fought in Ireland in the 1640s and early 1650s against the Irish Catholic forces and for a time he commanded a regiment of horse in Ireland, disbanded in 1653.

[361] Killaloe, County Clare, lies at the southern end of Lough Derg, Portumna at the northern end.

may prove wett, that the worke will not bee brought above water that summer, for wee have hadd this and the last sommer very dry, and it is observable that wee may not have two dry summers more.

My lord, the people of the cuntry is soe overjoyed at youre excellency's good intentions for a bridge, that they are exeedinge reddy to answere you in any thinge your honour will desier for the settinge it forward; I doe beeleeve to the makinge of the cauceway crose the meddow from the White castle in the iland[362] unto the high way towards Birr. As I have sayd, if I could bee thought worthy to know youre honour's resolution therein, my sone havinge ended collonel Coote, his house, and beinge come away thence, I would setle him to the finnishinge of Belamoe, and mysealfe and family would speedily setle unto the buissnesse at Portomna. That by this tyme twelve mounth I would, by Gode, His good assistance, be able to give youre excellency a greate and a good an accoumpt. If soe, then I shall bringe with mee many English and good familyes to setle there, which now with mee are aboute to setle in the county of Roscoman; and more with my three sones will folow after mee. And doe then crave that youre lordshipp would bee pleased to furnish mee with Derry iland, and the lands of Lehinch[363] over against the ferry place, which youre lordshippe was pleased when I parted with you to give mee a promise of them. I would take the Derry iland, the custome of the bridge, and all those lands that are ajatient there unto, for mysealfe, my sones and oure familyes, and those that shall setle with us, for which I shall give considderable. Cravinge youre lordshipp's pardon to minde you of youre promise to mee in that behalfe, and youre lordshipp's future favoure on my dependents.

My lord, since youre excellency's beinge here, my beinge absent hence, whilest I waited on you at Portomna and at Dublin, my worke heere hath binn very much delaied and protracted by reason that every man is buildinge, and the Irish workemen are runn away from mee, for since the oath of abjuration[364] is come amoungst them they had rather doe any man's worke than build places of strength, which may subdue and keepe them in obedience, and have skattered themsealves some 10, some 20, some 40 myles from mee. Soe that it is my humble desier that your excellency wilbe pleased, after my many and humble desiers, to

[362]Perhaps the castle that stands a little south of the road running out of Portumna towards Birr, at the north end of an isthmus or small peninsula of low-lying land on the north shore of Lough Derg. On some maps this isthmus is identified as Derry Island, and a second castle, further south and closer to the water's edge, as Derry Castle.

[363]Probably Lehinch/Lahinch, on the west coast of Ireland, in County Clare.

[364]An act passed in June 1657, aimed at discovering and then clamping down upon Popish recusants, required Irish Catholics to take an oath of abjuration, denying the Pope's power, transubstantiation, and the validity of the Roman church.

send youre orders unto the horse men that are here garrisoned with mee to assist mee in the bringinge them backe that are neere, and bringe others to worke, and houldinge them to the worke for theire pay. I am certaine that none that builds anythinge of quallity that gives soe much wadges as I doe, nor better pay. And alsoe for the better ease of the country and expedition of the worke, that 2 lynes may bee sent unto my lord president,[365] that those foote soldiers that shalbe sent heere may bee such oute of the company as are willinge and have desiered to bee sett unto laboure, which wilbe constant at theire worke and expedition in the same, and a good healpe for theire better mantainance and subsistence – I have some with mee, and might have more if theire officers were sent unto – and alsoe they wilbe redy to secure the place with theire duty as they ought. Not troublinge youre lordshipp from the more waitier afaires; takinge leave to crave youre pardon, and subscribe mysealfe in all dutifull obedience, as in all faithfullnesse shalbe found to bee,

Youre exclencey's most humble and faithfull servant at comand,

Daniell Thomas, senior

319. From Charles Fleetwood, 13 October 1657, 822, fos 216–217.

Deare brother,

It much troubles me that you showld still be disapoynted in the buysnes of Ireland, it not being setled. His Highnes indended as yeasterday to have given some resolution therin, but was prevented by other ocations. I know it must neads prove very inconvenient to your affayres that ther is no settlement. I shall be glade if it wer past. I know ther are many discourses about it, wherin I must have my share. But I have wholly declined my concerning myselfe therin to avoyde suspitions, though when I am called I shall, I hope, give my opinion with honesty and with a due respect to yourselfe. It is a buysnes of weight, and if the Lord gives a union in counsells, that nation will be happy. We have not received the return about the reducment, till which I shall endeavor that nothing be concluded heare. We have noe newes; the Lord continues us in much quietnes. We are labouring what we can to fortefy Mardyke, which surly is of great concerment to us. And if the lord embassedor Lockyer had not playde his part very well, we had bine in great danger of a baffle. But now the French army will remaine by us till that place be fortifyed. Wherin Sir John Reynolds' care and activity will, I hope, put his affayres into such a posture as to give him liberty, for some time, to return to his lady, who

[365] Sir Charles Coote, lord president of Connaught.

indeade seemes to be a very worthy person, and in whom, I hope, he will have a great blessing. This sommer hath very much weakned the Spanyard, who will hardly be able to get an army considerable, unlesse the empire be setled. The French are to quarter upon the borders of Flanders this yeare. Ther are strong endeavors to draw off all assistance from the Sweeds, and by a conjunction of the Popish interests to engage against the Protestant, which conjunction, if the Lord prevents not, will probably bring us into new troubles. I see no state maks it their buysnes to minde that interest except his Highnes, who hath a heart inlarged with seale for them and a heart fully sensible of their condition. The lownes of our treasury will prevent doing what may be expected from us and in his Highnes' heart to doe. With our humble service to youre deare lady, I am,

Your most affectionate brother,

Charles Fleetwood

320. From Daniell Thomas, Fort Fleetwood, Ballymoe, 14 October 1657, 822, fos 218–219.

May it please your excellency,

Youre servant is wholy and altogether devoted, not in complements to present his service unto your lordshipp, but in harty desier and true reality doth tender himsealfe and services with a serious resolution to performe the same, as it shalbe by God, His grace, apeare unto you from tyme to tyme, constant and faithfull, to serve you carefully to my uttmost abillityes if once imployed. And the more (if intrusted) I cannot but minde your lordshipp, as I did in the other letter, how much overjoyed the cuntry, on both sides of the Shannon, is in hopes of your lordshipp's good intentions concerning the buildinge of the bridge of Portomna. It will not only bee the publique good, but youresealfe cannot but confesse what provabillity of a good improvment there is like to bee on your owne estate on both sides the river, which will suddenly redowne thereby. That in 4 or 5 yeares tyme the improvment will pay for the building if it bee made with stone, which wilbe for ever, and but somethinge more then duble the chardge if it shalbe built with timber, whose defects and decayes will, in some particulars, yearly after apeare. And 2,000 tunns of timber will for ever destroy the woods there, and the dammadge not perceaved if 10 bridges were there to be bee built with stone, but the grownd and land much the better for it. Therefore if I might bee thought worthy, or some other person in the behalfe of the cuntry, as is theire desier, rather then the worke shall not goe on, to petition youre excellency and the councell, as you shall thinke it meete, for the prevaylinge of it, wheather I shalbe the undertaker or nott; yett it is 10,000 tymes to bee pittied that soe good a worke should bee necklected for any by ends. My lord, my education and practice, from my youth untill this warr, hath binn with the best of undertakers for buildinges in London; and cann make knowne my former performances before I came thence, as the buildinge of the Inne of Chancery, called Furnifalle Inn, Holborne; South Hampton House, behinde Grey's Inn; the Lord Grey of Warcke in the Charter House yard; the Charter House itsealfe,[366] for 20 yeares together untill the warre; and severall other good buildinges of my owne undertakeinge and performinge. I doe begge of youre lordshipp's pardon, to say that in this nation there is not another that will or cann performe with all abillityes as I shall, cann or will undertake; nor in another nation that cann or will performe in some abillityes, but in all or in any abillityes. They cannot performe better and with more or soe much expedition then mysealfe, for I have built with in 2 yeares' space the castle of Termonberry,[367] this of Belamoe,[368] collonel Rich Coote's and castle Coote,[369] and all at greate distances, which if they had binn together, and that I might bee constant in my buisnes, I would have performed as much more. And lett this my hand come in judgement against mee when I shall not performe in every particular as I have specified. And bee very well assured that, if I shalbe incurraged and finde favoure for the doinge of it, the slattinge of the house, the repairinge of the whole stable inwardly and other things which I know need full to bee done there, they shalbe expeditiously done. And as for the chardge, youre excelency shall not have occasion to take notice thereof. And what I have here specified, or shall here after doe, shee that lieth in my bosome, or any other

[366]All major properties in London, built or rebuilt in the early to mid-seventeenth century. Furnival's Inn, an inn of chancery attached to Lincoln's Inn, on the north side of Holborn, was taken down in 1640 and rebuilt to a design of Inigo Jones; Southampton House, on the east side of Chancery Lane, was built in 1639–1640 on a patch of previously open ground called Southampton Gardens; the Charterhouse, a medieval monastic foundation standing just outside the City of London, was partly demolished and substantially rebuilt in the period after the dissolution, especially after it passed into the Sutton family in the early seventeenth century and was altered to serve as a school, hospital, and chapel; and the adjoining Charterhouse Yard or Square, immediately to the south, contained a number of notable and elite residences by this time, including a property owned by William Grey, first Baron Grey of Warke, parliamentarian politician and briefly a rather ineffective officer in eastern England during the opening year of the civil war, who largely withdrew from public affairs at the approach of the regicide and played no part in national politics during the 1650s.

[367]Termonbarry, in County Roscommon.

[368]Ballymoe, in County Galway.

[369]The seat of the Coote family in County Roscommon, above the River Suck – a late-sixteenth-century fortified house acquired, improved, and strengthened by the Coote family in the opening decades of the seventeenth century.

person under the sunn shall ever know. Noe, nor my left hand shall know what my right hand doth. Cravinge your lordshipp's asistance in what youre lordshipp shall thinke meete, and two lines in answere to this particular together with your lordshipp's pardon, most humbly subscribinge mysealfe to bee,

Your excelency's most humble and faithfull servant in all dutyfull obedience,

Daniell Thomas, senior

321. From Robert Phaier, Rostelane, County Cork,[370] 15 October 1657, 822, fos 220–221.

My lord,

This is only to accquainte your excellencie that sicknes and windes hindred my returne out of England, within your excellencie's passe. His Highness (at my takeing leave) comaunded his love to be remembered to your excellencie and my ladie, which I make bold to doe in this paper, being not able soe soone to attend you. I intend sudainly for the county of Waxford and Carloe.[371] Theare, heare or any wheare, I am,

Your excellencie's most humble servant to commaund,

Robt Phaire

322. From Edward Whalley, Westminster, 15 October 1657, 822, fos 222–223.

Letter of request, noting that, while the Protector had given his son leave to go to France for a year, the period of leave granted by Henry Cromwell or Fleetwood was for just six months and was therefore about to expire; requests that the leave be extended to a full year, so that his son could remain in France and acquire the language until the following spring.

323. From John Godsnuffe, Kinsale, 16 October 1657, 822, fos 224–225.

Letter of request, recounting how, around 1651, he had married the widow of an officer killed at Drogheda who had lost her estate in Ireland to the native Irish but had preserved the record of arrears due to her late husband – Phaire Becher[372] – and his debentures; requests that, having spent over £150 moving his family from

[370] Rostellan, on the east side of Cork harbour and south of Midleton.

[371] Wexford and Carlow.

[372] Parliamentarian officer, though little is known about his military career other than that, in 1648, when he held the rank of lieutenant-colonel, he was appointed an assistant assessment collector in London and was dispatched to deliver letters to Ireland. He

England to Ireland and now rendered utterly ruined and destitute, he be allotted some poor land at Collonaloing in Baunrish parish, west Carberry, which had not been allotted to the army.

324. From Charles Fleetwood, 20 October 1657, 822, fos 228–229.

Deare brother,

I have received your letter with the abstract of musters, and canot understand what parts of the proposalls you most except against, and shall be very unwilling it showld be don contrary to your judgment. And as to that you mention concerning the revenue of Ireland, it is a great mistake the tythes[373] wer not in the least thought upon to be included, but the 50,000 per annum was of the rest of the revenue in Ireland. Which computation was not of mine, but of others, and from the notes you sent up hither. Therfor I am not to be blamed further then in my endeavoring to let others understand they have overvalued the revenue with you. And though I am for a full maintenance to all who give up themselves to the ministration of the gosple, yet if ther was as certeine a way as this of tithes I own it I showld, in my opinion, think it wer beter then in a way of such controversy. However, in this tithes was not in the least in intended. I am satisfyed in a full maintenance for a gosple ministery, which I think my duty to incourage and preserve, though in the way of tithes I confesse I showld be satisfyed if it could be put into another beter way. I know few of my actions passe without censure, yet from yourselfe I hope for a candid acceptation, and in this buysnes I was farre from such a design. We have don nothing as

presumably perished in the successful Cromwellian attack upon Drogheda in the autumn of 1649.

[373] After 1649, many tithes and other church lands in Ireland were forfeited to the state and the income therefrom became part of the overall state income, out of which state-appointed ministers and schoolmasters in Ireland were to receive salaries from the Irish treasury. In the course of 1657, these accounting procedures were changed and ecclesiastical income was kept separate and not included with the other general sources of income in Ireland – from secular land and property, customs, and excise. The change revealed that no more than half the cost of employing ministers and schoolmasters in Ireland was being covered by ecclesiastical income forfeited to the state and this, in turn, encouraged moves to return to the traditional system of parochial tithes in Ireland, thus reducing the financial burden on the central treasury. Henry Cromwell broadly supported these moves but Fleetwood, holding more radical religious views, was hostile to the traditional tithe system. When a meeting of ministers, convened in Dublin in the spring of 1658, proposed a return to traditional tithes in Ireland, Henry Cromwell supported the plans, writing to Fleetwood to allay his fears and defending the proposal as the best or only way properly to fund ministers already in Ireland and to encourage more ministers to come to Ireland to fill vacancies; he hoped it would 'not be lookt upon as an evil design, thus to settle the ministers, having regard [. . .] to those that do soberly, and not wantonly, scruple that way' (*TSP*, VII, pp. 129–130).

to the reducment since you cam. Our want of money will put us to great streigh[. . .][374] and our not sooner retrenching the charge will put us unto great necessityes. Since my last, my lord embassador Lockyer is com, by whom we understand a doubtfullnes what the issue of the buysnes of Mardike will be.[375] Though I hope we shall keepe it, the difficulty will be considerable, by reason of the stronge garysons which are on either side of it – Gravlin and Dunkirke. His lordshippe is suddenly to return, who is a very gallant person and hath managed his buysnes very handsomly. Mr Secretary gives you, I doubt not, an account hearof, and I shall not further adde then with what I am,

Your most affectionate brother and humble servant,

Charles Fleetwood

325. From Edmund Temple, London, 20 October 1657, 822, fos 230–231.

Letter of apology, reporting that he had outstayed his leave in order to attend his brother, Purbaikes,[376] who had been dangerously ill, but, in the light of his recovery, he was now making haste to return.

326. From James Murray, Earl of Annandale,[377] Scone, 22 October 1657, 822, fos 232–233.

Letter of thanks for favours granted over the past year or more, since taking leave of Henry Cromwell in Dublin in 1655; also expresses a hope of visiting Henry Cromwell in Ireland the following summer.

327. From Charles Fleetwood, 26 October 1657, 822, fos 236–237.

Deare brother,

I have not much to wright but know ere this time you will receive a full account of what is intended heare to be don, especially this night

[374] Edge of paper slightly damaged with possible loss of text, though the incomplete word is apparently 'streight' or 'streights'.

[375] Lockhart was carrying news of French proposals to abandon and demolish Mardyke, plans which were strongly opposed by the Protectoral regime and which the French dropped.

[376] Perbeck Temple, who had campaigned in Ireland in the late 1640s, held minor ecclesiastical and financial offices in England in the 1640s and 1650s.

[377] Scottish royalist peer and sometime supporter of Montrose, in 1652–1653 he was one of the Scottish representatives negotiating terms of a possible union with England and, in November 1654, Protector and council wrote to Fleetwood and the Irish council in his support, referring to him as a person of credit and worth and directing that, so that his Irish properties should not suffer, the native Irish tenants on his estates should not be subject to transplantation (Dunlop, p. 456).

being the concluding time as to the presant buysnes of settlement in Ireland, wherin, as the Lord pleases to make use of you as an instrument of good to the people of God, that will be your crown and glory. And be sure to let that interest you will stand and fall with be that of the people of God, and you will prosper. Your father hearin is an example. I meane it not as to any sort of such men, but as they are considered upon that generall and best account of union with our Lord Jesus. Let nothing prejudice against any of that number. I have hade late discourse with Allen and Vernon, who report very much your candidnes and favor towards them. I confesse I have found something as I thought of tartnes to myselfe, but I am sure they seeme very gratefull to you; and in that, I desire to rejoyce to finde your tendernes to good men, and though weaknes may appeare in some, yet to forbeare in that wherin publick prejudice is not, I think, that kind of tendernes will not return with losse to any who show it. I have nothing considerable to trouble you with, more then what you will have from another hand, only I think fit to let you know that the enimy, the cavileire, is at worke and their design very generall. The more carefull your men the better. The Secretary will give you a more full advertisment hearof, but I am sure this hint will be sufficient to put you upon the strictest orders to be carefull of their duty; which is all at presant from,

Your most affectionate brother and humble servant,

Charles Fleetwood

328. From the Commissioners[378] of Loughrea, Loughrea, [County Galway], 26 October 1657, 822, fos 238–239.

May it please your excellency,

Wee have now disposed of all the landes which wee were authorized to give out, although we could not soe farre finish that worke within the tyme limited by the councell, but that wee were necessitated to signe many orders since the expiration of our commission for possession of land sett out before. The transcription and perfecting of the bookes (for such use as your excellencie and the state shall direct), according to the former intimation of the councell, will take up some tyme, wherein wee cannot avoid the imploying of the clarkes, although we have no expresse warrant to incourage their attendance, which wee held it our duty to acquaint your excellency with. Humbly

[378]Commissioners, originally appointed in January 1654, for setting out land in Connaught and Clare for the native Irish and others who had been transplanted there (Dunlop, pp. 387–389, 521–523, 544, 571–572, 608–609).

expecting the signification of your lordshipp's further pleasure, wee are,

Your excellency's most humble servants,

Hen Greneway Will Edwards Char Holcroft

329. From Richard Hampden and William Barton, London, 27 October 1657, 822, fos 240–241.

May it please your excellency,

The reduceing of that brutish part of Monaghan (which wee have taken) into a compleate English plantation emboldens us to become your most humble suitors, that wee may be admitted tennants to those nineteene tates[379] of land mentioned in a petition, a copy whereof wee have presumed herein to inclose. We shalbe willing to improve the rent for the benefit of the publique. And if wee may be admitted tennants, it will preserve our owne just right, vizt, the fee farme rent which is unjustly detained, and wee feare is not to be obteyned without a suite in law, which to us at this distance would be very prejudiciall. Wee have sent the petition to colonell Tomlinson, who wee hope will present it to the right honourable the councell. Wee dare not farther trouble your honour, only are bold to subscribe ourselves,

Your excellencie's most humble and oblidged servants,

Richard Hampden William Barton

330. From Thomas Harrison, Dublin, 27 October 1657, 822, fos 242–243.

May it please your excellencie,

The same good God who hath in mercy gone along with your excellency hath also afforded His gracious presence to your family in their remove to their winter quarters.[380] My lady and the little ones are well and chearfull. We have yet no pacquet from England, through the want of a boate on the other side. Do what I can, I still finde myselfe like a weather-glasse, suffering my spirit, hopes and joyes to rise or fall according to the aire of newes and intelligence. Though I know it were an advantage as great as the duty to have our hopes (like the life of the saints) hid with God in Christ, sometimes I am troubled to see things coming on a little, and then seming to go as

[379] Tate: a measure of land in Ireland, equal to sixty Irish acres.

[380] The Cromwell family generally spent the summer at Phoenix House outside the city, returning to Cork House in Dublin for the rest of the year. Henry Cromwell was clearly still on his late summer and early autumn tour of Ireland, since this letter was addressed to him at Kilkenny.

farre backe againe. But I remember that I have bene upon the shore at low-water, observing the coming in of the tyde, and I have sene a little wave creeping forward, and then as fast and as farre retreating presently, and so another and another, so that I could not thinke the flood did at all increase, but upon setting a marke or standing neare the wash of the waves it was easy to see and feele that it was flowing water, and ere long insensibly it would be full sea. Thus it is with us in spiritualls; thus in temporalls.

I begge your lordship's pardon for this trouble, and am encouraged to hope for it because none can more fervently wish well to your lordship's person, and therin to the publique, then,

Your excellencie's most faithfull, poore servant,

Tho Harrison

331. From John Gorges,[381] Taunton, October 1657, 822, fos 244–245.

May it please your excellencie,

Your unvalluable favoures have soe perpetually ingaged my harte to your service that I professe I want expression to demonstrate my thainkefullnes and my syncere devotions to your comaunds. But truly, my lord, what I want in outard declaration I make up in most cordiall affection, and my weake braines are dayly, nay I may truly say howerly, contrivinge how I may give a testimony thereof. And that I may tender your lordshipp som account of my endeavours this way, I shall presume to acquaint you that I have presented the condition of Irland for want of godly ministers to the association of ministers in this county, att theire generall meetinge, where I informed them how much glory to God, and good to His church, one able, godly and discreet minester might bringe, havinge such countinance and incouragment from your lordshipp, which I assured was generally to all truly godly minesters given by you. The discourse I had with them and the arguments I used are too many to trouble your lordship with, but I hope the Lord will soe order thinges that I shall obtayne that favoure from them as to send you over as godly, learned, wise and moderate a divine as most in England, and as fitt for the worke of God in Dublin as any man. He hath bine the maine instrument in a very prudent manner to joyne the ministry of this county in such a firme bond of union that the name of Presbiteriane or Independant are not mentioned here.

[381] Parliamentarian politician and officer, probably a kinsman of Thomas Gorges, Henry Cromwell's secretary. He sat in all three Protectorate parliaments, in the first two for his native Taunton and Somerset, but in 1659 for an Irish seat – Counties Londonderry, Donegal, and Tyrone – by which time he was also lieutenant-colonel of Henry Cromwell's foot regiment in Ireland.

But I shall say noe more of his worth, but assure your lordship that if I either know your lordship or him, he is as highly qualified for your worke as can be imagined. I did perceive all the minesters att that meetinge soe senseable of your want, and soe expressive joyfull for your pious endeavoure, that I am sure hath bine since the occation of much prayer and many prayers to God. Wherefore I hope I need not doubt but this worthy devin will accompany mee to waite on your excellencie. For I must professe in this busines I playnly saw that text fullfilled: them that honor Mee, I will honor. For certaynly, my lord, if the effectuall fervent prayer of one rightious man avayleth soe much, your lordshipp will be incouraged on the consideration of thos many that I am confident are dayly put up for you: that God would carry you through thos great and waighty affaires that lies on you tendinge soe much to His glory. I shall attempt other asossiations of thes westerne parts, and shall give your excellencie an account of my proseedinges. But I now beginninge to blush at my tediousnes, and therefore cravinge pardon I humbly rest,

Your excellency's most humble, faythfull and cordiall servant,

Jo Gorges

I have incloased presented your lordshipp with the Somersett association, with theire adresse to his Highnes. I have allsoe sent coppyes of the same to the Scots minesters about Derry.

332. From John Reynolds, 2/12 November 1657, 822, fos 268–269.

May it please your excellency,

I cannot omit to acquaint your lordshipp with the late providence of God towards this place, into which I put myselfe for the mainetenance of his Highnes' interest therein.[382] It pleased the Lord to disappoint the enemy in his late attempt, wherein they lost severall officers of quality. The lord of Ormond had his horse killed under him by a greate shot. They threaten another assault, but our hope is that He who hath delivered us will farther owne His owne worke. In a little skermish neere this fort there was killed, by an English musketeir, Don Fernand Solis' brother, a considerable Spaniard. Our workes are in some forwardnes, and I trust the Lord will enable us to finish them contrary to the expectations of England or France. The latter councelled the demolishing it. My humble suite is that this garrison may not be made my prison this winter, but that I may leave it in a terible posture under the command of major-general Morgan or some other fit person, and have admission to attend your lordshipp in

[382] Under pressure from the Protector, Reynolds had accepted command of Mardyke.

Ireland. If this be denied I shall be enforced, like the rest of my fellow vagrants of this world, to returne to the place from whence I came, viz, Castle Campes, being the place of my birth. But I am neither willing to decline his Highnes' nor your lordship's services unlesse necessity requireth, being however resolved not to leave my wife to command Mardyke. I remaine, my lord,

Your excellencye's most obliged, faithfull and humble servaunt,
J Reynolds

333. From Charles Fleetwood, 3 November 1657, 822, fos 246–247.

Deare brother,

I shall still continue the freedom of that expression, notwithstanding what additionall honor the providence of God hath cast upon you in your being made deputy of Ireland, wherin I desire the Lord may still own you and make you a choyce instrument of much good to that nation, and especially to be as a nursing father to the people of God, your tenderness to whom the more you exercise it and as to such, the greater will be your mercy and that will return with a double blessing into your bosom. Your pattent and the counsell's instructions will suddenly be sent. The Lord unite your counsells and make you as a terror to evill doers and a prayse to them that doe well. I must desire you will please not to dispose of my 2 regiments. His Highnes, I presume, will have me continue the same for some reasons not so fitt for paper. I know you are constantly supplyed with all things from hence by another hand, and therfor shall only conclude with what I am,

Your most affectionate brother and humble servant,
Charles Fleetwood

I must intreat your forbearance of Mr Clarke for som time.

334. From Charles Fleetwood, Wallingford House, 3 November 1657, 822, fos 248–249.

Letter of recommendation, reporting that Protector and council had repeated their earlier order of 1656 (not at that time implemented by Henry Cromwell and the Irish council), and, in line with a bill considered but not completed by the second Protectorate parliament, they had directed that Major Walters[383] *be allocated land in Connaught or elsewhere in Ireland to satisfy his debt of £5,638 2s 3d incurred*

[383]George Walters, parliamentarian officer, was awarded land in County Cork and worked to establish an English settlement at Bantry (Dunlop, p. 366).

in public service, including the transportation of Irish recruits to serve in the Spanish army on the continent; since Walters had been pursuing this matter for two and a half years and since he and his family were now heavily in debt, land should speedily be provided for him and also some employment, so that Walters might be encouraged to carry over English families to settle in Ireland.

335. From Thomas Harrison, Dublin, 3 November 1657, 822, fos 250–251.

May it please your excellency,

I returne my most humble and hearty aknowledgments for the favour of your lordship's last letter. My lady hath of late bene somewhat indisposed by a cold, but (through mercy) recovers her freedome from it againe. My little lord[384] begins to stand better then ever, and little madam's[385] pleasant wit is the mirth and delight both of the family and strangers. About Thursday last[386] I was told that a gentleman came from Chester (when there wanted a boate to bring the pacquet), who affirmed that he came directly from London and that he was assured the settlement of Ireland had passed the councill, and that it was discussed there what the title should be and was fixed by one voice, but whether lord leiutenant or lord deputy was kept private.

I hope this pacquet, which we expect hourely, may put an end to these surmisings and suspenses; and though your lordship as to your owne particular may be but little (and desirous to be lesse) carefull about these things, yet the great concernment of the publique lying herein, God hath made it the duty of your place and condition to be concerned in it. I have often resembled the settlement of this nation to Daniell's vision, whereof the Holy Ghost saith that the thinge was true, but the time appointed was long (chapter 10: 1); and methinkes God still saith to us as to Israell of old (Isiah 7: 9): If ye will not beleive, surely ye shall not be established. God will never trust that which distrusts Him, I meane unbeleife. Tis good indeed often to sitt downe, to commune with our owne hearts, and to prepare for the worst, but still we must honour our good God by beleiving and waiting for the best. We say we doubt not His power, and we have as little reason to doubt His will. He whome God hath already received, on whome His love hath broken forth, how weake soever, shall be holden up, because God is able to make him stand (Romans 14: 1, 3, 4), and faith may and must be acted as well for temporalls as for spiritualls, according to

[384] Henry Cromwell's son Oliver, born in 1656.

[385] Henry Cromwell's daughter Elizabeth, born in 1654, before he went to Ireland.

[386] 29 October.

the generall grounds and incouragements in the scripture. That God is at hand, not to punish but heale our unbeleife by the convincing evidence of His fatherly care and love, is the fervent expectation of,

Your excellencie's poore servant,
Tho Harrison

My lady even now commands me to assure your lordship (with the tender of her love) that nothing but a cold hinders her ladyship from answering your lordship's letter. The pacquet is come this evening, but nothing with it publikely to put an end to our waitings.

336. From T. Billingsley, Whitehall, 7 November 1657, 822, fos 254–255.

Letter of request on behalf of his unnamed brother, reminding Henry Cromwell of an earlier order from the Protector that his brother be given employment in the service of the state.

337. From Henry Ingoldsby, Limerick, 7 November 1657, 822, fos 256–257.

My lord,

Yeasterday I received your commands that the forces in this precinct should bee putt uppon a watchfull posture and guard, which to the uttmost off my power I shall endeavor to effect and neglect nothinge off care to prevent all mischeivouse designes and attempts in these parts. But in order theareunto I must earnestly entreate that some course bee taken to supplye mee with one hundred pound contingent mony for the repayre off our severall cittadells, mountinge the gunns, provideinge lodgeings for the souldiers in them, and for severall other uses that I shall have necessary occations to disburse mony about. Tis counted indiscretion in a cuntriman to loose a sheepe for a halfe penny worth off tar. I hope those that steere the affayres off this nation will use theare thrift on a better account. I am sure itt concernes your lordshipp to prevent nigardly humors in such cases. The sooner I am answeared in these desiers, the sooner and surer expectations may bee answeared, thearefore I hope your lordship will speedily remember to order the supply that is heare sollicited for by, my lord,

Your excelency'se most firmely affectionate, humble servant,
H Ingoldesby

338. From George Monck, Dalkeith, 7 November 1657, 822, fos 258–259.

I have had intimation latelie of the vacancie of the clarke of the pels place[387] in Ireland by the death of that ingenious gentleman, Mr Cary, that has putt a great distresse uppon his wife and children, which is the occasion of the addresse I make att this time to your excellencie, to intreate you to bestowe that place uppon this bearer, Henry Monck,[388] a kinsman of mine, who is fatherlesse and one uppon whose familie the calamities of Ireland have had a great influence. But I shall nott desire your excellencie's favour in his behalf butt uppon condition that hee allow the salary of the office to the widdow for her support and content himself with such profitte as shall arise by the execution of itt, nor should I att this distance interpose in a businesse of this nature if I were nott well assured of his abilities and honesty, a character whereof your excellency may have of him from many in Dublin, besides my relation of him, for which I desire your excellencie's pardon to, my lord,

Your excellencie's most humble servant,
George Monck

339. From William Penn,[389] Macroom, County Cork, 9 November 1657, 822, fos 260–261.

May it please your excellency,

Haveinge received information that your excellency hath beene pleased to appoynt commissioners for setting his Highness his lands in those parts for some tearme of yeares, and for as much as seaverall parcells thereof are not onely contigious but (as I may say) interwoven with those (of that little interest) I have at Macrompe and Killcrea,[390] which should they bee lett unto any other would certainely bee my very great inconvenience and probably my discomfort, the prevention

[387]In the Irish exchequer.

[388]Parliamentarian officer and nephew of George Monck, by 1658 he was a cornet in Henry Cromwell's horse regiment in Ireland.

[389]Parliamentarian naval officer and admiral, in the mid- and late 1640s he campaigned mainly in and around the Irish Sea, with the title vice-admiral of Ireland, and from 1650 further afield, with a distinguished record in the Anglo-Dutch War. Loyal to the Protectoral regime, he had joint command of the 1654–1655 expedition to the West Indies. Following the initial failure of that expedition and his disgrace and the resignation of his commission in the autumn of 1655, he retired to Ireland. In 1644, he had married the widow of a Dutchman with property in County Clare and, in the early 1650s, he was allocated further Irish land in lieu of his wife's losses during the Irish rebellion. At this stage his main seat was at Macroom in County Cork.

[390]Kilcrea, County Cork.

whereof, with the hopes I have to tennant them with English (for which a former foundation hath beene layd) is the great advantage that I doe eye, for the obtayneinge whereof is heerewith very humbly presented the prayer of,

Your excellency's most faithfull and ever obedient servant,

Wm Penn

340. From Francis Bacon, Whitehall, 10 November 1657, 822, fos 262–263.

Right honourable,

Attending lately upon his Highnes, according to the dutye of my place,[391] I receyved directions for a new title to be added to your lordship of lorde deputye. How welcome the newes was to your lordship I know not, but I am suer it was very acceptable to the best affected heere, I meane the best affected to your lordship and the best affected to the peace of this nation and the setlement of this government, and to none more then to myselfe. For indeede, my lorde, your government is often represented heere and spoken of as wholye leading to the advancement of lerning, religion and government, which makes me whoe have ever bin in a greate part your lordship's now to be wholye yours. And I make it my humble sute to your lordship that you wold reckon me in the number of your faythfull servants amongst those that attend at Whitehall, in the number of which none shalbe more redy to obey your comands then, my lord,

Your most humble servant,

Fr Bacon

341. From Charles Fleetwood, London, 10 November 1657, 822, fos 264–265.

Deare brother,

I presume your being at Killkenny was the occation of this week's silence. Your pattent and instructions will, I hope, be sent you this weeke. The instructions are much the same as formerly. If you finde any defect in them, or the desire of an additionall supply, we shall readily grant the same, so farre as we have power. Your affayres have bine, I beleive, much put backwards by your want of settlement, wherin I have not bine guilty. But it being now setled so much to satisfaction will, I hope, alleviat the former omission. We have nothing of moment

[391] As master of requests.

to trouble you with, only our old enimyes are hard at worke, but through the timeous[392] discovery, I trust, will soone be prevent befor the hazard and danger appeares. Only they show their good wills, which I think we must never expect better. The Lord keepe us close to Himselfe, that we may not by any provocations of ours cause Him to withdraw, and we are well ynough. I suppose you heare of my lady Marye's marriage to my lord Faulkonbridg, which is now concluded on.[393] My lady Frances is tomorrow marryed.[394] The Lord grant that by this addition ther may be sutable blessings to the whole family; which that it may is the desires of,

Your most affectionate brother and most humble servant,
Charles Fleetwood

I beseach you cleare me in one thing which you know I am not guilty of, but am blamed by major Walker[395] as one who hath hinderd his preferment to be leiutenant-collonel to collonel Sadler. You know I never writt one word of it unto. My portion is much to suffer on all hands.

342. From Henry Greenway,[396] Loughrea, [County Galway], 12 November 1657, 822, fos 266–267.

May it please your excellency,

I thinke it my dutye to acquaint your excellency concerning the Irish in this province, who behave themselves very strangely towards us of the English on a sudden. They are growen very reserved in their discourse, and when they speake it savors much of discontent. Wee conceive they are much trobled about the oath which is to bee imposed upon them. Neither are they spareing to declare the cause, for in open sessions held lately in this place they declared that they would never take the said oath, but that they would loose all that they had first. I cannot heare of one person that is inclineing to it, soe powerfull are their preists amongst them to perswade them to the contrary. Here are many preists questionles in this province, and soe long as they can escape (when they are taken) with ymprisonment or banishment, they will not forbeare comeing into and resideing within this nation. There were good lawes formerly in force in England against preists

[392] Timeous: coming in due time; suitable or proper in respect of time.

[393] Mary Cromwell married Lord Fauconberg at Hampton Court on 19 November.

[394] Frances Cromwell married Robert Rich at Whitehall on 11 November.

[395] William Walker, parliamentarian officer, held this rank in Sadleir's regiment by 1659.

[396] Administrator in Ireland during the 1650s, in January 1654 he was appointed a commissioner for the allocation of land in Connaught to the transplanted native Irish and in due course he acquired property for himself in Connaught.

(especially in Queene Elizabeth's reigne) where it was treason for any preist to reside within the nation. Twas alsoe treason for any person to receive a bull or any autority from the Pope, or for any person whatsoever to perswade another to be a Papist. Now if those lawes were in force in Ireland the preists would presently withdraw themselves. And this would bee a meanes to procure obedience from this obstinate and perverse generation, who are soe hard to be brought into subjection to the English goverment, and to follow the English fashion and manners, that it is even as hatefull as death itselfe unto them. All which wee find by dayly experience that are magistrates and live amongst them. Another thing is humbly offered unto your excellency, that is concerning the saftetye of this towne of Loughreah,[397] which lyeth open, the walls being broken downe in many places, the gates whereof are not att all shutt in the night. Soe that if the Irish should attempt anything in these parts they might easily sett fire of our office and soe burne and spoyle all the records that concernes the transplantation. The generall greivance of the Irish is not the transplantation, for now they account sending into Conought and looseing their estates nothing in comparison of this oath, but yet they seeme to have some hopes by sending an agent into England to his Highnes and the parliament to suspend the oath. Thus craveing pardon for this boldnes in giving your excellency this short relation; humbly leaveing it to your excellence's consideration; committing you and yours to Him that is able to keepe you from the traps and snares of this wicked world; I take leave and rest,

Your excellense's most devoted and affectionate servant,

Hen Greneway

343. From Jane Fowke, 13 November 1657, 822, fos 270–271.

Right honourable,

I humbly returne you thankes (the poore widdowe's mite) for your remembrance of my deceased sonne in your ownings and actings for my grandchild. It was a greate presumption in the deceased person to tender what hee did. It is a far greater condescention in your honour to imbrace the tender.

My grandchild informes mee that you inquired whether I were in Dublin. My lord, I left freindes and cuntrie to enjoy my sonn, and nowe, being full of dayes, humblie desire that I may end them where hee left mee, and I knowe with that intent. As for the disposall of my grandchild, though his companie bee verie desireable in mine old age

[397]In County Galway, roughly midway between Portumna and Galway town.

(and I am informed by some that hee is fitter for a countrie life then otherwise), yet your and our noble freinds' better judgments muste bee submitted unto. My lord, an ould freind of my sonn's and mine explaines to mee, by an expresse from major Aston,[398] that there is order for sale of my sonn's goods att Chester, for discharge of funerall expences. I have the inventorie, and findinge the greatest part of the goods either to have beene used, or intended to bee used as apparell, which cannot bee sold att Chester butt at inconsiderable values, and not without much disparagement to the deceased person and his survivinge freindes, never anie of his kindred that I have heard of havinge had theirs sold uppon such account, I humblie begg that that order may bee altered, and some other course thought uppon (though to our greater prejudice) for the discharge of that debte. My lord, my sonn being a person whoe would have ventured life and fortune in and for your service makes mee thus bold, for which pardon beinge craved, I render myself,

Your honour's moste humble servant,

Jane Fowke

If your honour bee pleased to demand of Mr Adshed of Simon's Court, hee can sufficientlie informe you of our present condition att Ardee.

344. From James Sharland to the Irish Council, from on board the Kinsale frigate in Kinsale harbour, 13 November 1657, 822, fos 252–253.

Letter of enquiry, stating that he had sailed from Plymouth and now put into Kinsale harbour, to shelter from the weather, with fifteen days' provisions on board; asking whether he should come to Dublin to wait on Henry Cromwell or put to sea to give convoy to and protect six merchant vessels now at Kinsale bound for Bristol and the west of England.

[398]Probably William Aston, parliamentarian officer, who was major in Anthony Hungerford's foot regiment serving in Ireland from the late 1640s. This may suggest that the deceased man was a kinsman of the John Fowke, parliamentarian officer and politician, and MP for Counties Meath and Louth in both of Oliver Cromwell's Protectorate parliaments, who served alongside Aston as an officer in Hungerford's regiment in England and Ireland in the mid- and late 1640s. The deceased was certainly neither John Fowke himself (as he remained active in Ireland up to and beyond the Restoration) nor a brother of his, since John Fowke's mother was called Patience. In part, this note draws upon an unpublished article on John Fowke of Drogheda, County Louth, written by Dr Patrick Little for the 1640–1660 section of the History of Parliament. I am grateful to the History of Parliament Trust for allowing me to see this article in draft.

345. From Henry Lawrence, Whitehall, 17 November 1657, 822, fos 272–273.

My lord,

The counsell were this day enformed that a committee of themselves, to whom it is referred to consider how the publique charge of the commonwealth may be apportioned to the publique income of revenew, have heretofore sent your lordship some proposalls about the retrenching of some of the forces in Ireland, and have thereupon thought fitt hereby to desire your lordship to conforme to the wayes and proportions mentioned in the said proposall for retrenchment of some part of the said forces; or in case your lordship shall see cause to vary in your opinion from any of the rules thereby offered, then your lordship is desired to represent the same to the counsell, with your reasons.

Signed in the name and by order of his Highnes and the counsell,

He Lawrence, president[399]

346. From Charles Fleetwood, 18 November 1657, 822, fos 274–275.

Deare brother,

This bearer will bring you the pattent and instructions,[400] whearin I desire the Lord may appeare in owning of you and make you an eminent instrument of much good to that poore nation and His people in it. My time hath bine much prevented this day by an extraordinary occasion, which makes me lesse in a condition of wrighting what otherwise I might. Only shall acquaint you that the paper, which I sent you in order to a reducment, the counsell hath orderd a letter for the observing of what by me cam from the committee, so farre as

[399] Some rough notes have been jotted on the back of this letter, arranged as points numbered 1–5 and 7–8 (there is no 6), apparently thoughts by Henry Cromwell and/or the Irish council on how to respond to the English government's request to reduce the number of soldiers serving in Ireland:

'1st. Lookeing upon them were to be rather matters under consultation then of resolution

'2. Upon so slender a warrant as these unsigned papers were

'3. I received from other hands given in the late instruction received from your lordshipps the sum for our future maintenance for the safety of this place. If their bee anything in the noise about the caveleers stiring in England, withall considering the great distruction here occasioned by the oath of abjuration

'4. Disbandeing in 55

'5. So often does the postur of affaires change, that which was offered 3 m since may now require a new consideration

'7. Meddles with retrenchment, such matters from your lordshipps

'8. To object against them'

[400] The patent and instructions (Abbott, IV, pp. 665–667; Dunlop, pp. 672–673) were carried to Dublin by George Walters (*TSP*, VI, p. 628).

you are satisfyed in the reason of it; but whearin you differ from us you have a liberty left to make what proposalls you please in order to a better way of lessening the publick charge, which our necessityes inforce unto, the horse heare being 18 weekes in arreare and the foote 14 weekes, which you know canot but be a great inconveniency to us, the army not being suffered to live upon free quarter, but the officers are forced to ingage for their men and I doubt their credit is neare spent. And besids all this we are in want of £60,000 for the paying off our fleet, which we call in, and have no mony to defray thes charges; as allso the necessity that we shall be forced to run into by reason that our taxes will litle more then halfe reach our monthly charge. All of which I mention that you may rightly understand our condition, and endeavor the lessening of your charge so farre as may stand with safety, which at this time requires consideration, the common enimy being so hard at worke to make disturbance, which surly the Lord hath showed great mercy in its timely discovery, and will, I hope, be prevented in its consequence, though they are very confydent. Their disapoyntment will be our mercy; which that we may have hearts to wait upon the Lord for is the desire of,

Your most affectionate brother.

I shall beseach you that the place which I conferred upon alderman Preston[401] and Mr Allden may be now setled by you, which had bine don sooner but that Mr Scudamore was not provided for as intended; but now, I think, they are reasonable[402] well satisfyed. He showld be the 3d person for Ulster.

My lady Mary is to be marryed upon Thursday next.

347. From Richard Stephens,[403] Grange,[404] 18 November 1657, 822, fos 276–277.

Letter of request, asking that he be considered for service in the unit of 500 horse that the Protector had ordered to be selected from the army in Ireland for service in Flanders; sees service in Ireland and Flanders as equally godly, helping to destroy the power of Rome and the antichrist and enlarging the kingdom of God.

[401] John Preston, a prominent alderman of Dublin, who also served a term as mayor during the 1650s, had settled in Ireland in the late 1640s. A member of Winter's Independent group and a strong Cromwellian, he acquired substantial property and commercial interests in Ireland.

[402] Apparently a slip for 'reasonably'.

[403] Possibly the parliamentarian officer who, in January 1654, as a lieutenant-colonel, was appointed a commissioner for allocating land to the soldiers in County Kilkenny. The identification is unclear because there was an officer of that name who, by 1657, was serving as a major in Edward Doyley's foot regiment in the West Indies and so clearly cannot have been the author of this letter.

[404] A common place name in Ireland as in England.

348. From R. Preston, Athy, County Kildare, 23 November 1657, 822, fos 278–279.

May it please your excellency,

I have conferred with the soveraigne and others of this corporation touching this gentleman[405] and doe finde them soe sensible of your excellency's favour and care of them that they doe in all humility returne theire hearty thanks and they doubt not but (upon your excellency's recommendation) he is a person fitly quallified to discharg that great worke. But yet for the confirmation of theire judgments they humbly intreat that he may come hither againe to dispence his guifts for theire further satisfaction that they may with more maturity give their approbation to what they earnestly desire, which at present is all the account which can be given by, my lord, your excellency's most humble servant,

R Preston

349. From Martin Noell, London, 24 November 1657, 822, fos 280–281.

Letter of courtesy, praising Henry Cromwell and his record in Ireland, especially now that he had been raised to higher office in Ireland; and of request, reminding Henry Cromwell of the business that he had already put before him and about which both the Protector and Richard Cromwell had written letters of support; asks that captain Arthur and Mr Booth be admitted to confer with Henry Cromwell about his business.

350. From Robert Saunders, Youghal, 28 November 1657, 822, fos 282–283.

May it please your excellency,

Your excellency may remember that when I had the faviour of waytinge upon you att Dublin, I acquaynted your lordshipp that I had two letters from his Highness directed to your lordship and counsell for a lease of Ballindtor lands; butt I could not then present them because there was no counsell sittinge, only your lordshipp was pleased to promise to be my fren[...][406] in that behalfe.

[405]Possibly James Macc, who, in 1657, was listed as the salaried minister at Athy and Kilcullen, County Kildare.

[406]Paper slightly damaged with minor loss of text, though the incomplete word is apparently 'frend'.

And now, if your lordshipp stand not by me, I shall be putt outt of it by the lord of Broughall. I have bin a longe tyme designed agaynst by the cavalears of this county, and now theye have an opportunity to discover themselves, by prevaylinge with the lord of Broughall, to take from me the castell of Ballindtor with all the choyce lands thereto belonginge, notwithstanding I have had posession of it this seaven yeres. And this night the lord of Broughall tould me that he was resolvd uppon it, allthough his orders runs butt for two thousand plantation acars contigous to Ballamaloo,[407] which is as choyece a seate as Ballindtor; butt out of a designe to disposesse me, he takes butt halfe a plow land of Ballamaloo and coms with a narrow lane (it beinge three myles distance from Ballindtor) and takes in Ballindtor with all the choyce lands, the rest beinge butt of littell worth. This designe will not only be ruenous to me butt prejuditiall to the commonwelth, as also crosing his Highness' intended favour towards me, which your lordshipp will see to be very great att the perusall of the letters, it beinge granted me sence the parlament. I humbly intreate your lordshipp to owne my case herein, and if anythinge of this nature coms before your lordshipp and counsell, that your lordship would be pleased to stand my frend, for I have no other place in the country to remove my family and stock upon. The lord of Broughall tould me that he could take his proportion of land wherr it might be more adventagious for himselfe, only he pretened that it was not for his health, which is his only argument, which I humbly supposs will not be judged of wayt to com in competition with my undoeing.

I humbly conseave it may be prevented if your lordshipp please (in my behalfe) to request the lord Broughall to alter his course upon the formentioned grounds. I humbly intreat your lordshipp to excuse this, my great bouldness. I take leave to remayne,

Your excelency's faythfull, humble servant,

Ro Saunders

[407]Under legislation passed by the second Protectorate parliament in the summer of 1657, Broghill's precarious financial position was alleviated by a grant of £1,000-worth of forfeited land and an additional 2,000 acres in County Cork. This included the estate and house of Ballymaloe, a seventeenth-century mansion incorporating parts of a medieval castle, in south-east County Cork, roughly halfway between the town of Midleton and the coast at Ballycotton Bay.

351. From Thomas Belasyse, Viscount Fauconberg,[408] Whitehall, 30 November 1657, 822, fos 284–285.

My lord,

I am now humbly to entreate your pardon for not being more diligent in the tender of my service to your lordshipp, as well in respect of that immerited honor I was lately by his Highnesse's favour assumed to (in promoteing mee to the neerest degree of alliance with your lordshipp's famuly) as the reall vallue and esteeme I ever had for that personall merritt your lordshipp has so highly evidenced to all the world, boath which considerations thus happily united become a stricter tye upon me to employ what remaynes of my lyfe without the least reservation in your lordshipp's service, as becomes, my lord,

Your lordshipp's most reall, faithfull and obedient servant,

Fauconberg

352. From Mary Belasyse, Viscountess Fauconberg, Whitehall, 1 December 1657, 822, fos 286–287.

Dear brother,

I am in such a condision at present that I know not what to say for myself in that I have neglected making you aqueinted with my grat consern, which truly, dear brother, was not for want of that due sens I hav of your kindnes to me, but the love I hav her. In us you must neds excus, it being so sudenly concluded, as this busnes hath, has put me into so grat a confusion as that truly I could not tel how nor what to writ to any frend; and giv me lev to asur you, as you ar the person that I value abov any of my frinds, so also you ar the ferst that I hav writen to sens this afaer of min was known to me. You hav a great deal of resoon, I must confes, to think I ded not put that esetem upon you which I ought, if the sudenes of my maareg ded not spek for me, and therfor shal be selent, knowing you canot but pardon me, who I am sur hath as grat a respect for you as any of your relations; and gev me leav to tel you that my lord has as grat an estem also, and I wil asur

[408] Although from a royalist family – his grandfather, from whom he inherited the title in 1653, had fled to the continent after the battle of Marston Moor and converted to Catholicism – Fauconberg/Falconbridge convinced the Protector of his political and religious loyalty and won favour both before and after his marriage into the Cromwell family. He succeeded Lambert as commander of a horse regiment and, in the winter of 1657–1658, was nominated to and sat in the new second parliamentary chamber, one of the few members of the traditional nobility willing to do so. In 1658, he was also employed as ambassador extraordinary to France.

you, if ocation serv, you wil find him as mouh your frind and servant as I am, which you canot but be asurd is thus, which is frely yours, dear brother. As you hav a kindnes for me, let my consern for my lord beg also the sam for him, who I am asuurd if you knew – you ar a person of that understanding and worth – you nedd not my intretyes for it; and I hop Him which gives us an asurans of al things will let you se how much he merits the kindnes of al my relations, one in pertecular, yourself, who I can asur you he hath a pertecular kindnes for. I hop that God that hath by His provedens broat him and I into this near relation, and bles us and kep us in His own fear, that we shal not er but walk in the way He shal tech us. Dear brother, the grat thing that I hav to beg of you is your prayers for us, that God wil bles us and tech us our duty to ech other, so that we may live in lov and serv Him with our hart. I canot but hop God hath given me this as a blessing, in that He has ben peleased to despos of my hart so as that I have ben obedgent to my parents. In earnest, dear brother, he is a sober person, and on that desires after the best things, and God hath geven him a larg portion in the knowledg of them. The Lord mak him senseble of the improvement that his is to mak of so grat a talent, which I canot but hop that he wil. I shal beg your pardon for this troble, which I hav geven you, and belev that ther is non mor your afectionat sester and sarvant then,

M Foulconbridge

Dear brother, beg my pardon of my sester for not writing to her this post, and bee pleased to let her know that I intend next wek, if poseble I can, to gev her a pertecular account of this buisnes. I was maryed on Thursday next com fortneight, and truly, dear brother, to a person that hath a greater kindnes to me then ever I could and have expected. The Lord contenue it.

353. From William Lockhart, Paris, 1 December 1657, 822, fos 288–289.

Letter of recommendation on behalf of an unnamed brother,[409] *who had gone to Ireland to take up a grant made to him by the Protector.*

[409] Probably John Lockhart, parliamentarian politician, who sat for a Scottish seat in the second Protectorate parliament and who, upon the recommendation of the Protector to Henry Cromwell and the Irish council, was, in December 1657, admitted to the lease of a townhouse in Armagh and of nearly 2,500 acres of land in County Armagh (Dunlop, pp. 681–682).

354. From Robert Shapcote,[410] 1 December 1657, 822, fos 290–291.

May it please your excellency,

Beinge informed by Dr Gorges that you are pleased to have me in your thoughts as for my beinge in Ireland, and particularly as to the solicitor's place, soe I cannot but with all humble thankefallnesse accept of your favour and doe account it a very great happinesse that there is an opportunity given unto me wherby I may more really serve your excellency then hitherto I have bene capable off. Did not the meetinge of the parliament command my attendance here, beinge an unworthy member thereof, I should forthwith attend your commands, but this I hope will begge your excellency's excuse for some time, untill the end of the parliament; that beinge done, I shall make all possible speede to give my attendance and wayte your excellency's commands. In the meane I shall humbly take my leave, remayning,

Your excellency's most faythfull and very humble servant,

Rob Shapcote

355. From Edward Montague, Hinchingbrooke, [Huntingdon], 5 December 1657, 822, fos 292–293.

May it please your excellencye,

It hath beene my greate ambition to retaine that place in your esteeme, which your favor hath of longe tyme given mee the honor to hold, and havinge noe other matter (worth givinge you the trouble) but the presentinge my most humble dutye and service and constant assurance of my faithfull affection unto you, I have divers tymes begged the favor of my lord Broghill to doe it for mee, which I hope he hath performed. Att this tyme I find myselfe oblidged to give you the trouble thereoff by my owne pen, together with rendringe you my most humble thankes for your letter of the 18th of November, wherein I read such extraordinarye expressions of love towards mee that I dare not adventure by words to sett forth my recentments, but beseech you to expect more then cann be couched in them from my future actions (such as my poore, inconsiderable spheare may enable mee to offer unto you). None here would more heartily have rejoyced to have seene your person safe in England, nor could promise to themselves more particular advantage therebye; but the occasion of your stay beinge of greate publique concernement, and I hope of noe prejudice unto

[410] Parliamentarian politician, who sat for his native Tiverton from 1646 until his exclusion at Pride's Purge, and represented the town again in both of Oliver Cromwell's Protectorate parliaments. Although suspected of royalist sympathies, he became a firm supporter of the Protectorate, held local office in Devon, and, in 1657, was appointed solicitor-general for Ireland.

yourselfe (as my lord Broghill can better then I make out unto you), I can freelye denye myselfe therein, and am glad to find your lordshipp's resolution condiscendinge thereunto. Scince my cominge from sea,[411] I have obtained leave to see my sickly familye in the countrye, where I yett remaine, and therebye cann give your lordshipp little account of matters above, only I heare the list of the other house[412] is every day expected, but heare nothinge of the persons designed for it, but I make noe doubt your lordshipp will have a list of them as soone as this letter. Truly, the consequence of that affaire is very greate and what the constitution will proove I cannot imagine, unlesse my melancholy feares should make mee suspect the worst, because I doubt divers whom I could (and I beleeve your lordshipp also) wish were of it will not meddle, and noe doubt divers others will readily supply theire places. I heartily wish it otherwise. My opportunityes with his Highnesse are not manye, nor is my judgement fitt to advise him, but I have not spared to speake as occasion hath beene offered unto mee, and herein only I can boast that I have a hart true to the interest of the publique and his Highnesse' person and familye, nor shall cease to promote the same to my power. Your lordshipp will be pleased to excuse mee in this place for writinge of noe more matters; other, better hands will noe doubt plentifully supply you. And thus I here humble[413] take leave to subscribe, my lord,

Your excellencye's most humble, faithfull, affectionate, and obedient servant,

E Mountagu

The letter your lordshipp was pleased to command mee to convey, I have taken all care imaginable to have safely delivered, and I hope by my next to give your lordshipp an account of the receipt thereoff. If it be not too greate presumption, I begg the favor to have my most humble service presented to my lady.

356. From George Monck, Dalkeith, 15 December 1657, 822, fos 294–295.

May it please your excellencie,

I received your excellencie's lettre dated the 18th of November, and returne your excellencie most humble thankes for your kinde

[411] In October. He attended council meetings between 24 October and 17 November, but then was absent – this letter suggests he was with his family in the country – until reappearing in council on 14 January 1658.

[412] The new second parliamentary chamber, established under the revised constitution, whose founder members were being selected by the Protector.

[413] Apparently a slip for 'humbly'.

remembrance of mee, which I doe nott know how otherwise to expresse, butt shall bee alwayes ready in anythinge I may to serve your excellencie, wherin you shall nott finde mee to fayle uppon any occasion. Whensoever your excellencie hath any commands for mee, if you please butt to send your letter to colonel Cooper or to any one that commands in his absence, with a direction to send them to the governor of Ayre, they will soone come to my hands. Sir Arthur Forbes[414] was heere, butt hee seem'd to bee very much inclin'd to bee setled towards peace, and is now return'd againe into Ireland. I have very good caution for his peaceable living, and truly hee was very free in his expressions to mee that hee would live peaceablie, and soe I hope hee will. I looke uppon him as a man of honour, and I thinke hee will nott wronge his freinds that are bound for him, and breake his promises that hee hath made to mee. I returne your excellencie most hearty thankes for your respect to Dr Clarges. I have a great ambition to bee a planter under your excellencie if I could see his Highnesse a little better setled in his affaires, which, when I see done, I shall make bold to desire his leave to waite uppon your excellencie in Ireland; which is all att present from,

Your excellencie's most humble servant,

George Monck

357. From Charles Fleetwood, 22 December 1657, 822, fos 296–297.

Deare brother,

Since my last, we have considerd of the whole arreare which the 3 armyes are in, and it is found that you are lesse in arreare then what you wer in at the last parlament, and that now when you have received your assignations allready granted you will be about £70 or 80,000, which proportionably to the rest of the armyes are now wilbe lesse in ar[. . .]eare.[415] However, ther will <not> be any endevors <wanting heare> to answer your necessityes,[416] which I know are great; but you have lesse cause to complaine in that you are made equall with the

[414] Scottish royalist, who inherited from his father estates in Counties Leitrim and Longford and, in the wake of the 1641 rebellion, fought to protect them from the Irish Catholics. He campaigned for the king in Scotland under Montrose, was captured in 1645, and imprisoned for two years; after his release he continued to support the royalist cause in Scotland until captured by Monck in August 1654. Under the terms of his capitulation and release in 1655, he was allowed to return to his estates in Ireland.

[415] Paper slightly damaged with minor loss of text, though the incomplete word is apparently 'arreare'.

[416] Phrase originally read 'However, there will not be any endeavors wanting heare to answer your necessityes', but it has been amended thus, with 'not' clearly deleted and 'wanting heare' probably deleted.

rest. And if you showld not I think it would be very hard measure, and I hope my affection to your own person, as well as the desire I have to serve the publicke, will not suffer me to decline or neclect any thing which may be in my power to serve you or your affayres. If you did but know what a condition our forces wer in Scotland, as well as in England, you would see lesse reason of complaint. In Scotland they are forced to pay off thos they reduce with what moneys showld pay their standing forces, and to let it run in arreare upon the standing forces. We are preparing an account of the armye's and navye's arreares against the parliment's sitting, and therefor if you will please to have the full state of your arreare send up, ther shall be at least an equall care taken of you with the rest of the armyes; for be confydent of this, you shall not be in a worse condition then others. As for the reducment, the offence you tooke against me therin makes me I shall <not> very unwillingly meddle therin.[417] I have not seen the letter you writt to the counsell about it; I presume Mr Secretary hath it. The old enimy, the cavileire, is still at worke upon their former design, but the Lord is very gratious in the timous[418] discoveryes therof. His presance is our strength and will be still our preserver. Your care in Ireland will be answerable to what your danger may be, though I think the designe is at presant for England. We have continuall occation to see how litle probability ther is to gayn this sort of men, therfor the greater duty to be cautious of any thing which may give them the advantage lyes upon us. Which that we may be carefull to prevent is the desire of,

Your most affectionate brother and servant.

Charles Fleetwood

358. From Archibald Sproull, Raphoe, 24 December 1657, 822, fo. 298.

Letter of request, recounting how he had suffered in the service of England, as attested by certificates signed by Sir Bryce Coghran,[419] Sir Charles Coote, and

[417] Phrase originally read 'the offence you tooke against me therin I shall not very unwillingly meddle therin', but it has been amended thus, with 'makes mee' added and 'not' apparently deleted. The amended sentence appears garbled.

[418] Timeous: coming in due time; suitable or proper in respect of time.

[419] Bryce Cochrane, a Scottish officer, fought for the king in Ireland in the late 1640s but then came over to the parliamentarian cause, persuaded to do so by another royalist-turned-parliamentarian, George Monck, and admitted parliamentary forces into Carrickfergus in September 1648. However, he briefly flirted with royalism again, fighting for the future Charles II in Scotland in 1650. By 1657, he was in sufficiently good standing with the Protector to be given command of a foot regiment in Flanders and he probably campaigned there with his regiment until 1659.

Mr Harte,[420] *and had been promised by Henry Cromwell both land in Ireland for himself and £9 per year to fund his son's education; he is enormously grateful for this, but explains that he could not afford to support his son and that £9 was not enough to maintain his son, and thus requests an additional £12 per year to be paid out of tithe income appointed for charitable uses to help see his son through education; also requests from Henry Cromwell a clearer and firmer order to the commissioners for setting out land, directing them to allocate him land in Ireland.*

359. From Nathaniel Fiennes, Covent Garden, 28 December 1657, 822, fos 299–300.

My lord,

I have received severall letters from my brother, John Whithed, whereby I understand the greate favour your lordshipp is pleased to show unto him, which I must take in greate measure upon my accountt, saveing what doth flowe from your owne proper goodnes, which is verie comunicative to all that in any sort endeavour to render themselves worthy thereof. My lord, I have noe other buisines but what your lordshipp maketh me by the continuall obligations you are pleased to lay upon me and my relations, which we shall be most readdy to acknowledge upon all occasions that shall call us to account for the same. Wee have sent your lordshipp a writt of sommons to the other house of parliament, where though we shall want you much, yet we should want you more in Ireland;[421] and the benefitt which the commonwealth will receive by your service there will recompence the want that we shall have of your councell and company here, which would be most usefull and acceptable to all your friends, and very perticularly to, my lord,

Your lordshipp's most humble servant,

Nath Fiennes

360. From Philip Jones, December 1657, 823, fos 3–4.

May it please your excellency,

I had the honour this weeke to receive two of your lordshipp's,[422] the contents whereof I communicated according to your lordshipp's

[420] Identification uncertain, but perhaps the John Hart who was salaried Presbyterian minister at Taboyne, within the barony of Raphoe, County Donegal.

[421] Henry Cromwell did not, in fact, take his seat in the new second parliamentary chamber, either in the brief second session of the second Protectorate parliament in January–February 1658 or in the Protectorate parliament of his brother Richard in January–April 1659; instead, he remained in Ireland throughout the period.

[422] Almost certainly those at *TSP*, VI, pp. 651, 661–662.

commands.[423] I had hoped that the instruction sent your lordshipp and counsell impowering your retrenchmente of forces had taken off all expectation here of any such account upon the former order as you have bene pleased to mention. The referring to which instruction will on all such occations be the faithfull endeavours of your servants here. For your want of mony, I am sencible it must be very great, and must exceedingly add to your other great burthen, which hath bene doubtlesse greatly increased by the delayes of the settlement of that nation. I heartily wish I were in a better capacity to serve your lordshipp in that perticular; our wants here rendering mee lesse able then willing. But noe faithfullnes nor dilligence shall be wanting in mee to doe therein the best service I can.

I shall not wast your tyme with any account of our affaires here because Mr Secretary presents your lordshipp therewith weekely more fully then I can, which is the reason I have not the confidence to trouble your lordshipp oftner with impertinent letters. For when there is nothing left mee but the profession of my readines to serve you, I rather chuse to trust your noble charity for a beleife of that then to be soe injurious as to make such a thing the bussines of papers to interrupt your more weighty affaires, and begg your lordshipp's pardon that I have troubled you with soe many words as here I have donne to assure yow of a thing of soe litle vallue as my service. But as it is none shall be more sincere in it then, my good lord,

Your excellency's most humble and most faithfull servant.

[423] To his fellow-councillors Montague and Wolseley.

1658

361. From Charles Fleetwood, 4 January [1658], 823, fos 9–10.

Deare brother,

We have received your counsell's letter, and the counsell heare are very sensible of your condition and will not want desires and endevors to get you monyes. The assignments allready orderd you will, I presume, not make your arreare so great as a 100,000. We shall compare your account sent to collonel Jones with what the treasurers heare comput it at, and if you are not equally concerned and provided for with any of the other forces we shall soone remidy that difficulty, though the complaints from Scotland and the army in England are much to the same purpose, and really our case is so sadde that which way we shall be able to turn ourselves from the difficultyes we are under I know not; but I shall no more at presant trouble you and shall by the next have an exact account, and in the meane time we shall charge the 20,000 formerly assigned out of delinquents' lands upon the new buildings.[1] Our fleet and armyes are in a sadde condition. This army never hade such an occation to be tempted as they have now, yet are, and I trust will be, in a very stauch[2] and quiet condition. The Lord direct and manage the hearts of the parliment to such a consideration of the case of this nation that the issue may be for further settlement of thes poore nations, upon true and lasting foundations in preserving the libertyes of the people of God, and the civill libertyes allso, both of which we ought to have a due regard unto, though the 1st to have the preference. I think ther is much in the present goverment which conserves both, which that it may be most upon our hearts is the desire of,

Your most affectionate brother and most humble servant,

Charles Fleetwood

[1] By an act of parliament of June 1657, a one-off tax or fine equivalent to one year's rent was to be imposed on most new houses erected in the suburbs of London since 1620, payable in two instalments in autumn 1657 and spring 1658, with additional fines levied on new buildings erected there after September 1657. Although exceptions and exemptions were allowed, leading to petitioning, appeals, and disputes, by the autumn of 1658, a little over £40,000 had been raised by this means.

[2] Apparently a variant of, or a slip for, 'staunch': stout, firm, hearty, constant.

362. From Ralph King, 6 January 1658, 823, fos 11–12.

Letter of request, seeking an advance of a quarter's salary due to him as a commissioner for setting out lands, to help defray his charges into England,[3] citing the payment to major Symner[4] as a precedent.

363. From George Walters,[5] Waterford, 8 January 1658, 823, fos 13–14.

Letter of request, reporting that he and his afflicted, unsettled family had come to Ireland to take possession of the lands assigned him in Bantry and also the back rents due upon them, but he found that he had been allowed only six months' back rent, whereas the usual practice was to allow soldiers to collect rents due upon their allotted land from the time of the original allotment in or since 1655; therefore requests that those terms might be extended to him.

364. From William Jephson, Lubeck, 22 February 1658, 823, fos 17–18.

My most honoured lord,

It would bee an injurye to your candid nature, if I should indeavour to make fresh expressions to your excelence of the realitye of my affections to your service, since you have beene pleas'd soe often both by words and other actions to testifye your satisfaction in that particular. I shall therefore only give your excelence a short touch how affayres stand here. I am now thus farre in my way from Wismar (where I have spent most part of this winter) towards Denmarke upon a summons from the king of Suede to come into Funen Island to bee present at a treaty,[6] which hee hath consented unto with the king of Denmarke under his Highnesse's mediation, which the Dane had still refus'd untill the king of Suede was master of above 3 parts of his kingdome. Since I receyv'd the king's summons heare, hee hath taken in the islands of Langland, Laland and Faunsten, which last is within four English miles of Zealand, wherein the king of Denmark's chiefe citty (Copenhaguen) is scituate, not strongly fortifyed. Thither the king

[3] As MP for Londonderry and Coleraine, he sat in the second Protectorate parliament, which was due to reconvene in January 1658.

[4] Miles Symner, parliamentarian officer, major in Daniel Abbott's dragoon regiment in Ireland and one of a small group of officers appointed in 1656 to oversee the process of allocating officers and soldiers land in Ireland in lieu of their arrears. In 1658, he was also one of a small group of officers and civilians appointed to enquire into complaints from the adventurers.

[5] In October 1656, Walters had been allocated land in Connaught in lieu of more than £4,000 owed to him for his outlay in support of military operations in 1650 (*CSPI*, p. 832).

[6] The treaty of Roeskilde between Sweden and Denmark was signed on 27 February. As an agent of the Protector, Philip Meadows had played an important role in persuading Sweden to moderate her demands.

of Suede resolv'd to march over the yce the tenth of this month; and since I began my letter, one of the king's counsell was with mee, and assur'd mee hee had receyv'd a letter from the king's owne hand dated at Warburgh in Zealand, soe that the treaty is now like to bee de regno restituendo.[7] The successes of this king have beene prodigious this last two yeares. In the first hee made himselfe master of Poland, and being recal'd from thence by the king of Denmark's making warr upon him, hee hath still reserv'd Prussia, and this winter reduc't Denmark to his mercye. That which to mee seemes very remarkeable is, that the same extreamity of cold (which they say hath beene greater here this winter than hath beene knowne in the memorye of man) hath both furnisht him with bridges of ice to march over the sea with his army into all these islands, and hath likewise by the abundance of snow hindred his enemies in Poland and Muscovye from doeing him any considerable prejudice in his territories adjoining to them. I am making all the hast I can to the king of Suede, as conceiving his Highnesse not a little concern'd in these affaires, especially in the interest of the Sound and the trafique of the Baltique Sea. When this businesse is over, I hope I may have the liberty to returne home and come and kisse your excelencie's hands, and indeavour to expresse in all my actions with how much zeale and affection I am, my lord,

Your excelencie's most intyrely devoted, humble servant,

Wm Jephson

365. From Mary Belasyse, Viscountess Fauconberg, 9 March [1658], 822, fos 13–14.

Dear brother,

Having so good an opertunyty, I could not but expres the grat satisfaction I had in reseving yours, which you may imagen was an unexpreseble joy to me, although ther was somthing in it which mad me reflect upon myselfe. And when I had considred of my foolishnes in that you took notis of my taking il your not writing, and som other letel impertenat things I said in my last to my sester, I was extreamly consernd that I should giv you caus to expect that which was befor asurd of, and yet pleased that so dear a brother as yourself should tak the troble of satisfying me. I can say no mor but this, it being so layte, but that I am, dear brother,

Your ever afectionate sester and servant,

M Fauconberg

[7] This Latin phrase could be translated as 'about the restoration of the kingdom'.

366. From Richard Cromwell, Whitehall, 10 March 1658, 823, fos 21–22.

Deare brother,

I had hopes to have collected such matter as might have suited your cyphers, but I am yet constrained to waite, being as to materiall matter more in the darke then others, and by what I can guesse from countenances there are not any much in the light. Perhaps you may meete with a penn that may present you in trught, myne cannot. I can speake the feares of some, and the hopes of others, and should my penn saile betwixt boeth it might be as much mistaken and as ill guided as the phantassyes and apprehentions of those tow contraryes. We are promised that it will be shortely that somethinge will breake forth, and if I can but catche the shell cracked, bee assured I will make a discovery; the firste if possible to acquainte youe. For forreigne newes, you will understand it to be very considerable, and may prove advantadgious to England and its present ill condition. We live by providence; a very greate one it is if the successe of Sweedland upon Denmarke should briddle the angry Dutche, whoe hath too much connived at the assistants there merchants (much to our prejudice) hath made them against our affaires. I question not but you have been acquainted of our men of warre before Oste End meeting with 3 ships of bulke going in to help Charles Stewart, and though he is said to have 9,000 foote, and 500 horse, one and twenty ships hyred of the Dutche marchants, yet I hope they will be mett with by our fleete whoe are stricktly upon the watche. Your intirenesse in your army hath not produced any effect by example (though necessary) upon the English army as yet; we goe on slowely, and sometimes we can hardly see any motion. I hope God is oure pilote. That He may be your guide and helper is the earnest prayers of, deare brother,

Your most affectionate brother and servant,

R Cromwell

Doe me the favoure to present my respects and service to my deare sister. Excuse the hasty scrible of your brother.

367. From John Duckinfield, Carrickfergus, 15 March 1658, 823, fos 23–24.

May it please your excellency,

On Friday morneing arrived heere the Basing friggatt with the armes and amunition laid in her for this place, which was the same day received into the store. This morneing shee sett saile for Derry. I have heere enclosed sent your excellency artickles of a verry high nature, against ensigne Richard Baker, ensigne to my owne company. The[8] are crimes that I did but lately heere of, otherwise your excelency might have heard of them before this. The witness to prove this chardg are some of them att Mullengarr[9] and some heere. He is a person I could willingly have spared before now, and hope the court martiall will ease me of him, being a great prejudice to me and my company besides the charge against him. I humbly crave your excellency's favour (in case the ensigne should be casheered) on the behalfe of on William Parry, serjeant of my company, who is now a greatt propp and stay to my company and a person every way capable of the employment, that your excellency would honor me with the grant of a commission for ensigne for the said Parry, who is not a person given to any faction or other evill carridges which might render him uncapable of your excellency's favour towards him. He is a person of good quality and was necessitated to accept of his present employment till he could gett a better. I shall leave it to your excellency's consideration and remaine,

Your excellency's most humble and faithfull servantt,

John Duckenfeild

368. From Richard Hodges, Londonderry, 19 March 1658, 823, fos 25–26.

Letter of information, relating how, since sailing from Dublin bay, he had delivered munitions to Carrickfergus, sailing from there on 15 June, but then encountering bad weather; plans to wait upon Henry Cromwell shortly.

369. From Robert Stone, London, 19 March 1658, 823, fos 27–28.

Letter of request, asking to be allocated some Irish land still held by the state in return for £1,000, so that he could serve Henry Cromwell in Ireland, even though he now had employment in Holland; asks that any response be conveyed to him via his friend the judge-advocate.[10]

[8] Apparently a slip for 'they'.
[9] Mullingar, County Westmeath.
[10] Either Philip Carterett or Henry Whalley.

370. From James Standish,[11] London, 30 March 1658, 823, fos 31–32.

May it please your excellency,

After the presentinge of youre humble duety to his Highnesse and his earnest and very afectionat enquiry of youre lordship's, ladye's and children's welfare, I comunicated the grounds of my aplication pursuant to youre excellencye's comands,[12] and found a very favourable recentment, his Highnesse expressinge his concernement therin and that he would doe what in him lay for the efectinge therof.

And in order therunto, the businesse is referred to a committee of councill, and the treasurers at warre with myselfe ordered to draw up a state of the particuler for their view, which by reason of captain Blackwell's beinge out of towne yesterday and today will not be perfected untile tomorrow.

My lord Fleetwood, whome I have found very friendly and cordiale hearin, moved for this order, and at the same tyme alsoe that the £17,000 paid into the exchequer heer as advance by the farmers of the excise and customs of Ireland, or soe much therof as was undisposed, might be paid into the handes of the treasurers at warre, and what was disposed therof might be alsoe refunded and made good out of other cash for the Irish service, which was accordingly granted and an order framed to that purpose.

I finde alsoe by discourse with the treasurers at warre, a probability of a considerable summe in their handes, or that will shortly be, as remayninge of what hath binne assigned for us in England to the 25th instant, amounting to about £28 or 30,000. The certaynty as to the summe and when it may be ready I shall shortly know, unto which if his Highnesse and councile may be prevailed with to advance oure ould debt, but new demande of the £22,500 longe since charged for Ireland on Gould Smith's Hale,[13] youre excellency will not be farre

[11] Parliamentarian administrator, who served as deputy treasurer for the English army in Ireland in the early 1650s, as receiver general for the revenue of Ireland from 1654, and as deputy treasurer at war by 1658. In the process he acquired land and property in Ireland, especially in County Kildare.

[12] He had been sent by Henry Cromwell and the Irish council to explain the recently submitted Irish accounts and to plead for more money for Ireland, by stressing the dire financial situation in which the Irish government found itself, and the urgent need for £96,000 to pay off existing military arrears (*TSP*, VI, pp. 819–820, 862, 871–872; VII, pp. 21, 38, 55–56, 84–85, 176). He carried detailed instructions, dated 12 March, outlining the arguments and figures to be presented to the Protector (Dunlop, pp. 676–678). Throughout the opening months of 1658, the growing debts in Ireland and urgent requests for stronger financial support from England dominated Henry Cromwell's letters to Thurloe and others in London, though the Secretary offered little comfort, stressing that the London government was itself in a dire financial position.

[13] The London base of several parliamentarian financial committees, especially the committee for compounding.

off youre desires. Howbeit, there's nothinge shall be lost for want of askinge of all that you have given mee in command to doe.

I have had severall oportunityes with Mr Secretary, who hath binne very inquisitive in this particuler, and hath seemingly received with very much sattisfaction what I have informed him thearin, and hath assured mee of the utmost of his endeavoures to accomplish your lordship's desires with a spedy dispatch thearof.

My lord, theise are the buddes that have only as yett apeared. How they may blossom and come to perfection or be nipt, I know not, nor can I be assured. The lott is cast into the lap, but the disposure therof is from the Lord, to whose good protection and guidance I humbly committ your lordship. And prayinge for your lordship's welfare, remayne, my lord,

Your excellencye's most humble and faithfull servant,

James Standish

371. From Martin Noell, Old Jury, 9 April 1658, 823, fos 33–34.

My lord,

Having now transplanted much of my interest and affaires and relations into Ireland, I am bold to importune your excellencie's favour unto them, as often as I have any occasion to make addresses to your excellencie in their behalfe. The gentleman who presents this is my kinsman, sonn in law to colonell Grasevner,[14] who is somewhat upon my encouragement become concern'd in the farme and management of your customs and excize and hath now remov'd himself into Ireland principally to attend those affaires (as the treasurer thereunto) and some things which, as an ingenious and industrious person, hee hath an eie upon, being himself as well as I and a thousand more, ledd with greater hopes that waie, out of the exceeding satisfaction and expectation which your excellencie gives by your generous conduct and the prudence of your councells. The consideration of which makes him alsoe most desirous of being knowne to your excellencie that hee may have a reverence and obligation to your person as well as to your authoritie and may receive an influence from both, as it may favour him or his affaires. Which is heere my humble suite to your excellencie because in it I alsoe shall bee concernd and your good graces upon him will att the same time reflect upon, my lord,

Your excellencie's most humble and most faithfull servant,

Martin Noell

[14] Possibly Edward Grosvenor, parliamentarian officer, who commanded a horse regiment in Scotland in the early 1650s.

372. From Thomas Goodwin, London, 10 April 1658, 823, fos 35–36.

Letter of thanks for Henry Cromwell's favour in allocating him some lands in Ireland, in line with a ninety-nine-year lease granted to him by the Protector, as well as for his favour to Mr Molyne's son, whom he had recommended to Dr Harrison; would have offered thanks more promptly, but had only just heard the news from alderman Vincent[15] *of Irish Town.*

373. From John Hoddor,[16] Cork, 12 April 1658, 823, fos 37–38.

May it please your excellency,

The justices of the peace and other gentlemen of this county, intending at their quarter sessions next weeke to consider of addresses to bee made to his Highnes from this county, in relation to his happy government, were prevented by the paper herewith sent your lordshipp. And although the same was at first promoted and subscribed by private persons, yet since it carried in it the sence of the whole county, in other words then were intended, wee were soe farre from discountenanceing of it that it was thought fitt that the same should bee tendered throughout the county. I thought it my duty (in respect of my office) to informe your lordshipp of the progresse therein, and that it was subscribed with much alacrity, and that the inhabitants of the county have entrusted this gentleman, captain Betrige, to present the same, in regard of his zeale and diligence in the carrying it on at the first. I shall adde noe more but my prayers to Almighty God for your lordshipp's happines here and hereafter, being, my lord,

Your lordship's most humble servant,

John Hoddor

[15] Thomas Vincent, London merchant and alderman, a substantial adventurer who acquired lands in County Meath and Queen's County and who moved to Ireland in the mid-1650s.

[16] Military officer and local politician in Ireland, he supported and served as a victualling commissioner for the Protestant army in Munster during the early 1640s and also supported the Cromwellian campaign of 1649–1650. By 1652 he held the rank of major and was governor of Wexford. He was mayor of Cork by 1656 and it is in that capacity that he wrote this letter to Henry Cromwell.

374. From Richard Cromwell, Whitehall, 16 April 1658, 823, fos 39–40.

Deare brother,

Major Hazard[17] having offered to his Highnesse and the counsell a businesse of concernment to Ireland and the same being referred to your consideration and of such persons as you shall appoint, to have your opinion therupon. Although I make no question but that you will have a due reguard of his Highnesse's and the counsell's letter in that behalfe, as also continue the honnour of your former favours to the persone intrusted therewith, yett I shall, att his desire, recommend him and his said businesse to your favorable assistance; and your good offices done to him shall be owned by, deare brother,

Yours affectionatly,

R Cromwell

375. From James Standish to Robert Gorges, London, 17 April 1658, 823, fos 41–42.

Honnourd sir,

I perceive by yours his excellency hath received intimation from hence of a supposed stocke of cash that should be in the treasury, soe considerable as worth the sendinge downe in specie to be transported, which is a mistaken thinge, there beinge nothinge but what hath arisen and must out of our proportion of the assessments here to the 24th of March last. And you may see by the paper drawne up by the treasurers and myselfe, the coppy wherof was sent his lordship by the last post, how the account stood the 19 of February, what was then in cash here, what in arrear, vizt:

In cash	06,189	19	7
In arrear of the assessments to the 25th of December	14,184	09	8
In arrear to the 25th of March	24,000	00	0
	44,374	09	3
Out of which must be deducted to pay up the forces here to the 25th of March last	07,651	01	0
And that leaves	36,723	08	3

[17] Henry Hazard had presented to the Protectoral council various proposals concerning pilotage, lighthouses, and buoys around the Irish coast to improve navigation, which were referred by the council to Henry Cromwell and the Irish council on 14 April. In mid-June the Irish council replied to the Protectoral council, broadly supporting the proposals and recommending the erection of three lighthouses on the Irish coast and a fourth on the Isle of Man, though nothing, in fact, seems to have been done at this time (Dunlop, pp. 682–684).

And out of that all bills of exchange charged since the said 19th day of February, which as I guess is an amount unto the £16,000 and odde money. The certaynty you may quickly know from John Reeve, my clerke. And then there will remayne but £20,000, of which I am assured there is not 5, nay not 4,000, in the treasury at present, soe that bills of exchange will draw it as fast as it come in.

I did by my last desier Mr Short to stopp his hand in drawing of bills, but for the reasons before mentioned and what I have otherways comunicated to his lordship but now doe desier you to direct him to retourne to his usuale cause and pray lett him see this clause for his sattisfaction because I cannot write to him at present.

Your brother hath sent mee a coppy of a letter from his lordship about procuringe him advance for his ministry. He demands three hundred pounds. The letter expresseth noe summe. Lett me have a word concerninge this by the next. In the meanetyme, I have retourned him a civil answer and promised complyance soe farr as I can. And soe rests,

Your very humble servant,
James Standish

376. From George Griffiths,[18] Charterhouse, 3 May 1658, 823, fos 43–44.

Letter of courtesy and religious exhortation, praising Henry Cromwell's government of Ireland and the encouragement it had given to the sober and godly in Ireland and England, reporting that he frequently prayed for him and noting that he had been encouraged to write thus by Dr Harrison; also seeking an unspecified favour for his poor brother in Dublin.

377. From Hierome Sankey, Wallingford House, 3 May 1658, 823, fos 45–46.

May it please your excellencie,

I having the charge of sending away the inclosed to Ireland thought it my duty to present the inclosed to your excellencie, and to acquaint you that in the packquett I have sent another to Sir Charles Coot, collonel Lawrance and the officers att Dublin, which as I thought it a duty on the one hand to performe, so likewise on the other to acqueint your excellencie therewith accordingly as ingaged upon all obligations of love and duty. My lord, I may say without feignednes,

[18] Independent minister at Charterhouse, London, 1648–1661, who also served on various religious commissions during the Protectorate.

that there is not any person that lives who hath more cordiall affection and reall respect to your excellencie and his Highnes' family then I have, and will be more ready in much to evidence it in the most reall and justifiable demonstration thereof. Any my prayers morning and evening shall not be wanting for you, especially att this season when a so great a tryall,[19] especially upon a misunderstanding of these affaires and transactions here, may perplex the spirit. I shall adde no more but that I am,

Your excellencie's faythfull servant,

Hie Sankey

378. From John and Elizabeth Gauden,[20] London, 24 May 1658, 823, fos 47–48.

My lord,

The renowne of your lordship's goverment with such piety, justice and clemency as gives life and recovery to that state of Ireland, which was lately languishing and dying, this (just honor) hath made many your lordship's admirers, who (yet) are humbly observant of that distance wherein they stand to your lordship's eminent place and authority, noe lesse than your virtues. In this number I may owne myselfe and my wife, whose great content it is to heare of that happines which your lordship and your lady enjoy; and to find by that gentleman who lately came from your lordship, that wee alsoe are soe happy as to reteine some place in your memorys and favours, of which he gave us soe particuler assurance that wee have taken this confidence to expresse our thankfull sense of that honor your lordship and your lady are pleased to doe us, when you voutsafe to think a kind thought of us, as persons condemned to obscurity, never to bee releived, except by such a barren way of industry as is somtimes given mee by such sad occasions as that of my nephew William Russel's[21] and Mr Robert

[19] Perhaps his concern over the finances of Ireland or perhaps health worries, since both Henry Cromwell and his wife were ill during the spring (*TSP*, VII, p. 114).

[20] John Gauden, minister with close connections to both the Russell and Rich families. In the early 1630s, he taught Francis and William Russell at Wadham College, Oxford, and around 1640 he married their widowed sister, Elizabeth, becoming for a time vicar of Chippenham. In the late 1630s, he was household chaplain to Robert Rich, Earl of Warwick, and he remained close to the family, patronized by them and dedicating some of his published works to them. A moderate Episcopalian with Presbyterian sympathies, he supported or at least acquiesced with the parliamentarian cause but also retained links to royalist families, and his published works of the period reveal marked reservations about parliamentary religious policies.

[21] This is probably William Russell, eldest son and heir of Sir Francis Russell, whose death probably occurred sometime during the opening months of 1658 but is not mentioned in any of Sir Francis's own letters in this collection.

Rich's death.[22] To the urne of this last, I have beene invited by your lordship's sister, the lady Frances, to consecrate a litle monument; which possibly may (as marble) bee durable, though it bee fruitlesse, unlesse it bee productive of your lordship's favour and acceptance beyond that degree which it expects in England. The fate of books is like that of many trees, to bring forth nothing but leaves, being not read by many and veiwed by few, especially yf they strike upon just severitys, becoming all good, patiant and wise, to lay to heart. Noe discouragements in England have hindred mee from presenting my sense of others' death and my owne mortality to your lordship's view. The rather because I have heared that your lordship hath beene a noble assertor of Mr Riche's honor, even in Ireland, the vindication of which I willingly undertook against a great streame of vulgar credulity, being satisfied in this that I did the part of justice and gratitude to the dead. My ambition must bee to performe such actions as are their owne reward, among which, I hope, this is one. A copy of all I adventure upon your lordship's and your lady's acceptance, who in your highest secular advancements carry soe moderate a temper of minds and actions, as willingly reflects upon the end of all these momentary dreames. It is some recompense to my paines that I have hereby an oportunity to expresse to your lordship and your excellent lady how much wee are ambitious to live worthy of that favour your noblenesses were pleased to expresse to,

Your lordship's very humble servants,

Jo El Gauden

379. From Robert Beake,[23] London, 1 June 1658, 823, fos 184–185.

May it please your excellency,

I lately appeared before your excellency in the posture of a mendicant; the success of that address could not make me more yours then before, but your excellency has lay'd an obligation uppon a praying familey thereby, which I beleive will turne to your account. God make youe daylie more acceptable to His people. Now, my lord, I understand it to be your command that I should present myselfe

[22] Robert Rich, husband of the Protector's daughter Frances, died on 16 February and was buried at Felsted, Essex, on 4 March 1658, with Gauden delivering the funeral sermon, which he subsequently published as *Funerals Made Cordials*.

[23] Parliamentarian politician and officer, he fought throughout the civil war, campaigning in and around his native Warwickshire. By 1650, he held the rank of major and was serving as governor of Coventry and sheriff of Warwickshire. A keen opponent of sinful activities, he was very active in local and national politics during the 1650s, serving as councillor and mayor of Coventry, sitting on various Warwickshire commissions, and representing Coventry in all three Protectorate parliaments.

before you; my offering is the tideings of this day, which amounts to what follows. The courte of safety being sate,[24] there first appeared Dr Huet,[25] whose charge being read he was bidd to plead to it, but refused, yett entred into a confused speech declaring his resolutions to suffer rather then betray the rights of an Englishman, and therefore somwhat magisterially demanded oyer of the commission by which the courte sate. That being denyed, he pleaded to the jurisdiction of the courte; being over-ruled therin, he prayed counsell might be assigned him; then insisted uppon his tryall per pares;[26] after craved a coppy of the inditement; all these being denyed him, then he appealed to all the judges of the lawe (none being there present); but in conclusion the courte recorded his refusal to pleade, and remanded him from the barr. It's likely at his next appearance the courte will putt him to pleade againe, and if I mistake not, he will imbrace the opportunity. The confidence of this man was somwhat noteable and that litle sence he spake was to begett himselfe a name among his tribe, many of whom were spectators; and, setting asyde his adamant like diportement unbecomeing the gravity of a divine, there appeared nothing remarkable in him or from him.

Next comes upp Mr Mordant,[27] a gentleman debonaire enough in his carriage, and one whose case begott more pitty and compassion

[24] The special court, comprising more than 140 commissioners (though only around 50 sat), set up in accordance with an act passed by the second Protectorate parliament, which met between late May and early July to try those implicated in the recent royalist conspiracy. Hatched during the winter of 1657–1658 and drawing upon both royalists and disgruntled Presbyterians, it entailed Charles II and a royalist fleet landing at Yarmouth to draw away the army and then royalist risings in London, Kent, Surrey, and Sussex. However, divisions and poor planning, the efficient intelligence system run by Thurloe, and resolute action by the parliamentary fleet caused the plans to unravel and most of the leading conspirators were arrested during March and April. The final fling, a botched rising in London in mid-May, was also thwarted and a further clutch of conspirators were arrested.

[25] John Hewitt/Huet, clergyman and royalist conspirator, served as chaplain to various royalist families during the 1640s and, from the late 1640s, became minister and rector of two London churches, where his popular sermons attracted many royalists. His royalist activities and involvement in the conspiracy were well known to the Protectoral government and he was arrested on 8 April. His repeated refusals to plead and his challenges to the authority of the court availed him little, for he was found guilty, condemned, and beheaded on 8 June.

[26] This Latin phrase could be translated as 'by his peers'.

[27] John Mordaunt, royalist conspirator, had encouraged the royalist risings of 1648 and, after several years on the continent, returned to England around 1652 and was on the fringes of royalist conspiracy thereafter. In 1657 he pledged to provide 400–500 horse and help raise Surrey for the Stuart cause, and, early in 1658, he conferred with Ormond when the latter visited England to assess the viability of the plans. He was arrested on 1 April and initially released, but was rearrested in mid-April. At his trial on 1–2 June, he pleaded not guilty, spoke well in his defence, and was eventually acquitted on the casting vote of John Lisle, who presided over the court.

then the confidence of the other did gaine him applause, yett he also manifested noe squemish or dreading spirit. Soe haveing used the same play as Huett before him had donn (noe doubt they compared notes together), at last craveing the favours of the courte for direction in case of mistakes, he pleaded to issue. Butt before I come to the summ of his evidence, give me leave to observe to your excellency this passage, vizt, he praying the court to press his Highnes' counsell that they woud aleadge some presydents for tryalls of men of his quality without a jury, the sollicitor[28] presently replyed that the case of the queene of Scotts in 37th of the queene was home to the purpose. To which Mordant rejoined that there was noe parity in the case, for first the queene of Scotts was not under the protection of the lawes of England, and soe could not clayme Magna Charta, which was calculated for English men; 2nd shee was a queene and had not pares to be tried by; 3rd shee was an alien and a Scott and a tryal per indictatem lingue[29] was competent to such, and yet if admitted at that tyme would not effect the end proposed in the tryall. These observations of his, however they wanted there weight, yet wanted they not acceptation with the people as haveing a couller in them to discriminate her case from his.

The evidence amounted to this much, that he had animated Mr Stapleys[30] to declare for Charles Stewart's cause; that he had received lettres from him declaring his resolution to land in England; that he had dispensed 4 commissions which he received from him; that he had declared that in case the force of Sussex was in distress he would assist them with the force of Surrey. This was wrappt upp in the testimony of the two Stapeleys and the examination of one captain Mallory[31]

[28] William Ellis, parliamentarian politician and judge, sat in the Short and Long Parliaments and was a moderate parliamentarian, removed at Pride's Purge and playing no part in the regicide, but retaking his seat in the Rump later in 1649. He supported the Protectorate, sat in all three Protectorate parliaments, and was created solictor-general in 1654, in which capacity he played a prominent role in several of the state trials during the Protectorate, serving as chief prosecutor of the leading royalist conspirators in 1658.

[29] This Latin phrase could be translated as 'in which she refused to speak' or 'to defend herself'.

[30] Brothers John and Anthony Stapley. John, royalist conspirator and politician, and son of Anthony Stapley, parliamentarian officer and politician and a regicide who had died in 1655, represented his native Sussex in both of Oliver Cromwell's Protectorate parliaments. He was drawn into the royalist conspiracy, perhaps by promises of titles and honours, perhaps to expiate his father's guilt; he, in turn, drew his brother Anthony into plans to raise Sussex in the Stuart cause. He was arrested at the end of March and made a full confession to the Protector, implicating several of his co-conspirators and giving confused evidence against Mordaunt.

[31] Henry Mallory, royalist conspirator, engaged by John Stapley to assist him in Sussex. Arrested in April, he escaped at the end of May, shortly before he was due to give evidence

taken by Mr Scobell, which Mallory made his escape out of prisson. This was all the worke of the day.

By lettres received this day from captain Stokes[32] in the Levant seas, he adviseth that he has taken a Dunkerke man-of-warr of 26 gunns and 200 men; also from the Preston frigott, arived from the Southarne Cape at Plymouth, that shee and the Fagons had taken 3 shipps, 400 tunns apeece, laden with oyle and salte bound from Cales to Gallicia, and that about the Northerne Cape they had taken the Exchange of St Sebastian, commanded by the famous Beche,[33] the Irish pirate under James Stewart's commission, and with him in consortshipp 3 Irish captains more, all wich administer some content to us in the midst of our losses.

By lettres from Dunkirke this day wee understand that the enimy sallied out, horse and foote, on Thursday last and beate the French foote out of there trenches with some slaughter, but the English and Switz reinserted there stations and drive the enimy back with a wittnes, pursueing them soe closely that they mastered two smale workes pallisaded, and gayned the advantage of an approach within pistoll shott, at which distance they worke in a rowling trench and are not farr from the counterscarpe. The enimy is smarte and much animated; the French horse are likewise very dareing, but they now and then dropp for it. I cannot heare where the Spanish army is, nor indeed is there any talke as if it had a being. The last weeke we shippd over 500 of colonel Salmon's[34] regyment, and this day are in preparation for 500

against Mordaunt, though he was recaptured a few days later. He was tried on 10 June and sentenced to death on 15 June, but he was reprieved and remained a prisoner for the rest of the Protectorate.

[32] John Stokes, parliamentarian naval officer, campaigned around western England and the Irish Sea in the early 1650s, in the Anglo-Dutch War of 1652–1654, and then in expeditions to the Mediterranean in 1654–1655 and against Spain in 1656–1657. After the departure of the ailing Blake, he took command of a squadron of ships that campaigned widely in and around the Mediterranean in 1657–1658.

[33] Sir Richard Beach, royalist naval officer, proved a thorn in parliament's side. With a squadron of royalist vessels, he attacked and plundered English parliamentarian and merchant shipping in the early 1650s, though a determined parliamentary attack off the Scilly Isles in the spring of 1654 led to the capture or destruction of most of his squadron and his own imprisonment. However, he was exchanged soon after and, free again, he resumed his privateering activities and continued to harass English shipping for the remainder of the 1650s.

[34] Edward Salmon, parliamentarian officer, was lieutenant-colonel of Hardress Waller's New Model foot regiment from the mid-1640s, leaving the regiment in 1649 to become first deputy governor of Hull and then, in 1653, commander of a foot regiment of his own, succeeding the late Richard Dean. The regiment may have served in Scotland for a time in the 1650s, though Salmon himself seems to have remained in England as an admiralty commissioner. In the summer of 1658 he led much of his regiment to Flanders to assist in the siege of Dunkirk.

more. The want is onely infantry, the cavalry being numerous enough, and both (as I am crediby informed) makeing upp 3,200 effective.

The French courte is att Callais, and my lord Falconbridge[35] is safely arrived there though he had a most sadd passage by reason of the strong southerly winds we have had for some tyme.

D'Ruittar, the Dutch admiral, is out and was on Fryday with 22 men-of-warr and 3 victuallers in the Downes. His pretence is that he had by stormes spent some of his masts and wanted provission, and therefore prayed supply, his designe being for Portugall. But whether he had a good or a badd meaneing, his motion tis eyed, and yt – that is in our view – is his assayleing our shipps at Dunkirke to disturbe that seige. But to prevent that wee have ordered the conjunction of another squadron now out with general Mountague with that before Ostend, and then lett them doe there worse. My lord, I have bin too tedious. I wil not err soe heerafter, if your excellency will pardon this faulte and give me liberty to style myselfe,

Your excellency's most devoted servant,

Rob Beake

380. From Richard Cromwell, Whitehall, 2 June 1658, 823, fos 49–50.

Deare brother,

You set soe over a vallew upon common respects, that indeed I know not how to appeare in any thing. I would not that you should take notice of the gelding other then to waire him oute. I am certaine you have ingadged me by yore expressions to send my wishes after him, that he may delight you in youre sportes. Good horses, especially geldings, are very scarce, the Frenche hath dreined us; but I hope you will be in a shorte time able to furnish Ingland oute of Ireland. If not, be confident I shall lay oute untell you be in such a capacity for such an instrument for your pleassure. This letter was intended for my lord Fitzwilliams, whoe indeed appears to be a most civell person and I am perswaded is a person of honour, most ready to acknowledge the civilityes and obligations which he hath received from his Highnesse and youreselfe. His lordship is now upon his journey to waite upon you, and I could not deny him this trouble to his hand, for presenting my affectionate love to you, of which I have greate confidence you are assured, which is noe smale delight. My sister Elizabeth is yet under heavy afflictings.[36] The Lord sanctifie it to her and us all. Having

[35] Sent as ambassador extraordinary to the king of France, with instructions to urge the king to reinvigorate the siege operation at Dunkirk by his own presence there (Abbott, IV, pp. 809–810).

[36] The illness proved terminal.

nothing of moment, I only desire myne and my wyfe's services to my sister, my wyfe to youreself. I rest, deare brother,

Yours most affectionately,

R Cromwell

381. From Samuel Ladyman,[37] Clonmel, 5 June 1658, 823, fos 51–52.

May it please your excellency!

Being encouraged thereunto by your lordship's command, I am humbly bold to return this answere to what your excellency was lately pleased to propose concerning my removall to Dublin; and since my departure from your excellency, I have taken many occasions and set some time apart to seek the Lord and waite for His counsell in it. Some objections[38] I have met with, which I can call not other then temptations, as that a retired life in so populous a citty would scarce consist with the health of my craz'd constitution, though (Warbers[39] standing in an open, pleasant aire) even upon this account, as upon some others hinted by your excellency (viz, the larg extent of that parish and the quality of the persons dwelling in it), I have cause to be aboundantly thankfull for your lordship's choice of that place. I have also been tempted to thinke that here in the countrey I was in a fairer way to make some slender provision for my poor wife and family after my decease. But upon a more serious view I find these considerations so selfish, and attended with so much distrust of that good God who hath hitherto so plentifully and so mercifully provided for me, and with so much of ingratitude towards your excellency (considering how great, though altogether undeserved, your excellency's continued and tender care of me hath been) that I am very much asham'd of them, and through grace doe trust I have overcome them. But besides these, I do meet with many others which I neither can remove nor dare

[37] Church of Ireland clergyman, he was a preacher in Oxford in the early 1650s but, in 1652, he and Edward Wale went to Ireland with Fleetwood, serving as chaplains. He became salaried minister at Clonmel and supported Worth's Cork-based association of ministers in 1657. He was one of around thirty clergyman who, at Henry Cromwell's invitation, met in Dublin in the spring of 1658 to discuss and advise him on church matters, including the possibility of creating a formal structure for the Protestant religion and church in Ireland, and of finding a new way to support ministers there, Henry Cromwell commenting that the existing financial arrangements were 'grown to that scurvy pass' and were 'a mongrel way between salary and tythes' (TSP, VII, pp. 21–22, 101–102). However, in this letter he appears to be declining an invitation from Henry Cromwell to relocate permanently to Dublin and to accept a parish there. Indeed, he remained at Clonmel throughout this period and well beyond the Restoration.

[38] Word written larger than the surrounding text and with very thick strokes of the pen.

[39] Perhaps an abbreviated reference to the parish of St Werbergh's in Dublin, where Stephen Charnock had been minister in the mid-1650s.

neglect; I am very fearfull least Mr Charnock's so suddain leaving his charge and my leaving mine should be improv'd to the Lord's great dishonour, by too many who will rejoyce to catch at any thing that may but seem to give them an occasion to slurre the worke in our hands. Againe, as I do justly bear a great affection to this people among whom providence hath fix't me, considering their continued respect towards me (notwithstanding for want of ordination, I was uncapacitated for more then 5 yeares to answer their just and necessary expectations), so am I very desirous (if the Lord see it good) to reap some fruit of what seeds I have here scattered (though but with a withered hand) and am very loath to leave the great hopes I have of sharing in such an harvest, being now more compleatly furnish'd for and solemly set apart to my work, and promising myselfe (not without good ground) very much assistance in it from our present governour, for whom this place hath still cause to blesse the Lord and to be thankfull to your excellency. Again, I am very sensible of my own weaknes, how that it doth render my body unable for much study and my lungs for much discourse; and for me to prove a broken staffe in your lordship's hands, as it would be my sore burthen and unspeakable greife, so to your excellency a most unhandsome disappointment. But about all that call, that cleare and reiterated call which I have had to this place and people is such that I am affrayed to leave them; and should I do it, am strongly jealous that God would blast my poor labours in any other place.

Labouring under all these discouragements, let me beseech your excellency to pardon me, though I am forc'd to make this return to your late gracious motion (for I know it proceeded from your lordship's undeserved respect, not from any defect of others more able for that service) that I cannot but humbly entreat your excellency and earnestly beg it of the Lord, that it might consist with your excellency's good pleasure still to leave me here. Because (though I cannot free myselfe from the same secret itch after honour with others) in the integrity of my heart I do judg that I may here be most usefull. Now, that the Everlasting Councellour would continue to direct your excellency in the management of your great and weighty trust; and bear up your spirits amidst the many discouragements which will attend its faythfull discharge; and that the same God would recompence a thousand-fold into your lordship's bosome your unwearyed labour of love for His ministry, His church, His ordinances; and would still vouchsafe a descending blessing upon your excellency's honourable relations, family, person and authority, shall be the earnest and constant prayer of,

Your excellency's most unworthy, yet most obleiged servant,
Sam Ladyman

382. From Edward Whalley, 7 June 1658, 823, fos 53–54.

May it please your excellencye,

I have sent my sonne Henry to wayte upon and attend your excellencye's commandes. Hitherto, both beyond the sea and at home, he hath beene of a blamelesse conversation. May he but by his good deportment receave the[40] testimonie of your excellencie's approbation, it wilbe a great contentment to his mother and myselfe. My councill to him is, and prayers for him are, that the Lord would inable him in the first place and above all things with a sincere heart to serve Him, and then I am sure he shall not want a due respect from your excellencie. My sonne John[41] desired me to acquaynt you with the date of his commission here, which is the 12th of Aprill last, that so no stop may be put to his warrants to that time. The reason of his request to me is that by a duell with the earle of Chasterfeild,[42] receaving a small hurt, he is not able to write himselfe. I am sory I should have occasion to write so much, but though a meere stranger to the earle, meeting accidentalye with him at the hie court of justice, and the next morning receaving a challenge from him, which my sonne unwilling to beleeve went to his lodging immediately to him to have avoyded it yf possibly preserving his honour, but being further provokt, my sonne refusing to have a second, and unwilling to involve any freind into an evill that in could blood he condemned himselfe for, as also as unwilling to expose the person or estate of any to hazard, they ended theyr controversie at the Isle of Dogges. My sonne Henry will give your excellencie a more full account of it. I shall onely add this, that amongst men meerely morall hee hath gayned honour, that it could be so accounted or worth anything, Christians censure him very favourably and his Highnes thinkes he was very highlye provokt. Yet the law makes him as hie an offender as the other. I have bin very much displeased, and some thinkes too much with him, for I hope the Lord will give him

[40] Word repeated in error.

[41] Parliamentarian officer and a cornet in Henry Cromwell's horse regiment, he was for a time held in the Tower as a consequence of fighting this duel and, in 1659, was dismissed from his regiment.

[42] Philip Stanhope, second Earl of Chesterfield, royalist courtier and politician, spent most of the 1640s and early 1650s on the continent. He was in England in the early 1650s, returning abroad in 1655 following the death of his wife and young child. He returned to England sometime late in 1657. Duelling was in his blood: in 1649, he was expelled from a Paris academy for duelling; in February 1658, he was arrested in London to prevent a duel; and he spent some time in the Tower as a result of fighting this duel with Whalley, returning there in the summer of 1659 on suspicion of involvement with Booth's royalist rising. In January 1660, he fled England after killing the son of a Hammersmith doctor in a duel fought over the price of a horse.

to make a good use of. And so craving pardon for this troubling you with an impertinent relation, I take leave and remayne,

Your excellencie's most humble and faythfull servant,
Edw Whalley

Pardon the boldnes of the postscript, my wyfe having a great desire to present her most humble service to your excellencie and virtuous lady.

383. From Anne de Burgh, Marchioness of Clanricarde,[43] 8 June 1658, 823, fos 55–56.

My lord,

I assure myselfe your excellencie hath already notice of the death of my deare lord, which is the sad occasion I have of making this humble adresse to you, because I am thereby intitled unto the joynture setled at my mariage, wherein Portumna is included. My sexe and fortune renders me uncapable of distrusting my right, and your excellencie's generous goodnes maks it needlesse, because experience shewes you are not only ready to afford justice, but favours also, to all that have a title to pretend them from you. I shall therefore humbly offer my right and estate in Portumna and the lands adjoyning unto your excellencie, beseeching you to allot me such recompence in leiu of them as you thinke fitt; it being intirely submitted to by, my lord,

Your excellencie's humble servant,
Anne Clanricarde

This bearer, Sir William Usher (my honered freind), will upon occasion shew forth my joynture and convey your excellencie's commandes to me.

[43] Lady Anne Compton, daughter of the Earl of Northampton and widow of Ulick de Burgh, Marquess of Clanricarde, Irish landowner, courtier, royalist, and politician, who had extensive estates in Ireland, including the Portumna estates that Henry Cromwell now held. Clanricarde surrendered to the English regime in the autumn of 1652 and, with most of his Irish estates deemed forfeit, he spent his closing years of ill health in London. The date of his death is unclear and perhaps occurred in the summer of 1657, but spring 1658 seems more likely and is more consistent with this attempt by his widow to recover, or at least to gain some compensation for, those parts of the estates that had been settled upon her at her marriage. In 1656, she had petitioned for the return of 4,000 acres of her husband's estates (Dunlop, p. 629; *CSPI*, pp. 654–655, 832, 848, 855).

384. From John Heart,[44] Taboyne,[45] 8 June 1658, 823, fo. 57.

May it please your excellencie,

Necessity constraineth me to adventure the utering of a few things to your lordship by way of grievance, the remedie of which as it can not be expected from any to be so effectuall as from your lordship, so also not so readily and willingly to be applied by any as by your lordship. The experience of all the godly who have been acquainted with your lordship can give testimonie to this thing, so that I can not but say it (without flattrie God knoweth) your excellency may be called a repairer of breaches.

May it please your excellency, I have been constrained in my conscience at the late convention of ministers who we[. . .][46] assembled at Dubline by your lordship's authoritie,[47] to give in a great many scandalous, insufficient and negligent ministers in the countrey where I live, through which I have brought the hatred of many wicked men upon me, whose tounges will be set on fyre of hell to speake mischievous things and things full of fasthood against mee, which may be readily credited by some about your lordship. I humblie therefore begg of your lordship that in what I may be charged with by any whatsoever to your lordship, I may have the libertie to answere for myselfe before the things be hearkned unto that shall be spoken against your lordship's unworthie servant, for I doe know that men have vowed to cast mee out of your lordship's favour per fas aut nefas,[48] meerlie upon the account of my discharging a good conscience. I am affraied to be judged too presumptuous in this my desyre, but I pray your lordship to pardon my weaknesse in this thing, for I flee to your lordship as the common sanctuarie (under the great Governour of heaven and earth) of the godlie of the nation in there distresse.

If it may please your excellency to heare mee a litle further. The complaint of a poore people dwelling at Rapho, who have a godlie minister amongst them[49] and have sett up the Presbyterian way of discipline to which they adhere, is very sadde, and they have requested mee to represent it to your lordship. There is a prelaticall pairtie in that parish, who endeavour to hinder them in the excersise of there

[44] Presbyterian minister, occasionally employed as an intermediary between Henry Cromwell and the Presbyterians.

[45] Probably Tabone, Raphoe, County Donegal.

[46] Paper damaged with some loss of text, though the incomplete word is probably 'were'.

[47] The series of meetings had ended on 26 May, with the ministers passing to Henry Cromwell, just before their departure from Dublin, 'a large paper in referrence to several matters offered by me to their consideration' (*TSP*, VII, p. 145).

[48] This Latin phrase could be translated as 'by fair or unfair means' or 'justly or unjustly'.

[49] John Crookshanks, minister at Raphoe and a fellow Presbyterian.

discipline, as when they by deacons collect the money for the poore at the church door, they come and interrupt them by there churchwardens, yea and have proceeded this farre upon the sabbath day to beat the elders of the church, and in other places the scribes of the particular elderships are bound over to the assizes for the lawfull exercise of discipline. If I should complaine to any other then to your lordship I know I could not be heard, it would be thought my reflection upon Doctor Lesslie, late bishop of Rapho.[50] But thanks be to God through Jesus Christ, who hath us a magistrate that will heare us when we call, I mean when we call not idly and foolishlie but rationally. The justices of peace in the countrey having warning from your lordship may helpe all this.

That your lordship may waxe greater and greater, and that your heart may be lift[51] up in the wayes of God yet more (for what is allready the hearts of His people are glewed unto yow) is, and God willing, shall be the uncessant prayer of, my lord,

Your excellency's most humble and obedient servant,

Jo Heart

385. From Nathaniel Waterhouse, London, 8 June 1658, 823, fos 58–59.

May it please your excelency,

His Highnesse hath been pleased to bestow on my brother, Doctor Waterhouse, as a signall of his favour for his former service as phisitian to the army in Ireland, two hundred markes per annum for one and twenty yeares out of certaine lands lately belonging to the bishopp of Derry.[52] May it please your excelency, my humble request is that your excelency would be pleased to aford him what lawfull favour you can in it, in regard he is, as I am informed, out of his former imployment as phisition of the army. And soe with the humblest of my duty to your excellency, I begg pardon for this bouldness and shall ever rest,

Your excellency's most humble servant,

Nat Waterhouse

[50] John Lesley, bishop of the Isles, 1628–1633, and of Raphoe from 1633, who, despite his royalist and Episcopalian views, remained in Ireland during the 1650s, actively seeking and often obtaining payment from the English parliamentary regimes.

[51] Apparently a slip for 'lifted'.

[52] John Bramhall, bishop of Derry from 1634, began his career in Yorkshire and crossed to Ireland in 1633 with Sir Thomas Wentworth. A strong supporter of the king's and Wentworth's handling of Ireland, he was very active in advising on and seeing executed the religious policies of the period. Although impeachment proceedings against him in 1641 stalled, he effectively lost power and influence in Ireland and, apart from a brief return visit in 1649–1650, spent the 1640s and 1650s either in England as a supporter of the royalist cause or in exile on the continent.

386. From Bryan Smyth, Coleraine, 9 June 1658, 823, fos 60–61.

May it please your exelencye,

I being come into the country have, according to my dutye, visited the severall quarters of the regiment I belong unto, and am in the worke. I doe find that the Irish in the Glines and Red Bay[53] are very high and insolent, speaking out their hopes of some suden chainge, as the country informes mee. Amoung other that are bould, there hath bin latly one Randall MaDonnell, who is some litle kin to my lord of Antrim, who hath noe constant residence, hath set fier on a house nere Red Bay, sorely wounded the man of the house, a Scotsman, who got the warant of a justice of peace to apprehend the said MaDonnell, but hee sculks about and cannot bee had. Besids some prists ar, as I here, come over from Spaine, who say mas upon the mountaynes and yet are soe covertly harboured by the Irish that they cannot bee had. I humble[54] offer to your lordships as my oppinon that the country cannot bee safe unles thes desperate Irish bee removed, or compeld to bring in the prist, and such others as commit insolency dayly, but cannot bee found by us throw their mens. Wee can hardly get ether English or Scot to take the office of a constable upon them for feare of these desperate Irish, who are indeed numerous. Ther is on Neale Oge MaColley, nere Red Bay, who is said to harbour the prist, and alsoe the foresaid man that burned the house, but hee is soe sutle a vilane that noe man who would can make a throw discovery and profe against him. Hee is a most notorious, swering, dronken man. Luitenant-colonell Dukingfield hath knowledg of him; but noe good can bee done with them, they are soe sutle and false, without removeing. I am confident they were acquainted with the late hored plot in England, for sence ther seeme some alteration as to thir hight. I leave the consideration of this matter to your excelencye. I have one request to your excelencye in the behalfe of a soldier in my company, one Richard Godman, who desires your excelency's discharge, being a tradsman and not able to mayntayne his wife and children as a soulder without neglect of his duty. And let mee beg your excelencye to admit one Samson Williams, an ould and honest redused souldier to come in the said Godman's steed. Pray pardon my lenth. I shall only crave leave to wish your excelency the constant guidance of God's spirit that you may doe His will, and cary on His interest, and love His people, and hate His enimyes, and bee eminent for godliness, and doe nothing that may displese Hime upon any account; that you may cast noe discoragement upon any one that God would not have

[53] On the east coast of County Antrim, by Cushendall.

[54] Apparently a slip for 'humbly'.

discoredgd; that you may have a deserving spirit, and much of the dred and feare of Hime who is the santury of His. Soe rest,

Your excelencye's servant,

Bry Smyth

387. From Robert Beake, 15 June 1658, 823, fos 62–63.

May it please your excellency,

That anything I can doe finds acceptation with yow is attributeable onely to your noblenes; that yow make signification of your acceptance is to be ascribed to your condescency. It was your excellency's trouble to write a letter, it was my honour to receive it, which I mention with all humble expression of thankefullnes.

From Thursday last till this day we had litle from the French campe to discourse off. That which silently crept among the French to our reproach was the permitting of a billander[55] to goe into Dunkirke and another vessell to come out thence with intelligence; but our plea is good as to both, for the billander was not distingwishable from other vessells that came with provisions to supply the leaguer, and the other swimd on shole water where our shipps could not ride; this litle was made much.

Monesieur Chattelleon,[56] a marshal of France, was very lately wounded and some say mortally. I shall mention to your excellency two things worthy remarque. One is a passage in my lord Lockart's letter to his Highnes concerneing the gallantry of the English foote in the late fight. Saith he, marshall Turin and others non-concerned affirme the English to have acted the parts of more then men,[57] and the English under Charles Stewart less then men, for they first shrunke in the fight. Soe great a discrimination doth a good cause make among men of the same clymate. Another observation is that of the enimy (being taken), who cryed out that they never knew any use of the muskett but at one end, but the English had found the use of both ends, soe ready were there stocks about.

But the news brought by an express at 5 of the clocke this day lays aside the further mention of perticulers of this nature, to make a way for the tydeings of Dunkirke's surrender.[58] My lord, the sence of God's goodnes heerin doth almost fill us with astonishment. To His name be rendred all the glory. The Lord's day the king of France came

[55] Bilander: a double-masted coastal vessel.

[56] Jacques, Marquis de Castelnau-Manvissiere, commander of the Flemish army in the absence of Turenne, subsequently died of the musket wound he received outside Dunkirk.

[57] Word heavily amended and poorly formed.

[58] The town surrendered on 14 June.

from Callais to Mardike uppon intimation of a treaty offered by the towne. The articles concluded on were that night caried by marshall Thurin to the king at Mardike. He imediatly then gave order to the English generalls, sea and land, to signe them with him, which they did accordingly, and the articles were under hand and seale when the messenger came away. He speakes not to the actuall surrender of it, but saith that Sir Brise Cockram was treated with some other gentlemen (English) uppon theire workes with al possible civillity and honor, looking uppon themselves as comeing under the wings of the English Protector. The articles are not knowne as yett to his Highnes. The towne was reduced to great streights for all things, and we were ready to spring a myne (which they forsaw would take, and was not preventable), and these considerations brought there hearts downe. As for the Spanish army, there is noe mention at all of it, nor knowne where it is. About 4 of the clock this afternoone my lord Pikering, Hubbard and Howard,[59] with 3 score and tenn coaches, with 6 horses in each, besides a greater number that had fewer horses, went to meete the duke of Crequi and monsieur Mancini,[60] the king and cardinal's two favourits. They landed at Towre and were brought to Brooke House.[61] There retinnue was but ordinary.

This day the high courte of justice sate in the Painted Chamber in order to pronounce judgment on captain Mallory, Sir Humphrey Bennet and Mr Woodcock.[62] It is now about 7 at night and they are not gon out of the Painted Chamber yett. It is certaine when they sitt, which will be this night, the sentence will be death to Mallory and acquittall to the other two.[63] Evidence falters exceedingly and Stapelely shuffles abhominably, and at some streight things seeme to be as to further proceeds, yet it's not doubted but the London trayters wil evidently appeare such uppon there tryall.

[59] Sir Gilbert Pickering, Sir John Hobart, and Charles Howard, all of them 'lords' in the sense that, in the autumn of 1657, they had been named to the new second parliamentary chamber.

[60] Charles, Duc de Crequi de Blanchefort and Philippe-Jules Mancini Mazarini, Duc de Nevers, had been sent by the king of France on a diplomatic mission to the Protector in response to Fauconberg's mission to him.

[61] In Holborn, built in the early seventeenth century by the Earl of Bath, and acquired by Fulke Greville, Baron Brooke.

[62] Royalist conspirators arrested in connection with the recent plot. Bennet and Thomas Woodcock had both been recruited by Stapley in the Sussex element of the conspiracy, and both were tried, with Mallory, on 10 June, with verdicts and sentences handed down on 15 June.

[63] In fact, Henry Mallory was convicted and sentenced to death but reprieved, Woodcock was acquitted, and the case against Bennet was dropped.

Advise came that my lord Richard was safely arived at the Bath on Fryday last.

Your excellency's in all humble observance and duty,

Rob Beake

388. From Elizabeth Butler, Marchioness of Ormond, Dunmore, 16 June 1658, 823, fos 64–65.

My lord,

Hearinge latlie of the confinment of Mr Lesslye, a devine and one whoe upon the recomendatione of severall of his owne professtione and others of qualitye livinge in thous parts where hee did, to bee a persone learned, of peasebell and seville conversatione, and a singell man, I did promise to entertayne at my beinge last at Dublin to bee my housold chaplin. Aganst whom I understand that ther is some offense takene, but what the perticulars are or may bee, I am as ignorant as innosent of beinge anye ways an acsesarye unto what may bee made his crime, if anye hee shallbee found gilltye of. Soe as my humbell desier unto your lordships is that noe part of the displeasure aganst hime, whoe is to mee a stranger – more then that I doe remember to have siene hime at Dublin aboute twelfe years sense and then heard hime preach, hee beinge at that time under the notione of one of my lord's chaplenes, yet never had unto the best of my remembranse, but at my comminge last from Dublin, in all my life anye discourse with hime – may not involve mee and consequentlie prejudis mee in your lordship's estime, whoe singlie without the othoritye of the plase you hould, I carrye to great a respect for to intrest myselfe for anye aganst whom your lordships may ethar in your private or publicke capasitye have anye exseptionse aganst. Soe as unles your lordships shall become sattisfiede of his beinge as innofensive as hee was carracterede, and I belevede hime to bee, I shall declyne the entertayninge of him, as I hope your lordships will the admittinge anye beleufe to my prejudis in this or anye other perticular. To which other's offense, and not my owne, may by my ill-willers bee agrevatede to my disadvantage, whoe, notwithstandinge all that the unhappenes of my condistione cane throw upon mee, your lordships shall never find, but allways redye to testifie myselfe, my lord,

Your lordship's most humble servant,

E Ormonde

389. From Frances Rich, 19 June 1658, 823, fo. 66.

Deare brother,

Though I know myself to be very geulty of neglect to you, yet give me leve to hope this paper will beg your pardon for my so long silance. I can with confidence declare and without complement that non would be more rejoused if in anything I could expres the love and deare affection I have for you then myself.

Deare brother, I could fil this papir with giving you an account of the aflections I have mett with, but I shall not give you that truble now, only let me tell you I have lost a dear husband; the Lord helpe mee to mack a sanctyfied[64] use of it and all His despansations to me. Tis tru I have grat marcys left me in my relations, that many of God' presious ons want, though I think that nothing in the world can repair my loss, and inded doe not desire any thing in it below Crist. I hope it is my earnest desire to gett Him for my husband that will never dey. Pardon thes poor, broken, imparfact lines and belive thay com from her that desirs to aprov herself to be your deare sister and sarvant,

Frances Riche

I beg of you to present my sarvis to my deare sister, and tel her that I should have trubled her with my rud lins but that my sister Elizabeth's goeing into the country tomorro I had no tim. She hath bin very ill, but blesed be God we hop she is in the mending hand.

Pray burn it.

390. From John Jones, Chelsea, 22 June 1658, 823, fos 67–68.

Right honourable,

Haveing received information that one Mr Dutton of Denbigheshire is now prepareing to come over to Ireland to serve your lordship, I conceive it a duety incumbent upon mee to give yow some accompte of him. Hee is a man that hath beene an enemie and hath suffered for it in that countrey. His sonne hath beene now for a longe tyme a prisoner in the Tower. His wife is the daughter of a woman that hath had five or six bastards, and is of the most infamouse familie in that part of the land. Truely, sir, I affect not to bee an informer, but my affections to your lordship and your honourable familie forceth me to give you this intimation to prevent any occasion of offence, which many times are extended beyond their due limitte by zealouse men of contrary principles. Findeing that my little concernement in Ireland goes on but very slowely towarde a settlement, and my wife's great desire to waite on your lordship and your most honourable lady (for whom she hath aboundance of affection), and the Lord haveing restored her to a competent measure of health, wee are both very easily inclined to come over to Ireland sometime this summer, if the Lord please, haveing not yet in our view any impediment to

[64] Word heavily amended and poorly formed.

divert us. Wherever wee are, your lordship will finde us very sincere and faithfull to your interest and service, and ready as opportunitie shalbee presented to approve ourselves,

Your lordshipp's most humble servante,

Jo Jones

391. From Nathaniel Fiennes and John Lisle, Westminster, 28 June 1658, 823, fos 69–70.

My lord,

Upon the instance of Robert Reynolds esq complainant before us in the chancery here against Sir James Calthorpe and dame Dorothy, his wife, for the proveing of the will of Sir John Reynolds,[65] deceased, wee thinke fitt to informe your lordshipp that the defendants did demurre to the jurisdiction of the courte of chancerye here, which demurrer upon a solemne debate and argument before us is overruled, and the defendants ordered to answere the bill in cheefe, soe that the courte of chancery here is duly possest of the cause, which wee referre to your lordship's consideration, and remaine,

Your lordship's most humble servants,

Nath Fiennes John Lislees

392. From Robert Reynolds, London, 29 June 1658, 823, fos 71–72.

My lord,

The lords commissioners of the great seale of England have that high and due esteeme of your lordshipp's wisdome and justice, that it being in debate with them touching the securing the possession of Carrick in the same handes and plight it was when my brother died, untill a legall eviction (which is according to the common course of all courts of justice), thought it sufficient (without seeming to impose upon your lordshipp's government) to certifie under their handes how farre they are possest of the cause depending before them, wherein I am complainant against Sir James Calthorp and his lady for the

[65] Reynolds had drowned on 5 December 1657, when the boat in which he was returning to England was wrecked on the Goodwin Sands, Henry Cromwell reporting his sadness at the loss (*TSP*, VI, p. 683). As he had no children, his new wife, now widow, had only a life interest in his personal estate. Instead, his will of May 1657 and administration of the estate were disputed between his half-brother Robert on the one side and his sister Dorothy and her husband Sir James Calthorpe/Calthrop on behalf of their children (named in the will as heirs to his Irish lands) on the other; in January 1658, Henry Cromwell recommended a compromise settlement in preference to a long and costly legal dispute (*TSP*, VI, p. 761). In 1658, administration was at length granted to Dorothy, but the case was far from resolved and it came before the restored Rump in 1659.

making good of my brother's will and asserting my undoubted right to Carrick, which when recover'd I shall lay downe at your lordshipp's feet, my cheife aime being to vindicate the honour of my brother, that hee was not so weak, so unnaturall, so incogitant[66] as to dye without a will which is an unhandsome returne where hee hath shown so much affection. My lord, haveing done my duety herein, I humbly crave your lordshipp's effectuall commands to Mr Wilson to preserve the possession untill a lawfull decision of the right, and hast to subscribe as I am and shalbee,

Your lordshipp's most humble and faithfull servant to honour you,
Robt Reynolds

393. From Nicholas Lockyer,[67] London, [June 1658],[68] 823, fos 1–2.

My lord,

Pardon that I presume to salute you in these underlines; you will not oft find me faulty in this kinde of boldnes. Blessed be our God that hath fetched you from the gates of death, and will please to spare instruments of hope yet unto us. I am oft refreshed by good Mr Gorge with many good things he writeth of your lordship's industry to encourage and advance all the good of men and Christians you can; in this the Lord make you skilfull, strong and prevailying. Every place of trust hath tryall, but the greatest trusts have the greatest tryals; the Lord will gird you with the spirit of wisdom and might and of feare of His name, and He will hold your hand and make crooked things straight and rough things plain before you. You are not yet accustomed

[66] Incogitant: thoughtless, careless, inconsiderate.

[67] Independent minister, who supported the parliamentarian cause and preached several times before the Long Parliament. In 1649, he became one of Oliver Cromwell's chaplains and rose under his patronage, becoming a fellow of Eton College and a preacher at Windsor Castle, being given a parish in Buckinghamshire, attending the parliamentary commissioners in Scotland in 1651, and regularly preaching both in London and before the various parliaments and councils of the 1650s. He became, in effect, one of the Protector's chaplains.

[68] The dating of this letter is a puzzle. The contents most obviously place it in late June 1658, because Elizabeth Claypole's final child, born in June 1657, died in mid-June 1658 (*TSP*, VII, p. 177), Elizabeth Claypole was seriously ill by this time (despite enjoying interludes of apparent improvement, as noted here), and the reference to God saving Henry Cromwell from the 'gates of death' could well be a somewhat dramatized and exaggerated reference to the sharp illness that he and his wife suffered in the spring of 1658. On the other hand, the letter is clearly dated '28 December' (there is no year given on the letter or endorsement) and to write 'December' instead of 'June' is a curious slip of the pen. It is, therefore, just possible that this letter could be placed in late December 1655, if we attribute Claypole's poor health at that stage to a difficult pregnancy from which she then recovered but which had ended in a miscarriage, stillbirth, or birth of a very short-lived child (see nos 33 and 34).

to such a yoake, but Christ will boare your eare to hard service and annoint with fresh oile, and you will be learning still much from living volumes of men and actions which will recompence much all durance upon you. I rejoyce, sir, with you that you yet live, and that you have a place not onely in our land of the living, but in the hearts of that people over which you watch. I pray the Lord to blesse them to you and you to them, and that what ever you doe may please God and yf possible all the people too. I am still yours in my poor prairs, which is, sir, such as I have, and indeed all I have, where with as a prophet to blesse you and yours. Touching my condition in this world, my lord, which I did a litle open to your lordship before you went, and which you were so gratiously pleased to licen to. What the state gave mee almost three yeres since for two hundred pound a yeere, which not till within this halfe yeer I could come to posesse and look into, proves but 60 pound per annum; so that the state was pleased to resume it, and to give mee two thousand pound, which I am now endevouring to apportion to my seven children as well as I can. And, my lord, I thought good to offer it to Mr Gorge to lay out five hundred pound in Ireland to be one child's portion, that it may seem good to your lordship to give him your countenance and help in my behalfe. You will in this, sir, help ones very helples, and lay bonds upon,

Your most humble servant,
Nicho Lockyer

I strengthen your hand, sir, with your father upon all occasions, and find it but needfull.

Our family is all well; my lady Claypool drawes to health, but her child last borne is dead. My humble service to my lady.

394. From Robert Beake, [early or mid-July 1658], 823, fos 187–188.

May it please your excellency,

There is litle of moment now communicable. The state of Flanders has not passed under any considerable alteration since the takeing of Bergen. The forte of Linke has bin reported to have bin taken 3 dayes agoe, but the last messenger left it onely in treaty for surrender. On Fryday last the body of the Spanish army were in and about Newport, where also was Don John, the dukes of Yorke and Glocester, the marquiss of Caracene, with divers other eminent persons, the prince of Condy at a pass not farr distant from them. Towards this body, the French army mooved the same day. The Spanish strength was in horse, whose number equalls those of the French, being as is sayd 12,000; but few or noe foote. To the French came this last weeke a body of 7,000 recruits; and it's necessary ours should be recruited also for the 8 English regiments are very thin. It is bruited as if the Spainard had foyled the French before Rocroy and forced them to rise, but it's beyond dispute that that part of the army drawes to the maine body, and La Ferte has gott a wounde in the back, whether fighting or flying I yet understand not. The French king has bin almost sick unto death, but a litle recovered at this tyme. My lord Mountague in his passage to the Downes was invited by the cardinal to come to Callais, where he went and was entertayned with all termes of noblenes. We understand also from France that the enimy has quitted Ferne.[69]

The comission for the counsel of Scotland renewed for 3 years; noe alteration made in men or instructions. Sir George Ascue is bound for Sweden to be admiral of those seas for the Swedish king. Major-generall Jepson is now in his passage from his courte. Mr Peters is gon over to Dunkerke compassionating much the want of the English souldiery in respect of ministers. I crave your excelency's pardon if I subscribe myselfe,

Your excelency's most devoted servant,

Rob Beake

I am bound for the country for 3 weekes; I hope it wil excuse this kinde of service.

395. From Timothy Taylor and Essex Digby,[70] Kilroot, County Armagh, 12 July 1658, 823, fos 73–74.

May it please your excellency,

The bearer hereof, Mr Buckworth,[71] is one of those two ministers which were presented by the late convention of ministers att Dublin to your excellencie as both (by publick authoritie) officiateing in Maghralin in the county of Downe. Mr Wattson,[72] the other minister,

[69] This account of events and developments in Flanders firmly places this undated letter in the first half of July 1658. Bergues fell on 1 July, while the fall of Furnes, news of which was just filtering through to Beake, occurred on 3 July.

[70] Ministers in Ireland. Taylor held livings in Herefordshire, Shropshire, and Cheshire before crossing to Ireland around 1650 and becoming minister at Carrickfergus; in religion, he shifted from a Presbyterian to a more Independent stance, strongly supported Henry Cromwell, and advised him on his religious policy. Essex Digby was in Ireland rather earlier, by the 1640s, but he was driven from his parish of Geashill during the Irish rebellion; by 1654, he was a salaried minister in Belfast, displaying clear Episcopalian sympathies.

[71] Anthony Buckworth, minister in Ireland, was, during the mid-1650s, a salaried minister first at Newry and then at Magheralin, County Down; he, too, was an Episcopalian.

[72] James Watson, minister in Ireland, who was originally an Episcopalian but who conformed to the Presbyterian system and moved towards that faith. In the mid-1650s, he was also based at Magheralin, where he allegedly clashed with Buckworth, though by 1659 he was minister at Loughgilly, County Armagh.

hath (as I understand) obtained an order from your excellencie to be the preacher at Magheralin. And about this same time God soe ordered it in His good providence that the inhabitants of the parrish of Kilree[73] in the countie of London Derry desired us to recommend a minister to them. Wee forthwith sent unto them Mr Buckworth, who after he had preached two dayes and conversed with the people, received as a testimony of the approbation of all the well affected English inhabitants a petition directed to your excellencie and the councill on his behalfe. Wherefore wee humbly desire your excellencie that the aforesaid Mr Buckworth may receive all due encouragement and may be sent downe to preach the gospell att Kilree. That God would preserve your excellency and make you an instrument of much good to His people in this nation shall be the prayer of,

Your lordshipp's most humble servants,

Timothie Taylor Essex Digby

396. From William Malyn, Whitehall, 13 July 1658, 823, fos 75–76.

May it please your excellencie,

I have hereinclosed sent a graunt from his Highnesse to captain Gregory of the mannor of Emly[74] ______ ______; his Highness hath set downe the terme, but as to the rent his Highness leaves that to your lordship. His Highness is willing at your lordship's desire to doe captain Gregory a kindnes, and not knowing whither the present rent may be too little or too much, his Highness doth rather chuse to leave it to your lordship's determination. My lord, I was verie glad to receive a lettre from your lordship, for I could not but conclude that I did lye under a censure in your lordship's thoughts (and that justly) of a great neglect towards your lordship in that I have not written to your lordship soe long time, and therefore did feare that your lordship would not vouchsafe to honour me with any of your lordship's commaunds. But truely, my lord, it hath not been out of the least disrespect or withdrawing of that duty which I owe to your lordship, but the true reason thereof is (as I hinted to Doctor Harrison) I have nothing to write, but what is publiqe and comon, which your lordship will have from other hands enough. I do not love to be over inquisitive; only I desire the cause of God may prosper and that it may goe well with Syon, and that we whome God hath owned and done great things for, may be found faithfull doeing the will of God in our places and generation.

[73] Kilrea, County Londonderry.

[74] In County Tipperary. Malyn drew two lines after the name of the manor, perhaps to indicate the missing or unknown county.

I presume your lordship hath heard that the lady Elizabeth hath been long exercised with extreme sharpe paynes, and hath still very sharpe fitts. His Highness and especially her Highness are much affected and afflicted therewith. I am perswaded God is dealing with her spirit and hath done her much good, and I trust will still goe on untill He hath perfected His good worke in her. Your lordship cannot but have heard the great successes which God hath been pleased to give to our forces in Flaunders. I pray God to give us hearts wisely to improve our mercies, and to walke suteable thereunto. The lord Richard is sent for from the Bath, and Dr Goodwyn is also sent for from Oxford, and it is whispered by some that something of great importance is to be done, and it is in the mouthes of many that there wilbe another parliament shortly called. I pray God to be with his Highness in an extraordinary manner in assisting him with a spirit of wisdome and councill at such a time as this, when I thinke he hath but little helpe in that kind to leane on, and it may be God will have it so, that soe He may be more sought to and owned.

My lord, I doe much rejoyce to heare so good a report of your lordship and of your goverment. I pray God that you may still goe on to doe yet more worthily in Israel. The lord give you wisedome from above to manage the great affaires committed to your charge. Surely, the main and cheifest point of wisedome in rulers and those in power, especially in these latter dayes, wilbe to owne and set up the soe solempne and serious worship and service of God and to imbrace the Lord Jesus Christ and to advance and promote His kingdome and interest. I am,

Your excellencie's most obleiged and faithfull servant,
Will Malyn

397. From William Wentworth, Earl of Strafford,[75] London, 13 July 1658, 823, fos 77–78.

Letter of business stating that, having heard that Henry Cromwell might be interested in his lands at Newcastle, County Wickloe, he was offering to lease them to him for 31 years at a rate to be determined by Henry Cromwell.

[75] The son and heir of Sir Thomas Wentworth, first Earl of Strafford, who was executed in 1641, he spent the 1640s and early 1650s in exile on the continent, returning to England in the winter of 1651–1652. Although most of the family's estates in Ireland and England had been sequestrated by parliament, he did manage to retain or recover some of the lands his father had held.

398. From Edward Worth, London, 20 July 1658, 823, fos 79–80.

May it please your excellencie,

I have been both at the commencement at Cambridg and act at Oxford, where God was pleased to give me the opportunitie of conversing with many of eminencie, both for learning and pietie; to whom I communicated the copie of your excellencie's speech and the returne therein made by the ministers.[76] The satisfaction which they expressed thereat was very great, not onely on the accompt of the things themselves but alsoe of the tendencie thereof to make brethren one. And truly (my lord), I doe positively affirme that (through God's goodnes) there is such a uniting spirit breathed forth among those Presbyterians that they said with one accord they could freely close with the Congregationall brethren on the termes humbly presented to your excellencie by the Dublin convention. I have been earnestly sollicited as well by the heads of both the universities as by the London ministers, to print those papers, or to give them copies thereof; but I dare doe neither untill I have received the Secretarie's apprehension concerning them, to which end I delivered them to him when first I came hither, but his multiplicitie of publique affaires hath hitherto deferred their perusall.[77]

I bless the Lord for any publique service He ever inabled me to performe; but I am not conscious that ever I was inabled to doe soe much service for the publique in any kind as hath been done by these papers in the generall satisfaction they have ministered, the fruit whereof is soe much more because most conclude that your excellencie's proceedings in Ireland derive their influence from

[76] The speech with which Henry Cromwell opened the Dublin convention of ministers of 23 April 1658 and the address that the ministers presented to him in response. The latter praised Henry Cromwell and referred glowingly to his opening address as 'those high concernments your excellency was pleased to instance as the grand intendment of the present convention, tis to us as life from the dead' (BL, Lansdowne MS 1228, fo. 13). Worth's conservative plans, for organizing the religion of the Protestants in Ireland along broadly Presbyterian lines, were generally endorsed by Henry Cromwell and, with support from ministers from Ulster, gained majority support at the Dublin convention. In its wake, Worth was sent over to England by Henry Cromwell to present his ideas to the Protector. However, although Henry Cromwell repeatedly sought to stress the mutual understanding and unity shown at the Dublin convention and the broadly based support for the final proposals, playing down opposition, by early June, Thurloe had picked up rumours that the plans had in fact proved divisive and were being opposed not only by those 'inclyned to Anabaptism' but also by 'the soberest Independants' (*TSP*, VII, pp. 145, 153, 161–162).

[77] Worth was carrying a letter of recommendation from Henry Cromwell to the Protector, dated 9 June, which ended up amongst Thurloe's papers. In it, Henry Cromwell warmly supported both Worth and the 'address of the ministers which he presents' and defended him against those who had recently 'misrepresented' him in England (*TSP*, VII, p. 162).

England. I came from Oxford to Hampton Court the fifteenth of this instant, and waited on his Highnes, but gave not any particular accompt of these papers, because I expected the result of the Secretarie's thoughts first.

On Thursday I shall againe attend his Highnes and humbly present the paper of the Ulster Presbyterie (which I received not till this day by reason of my absence) and therein the concurrent judgment of the universities and London ministerie, which being done I shall humbly crave your excellencie's leave to returne for Ireland.

The address of the inhabitants (especially that of Corke) was very acceptable to his Highnes.

Of other instances what the publique wants are, and what means consulted on for supplie, I am sure your excellencie will receive an accompt by better information; and therefore in duty I pretermit[78] further to trouble your excellencie with the importune apprehensions of,

Your excellencie's most obedient, most faithfull and most humble servant,

Edw Worth

The blessing of God Almightie be with your excellencie in your publique and familie relations.

399. From Richard Cromwell, London, 29 July 1658, 823, fos 81–82.

Deare brother,

Had I been my owne when att the Bathe[79] I thincke I should not have returned withoute vissitinge you; for I can assure my affections often imployes there sailes for Ireland, but oure bodyes are too heavy for our soules, and it muste be contented with its clogg while in this world; that being the very reason of my not seeing you will, I am confident, excuse me. I have for some time ommitted writing to you, and were I withoute an excusse I might very well lye under your senssure, but the trught of it was that I could not write any thing worth youre trouble as to publique affairs by reasson of my absence from the fountaine head and the drynesse of it in this our drought; or could I furnish you with any thing domesstick that was pleassant, or might suite youre spiritts that had full imployment in all kinde of worke in a troublesome age. Youe have been (I supposse) by severall hands, and at severall times, informed of my sister Elizabeth's illnesse, whoe

[78] Pretermit: omit, interrupt, halt, intentionally let pass.

[79] During July, he and his wife had been on a grand, almost semi-regal, tour of the west of England.

began it some weeks before my leaving London, and at my returne (which was some space of time) was founde at Hampton Courte in a very ill state of body; but Satterday laste she fell into high convulsive fitts, such as made boeth physictians and freinds to dispare of life, there being nothing left but a poore low hope; for from Munday night untell Fryday following aboute 4 a clocke in the afternoone there was not as any could discover soe much as the clossing of the ey leads. Such an amaizement it strocke amongst us, that we are under the greate mercy of God in a still wonderment, and cannot put oute of our eyes the sad spectackle she was unto us. And now we have some more hopes, and her physictians are somewhat revived, and beginn againe to renew there working, seeing that God begann where theye were at an end, boeth of there readings and practices, for nothing ded opperate; but now things beginn to have a blessing put unto them, that our darke and disconsolate famuly may once againe revive and live, I hope to the praise of God. This account (though unpolished) I thought good to send you, that you may have your hopes with those of your freinds here refresshed. His Highness having soe much afflicted himselfe is not very well, but I hope by the next oppertunity to write better newes. My service to my sister, with those of my wyfe's to you boeth. I rest,

Your affectionate brother and servant,

R Cromwell

400. From Nicholas Bernard, Gray's Inn, 1 August 1658, 823, fos 83–84.

May it please your excellency,

The great respect which I have ever observed your excellency hath had towards the late archbyshopp of Armagh, hath mooved me to present this book of his, which is his Annales translated into English, done with his owne consent in his lifetime.[80] And the conveniency of the bearer, Dr Worth (who hath taken the care of it), doth the rather invite me, which I beseech may be accepted from,

Your excellencie's most humble and devoted servant,

N Bernard

[80] *The Annals of the World deduced from the origin of time, and continued to the beginning of the Emperour Vespasian's reign and the totall destruction of the Temple and Commonwealth of the Jews* (London, 1658).

401. From Robert Beake to ?,[81] [late July or very early August 1658],[82] 823, fo. 186.

Most honored sir,

There past but one post since I came to towne and by that I writt to you, therefore hope you are not angry, but in sadnes I am indisposed to write whilst matterials are wanting; the wind blowes noe news from any corner of the wordle. Noe man can be an intelligencer but he must somtymes make minute observations, such must myne be at this tyme. Whilst it's in my thoughts lett me acquainte you that Dr Worth doth his excellency heere great[83] service, he has rooted such a good opinion of his goverment and especialy of the economy of his owne house in the hearts of our ministers that they rejoice much and bless God on his behalfe; yett some muttering there is as if Dr Winter came over uppon another errand.[84] The lady Claypole is fetched back from the grave and very likely to recover. His Highnes has bin ill these 3 dayes but now on mending hand. The Flemish affaires moove slow, Graveling remaynes still begirt. The new emperor is upon returneing to his hereditary countrys. Count Pignoranda and after him (as it's said) Leopoldus wilbe sent to head the Flemmings, Don John being perfectly hated by man, wuemane and child. The last weeke the Portugal embassador had his first conference with the deputyes of the states general, he offers al imaginablye pecuniary satisfaction but as to Brazeele it was not in the power of his master to dispose off. The Dutch are allarmed on al sydes, therefore in al hast they lately posted

[81] The letter was probably not addressed to Henry Cromwell, as he is referred to in the third person as 'his excellency'. The style and opening address to the recipient as 'honored sir' are consistent with Beake's letter to John Bridges of 15 February 1659 (no. 470), so this letter may also have been intended for Bridges.

[82] The letter is undated, but the reports of domestic and foreign developments place it firmly in late July or the very beginning of August 1658. Thus Beake refers to Elizabeth Claypole's severe illness, though the report that she was getting better and likely to recover proved far too optimistic, as she died in the early hours of 6 August, as well as to the onset of what proved to be the final illness of the Protector, which first afflicted him in late July. Abroad, he refers to the siege of Gravelines, which ended with its capture on 17 August; to the new Holy Roman emperor, Leopold I, who was elected on 8 and crowned on 25 July; and to a meeting between the Portugese ambassador and the Dutch states general, which took place on 12 July.

[83] Uncertain reading of a very poorly formed and apparently abbreviated word, which could alternatively be read as 'K^{t}' (an abbreviated form of 'knight').

[84] Winter had found himself outmanoeuvred and outvoted by Worth and his allies at the Dublin convention of ministers over a number of issues, but especially over the restoration of traditional tithes in Ireland: Worth and the conservative majority supporting the proposal, the more Independently minded Winter strongly opposing it. There were rumours that Winter and his allies would cross to England in an attempt to put their case to the Protector and to counter Worth's mission to the Protector. In early July, Henry Cromwell wrote to Thurloe warning him against Winter 'and such credulous weak men' (*TSP*, VII, p. 243).

Opdam to sea. I spake with Mr Jessopp[85] who tels me as yet no man has cald for your papers. I am in doubt whether I should rejoice or be sorry that Mr Roberts is with yow. His abillitys wil teach you to prize him. I am,

Your affectionate servant,
Rob Beake

I was in hast.[86]

402. From Richard Cromwell, Hampton Court, 12 August 1658, 823, fos 85–86.

My lord,

I have been advertised that there are three gentlemen in your service in Ireland who are actuall fellowes of New College in Oxford: Mr Chernock, Kent and Fairfax,[87] and that the first of these enjoys the benefitt of a very liberall mayntenance. My lord, if it shall please you by your interest to dispose eyther of them to a resignation of theyr fellowship there, to ______ Lane,[88] the son of a worthy and pious divine, who has expected this utmost period in the colledge neere Winchester, and who (without such a provision will lose this hopes of perferment), it will be a favor to be own'd and always acknowledg'd by,

Your affectionate brother and servant,
R Cromwell

[85] William Jessop, parliamentarian bureaucrat and politician, was patronized by the Earl of Warwick and was connected with many of the leading parliamentarians of the 1640s, through his role as secretary to the Providence Island Company in the 1630s. He held a range of offices in the military and naval parliamentary administration and, although he was dismayed at the abolition of the House of Lords in 1649, he retained office. He strongly supported Oliver Cromwell and, during the Protectorate, was promoted to become assistant secretary of the Protectoral council and treasurer of the Protector's contingencies, as well as sitting on assorted commissions and committees. He represented his native Stafford in the third Protectorate parliament.

[86] Indeed, it appears to have been written very quickly, with many poorly formed words and letters.

[87] Stephen Charnock, fellow of New College from 1650; John Kent, fellow of New College from 1649, who served as captain of a troop of horse in Ireland in the mid- and later 1650s; and Thomas Fairfax, probably a cousin of the former parliamentary lord-general Sir Thomas Fairfax, and fellow of New College from 1650.

[88] Identification uncertain, not least because his first name has been omitted and a line drawn in the letter to indicate the missing or unknown forename, but perhaps Francis Lane, possibly the son of Samuel Lane, minister at Northrepps, Norfolk.

403. From Edward Worth, Hampton Court, 17 August 1658, 823, fos 87–88.

May it please your excellencie!

Though scientia mali be not mala,[89] yet I could neither last weeke nor the weeke preceding force myselfe to be the messenger or relater of the sad news which afflicted both the publique magistrates and private Christians. It hath now pleased the Lord graciously to dispell those clouds and to shine in mercie on us; this day his Highnes rode abroad in his coach, but as yet the physitians disswade him from interposing in any publique buisines. Truly (my lord), the sense of our sin on both extremes: on the one, in trusting too much on that eminent instrument of our mercies as if the fountaine could not continue running though a pipe were removed; on the other, in murmuring and repining at the mercies we enjoy as if all we injoy were noething whilest we apprehend any thing wanting which we desire. The sense of these sins did very much increase our feares least God in justice should take His Highnes away from an earthly to an heavenly throne. And these feares inlarged the hearts of men generally fearing God to wrestle at the throne of grace on this accompt. The Lord hearing prayre is now returning answer. Oh that we may not relapse to our former folly.

Dr Winter is chosen by his old parishioners to be minister at Cottingham,[90] and I am informed that he and some of the most eminent professors among them will this weeke come to London in order to an address to his Highnes for a settlement. I shall be willing to stay some time here to observe his motion, if once I can be certaine of his resolution.

One colonel Ker[91] is here out of Scotland with a petition from a synod there to prevent the assessment of the ministers' maintenance. He is a sober man, and assures me that the ministers of that nation doe bless the Lord on your excellencie's behalfe. But another synod there hath subscribed a testimonie against toleration of heretiques, and with them colonel Ker (which is very ill rescented). However, it is thought neither he nor his buisines will suffer any prejudice.

[89] This Latin phrase may be translated as 'the knowledge of evil be not evil'.

[90] In Yorkshire, where he had been minister from 1643 to 1651, perhaps suggesting that Winter was considering leaving Ireland at this stage, though this may have been wishful thinking on Worth's part.

[91] Gilbert Kerr, Scottish officer and a leader of the hardline covenanter 'western association' army formed in west and south-west Scotland in the summer of 1650. He took a very firm and narrow line in religion and was imprisoned by Monck for his actions in supporting and presenting this petition from the presbytery of Jedburgh.

Saturday last[92] was kept at Hampton Court as a day of solemne humiliation for his Highnes' distemper. Yesterday the like was observed in many places of London, but privately. Surely that God who hath begun to answer before these solemne exercises will perfect the worke He hath soe begun.

The Lord prepare your excellencie for whatever His providence hath determined. That Christ may be your anchor-hold under all dispensations, soe prayes,

Your excellencie's most obliged, most devoted and most faithfull servant,

Edw Worth

The blessing of God be with your excellencie.

404. From Richard Cromwell, Hampton Court, 24 August 1658, 823, fos 89–90.

Deare brother,

Sence oure late, greate stroacke,[93] of which I know you beare a share, it hath pleassed God to vissett our sorrowes with greater feares, for it is one thinge to have the greatest bowe lopt offe, but when the axe is layed to the roote, then there is noe hopes remaining; such was oure reall feares, grounded for certainty upon the moste propper judges, not only by the physistians, but alsoe an inwarde feeling of the patient, and such a one that created noe fancy in the case. And to make it to appeare, upon her Highnesse's and his childrens' comming after dinner to him, he broake out his more seacrett thoughts, assuring us of [. . .][94] danger, and that we should live upon the covenant, and that he intended to setle his broken private fortune, having sent for his stewards and officers, desiring us to withdrawe and to be in readynesse to be called in as he should have occation in our particuler concernes. I doe not write thus particuler but suppossing you may wante it in these cercumstances, and that you may have only generall illnesse rendred unto you; and I am the more willing thereby the premisses of youre speciall concerne may be alsoe put up, which I am confident carryes up with them affection. And were I not swallowed up with amaizing considerations of these late threatning daingers, over nation as well as oure famuly, and somewhat more speciall myselfe, I should give you an accounte how deservings had like to have remedied roote and branche

[92] 14 August.

[93] The death of their sister Elizabeth Claypole.

[94] Edge of the paper damaged with possible loss of text. There is evidence of an upward stroke of the pen at the start of a short word, now lost. The sense of the sentence suggests that the lost word could be 'no'.

of all concernes; but God is still good, blessed be His name, and hath resspited His seveere displeassure, having shooken His rodd over us to make us more complyable and closer in our dutyes to Him. We are a sinnfull famuly, and the nation a murmering generation, therefore it is good (though greivous) that we have been afflicted. Nay, we are (though we are not soe lowe in our hopes as we have been) still in feares, for though his Highnesse remaines ill, yet that the disstempir is more appairant (it being sett in a tertian with the change of ayre, which is supposed to be for London this day in the intervall of fitts) the dainger is not soe greate. It is God that hath removed his more dreadfull illnesse to this more common, and it muste be His greate power to check and abandon illnesse. He by His dispossing providence makes His soverraignety good to Himselfe. We have had greate prayer and faith acted of late in our famuly, the Lord make it bennificiall unto us.

I feare I may be troublesome to you, and my haste forces me to stop upon this subject, having somwhat to say in the behalfe of this worthy person, Dr Worthe, whoe hath exercissed a greate deale of affection to our famuly. I am not giving him a carrector, he being better knowen to yourselfe; but I may assure you he is the same for you in Ingland as in Ireland, and withoute doubte he is a moste serious Christihian. But you will give me leave to acquainte you with the causse of his soe long stay, which was that he might be rather a messenger of glad tydings, then of ill; which makes way for me to desire youre thancks to him for his love to oure famuly in this time of our sadnesse. We have been a famuly of much sorrow all this summer, and therefore we deserve not the envy of the world; to be a famuly of trouble is suffitient, but to have it loaded upon with afflicting, killing and distroying sorrow makes for pitty instead of anger. We shall still truste in God, whoe is our rocke, upon whome as a suer foundation I recommend your feete; and rest with my service to my d[…]s[95] alsoe to my lord and lady Russell,[96]

Your affectionate brother and servant,

R Cromwell

My lord, this inclosed should, as the date will make it appeare, have waited upon you before now; but if it may finde your favourable countenance and assistance (it being on the behalfe a worthy person, whoe is in want of an act of charrity) it will not only redeeme its loste time, but obleige your affectionate brother to serve you in the like kinde.

R C

[95] Paper damaged with some loss of text, though the incomplete phrase may be 'dear sister as'.

[96] They were on a private visit to Ireland at this time.

405. From Joseph Eyres,[97] Cork, 27 August 1658, 823, fo. 91.

May it please your excellency,

What your excellency suggested to some ministers at Corke, concerning the obstructing the worke of Christ occasioned by some men of unsound principles and unsavoury practises in the ministeriall imploiment, is a serious and sad truth, of which (to my greate griefe) for divers yeares I have had experience. Of which grand inconvenience, as an expedient, certaine instructions came[98] some justices of peace in the county, which proving ineffecttuall it was humbly hinted and desired that some ministers might be added to the justices as assessours and assistants. For ministers alone to be ingaged in a worke of that nature would bring too greate an odium uppon them. The practice in England is a good precedent. Though in that land they, to whome such a commission is directed, have power of ejection; yet I am perswaded it would be better that in this land they be restrained to information and representation. If the justices have not power to examine uppon oath, none will dare to informe or very few, because the persons peccant are so high in the esteeme of many. As for justices of peace fit to be ingaged in the worke, I humbly offer: the mayor of Corke,[99] the recorder, Mr Bathurst, Mr William Hawkins, Mr Savadge of Bandon, Mr Mordocke of Youghall, Mr Walter Cooper. As for ministers: Dr Worth, Mr Stawell, Mr Child, Mr John Hall of Clonokelty, Mr Powell, Mr Burston, Mr Edward Eyres my father, Mr Wells,[100] I apprehend as fit to be concerned. And because the ministers in sallary were considered by the minist[...] lately assembled at Dublin by authority from your ex[...], I humbly conceive that all other ministers that have the a[...][101] of tyths, or preach on the people's incouragement, are fit to be taken into consideration. It's of greate concernement that some minister be setled at Dublin, who understands the state of the country, and will be active and industrious in improving that

[97] Minister in Ireland, from 1653 he was salaried minister of Christ Church in Cork and became a member of Worth's Cork-based association and a firm ally of Worth; he demonstrated both Episcopalian and Presbyterian leanings.

[98] Word – probably 'to' – apparently omitted.

[99] John Hoddor.

[100] Jonas Stowell, minister at Kinsale; Robert Child, minister at Bandon; John Hall, minister at Clonakilty; Richard Powell, minister at Timoleague; Daniel Burston, minister at Tallow and then at Waterford; Edward Eyres, prebendary of Timoleague; and probably Edmund Wells, who, during the 1650s, was minister first at Kinsale, then at Bandon, and finally at St Finbarr's, Cork.

[101] Edge of the paper damaged with some loss of text, though the two incomplete words are probably 'ministers' and 'excellency'; there is less indication what the missing word or words preceding 'of tyths' might be, though 'allowance', 'allocation', or 'allotment' would be plausible.

his knowledge. The Lord blesse your excellency and incourage your heart, and strengthen your hands in His owne worke. I am, my lord,

Your excellency's most humble, obedient and faithfull servant,

Joseph Eyres

406. From Philip Jones, 7 September 1658, 823, fos 92–93.

May it please your excellency,

We are now under the sad dispensation of the losse of your deare father, our lord and master. He is gonne to heaven imbalmed with prayers and teares, and that of many who had not learned his value till God was calling him from us. I wish they may be soe farre gainers by his death as to know the good he intended them while he lived.

Such crys and teares from good people have not be[102] knowen in any style for any person or thing as for his life. God hath ben pleased to deny it, yet He hath afforded us this mercy (as to David) that he hath this day a sonne upon his throne and that with great unanimity, but he is not without his great difficultys, which I hope the God of his father will carry him through. The perticulers I shall leave to other dispaths and to the bearer, but could not omitt this opportunity of sending this my humble duty to your excellency, and in most intire sincerity to subscribe myselfe, my lord,

Your excellency's most faithfull and humble servant,

Phi Jones

407. From William Malyn, Whitehall, 8 September 1658, 823, fos 94–95.

Letter of condolence and consolation, expounding and expanding at length on the God-given blow of Oliver Cromwell's death and on the terrible loss that the godly people and whole nation as well as his own family had suffered; seeks to comfort himself and Henry Cromwell through biblical exposition and religious exhortation.

408. From Brian Smyth, Dublin, 15 September 1658, 823, fos 96–97.

May it please your excellency,

It was betwene the Newry and Drogada before I received the sad news of his late Highnes' death, whose memory is never to be forgoten by any good man; and indeed, my lord, it surprised and filled my hart with reall sorrow. And oh that myselfe and all God's people may lay it to hart as the sadest breach that ever Hee made upon us. It was alsoe

[102] Apparently a slip for 'been'.

another reall ground of troble to mee it should soe fall out that I mised the first post touching the proclayming the now lord protector, your most noble brother.[103] I am, indeed, soe trobled that I will not see your face without your comands to mee, nor abide here tho it's long sence I saw my dear wife, but begon exept your excelency bee pleased to give mee only two weekes tyme, tho I have your passe for my coming. I have bine carfull as sone as I herd the news to post away letters to our companys to bee more then ordinary wachfull, and to yeald cherefull obedience to comands in my absence, which I am sure of. I beseech your excelency to excuse this troble put upon you in your mornfull condition, in which I will to my utmost helpe you and hartilye bege a santified use of this sad stroke, boeth to you and us.

I am, indeede, youre excellency's obedient servant,

Bry Smyth

409. From Francis Russell, Beaumaris, 16 September 1658, 823, fos 98–99.

My deare lord,

It hath pleaseed God to bring us safe to Beaumorris; our passage by sea was very pleasant. Tis good for us to be thankfull, and towards every thing to have the eyes of our understanding open. The fooleish onely perish by reason of ignorance. My deare lord, I must never forget your love, and I hope your lordship shall find that you have not bestowed your favours on the unthankfull. Let nothing of this world ly to heavey upon your mind and spirit. Whatsoever you find in your hart to doe, that doe. While you are subject to God onely, and right reason in a sober, humble, selfe-denying spirit, you will have power both in heaven and on earth, and the princes, wise or great ownes[104] shall serve you, and be glad so to doe, for wisedome commands and can doe all things. I am very confident that if you have a mind to it you may be in England with your freinds before Christmas. All your commands I shall observe, and give your lordship a constant account how much I am and allways shall be, my lord,

Your lordship' to be commanded,

Franc Russell

My love to your wife.

[103] The news of Oliver Cromwell's death and of Richard Cromwell's succession reached Dublin on 10 September, and the new Protector was immediately proclaimed there (*TSP*, VII, p. 384; Dunlop, pp. 685–686).

[104] Word originally written 'ones' but the author has then added a 'w', probably in error.

410. From Edward Whalley, 18 September 1658, 823, fos 100–101.

May it please your excellencye,

The officers here in towne, as well those of Scotland and those of Ireland under your excellencie's command, as those here in England, this day presented an humble addresse to his Highnesse, which as it did, I doubt not, exceedingly satisfye him, so what he was pleased to say upon the reception of it did abundantly satisfye them. I hope it is a good wellcoming him to his governement and hath a great tendencye of uniting his Highnesse and his officers' heartes together. Your excellencie will very shortly be presented with a coppye of our addresse, with a desire of your and your officers' concurrence in the same. My lord, I returne your excellencie my humble and heartie acknowledgments of your great respects to my sonne. Both hee and I have nothing to repay but our continued faythfulnes, which as I hope, the Lord directing him, he wilbee readye upon all occasions to evidence; so hee likewise that is,

Your excellencie's most obliged servant,

Edw Whalley

411. From Samuel Desborough, Edinburgh, 21 September 1658, 823, fos 102–103.

May it please your excelency,

Allthough the obligations your goodnes hath layd upon me both of an old and later date might justly call for frequent acknowledgments, but my naturall aversment to often writing, especially to persons of such eminency as your lordship, lest I should bee esteemed a complementer (or worse) hath hindred mee from troubling your lordship with my lines. But now having so fitt an opertunity by this gentleman, the bearer hereof, I could not satisfy myselfe without presenting my humble service and tell your lordship that I have a heart as ready to serve you as any, but not being in capacity to doe it, I desire to looke up to heaven that all graces and mercyes may bee comunicated to your lordship sutable to your high imployment, especially spirituall blessings in Christ Jesus. That you may bee a true and living image of your blessed father, whom the Lord hath now sett above those vexatious troubles he was loaded with here below and put into a state where hee shall never know what sin nor sorrow means more, you have cause (great cause) to lament, but not to murmurr; God hath given us cause to mourn and that with a greivous mourning for the loss of such a pretious pious prince, but we must not repine because the soveraigne Lord hath don it, in whose hands is our life and breath, who gives not an acompt of His actions to the sons of men. Therefore wee ought to bee dumb and not open our mouth, but sit silent before Him, wayting for His salvation as in times past, for though men and means fayle, yet our God is the same yesterday, today and for ever. And Hee hath not left us in this sad and darke day without som token for good and given us matter of prayse in the midst of sorrowes for that unanimity which apears amongst the armyes in the three nations, of which to heare and see is to mee a matter of joy and hope that God may yet give His people rest and peace. But however it bee in this world, if wee have assured hopes upon good grounds of rest in another, it's sufitient. The God of all grace and peace bee with your lordshipp evermore. Soe praieth,

Your lordship's most affectionately obliged, faithfull and humble servant,

Sa Disbrowe

412. From Gilbert Mabbott,[105] 21 September 1658, 823, fos 104–105.

May it please your excellency,

By lettre from the king of Sweden to the lord George Fleetwood[106] heer, tis certefied that on the 7th instant the Swede tooke Cronenburgh castle, which comaunds the Sound, and is in possession thereof. They have also 36 sayle of men of warre rideing before the castle to secure the Sound, and the king lies with his forces before the towne of Coppenhagen. From Flannders newes is come that Ypre is taken,[107] and all things being securely settled there, marshall Tureine is marched with his forces towards Newporte. On the 10th instant his Highnes the lord protector was (with all usueall ceremonies and much joye and satisfaction of the people) proclaymed att Edenburgh. Friday last[108] in the afternoone a generall meeting of all the common officers of the army of the three nations (now resident about London)

[105] Parliamentarian writer and reporter, who, via John Rushworth, assistant clerk of the House of Commons, became attached to the secretariat of the parliamentarian army during the 1640s, and who thenceforth acted as the army's London agent and correspondent, writing and dispatching letters and newsletters to army commanders and other contacts in the English provinces and in Scotland. This is the first example of a stream of newsletters of this type addressed to Henry Cromwell in Ireland during the Protectorate of Richard Cromwell. Mabbott probably also contributed to several parliamentary newspapers of the period, and may for a time have edited one or more of them.

[106] Military officer in the employ of Sweden and a baron in the Swedish nobility, he was the elder brother of Charles Fleetwood and cousin of the George Fleetwood (with whom he is sometimes confused) who was a parliamentarian officer and a regicide. This George had fought for Sweden since the late 1620s, and from 1655 he was Swedish envoy extraordinary to London, working to cement ties between Sweden and the Protectorate and to recruit troops for Swedish service.

[107] On 14 September.

[108] 17 September.

was held at Whitehall. The lord Fleetwood first acquainted them with the intent of their meeting, namely, to consider of an addresse to his Highnes, which being read unto them, it was unanimously consented unto and signed by them all, being in number above 220; and on Saturday last betweene 11 and 12 it was presented to his Highnes by the lord Fleetwood attended by all the subscribers. And his Highnes (by a speech to them) was pleased to testefie his gracious approbation thereof; and now tis supposed a parliament will bee suddainely called. Consideration is had by the councell of raiseing more moneys for present supplies. The lord Mountague hath a regiment of horse given him.[109] I humbly subscribe myselfe, my lord,

Your excellencie's most humble and most obedient servant,

G Mabbott

413. From George Monck, 21 September 1658, 823, fos 106–107.

May it please your excellencie,

I received your excellencie' by Mr Robert Wood, for which I returne your excellencie most humble thanks; and these are to acquaint your excellencie that although it hath pleased God to give us a sad stroke in taking away his late Highnesse your father, and my deare friend (for which truly heere are many sad hearts), yet it hath pleased God to give the people heere very chearfull spiritts in the proclayming his now Highnesse to bee his successor. And for the officers and souldiers under my command, I see in them a chearfull inclination of serving his Highnesse. And to testifie their obedience and faithfulnesse to him, they are to meet on Wednesday next to agree uppon the draught of an addresse to his Highnesse, which all commission officers are to signe, which I doubt not but they will very chearfullie doe. And I am very glad to heare that the forces under your excellencie' command are soe united, which is very good newes to us heare. All thinges are heere very quiett and peaceable at present, I praise God for it. I should oftner write unto your excellencie had I any thing worthy the troubling your excellencie, but the condition of this country has been such that it has affoorded very little newes, but when ther shall anie thinge happen that is worth your excellencie' knowledge I shall acquent you with it. I shall desire[110] your excellencie to bee assured that ther is noe man shall bee more ready to serve you then him who is,

Your excellencie' most humble servant,

George Monck

[109] The New Model horse regiment previously commanded successively by Thomas Sheffield, Thomas Harrison, and Stephen Winthrop, the last of whom had died in the spring of 1658.

[110] Word repeated in error.

414. From Vincent Gookin, 27 September 1658, 823, fos 108–109.

Letter of request, on behalf of his kinswoman, sister of Edmund Ludlow,[111] *who, on Gookin's advice, had invested a legacy from an uncle buying a farm in Ireland, which had failed, and had then used what money remained to buy up a debenture from captain Campbell*[112] *and so gain 350 acres of land around Drogheda, an area set aside for settling military claims; recounts that even though her ownership was confirmed by the Irish exchequer, those lands were now claimed by Sir Anthony Morgan, who had an order from Henry Cromwell and the Irish council for their possession; sets out long and detailed arguments in support of his kinswoman's claim, both as the purchaser of Campbell's debenture and in her own right as a pious and loyal woman, of a good family, and with a family to support, who had acted in good faith throughout but was now wholly reliant on these lands; finally, argues that Morgan, who had no debts or children to support and who had already been handsomely rewarded, might be allocated land in County Cork, which could be deemed to fall within the areas set aside for settling military arrears, or alternatively that, if he should be confirmed in possession of the land around Drogheda, then Gookin's kinswoman should receive land in County Cork instead.*

415. From John Honner, Boffin,[113] 27 September 1658, 823, fos 110–111.

My lord,

Here hath been one Mr Kitt who brought your excellency's order to doe him all the lawfull favour I could in trieing for the fishing in those partes, which to the utmoste of my power I did my best, and did summone in all the countrey and islanders that knew what belonged

[111] Parliamentarian officer and politician and a regicide, he campaigned around his native Wiltshire during the civil war, from 1644 commanding his own horse regiment. Elected to parliament in 1646, he became prominent in the later 1640s in parliamentary and army politics, his radical political and religious views leading him to support Pride's Purge and the regicide. In 1650, he was appointed both a parliamentary commissioner for the civil government of Ireland and second-in-command to Ireton as lieutenant-general of the horse. Although not given overall military command on Ireton's death in November 1651, he effectively led the mopping-up operation of 1651–1652 before Ireton's successor, Fleetwood, crossed to Ireland. His republican principles led him to oppose the Protectorate and, in 1654, he resigned as commissioner for the civil government, although he sought to retain his military position. Despite orders to the contrary, he crossed back to England in the autumn of 1655, was arrested and imprisoned and forced to relinquish his command after an interview with the Protector. He spent the remainder of Oliver Cromwell's Protectorate in uneasy semi-retirement in Essex, though he returned to the fray in Richard Cromwell's Protectorate parliament, prominent in the republican opposition to the tottering Protectoral regime.

[112] John Campbell, parliamentarian officer, served in Ireland during the 1650s as a captain, initially in Sir Charles Coote's horse regiment and then in Henry Ingoldsby's dragoon regiment.

[113] Inishbofin.

to fishing. And he tooke his choice of some two and twenty men with their botes for twelve dayes and went away and did not give them any reasonable satisfaction for their paines. And I was desired by my lord president[114] and collonel Sadler to let him have the state's friggat for some small time, which I did with all her men according to his desire, and she was waiteing on him some one and twenty dayes for which he left but eighteen shillings to the great hindranc of the commonwealth in not paying the men for the time they were in his service. And I did desire him and all those that did belong to him, if there was anything that I could doe for them, I should be ready at all times.

And now I am informed from Gallway that he did intend to complaine of me for not haveing civell respects when he was in Boffin, which I wonder at, for I thanck God as yet I never was so uncivell to any in all my goverments and proceedings, both in England and Ireland, as to have any complaint, and should be very lothe now to have anything that is unjust against me. So I doe crave your excellency's leave not to beleive any ill reporte of me that may arise by Mr Kitt or any other untell you doe hear further from your servant, which will be as soon as the masons give over their worke in the forte, which will not be long and then I doe intend, with your excellency's leave, to see you at Dublin. These partes are in as quiet a posture as any partes in the three nations, and in a thriveing condition, and doe pay a good contribution. And my desire is that I and my souldiers may have the islands of Boffin and Clare for this year as all other men doe in these partes, paying for them as they were canted[115] for the last year. I am very sorry for my olde friend's death, my Lord Protector. But the Lord be thancked for so hopefull a vine from him, which I and my companey afferme with what might God doth inable us. Which is all but to desire to remaine,

Your excellency's faithfull servant,

John Honner

416. From Simon Rudgeley, London, 27 September 1658, 823, fos 112–113.

Letter of thanks for past favours and of courtesy, apologizing for his long silence, dismissing rumours of his death, and offering his services to Henry Cromwell.

[114] Sir Charles Coote.

[115] To cant: to sell by auction.

417. From Daniel Abbott, Nenagh, County Tipperary, 28 September 1658, 823, fos 114–115.

Letter of condolence and consolation on the death of Oliver Cromwell, expressing great faith in the sons he had left; reports that he was sending to Gorges an address of loyalty to the new Protector cheerfully signed by all the commissioned officers of his regiment.

418. From Gilbert Mabbott, 28 September 1658, 823, fos 116–117.

May it please your excellency,

The commissioners of the militia of London and officers of the trayned bands and the officers and souldiers of the garrison at Kingston upon Hull have presented the like addresses to his Highnes as was lately presented to him by the officers of the army heer; and severall regiments of the army are preparing to doe the like. Commissions are issued out to the lords commissioners of the great seale, to all the judges and to the receivers and auditors of the publique revenue. Friday last[116] the commissions of the generall and councell in Scotland were renewed. The councell likewise passed a declaration for a day of publique humiliation to bee observed on the 13th of October next throughout England and Wales for the much deplored loss of your renowned father and to seeke the Lord for a blessing upon his Highnes and that the Lord will bee pleased to remove from us the late epidemicall sicknes. This day the commissions to the judges in Ireland were renewed. Instructions are given for reneweing the commissions to the councell of Ireland and to your excellency by the tytle of lord lieutenant of Ireland.[117] Severall orders are passed to putt a stopp upon all the treasuries from payment of any moneys, but onely to defray the charges of his late Highnes' funerall, the glorious solemnity whereof will bee much after the manner of the late king James's. I humbly subscribe myselfe, my lord,

Your excellencie's most humble and most obedient servant,
Gilb Mabbott

[116] 24 September.

[117] Mabbott has written Henry Cromwell's new title in large letters, so the words stand out from the page. At the beginning of November, Henry Cromwell himself wrote that, upon receiving the formal documentation from the Protector, 'I had great strivings within my breast, before I could prevail with myself to accept and open the commission' (*TSP*, VII, p. 492).

419. From Abel Warren,[118] Lodge, 30 September 1658, 823, fos 118–119.

Letter of request that, in light of a favour recently granted to colonel Redman,[119] he be promoted to the rank of major, supporting his claim by pointing to his sixteen-year military record under the late Protector, as well as to his desire to serve Henry Cromwell.

420. From Edward Wale, [early October] 1658, 823, fos 134–135.

May it please your excellency,

Upon the receipt of your lordship's declaration for the setting apart Thursday the 14th of this instant October as a day of solemne humiliation throughout this land, I saw great cause of comfort and reviving after our sad and heavy losse of his Highnesse of blessed memory. For though for the sinnes of all degrees and ranks of men among us this great affliction is come upon us, which cannot but sorely wound the hearts of all in this and the neighbour nations which truely feare the Lord, yet when we see the care of religion surviving in his successours it cannot but be a cheering cordiall to all that love the trueth and pray for the happy progresse of a gospell reformation, because this care and zeale for religion is of God, and the best and most assuring evidence that still He beares a favourable respect to our nation and that He will not take His peace from this people. And indeed without this care for religion and encouraging of a gospell ministery here, this land is likely in the next age (which God prevent) to degenerate into meere brutishnesse and barbarisme. But having seene your excellencye's fervent desire to enkindle and preserve the life of religion and godlynesse in this nation, I thought it my duty to give your lordship account of what is done here.

Having preached for some time in this place, not altogether without fruite, I thought it my duty to draw such Christians as were knowing and blameless to pertake in the Lord's supper and other ordinances of Christ, as well as in hearing the word. This practise I continued for some yeeres, but seeing the slacknesse of the people to seeke communion with us (some thinking the way we were in to be too strict, others too loose, and others mistaking my intentions and purposes), I

[118] Parliamentarian officer, he first shows up in the military record in the late 1640s as a cornet in Edward Whalley's New Model horse regiment and by 1650 was a captain in Oliver Cromwell's horse regiment in Ireland. He may also be the Warren who was earmarked as major of a new foot regiment to be raised for service in Ireland in 1650–1651, but the plans were abandoned.

[119] Daniel Redman, parliamentarian officer, the long-serving major of the late Protector's horse regiment in Ireland, had recently been given command of the horse regiment in Ireland formerly commanded by the late John Reynolds.

have seene it my duty to exhort them to communion, and to presse their baptisme as an ingagement upon them to seeke after the sealing ordinances. And I have declared to them that none shall be refused that shall be found qualifyed according to what is written in this paper, which here I send enclosed to your excellency.[120] For as I would not shut out any of the least of Christ's members from their just priviledges, soe I would not incourage any loose or profane person to take what is none of his, to the dishonour of Christ and his owne hurt. I know that aswell overmuch strictnesse, which disheartenеth the weake, as a loose and dead formality, which offendeth the strong, are displeasing to Jesus Christ. I have also set upon the worke of catechizing publiquely on the weekeday, and the people come and bring their children in some competent number. But fearing to be too troublesome to your lordship, I humbly crave pardon for this boldnesse and take my leave, not ceasing to pray for his present Highnesse's and your excellencye's happy goverment, and that the humiliation and reformation intended may be soe directed and assisted from heaven that it may finde acceptance there. I continue,

Your excellencye's humble servant,
Edward Wale

421. The paper of necessary qualifications, [enclosed in letter no. 420], 823, fos 136–137.

After my exhorting the people to seeke after the sealing ordinances, I have told them that none should be refused.

1. That can and will professe these things as in the presence of God, viz:

   That his heart is drawne off from sin and the creature to seeke his rest and satisfaction in Christ alone.
   And that he loves God's name, His word, His ordinances, His wayes, His people, and those most that are most holy and strict in their lives.
   And that he unfeignedly desireth to be under the watchfull care of God's ministers and people, and to be exhorted by them and helped on in godlynesse.

2. In whom these things are really found, viz:

   That he hath a competent knowledge.
   And that he is a frequenter of religious exercises in publique and private.

[120] No. 421.

And that he hath set up the worship of God in his family.
And that he instructs his children himselfe, and brings them to be catechised, if he hath any.
And that he is a strict observer of the Lord's day.
And that he is free from (at least grosse) errour in his judgment, and from scandall in his life.
And that he submitts himselfe to Christian discipline.
And that he will renew his covenant with God in the presence of His people.

422. From Francis Russell, Whitehall, 5 October 1658, 823, fos 122–123.

My deare lord,

Allthough I have not bin long in this towne and place, yet I have not bin wanting to serve you and your desires. It was but the last night that I came from Chippenham, haveing bin very ill since I left Ireland. The last night I waited on your brother, his Highnes, and this day on my lord Fleetwood. I have bin very free and plaine with them both about your comeing for England.[121] The perticulers of our discourse twill be needlesse to mention, and indeed time now will not give me leave. Your lordship well knows my way and manner of plainenes of speech, and truely I have not bin wanting to speake my mind as I ought to doe. They have had both of them my thoughts concerning you. I am ill at hideing myselfe when I think there is a just occation to pull of all coverings. His Highnes, as I suppose you will understand by others if not from himselfe, is very desireous to see you here. He told me he was very sensible of your love towards himselfe and that the sooner you came into England it would be the better. My lord Fleetwood did expresse a most reall love and respect that he had for you and sayed that he thought it of much advantage to affaires as they now stand that you tow might meet and understand each other, and that if any jealousys should ly whispering and swelling betwixt you, they might be taken away by love and plaine dealeing with each other. He hath promised me to move you[122] comeing over to some of the counsell and

[121] Henry Cromwell was angling for permission to return to England at this time, for either a brief visit or a more extended stay, partly on grounds of ill health, partly so that he could see and confer with his brother. His return came to be opposed by some inside and outside the council and the army, particularly those who had reservations about Richard Cromwell's government and did not wish to see him strengthened by his brother's presence, and those who did not want Henry Cromwell to gain influence or high position in the army in England (*TSP*, VII, pp. 423, 438, 453–454, 454–455, 463, 490, 492, 493–494, 497, 510, 528–529).

[122] Apparently a slip for 'your'.

I suppose twill be to those who are for your tarrying in Ireland. If I can guesse at things, generall Disbrow is the person most against your comeing over; I will say no more. Truely, my lord, if you will take my counsell I should advise you to stand to your desires of seeing England and to signifie the same to his Highnes and your brother Fleetwood by wrighting unto them. And pray take this as my thoughts (and I think I doe well understand what I say) if you have a mind for England resolve it stoutly and I am confident nobody will dare to hinder your comeing. Let them talke and rant never so high, tis time for you to live above all those things and not to be concerned what the world either sayed or thinks. You have here many good freinds and considerable ones, and that would be glad to see you. By the next post I hope to give your lordship a better and more full account of things here. Let the feare and love of God guide your mind and spirit, truely I have no better counsell for you. The Lord blesse you and all yours. My love to your wife. I must allways be, my lord,

Your lordship's faithfully to serve you,

Franc Russell

If your lordship comes not over to us suddenly I have thoughts of leaveing both court and citty. I will be a lord[123] no longer but a country man; follow the plough and beg your leave that Francis[124] may come over to follow my busynes here.

I doe beg two or three in your next letter to my lord Fleetwood in the behalfe of my sonne Jack.[125]

423. From William Lockhart, Dunkirk, 5/15 October 1658, 823, fos 126–127.

Letter of condolence and consolation on the death of Oliver Cromwell, though noting that the future already looked brighter; says he was enclosing a copy of the address of loyalty to the new Protector sent from Dunkirk; offers his services to Henry Cromwell.

[123] He was a member of the nominated second chamber of parliament.

[124] Following William Russell's death sometime during the winter or spring of 1658, Francis had become the writer's eldest surviving son and heir.

[125] John Russell, probably the third son of Sir Francis Russell, but, following the deaths of his brothers William and Francis (who died in 1659), he became the eldest surviving son and eventually succeeded his father to the baronetcy in 1664, a year after he had married Oliver Cromwell's daughter, Frances, widow of Robert Rich.

424. From Charles Whalley, 6 October 1658, 823, fos 124–125.

Letter of request, seeking Henry Cromwell's help in a long and expensive legal case brought against him by Lord Fitzwilliam,[126] *being heard at the chancery in London; recounts how, many years ago, before the Irish rebellion and at the request of colonel William Edwards,*[127] *he had become joint surety with Edwards for payments due on some Irish land held by Sir Edward and John Trevor, father and son, both now dead; in fact, no rent was paid for many years, since the land was effectively worthless during the rebellion, but nonetheless he was now being pursued at law by Fitzwilliam for payment; asks Henry Cromwell to mediate.*

425. From Bryan Smyth, 15 October 1658, 823, fos 128–129.

Letter of request and recommendation, urging Henry Cromwell to employ as a messenger Timothy Avery, a godly but indebted young man who had a family to support, and in some other minor office Mr Renes of Derry, an honest man with a wife and many small children to support, who had been reduced by the hand of the Lord from a comfortable to a straitened condition.

426. From Hugh Peters, 26 October 1658, 823, fos 130–131.

My lord,

Upon the death of your father I writ and know not whither my dispicable lines touched your lorde. And yet such hath bin my constancy to your lordshipp that fawning nor frowning have taken place with mee to make me fearfull or careles in reference to yourselfe or your affayres; but cannot bee a courtier (as they say). You had long since my thoughts in writing, nor am I doubtfull of the good effect they tooke, and I wish the Lord would please to keepe you every way to His praise in Christ.

Your lordshipp's worke is your owne salvation for ever, and the serving the Lord's interest whilst you are here. Your last synod there of ministers hath not a little affected and afflicted us here.[128] Doubtles the world is one thing and the church another. If this distinction bee slighted, farewell God and goodnes. I am not so uncivill to aske an

[126] Probably William, second Baron Fitzwilliam of Lifford in the Irish peerage, who sat as MP for Peterborough in the Long Parliament until excluded at Pride's Purge. He died in February 1659.

[127] Perhaps the parliamentarian officer of that name who came to Ireland in 1647 as an officer in Anthony Hungerford's foot regiment and who, during the 1650s, served on several commissions relating to the distribution of land in Ireland.

[128] As a religious radical and a strong critic of tithes, Peters took a dim view both of the generally conservative tone struck at the Dublin convention of ministers held in the spring of 1658 and of the proposals that Worth carried to the Protector in the summer.

account of your Highnes, alas what am I? But if I love you, then I must doe. Flatterers never loved you; frends doe that are playne.

I wish you never heare unam partim[129] only: see who are about you, noscitur e socio[130] etc, servants and companions till any new constitution. I gave you a hynt of Dr Worth. Your father dyed as he lived, an Independant. Presbytery and Independancy are all the consistency in religion. I am your lordshipp's if anything.

HP

I feare your horrid excise will shake your country.

427. From Thomas Adams,[131] Kilkenny, 30 October 1658, 823, fos 132–133.

Letter of request, praising Henry Cromwell's government in Ireland and seeking employment in his and the Lord's service.

428. From Francis Russell, Whitehall, 1 November 1658, 823, fo. 138.

My deare lord,

For my love and desires to be faithfull unto you, I find I have got not onely scratches but wounds, but being they were honorably got in your service I shall looke upon them as onely markes of honor. I am goeing home to dresse them, not knowing when I shall returne hither againe unlesse it be to meet and wait upon your lordship, for I cannot but hope but that some of[132] endeavours will worke a good effect in time. Indeed, I have great need to retyre myselfe, haveing had some unpleasant houres here. Hir Highnes, your mother, is much troubled that she is not likely to see you so soone as she thought for, and commanded me to wright so much to your lordship. I find she loves you exceedingly and told me that she would speake to his Highnes againe about your comeing over. I find it not wisedome for me to speake freely about your desires, but onely to my lord Fleetwood, who I know was ignorant of the late stop made to your seeing England, of which you will have an account from himselfe, who I am confident loves and values you exceedingly, as I found in a large discourse with him about you, and as we were parting sayed (in these words) my lord Henry must come. I have had great experyence of men since I last saw you, and I doe beleeve you have had no lesse, and will have

[129] This Latin phrase could be translated as 'one part' or 'one side'.

[130] This Latin phrase could be translated as 'one is known by the company one keeps'.

[131] Possibly the Thomas Adams of Kilkenny, referred to as a major, who, in 1654, was appointed a commissioner for setting land for disbanded soldiers in County Kilkenny.

[132] Word – perhaps 'my' – apparently omitted.

more dayly. By wisedome, patience, love and the feare of God, I hope a good understanding will be giveen you, that you may be able to discerne things that truely differ. Will Perepoint hath bin twise of late at my lodgeings. He is most faithfully your freind. In our discourse togather I did as to some things and perticulers open his eyes. He did professe to me that the onely reason he had for your not comeing as yet was least the army should prove unquiet. Wherein I told him freely that I did beleeve he was mistakeen, so that he seemeed to be satisfied. Some of your freinds here I have (if I mistake not) found to eb and flow as to your comeing. Amicus certas in re incerta cernitur.[133] My lord Claypoole told me the last Sunday that he did beleeve you would be sent for ere long. He mentioned not the time, neither was I curyous to know. Tis neere a fortnight (as I take it) since I had any discourse with his Highnes about you, for himselfe not offering it (as he had done formerly) I tooke it to be wisedome to forbare.

My deare lord, in one of my late letters to you I told you that I thought God in His love, time and goodwill would satisfie your desires before men, so that you should be beholding to Him onely. While you looke upwards you shall be safe, but if downewards you will find men to be but as they are, neither so freindly, loveing and faithfull as our good God and Father is, whose onely nature is love and pitty, full of kindnes, gentle and easy to be entreated; therefore delight yourselfe onely in Him, consult with Him dayly and hourely. Oh that you might be found such a one as I have boasted of you to be: that is, feareing the Lord, faithfull to what you have received from Him, walkeing honestly accord[134] to your light and knowledge, noble, civill, courteous, without designe or ambition as to earthly, worldly things. My deare lord, if the crosse be at present offered you as your portion, kisse it, tis the onely way to life and resurrection and the same path that your captaine, the Lord Jesus, is gone before you. Indeed, now I must love and honor you because I see your wisedome, love and patience tryed, and I hope in this tryall I shall never deny you or say I knew you not. Since I begunne this letter, I have met with some discouragements as to my hopes of your comeing; from the doctor[135] you will receive them, therefore I will be silent. While you suffer I shall bare you company, and when you rejoyce I shall be glad. My lord, if you can trust my love and faithfullnes, let it be so likewise betweene my lord Fleetwood and yourselfe. Be not to wise but trust a foole once, considering you will find in time that the wise will leave you. My experyence of men is

[133] This Latin phrase could be translated as 'a true friend shows himself in uncertain times' or 'things' or, more colloquially, as 'a friend in need is a friend indeed'.

[134] This word has been split at the line end and the writer has evidently forgotten to add the 'ing' at the start of the next line.

[135] Probably William Petty.

as great as yours and being and[136] old beaten soldyer I can say so. My love[137] your wife. I hope your love, wisedome and strenght will support hir as the weakeer vessell. If your lordship please, I beg againe that Francis may come for England, not that[138] intend in the least he should desert you or your service, but onely that in my retreat and retyrement he might follow my busynes, he being my eldest sonne and without whose presence here I shall not be able to doe some kind of busynes, my estate being entaileed upon him. I beg your letters as your leisure will give leave, and that they may be inclosed in my lord Fleetwood's packet or Doctor Petty's, captain John[139] being turneed country-man, where I must follow him. The Lord blesse you and all yours. I doubt our letters sometimes miscarry, because I doe so seldome heare from you, and that haveing written unto Doctor Gorge I never had any answer. I am and allways must be, my deare lord,

Yours in true love and all faithfullnes,

Franc Russell

Since I finished this letter I am told tis likely you will be sent for.

Trust not to much your wise freinds, for they, like swallows when your sommer's done, will fly and seeke some warmeer sun.

Experto credo Francisco.[140]

429. From Timothy Taylor, Kilroot, County Antrim, 1 November 1658, 823, fos 139–140.

Letter of request, pointing out that his salary as a minister was in arrears, because he had received just £25 since 25 March and so was owed a quarter and a half quarter's salary, but also requesting that the quarter's salary due on 25 December be paid in advance; reports that it was an expensive time for him, because his wife had fallen from a horse over the summer and been housebound as a result and even now could only get about on crutches.

430. From Gilbert Mabbott, 2 November 1658, 823, fos 141–142.

May it please your excellency,

Wee have yet noe certeine news of the surrender of Coppenhagen, but undoubtedly expect to heare of it every day, the greate probability

[136] Apparently a slip for 'an'.

[137] Word – perhaps 'to' – apparently omitted.

[138] Word – perhaps 'I' – apparently omitted.

[139] John Russell, a parliamentarian officer whose military career is thinly recorded but who reputedly fought at Marston Moor in 1644, was one of Sir Francis Russell's younger brothers.

[140] This Latin phrase could be translated as 'I believe the experienced Francis'.

thereof being confirmed by very many. The Dutch embassador is preparing to departe. Sir George Aiscue is dispatcht (with 2 vessells for convoy) to joyne with the Swede. About 200 English and Scotts comeing lately from Bulloigne were all (except 2 or 3 officers, who escaped on horsebacke) slayne and taken by the enemy neere Mardyke. Friday last[141] the officers mett at Jamese's, spent the whole day in prayer and appointed to meete there againe on Friday next, and their meeting then to continue but 3 houres. Judge Hales[142] refuseth to sitt till hee bee satisfied in one pointe of the judges' oath, and excused from sitting upon life and death. The councell have ordered a monthe's pay extraordinary to the regiments of his Highnes, the lord Falconberge and Sir Phillip Twisleton,[143] who are to marche to Scotland. A comittee is appointed to consider of a way to prevent indicteing of ministers for not administering the sacrament. Captain Hart[144] is appointed by advice of the councell to bee major to the lord Mountague's regiment. Yesterday his Highnes had debate with certaine feild officers about raiseing of moneys to pay parte of the souldiers' arreares. The high court of justice mett, but suspended their sitting till further empowered by new commission. The Portugall's army have lately received a greate defeate. The duke of Curland refuseing to lend the Swede the like somme as hee lately lent to his brother in lawe (the duke of Brandenburgh), major generall Douglas thereupon marcht into his dukedome, tooke his person prisoner and therewith secured £200,000. I humbly subscribe myselfe, my lord,

Your excellencie's most humble and most obedient servant,

Gilb Mabbott

[141] 29 October.

[142] Matthew Hale/Hales, judge and legal writer, remained in London during the civil war and worked with the parliamentarian regimes of the period, though it is noticeable that he was frequently assigned to defend prominent royalists in state trials. In 1652, he was a member of a commission appointed by the Rump to consider legal reform and he chaired the opening two sessions. In 1654, he accepted office as a judge in the court of common pleas and was elected to the first and third Protectorate parliaments, but he was not a committed Cromwellian and, in 1658–1659, prevaricated about continuing to serve the Protectorate.

[143] Parliamentarian officer, by the mid-1640s he was an officer in Edward Rossiter's New Model horse regiment and in 1647 he replaced Rossiter as its colonel. He and his regiment were frequently in Scotland, campaigning there in the autumn of 1648, under Oliver Cromwell in 1650–1651, and again in 1652–1654. He seems to have remained in England in the later 1650s, even though his regiment returned to Scotland once more in the autumn of 1658.

[144] Theophilus Hart, parliamentarian officer and a long-serving captain in Twisleton's regiment, became major in Montague's New Model horse regiment.

431. From Jeremy Benton,[145] Nantwich, 3 November 1658, 823, fos 143–144.

Right honnorable,

No sinister respects, no expectation of better preferment, no dissatisfaction with your governement have mooved mee to leave Ireland, and therefore I am in hope thereby to gayne your pardon for my not acquaynting you with it. I desire of you, my lord, not to bee displeased with mee, for many urgent reasons prevayled with mee thereunto, of which I have given an account in a letter to Dr Gorges, whom I desyred to acquaynt your lordship therwith. I humbly thanke your lordship and council for granting an order for my sallary due on midsummer day last, for Trim was supplyed by myselfe and at my charge til that time; and I most earnestly implore your favour, that you would bee pleased to give life to it, and to make it effectual, that so my wife and family may bee no longer detayned (whiles looking after it) to my great prejudice, if not ruine. My lord, your favour and respect to the ministery is so wel knowne that I thinke you cannot want supplyes, and I perceive ministers are comming over frequently and that Trim is provided for. I beseech you, let not mee bee the first you deale hardly with; had I but the opportunity of one halfe houre's speech with your honour, I question not but I should satisfy you fully as to the causes of my stay in England. That litle estate I have is in other men's hands, and I could find no freinds in my absence that would looke after it carefully, and I am necessitated therefore to mynd it myselfe, else must loose it. And I could not tel what to doe for a dwelling in Trim. I payd a great rent for an house there, that wee feared would fal on our head in every great storme, and I had litle incouragement since major Stanly left the place. And I know not what to doe about the sacrament there, beeing divisions amongst them. This is the great bone of contention everywhere almost. Besydes a brother and sister of myne are dead lately, and left many litle children and nothing to manteyne them and if I take not care of them they may perish. The getting of the present sallary is one of the greatest busynesses that deteynes my wife in Dublin; I doe therefore once more begge of you that you would be pleased to send some special order to the treasurers that so this remora[146] may be taken away that hinders her comming over to mee. May the Lord of heaven make you stil instrumental more and more for the good of His church and blesse you and yours with al

[145] Salaried minister at Trim by 1656, he may be the Jeremy Benton who was minister at parishes in Surrey and Essex in the early 1650s.

[146] Remora: a sucking fish once believed to slow or stop ships, and hence more generally a delay or hindrance.

temporal and eternal blessings, is and shalbe the dayly prayer of your honour's

Most humble servant,

Jeremy Benton

432. From Thomas Gorges,[147] London, 9 November 1658, 823, fos 145–146.

May it please your excellency,

Although I well know your more weighty affayres cannot easily admitt of such diversions and trouble as my lines offer you, yet the meanest of tributes proceedinge from gratitude hath ever bin by the highest of princes accepted. I am therefor to pay your excellency as much duty as your high obligations layd on me and my neer relations bindes me unto, but (my lord) I know my own incapacitye streightns me and gives me only an heart full of devotion to serve your person and interest. I shall not dare to offer your excellency any of our occurances; I sit at distance from the arcana imperii[148] and may err in the information. Only this I presume to assure your excellency, that every day new manefestation of loyaltye, affection and service is espoused unto his Highness, whose eminencye nothinge but an hand from heaven can ecclipse. He gayns exceedingly on the sober party, which gives a checque to specious pretences or designs of some persons who as yet have noe apparent footinge.[149] All interists naturally will struggle for breath, but our great rejoycings are in that happy union Ireland injoys under your excellencye's most prudent conduct, which hath soe powerfull an influence here that mallice itself (although full of detraction) can finde noe just cause of quarrell. I humbly present your excellency a paper inclosed in this packet, which carryes with it

[147] Parliamentarian politician, brother of Henry Cromwell's secretary, Dr Robert Gorges, he held a number of minor financial offices during the Protectorate and represented Taunton in all three Protectorate parliaments.

[148] This Latin phrase could be translated as 'the hidden things of the ruler' or 'government' or 'the mysteries of state'.

[149] Gorges is probably alluding to questions about Richard Cromwell's power and position, which began to circulate, especially in military circles, within weeks of his succession. By the beginning of October, many junior and some senior officers were questioning his right to command the army and were suggesting or petitioning that a military figure, perhaps Fleetwood, should be appointed commander-in-chief. Regular meetings of the officers were held during the autumn, some chaired by Fleetwood, who was ostensibly steering a middle course, keen to maintain his dominant military position while also professing loyalty and obedience to the Protector, some attended and addressed by Richard himself, who spoke at meetings on 18 October and 19 November to stress his constitutional and God-given power as commander-in-chief, while pledging to work for the army and with Fleetwood as lieutenant-general of the army under him.

somwhat of high demands, yet good use may be made of such persons, and if your excellency shall judge any part of it worth the consideration and command my service in it, I shall welcome that opportunity that may any ways declare me,

Your excellencye's most humble servant,

Tho Gorges

433. From Gilbert Mabbott, 9 November 1658, 823, fos 147–148.

May it please your excellencie,

The councell have ordered a draught of an establishment for Dunkirke to bee prepared. Six sergeants of the six regiments to waite upon and assist the receivors of the moneys upon new buildings, which is propounded to bee towards satisfaction of the souldiers' arreares. The duke of Bucks[150] (being sicke) hath liberty to staye at Yorke House 20 daies longer. The officers mett againe Friday last[151] at Jamese's and (about 3 houres) prayed and expounded severall places of scripture and appointed to meete againe Friday next for the same purpose. From Denmarke tis certefied that the Swedes were possest of the island of Amacke, the cheifest support for supply of provicions to the besieged in Coppenhagen, but the enemy upon a salley regained it and had taken the person of the king of Sweden prisoner had not halfe an old boate (which partely supported his body) and his dextrous swimming prevented it. The Dutch ambassador (waveing his owne private affaires) is not yet gone, nor goeing; but Sir George Aiscue tooke shipping on Friday last for Denmarke. The funeralls of his late Highnes (intended to have beene solemnized on this day) are putt of till further order. The gentlemen of the long robe and the lord president,[152] lord chamberlaine[153] and members of the house of lords[154] are to bee in close mourning gownes. Wee heare nothing of Coppenhagen, onely the merchants say that the Swedes are 32 sayle strong to fight the Dutch and therefore they desire a treaty with the

[150] George Villiers, second Duke of Buckingham, supported the royalist cause in the late 1640s and early 1650s and then spent several years abroad, but, by the mid-1650s, he may have been attempting to build bridges with the Protectoral regime and was not initially arrested on his return to England in 1657. However, his marriage later that year to the only child of Sir Thomas Fairfax, himself now suspected of royalist learnings, greatly alarmed the Protectoral regime, and Buckingham was arrested and held either in the Tower or, for the benefit of his health, in more comfortable house arrest in London until being released in February 1659 and allowed to return to the Fairfax estate in Yorkshire.

[151] 5 November.

[152] President of the council, Henry Lawrence.

[153] Sir Gilbert Pickering.

[154] That is, the new, nominated, second parliamentary chamber, established under the revised constitution of 1657, which carefully avoided using the title 'House of Lords'.

Swedes for an accomodation. His Highnes gives greate satisfaction in his answeares to those persons who make daily addresses to him from the severall counties and corporations in England and hath promised to pay of all the arrears of the foote souldiers, which makes them not a little joyfull in his favour. I humbly subscribe myselfe, my lord,

Your excellencie's most humble and most obedient servant,

Gilb Mabbott

434. From William Sedgwick,[155] Fulham, 9 November 1658, 823, fos 149–150.

Letter of thanks for giving employment to his unnamed kinsman, who had exhausted his trade and estate in England, and who had been recommended to Henry Cromwell by Sir Francis Russell; also expresses his joy in hearing of Henry Cromwell's godly government of Ireland and urges him to continue to work with and for the Lord.

435. From Methuselah Turner, London, 9 November 1658, 823, fos 151–152.

May it please your excellencye,

About July, August and September 1656 I became an humble suplicant unto your excellencye in the name of the committee for claymes, prayeing that the lands assigned to them for their service might bee sett out, possession given, the grant passed and the rent ascerted according to his Highness' letter. It seemed good unto your lordship then to order the possession only of 1,500 acres and to respite the remainder, as also passing the grant untill his Highness should signifye his farther pleasure therein. Whereupon it pleased his Highness, by his letter dated December 4 following,[156] to order:

That the said whole 3,000 acres survayed by your excellencye's direction and exprest in the inclosed survay, which came in your letter, bee sett out to the concerned.

That possession bee deliverred them or their assignes of the whole.

That the rent reserved bee foure pence per acre.

That a grant bee passed of the premises for the terme of 99 yeares.

[155] Minister, an opponent of Charles I's religious policies, he supported the parliamentarian cause and, during the early 1640s, he preached several times before parliament and also had short spells as a military chaplain; from 1645 to 1649 he was minister at Ely cathedral. However, his subsequent criticism of the army and of the regicide led some to suspect him of royalism, just as his intense spirituality and doom-laden prophecies led many to question his sanity, and he adopted a less prominent role during the 1650s.

[156] Dunlop, p. 646.

Pursuant wherto it pleased your excellencye about the end of July last to signe the contract and grant a warrant for the particuler in order to its passing the great seale.

Notwithstanding all which, it is signifyed that an obstruction hath very lately happened wherby the concerned are like to bee deprived of that proportion of lands lyeing neare unto Kilmallock, being part of the 3,000 acres exprest in the survey sent unto and confirmed by his Highness in his said last letter.

Now soe it is may it please your excellencye:

That through the hope I had of the good issue heereof, I have in purchase of my other partners' proportions expended the very all of my estate, soe that the deteynment of this proportion may prove a sadd dammage to mee and to mee only.

That by reason of publique service relateing to the hospitalls of the Savoy and Ely House,[157] I am incapacitated at this tyme to attend in person on this matter.

That ther is none unto whom I can with that assurance fly for succour as unto your excellencye, being encouraged therto by my former experience of the many favours you have been pleased to allow mee. Wherfore I doe most humbly supplicate your excellencye, even for the love of justice, that you would bee pleased to releive mee heerin by interposeing between mee and this endeavored prejudice, verilly hopeing and beleiving it will never bee a greife of heart to you that you have soe done. In hummillity craveing pardon for this great presumption I remayne,

Your excellencye's most humbly and faithfully to serve,

Mathuselah Turner

436. From Francis Russell, Whitehall, 16 November 1658, 823, fos 153–154.

My deare lord,

The hopes and desires I had of seeing your lordship as yet in England being in my opinion at an end, I am goeing home to Chippenham. My lord Claypoole tells me that he is to wait on your lordship, and I suppose will bring you the reasons both by letter from his Highnes and word of mouth why tis not convenyent for you to leave Ireland at this time. My lord, haveing now thoughts to retyre and withdraw hence to a private retyreed life, tis my request to your lordship that Francis may come over to me this winter to follow my little busynes,

[157] Savoy House, or simply The Savoy, on the south side of the Strand, a medieval palace largely rebuilt in the early sixteenth century; and Ely House in Holborn, a medieval ecclesiastical hostel of the bishop of Ely, largely rebuilt in the later sixteenth century. Both served at this time as military hospitals for sick and wounded parliamentary troops.

and, if you shall so please, I shall send Jack over about the spring to your service in Ireland, finding it difficult to get him into the army here, allthough I have tryed what I could doe therein with as much modesty and wisedome as I could. My lord, I think and am confident you know me well to honor and serve you allways in my poore sphere. None shall be more faithfull. When your occations will give you leave, I shall be glad sometimes to receive a letter from you. If you wright at any time to me be pleaseed to put your letters into my lord Fleetwood's packet or Doctor Petty's because my brother Jack is leaveing Whitehall and intendes to turne country-man with me. I shall as often as I can trouble you with my letters. Tis some tryall to my spirit that I have so little hopes left of seeing you in England, but the will of God I desire to rest in and to submit to His pleasure. He onely knowes what is best for us all. We are poore, ignorant, simple creatures. The Lord in His love and mercy pitty us all and remember whereof we are made. My love to your wife. The Lord blesse you both and all yours. I am and must allways be, my dear lord,

Your lordship's in all true love and faithfullnes,

Franc Russell

437. From the mayor and aldermen of Gloucester, Gloucester, 17 November 1658, 823, fo. 155.

Letter of thanks, acknowledging Henry Cromwell's continuing affections for Gloucester and his gift of £50, which would be put to good use by the town.

438. From George Monck, Dalkeith, 23 November 1658, 823, fos 156–157.

May itt please your excellency,

I make bold to returne your excellencie most humble thankes for the favour you have bin pleased to shew to my kinsman Henry Monck in giving of him a cornett's place, which in a letter from my lord Broghill hee was pleased to informe mee of. I know nott how I shall bee able to requite those many favours I have received from your excellencie, butt thus much I shall desire your excellencie may know, that your favours and worth have soe obliged mee that you may bee assured of mee as your faithfull servant. I prayse God all things in these parte are quiett and well, both in the army and Scotts nation and I hope will continue soe, and I am very glad all thinges are soe under your excellencie's command. Soe desiring the Almighty God to blesse you and goe alonge with you in all your proceedinges, I take leave and remayne,

Your excellencie's most humble and faithfull servant,

George Monck

439. From Simon Rumney,[158] Tralee, County Kerry, 29 November 1658, 823, fo. 158.

My lord,

Your excellencie's servuant especially in the gospell and faithfull to your just interest every way humbly prayes liberty for a few words, though as from a shrub to a cedare, especially because the present patrone to most of the transported ministry in Ireland. I solicited your excellencie by petition at Lissmore in your progresse for my salary then due, alledging reasons of some weight for expedition, whereupon your excellencie (as I was informed) appoynted Doctor Gorge to make a dispatch to Dublin about it; although then I was by your excellencie enformed of some suspicion of missdemeanour by me (which since hath beene found causelesse) with your promise that the matter should shortly be tryed at Dublin. In order to which I have since passed the tryall, and beene approved of by the commissioners appoynted in Kery to try all matters of scandall concerning me, and by the ministers in Limerick to try my ministeriall sufficiencie, which approbations I hope are long since returned to your excellencie and honourable counsell, whereby your excellencie may perceive mallice or ignorance to be the (but bad) enformers, but cleered innocency the product. Yet this remora[159] to my salary hath beene such dammage to my subsistence that, if it be not speedily removed and order with effect taken for my receiving of my salary, my present want is like to be unsupportable. I haveing not received a penny due since March last, soe that there is due to me within a month after the date hence of one hundred and five pounds, for three quarters salary, of which I am indebted above fifty pounds, and where to borrow more I know not nor with modesty can I, which is, I thinke, a deplorable case for my chargeable famuly. I haveing nothing but by the penny, which course if not prevented will force me either to have thoughts for England againe or to take some other employment here and not betray my famuly to want. I beseech your excellencie to pardon my enforced plainenesse and to speed effectuall order for my supply and prevention of my like future want. But especially let me for the Lord's sake beg of your excellencie in the behalfe of starveing soules in Kery to send if possible some more godly ministers. Prolixity, though forced, shameth me, therefore I take

[158] Minister in Ireland, working at Tralee by 1656. At the Dublin convention of ministers of spring 1658, he was one of thirty-one salaried ministers in Ireland listed as under suspicion of scandal or insufficiency.

[159] Remora: a sucking fish once believed to slow or stop ships, and hence more generally a delay or hindrance.

leave with affectionate prayers for your excellencie's and counsell's grace, safty, honour and happinesse, as the desire of,

Your excellencie's servant in the gospell,

Simon Rumney, minister at Traley in Kery

440. Francis Russell, Chippenham, 6 December 1658, 823, fos 159–160.

My deare lord,

I hope none of mine to your lordship have miscarryed, yet I dare not be to confident of it, haveing written unto you allmost every weeke since I came out of Ireland, and not received above three of yours. Being now retyreed home, I can but tell you how wee doe, and how glad we should be if twere though[160] fit that you might have your liberty and not be confineed to Ireland. Surely you have deserved better. By your patience now I hope you will get experyence and see into that kind of wisedome which may make you wise indeed. My love and faithfullnes for you hath bin such as did become a true freind, for which it may be I doe suffer with you and am not asshameed of it. Pray as often as you can, let me receive of yours. If you come not for England this winter I have no thoughts of stiring from home, allthough I be summoned by writ to the parliment.[161] Surely I have served my country and freinds long enough at my owne charge and trouble, for which I might at least have expected a recompense of poore love, but finding not it, I must grow wise before it be to late. Really, my lord, I am at a stand what counsell to give you, not being able to judge of your present frame and temper of spirit, but this I say and must affirme as wisedome, that to take a kind of banishment from my freinds and country would by no meanes agree with me. Your tryalls have begonne with you betimes, and it may be you must bare that crosse to the grave. Me thinks it seemes to be appointed for you as your portion, therefore take it up with wisedome and patience. Yet a man-like wisedome will become you and is not to be neglected. To serve any body and not to be recompenced with love me thinks is below a man, though never so humble and selfe denying. If the men of this world needed not me, why should I make myselfe theyres. My brother Jack you are never likely to see againe. Doctor Eade hath little hopes of his life, but seemes to give him over. I doe wish you here at Chippenham with us, haveing my mind full of thoughts about you.

[160] Apparently a slip for 'thought'.

[161] Summoned as a member of the second chamber to sit in Richard Cromwell's Protectorate parliament, due to meet in January. Despite his comments here, Russell did take his seat.

They are not fitt for paper, but belong to yourselfe onely. Surely I ly not if I should say you can have no freind so truely loveing you as doeth, my deare lord,

Your lordship's most faithfull freind,

Franc Russell

My love to your wife and my Lord Aunger.[162]

441. From Peter Wallis,[163] 6 December 1658, 823, fos 161–162.

Maye it please your excellincie,

Since the busines depending before your excellincie and councell is become matter of competition and the opponents pleading right from theire great deserveings (evidenced by a confident pen) and suggesting that my undertakeings are out of prejudice to them, that I humbly crave your excellincie's favour and leave (though I dare not pleade merritt, haveing a due sence of my owne undeserveings and shortenes in the performeing of anye duty committed to my trust) humbly to assure your excellencie of that trueth (which I hope you allreaddy do beleeve) that when I have evidenced the practicablenes of what is propounded and thereby brought it into a waye of profitt, that I shall not onely give your excellincie a true accompt thereof but shall allsoe most cherefully give and resigne my intrest unto your excellencie's disposse. And if your excellencie shall, notwithstanding what hath bine sayd, thinke fitt to lett them (by what hath bine offred by me) have a further opperttunitie to magnifie themselves and throw contempt upon me, it's a portion I desyre to learne to beare with more profitt then yett I have don, allthough I am sincible how I am a suffrer in my reputation by theire undue (nay false and scandolous) reports and representations of things even beyond collor of trueth. And surely it's strange modestie that a person soe faulty as captain Gookin

[162] Francis Aungier, third Baron Aungier, came from an English family that had acquired property in Ireland in the early seventeenth century. He began his political career at the very end of the Protectorate, sitting for Counties Westmeath, Longford, and King's in Richard Cromwell's Protectorate parliament and becoming a London correspondent of Henry Cromwell during the latter's final weeks in Ireland. Aungier's political career in both England and Ireland unfolded and flourished after the Restoration.

[163] Parliamentarian officer, a corporal in Oliver Cromwell's horse regiment in the early 1640s, by the 1650s he was major of Henry Cromwell's horse regiment in Ireland and seems to have had effective command of that regiment when Henry Cromwell returned to England in 1652; he was given full command as colonel after the fall of the Protectorate. He was appointed to many commissions during the 1650s, especially in County Cork, and was active in the business of transporting Irish for the service of Spain, in making good articles of war, in the setting of land for military debts, and in the approbation of ministers. In religion, he either was a Quaker or at least showed strong Quaker sympathies.

is in refferrence to the losse and sufferrings of the commonwealth should pleade merritt and right of prefferrence as he doeth both in the busines of Rosse and in the case depending. The 1st of which I offer to make evident is at best an unnecessary expence to his Highnes and commonwealth of at least £2,000. For that I had, some monthes before his undertakeing at Rosse, repaired a castell about a mile from Rosse which contained and was fitt to accomadate more men then wee could ever spare to attend that post of our quartere or admitt Rosse be somthing more convenient for a garrinson.[164] I doe affirme that £150 would have made accomadation for more men then ever were placed or could be spared to attend the service of that post as aforesaid. And surely I thinke his best arguement for the prefferrence to beere must needs be his having the benifitt of keepeing 100 Irish famalyes there two yeares without anye benifitt to his Highnes and commonwealth. I am troubled that I am soe troublesome unto your excellincie, but haveing experiencie of theire dominering temper and spiritt and resolveing this to be my last asaye in such cases (unlesse called thereto) have humbly presented unto your excellincie's clemency; and with this humble caution to your excellincie's memory of my humble petition to your excellencie not to appeare in the thinge unlesse your excellincie weere resolved I should have it offreing candidly what might be fitt, I submitt the resolution of the case unto your excellincie's owne brest (the councell are strangers to the necesarynes of the worke) and shall have more satisfaction in your excelincie's appoyntments (haveing had this liberttie of logeing the case before your excellincie) then in my owne election of anyethinge. I am heartily ashamed of soe great trouble, therefor againe most humbly sollicite your excelincie's pardon and subscribe,

Your excellincie's most obedient, poore servant,

Peter Wallis

442. From Gilbert Mabbott, 7 December 1658, 823, fos 163–164.

May it please your excellency,

The councell have ordered supplies for the garrison of Portsmouth, a monthe's pay to the army in England out of the treasury for new buildings. Tis referred to a committee to consider of the speedy bringing in of the arreares of the farmes of excise. Severall moneys

[164]There appear to be no further details extant to throw light on this issue and even the location is not entirely clear, although the writer is probably referring to the walled town of Ross or New Ross, County Wexford, and to a fortified building a little outside the town – perhaps Mountgarrett Castle, a fifteenth-century tower house, which stands about one mile north of Ross, east of and overlooking the River Barrow.

are ordered to the commissioners for new buildings for satisfaction of officers and contingent charges of that affaire. The committie of the army and treasurers at warre to bee contynued for the next six monthes as formerly. Instructions are sent to our agent in Holland toucheing the losses of the English by the Dutch in the East Indies. Tis referred to a committee to consider of the transportation of horses to Mardyke for those that loose horses in that service. The duke of Bucks hath 3 monthes longer tyme to staye at Yorke House. It is offered to his Highnes as the advise of his councell that his Highnes will summon a parliament to meete att Westminster the 27th of January next. The same qualifications are to be observed in the election of these members <for Ireland and Scotland> as of those in the last parliament. Writts are likewise to issue for electing members for Ireland and Scotland. The Dutch fleete are returned home from Coppenhagen. The Swedes are alsoe in safe harbour and our 20 sayle that went lately towards Denmarke are returned into Solebay (an English porte). I humbly subscribe myselfe, my lord,

Your excellencie's most humble and most obedient servant,
Gilb Mabbott

443. From William Goffe, Westminster, 10 December 1658, 823, fos 165–166.

May it please your excellency,

You will perceive by the inclosed that greate and undeserved favour it hath graciously pleased his Highnes to cast upon me,[165] which allthough I did not dare to use the least or most remote indeavour to obtaine, yett being freely tendered I could not but acknowledge it as a very good providence of God towards me and my wiffe and children, for whom I have hetherto made very slender provission. This favour of his Highnes would be there cheefest subsistance if it should please the Lord to take me from them. And therefore as I doe receive it as a blessing from God, soe I hope I shall ever retaine a thankefull and dutyfull sence of the greate kindnes of his Highnes, who is the cheefe instrument of handing that blessing to mee, which yett is to be compleated by the hand of your excellency of whose love and kindnes I have (though most unworthy) had soe much former experience, that I dare not now make the least question but what lieth on your parte to be done for the perfecting of his Highnes' favour will not be wanting. Only I beceech your excellency to be confident that what kindnes yow shall be pleased to shew in the effectuall execution of this affaire will

[165]A grant of lands in Ireland to the value of £500 (*TSP*, VII, pp. 504–505).

ever remaine as a strong oblegation upon one who is willingly oblidged to be your most faithfull and affectionate servant, which truely, sir, I have not found my hart soe free in as to many persons in the world beside. It is now seaven yeere agoe since the Long Parliament did bestow severall gratuities upon some of my fellow officers and I was then proffered a kindnes by one of the most considerable members of that house if I would but have shewed a willingnes to be oblidged by him, but being resolved not to begg a favour of that kind of any man nor willing to be oblidged to any person but his late Highnes (of glorious memory) I missed that opportunity. But I have esteemed my freedome greater riches, it being a sore evill to be oblidged to those whom a man cannot cheerefully serve. Yett I ever thought to be fast bound to his late Highnes was perfect freedome, for in being faithfull to him I knew I pleased God and served the interest of His people and I thinke the same thing as to his present Highnes, whom the Lord hath beene pleased by a wounderfull providence to sett up in his roome. And therefore, though he should give me a mountaine of gould, he could not thereby engage me to be more faithfull but might hapily make mee more able to doe him service, being fully sattisfied in my jugement and conscience that whoever will be and continue a freind to that glorious cause wee have beene engaged in must not be unfaithfull to his Highnes, but ought to give there utmost assistance to him in that greate trust that God hath for the good of His people reposed in him. I beceech your excellency to pardon these rude expressions and looke upon me as a one who (though most weake yett) desireth with all his abillity to serve his Highnes, your excellency and all the rest of that noble and religious family, unto whom not only myselfe but these nations and especially the people of God in them (upon your deare father's account and your owne) are more then ordinarily oblidged. But your cheefe reward is with God who will not faile (as long as yow love and feare His name and walke in His waies according to the example of your blessed father with a perfect hart) to uphould and preserve yow against all opposition whatsoever, which that yow may doe and bee is and shall be the continuall fervent prayer of, my lord,

Your excellencye's most humble and faithfull servant,
W Goffe

My lord, allthough I doe wholy cast myselfe upon your excellency's favour in the ordering of this bussines to the best advantage, yett I shall humbly desire yow to give Dr Harison leave now and then to put your excellency in mind of me.

444. From Edmund Temple, Borestall House, 12 December 1658, 823, fos 167–168.

My lord,

I have rather chose to be an informer then a seconder of the sad newse of major generall Jephson's death.[166] His person and losse is too well knowne to your lordship for me to adde anything by all that I can say, and I know your lordship has so greatt a proportion of religion and reason (and have too lately had too great and too sad occasion to make use of both) that you well know how to make the best gaine of the losse of your dearest freinds. And certenly, my good lord, this great gathering of late canot but make you and all good people looke up with astonishment on the wonderfull wayes and workeings of the great Dispenser of all things, who best knowes what is best for all.

My lord, on his death bed, relying on your goodnes, in the presence of my lord Wharton[167] and collonel Norton, for want of a fitter legacy he has dedicated his eldest son[168] to your lordship, hopeing through God's blessing he may suddenly prove worthy your lordship's owneing and acceptance and to deserve the honor of some service neare your lordship's person, for which there is care taken to fit him with all possible speed. Collonel Norton is joyned with your lordship to take of all manner of truble more then your owneing and countenanceing him so far as his virtue shall meritt and your lordship's love to his father induce you; but of this your lordship will very suddenly heare more from collonel Norton, and also from his Highnes, who has beene exceeding kind to the major generall and has promised the continuance of it to the sonne. My most humble petition to your excellencie for the present is that the troope and company may not be disposed of tell you have considered of his Highnes' intentions to gratifie his sonne and brother and of some other reasons to long to truble your lordship with at present, but such as I presume your excellencie will not deny granting your old, deare, deceased freind and servant.

My lord, I confes without this sad occasion I have dayly and howerly many of my owne to render my humble duty and thankes for your great goodnes to me, but I durst never give myselfe the liberty of presumeing to truble your lordship with my impertinent lines. And

[166]He returned to England in August 1658 and died at his house at Boarstall, Buckinghamshire, on 11 December.

[167]Philip Wharton, fourth Baron Wharton, parliamentarian officer and politician, who played a brief and inglorious military role early in the civil war as commander of a foot regiment but whose main contribution to the cause during the 1640s was as a politician and administrator. However, his enthusiasm waned with the regicide and abolition of the House of Lords and he held aloof from the regimes of the 1650s, courted by Oliver Cromwell but keeping some distance from him and declining to take his seat in the new nominated second parliamentary chamber established in 1657.

[168]Probably John Jephson.

now I no souner apeare before your lordship in paper but the cause of my comeing and stay pleads with your great goodnes (that boyes me up and hath brought me afresh into the world) for my pardon; and now your lordship shall quickly see twas my dear freinds, not any busines of my owne, brought me and keep me heare, for I shall now no souner have made my aplication to his Highnes for some of his concernements but I shall returne to the centure of my hapines. Your excellencie's presence and comands to live and die in which is the greatest ambition, content and hapines that in this world can befall, my lord,

Your lordship's most humble and most obedient servantt,

E Temple

445. From Matthew Tomlinson, 14 December 1658, 823, fos 169–170.

Letter of apology, explaining that he had to remain in England for a while longer, because he was involved in a legal case against an unnamed person to whom he had entrusted the care and administration of his modest English estate but who had proved untrustworthy.

446. From Henry Scobell, Whitehall, 15 December 1658, 823, fos 171–172.

May it please your excellencie,

Being commaunded to send the writts of summons and election to parliament by a messenger, I have presumed to take the opportunity to present your excellencie the tender of my most humble service, praying the Lord to supply you with abundance of his grace and wisedom, that your excellencie may doe worthily for God and His people and adde a further lustre of honor to that name which God hath made to be renowned through the world, which is the hopes and wilbe the rejoycing of, my lord,

Your excellencie's most humble servant,

Hen Scobell

447. From William Hetley,[169] Cambridge, 16 December 1658, 823, fos 173–174.

My lord,

Your excellency haveing commended Sir Anthony Morgan to this university as theire burgesse in this next succeeding parliament,

[169] Of Brampton, near Huntingdon, and an associate or servant of Edward Montague. He was also distantly related by marriage to Henry Cromwell, because his wife, Karina, was the daughter of Henry Cromwell, cousin of the late Protector, Oliver Cromwell. He was not returned to Richard Cromwell's Protectorate parliament.

supposing then that there would be none chosen out of Ireland, whereupon the generallity of the university did very freely ingage theire voices, and I being desired from some well affected persons (his Highnesse haveing declared his approbation before upon theire motion in case the university were willing to chuse me) to stand with whomsoever els was named, I was resolved to joine with Sir Anthony. But the Secretary being named,[170] I withdrew and went out of towne; but your lordship haveing countermanded your former request, not doubting but he would be chosen for Ireland, the vice-chancellour, Dr Bond,[171] was requested to joine with the Secretary, which he has don with this[172] reservation, that if your excellency shalbe willing that Sir Anthony shalbe chosen here,[173] notwithstanding your former countermand upon some second thoughts, he is willing to lay downe and the rather finding some inconveniency to be absent soe long from the university and withall has promised to deferre the choice till I heare from your lordship if he can possibly. Whereupon I made bold to trouble your excellency with his offerre and I doubt not but if your excellency will intimate your pleasure to any of the heads or whom elce you thinke good, but we shalbe able[174] effect your request without any difficulty and I shalbe very ambitious to approve myselfe,

Your excellency's faithfull servant,

Will Hetley

If your letters be directed to Daintry post-master he can easily and speedily convey them hither.

I am now ingaged for Huntingdon.

In greate hast.

448. From Gilbert Mabbott, 21 December 1658, 823, fos 175–176.

May it please your excellency,

The establishment for Dunkirke is passed to comence 25 December instant and severall provicions are ordered to bee sent thither. It is left to the lord Lockheart to call in the five companies which are in the

[170] Thurloe was elected by Cambridge University and chose to sit for that seat, though he was also returned elsewhere.

[171] John Bond, academic and parliamentarian politician, elected to the Long Parliament in 1645 as MP for Melcombe Regis in his native Dorset, though he was excluded at Pride's Purge. In 1645, he became master of Trinity Hall, Cambridge, and, in 1650, professor of law at Gresham College and a master in chancery; in 1658–1659, he served as vice-chancellor of Cambridge University.

[172] Word repeated in error.

[173] In fact, Morgan sat for Irish constituencies in all three Protectorate parliaments, representing Counties Meath and Louth in 1659.

[174] Word – perhaps 'to' – apparently omitted.

feild into the garrison of Dunkirke if hee thinke fitt. The writts for a parliament are all sealed. Those for Ireland and Scotland are sent by messenger of the councell. Wednesday next[175] is appointed a day of fast for his Highnes and his family and the officers of the army; Wednesday following for all England and Wales; and Wednesday three weekes for Ireland and Scotland. Divers memorialls presented from the lord embassador Newport about the Dutch shipps stayed by captain Stoakes in the Streights referred. Satisfaction is instantly demanded by the councell from the Dutch embassador for the injuries susteyned by the English in the East Indies. His Highnes' youngest daughter is deceased.[176] News is come that the Dutch fleet is in the Sound, and tis generally beleeved that ours is (since) arrived there alsoe. Wee daily expect to heare of an engagement betweene them. Coppenhagen is in a very lowe condition for want of provicions. The Dutch embassador proposes (at a distance) an amity between the Swede and the Dane according to the last articles agreed on betweene them. Wednesday last John Napper (clarke of a troope) and John Reynes (trooper), both of the lord Fleetwood's regiment, were casheired by a court marshall of the army for endeavouring to carry on an unlawfull petition for arrears and increase of pay. I humbly subscribe myselfe, my lord,

Your excellencie's most humble and most obedient servant,

G Mabbott

449. From Claudius Gilbert,[177] 24 December 1658, 823, fos 177–178.

May it please your excelency,

I understand that the committee hath presented my name (with those of other ministers to be settled in Dublin) for the parish of Michaele[178] to your lordshipp and the council. The thoughts of so

[175] 22 December.

[176] Dorothy Cromwell, born on 13 September 1657, died at Hursley on 14 December and was buried there two days later.

[177] Minister in Ireland, by 1652 he was the salaried preacher at Limerick, perhaps encouraged to settle in Ireland by his uncle, Henry Markham. He was evidently held in regard by the English regime, for his salary was raised and he was placed on various commissions. His publications of the later 1650s reveal his conservative religious viewpoint, condemning Baptism and Quakerism and supporting governmental control over religion, in part exercised through associations of ministers conforming to a set confession of faith. Such views were close to those of Henry Cromwell and of Edward Worth's Cork association of ministers.

[178] St Michael's in Dublin. Its incumbent, William Pilsworth, had long been held in low regard by the English government in Dublin, both as a non-approved minister and as one suspected of using the old prayer book, and the opportunity was now taken to remove him and promote the favoured Gilbert.

favorable an approach cannot but much rejoice my heart, promising the opportunity of being really much more serviceable there to your excelency and the publick then I could be here. My wif's continuall indisposition in this place occasioned by the unsutablenes thereof to her temper cannot but render Dublin much more acceptable, it having agreed very well with her. Her desires also of removing to England for health's sake, which I was necessitated to promise her (in case providence offered no better way), may be satisfied by this expedient, and I thereby put into a better capacity of attendinge Christ's worke and your excelencie's commands, which is the chief longing of my soule to the utmost of my poor abilities. I doe also find much lesse need and use of me in this place then formerly. However I be disposed of, it shall be my constant designe and delight to approve myselfe by the grace of Christ,

Your excelencie's cordially obliged and humbly devoted,
Claudius Gilbert

450. From Francis Rous, 24 December 1658, 823, fo. 179.

May it please your excellency,

This bearer gives not only an oportunity but a reason of making an humble and gratefull acknowlegment of your favors. For when your excellency was pleased to remember him, I ask leave to presume that you did not forget mee. I hope and beleeve that he will be a faythfull servant, for otherwise his kinred with mee would be soone at an end. Hee hath made some staye with mee and some with an onely brother planted in the West Indyes, but having lately come over is now returned, whom he is never likely to see agayne.

As for myself, I have bene visited with a long infirmity which hath detayned mee against my desire from publick services. But it pleaseth the Divine Goodnes to give mee some degrees of recovery, which yf they shall be brought to perfection, I shallbe ready to expresse my willingnes to do service for the publick, the greatnes of the worke expected needing earnest endeours, but especially requests to the God of peace that He will continue the peace which He hath thus gratiously begun to create.

And now praying that your excellency may make a long and happy progresse in the way of godlynes, righteousnes and prudent government, wherin you have begun so fayre a race, in this devotion, resting, I desire to be esteemed that which I truly am,

Your excellencye's most reall, constant and humble servant,
Francis Rous

451. From Gilbert Mabbott, 28 December 1658, 823, fos 180–181.[179]

May it please your excellencie,

The dutchy chamber and court is assigned to keepe the records of the house of commons. The regiments of foote in England are reduced to 750 in each regiment and 500 of those reduced are sent to Flanders and collonel Gibbon's[180] and collonel Salmon's men to returne. The establishment for the garrissons in Flanders is passed. Major James Russell is constetuted governor of Nevis. A comittee of the councell to consider by what authoritie the opera in Drury Lane is showne in imetation of a play and what the nature of it is. £160 per annum for liffe is setled upon collonel Marckworth's[181] widdow. Jamese's House is ordered to be made ready for her Highness dowager[182] and that garrisson to be removed to Berckeshire House. Major generall Harisson[183] is allready chossen a member. The maior of Reading with the towne clerke soe much displeassed the townsmen on Tuesday last[184] in proposeing 2 gentlemen to be chossen for that

[179] Another version of the majority of this newsletter, with minor variations in the text, is found in a newsletter by Mabbott, dated 25 December, which survives amongst the Clarke Papers at Worcester College, Oxford, and which is printed in *Clarke Papers*, III, p. 171.

[180] Robert Gibbon, parliamentarian officer, rose to prominence in the mid- and late 1640s as first a captain and then major in Henry Ireton's New Model horse regiment. In 1650, he was commissioned to raise and command a new foot regiment to counter the Scots, but it never actually campaigned in Scotland and was disbanded the following year. In the mid-1650s, he was governor of Elizabeth Castle on Jersey. In the autumn of 1656, he was again commissioned to raise and command a new regiment of foot, most of which campaigned in Flanders from late 1657 until the end of 1658.

[181] Humphrey Mackworth, parliamentarian officer and politician, campaigned for parliament in his native Shropshire and, in 1645, holding the rank of colonel, became governor of Shrewsbury. He held a string of offices in Shropshire and adjoining regions including, from 1648, the attorney-generalship of North Wales. In February 1654, he was added to the Protectoral council and later in the year he sat for Shropshire in the first Protectorate parliament, but he died suddenly and intestate in December 1654.

[182] Elizabeth Cromwell née Bourchier, widow of Protector Oliver Cromwell.

[183] Thomas Harrison, parliamentarian officer and politician and a regicide, had a distinguished military career, first as a major in Charles Fleetwood's horse regiment and then, from 1647, as colonel of his own New Model horse regiment, which fought in northern England in 1648. He and his regiment remained in England and Wales in the early 1650s and did not campaign in Ireland or Scotland. As a political and religious radical, prominent in religious circles, in army politics, and in parliament after his election in 1646, he strongly supported Pride's Purge and the regicide and, becoming disillusioned with the Rump, also supported its ejection and the establishment of the Nominated Assembly, which he joined as a co-opted member. However, he viewed the Protectorate as a betrayal of the radical cause and spent the period out of office and under suspicion, repeatedly arrested and questioned, with spells of imprisonment or house arrest. He had not been returned to the first or second Protectorate parliaments and, despite rumours and reports at this time of his election for Stone in his native Staffordshire, he does not appear to have been a member of the third Protectorate parliament.

[184] 21 December.

place that they imediately tooke away the mace from the maior and elected another maior and towne clearcke in thire steedes. Our 20 sayle are returned home, but whether Sir George Ascue bee gott into the Sound wee heare not yet. Mr Scott[185] hath lost the vote for being a member for Alisbury and Sir James Whitlocke[186] and another[187] is chosen. Begging your excellencie's pardon for this hasty coppy, I humbly subscribe myselfe, my lord,

Your excellencie's most humble and most obedient servant,

G Mabbott

452. From William Lockhart, Dunkirk, 30 December 1658, 823, fos 182–183.

Letter of courtesy, praising Henry Cromwell and his government of Ireland as a more suitable memorial to his late father than any statues or monuments, and apologizing for not writing to him during his recent, short visit to London; gives thanks for Henry Cromwell's recent favour to his brother and requests that, if some land that his brother now held around Armagh be allocated to the town and townspeople, he might be allocated land of equal value elsewhere.

[185] Thomas Scott, parliamentarian politician and a regicide, was prominent in the Long Parliament and its Rump from his election in 1645 onwards, strongly supporting the regicide and effectively serving as state intelligence chief under the Rump. He strongly opposed the ejection of the Rump, seeing it as a betrayal of the cause, and his radical and republican principles led him to criticize and oppose the Protectorate. Elected to the first two Protectorate parliaments, he was excluded at or soon after the start of the session. Although he missed out at Aylesbury, he was returned to the third Protectorate parliament for Wycombe in his native Buckinghamshire and he proved to be a leading parliamentary critic of the Protectoral regime.

[186] Parliamentarian politician, the only son of Bulstrode Whitelocke by his first marriage and elected through his local influence.

[187] Thomas Terrill/Tyrell.

1659

453. From Gilbert Mabbott, 4 January 1659, 823, fos 195–196.[1]

May it please your excellency,

The last weeke Mr Secretary Thurlowe and Doctor Slater were chosen for Cambridge and for other parts Mr Charles Rich, Mr Turner (of Greys Inn), Mr Barrington (one of his Highnes' bedchamber), Mr Brewster, collonel Matthews, Mr Herbert (earle of Pembroke's brother), major Ludlow, Mr Hill, Sir John Carter and Mr Manley.[2] Wednesday last his Highnes conferred the honour of knighthood upon collonel Hugh Bethell.[3] Such of our fleet lately returned from the Sound and not prejudiced by the ice are ordered to remaine in the Downes and the rest to come into harbour. A booke entytuled Breife Directions how fitt a popular Governement may bee made, referred to a comittee to finde out the author thereof. Upon complaint of the Dutch embassador against 2 books, entytuled Mercurius Anglicus and The Dutch Charactarized, referred likewise. The king of Sweden intends to leave a sufficient leaguer before Coppenhagen and to joyne with 10,000 of generall Wrangell's forces intrenched neere Fredericks Ode[4] and in order thereunto 5,000 men are marching to him out of Pomerania. Sir George Aiscue is certainely gott into the Sound with his 2 shipps. A flood hath lately happened which hath overrunn 3 villages in the north of Holland. I humbly subscribe myselfe, my lord,

Your excellencie's most humble and most obedient servant,

Gilb Mabbott

[1] Another version of part of this newsletter, with some variations in the text, is found in a newsletter by Mabbott, dated 1 January, which survives amongst the Clarke Papers at Worcester College, Oxford, and which is printed in *Clarke Papers*, III, p. 172.

[2] John Thurloe and Thomas Slater, MPs for Cambridge University; Charles Rich for Essex and probably Edward Turner, also for Essex; John Barrington and Robert Brewster for Dunwich; Joachim Matthews for Maldon; either John Herbert for Wilton or his brother James Herbert for Queenborough; William Ludlow and Richard Hill for Old Sarum; Sir John Carter for Denbighshire; and either Thomas Manley for Bedwin or John Manley for Denbigh.

[3] Parliamentarian officer and politician, he campaigned under the Fairfaxes in Yorkshire during the opening stages of the civil war and remained active in northern England, commanding a regiment of northern horse during the last year of the war and again in the renewed fighting of 1648. He sat for Yorkshire in both of Oliver Cromwell's Protectorate parliaments. According to this report, he was knighted on 29 December.

[4] Perhaps Fredrikshald.

454. From William Lockhart, Dunkirk, 7 January 1659, 823, fos 197–198.

Letter of courtesy, praising Henry Cromwell and expressing affection for him.

455. From John Lockhart, London, 18 January 1659, 823, fos 199–200.

Letter of courtesy, expressing regret that he would be unable to visit Henry Cromwell in Ireland that winter because he was required in London both to serve the Protector and to sit in the forthcoming parliament; and of request, seeking the renewal of his existing lease on unspecified lands in Ireland or, if some of those lands be disposed of to others, some land elsewhere to restore his holding; both Dr Petty and an unnamed friend of his, known to Dr Petty, had been briefed on this business and could give Henry Cromwell full details if necessary.

456. From Vincent Gookin, Kinsale, 21 January 1659, 823, fo. 201.[5]

May it please your excellency,

Having your excellencye's free leave to attend this parliament or chuse another in my place, I picht upon Doctor Petty upon these grounds: 1st hee is a person of excellent parts; 2ly noe person I thinke in the 3 nations can doe more to the setlement [...][6] the army and adventurers than hee; thirdly the good the army will[7] certainely receive by his management of their affayres in the house will convince them that they can not harme him without injuring themselves and possibly that they doe ill if they love him not; 4ly hee is (I humbly conceive) fit for such a worke and will goe through with it, which is too hard for such as I am and many others noe wiser than myselfe to deale with; 5ly his abillity and honesty, joyned with the good will and honesty of the other two parliament men chosen for this county and the citty of Corke, will contribute much to the good of these places and make us love him who, I conceive, deserves it.

When I came to Corke, I found my lord Broghill had engaged some of the wisest of Corke corporation, without the consent of the brethren and the freemen of the citty, to chuse lieutenant colonel Foulkes; and that Bandon and Kinsale had in their owne courts chosen mee. Those of Corke and Youghall, upon my propounding desire to keepe themselves free till they had consulted with the other townes about

[5] This letter is now very badly foxed, making some sections of the text little more than semi-legible. However, it has been reproduced, with other documents relating to this election dispute, and the whole dispute analysed, by T. C. Barnard in 'Lord Broghill, Vincent Gookin and the Cork elections of 1659', *English Historical Review*, 88 (1973), pp. 352–365.

[6] Paper damaged with some loss of text, although the missing word is apparently 'of'.

[7] Paper damaged at this point and the word is only semi-legible.

their members, bemoaned the losse of their liberty, but however those that were bound gave those that were not encouragment to keepe their liberty till they heard more from mee. From Corke I went to my lord Broghill, desired his assistance that Corke might be perswaded to chuse Doctor Petty, and Kinsale and Bandon to chus Pen. The last he consented to; the first hee refused, alleadging it could not be done without dishonouring him, though I made noe question but to get lieutenant colonel Foulkes his consent to it, which if lieutenant colonel Foulkes should grant, his lordship sayd hee would take very ill from him. Therupon I gave of thinking to doe anything in Corke and repayred to Kinsale and Bandon, propounded Doctor Petty to them, shewing them that their election of mee obliged them to mee and their chusing Doctor Petty at my request obliged him too; to which, upon the arguments used by mee and their confidence in mee, they consented, provided yf Corke and Youghall would chuse mee, I would serve them; to which purpose they wrote a lettre to those of Corke and Youghall, which I delivered them, and in open court told them that in performance of my engagment I would serve them if they thought fit to chuse mee, but withall advized them to consider of their engagment and that I desired it not from them unless they thought fitt; and untill that time I never told them or any of them, or any other, that I had any purpose to propound myselfe to their election.

This was Tuesday last in the morning.[8] It was the Thursday before that I was with my lord Broghil, who in the meane nigted[9] about 2 dozen of his to Corke to engage them for Foulkes, and had apointed particular agents to consult with every freeman in the citty, which they did at the law offices and other such like eminent places. All this while I was not [. . .]hought[10] of; but when I came to be thus offered such a distinction [. . .]en[11] that greeted mee,[12] his lordship upon this alarme came soe frighted to Corke that hee prevented mee in shewing him how I intended his lordship noe harme in it, and that his speaking but one word to Kinsale and Bandon people, to have quited mee of my engagment to stand for Corke and Youghall, had absolutely removed mee out of his way, who was as much afrayd of goeing to the parliament as his lordship was of my election. His lordship, as soone as hee came

[8] 18 January.

[9] Uncertain reading of a very poorly formed and semi-legible word. Barnard transcribes this phrase as 'in the meane wrote about 2 dozen of l[ette]rs to Corke'.

[10] Paper damaged with minor loss of text at the start of this word, which apparently read 'thought'.

[11] Uncertain reading of a poorly formed and incomplete word, the first part of which has been lost because the paper is damaged.

[12] Barnard transcribes this phrase as 'when I came to be thus opposed, such a distraction grew that grieved mee'.

to Corke and the solemnityes of his comeing performed, went to the court and there rayled upon mee and magnified his owne services. Wheather his lordship did himselfe any good in it or mee hurt, others more indifferent to judge will ere long informe your lordship.

Upon the coming of Bandon and Kinsale people to Corke, I desired them for quietnes sake to free mee from my engagment, which they (unspeakably kind to mee in every way) granted, and therupon I signified soe much to the citty, all which notwithstanding I assure your lordship that in the towne hall at the election of lieutenant colonel Foulkes, his lordship had not with him but one alderman upon the bench and one in the crowd, and not above 30 of 400 freeholders in the citty at the election, but his lordship's owne people cryed up lieutenant colonel Foulkes; and I doe profess to your lordship that I did not in all that time by myselfe or any other in the least measure interpose in the election or speake to one person on my behalfe, though his lordship doubting mee, sent to his owne lodgings for more than 100 of the freeholders, man by man, and engaged some; others refused. This much I have presumed to aquaint your excellency with because I know his lordship will endeavour to prejudice mee. There are many particular passages in the carying on this business by which, when I have the honour to waite on your excellency, I shall make it apeare that I designed the election of Doctor Petty without offering in the least to prejudice his lordship's honour or thwart his purpose, unless against Doctor Petty, which I confess I should have done and did and doe hope I have not done amisse in it. I know, my lord, I have not bin in my lord Broghill's favour these many yeares. Hee now tells the people but what I knew before: that hee is my enemy.[13] I beseech your

[13] Although some parts of this letter are now damaged with loss of text and much of the surviving text is now very difficult to read, permitting alternative readings of some words and phrases, the overall situation described in the letter is clear and is fully discussed by Barnard in his article. Lord Broghill was active in the County Cork elections, seeking to ensure that his relations, allies, and clients were returned for all three seats – Maurice Fenton for the county seat, Francis Foulkes for Cork and Youghal towns, and William Penn for Bandon and Kinsale towns. On 22 January, he wrote to Thurloe, reporting that he had the previous evening attended the elections for County Cork and for Cork and Youghal towns, where 'There were greate endeavors to have had som chosen, that I was not very sure of; but their designe was defeated, and thos two I propounded, without six negatives, chosen' – for the county 'my owne cosen german' and for the towns 'a gentleman [. . .] always bred with me; and for both thes I ingage' (*TSP*, VII, p. 597). Broghill had clearly been angered to find Gookin intervening, claiming support from Henry Cromwell, in order to have himself elected at Cork and Youghal and to promote William Petty at Bandon and Kinsale. Gookin may have acted thus because he genuinely believed he had Henry Cromwell's blessing or active support, although he may also have been trying to protect himself – he was probably aware that Hierome Sankey and Benjamin Worsley were preparing an attack on Petty concerning his involvement in the Irish land settlement and may have believed that, if the assault upon Petty succeeded, he, as surveyor general, might be next in the firing line, and

lordship to suspend your judgment of this difference till you heare mee speake for myselfe, who am, my lord,

Your lordship's obedient and faythfull servant,

Vin Gookin

457. From Maurice Fenton,[14] Cork, 21 January 1659, 823, fos 202–203.

Letter of request, seeking permission to travel to England to sit in parliament as MP for County Cork, noting that, because of his recent appointment as an officer in the army in Ireland, he required such permission before he can go; also enquires whether, if permission was granted, Henry Cromwell had any commands for him and promises obedience to them.

458. From Matthew Tomlinson, 1 February 1659, 823, fos 204–205.

May it please your excellency,

Upon Thurday last,[15] after a sermon preacht by Doctor Goodwyn, both the houses mett. His[16] made a very substantiall discourse to them, after which the house of commons withdrew and beinge assembled chose Mr Chute[17] the lawyer theire speaker. There hath not yet anythinge beene done considerable in either house, the time only giveinge oppertunity to appoint comittees for priviledges

so was strongly supporting Petty and trying to ensure that they both won parliamentary seats. But the electoral clash was not primarily about policies or political principles, since all the candidates were drawn from the old Protestants in Ireland and all of them broadly or strongly supported Henry Cromwell in Ireland and the Protectoral regime. Instead, this dispute mainly sprang from a squabble over status in Irish provincial society, because Broghill was angered that someone well below him on the social scale was effectively challenging his position in County Cork and questioning his electoral and political control. In the end, Fenton was returned without challenge for the county seat, Foulkes for Cork and Youghal, and Gookin for Bandon and Kinsale. Petty was returned for another Irish constituency, and for West Looe in Cornwall, and chose to sit for the latter.

[14] Parliamentarian officer and politician, he was the son-in-law of Sir Hardress Waller and a cousin and ally of Broghill, whose influence was probably vital in his return for the County Cork constituency.

[15] 27 January.

[16] Word apparently omitted. Clearly 'His Highness' is intended, since the Protector made a brief but effective opening speech, which was widely praised at the time.

[17] Chaloner Chute, parliamentarian politician and lawyer, acted as defence counsel for several royalists prosecuted by the Long Parliament during the 1640s, although he also broadly supported or at least acquiesced with the parliamentarian cause, and was several times considered as a possible commissioner of the great seal, though that post was apparently offered to but declined by him in 1653. He was elected to, but excluded from, the second Protectorate parliament. Returned to serve for Middlesex in Richard Cromwell's Protectorate parliament, he was elected speaker at the outset, but his health soon broke down; he effectively resigned the speakership in early March and died on 14 April.

and elections. The other house of lords hath indeed apointed a comittee to consider the defects in the lawes for punishinge drunkenes and swearinge and profaninge the saboth; and yesterday an act for recognition of his Highnes was first read, and this day upon the second readinge was comitted accordinge to usuall forme; the like bill for recognition was this day read in the house of commons. Some question yesterday in that house concerninge admittinge Scotsh and Irish members, but upon debate, though I doe not heare there was a vote, yet the generall sence rann for the affirmation. My lord, I cannot but give your excellency this account, that havinge receaved a summons[18] I durst not withstand my appearance thereupon, though indeed with very much hesitation in referrence to my owne unfittnes. But if in this station I may be anywayes serviceable to your excellency or the affaires of the countrye under your goverment, I shall account it greatly my duty to improve all oppertunityes for these ends. My lord, I begge your pardon for this trouble and humbly remaine,

Your excellency's very faithfull and humble servant,

Math Thomlinson

459. From Henry Ingoldsby,[19] Beaumaris, 7 February 1659, 823, fos 206–207.

My lord,

Throw mercy wee landed safe yeasterday att this place, beinge transported and convoyed heither by your excelency'se favors in the Paradoxe frygott which, beinge againe returninge for Dublin, I could not deny myselfe the satisfaction off acknowledging the honour and kindnesse you placed on my wife and selfe thearein with thankfulnesse. Wee are with the most speed wee can for London, wheare those commands you entrusted mee with to his Highnesse shall bee faythfully remembred and communicated to him by, my lord,

Your excelencye'se most thankfull, obleidged and very humble servant,

H Ingoldesby

460. From Richard Norton, 7 February 1659, 823, fos 208–209.

My deare lord,

Though I have not trobled you with my pen, many heere can beare wittnesse of my affection and respects to your lordship. I know what

[18] Tomlinson had been summoned to sit in the nominated second chamber.

[19] Ingoldsby had been returned to Richard Cromwell's parliament as MP for Counties Kerry, Limerick, and Clare.

I can say must be impertenent when I have noething of businesse and that makes me forbeare, choosing rather to deny myselfe the honnor then to bee troblesome. The occasion of my boldnesse at this time is that I may performe my promise to your lordship's affectionate servant and my deere freind, Will Jephson, who as he was a faithfull friend to your family while he lived, thought he would doe something to expresse his great affection to and confidence in your lordship at his death, as his last act; with the greatest satisfaction that ever I saw, desired to bequeath the care of his sonne and heire to your lordship's wisdome, goodnesse and protection, hopeing (and truly on good ground from the youth's ingenuity) that he cannot miscarry under your advice. I know not how pleasing this troble may be to your lordship and therfore had it not been the request of a dying friend, I should have first made enquiry into your lordship's inclination to it, but it is that we his friends are tyed thereto, therfore I am the more bold to importune throu that friendship you bare to his person that is gone, and, my lord, throu that score of friendship your lordship hath been pleased to expresse to me, your unworthy servant, that you will be pleased to accept of it. His Highnesse told me he would write to you to presse you to it, but I know there is soe much goodnesse and noblenesse in your owne nature that I rely on that confidence and assureance rather then that I will troble his Highnesse in it further. And now, my lord, being assured that you will owne him (who truly, I must say, is well worth the owneing, being a very ingenious youth) I must lett your lordship know that it is the desire of his grandmother and all his friends that he may be continued in Oxford yet for one yeare. We cannot but with great sence of your lordship's goodnesse take notice of what you have done already for him in bestowing the troope on him. He will soone be ready for it. And if I may not be to bold, poore Will's relations and friends would looke on it as an act of charity, soe a great obligation on us, if your lordship would conferr on his uncle, John Jephson,[20] the foot company. And we hope your lordship will owne collonel Temple in all his undertakings for the family, perticulerly for Mr Jephson's arrears, as alsoe in the wine office, and that he may have the remaining part of it by lease on reasonable termes that the other part may be usefull to my young cosins.

My lord, I hope I have said enough on this subject, beleeveing soe much in your noblenesse that I might have spared most of it. My lord, we are heere lanched into the ocean and when we shall come to land I know not. Noe man can give any certaine guesse at our composure in the house; but if I can guesse any thing, we are not like to incline

[20] Younger brother of the late William Jephson, his military career (if any) is obscure and poorly recorded.

to republicans, nor truly to the new house, and that I can gather yet noe otherwise but by a gentleman's speaking this day when, in the midst of his speech, he was sharpe against that fagge end of the Long Parliament and spake for the old lords. The house gave a humme. We are but this day entred into the debate of the governement and I see noe doubt of their owneing his Highnesse, but I know not what to say to the other house, soe that I beleeve Sir Mathew Tomlinson and had best stick to that title. What they will doe abroad or how we shall relish with the army I know not yet. Give me leave, my lord, on this remainder of paper to expresse my affections to your lordship and my deere lady. Although I have not made any returnes, yet the expressions of kindnesse I have heard of from your lordship towards me have filled me soe full that I am ready to burst out and shall in thankfullnesse, on any occasion wherein I may, manifest that I am your true servant,

Rich Norton

461. From Nathaniel Brewster, Norwich, 8 February 1659, 823, fos 210–211.

Letter of apology for his long stay in England, held up by the requests of people for him to remain, but he now intended to return to Ireland and to wait upon Henry Cromwell there.

462. From Gilbert Mabbott, 8 February 1659, 823, fos 212–213.

May it please your excellencie,

The last week a recognition or bill for owening his Highness and the present government as it is now constituted was read the first time. Wednesday[21] the election of Mr Henrey Nevill[22] was approved and other elections decided. Thursday they comitted Major Audley[23] to

[21] 2 February.

[22] Henry Neville, parliamentarian politician, spent the war years abroad, returning to England in the mid-1640s. He was elected to the Rump as MP for Abingdon in the spring of 1649 and soon proved himself to be an active and radical member. His republican sympathies led him to oppose the Protectorate. He failed to secure election in 1654 or 1656, but he was returned to Richard Cromwell's Protectorate parliament as MP for Reading. His election was questioned but confirmed, although, soon after, he also faced accusations of blasphemy and atheism.

[23] Lewis Audley, parliamentarian officer, first shows up as a captain in Sir Thomas Fairfax's New Model foot regiment in 1647. By 1648, he was a major, active in suppressing royalism in Surrey, and in 1650–1651 he was working on the Anglo-Scottish border, helping to raise and deliver recruits for the Scottish campaign. As unsuccessful parliamentary candidate for Gatton in Surrey in 1658, he was condemned and briefly imprisoned by parliament for abusing his successful opponents and trying to provoke one or both of them to a duel.

the Tower for villifying Mr Bish,[24] a member of their howse. They ordered collonel Overton's[25] person to be brought by the governor of Jersey to the parliament with the cawse of his comittment. Every Monday in the afternoone sitts a grand comittee for religion; every Wednesday for grievances and courts of justice; and every Friday for trade. Friday was kept a day of humiliation. The ministers had thankes given them. Saterday they remitted the fine of £3,000 formerly imposed upon lieutenant-collonel Lilburne's[26] estate. They comitted one King,[27] a vintner in London, for sitting 3 dayes in parlament, hee beeing no member thereof. A comittee was named to examine how the revenuw in North Wales, South Wales and Monmouth for maintenance of the ministry there (for which major general Harrison was formerly questioned) is expended and in whose hands it remaines. Yesterday Sir Arthur Hesilrig[28] spake 2 houres together, Mr Scott

[24] Edward Bysshe/Bishe, parliamentarian politician, was MP for Bletchingley in the Long Parliament, although he absented himself in the wake of Pride's Purge. He sat in the first and third Protectorate parliaments for Reigate and Gatton respectively.

[25] Robert Overton, parliamentarian officer, campaigned under Sir Thomas Fairfax in northern England in the early and mid-1640s. In 1647, he became colonel of a foot regiment and, from 1648, he was governor of Hull. He campaigned in Scotland under Oliver Cromwell in 1650, staying on there both as governor of Edinburgh and to help mop up the highlands and islands in 1651–1652. His loyalty to the Protectorate was uncertain, however, and in late 1654 he was drawn into a circle of military insubordination and possible conspiracy. He was arrested and imprisoned, and, although no charges were brought or trial held, he spent over four years in captivity in the Tower and then on Jersey. Given a hearing by Richard Cromwell's Protectorate parliament, his release was ordered in mid-March 1659.

[26] John Lilburne, parliamentarian officer, political radical, and prominent Leveller, had been charged with treason by the Rump, condemned in absentia in January 1652, fined £7,000 – £3,000 of which was to be paid to the state, the remaining £4,000 to various individuals – and banished. Upon returning to England in 1653, he was arrested and tried for, but acquitted of, treason, though he spent parts of his last years in prison. He died while on parole in Kent in August 1657.

[27] William King, who was agitating against the Protectoral regime and in support of the Rump.

[28] Parliamentarian officer and politician, he campaigned from the outset of the civil war, initially in southern England in Sir William Waller's army. In 1647, he became governor of Newcastle and, during the late 1640s and early 1650s, he was almost regional governor of north-east England, dominating military affairs in that area, raising and commanding regiments there, and giving strong support to the English campaign in Scotland. Although absent from London during the winter of 1648–1649, and so playing no part in the regicide, he took his seat in the Rump in the early 1650s and became very prominent in that parliament. He condemned Oliver Cromwell's ejection of the Rump and became a fierce republican opponent of Cromwell and the Protectorate. He was elected to all three Protectorate parliaments for his native Leicestershire and, although he was excluded from the house at or soon after the opening of the first two, he was very prominent in Richard Cromwell's Protectorate parliament as a leading opponent of the Protectoral regime.

above an houre and collonel White[29] about halfe an howre against the recognition, and were briefly and fully answeared by Mr Bunckley,[30] major Beake[31] and sergeant Maynard.[32] At this rate the howse cannot come to a question in a fortnight's time, but it will bee this day endeavoured to perswade the members to speake thereunto without circumlocation and keepe close to the matter in question, that other business of publique concernment may bee heared likewise. This was the first day of the lord Falkeland's[33] and Sir Henry Vane's[34] sitting in the howse. The dangerous petition from some thowsands in the city so much spoken of here was yesterday expected but came nott. This day Mr Samwell Moyer[35] (law chaireman of the comittee of Haberdashers Hall) with about 20 more citizens came downe with the said petition, but the howse being very busie in debating the recognition, there was no opportunity to present the same. The house sat till 3 of clocke upon

[29] Probably William White, parliamentarian politician, elected for Pontefract in 1645, who sat in the Long Parliament and Rump and resumed his seat in the restored Rump in 1659, playing a prominent role in financial business. He appears to have sat, perhaps for Clitheroe, in Richard Cromwell's Protectorate parliament, strongly opposing the Protectorate. I am most grateful to Dr Patrick Little for his help in identifying this MP.

[30] John Bulkeley, parliamentarian politician, MP for Christchurch, and a very experienced parliamentarian, elected to every parliament of the period 1640–1661.

[31] Robert Beake, parliamentarian officer and politician, MP for Coventry.

[32] Sir John Maynard, parliamentarian politician and lawyer, was elected to both parliaments of 1640 and was active in the house and as a prosecutor in state trials, but he withdrew from parliament during 1648 and took no part in the regicide. He was created a serjeant at law in 1654 and Protector's serjeant in 1658. He sat in the second and third Protectorate parliaments, for Plymouth and Newtown, Isle of Wight, respectively.

[33] Henry Carey, fourth Viscount Falkland, was returned as MP for Oxfordshire and, although the election was disputed, a proposal in early February to rerun the election won little support and his return was confirmed; this was his first parliament.

[34] Sir Henry Vane, junior, parliamentarian politician, one of the leading and most committed parliamentarians of the 1640s, played a prominent political role in the Long Parliament and, even though he held aloof from the regicide, he retained his position as a leading member of the Rump. His radical and republican principles led him to break with Oliver Cromwell over the latter's ejection of the Rump and he became a strong opponent of Cromwell and the Protectorate. Out of office and viewed with suspicion during Oliver Cromwell's Protectorate, he was returned to Richard Cromwell's Protectorate parliament as MP for Whitchurch, Hampshire and became a leading opponent of the regime.

[35] Samuel Moyer, parliamentarian financier, merchant, and politician, strongly supported the parliamentary cause during the 1640s and early 1650s and sat on many, mainly financial, commissions over those years. A political and religious radical, he became disillusioned with the Rump, welcomed its ejection, and sat in the Nominated Assembly as a radical member for London. He strongly opposed the Protectorate, seeing it as betraying the radical cause. He was a leading light in reviving and presenting to the third Protectorate parliament a radical, subversive petition, originally drawn up in January 1658, aimed at bringing together the army and radical religious groups to remove the Protectorate and to restore either the Long Parliament or some other republican regime.

the said debate but when they come to a question thereupon is very uncertaine. I humbly subscribe myselfe, my lord,

Your excellencie's most humble and most obedient servant,

G Mabbott

463. From Hierome Sankey, Wallingford House, [8] February 1659, 823, fos 231–232.

May it please your excellencie,

I hope my wife hath excused my rude departure from your excellencie, occasioned by the sudennes of my resolution upon Wednesday was se'nnight, incited therto by a faire gale and an appearance of setled wether. I blesse God we had an easy and speedy passeage and I came hither betimes on the Tuesday following.[36] On Wednesday I waited on his Highnes, to whom (according to your commands) I presented your excellencie's service and communicated your desires. He was glad to heare that your excellencie was in any measure recovering in your health, and cannot but be desirous to see you, but is confident that your deare father's example, who wore out himselfe for the serving of others, will be a patterne to him and your excellence to prize that service above health or anything that is dearest to you rather then the publique affaires should suffer any damage. My lord, I am most confident of his Highnes' willingnes to comply with you in your desires as to your intended or desired journey hither as soone as the season can be inviting to such a busines. Next day[37] was a solemne fast in the house. Dr Owen preached first and very seriously asserted and pressed the whole cause and interest. Dr Reynolds[38] followed; pressed hard to unity. Mr Calamy[39] followed.

[36] The subsequent details of parliamentary developments date this undated letter to 8 February. Thus this would appear to be Tuesday 1 February.

[37] In fact, this occurred on Friday 4 February.

[38] Edward Reynolds, parliamentarian minister, frequently preached before parliament and its councils during the 1640s. In 1648, he was appointed dean of Christ Church, Oxford, and vice-chancellor of Oxford University, but he lost both offices in 1650–1651, in the wake of his opposition to the regicide and his ambivalent attitude towards the republican regime. A moderate Presbyterian, he became prominent once more during the Protectorate of Richard Cromwell, attempting to reach an accommodation with that regime.

[39] Edmund Calamy, parliamentarian minister and one of the most popular and influential preachers of the period. During the 1640s and early 1650s, he frequently preached before parliament and its councils, was appointed to various religious bodies and committees, and became a leading light of Sion College and one of the most prominent London Presbyterians. His opposition to the regicide, and more particularly to Oliver Cromwell's ejection of the Rump, led him to keep slightly more distant from the regimes of the 1650s, but he retained influence during the Protectorate.

Those two were very moderate. Mr Manton[40] concluded, who was the most earnest of them as to church worke. On Saturday I waited on her Highnes dowager, who was very glad to heare from you and indeed most earnestly desires to see you. My lady and the children making many particular enquiryes after you all and would needs know what answer his Highness made as to your coming over and whether he doe not intend that it shuld be speedy. All the rest of your relations through mercy are in good health and would be glad to see you. Last weeke produced not much in the house, save settling comittees and some small busines about the members that were dubiously returned, about which there are the greatest number of controversies that I beleeve have ever hapned in any parliament.

Yesterday the recognition act for recognizing his Highness was read the 2d time. The commonwealthmen were for laying it aside; others some for mending it att the table; others for committing of it, some to a grande committee, others to a particular one. This day the 1 question was more particularly stated (viz) whether his Highness shuld be declared to be the rightfull and undoubted lord protector of this commonwealth etc and prest that this might particularly passe and then the bill might be committed. And after some houres' debate it was propounded with the expedient that in the parliament 54, after 7 daies' debate, judge Hale propounded under the gallery (if your lordship remember) viz that his Highness shuld be declared to be the lord protector of the commonwealth of England, Scotland and Ireland and teritoryes thereto belonging, to be qualified with such limitations and authorityes as shuld be agreed on by this house.[41] The former was urged by Mr Trevor, Birch, Swinfen,[42] with many lawyers and a great many others. The expedient brought in by Mr Weaver[43] and spake to

[40] Thomas Manton, parliamentarian minister, was, from the mid-1640s, a prominent, London-based preacher, who frequently preached before parliament and its councils. He opposed the regicide and was largely out of favour during the early 1650s, but he supported the Protectorate, advised both Oliver and Richard Cromwell on religious matters, and was favoured by them. He, too, is best described as a moderate Presbyterian.

[41] This had been proposed by Hale during the early days of the first Protectorate parliament, in which Henry Cromwell had sat. He made the proposal on 11 September 1654 (*Burton*, I, xxxii), after the opening, divisive week, during which republican MPs had bitterly attacked the Protectorate and its constitution. Although it seemed to gain some support, it was not enough to head off the looming crisis, for, on 12 September, the Protector briefly closed the house and imposed a new test on members.

[42] John Trevor, MP for Flintshire; John Birch, MP for Leominster; and John Swinfen, MP for Tamworth.

[43] John Weaver, MP for Stamford. He supported the parliamentarian cause in the civil war in an administrative role, serving as treasurer of the Eastern Association, and in 1645 he was elected as MP for Stamford, sitting in the Long Parliament and its Rump (though he held aloof from the regicide), and in 1649 he was appointed a parliamentary commissioner

by Godfrey, Brinkley, Groves, Nevil[44] and many others. The difference is wholly de modo,[45] his Highness having the hearts of all; Sir Arthur[46] himselfe having excedingly commended him, looking upon him as a person of great worth and according to his owne expression, without guile or galle. The debate held till about 3 a clock and is now adj'rnd till tomorrow morning. The house is exceeding full, there being above 400 in it and many more members then can sitt downe. The elections for Ireland and Scotland, I am perswaded, will stand, but there will be a consideration had speedily of them, and your lordship will do well to hast away your members. I wonder Sir Anthony Morgan and Mr Anesley stay so long.[47] We have had no post thence this fortnight. Most part of Saturday was spent about lieutenant-general Ludlow, who sitts in the house without the oath prescribed;[48] and after 2 or 3 houres spent in the debate there was a madman (but had the appearance of a sober man) discovered by the sargeant to be no member, having sate 3 daies in the house, was call'd to the barre and adjudged to Newgate, but it tooke up so much time that it was too late to reassume the debate. But I am perswaded it will not <att present> for some time be reassumed in regard Godfrey, Bamfeild, Sir George Booth, Ned Cooke[49] and others are in upon the same accompt and ther's none of them but have some freinds or other who will be tender of them; besides it was much prest that they had much more right to sitt than the members for Ireland and Scotland, and therfore desired that might be first insisted upon.

And now, my lord, I thinke I have wearyed you out. Tis the Lord above who must manage those counsells for His people's and the nation's good. Lett our eyes be upon Him and our hearts lifted up to Him. I have presumed upon this freedome with you in regard you know the persons and things. Me thinks I see the wisedome and expectation even of the wisest man failing as to the result of their wisest contrivances. Ther's much lesse of boysterousnes in this house hath appeared as yett then used to be upon such debates. We find a

for the government of Ireland. His republican sympathies led to his estrangement from the Protectorate and, although he was returned for Stamford to Oliver Cromwell's two Protectorate parliaments, he was excluded from both at or soon after the start of the session.

[44] Lambert Godfrey, MP for Romney; John Bulkeley; Thomas Grove, MP for Marlborough; and, probably, Henry Neville.

[45] This Latin phrase could be translated as 'about form', 'manner', 'measure', or 'extent'.

[46] Hesilrige.

[47] Morgan, MP for Meath and Louth, and Arthur Annesley, MP for the city of Dublin.

[48] Edmund Ludlow, MP for Hindon, had slipped quietly into the house without taking the oath required by the 1657 constitution, in which MPs swore to be true and faithful to the Lord Protector and not attempt anything against his person or powers.

[49] Godfrey; Thomas Bampfield, MP for Exeter; Sir George Booth, MP for Lancashire; and Edward Cooke, MP for Tewkesbury.

necessity of waiting upon God as to every daie's result; other refuges will faile. The good Lord keepe up your spirit in dependance on Him. Thus prayes,

Your excellencie's most obliged servant,

Hie Sankey

Sir Henry Vane was up this day but hath not yett spoke, but is to begin tomorrow.

464. From William Duckenfield,[50] 14 February 1659, 823, fos 214–215.

Letter of request, noting that his company of foot in Henry Cromwell's regiment was then serving in England but was due to return to the rest of the regiment in Ireland, while a company of foot in Hewson's regiment was then serving in Ireland, though its officers were keen to return to England; thus suggests to Henry Cromwell a straight swap or exchange of companies, so that Hewson's company could stay in Ireland under the writer and his fellow-officers, while Henry Cromwell's company could remain in England under Hewson and so allow Hewson's company officers to leave Ireland and return to England.

465. From Arthur Annesley, London, 15 February 1659, 823, fos 216–217.

May it please your excellency,

I hould it my duty to give your excellency the first account of my safe comeing to London, who have deservedly the greatest interest to command my services in all places. I was here within six dayes after I tooke leave of your excellency and soone after attended his Highnesse with your excellency's letter, which he hath been pleased to promise me the fruit of and expressed himselfe very gratiously towards me, which I must acknowledge the product of your excellencye's favourable character given of me, wherewith his Highnesse was pleased to acquaint me. I was not in the house till yesterday, where we happyly put an end to six dayes' high debates with a question passed nemine contradicente,[51] whereof I send your excellency the coppy inclosed, which will give some judgment of the likelyhood there is that this parliament may be instrumentall towards our settlement. The humble petition and advice is upon the matter laid aside, and I beleeve some other acts passed at the same time will undergoe a renew

[50] Parliamentarian officer, whose military record is obscure but who was apparently an officer in Henry Cromwell's foot regiment.

[51] This Latin phrase could be translated as 'without opposition', or 'without anyone speaking' or 'voting against'.

if not repeale. The other house is not at all owned, yet there is ground to beleeve a house of peeres will be settled. There was a meeting this day of the officers of the army at Wallingford House, but it's thought the votes passed yesterday have left them little to offer. A petition from the commonwealth party in the citty tooke up this whole morning in the house and had no other answere but that some particulars thereof were allready under consideration, that what else in it was fitt for the house to consider should be considered in due time, and that the house according to the expression in their petition did expect they should acquiesce in their resolutions. They were the more cautious in this answere to pravent multitudes of petitions which might probably be offered of different and contrary straines. Your lordship sees how free I am to open myselfe to your excellency, wherein if I receive your lordship's approbation, I shall continue my weekely service in the same kind or any other way that may most effectually expresse me, may it please your excellency,

Your excellency's most obedient servant,

Arthur Annesley

My father[52] presents his most humble service to your excellency and acknowledgment for your excellency's letter to his Highnesse in his favour.

466. From Francis Aungier, London, 15 February 1659, 823, fo. 218.

My lord,

I should verye hardly have attempted to give your lordship the trouble of a lettre amidst the many serious afayres wherein I knowe your lordship to be involved. But that I can find no other way to sapresse that gratitude and high sence which I have of your lordship's favours to me then by yeilding (as farre as I am capable) a just obedience to your lordship's commands.

This day was the first in which I was able to obteine the honour of beeing admitted to tender your lordship's lettres to his Highnesse, from whome, as also from my lord Faulconberge, I receaved so gratious, soe obligeing an acceptance that had not my addresse beene wholy grounded upon so strong a bottome as your lordship's favourable recommendation I should have tottered, nay sunke under so greate a

[52] Francis Annesley, Viscount Valencia and Baron Mountnorris, politician, attained office, reputation, and land through his work in the colonial government of Ireland in the opening decades of the seventeenth century, but he fell from favour and lost office in 1637, spending the 1640s and 1650s in semi-retirement on his estates in England and Ireland. He died shortly after the Restoration.

loade of obligations which I there receav'd, and for which I must ever acknowledge myselfe to stand endebted unto your lordship.

Yesterday (my lord) I entered into that place[53] into which nothing but my desires to serve his Highnesse and your lordship could have carryed me and from which I should make a verye suddaine and glad retreate if my present inclinations might be countenanced by your lordship's allowance. Not that I am or ever can be wearye of endeavouring to serve so good a master. But when I find reason to suspect that my litle inconsiderable industryes will be rendered ineffectuall by the opposition of such vast forces as I perceave mustered together with a resolution to contradicte those interests to which my reason and dutye have commanded my adherence, I hope your lordship will not wonder if I say I have an aversion, since nothing can appeare more insupportable to my yeares and temper then to meete with an opposition in my affections, which I must despayre of being able to graple with. I find (my lord) three severall compositions in this fabrick. The best is that which I feare to be the lightest, not that it is the least in bulke, but that I suspect it will prove the least in capacitye to effect what it intends. The midle region is that which will in probabilitye give the lawe to both the others. They are strong, they are adhesive to what they intend and extreamely indefatigable. The last and least is the worst; they are made up of gall and wormewood; they are industrious and vigilant but too sowre for either of the other perfectly to intermixe with. It is this which would drawe all downewards and dissolve theyr litle world into its former chaos. But these as they stand distincte are not so formidable as I heretofore apprehended. Yet I must say that this in conjunction with that which in my observation I placed in the midle spheere will totally hinder and barre those high inclinations to which the first were levelled. Nay, if they cannot compasse theyr owne sullen aymes, I perceave they will be content (in order to doeing mischeife) and take pleasure to frustrate the expectations and ruine the hopes of those against whome they are opposed. In fine, the conjunction of these twoe in this particular may be as fatall to the other as if themselves were prevalent. For if I should fall into the hands of robbers where I should find some incline to cutt my throate and others (pretending themselves more moderate) should perswade them to satisfye theyre crueltye by cutting of my hands and putting out my eyes, I should hardly be able to determine that there were a melius eligendum[54] in that condition. But it may be (and I could heartily wish the issue may prove so) I am too apprehensive in my feares and I easily grant that this passion may as well blinde me as it hath don thousands who

[53] He sat in this parliament as MP for Counties Westmeath, Longford, and King's.
[54] This Latin phrase could be translated as a 'better choice' or 'option'.

have beene more prudent. However, if I doe erre, I cannot suspect it an unpardonable crime since it takes its rise and origen from my affections which I cannot but cherish. But while I am discoursing of this I have left no place in this narrowe paper to give your lordship an account of our parliamentarye proceedings, for which I must beg your lordship's pardon that I give them in the particuler enclosed,[55] since I am resolved that this shall have no farther or other chardge then to tender unto your lordship, my lady and Mrs Russell[56] the humblest devotion of (my lord)

Your excellencye's most humbly, faithfully, cordially devoted servant,

Franc Aungier

467. From Francis Aungier, [enclosed in letter no. 466], 823, fos 219–220.

February the 14th 1658

Resolved:

That it be parte of this bill to recognize and declare his Highnesse Richard, Lord Protector, to be Lord Protector and cheife magistrate of the commonwealth of England, Scotland and Ireland and the territoryes and dominions thereunto belonging.

Before this was passed, the word recognize was debated 6 howres whether it should stand in that parte of the bill and when it was putt to the question it was carryed in the affirmative by 23 voyces. The negative was headed by Sir Arthur Hazelrigge, Sir Henry Vayne, Ludlowe, Lambert, Scott, Sir Anthony Ashley Cooper,[57] Nevill and all that gang. When this was pass't, the next question was whether there should be any additions to this previous vote, concerning the

[55] No. 467.

[56] Identification uncertain, but perhaps Katherine Russell, the younger sister of Henry Cromwell's wife, at this stage an unmarried eighteen-year-old.

[57] Parliamentarian officer and politician, though he initially fought for the king in and around his native Dorset; he did not join the parliamentary forces until 1644, although thereafter he was active for parliament in regaining and then running Dorset. He held local office in Dorset and Wiltshire in the late 1640s and early 1650s, but he was not an MP and had no connections with the regicide. He sat in the Nominated Assembly, allied to the moderates, and he initially attained high office during the Protectorate, as a founder member of the Protectoral council and member for Wiltshire in the first Protectorate parliament. However, for reasons that are not entirely clear he broke with the regime at the end of 1654, lost or left office, and, although again elected for Wiltshire, was excluded from the second Protectorate parliament. Returned once more for Wiltshire, he was a prominent opponent of the regime in Richard Cromwell's Protectorate parliament and allied himself with its republican critics.

exclusion of the militia, negative voyce, the rights and priviledges of parliament and the libertyes of the people. But this was carryed in the negative by 89 voyces, though the worse and worst (I meane the midle and last) partyes joyned in the opposition.

The last vote was, that before this bill be committed, this house doe declare such additionall clauses to be parte of the bill as may bound the powre of the cheife magistate and fully secure the rights and priviledges of parliament and the rights of the people, and that neither this nor any other previous vote that is or shall be passed in order to this bill shall be of force or binding to the people untill the whole bill be passed.

February the 15th 1658

This day there was a petition from some of the cittye, only those of Prayse God Barebones'[58] gang, sign'd by thousands of hands at least (the contents whereof was for our returne out of the state we are to a commonwealth without a supreame magistrate) and presented to the house, but it was so ill resented by the house in generall, though Sir Henry Vayne, Sir Arthur Hazellrig, Lambert and others moved that thankes might be given them for theyr good affections, that they receaved no other answere but that the house had taken notice of and read theyr petition, parte whereof they had then under theyr consideration and as much of the rest as they should thinke fitt they would in due time consider hereafter. In the meanetime the house did expect that according to theyr promise mentioned in the close of theyr petition they should acquiesce in the resolution of the parliament. This was eisdem verbis[59] the answere to the petition after it was voted that the mention of thankes and good affection should be left out of the answere. Tomorrowe we shall fall upon the other parte of the bill that relates to the militia and negative voyce, which I guesse the parliament will endeavour to engrosse to themselves.

468. From Gilbert Mabbott, 15 February 1659, 823, fos 223–224.

May it please your excellencie,

The parlament on Wednesday and Thursday last[60] was in debate of the recognition and ordered that before the committment of the bill

[58] Praisegod Barbon, parliamentarian politician and preacher, was a London-based religious radical, millenarian, and strong supporter of religious liberty, who held local office in London but who achieved wider notice in 1653 as one of the more influential radical members of the Nominated Assembly.

[59] This Latin phrase could be translated as 'of the same words' or 'almost word for word'.

[60] 9 and 10 February.

there should bee a previous vote that his Highnes is the undoubted Lord Protector and cheife majestrate of England, Scotland and Ireland and the dominions and territories thereunto belonging. The question was whether to this question these words should bee added, vizt with such limitations and restrictions as the parlament should thincke fitt, and it was resolved in the negative. Friday the house was againe in debate of some other addition to this previous vote but came to noe resolution. Saturday they expelled Mr Villers[61] (whoe now calls himselfe D'Anvers) and Mr Jones[62] (attorney generall for North Wales) for being in armes against the parlament. Mr serjeant Glanvile[63] wrote a lettre to the speaker desireing that another may bee elected in his stead, hee being not quallified to sitt in the howse, which was ordered accordingly. The commissioners of his Highnes had a meeteing this weeke with the commissioners of the king of Sweden. That night there was a presse of watermen and mariners upon the river. The councell ordered that the commissioners of the navy should put in execution all the powers committed to them for the speedy puting forth the fleete to sea. Severall officers mett this weeke at Wallingford Howse to consider of the heads of a petition to bee presented to parlament. His Highnes was pleased to come to them and give them some cautions and admonitions in the pening the said petition, which they have since referr'd to a committee of officers. Yesterday the parlament debated againe the recognition and past there 2 votes thereupon, vizt that it bee part of this bill to recognize and declare his Highnes Richard Lord Protector to bee the Protector and cheife majestrate of this comon-wealth of England, Scotland and Ireland and the dominions

[61] Born the illegitimate son of the wife of Viscount Purbeck, he was known or styled himself variously as Robert Wright, Howard, and Villers/Villiers, as well as second Viscount Purbeck. Raised in France as a Catholic, he returned to England in the early 1640s and fought for the royalists, although by the later 1640s he had gone over to parliament and converted to Protestantism. He claimed the surname Danvers after marrying into that family, though he renounced any claim to the Purbeck title after the death of his mother's husband in 1657. He was returned to Richard Cromwell's Protectorate parliament for Westbury but was expelled on the grounds of his former delinquency, although a motion to imprison him failed.

[62] Edmund Jones, parliamentarian politician, attorney-general for South Wales and returned for Breconshire to the first and third Protectorate parliaments. Despite arguing his innocence and pointing to his loyal service to parliament since the late 1640s, it emerged that, during the 1640s, he had compounded for his alleged delinquency and so was expelled from the house.

[63] Sir John Glanville, politician and lawyer, supported the king's cause in the civil war and presided over trials conducted by the royalists at Salisbury and Exeter. He surrendered to parliament in 1644 and was imprisoned until 1648; he compounded for his delinquency, was disabled from sitting as an MP and expelled from the Long Parliament. When returned to Richard Cromwell's Protectorate parliament for St Germans, he did not try to take his seat, was deemed unqualified, and a new election was ordered.

and territories thereunto belonging; 2ly resolved that before this bill bee committed the house doeth declare such additionall clawses to bee part thereof as may bound the power of the cheife majestrate and fully secure the rights and priviledges of the parlament and the liberties and rights of the people and that neither this nor any other previous vote that is or shalbee passed in order to this bill shalbee of force or bindeing to the people till the whole bill bee passed. This day Mr Moyer and about 20 more came downe with the petition, signed with some thousands of disconted[64] persons. The petitioners were called in and the speaker tould them that severall of the particulers contained in the petition were now under the consideration of the howse, and others would fall in upon their further debates, and for the rest the howse did expect that they would acquiesce in the judgment of parlament. The petitioners withdrewe and were not a little troubled in that they had not the thanckes of the howse (for their petition they could not expect) for their good affections, which upon a division of the howse was carried by 100 voices in the negative. I humbly subscribe myselfe, my lord,

Your excellencie's most humble and most obedient servant,

G Mabbott.

469. From Hierome Sankey, Wallingford House, 15 February 1659, 823, fos 225–226.

May it please your excellencie,

The debate which I gave you an accompt of by the last continued till last night att nine of the clock, save that Saturday was spent in throwing out cavilleers, one Jones of Wales, formerly the king's atturney, and lately his Highness' for South Wales, and Villiers that goes by the name of Danvers, and one Street[65] of Worcester to be heard on Tuesday next, his witnesses being not ready. The debate continued for six daies and most spent till 3 or 4 a clock. The 2d question was brought in by Mr Annesly and though a great member of the House contended for the conjunction of the votes, yett after it was carryed that there should be no addition to the first question, yett they that carryed the

[64] Clearly written thus, though apparently a slip for 'discontented'.

[65] Thomas Street, parliamentarian politician and lawyer, was too young to fight in the war but, having gone up to Oxford University in the spring of 1642, he remained there, and thus at the king's headquarters, during the war years, and was arrested and briefly imprisoned by parliamentary forces upon returning to his native Worcester in 1645. Elected for Worcester in Richard Cromwell's Protectorate parliament, his first parliament, Street fought off accusations of active, wartime royalism and retained his seat.

first question, very rigourously[66] and fairly assented to the 2d, which passed without one negative.

Truly, my lord, this is through God's mercy a comfortable beginning in the conclusion of the debate, though it was not carryed on without much heates etc that might better have been spared. Tomorrow the house goes on to the militia and to the negative voyce. I hope through God's mercy the foundation of a settlement indeed will be layd. I make bould to present your excellencie with this briefe accompt, not but that I know you have larger from other hands, but yett it becomes me to pay my tribute. And if your lordship have any commands to lay upon me, there's none shall be more ready to observe them then, my lord,

Your excellencie's most faythfull servant,

Hie Sankeye

470. Robert Beake to John Bridges, 15 February 1659, 823, fos 221–222.

Honoured sir,

The last night (at 10 of the clocke) closed the debate begunn the 7th instant, vizt a previous vote for recognizing his Highnes to be Lord Protector and cheife magistrate of England, and in order to the comittment of the bill for recognition, it was carried at last in the affirmative by 223 voices and the negatives were 133. It's wonderfull to consider with what heate this was attayned unto. That which made it sticke was a desire of haveing the rights and libertys of the people to goe hand in hand with this vote, and in this the republicans were the onely zealotts, the Presbyterians with vigor driveing t'other way. The militia and negative vote were two of the cardinal hinges upon which the people's liberty depended and these were the topicks whence they deduced al there arguments to batter downe the previous votes. To such a height were these libertynes growne that one while they would averr the ould parliament was in being, another whyle that they had the sole legislature in themselvs, another while they question whether his late Highnes had animum dispenendi[67] when he named his successors, and yet agayne whether he was compos or non compos[68] and what legal testymony was extant of the right of his Highnes' succession. And theis are soe much the more to be wonderd at if we consider the tye and obligation they layd uppon themselves at the doore in their first

[66] The first letter of this word is poorly formed because of an ink blob and attempted correction and it could alternatively be read as 'vigourously'.

[67] This Latin phrase could be translated as 'a mind', 'passion', or 'feeling to dispose' or 'to order'.

[68] These two Latin phrases could be translated as 'sound', 'sane', 'in possession' or 'in control'; and 'not sound', 'not sane', 'not in possession' or 'not in control'.

entrance and yet some ventured without the oath to take their places: Sir Henry Vaine, lieutenant generall Ludlow, Sir George Booth, Mr Bamfeild and others of such perswasion, and because the excepting against the first would involve the other, therefore they are all winked at. The other house doe litle, nor doe wee take notice of them. The commonwealths men are against the thing itselfe, the Presbyterians are for addition of some lords. It's talked as if the army would stirr, but his Highnes has a severe eye upon them and is resolved he wil not interupt the parliament. After the previous vote, last night passd another to secure the people's rights and the priviledges of parliament and this was mooved by your freinds when (upon the carieing of the other question) the tribunes of the people would not (because of their doggednes) aske that in the second place which they could not gayne in the first. This vote speakes men true patriots, as the other (the party that caried it) truly desirous of peace and setlement. There was not a negative in it. Sir, I am,

Your affectionat servant,

Rob Beake

471. From Thomas Gorges to Robert Gorges, the Speaker's Chamber, 15 February 1659, 823, fos 227–228.

Good brother,

I have sent you yesterday by collonel Temple a few lines and but few because he is able at large to inform you. Our 6 days' debate came last night neer 9 of the clock to a resolution, which is to recognize his Highness Richard, Lord Protector, to be the Lord Protector and cheif magistrate of the commonwealth of England etc. This as part of the bill

Resolved: That before this bill be committed, this howse doe declare such additionall clauses to be part of the bill as may binde the power of the cheif magistrate and fully secure the rights and priviledges of parliament and the rights and liberties of the people, and that neither this nor any other previous vote that is or shalbe passed in order to this bill shalbe of force or bindinge to the people untill the whole bill be passed.

This day the petition formerly tendred and put off was agayn presented. The petition was ushered in by Mr Samuel Moyer, commonwealths men, Leveller, 5th Monarchs attending them, and the same petition which was intended for the last parliament a short tyme befor theyr dissolution. It is very high, cajolinge the army, owning noe power but the representatives in parliament, which created this vote as the answer to the petition:

That this house have read the petition, that some of the particulars this house hath already taken into consideration, and such others as are fit for the howse to take into consideration they will in due tyme consider of, and doe expect you shall acquiesce in the determination of this howse accordinge to your own expressions.

This petition was in the name of divers cittizens and inhabitants of the City of London.[69]

That you see this answer is parliamentary and wheras it was added that the howse did approve of the petitioners' good affection, it was layd aside by a vote of 100 and odd voyces difference. By this you may somwhat judge of the sence of the howse which, notwithstandinge as much of craft and specious designs are used imaginable, yet we shalbe safe within doors and I hope we have not much reason to fear abroad, for the army is (after much workinge uppon) resolved to own the 2 howses with the single person, and wilbe satisfyed with some negatives as to the constitution and probably to religion, and in other bills only some days or weeks of advise and then to pass for laws, a coordination in the militia, sittinge a parliament, in him and the parliament, and in the intervalls in him and the councill. Those things may secure all partyes and settle his Highness better then much struglinge may. I give you not my sence now on these things. I am glad we can reach anythinge that hath safty in it, and we must observe seasons and tymes as well as things and persons. I pray acquaynt Shapcote[70] with the contents of this, and assure him he hath many frends here and I presume he may be shortly intitled to the attorney generall's place.[71] I am now attendinge about his Tiverten buisness[72] and as far as I can look into the thinge, it will beget a new writ and then he may rest assurd.

My collonel Cook and your good frind tells me he writ formerly unto you concerninge his cosen german Mr Walter Scudamore,[73] formerly related to the lord chief justice Pepis. His desyers are yours and Shapcot's assistance accordinge to the merits of the gentleman and Hoppar[74] and applications he makes unto you. The collonell

[69] Sentence added in the margin at this point.

[70] Robert Shapcote had sat for Tiverton in the first two Protectorate parliaments and was seeking to represent the town again in Richard Cromwell's Protectorate parliament, though his return was being disputed.

[71] He was already solicitor-general and was seeking the attorney-generalship of Ireland (*TSP*, VII, p. 627).

[72] In early March, the privileges committee finished considering the disputed election for Tiverton, and, on 10 March, the house supported the committee's final report, which found against Shapcote.

[73] Fleetwood had written to Henry Cromwell at the beginning of February on Scudamore's behalf (*TSP*, VII, p. 604).

[74] Uncertain reading of a poorly formed word.

would have written to Shapcote and soe would I, but we want tyme. I must hasten into the howse wher the committee of priveledges sit to hearken after my comrade's commands. I am,

Yours,

T G

I heer shall send you the bond. My comrade's buisness is not likely to come on this night.

My last tould you of payinge captain Owen and that hee sent you Mr Maund's letter, which tells you that he hath returned the monyes for Ireland, soe I have but £50 towards our excellency's £100 and you owe some somes here fitting to be payd.

472. From Arthur Annesley, London, 22 February 1659, 823, fos 229–230.

May it please your excellency,

Though there occurres little to write since my last, yet that my dutyfull observance of your excellencye's commands may appeare, I shall acquaint your lordship that the last weeke the house of commons resolved that it be part of the bill of recognition to declare the parliament to consist of two houses and to state the bounds and powers of another house; and this day we were in further debate thereof, but have adjourned the debate till Thursday next. I beleeve no house will passe but with admittance of the ancient peeres that have not forfeited. How farre the army will approve thereof I may question in a letter, though we abhorre the thought of it in our house. We have another great businesse tomorrow, which was entred upon yesterday and adjurned. Tis concerning the sending a fleet to the Sound, which is like very shortly to be disputed betweene the two crownes of Denmark and Swede and their confederates. The Hollanders have a 100 large shipps ready; we fifty. My opinion is we shall recommend it to his Highnesse' care to send a strong fleet with caution to endeavour peace betweene those crownes and to avoid any breach with our friends and allyes as they both are.

Letters are sent to your lordship by our speaker for the state of the revenue and charge in Ireland. It will be good that a returne be hastned, that we may make the best use we can for a supply hence. Wherein and in what else your excellency shall command my service, I will ever manifest myself, may it please your excellency,

Your excellencye's most humble servant,

Arthur Annesley

473. From Daniel Abbott, Kilkenny, 1 March 1659, 823, fos 233–234.

May it please your excellency,

Just as I was coming forth of Dublin, I had notice given me by one belonging to colonell Pritty[75] that the said colonell intended a triall at Clonmell the next assizes for the 200 acres of land belonging to the silver mynes. And upon a serious consideration had thereof, I humbly conceive that if colonell Pritty gaine this particular plott of land by a triall at the common law, it wilbe impossible to recover it for the use of the said mynes and without which the state will never have benefitt thereof, though upon a readmeasurement the said colonell Prittye's lott be found to be an overplus of neare double what he ought to have. The judge before whom this triall wilbe is the recorder of Dublin,[76] who hath bin his only councell to putt him forward in going to law and most pleaded his cause at the late triall before the lord cheife barron.[77] My lord, wee have nothing to plead against his recovering this land but that it was not admeasured and given out unto him according to rule, and that it was so is an undenyable truth. And though the attourney generall and solicitor generall[78] both pleaded it, the lord cheife barron seemed to take little notice thereof, but decreed the land to colonell Pritty. And no doubt the recorder will doe the like if something be not done by your lordship or the councell to prevent the present tryall (which wilbe the 10th or 11th of March) by letting the recorder know that you are credibly informed the particular lott of colonell Pritty hath neare double its proportion of acres that of right belonges to the said colonell and that it is your lordship's and the councell's intent to have it admeasured and sett out unto him according to rule and till then there can be no legall proceedings in law. If this or any other way by your excellency shalbe thought fitt at present for the stopp of the said triall, it's like that the said colonell Pritty may be brought to some reasonable composition and so the state's interest in some measure preserved and the pattentees encouraged to proceed in carrying on the works, which otherwise wilbe wholly left to colonell Prittye's mercy

[75] Henry Pretty, parliamentarian officer, went to Ireland in 1649 as a captain in Henry Ireton's New Model horse regiment, though soon after he was promoted to be major of Oliver Cromwell's horse regiment in Ireland. When that double regiment was divided into two new regiments, Pretty was an officer in the regiment initially commanded by Henry Shelburne, but, on Shelburne's death in 1651, Pretty became its colonel; around the same time he also became governor of Carlow.

[76] Probably John Bisse/Bysse, who, claiming Henry Cromwell's support, had been returned by the city of Dublin to the second Protectorate parliament and who, after there had been initial thoughts of excluding him, had been admitted and played an active role in that parliament (*TSP*, V, p. 477).

[77] Miles Corbet.

[78] William Basil and Robert Shapcote respectively.

to their damage, neare £1,500 already expended, besides they and the state being debarred of any future profitt to be expected from the said mynes. After this triall the pattentees wilbe putt out of possession of their smelting mills, the poore workmen out of their howses which they have lately built, and so be necessitated to returne for England, from whence it cost us very deare to gett them over, and so the whole worke rendred uselesse and the undertakers remedilesse. If what is proposed or any other way shalbe thought meet by your lordship or the councell to be done by way of prevention for the aforesaid reasons, some one or other must be speedily dispatched away to be at Clonmell by the 10th of March to make affidavit in the court of what shalbe tendred, otherwise it wilbe of none effect in the court. Thus humbly craving your lordship's pardon for this trouble, being urged thereunto in discharge of my duty as employed in the behalfe of the pattentees, as also the concernment of above £500 to myselfe, I take leave and remayne,

Your excellencye's most humble servant,

D Abott

Being thus surprized in matter of time, I am perswaded there will not be one councell that goes that circuit but is already retained for colonell Pritty.

474. From Thomas Gorges, 1 March 1659, 823, fos 235–236.

May it please your excellency,

The encouragements I have receaved by the hands of your servant, my brother, not only gives me this boldness but an assurance of pardon for all other errors that may escape my pen, and seinge you will accept of the trouble, I shalbe constant in it and in those slender collections I present your excellency, withall I shall only state matter of fact and the reasons on which they are grounded, rarely intreposinge my own thoughts.

I need not tell your excellency that we are met with as many divisions naturally planted in us as our particular interest leads unto, and wher ther are such fundamentall contradictions it is noe wonder if debates are longe and dubious. We have past one great mountayn, the owninge the single person, but doubtless shall exceedingly dispute the bounds and soe far endeavour to restrayn him that he shall have vox praeterea nihil[79] and the duke of Venice shall prove more absolute then our English Protector. Noe negative, noe title to the militia, less to the army (as divided from the militia) is what some aym at. Others are

[79] This Latin phrase could be translated as 'a voice (and) nothing more'.

for a negative as to the constitution, revenew when setled and matters of religion, others to the powers admitted in the petition and advice, and some for larger; but as farther debates arise, soe I shall give your excellency the result of them. The consideration of the present state of affayrs in the Baltick Sea hath taken up some tym, and indeed will call for more. If the English loose theyr interest ther they must expect laws from the Dutch, who court with us the same mistress trade, and cannot but be jealous of us, as well as bearinge a revenge unto us. The gentlemen whose principles are for a commonwealth oppose very strongly our interposinge ther, especially as a frend to Sweden. Theyr reasons are: the tenderness of blood, wastinge of treasure, dissatisfaction on the Swede's cause especially his last invasion of Zealand, and his swellinge power in case he becomes absolute in the Sound, wherby he may impose what terms he please on Christendom, whereas if it remayns in divided or weaker hands, our interest is safer and our terms better. This debate on Wensday last[80] begot this resolution: that a very considerable navy be forthwith provided and put to sea for the safty of this commonwealth and for the preservation of the trade and commerce therof. On Thursday the debate ran in whose hands the managment of this fleet shalbe, and beinge prest to be in his Highness and councill, it was highly opposed, first because it tacitely gave him the right of the militia, 2dly it gave him the power of peace and war, 3dly it owned his councill and imployed them, and at 11 that night it was resolved that it be referd to his Highness to put the vote of the house in execution for the preparinge and puttinge to sea a considerable navy etc, savinge the right and interest of this howse to the militia and to the makeinge of peace and war. What his Highness will doe by virtue of this vote I know not, for it signifyes litle, and yet I hope he will not omitt this seasonable opportunity in appearinge at least as a powerfull mediator for peace between those princes. The Dutch have provided 100 noble ships of war with 10 fier ships and 10 advisoes[81] and have 16 more on the stocks almost ready. The howse adjourned till Saterday.

Saterday the howse discharged one Portman,[82] beinge committed to the Tower on his late Highness' warrant as beinge a principall actor in the insurrection amonge the 5th Monarchy men. This imprisonment is voted illegal and unjust. Thus your excellency sees that the indulgence

[80] 23 February.

[81] Adviso: a dispatch boat.

[82] John Portman, a Fifth Monarchist or Fifth Monarchist sympathizer, was arrested and questioned several times during the Protectorate. Imprisoned since February 1658, in February 1659 he petitioned parliament for his release and, having heard him, on 22 February, parliament declared his imprisonment illegal and, following a further debate, ordered his release on 26 February.

of your renowned father hath another interpretation uppon it. Had his Highness proceeded with that sort of men as he did with another generation, he had better secured the nation from those vipers that gnaw his blessed memory with the most poysoned teeth of design and mallice.

Yesterday we reassumed the debate of the other howse. Many questions started as to the bounds of them, but much prest to know the persons first and then declare theyr powers, but answered if the persons be concluded to be the ould nobillity, it will after that prove too late to bound them, for they beinge restored to theyr primitive rights are sole judges of it themselves. Much debate whither by the petition and advice ther is any power given to the successor to call another howse, but the 8th paragraph and the explanation on the 5th and the oath to be taken by both howses satisfyes that it was soe intended; but in the meantyme that poor petition suffers more tortures then Lawrence Sabastean or any of the martyrs in the Romesh legend ever did, it beinge severall tymes sayd, had Alexander the 6th, Ceasar Borgia and Matchiavill met to have created a platform of tyranny they could not have paralleled this peece. The howrly objection that it was made by a forced parliament, because many were kept out, is allmost dispelled, because it must be a parliament to declare the force and retorted on the[83] those gentlemen that used it because it will anull all the acts made from December 1647[84] till 1653, they then sittinge under a greater force. But I trouble your excellency with my undigested and hasty lines. At 3 of the clock this afternoon (we haveinge shot all day at rowens),[85] it was resolved that tomorrow the debate shalbe whither this howse will transact with the other howse now sittinge as an howse of parliament, which indeed will in a short tyme bringe us a consistency or dissolution, and I humbly conceave it better to break heer then on any other poynt.

The armye, we hope, sit down quiett and resolve soe to doe; if otherwise we rejoyce in that union that is under your excellencye's government which wilbe able to ballance any disordered passions heer. I am now to beg your excellencye's pardon for my ill pen, worse method and longe tryall of your patience to read both, and your opinion that I am,

Your excellencye's most humble servant,
Tho Gorges

[83] Superfluous word or word then omitted.
[84] Presumably Pride's Purge of December 1648 is intended.
[85] Rowen: a second crop or an aftermath.

475. From Thomas Grove, Westminster, 1 March 1659, 823, fos 237–238.

Letter of recommendation on behalf of his unnamed brother, a poor man with many children to support, who intended to seek a new life in Ireland; requests that his brother, a godly and sober man, be given a place or office which would yield him a reasonable income; praises Henry Cromwell for his good and godly work in Ireland.

476. From Arthur Annesley, London, 8 March 1659, 823, fos 239–240.

May it please your excellency,

I received the honour of your lordship's letter, which warrants me to continue this weekely information of what passeth here, which I once apprehended I should not have been able to doe this poast, but the speaker falling so ill about nine of the clock this night, we could not come to the maine question,[86] which would have held us till one of the clock at night as it did yesternight. The house adjourned and I have gotten a few minutes to let your excellency know what is done and what we are like to come to. Your lordship hath inclosed the question that hath imployed the house allmost these ten dayes and been debated pro and con with a great deale of judgment and consideration, but whither it will yet passe is uncertaine, though the latter part concerning the ancient peeres was added this night to make the question more passable, ther right being asserted in the house so unquestionably that no question could passe without a provision for it. The passing of this addition somewhat tryed the pulse of the house for they were devided upon the question and those in the affirmative were 195 and those in the negative 188. So that with the speaker and 4 tellers your excellency may see that there were in the house this night 400 wanting twelve. And it's very probable the maine question, with the addition to it, which is to be put tomorrow, will passe in the affirmative and then some hope businesse may goe on more smoothly with two houses. But I must further acquaint your excellency that those in the negative this night, doubting the question would be carryed against them and observing that most of the members of Ireland and Scotland voted for it, they sett on foot the debate about the illegality of their sitting and proposed they might withdraw and give no vote in a question that might be so fatall to England. How the house will proceed herein tomorrow I know not, but it's cleer if the question passe the members

[86] Whether to do business with the other house and so recognize it as a house of parliament.

of those two nations carryes it, which gives great discontent. The Lord quiet all men's spirits towards settlement. Our fleet is not yet gone to sea. Here are some rumours of a late defeat given the Swedes. Your lordship will, I hope, pardon my hasty scrible and still owne me as, my lord,

Your excellency's most obedient servant,

Arthur Annesley

477. From Francis Aungier, London, 8 March 1659, 823, fos 241–242.

Letter of courtesy, profusely thanking Henry Cromwell for his letter and his affections and heaping praise on Henry Cromwell, his family, and his government of Ireland; apologizes that, because he was unwell and forced to keep to his chamber, he had very little news to report.[87]

478. From Thomas Gorges, London, 8 March 1659, 823, fos 243–244.

May it please your excellency,

I conclude ere this you have receaved the trouble of my last lines, and I can add but litle to what the last poast conveyed you. Ever since that date we have ben on the same dispute, whether to transact with the other howse now sittinge as the other howse of parliament. The arguments have ben passionate and pressed suitable to interest, but noe resolve as yet obteyned. But those gentlemen that are for owninge them, findinge themselfs overpowred and indeed outwitted by the commonwealths men (who have cajold many of the yonge gentlemen on particular disgusts as to the persons of the present lords) wer inforced to move for additions to the question, and findinge the yonge gentlemen very zealous to preserve the rights of the anteant lords, added a salvo to the rights of the aunteant peers that have contenued faythfull to this commonwealth when duly summond by writ to sit in the other howse of parliament. The howse on these disputes sate till one this morninge and met at one this afternoon and about 8 put the addition and divided, the ayes 195, the noes 188, and then we rationally expected the mayn question, but instead of that the gentlemen that lost theyr hopes interposed the sittinge of

[87] Indeed, the only mention of parliamentary business in this letter is a brief paragraph added at the end: 'The speaker's unexpected indisposition has ajourn'd the debate of the other house till tomorrowe, when I feare it will not be determin'd, for those that have interpos'd this last weeke past have the same mind still and will oppose, though they make repetition of theyr arguments. The armye, I am inform'd, are disgusted at this hesitation, but the house, though they have beene told so, will take no notice of it.'

the members of Scotland and Ireland and debated it for longe, till the speaker through much weakness sanke in the chayr and soe we adjourned till toomorrow 10 of the clock. By this your excellency may judge with what high disingenuous proceedings those gentlemen lead the howse who, I hope, begin to see the anguis in horba.[88] It is very late, yet I could not suffer my akinge head to take any rest till I had given your excellency this trouble, and havinge begd your pardon for it and opinion of me as I rest, my lord,

Your most humble servant,

Tho Gorges

479. From Anthony Morgan, 8 March 1659, 823, fos 245–246.

May it please your excellency,

Soon after my coming hither I presented the letters your lordship gave me and was every where received with a great deal of kindness, and his Highness spoke many loving words of the mutuall affection betwixt himselfe and your lordship. Nothing hath yet occur'd worth writing. Mr Secretary (with whom I have yet had no discourse) hath this day invited me to dine with him, being as he says the best opportunity he can give. Wee have spent 4 daies in debate of the question whether wee will transact with the other house as house of parliament. Last night the house, intending to come to a question, shut the doores and about 1 a clock at night wee adjorned without putting any other question then that for adjornment till 1 a clock next day, upon which question the house being divided there were in the House 391 besides the tellers. The great number makes things very tumultuous and the house so hot that I doe not see how it can be borne in summer. I know not whether that will be amongst the reasons of our not sitting so long. Mr Secretary in his speech, amongst other ill consequences, said wee should fall into a sneaking oligarchy. Sir H Vane said no, that was not the matter but that some sneaking counselors feared least this house should have the eare of his Highness.

The commonwealth party are weak yet like to carry this great question by the accession of such as dislike the persons of which the other house is composed, or else are violent for the old peerage under which cloke some carry Charles Steward.

[88] This Latin phrase could be translated as 'snake in the grass'.

Collonel Ashfeild[89] and lieutenant collonel Gough[90] walking in the hall, lord Whally[91] passing through to the other house fell in discourse with them. Ashfeild seemed against the government, Whally for it. Ashfeild told Whally what he said was not true. He replied, sir, you have in effect given me the lye 6 or 7 times and with so much insolence that were it in another place I'de cut you one the pate. Goffe answered, if he went to that he might have cutting enough. Whaly went away, they followed him. Whaly turns about and desires them not to follow him. Ashfeild turnd his back and replied he scorned to follow him. Whaly complains to his Highness. All parties are sent for. Ashfeild denies, collonel Mills[92] prove Whaly's complaint. His Highness orders Ashfeild should give satisfaction to Whaly by acknowledgment or else it should be referred to a court marshall. Next day Ashfeild excuses himselfe and is loth to betray his own inocency. They withdraw. His Highness with advice of some officers refers it to a court marshall, and the charge is now preparing against Ashfield and Goff. The originall of this was upon the late meeting of officers of about 30 where Whaly opposed and disliked there meeting, at which meeting some papers were prepared and committed. What they were I know not yet. All this account I have from Whaly.

All our Irish members seem much startled at the proceeding with Lill,[93] taking it for a rule that no tryall ought to be for life by a court martiall when the civill courts are open, and seem to have been confirmed in their opinion by all wise men here. They are glad to

[89] Richard Ashfield, parliamentarian officer, during the 1640s served as a captain, then major, then lieutenant-colonel, of Philip Skippon's New Model foot regiment. He campaigned under Oliver Cromwell in Scotland and, in the course of 1651, was promoted to colonel and gained command of the regiment. It remained in Scotland throughout the 1650s, though Ashfield himself seems to have spent time in London, away from his regiment. He became prominent at this stage as one of the London-based officers supporting Fleetwood and increasingly hostile towards the Protectorate and the Protectorate parliament.

[90] William Gough/Goffe, parliamentarian officer, who must be distinguished from the colonel William Goffe who served as a major-general in 1655–1657. This William Gough was a captain, and later lieutenant-colonel, of the New Model horse regiment of Stephen Winthrop, and later Edward Montague, which served in Scotland in the mid- and late 1650s, although he too seems to have spent time in London, away from his regiment, and become a strong supporter of the army's moves against the Protectorate and Protectorate parliament of Richard Cromwell.

[91] Edward Whalley, styled 'lord' because he was a member of the other house.

[92] John Mill/Mills.

[93] Apparently a parliamentarian officer or soldier, though his military record is obscure, he had reportedly been convicted of murder or mutiny and condemned to death, but by a court martial rather than by a regular civil court, leading to questions about the legality and wisdom of executing him. The case seems to have caused considerable controversy and to have taken up an inordinate amount of time, evident not only in this and subsequent letters in this collection but also in correspondence passing between Henry Cromwell and Thurloe during March (*TSP*, VII, pp. 635, 636).

heare the warrants for his execution is suspended. I have not yet had time to search into this matter but thinke your excellency is in a safe by suspending the execution. Somtimes I almost thinke it a matter fitt for the determination of parliament sed quere.[94]

Last night about 12 a clocke, Mr Knightly[95] having asked leave to goe home, not being well, soon after returned and complaind to the house that he was told the house would be dissolved next day if the question about transacting passed in the negative and that the soldiers had affronted him and when he said he was a parliament man then they flew more violently upon him. The house presently cryed out adjorne. Sir John Northcot[96] moved the matter might be referred to examination, but it died.

Since my writing this, I had an hower's discourse with the Secretary, the particulars not worth writing, only he told me he was much importuned by some Irish members (named Ingoldsby)[97] that Mr Booth[98] might be solliciter generall and asked my opinion. I told him that if he would promise me that whosoever I named should be the man, I would say it should be who my lord lieutenant would name, for thought he might reasonably expect that as a civility even though his councell was thought useless and it seemed strange to me that at least that ceremony was not used towards him in the late disposition, since he must either take upon him the reproch of a thing the people thinke ill done or proclaime how little regard was shewed to him here. The 1st he said should surely be mended, the other was occasioned through the importunity of Sir William Bury's[99] lettre and others crying out as if all were lost if sombody were not made presently and none could be got from hence. He thinks it very reasonable your excellency should

[94] This Latin phrase could be translated as 'but why' or 'but for what reason'.

[95] Sir Richard Knightley, parliamentarian politician, sat in the Short and Long Parliament and was very active in the parliamentary cause in the early and mid-1640s, but he was excluded and briefly imprisoned at Pride's Purge and took no part in national politics in the wake of the regicide. He made a cautious return during the Protectorate and was elected for his native Northamptonshire in Richard Cromwell's Protectorate parliament.

[96] Sir John Northcote, parliamentarian officer and politician, was elected to the Short and Long Parliaments in 1640, campaigned in his native Devon during the opening phase of the civil war, and was captured when Exeter fell to the king. Released on an exchange, he resumed his Commons seat in 1645 but absented himself at Pride's Purge. He was elected to represent Devon in all three Protectorate parliaments, although he was excluded from the second, probably on suspicion of royalist leanings.

[97] Either Henry Ingoldsby, MP for Counties Kerry, Limerick, and Clare, or George Ingoldsby, MP for Limerick and Kilmallock towns, or perhaps both of them.

[98] Probably Robert Booth, a lawyer practising in Dublin by the later 1650s; nothing came of this suggestion at this stage, although he became a judge in Ireland and then England after the Restoration.

[99] William Bury/Berry, the Irish councillor.

come over but went of from that point, which I easily suffered, having only stirred it obiter.[100]

From hence wee went to the house, carryed an addition to the question by 18 voices, owrs beinge 203 besides the tellers. Then the main question being to be put, the other party by the division upon the addition being sure they should loose it, excepted against the Irish and Scotch. Much wrangle ther was about it, whether the motion was then regular being stirred only to stop the question. The speaker was sick and the house adjorned in some confusion till tomorrow 10 a clock. Sir Hierome Sankey made his election (some say very unseasonably), said he was chosen for Tipperary and Woodstocke, and he would sticke to his election in England (with an emphasis) and divides with the commonwealthsmen; and so does Mr Ansley, who declares the petition and advice is no law etc.

I remain your lordship's faithfull servant.

480. From Hierome Sankey, Wallingford House, 8 March 1659, 823, fos 247–248.

May it please your excellency,

The question that has bene the matter of the debate this ten dayes and more I have here inclosed sent you. The reasons of the lenght of the debate were upon these accompts: many of the contry gentlemen have bene very earnest in assertinge the right of the old peers upon supposition that the vote mentioned would wholy exclude them. The cheife of which was Sir George Booth, Mr Hungerfoord, Mr Knightly, Mr Anesly, Mr Turner, Mr Tirrell, Mr Maurice[101] and severall of great interest and reputation, who in this vote upon another accompt fell in with the commonwealth party, who have a great many able men, who have noteably bestired themselves against the petition and advice (viz) Sir Henry Vane, Sir Anthony Cooper, John Sadler, Sir Arthur Haselridge, Mr St Nicholas, Mr Boscowinge, Mr Robert Reynolds, Mr H Nevil, Mr Weaver, Mr Morley, my lord Lambert,[102] cum

[100] This Latin word could be translated as 'by the way', 'in passing' or 'cursorily'.

[101] Sir George Booth, MP for Lancashire; Henry Hungerford, MP for Great Bedwin; Sir Richard Knightley, MP for Northamptonshire; Arthur Annesley, MP for Dublin; probably Edward Turner, MP for Essex; Thomas Terrill/Tyrell, MP for Aylesbury; and William Morrice, MP for Newport in Cornwall.

[102] Sir Henry Vane, MP for Whitchurch; Sir Anthony Ashley Cooper, MP for Wiltshire; John Sadler, MP for Yarmouth, Isle of Wight; Sir Arthur Hesilrige, MP for Leicestershire; Thomas St Nicholas, MP for Canterbury; either Hugh Boscawen, MP for Cornwall, Charles Boscawen, MP for Truro, or Edward Boscawen, MP for Tregony; Robert Reynolds, MP for Whitchurch; Henry Neville, MP for Reading; John Weaver, MP for Stamford; Herbert Morley, MP for Sussex; and John Lambert, MP for Pontefract.

multis aliis.[103] Both parties bringe in there arguments, both as to the constitution and the persons now sitinge (viz) that the members in the other house had two and twenty regiments under there commands; that there were seven judges, soe that there could be noe proper appeales from the courts at Westminster Hall, seaven judges being members of the house; that ther was likewise sixe and thirty sallery men members in that house, as likewise conserninge the power and moneys etc, which collonel Morley,[104] Mr Weaver and others, not so much in a commonwealth accompt as these men named, were dissatisfied withall. The addition to the question was brought in and urged by such Presbiterians as I am perswaded thought themselves they were bound not to prejudice the peers upon the accompt of the covenant, upon which accompt Mr Bunkley, Mr Groves, Mr Swinfeild, Mr Bamfeild, Mr Godfrey[105] and severall others fell in with the court part. Mr Secretary told me he liked not the addition, but could not tell how to helpe it, unless to bringe in confusion by the loss of the question, and I beleive Mr Trevor, sargeant Maynard, Mr solicitor, Mr atturney generall,[106] etc were of his mind. The addition to the question was put above an houre since. The ies were 195, the noes 188. After the addition to the question was put and carried in the affermative, exceptions were made against Scotch and Ireish members and very many of the noes, though against the useuall order of the house, urged the house to judge of the right of there sitinge. Others moved for other additions to the question, but the speaker beinge ill and ready to faint away, haveing bene ill all this weeke by excessive toyle, Mr Bunkeley haveinge moved for Sir Lilburne Longe[107] to take his place for a weeke,

[103] This Latin phrase could be translated as 'with many other things' or 'with many others'.

[104] Herbert Morley, parliamentarian officer and politician, campaigned for parliament in southern England during the opening years of the civil war and had allied with the radicals in the Long Parliament and its Rump, even though he did not attend the trial of the king or sign the death warrant, and he consistently opposed both Oliver Cromwell after the ejection of the Rump and the Protectoral regime in general. Elected for Sussex to Oliver Cromwell's two Protectorate parliaments, he sat in the first and was not one of those excluded – or who excluded themselves – after 12 September 1654, but he was excluded from the start of the second.

[105] John Bulkeley, MP for Christchurch; Thomas Grove, MP for Marlborough; probably John Swinfen, MP for Tamworth; Thomas Bampfield, MP for Exeter; and Lambert Godfrey, MP for Romney.

[106] John Trevor, MP for Flintshire; Sir John Maynard, MP for Newtown, Isle of Wight; William Ellis, solicitor-general and MP for Grantham; and Edmund Prideaux, attorney-general and MP for Lyme Regis.

[107] Lislebone Long, parliamentarian politician and lawyer, held local office under parliament in and around his native Somerset during the early and mid-1640s and was elected as MP for Wells in 1645, surviving Pride's Purge and sitting in the Rump, but absenting himself during the period of the regicide. He sat in all three Protectorate parliaments (as MP for Wells, Somerset, and Wells respectively), held other offices during

the house adjourned till tomorrow morneinge. Your excellencie's I received and shall observe your commands. I begge the excuse of very short time. I comitt you to the Lord's protection and rest,

Your excellencie's most humble servant,

Hie Sankey

481. From Adam Molyneux, 11 March 1659, 823, fos 249–250.

May it please your excelencie,

Bonaventure O'Cahan, an Irish bishop, was (about three monthes since) imployed from Spayne heather to inquier the state and condition of this nation in order to sum proposalls which I doubt not your lordship remembers were sent heather last summer from Charles Stuart, in which matter he hath conferred with most of the popish clergie, amongst whome noe particuler matter or sercomstance was contrived for our disturbance other then comfortable hopes of releife by midsummer next, and that wholy dependinge on the expected peace betwene France and Spayne. This Bonaventure is now gon to London to compare nootes with Edmond Reley, bishop of Ardmagh and primatt of Ireland, whoe is now there with the French ambassador. Many frivolus and longe discourses I am often troubled with, as likewise severall letters of coraspondence that pass betweene the popish clergie from London to Dublin and soe to these partes, that importe nothinge but foreine and publicke transactions not fitt to trouble your lordship with, but this (togeather with summ charitable collections for the distressed clergie) I am confident is the utmost of this winter's consultation amongst them. Of which I thought myselfe obliged to give your lordship this accompt. Beginge pardon for this bouldness, I rest as in all duty bound,

Your lordship's most faithfull and obedient servant to be commanded,

Ad Molyneux

482. From Arthur Annesley, London, 15 March 1658, 823, fos 251–252.

May it please your excellency,

Though the little that hath been transacted in parliament this weeke affords no great matter to write of, yet my duty calls upon me to let your excellency know that the whole weeke hath been spent upon the subject my last gave your lordship a hint of, viz about the right of the

the Protectorate, and became recorder of London in 1655. Elected speaker on 9 March, Long soon fell ill himself and died just a week later, on 16 March.

members of Scotland to sitt in parliament, and though it hath been hotly and with great reason disputed against, yet I am of opinion, though with some difficulty, it will be continued to them, and Ireland I beleeve will follow their lott.

The other house are a little impatient at our delayes, which have been unavoydable, these last two dayes having been lost by the new speaker's disposition equall to the other, which made us adjourne yesterday as soone as we sate till tomorrow morning, and if he be not then well we must choose another, unlesse Mr Chute be in ease to take the chaire againe.

If your lordship have it not from other hands, it will not be improper that I let your excellency know that Dr Owens hath gathered a church in the Independent way and that lord Fleetwood, lord Desborrough, lord Sidenham, Berry, Goffe and divers others were admitted members since my last, which hath divers constructions put upon it and is not, that I can heare, very well liked at Whitehall.

Your lordship will, I hope, pardon my freedome and owne me to be, may it please your excellency,

Your excellencye's most obedient servant,

Arthur Annesley

483. From Henry Whalley, Westminster, 15 March 1659, 823, fos 253–254.

Letter of request, asking Henry Cromwell to keep a close eye on his son, Lieutenant Whalley, who had reportedly developed bad and ungodly ways, urging him to give his son a reproof as well as good counsel, so that he might be reclaimed; also reports that the Protector had appointed Carterett to be judge advocate in England and the writer to be judge advocate in Ireland and so hopes that he might do good service both to Henry Cromwell and to Ireland.

484. From Anne Bodville,[108] 21 March 1659, 823, fos 255–256.

My lord,

Your lady lying in makes me to give you the trouble of reading these two or three lines. I desired her to present my lord Fiennes and his ladye's humble service to you, who often acknowledge themselves very much obliged to you in the behalfe of her brother, Mr Whitehead, which I understand by them is one of your lifeguard. They have desired me to petition you on his behalfe, that if there be any new officers

[108] Anne Bodville née Russell, the estranged wife of John Bodvill/Bodville/Bodvel, MP for Anglesey in the opening years of the Long Parliament, sister of Sir Francis Russell and so the aunt of Henry Cromwell's wife.

made, as they are informed there is to be, that you wilbe pleased to take him into your thoughts, if there be any preferment that you thincke him capable of. For which my lady Fiennes desired me to tell you, she shall take it as a great favour and acknowledge herselfe very much obliged to you.

Pray present my service to your lady. I will write to her at large. My dearest lord, farewell. So begging your pardon for this trouble, being alwaies ready to acknowledge myselfe infinitely obliged to you, I rest, my lord,

Your faithfull freind and humble servant,
A Boduell

485. From Nathaniel Fiennes, Covent Garden, 21 March 1659, 823, fos 257–258.

Letter of courtesy and of thanks for continuing favour to his brother-in-law, John Whitehead; also seeks acknowledgement that the bearer of his previous letter, his cousin Edmund Temple, had arrived safely in Ireland, since there had been worrying rumours that he had been captured by pirates and had escaped from their hands only with great loss.

486. From Arthur Annesley, London, 22 March 1659, 823, fos 259–260.

May it please your excellency,

Though the honour of your excellencye's letter of the 16th of this month doth ingage me to increase of diligence in giving your lordship an account of transactions here, yet the present sad condition that my aged father lyes in by the dead palsey, which fell on him since the last poast, which hath taken away his speech, hinders me from being so large in the present dispatch as I intended. But the inclosed will shew your excellency how slowly we proceed, but I hope we shall now goe on faster. Tomorrow is appointed for to debate the sitting of the members for Ireland, who I doubt not will have the same vote passed for them.

And then we shall resume the question which I formerly sent your lordship concerning transacting with the other house, who are preparing the way for us, having allready laid aside in compliance with the house of commons a bill which was brought in by one of the other house against their being hereditary peeres.

They have also taken into consideration the reduceing those acts which settle excise and customes perpetuall to a certaine number of yeares, to answere the commons' great objection that the purse of the people is taken from them.

There is great probability of the Spaniard and French agreeing. And the Swede hath certainly received a blow. Your lordship will, I hope, pardon me that, having intrusted one Alexander Eustace in my absence with the care of my concernments in the county of Kildare, he being neither proprietor nor one that was in armes, I may beg his freedome from transplantation till my returne, I ingaging for his good behaviour, for I should suffer very much if I should be deprived of him till I were there to dispose of my affaires and get another in his place. Your excellencye's direction herein to Dr Gorge will further oblige, may it please your excellency,

Your excellencye's most humble and obedient servant,

Arthur Annesley

487. From Thomas Gorges, 22 March 1659, 823, fos 261–262.

May it please your excellency,

Findinge your favourable acceptance of my unpolished lynes, I take the boldness to contenew your trouble. My last informed your excellency that when we came to the question of transactinge with the other howse, an interposinge question concerninge the sittinge of the Scots and Irish members broke in uppon us, which yet is our debate as to the Irish. The Scots with much difficulty came last night to a resolution of continuance. The debates have run on theyr right either as legall, equitable or prudentiall. The legallity rested on his Highness' ordinance of union confirmed the last parliament;[109] the equity on the intended union by the Longe Parliament, whose bill was twice read and whose declarations invited that nation to a brotherly unitinge far from terms of conquest; prudence would not at this tyme give a nationall discontent and cast out those this parliament that have sate the two former, agaynst whom nothinge could be objected but the destribution to which that nation had submitted accordinge to his late Highness' ordinance (which beinge not confirmed was the only ground of dispute). Yet the same argument lyes agaynst England on poynt of distribution, it beinge left imperfect in the petition and advice. Next, if the Scots are not admitted with us on the union, necessity requyers a new treaty and till it takes effect noe assessment could be imposed on them and they wer to seek whither they should be treated withall as bretheren or vassals. But the gentlemen of the commonwealth profered on theyr present expulsion a bill to be prepared to confirm the union and to give them power to send members hither, but every gentleman saw the impossibillity of that this parliament, especially

[109]The ordinance of Protector and council of April 1654 had been confirmed by the second Protectorate parliament at the end of its first session, in June 1657.

after Sir Henry Vane had declared that this nation could not receave them till we ourselfe wer capacitated for it, for by our declaration and the former intended act they wer to be admitted unto us as a free state. A longe debate was on theyr withdrawinge and much pressinge on poynt of ingenuity and modesty, but they resolutly tould the howse that theyr modesty and ingenuity should rather suffer then theyr fayth and justice to the nation, and on Fryday night[110] the question was put whither the question should then be put for the Scots members to withdraw. It was carryed in the negative by many more then the number of the Scots and Irish; and the mayn question on withdrawinge being put, the house divided, but the commonwealths men (beinge willinge to preserve a dyinge reputation and to stayn all our votes as carryd on by the strength of the Scots and Irish) refused to tell, but yeelded. I dare assure your excellency we carryed it by 50 English at least.

Yesterday the mayn question was put, that the members now returned to serve for Scotland should continew to sit in this present parliament, and carryed in the affermative by what voyces I know not for they betook themselfes to theyr former art, but on that question whither it should be put we wer 211 and they 120, of which number I may with confidence say they lost many on the question. Yet as we wer ready to put the question, collonel Salmon, a collonel of the army and commissioner of the admiralty, moved for the addition to the question, vidzt: as havinge not legall right, which seemed exceedingly disingenious, yet the ball beinge up it was soe kept for some tyme, but with scorn layed aside.

Toomorrow we fall on the Irish members, and the question was propounded in order to the debate whither the Irish shalbe continued to sit in this parliament. Others moved that the words, that they have a legall right, which by a question was layd aside.

Major generall Overton is released and his imprisonment voted illegall and unjust.

Thus your excellency sees how we get all by inches, and with that party joyns the yonge gentlemen. I would not beleeve they had any cavaleer principles in them, but this I dare aver, if ther be not a preservative by the means of another howse to have a checque on this, a few years will fill this howse with cavaleers, for the yonge gentry generally are bred dabauched and more close with that interest then with what God hath and will own amonge us. But I am too tedious to detayn you from your more weighty affayres, and therfor beg your pardon and opinon of me as,

Your excellencye's most humble servant,

Tho Gorges

[110] 18 March.

488. From Francis Aungier, London, 22 March 1659, 823, fos 263–264.

Sir,

The lettre with which you were pleased to honour me of the 9th instant comeing to my hands after the departure of the last poast puts a necessitye upon me of acknowledging a double obligation. Namely for that and the other of the 18th instant in one single answere, which otherwise had beene a rudenesse that I could not have pardoned even in myselfe.

I will not be uncivilly sollicitous to knowe what acceptation my lettre found with that lady to whom my person was so ungratefull, but shall beseech you to beleeve this truth, that the power of keeping me in my present station or of placing me in any other shall and must be in your sole commands, I haveing long since wholly resolved myselfe to be at your disposition as becomes your servant. And if your perticular favours doe not make me forgett myselfe or render me soe presumptious as to exceede the bounds and limmittes wherein my duty ought to be confined, I shall conclude myselfe wholly out of danger. But as you are more then ordinarily indulgent, so I hope you will not neglect what shall appeare necessarye for the advantage of those who are under your obedience. He who intends to throwe of an uselesse servant with disgrace will permitt him to committ absurdityes and heape errours upon errours untill his improvidence hath left him without excuse. But where he intends a continnuation of favours, he purges those humours by restrayning them from an increase. And I shall humbly beg that you will please to observe this method with me when you shall find it necessarye. When I undertooke to give you a weekely account of the expences and other passages of our family, I apprehended that it would be much more satisfaction to you to receave my sence (though never so inconsiderable) of our affayres then a bare and naked observation of providence as to matter of fact. This perswaded me to trouble you with something more then the steward's bills and put me upon an endeavoer to vary from the method of a gazett, who only tells us that such a thing is now upon action without delivering us the reason upon which those persons move who mannage the designe, or which way it is to be avoyded if inconvenient. And I cannot but still continnue to hope for pardon for the troubles which you will from hence receave, since it is in your power with one word to divert what was only intended for your mirth and pastime as you will evidently discerne this and my other lettres to have beene, wherein I must needs appeare apish by attempting to personate the polititian. I beleeve providence to have as great a care even of our little private concernes as she hath of nations and empires. Yet while we consider how impossible it is for us to discover her intentions and how highly she is delighted with our cooperating with her, I have never esteemed endeavours to be unpleasing to heaven. Nor could I ever imagine that the Creatour of all things intended man to be an inactive and silent observer of providence, while He endowed him with reason and understanding. We must therefore eye providence with an eye that shall be provident to ourselves. I did not (sir) undertake to judge of either the right or meritts of that person whom I presumed to mention, and for whom I am no otherwise concern'd then purely with relation to your interest. Seriously it was solely my regard to that which gave me the confidence to suggest what then occur'd unto me without haveing any appeareance of unreasonable. I easily confesse that favours are not favours if taken by storme. But where I have reason to beleeve that an almes will reconcile my enemy, I thinke I should hardly suppose myselfe obliged to trye whether I can defend my purse or persons by my longer weapon. Nor doe I yet discerne how such a gift can enslave the giver, unlesse he become so prodigall as to give his enemy his sword or make him master of his army. He who shall sollicite for such an almes teacheth the person to whom he sueth in what method he shall returne his answere. But in affayres which are no way military, I doe very much question whether the receaver be not more enslaved then the giver. As I durst not presume to determine a right, so neither dare I judge the consciences of others. Nay I shall hardly undertake so much as to define what is meant by conscience according to the true sence of politicks. This only I dare affirme, that the consciences of men are so often veyled with the curteines of theyr own interests that for strangers to steere by them, there will be required more judgment then I shall ever hope to be capable of, without you will vouchsafe to worke in me a miracle by your instructions. This considered, I thinke we may be carefull and industrious without sinning either against charitye or conscience, of both which I shall be equally tender as of my owne soule or of your interest, which I value at the same rate as I doe my life.

Thus (sir) I have made you my confessarius.[111] I have opened unto you that doore which useth to secure my most secrett and retired thoughts and doe humbly submitt both those and him (who will no longer owne them, then you shall esteeme them current) unto your freindly censure. I hope I shall not be found guilty herein of anything which can offend my Maker, though the idle vulgar would looke upon these maximes (when asserted otherwise then by the actions of theyr deare Sir Harry[112] and others theyr beloved leaders) as irreligious if not worse. But I knowe the person to whom they are addressed and

[111] This Latin word could be translated as 'confessor'.
[112] Vane.

whose better judgement shall easily overrule me so soone as you shall please to intimate that my oppynions are extravagent. But to the end yourselfe (who is best able to judge of our affayres) may proceede to drawe your owne conclusions, I shall returne to give you a continnuation of our domesticke occurences, which begin now to looke with a more chearefull countenance since our master hath had the additionall assistances of those freindes of ours, who came last to England. One grand difficulty we have removed this weeke, and I am noe way doubtfull but that tomorrowe will remove another of the like nature. So that our dissenting kinsmen will be overruled and enforced to joyne us with themselves in the carrying on of the worke of our master. But we are put to more then ordinarye labours in this affayre. We cannot obteyne one kindenesse without suite or reference and had not equity on our side in favour of the heyre, doubtlesse these men would effect what they so strictly labour for and reduce all things unto theyr originall chaos. Yet if we can obteyne a judgement upon our grand affayre in relation to our neighbour famuly (with whom we must either speedily unite or incurre a mischeife), I shall looke upon our howse as grounded upon a foundation without which it cannot long continnue. I doe not find that our opposors have many games more to play after this is over, in regard our master with that allyance will grow beyond theyr reach. Yet I cannot thinke they will leave one stone unmoved which they shall find themselves able to loosen. And if they cannot hinder us from setling, at least they will endeavour to make us as unsteadfast as they can by theyr malice and contrivance. But my desires to expresse my duty have carryed me beyond the ordinary compasse of a lettre, which I can no otherwise excuse then by protesting that I am secure of pardon if you could but receave halfe so much pleasure in reading as I doe in writing this, which comes to Dublyn to give you an assurance how constantly I am and ever will be, (sir),

Your most obliged, humble, faythfull servant,

T L[113]

[113] This is the first of two letters in this collection (nos 488 and 504) signed 'T L' and endorsed 'T L Lord Angier'. They were clearly written by someone familiar with developments in the House of Commons and probably by a member of that house, and their tone and style is in many ways broadly consistent with the three letters in this collection that are signed by Aungier (nos 466, 477, and 507). It is curious that these two letters are not signed by him but instead bear initials which are not his, and that they are written in a hand which is both distinctive and certainly not the hand in which the three letters signed by Aungier have been written. Despite these differences and oddities, the contemporary endorsement does firmly identify Aungier as the (sole or joint) author of both these letters and so, although some doubts persist, both have been ascribed to Aungier.

489. From Anthony Morgan, 22 March 1659, 823, fos 265–266.

May it please your excellency,

Last night my lord Broghill told me that he had received by Dr Clarges a state of Lill's case and that he would goe with me to his Highness to acquaint him with it, but wee thought it advisable 1st to agree what wee should desire from his Highness. Mr Secretary (when I told him that your lordship had not lately received any lettres from him) said twas true he had not written the 2 last posts and indeed he had lost your cipher and to write without yt were to little purpose or dangerous, and for Lill he adviseth you should put him over to be tried by the common law, for (said he) they begin to talke of it already that a man guilty of murder should be kept from justice because you favor him. I could hardly beleive I understood what he said and therefore I made such replies as the occasion and place would admitt (it being in the parliament house). I asked him whether I should give you his opinion of leaving him to the common law as taken up upon an express deliberation and advice with others or as a thing he had only leasure to think on when he was put in mind of it by me. He said he did never set any time apart to consider it. He promised to give me a paper in which is the opinion of Dr Walker,[114] but I can not yet get it. He sais he will write this post. The Scotch business is over and carried, I think, by a 100 voices. The Irish came on today and I think will fare no worse, but they have taken me up so wholly that I have not seen Whitehall since my last. Margetts[115] is judge advocate for Scotland, Whaly for Ireland and Cartwright[116] (for whose integrity lord Whaly sais Mr Secretary undertakes to answer) for England. Lord Philip Jones complained to his Highness that one Morgan, a servant in Whithall, had injured him by reporting that he had bought a great estate with the mony received for tithes in Wales by color of the comission for propagating the gospell there. Morgan was summoned, tells his Highness that he knew nothing, but that one Davy Morgan,[117] now a member of parliament, and collonel Freeman[118] could make it appeare to be true. His Highness sends for Davy Morgan and in the presence of the lord Philip Jones askes what he could say. He replied

[114] Identification uncertain, but probably Walter Walker, parliamentarian administrator and lawyer, who was judge advocate to the court of admiralty.

[115] Thomas Margetts.

[116] Philip Carterett.

[117] David Morgan, parliamentarian politician, MP for Carmarthen in Richard Cromwell's Protectorate parliament, and probably the David Morgan who was named to various Carmarthenshire commissions during the 1650s, although he had not been appointed a commissioner for the propagation of the gospel in Wales established by the Rump in 1650.

[118] Identification uncertain.

he beleived it would appeare sombody had a good some of that mony and had reason to thinke lord Jones to be the man in regard he had alwais obstructed the bringing that matter to account and instanced in some particulars and said that the matter was now under examination before a comittee of parliament and ere long the truth would appeare. His Highness said he could take no notice of that, but so farr as it made any troble in his family, twas fitt for him to enquire into it and said lord Jones was an honest man and had been alwais so reputed.

This is the summ of a long storie which I heard Davy Morgan tell, and collonel Freeman was sent for before his Highness and (as he related) said much to the same purpose. When a faction breaks out in Wales it seldome dies.[119] I give your lordship these little Welch stories to entertain you in the place where you use to read diurnalls, being all the service I can doe. I write to your lordship often, but should be trobled if that should occasion your lordship to write to me unless upon express business. I thanke your lordship for doing me that right to beleive I doe not measure your lordship's favor by the length of your letters. Neither am I so ridiculously womanish as to thinke it the less if you never write at all. I know you are not at leisure to trifle. I remain,

Your lordship's faithfull and obedient servant,

A Morgan

I am, it may be, too apt to suspect people here may be byassed in Lill's case; but I thinke the better opinion is they are unskilfull or timerous. I hope by the next to speake more positively.

490. From Henry Whalley, Westminster, 22 March 1659, 823, fos 267–268.

Letter of apology, noting his recent appointment as judge advocate in Ireland and pointing out that, because of his parliamentary duties, he would be absent a while longer; requests that, during his absence, Mr Alden, the existing deputy advocate, might continue to act in his stead.

491. From William Pierrepont, Lincoln's Inn Fields, 25 March 1659, 823, fos 269–270.

Letter of courtesy, praising Henry Cromwell and offering to serve him; reports that he had obeyed Henry Cromwell's instruction to him as set out in a letter delivered by Sir Charles Coote and had now given his views on the matter to Coote.

[119] Indeed, the criticisms of Jones were gathering strength at this stage and had probably been boosted by the successful attack upon his crony, Edmund Jones, recently expelled from the house. The attacks on Philip Jones resumed later in 1659 and, by the end of the year, he had lost almost all his central and local offices.

492. From Edward Montague, Sole Bay, 25 March 1659, 823, fos 29–30.

Letter of courtesy, expressing his admiration for Henry Cromwell and his desire to serve him; notes that he was then with the fleet and about to set sail for the Sound.

493. From Charles Coote, London, 29 March 1659, 823, fo. 271.

May it please your excellency,

On Fryday laste[120] I waighted on Mr Perpoynte, with whom I had a large discourse concerneing your lordship's affayres, who was pleased the next day to send me the inclosed to be transmitted to your lordship. He commanded me to signifie unto your lordship that it was cleere against his judgement that your lordship should thinke of comeing into England for severall waighty reaons, and soe much he desyerd my lord Russell for to acquainte your lordship with formerly and he is now more confermed in the same then he was. He seemes to be much affected with the condition your lordship is in and with those hardshipps your lordship labors under, especially the present constitution of your counsell and the little interest you can pretend in them, which must nessesarylye render your lordship' life very uncomfortable. He assured me he would make it his worke for to serve your lordship and if your lordship would have a little patience, he did not doubt to gett that done which would be highly to your lordship' sattisfaction. I assure your lordship, you have a very high place in his esteeme and in a multiditude of sober, good peoples, who on all occations manifest thayre respects unto your lordship to your advantage and looke uppon you as the person that hath reduced Ireland unto a happye condition.

Though I am confident your lordship hath had it from a better hand, lett me humbly acquaynte your lordship that his Highness remonstrated such an affection and regard for your lordship lately as startled some and will undoubtedly prevent others from any atempt of doeing your lordship any ill offices, either directly or colatterally.

The laste weeke the vote paste for the members of Ireland sitting in this present parliament as well as the Scotts, and yesterday the vote paste likewise for the howse's transacting with the other howse dureing this parliament, with a saveing of the right of the ould peerag who had bine faythfull to the commonwealth. These things hath taken upp all the time hether unto, and blessed be God, notwithstanding affayres had a very sadd aspecte when I came hether first, they begine to grow more serene, and if the Lord have not a controversy with the

[120] 25 March.

nation, we are in a probable way of building on such a basis as may be comfortable and permanent.

My lord, it is the humble advice of severall of your lordship's good frends that you make it your greate worke to gett over as manye able, good ministers as it is possible, that your lordship indevor the settlement of a godly and sober minestry there, which will not onely bring a blessing from God but stopp the mouthes of malitious men and conferme the good oppinion of those that truly feare the Lord, and that in order hereunto your lordship doe write frequently for minesters hether.

Sir Jerim Sancky, with the highest preludium[121] agrevated with all the oratorye he had, brought in a most formidable charge against Doctor Petty into the howse of commons[122] and in the close of his harange declared how nobly and prudently your excellency had caryed yourselfe in that affayre; that on some rumor of Pettye's miscariage had called the principall officers of your armye together, and signified unto them that if Petty had not acted faythfully in his trust, your lordship would be soe farr from protecting him as that you would contribute your assistance to the bringing him to condigne punishment. When he had done, Sir Anthony Morgan layd open your lordship's proceeding therein to the greate sattisfaction of the howse. Petty is ordered to appeere here and is like to finde few frends. And I beseech your lordship, as one who tenders your honour, that your lordship will not any wayes interpose in this matter, the howse being highly dissattisfied with him. If he can justifie himselfe it will be his honour, his future safety; if otherwise, noe punishment can be sufficient for him or to dehorte[123] others from the like impious acteings. Pardon, I beseech your lordship, this playneness, being nether more or less then the advice of some of your lordship's best frends here. I shall not truble your lordship further at present then to assure you that I am, my lord,

Your excellency's most humble, faythfull and obedient servant,

Cha Coote

[121] This Latin word could be translated as 'prelude' or 'sign of what is to come'.

[122] Sir William Petty, who sat in Richard Cromwell's Protectorate parliament as MP for West Looe in Cornwall, was open to attack from the impatient, the disappointed, and the jealous, who criticized his role in surveying and redistributing Irish land and who were aware that Petty himself had acquired both property and money in the process. But Petty was probably also attacked because of his allegiance to Henry Cromwell, and thus as a means to assault by proxy the conservative Protectoral policies and regime in Ireland. In fact, Petty resolutely defended himself, and the dissolution of parliament effectively killed off this attack. On 11 April, Henry Cromwell wrote to Thurloe strongly supporting and defending Petty – 'if Sir Hierom Sankey does not run him down with numbers and noise of adventurers, and such other like concerned persons, I beleive the parliament will finde him, as I have represented him' – and noting that Petty was not the real target of this attack (*TSP*, VII, p. 651).

[123] To dehort: to dissuade.

494. From Thomas Belasyse, Viscount Fauconberg, 29 March 1659, 823, fos 272–273.[124]

My lord,

Yesterday by above 60 voyces the maine question was carried to transact with the other house as an house of parliament during the sitting of this present parliament. Without dores allsoe things seeme to have a fairer temper then formerly, so that all sober, honest men begin now to renew their hopes of a settlement, which God grant.

The charge that was brought in against Dr Petty I suppose your excellency has from other hands a full account of, only this I must acquaint you with: the Protector ratled Sanchy and told him whosoever endeavoured to blemish in the least his deare and onelw[125] brother hee would esteem him his greabest[126] enemy.

My bad eys will not let me give your excellency farther troble then of reading this fresh protest that I make of being unalterably,

Your excellencye's most affectionate, faithfull and ever obedient servant,

Fauconberg

495. From Thomas Gorges, 29 March 1659, 823, fos 274–275.

May it please your excellency,

By the last poast I informed you of the resolve for the sittinge of the gentlemen returned to serve for Scotland. On the next day those that serve for Ireland wer taken into consideration and resolved as for Scotland. The gentlemen of thos nation[127] prest for parliaments amonge themselfe and wer not unanimous in the vote, yet the affirmatives wer 156, the negatives 106.

[124] This is the first of two letters in this collection by Fauconberg (nos 494 and 505), of March and April 1659, which he has written partly in code. The code is broadly similar to others in use at the time, with each number standing for an individual letter, plus occasional letters of the alphabet standing for a person or group of people. The second encoded letter (no. 505) has been largely decoded by its recipient – the letters and words have been entered above the numbers in a seventeenth-century hand – and further decoded letters by Fauconberg of the period August 1658–February 1659, surviving among Thurloe's papers (*TSP*, VII, pp. 365, 413, 528, 612), reveal more of the code. Accordingly, in these letters those parts of the text which can reliably be decoded have been reproduced in that form and only where the meaning is uncertain or unclear has the letter been left in its original coded form and possible or probable meanings indicated in footnotes.

[125] Code slightly garbled – clearly 'onely' is the intended word.

[126] Code slightly garbled – clearly 'greatest' is the intended word.

[127] Originally written 'that nation', but then amended imperfectly to a partially plural form.

On the 24th instant Sir Jerom Sanchy impeached an eminent servant of your excellencye's, Dr Petty, for bribery, breach of trust, and the doctor is to be summoned by the speaker's lettre to attend that day month.

Fryday and Saterday wer spent on private reports and cases, especially on major generall Brown,[128] who is restored to his dignity of alderman and the vote made in the Longe Parliament against him vacated and a committee appoynted for his reparation.

Yesterday the grand question was reassumed of transactinge with the other howse as the other howse of parliament, but befor we could come to any resolution many interveninge additions wer offered: as first, whither this howse should not approve them before they transact. The afermatives 146, the negatives 183.

The next, that this howse shall first bound them, which was layd aside by a question without dividinge. 3d, that this howse will transact with them duringe this parliament: resolved. The words, and noe longer except they are confermed by act, being an addition to an addition and incongruous in itself, wer layd aside and neer 5 of the clock (without any adjourment for refreshinge) the mayn question came to a resolution, which is:

That this howse will transact with the persons now sittinge in the other howse as the other howse of parliament duringe this parliament, and that it is not heerby intended to exclude such peers as have bin faythfull to the parliament from theyr priviledges of being duly summoned to be members of that howse.

The ayes 198, the noes 125.

I hope this vote will set the wheels in motion. The commonwealthsmen crye out on slavery and write an Ichabod[129] on the freedom of England, which they would willingly recommitt to the keepers of theyr libertyes, but England is too sencible to be betrayed or cajold to a second slavery under them.

[128] Richard Brown/Browne, parliamentarian officer and politician, was prominent during the civil war in maintaining order and quelling royalist activities in London and southern England, often working with Sir William Waller, until the two fell out in 1644. In 1646, he was returned to the Long Parliament as MP for Chipping Wycombe, but in the later 1640s he became a prominent Presbyterian opponent of the army and was excluded from parliament at Pride's Purge. Returned for London to the second Protectorate parliament but excluded from the house, he took his seat, again for London, in Richard Cromwell's Protectorate parliament. There he complained about his treatment in the years following Pride's Purge, alleging five years' cruel and close imprisonment in Wales, together with the loss of offices and income.

[129] Biblical reference to how, in the aftermath of the defeat of the Israelites by the Philistines and the loss of the ark of God, the wife of one of the Israelite leaders killed in battle gave birth to a boy, who was named Ichabod, signifying 'no glory' or 'the glory has departed and been lost' (1 Samuel, chapter 4).

After this vote they moved for a self denyinge ordinance, that noe person under any sallary should sit in either howse.

This day a bill was brought in by Mr Buncley proposing the excise and new impost for ______ years, except longer tyme admitted by act of parliament, and the customes with tunnage and poundage for ______[130] months after his Highness' death. This took up this morninge, the commonwealthsmen beinge for wreckinge it, although it was the only obstruction to transactinge with the other howse, that they had a perpetuall negative on the purse beinge £1,300,000 per annum and they themselfs payd out of it, but it came to a resolution for the 2d readinge on Thursday. By this your excellencye may not only judge the ingenuity of those gentlemen but alsoe conclude us under tedious and doubtfull debates. The issue is only in the Lord, to whom your excellency's person and goverment is daily presented by,

Your humblest servant,

Tho Gorges

Some heat arose in the howse this day in relation to words spoken by Sir Henry Vane, who sayd this howse was rather a prudentiall constitution then a parliament. Mr Grove called him to the bar, but on other proposalls for moderation it was layd aside.

496. From Gilbert Mabbott, 29 March 1659, 823, fos 276–277.

May it please your excellencie,

Wednesday last[131] the house, according to Tuisday's result, resumed the debate of the Ireish members and resolved that the members returned to serve for Ireland shall continue to sitt as members dureing the present parlament. Thursday a charge of very[132] misdemeanor was exhibited by Sir Hierosme Sankey against Doctor Petty, which was read, debated and a coppy thereof ordered to bee sent to the said Doctor Petty, whoe is to give his answer within six weekes. Major generall Packer's[133] election was then made voyd. Friday a petition was

[130] Lines have been drawn in the letter here and before 'years' to indicate the omission of figures specifying durations.

[131] 23 March.

[132] Word – perhaps 'great', 'serious', or 'high' – apparently omitted.

[133] William Packer, parliamentarian officer and politician, was an officer in Oliver Cromwell's horse regiment in the early 1640s and later in Sir Thomas Fairfax's New Model horse regiment. He campaigned under Oliver Cromwell in Scotland and remained with the regiment in Scotland as its commander in all but name. In the mid-1650s he became deputy major-general (under Fleetwood) of the north-western Home Counties. He was elected to the second Protectorate parliament for Woodstock, but his radical religious and political views led him increasingly to oppose the Protectorate and he was dismissed from the army by the Protector early in 1658. He was returned to Richard Cromwell's

presented in the behalfe of some persons that were in the late plott,[134] whoe were transported from Exeter goale to the Barbadoes, in which petition severall members were charged, namely Mr Secretary, Sir John Coppleston, Mr Noell[135] and severall others; and the petition, beeing received att the grand committee, was reported to the howse, and some exceptions beeing taken att it that any committee should receive a petition wherein members were concerned and report it without hearing them. The debate lasted all day and soe for the present the thing fell. A motion was read upon the case of Sir Sackevilt Crowes[136] and it was referred to a committee to consider how the bonds entred by him in the Long Parlament may bee delivered up. The committee for grievances have received severall petitions: one against major generall Boteler,[137] whose proceedings they have voted unjust and illegall; and likewise another against the farmers of the excise in Ireland, which is referr'd to a subcommittee. The councell have ordered the regiments of foote hereabout the towne to bee paid up on the first place. Monday last the howse resumed the debate for transacting with the other howse as an howse of parlament. The question was putt: That the howse will transact with the persons sitting in the other howse as an howse of parlament. The question beeing putt that these words should bee added to the question, vizt: (after they shall bee approved by this howse) and it was carried in the negative. The question beeing putt that these words (after they shall bee bounded by this howse) should bee part of the question, and it was passed in the negative. The question being putt that these words should bee added (dureing this present parlament) it was carried in the affirmative; and so upon the maine question it was resolved: that this howse will transact with the persons sitting in the other howse as an howse of parlament dureing this present parlament, and that it is not hereby intended to exclude those peeres that have beene faithfull to the parlament from their right of beeing duly sumoned to sitt as

Protectorate parliament in a disputed election for Hertford but, on 24 March, after some debate, the House decided to support the recommendation from the privileges committee, declaring against Packer's election and excluding him.

[134] Penruddock's rising of spring 1655.

[135] Copplestone, MP for Barnstaple, and probably Martin Noell, MP for Stafford.

[136] Sackville Crowe, royalist entrepreneur and diplomat, had held office at home and abroad during the pre-war decades, from 1633 serving as ambassador at Constantinople. In 1647, he was displaced by parliament's appointee and arrested, and, from 1648 until the mid-1650s, he was imprisoned in the Tower, eventually gaining limited freedom only by giving a bond and other securities.

[137] William Butler/Boteler was under fierce attack for his record as a major-general in the mid-1650s, with MPs proposing a range of punishments, including dismissal from his military and civil offices, although the abrupt dissolution of parliament saved him from the worst of parliament's vengeance.

members in that howse. This day was spent on debate of a bill for continueinge the excise for 3 yeares longer and the customes dureing the life of his Highnes and 8 moneths after, which was read the first time. I humbly subscribe myselfe, my lord,

Your excellencie's most humble and obedient servant,

G Mabbott

497. From Anthony Morgan, 29 March 1659, 823, fos 278–279.

May it please your excellency,

Yesterday the question of transacting etc passed in the affermative by 73 voices. As soon as the house rose lord cheife justice Glin, Mr Pierpoint, sergeant Maynard, lord Broghill, Sir Charles Coot and myselfe met together in our private capacities and after 2 hours' debate agreed that no adequate remedy could be found in the case[138] whereof your excellency desires a solution. It was said that the laws of the land admitted no martiall law (unless the ordinance for confirmation of the articles of warr be yet in force, and aptly penned to answer times of peace and Ireland, but wee wanted that and therfore made no judgment of it). That if it should be excersised in times of peace his Highness would be damnified, because that gives no forfeiture nor corruption of blood. The people would be prejudiced not knowing how to seek for remedy against injuries offered by soldiers, by the laws by which themselves are governed. The soldier himselfe would lose the priviledge of chalenge to jurors, etc.

On the other side, if the soldiers by sea and land once know that they are liable only to the civill judicature, the meanest soldier may beard the generall himselfe and you can not say you have an army etc.

It was once said that the exception to martiall law lay only in case of life, but that was soon yeilded and twas concluded that if any one article were good, every one is soe.

Mr Pierpoint thought you should transmit corpus cum causa[139] to the common law. Twas objected that could not secure you, but you would be lyable to censure for that which was one of Strafford's highest crimes and was affirmed to be one of the articles of his charge is for condemning Mountnorris.[140] Since it could not now be undone and

[138] Lill's case.

[139] This Latin phrase could be translated literally as 'the body with the cause' or more loosely as 'the defendant and the case'.

[140] In the mid-1630s, Francis Annesley, Viscount Valencia and Baron Mountnorris, fell out with Sir Thomas Wentworth (later Earl of Strafford), the king's chief minister in Ireland, and insults and accusations were exchanged. In 1635, Wentworth moved to crush his opponent,

might rise against you hereafter, Glin advised you should transmit it to the parliament for their pleasure in it. Twas said the temper of the ______[141] was not fitt for a question of that nature. Certainly they would resolve it negatively and then the consequence is obvious and the most prudent part of the parliament would be trobled that they should be put upon it to declare either way in a matter of that weight. Then twas said what generall would be so unwise to excersise a charge with the hazard of his own head.

Upon the whole twas resolved by all as adviseable that noe warrant should be given by your lordship for his execution. And it was proposed as the best present shift that your lordship should by advise there transmit the case to the members serving for Ireland to be communicated to the parliament for their judgment.

That an entry should be made there which might remain as on record of your transmitting it.

That those to whom you send it should take a liberty (not by your direction but their own discretion) to represent it or let it sleep. And if the parliament give no judgment in it before they rise, tis thought you may then more safely execute him or take upon you to give your own judgment in the case by transmitting him to triall at law.

A day or 2 before this meeting, I being with his Highness, he told me that some pastors of churches had been with him about collonel Ashfeild and asserted that there was no court marshall in England etc, but he said he would let goe his hold soe and that he told them that unless he gave publique satisfaction he would not remit the offence, since the affront to Whaly was publick (for they offerred privat satisfaction). He alsoe told me that if there was no court marshall, either there was no army or a lawless one, which was worse then none. Then I tooke occasion to state our case and told him that if he would say the word, it would doubtless be excersized by his generalls. He said, nay, but wee must not hazard both brothers at once.

I made a visit to lord Falconberge. He said let the parliament vote what they would, nothing could be soe bad as breaking, for then wee know who will rule. While they sitt they will be a ballance and nothing less then a parliament can be soe.

I have not stirred the busines of your comming over, thinking it advisable 1st to make my access easy. But I will soon be at it.

using Mountnorris's position as an army officer as a means to have him tried by court martial on a capital charge, before a council of war at Dublin Castle, with Wentworth appearing in person as suitor for justice. Mountnorris was duly condemned to death, though the sentence was commuted. Wentworth's partial and inflammatory role in this affair was, in turn, used against him in 1641.

[141] A line has been drawn in the letter at this point to indicate the omission of a word or words.

By all I can guess, by such as I converse with abroad, Mr Secretary is the man of the most absolute power.

Sanky exhibited a charge in the house of commons against Petty for bribery, breach of trust of so high a nature as was (as he said) without president and that he had many thousands of acres he had no right unto and many £1,000s of the state's mony. Sir Charles Coote told me before he moved yt he was about to doe it, and spoke to me to advise him against it. I did so in this manner: I told him twas against the orders of the house to move it then, being between the putting of an addition and the main question, thinking it easier to delay then divert his mallice. He told me I knew not what he had to move and desired me to lett him alone.

The house ordered Petty should be sent for, as you will perceive by the speaker's lettre with a coppie of his charge. Others, I suppose, will write all particulars either to your lordship or him. I am told that yesterday Sanky went hence for Ireland, I suppose to make good his charge. I pray God Petty doe not rely too much upon orders of the councell, though never so just, least your lordship's name be tossed about. I am sure your reputation is (I thinke I may boldly say) the clearest of any man's in the 3 nations. I love him well but I have a zeal for your honor as becomes him that is,

Your lordship's most obliged and most faithfull servant.

This week's packet is not yet come. I write no more to my wife till I see her. Lady Reynolds went out of town yesterday. All at Chippenham are well.

498. From Francis Hervey, Wexford, 2 April 1659, 823, fos 280–281.

My lords,

I humbly conceive it to bee my duty to make knowne unto your lordshipps that this roade is very much troubled by the pirates who have surprysed sixe small vessells of this towne within 15 dayes, whom they plundred at ther pleasure and afterwards brought them into the Bay of Grenore[142] and uppon easy composition gave them freedome. Ther was two small barks rann on ground nigh the shoare, but the enemy was so bold as at high water pursued them with ther long boate and caryed them off and the country could not oppose them. Ther ar two small shipps of about 6 gunns with 30 men in each who Wednesday last[143] were in our bay for som space of 24 howres and went northward. I posted advise to the governor of Duncanon to give notis to any of the frigotts in that river but could heare of none to

[142] Adjoining Greenore Point, south of Rosslare.
[143] 30 March.

pursue these spoylers. They ar so buisy as doe alltogether impedite the small trafficqe of this poore place. Not having else, but emploring your greatious ayd and assistance herein, doe in all humilitie take leave and remayne, my lord,

Your lordshipp's obedient and humble servant,

Fra Harvey, mayor

499. From Joseph Waterhouse, 2 April 1659, 823, fos 282–283.

May it please your excellencye,

The lawes of God and man obleigeing one to have a care of himself, I hope your lordship will excuse this intrucion upon your more serious affaires. While your excellencye was abroade upon recreations, I would not make any breach thereof, nor could I in civillitye. Neither now should I bee just to myselfe, those repassers being pass'd, should I passe in silence to relate the state and condition (I might rather say the noe state and noe condition) of my present being. And how little I have deserved itt, your lordship's perusall of the enclosed will make appeare. That when twoe phisitians by the establishment were appoynted for the armye then to march for Ireland under the conduct of his late Highnes your royall father, none adventured upon the serving of his Highnes, of his countrye, while hazards and daunger attended, save onlye the now forlorne myselfe; att which tyme I performed the dutye of twoe phisitians and in such a tyme when townes were more depopulated by the plague, pestilence and famine then by the sword. Yett my service attended not onlye those daungers but the sword and cannon alsoe, for which my faithfull service performed throughout the whole armye in generall and perticularlye for some to his late Highnes (according to his promise to mee in England to better my then condition), hee gave mee the custodium of Cloyne[144] in the countye of Corke, which was as unhandsomelye taken from mee, as my place of being phisitian to the armye, boeth which I justlye deserve, and have his late Highnes' hand for them, and never justlye ejected from either. But when the daunger of the warr etc was over, the councell of England sendes severall phisitians over att twenty shillings per diem. This emboldened mee to desire of the graund comissioners the like favour, which att first (as good reason they had for itt) they graunted, but (like Marjere good-cowe) they tooke the custodium of Cloyne from mee. Thus used, continued I in my dutye and imployment when I was againe reduced to tenn shillings per diem (o monstrum horrendum!)[145] but then the good late Lord Protector liveing would

[144] Town and ecclesiastical centre in the south-east of County Cork, to the east of Cork harbour.

[145] This Latin phrase could be translated as 'dreadful monster', 'monstrosity' or 'portent'.

not see soe horred an abuse take place one him (whoe next under God was instrumentall to preserve his life, witnes att Ross),[146] and therein, if dulye regarded, the whole three nations, I say the state of all, the state of each of the three nations ought not in honour to see and suffer that person now to be nothing)[147] whereupon these enclosed letters[148] were writt to reestablish mee in my former pay. Which (oh sad) thougth hee bee dead, methinkes his lynes (for his sake) should ever live and his commaunds therein bee still in force. Yett for all these, my place was inforced from mee and noe place since conferred on mee. A greivious case, woundered att and lamented by her Highnes dowager, by all freinds in England and Ireland; and his now Highnes, pittyeing my condition, expressed a remedye not long since in lynes to your excellencye, when you were pleased to expresse unto mee that upon the settlement of the civill officees you would not fayle to bee myndfull of mee and settle mee in one. But this promise was not of soe much waight to mee as when att Corke House upon an occasion your lordship ledd your ladye into your dressing roome, where your excellencye had left mee bemoaning my sad condition, when hand in hand you came upp towards mee and then and there gave mee your hand, an engagement that you would reallye doe for mee and conferr some worthye imployment one mee. I had then your word for itt and now latelye your verball graunt of a place I mentioned unto you, upon which I made freinds acquainted therewith, and these attend your excellencye onlye att present to make that good, that there may bee noe dispute with Mr Woodes, who cannot in anywise pretend preference with mee. And that your lordship would bee pleased seriouslye to take to hearte my former servicees, my former and present suffereings and use some meanes of redresse and make the world knowe you owne mee as reallye I am,

Your excellencye's most faithfull, though poore servaunt,

J Waterhouse

500. From the Irish Commissioners, 28 May 1652, [enclosed in no. 499], 823, fo. 284.[149]

Ireland, by the commissioners of the parliament of the commonwealth of England for the affaires of Ireland.

[146] Oliver Cromwell had spent most of November 1649 at New Ross, suffering from a malaria-type disease.

[147] The parenthesis closes without having opened.

[148] Nos 500–502.

[149] This letter appears to be a copy, with the main text and all three signatures appearing in a single hand.

Whereas Dr Joseph Waterhouse, physicion to the armye, hath beene in the service of the parliament as phisitian to the armye ever since the said armye came over under the conduct of the lord leiutenant, in which service hee hath undergone much hazard and hardshipp by his constant attendance in the feild in sommer and att the head quarters in winter, in which tyme many dangerous diseasees raighned in the armye and garrisons, for which service hee hath received onlye 10s per diem and £80 per annum for two yeares, being the profitt of a farme granted him by the lord leiutenant. And whereas the councell have of late ordered that Dr Denham and Dr Goldsmith, phisitians appointed for the service of the armye in Ireland, should have an allowance of 20s per diem for theire entertainement and intended to send over more phisitians upon the same termes, upon due considerations had of the former service of the said Dr Waterhouse and the intention of the councell for the incouragement of able men of that profession to serve the state in Ireland, it is ordered that Dr Joseph Waterhouse be allowed 20s per diem from the first day of this instant May for his entertainement as phisitian to the armye and that the same bee paide unto him monthly out of the grand treasury sent or to be sent from England for the pay of the forces in Ireland and the incident chargees thereof and continued unto him untill further order. And itt is further ordered that the interest or clayme of the said Dr Waterhouse to the house and lands of Cloyne in the county of Corke, by vertue of an order of the lord leiutenant of Ireland, bee from the said first of May last, and hereby is determined and the commissioners of the revenue att Corke are hereby ordered and required to lett the said house and lands according to theire instructions for the best advantage of the commonwealth. Dated att Corke, 28th May 1652.

Miles Corbett
Edm Ludlowe
Jo Jones

501. Oliver Cromwell to the Irish Council, Whitehall, 12 September 1654, [enclosed in no. 499], 823, fo. 285.[150]

My lordes and gentlemen,

Dr Waterhouse haveing represented his case to us, much whereof is perticularly knowne to ourselfe, vizt that hee was the onlye phisition (although two were allowed by the establishment) that went over with

[150] This and the following letter (no. 502) were transcribed and printed with commentary and annotations by Clyve Jones, 'Two unpublished letters of Oliver Cromwell', *Bulletin of the Institute of Historical Research*, 46 (1973), pp. 216–218. Both letters are clearly copies and neither the texts nor the signatures are in Oliver Cromwell's own hand.

the armye under our conduct into Ireland and after our being some tyme there takeing notice of his services and the trouble and harards which was undergon by him and of his care and diligence as to others, soe perticularlye towardes ourselfe, wee did thinke fitt for his further encouragement (his pay by the establishment being but tenn shillings per diem) to graunt unto him a custodium of the value of eightye pounds per annum. Which, when hee had received two yeares' profitt, was, as wee are informed, upon the settlement of that countye, otherwise disposed of. After which the councell of state, findeing itt expendient to send over more phisitians, they allowed to each of them 20s per diem and thereupon the commissioners in Ireland did augment Dr Waterhouse his paye to 20s per diem, likewise which, as hee sayeth, hath for about a yeare last past bene againe reduced to 10s per diem. Wherefore in respects Dr Waterhouse bore the maine brunt of the trouble and harared in that kinde, boeth as to the feild in the warr and alsoe to infectious diseasees in the garrisons, and he haveing nothing of arreares to clayme, his pay being wholye expended in his necessarie support and maintenance, wee doe think fitt some additionall allowance be made to his present pay as a reward of his former services and for his future encouragement in such way as to you shall seeme meete, which wee recommend to your care and remaine,

Your loveing freind,

Oliver P

502. From Oliver Cromwell to the Lord Deputy and Council, Whitehall, 26 March 1655, [enclosed in no. 499], 823, fo. 286.

My lords and gentlemen,

In our last letters wee sent unto yow concerning Dr Joseph Waterhouse, dated the 12th of September last, for the reasons therein expressed wee desired his pay might bee made equivalent with 20s per diem. And our meaning and desire was and is that itt bee soe made unto him from the last of his abaitement thereof and soe forwarde. The way and manner wee leave to yow and remaine,

Yours,

Oliver P

503. From Arthur Annesley, London, 5 April 1659, 823, fos 287–288.

May it please your excellency,

This weeke hath produced nothing of moment but a declaration for a fast to be kept 18th of May in the three nations, which when your lordship sees you will wonder should cost three dayes' debate, but the great opposition to it was in regard it's intiled a declaration of his Highnesse and both houses and we have resolved to desire the other house's concurrence to it and tomorrow we are to debate the manner of transactinge. Another ground of opposition to the declaration was that it asserts the power of the magistrate in maintayning religion and punnishing offenders against the second table.[151] The rest of the weeke was spent about the bill concerning the limiting excise and customes to a few yeares, which is yet at a stand. There is now a committee appointed for the affaires of Ireland and some bills by their order are in preparation. If your excellency and the councell, who best know what lawes are wanting, shall transmitt your sence therein, I hope we shall now have an oportunity to doe good for that poore nation. We sate so long this day in the house that I must beg your excellencye's pardon for my brevity and hasty scribble, resting ever,

Your excellencye's most obedient servuant,

Arthur Annesley

504. From Francis Aungier, 5 April 1659, 823, fos 289–290.

Sir,

The motions of our referrees are so extreamely slowe that they hardly administer sufficient matter for a weekely intelligencer, unlesse the impertinences of the persons who designe to be impertinent that they may keepe of action were inserted to create your mirth for want of discources to satisfye your curiositye. They goe on still at the old rate, in which the factions keepe theyr constant stations as if from meteors they had expectations of becoming fixed starres in the heaven of our disturbed famuly, whose inheritances they are as industrious to usurpe or ruine as we are to preserve and cherish. But I cannot doubt of makeing our labours successefull if we can become masters of as greate a share of patience in the mannagerye of our worke as they appeare to practize for compassing of theyr malicious aymes. This in the meanetime they use for the support of theyr neare-expiring hopes that if they can but in any one perticular gaine an award for theyr advantage, they shall so farre become victorious as to frustrate the expectations of our master. And with theise crutches they goe on so chearefully that though they meete with difficultyes, yet are they as seemingly contented as if the game played altogether for theyr owne advantage. This I have sometimes a more then ordinarye oppertunitye to observe, by mixeing in theyr companyes. Nor are they so very shye

[151] The second table of the Ten Commandments, relating to offences against one's fellow man. The leading republicans had opposed this part of the declaration on the grounds that it might limit liberty of conscience.

of me as they are of many others. Their overhott zeale prevailing with them to beleeve that those persons who are not noated for discoursers are not to be accounted as theyr mortall enemyes but especially (if they want yeares of judgement) may be overcome by the vanityes of theyr pretentions. What theyr meanes are of comeing to theyr journeys' end are neverthelesse preserved as the arcana[152] of the state of Venice. The grand designes at which they drive are generally contracted into a determinate number, which they represent in few words and with a very great stock of confidence, that they may seeme the more reasonable and the lesse questionable upon the debate with the more inconsiderate whom they labour to ensnare. That which they offer is breifely thus: first, they will secure themselves and then they will provide for the necessityes of theyr master. But in the interim they conceale that those things which they call theyr owne securityes are the only mediums which they prepose for his destruction and that the deferring to provide for the discharging of his debts and his present maintenance must render him obnoxious to those inconveniencyes which they wish may happen. Secondly, in provideing for themselves they say they are so extreamely modest that to denye them satisfaction (and that in the first place) were to proceed contrarye to the former sences even of our owne relations. We aske no more (say they) then the nomination of councellours at lawe and equitye for our master's businesse (which was, as they affirme, assented unto by that person of whome our master's father recovered the inheritance) and that these in our owne absence shall be either absolute to dispose of all things or at least that our master shall have no authoritye without theyr full consent. But that you may see (they adde) how much we affect the interest of the heyre and his estate, we will appoynt him such as shall engage never to take any salary or fee for theyr advices. This proposall they thinke unanswereable, but they are too cautious to discover that they solely intend themselves his councell and in that his masters, armed with an absolute uncontroleable authoritye to embezele his estate at pleasure. Lastly, to preserve him entire (say they) we will, by the dammages which we expect to recover against those whom we have and yett intend to sue (a reckoning without theyr hoast) and otherwayes, rayse a considerable summe of moneys for the satisfaction of his debts, yet with so greate a thrift that the cheifest of creditors shall be compelled to accept of halfe pay by way of composition for what hath beene so long and with so much patience on theyr partes expected to be satisfyed. But here also they keepe theyr divell in the darke and are wholly silent in discourseing the mischeifes which would fall upon our master by depriveing him of his choycest servants (for

[152] This Latin word could be translated as 'profound secrets' or 'mysteries'.

those are the persons whome they sue) because the opposers of the ambitions of this faction, and the inconveniencyes in which he should inevitably be involved if his creditors should find noe way to be releeved but by these persons whom they can never satisfy otherwyse then by complying with theyr endeavours to devoure the fortunes of the heyre for the satisfaction of theyr hate and avarice. These (sir) are the bases on which our adversayes are mainely founded and though they are so evidently villanous and unsuitable even to theyr owne professions if duely pryed into, yet doe I find them proposed with such a semblance of plausible reason to the ordinary sorte of men that it may verye well admitt a doubt whether by some surprize they may not wound us when we thinke ourselves secure. But I am only able at present to deliver the substance of things in short and to give my opinions at randome according to what I have gleaned amongst that partye. I shall hope that in some time I may be able to feele the bottome and to give you a more satisfactorye account of my care in these affayres wherein I knowe your concernement so strictly interwoven. In this, I hope you will beleeve me prepared to use my greatest industrye, consideringe me, in a more perticular manner then others, obliged to preserve your interest, who in a more perticular manner then others have endeared, (sir),

Your most humble, faithfull servant,

TL

505. From Thomas Belasyse, Viscount Fauconberg, 12 April 1659, 823, fos 291–292.

My lord,

Had I not beene out of towne, your excellency should the last post have had the troble of mine, tho I know very well F[153] tells you all and more then I can. The armye's representation[154] I suppose your excellency receives by this post. Tho Fauconberg did not signe it, hee was at the council and can tel you how twas carried on. The heads agreed on were three: indemnity, pay and security from cavaliers. But when this came to be refered to a committee for wording, the under-officers (for all the rabble were present) cryed up Lilborne, Ashfeild

[153] Almost certainly 'Broghill'.

[154] The army officers' document, issued on 6 April and conveyed that day by Fleetwood to the Protector, was entitled *The Humble Representation and Petition of the General Council of the Officers of the Armies of England, Scotland and Ireland.* As well as calling for the settlement of the army's material grievances, such as arrears of pay and indemnity, it claimed that the good old cause was under threat and proclaimed that the army would assist Protector and parliament in the work of uncovering and removing all those deemed to be 'wicked'.

and such like, who brought the thing pend much wors then you find it, and wee were too few to alter the whole, onely with some difficulty it was amended in several places (which yet is hardly credible). It has ben brought before the house, is much disrelisht there and the rather in regard of a fast held tomorrowe by the officers and another consultation appointed on Thursday, the end (it's supposed) is to make the approving the late king's death a touchstone or test for members of the army and council. A friend of Fauconberg's saw a bil to this purpos in the hands of V.[155] Many sober men are leaving the parliament; if others doe so all wil be left a prey to commonwealths men and the dregs of the army.

This day the house has beene very severe with major Butler, which will, I feare, dissatisfy some. I shall not now give your excellency any farther troble then by reading this assurance that I am,

Your most affectionately faithfull and obedient servant,
Fauconberg

506. From Anthony Morgan, 12 April 1659, 823, fos 293–294.

May it please your lordship,

I write only to shew that I doe not forget my duty. The representation of the army hath put such a damp upon that which before was the prevailing party in the house that all seems to goe at haphazard. Wee trifle away time and tis hard to say what wee are doing. That which seems to be in agitation is how to pay the army in England for 3 months, that they may have time to consider the debts and supplies necessary. Major generall Butler, if the question had been put, had doubtless been voted uncapable to beare any trust, military or civill, for acting upon (some say beyond) a lettre of his late Highness. The question was with much difficulty diverted and a committee named to consider how to proceed against him, but yet they voted him out of the office of justice of the peace. The commonwealth party appeared most in the prosecution, some think to the end the army may be disatisfied with the parliament, many of them being in like danger and so cause confusion, which some of the commonwealth party have said was the only way to their ends. The enclosed libell, being the latest I have seen, may be as acceptable as a diurnall. The Irish packet is not yet come. I remain,

Your lordship's most obedient and most obliged servant,
Ant Morgan

[155] Almost certainly 'Desborough'.

507. From Francis Aungier, London, 18 April 1659, 823, fos 295–296.

My lord,

I have at present so litle and yet so much to say to our present businesse that I am resolved to say just nothing. Our trustees were yesterday employing theyr whole day in labouring to make theyr servants understand theyr dutyes unto those from whom they must exact theyr wages. And really I thinke they have gon verye farre in that designe. But in regard I am ignorant of what is like to be the issue of so sharpe a conflict and am not in the number of those who dare lay clayme unto the spiritt of prophesye, I shall wave perticulars untill the next returne and probably you will command me before that to give your lordship a totall release from my hitherto weekely troubles, considering that your lordship will be now secure of receaving informations from a better (I may justly say, the best) hand and from him who, omitting all impertinencyes, will trouble you with no more then what is truly fitting and worthy your lordship's observation. I had the happynesse this morning to kysse the hands of our freinde[156] who is preparing for his encounter with his new dipt adversarye.[157] All that troubles me is to consider that a person so rarely qualified as is our learned doctor should be necessitated to trifle away his time (like Don Quixot) in giveing battayle to wyndmills and barbers' basons. But since it must be thus, I could heartily wish that your lordship's affayres would have permitted you to have been present at the scuffle. Infallibly it will be a comedye beyond comparison. Our walls will certainely preserve the doughty gallant from the Thames, though not from practizing his beloved principles. For certainely he will be putt into a capacity of rebaptizing himselfe in the holy waters of his more pretious and saintelike sweate. Your lordship need not feare a crowde or noyse to eclipse the courage of our freind. I doe not question but that he hath more freinds then enemyes and amongst the number of his freinds many whom (though strangers to his person) his partes and meritt have commanded to his service. I forbeare to recount unto your lordship my owne endeavours for his good. It will be enough to begett a beleefe in your lordship that I am not idle while I proclaime him for my freind. But I shall hope you will then beleeve that I have don my uttermost while I have considered him as a servant to my most noble master, whome I esteem I am then serving best while I serve those servants of his, who are best able to doe him service. And this I hope

[156] Petty.

[157] Here and later in this letter, Aungier makes sarcastic references to Sankey's alleged Baptist beliefs, which included support for adult baptism through total immersion.

your lordship will conclude the readyest way to expresse myselfe, my lord,

Your lordship's most humbly, most faithfull devoted servant,
Franc Aungier

508. From Dudly Loftus, Westminster, 19 April 1659, 823, fos 297–298.

May it please your excellencie,

This last weeke the house of comons hath bin more active then formerly, they haveing not onely transacted with the other house but allsoe voted yesterdaye the dissolution of the generall <meeting> assembly of officers at Wallingford House, in pursuance whereof it was voted in the house of comons that noe officer or souldier should continue in place of command or trust in the armie or navie whoe should hinder the meeteing of parliament or any members thereof. Mr Stevens,[158] a member of our house, was this day sent in a message to the other house whereby was desyred their concurrence to these votes, whereof we doe not doupt. Immediatly after we had soe voted the asembly of officers to be dissolved, his Highnesse haveing sent for them into his presence did declare their assembly dissolved and inhibited them to assemble againe. This act of his Highnesse is very satisfactory to the house and well pleaseing to most people and particularly to the Citie of London, whoe in their affections ar firmly united to his Highnesse and to the parliament, and will readyly manifest the same as cause shall require. I doupt not but these votes will prove a stable foundation of a lasting settlement for the honour of his Highnesse and the just liberty of the people. I shall take leave to acquaynt your excellencie that most of the members of Ireland are faithfull and serviceable and soe reputed to be. Severall bills are prepared for Ireland: an act for settlement for the ministry of Ireland upon legall titles and increase of mayntenance wher their tithes and gleabs are defective; an act of union; an act for probat of wills, which I have soe drawne up as to put the disposall of all offices relateing thereunto in your excellencie. I doe infinitely rejoyce that the Lord hath given your excellencie another sonn[159] and that your excellent lady is soe well recovered. I bessech God to multiply His blessings upon all the parts

[158] John Stevens, MP for Gloucestershire.

[159] None of Henry Cromwell's sons who survived infancy was born at this time – his second son, Henry, had been born in Dublin in March 1658 – so, although his wife had undoubtedly been pregnant (see *TSP*, VII, p. 492 and letter no. 484), this report must relate to a child who died soon after an apparently successful birth.

of your excellencie's family and make me as able to serve them as I doe unfeinedly avowe myselfe to be, my lord,

Your excellencie's most humble and infinitely obliged servant,

Dud Loftus

509. From Gilbert Mabbott, 19 April 1659, 823, fos 299–300.[160]

May it please your excellencie,

Wednesday last the howse resumed the consideration of the excise and afterward voted that none of their proceedings should bee hereafter published in the weekely printe. That whole day[161] was spent by the army in prayer and preaching att the lord Fleetwood's howse and carried on by Mr Griffith, Mr Peters and another minister. That day the howse agreed to the declaration for a fast and sent it up to the other howse for their conccerrence (by Mr Grove).[162] Their lordshipps sent answer that the howse would speedily consider thereof and send answer by messengers of their owne. That afternoone[163] a generall councell of the army mett att Wallingford Howse and agreed to declare against Charles Stewart and his interest and for the Protector and parlament, to protecte all such persons as have beene ingaged in his death[164] and to admonish the army to amyty and unity and a strickt walking before the Lord. It is observed that when Mr Growe was called in, all the other howse was bare to him and the 50 that accompanied him and soe mett them againe att their barre att their lordshipps delivering the answear. Friday the howse ordered Mr Bampfeild[165] their speaker (Mr Challenor Chute, their first speaker, beeing lately departed).[166] Saterday was spent in debate of a paper of grievances from the Quakers directed to their speaker, whoe they desire would read to the howse. They began thus (friends): after it was

[160] Another version of parts of this newsletter, with some variations in the text, is found in newsletters by Mabbott, dated 14 and 16 April, which survive amongst the Clarke Papers at Worcester College, Oxford, and which are printed in *Clarke Papers*, III, pp. 189–190.

[161] 13 April.

[162] Thomas Grove, MP for Marlborough.

[163] 14 April.

[164] The regicide.

[165] Thomas Bampfield, parliamentarian politician, was deputy recorder and then recorder of Exeter and played an active role in Devon local government during the 1650s. He sat for Exeter in all three Protectorate parliaments, and, although not very prominent in the first, he was much more active in the second, pushing for the independence of parliament against executive interference and taking a generally 'country' stance. It was probably this that made him broadly acceptable to the various groups in the third Protectorate parliament and led to his brisk and efficient but brief service as speaker in the closing days of this parliament.

[166] He died on 14 April.

read 2 of them were called in and the speaker tould them that the howse expected that they should retorne to their severall homes and live peaceably and with submission to the lawes of the nation. The lord Fleetwood is (with such officers as he thinkes fitt) draweing up the last heads agreed upon against the next meeting, 20th instant. Yesterday about 2 of clocke the officers, according to his Highnes' command, attended him att Whitehall, where he made knowne his pleasure that from henceforth the meeting of the officers in generall councell bee dissolved (the parlament haveing their desires under consideration). The parlament that day lockt themselves close up, not alloweing a member to come out till 4 of clocke, and ordered that there shall bee no generall councell of the officers of the army without direction, leave and authority of his Highnes and both howses of parlament, and that no person shall have or continue any command or trust in any of the armyes or navyes of the 3 nations whoe shall not subscribe that he will not disturb or interrupt the free meeting of parlament of any member of either howse of parlament or their freedomes in their debates and councells, and that the concurrence of the other howse bee desired therein. It was referr'd to a committee to consider how his Highnes, the parlament and the 3 nations may bee secured against the cavaleire party. Another committee was appointed to prepare a bill to indemynify such persons as have served the comonwealth. The speedy payment of the arreares of the army and navy to bee considered of tomorrow. This day the 2 first votes were sent up to the other howse; the declaration against the cavaleeres debated; and severall frigatts to preserve trade appointed. I humbly subscribe myselfe, my lord,

Your excellencie's most humble and most obedient servant,

G Mabbott

510. From Anthony Morgan, Colchester, 19 April 1659, 823, fos 301–302.

May it please your excellency,

Since my last I received 3 letters from your lordship. The 1st was the chiding letter, which pleased me very much because it gave me evidence that your lordship will give me oportunity to amend my oversights by telling me of them whensoever I offend. When I shewd the lettre to Charles Coote he told me he had written to your lordship an account of all that I said in the house upon that occasion. But whether he did so or not, I am sure I said all that your lordship wonders nobody would say and Charles Coote protests there was nothing keept him from saying the same but that I had said it before he had oportunity to stand up.

The 2nd was by Petty, who came to town on Sunday night last.

The 3d by the post, in which was one enclosed to lord Russell, which I sent away to him. The enclosed was the last I received from him.

Yesterday morning his Highness ordered that all the officers who had mett at Wallingford House should attend him at 3 afternoon in Whitehall, where he told them (as I was informed by one present there) that he had acquainted the parliament with their representation, that the desires in it were under their consideration, that it was not needfull they should continue their meetings in expectation of an answer, that therefore they should not meet on Wednesday next as they had appointed but should all repaire to their charges. He added 2 reasons: one that many members of parliament were dissatisfied with such meetings sitting the parliament, the other that the cavaleer was arming in order to some new attempts. General Disborough replied he wondered that any honest man should be offended at their meetings to regulate disorders among themselves. His Highness affirmed his 1st orders and withdrew. General Disborough and divers others went out with him towards his chamber and as they went general Desborough said to his Highness, but sir, the meeting is not dissolved for all this, for they adjorned themselves to a meeting at Wallingford House and not to this place. His Highness replied, sir, I say they shall not meet there nor anywhere else. Collonel Ashfeild step in and said, sir, this suddain order will put us to great inconveniences and when wee come to our soldiers without mony, wee shall not know what to say to them, besides there are divers officers but newly come to town. His Highness replied, sir, you of all men have least reason to except against this order, having been 2 years from your command, and I beleive those who came lately to town will be willinger to returne then those who have been longer here.

The same day betwixt the time of the order issued for the officers to attend his Highness and the hower he dissolved the meeting, the commons voted that no generall councell should be held during the sitting of the parliament without leave from his Highness and both howses, that no person should beare any office or trust in the army who should refuse to subscribe that he would not interrupt any member of parliament in his duty, etc, that a declaration should be published to banish cavaleers from London, that tomorrow they would take into consideration how to pay the arrears of the armies and navy.

They sent the 1st vote this day to the other house for their concurrence.

The commonwealth party were much against the 1st vote against generall councells and alsoe against the providing mony for the soldiers, some think because their only hopes are in confusion of affaires. I am,

Your excellency's most obedient servant,

Ant Morgan

511. From Robert Saunders, Kinsale Fort, 24 April 1659, 823, fo. 303.

May it please your excellencye,

The Paradox friggott came into this harbor Aprill 24 about eleaven in the morning, captain Cowes[167] comander, and brought in with him a galeott[168] of St Sebastians of two guns and thirty-five men, which had very much infested this coast this spring, chasing some merchant ships to this very harbor's mouth. This action of his hath highly sattisfyed the merchants heare and much encouraged traders in thes parts. I have received twenty-six prisoners of him (the rest were sent home with an English vessell which they had taken) and have sent them to the county goale to be secured till your excellency shall please to send order for ther further dispose. In the meanetyme humbly desire your excellency to give your speedy orders to the treasury that they may have for ther maintenance the usuall allowance for prisoners. As for the captain (whose name is Nicholas Johnson, comissionated by James Stewart), captain Cowes reserves to present, with the ship, to your excellency as soone as wind and weather will give him leave to waite on your excellency at Dublin. So humbly take leave to remain,

Your excellency's most faithfull, humble servant to comand,

Ro Saunders

512. From Gilbert Mabbott, 26 April 1659, 823, fos 304–305.[169]

May it please your excellencie,

Wednesday and Thursday last[170] the howse debated the settlement of the militia. Thursday att night all the regiments here both of the horse and foote were in armes, that of the late lord Pride marcht into Whitehall without opposition. His Highnes gave orders to collonel Hacker's[171] and other regiments to march to Whitehall for

[167] Richard Cows/Cowes, parliamentarian naval officer. On 24 April, he wrote a letter to Henry Cromwell about this action (*TSP*, VII, p. 664).

[168] Galiot/galliot: originally a swift Mediterranean galley; by the seventeenth century, the term was also used for a light, single-masted, flat-bottomed Dutch merchant vessel.

[169] Another version of much of this newsletter, with some variations in the text, is found in a newsletter by Mabbott, dated 23 April, which survives amongst the Clarke Papers at Worcester College, Oxford, and which is printed in *Clarke Papers*, III, p. 193.

[170] 20 and 21 April.

[171] Francis Hacker, parliamentarian officer and politician and deemed a regicide, campaigned extensively in and around Leicestershire during the civil war, raising and

the preservation of his person, but haveing before received other order from the lord Fleetwood they (with all the rest) obeyed his excellencie's rather then those from his Highnes. All this was done without seizeing any man's person, shedding a dropp of blood or makeing the least confusion in the City and suberbs. Friday his Highnes signed a commission to dissolve both howses. The other howse sent the blacke roadde 3 times to the commons to meete them for that purpose, but because it was not brought by a member of their owne, they refused to admitt thereof by the messenger against whom they lockt their doores, who thereupon by order of the other howse brake his blacke rodde att the doore of the commons in testimony of their dissolution. Yesterday Sir Arthur Haselrig and about 40 or 50 more members went to the commons howse doore, which they found lockt against them and not haveing admittance upon their knocking retorned into the hall. The articles of peace betweene France and Spaine are concluded for 14 yeares. Wee heare nothing of acion from our fleete in the Sound. The councell of officers hath beene consideringe of a future government, whether by the petition and advice, the calling of the Long Parlament or by a government of a new constitution; they are not yet agreed upon any of them. I humbly subscribe myselfe, my lord,

Your excellencie's most humble and most obedient servant,

G Mabbott

513. From Francis Russell, Chippenham, 29 April 1659, 823, fos 306–307.

My deare lord,

Your lordship's last to me tarryed somewhere by the way, so that I could not give you an answer sooner. My daughter Reynolds, I suppose, hath giveen your wife an answer to hirs, which is upon the point an answer to your lordship's last to myselfe, besides these times forbid the change of any single condition. My being here at home cannot furnish you with any exact account of these times and thire changes, but I suppose you have it from better hands we haveing onely a great noyse that the parliament is dissolved to thire great

commanding horse units there, though he twice fell prisoner to the royalists. He was entrusted with custody of the king at the time of his trial, signed the order to the executioner, and oversaw the execution itself. In 1650, he was made colonel of a newly formed horse regiment, which campaigned in Scotland under Oliver Cromwell. From 1652 onwards, he and much of his regiment were based mainly in England, although the regiment returned to Scotland in 1657–1658, and Hacker proved a loyal supporter of Oliver Cromwell and his Protectorate, returned for Leicester to the second and also the third Protectorate parliaments. But, in April 1659, he was one of those senior military commanders with regiments in and around London who chose not to obey or support Richard Cromwell.

disapointment. My lord, there is no new thing under the sun but we may easyly beleeve that where the power of the sword is, it will and must doe its appointed worke. Onely I could have wished that the wisdome of some of your freinds would have giveen you leave to have viseted England three or four months since. For my part, I foresaw that theyr policys who would not have you here was not simple enough to thrive or bring their ends to passe, but I was a foole than; but what are they now? Judge you betwixt us. When I strove to bring a good and a right understanding betweene my lord Fleetwood and yourselfe, I was thought a knave by some and a foole by others, and with those two markes of honor I was forced to retyre home. Oh how pittyfull a thing is this worldly policy, but every one must reape what they so. I am sure that is but rationall and reasonable to beleeve. Many who I thought to be your freinds (yet I had my jealousys of them) I shall never trust againe, both as to their wisedomes and honestys. I dare be confident had you bin here three months since (and would have sometimes bin but adviseed by such a foole as I am), things in England had not bin as they are. Yet I can call nothing bad that comes to passe by the providence of God, for He onely is good and wise in all His ways. If at any time I have bin melancholy or thoughtfull, I had a deepeer reason and ground for it than was understood. It may be I saw further into the millstone with one eye than all your freinds did with both theyres; but you know what became of him that by wisedome did save the citty, was not he dispiseed because poore? My lord, let nothing of this world trouble you, the glory of it is but like the flower of the grasse. The kingdome of heaven within us is that which a wise, good man onely aymes at. Your father's honor and greatnes in this world is allmost forgotten. By that you may see what earthly crownes are. Your brother, while he lives, may cry all is vanity, trouble and vexation of spirit. Oh my deare lord, covet onely that wisedome which is from above and remember allways that the wisedome of this and for this world is but fooleishnes. My love to your wife and pray as often as you can let me heare from you. Have a care of the subtle crafty ones who have love for none but their ownes ends. In patience posses your soule and let not anger, wrath, malice or revenge have any place in your hart. I am, my deare lord,

Your lordship's allwayes truely to serve you,

Franc Russell

Love and wisedome are stronger than any weapons of war and yet will doe greater things than we think of.

514. From Gilbert Mabbott, 2 May 1659, 823, fos 308–309.[172]

May it please your excellencie,

The last weeke a councill of officers sat at Wallingford Howse, consisting of these lords, vizt: Fleetwood, Disbrowe, Sidenham, Cowper, Hawson and Berry, collonells Hacker, Ashfield, Lilburne, Sallmon, Baxter,[173] Clerke, Kelsey[174] and Sancky. Lord Lambert, collonel Okey,[175] collonel Sanders[176] and others lately added. They have spent much time in consideringe of a government and incline to the calling of the Long Parlament and nominating a councell, whoe are said shall have a checke or negative upon them, others say not. On Thursday last[177] the councell ordered that the lord Lambert shall command the lord Falconbridge his regiment, collonel Okey the lord Ingoldsbye's, collonel Sanders which was formerly his owne, Sir Arthur Haselrig

[172] Another version of parts of this newsletter, with some variations in the text, is found in newsletters by Mabbott, dated 30 April and 2 May, which survive amongst the Clarke Papers at Worcester College, Oxford, and which are printed in *Clarke Papers*, III, p. 196 and IV, pp. 2–3.

[173] John Barkstead, parliamentarian officer and politician and a regicide, fought for parliament in the civil war, mainly in the south-east, and was governor of Reading from 1644 until 1647, when he was given command of a New Model foot regiment previously commanded by Richard Fortescue. He strongly supported the regicide, was active in keeping order in and around London during the 1650s, and was, from 1652, lieutenant of the Tower. He sat in all three Protectorate parliaments, from 1658 as a member of the unelected other house, and also served as major-general of Middlesex and Westminster in 1655–1657.

[174] Thomas Kelsey, parliamentarian officer and politician, served in the civil war as an officer in the foot regiments of Edward Montague and Richard Ingoldsby and, from 1646, as deputy governor of Oxford. Although he played no part in the regicide, he strongly supported the regimes of the 1650s, becoming colonel of a dragoon regiment and governor of Dover. He was very active as major-general for Kent and Surrey in 1655–1657 and sat in all three Protectorate parliaments, though by 1659 he had become disillusioned with the Protectorate and supported its removal.

[175] John Okey, parliamentarian officer and politician and a regicide, served in the civil war as an officer under the Earl of Essex and Sir Arthur Hesilrige and in 1645 was given command of a New Model dragoon regiment. Having supported the regicide, he campaigned in Scotland in 1650–1651 and again in 1654. However, by that time he had become critical of the Protectorate and, during the first Protectorate parliament, to which he was returned for a Scottish seat, he helped draw up a military petition critical of the regime. He was court martialled, sentenced to death though reprieved, and dismissed from the army. He spent the remainder of Oliver Cromwell's Protectorate in retirement, under suspicion and arrested and questioned from time to time. He was elected to Richard Cromwell's Protectorate parliament and was restored to his command after the fall of the Protectorate.

[176] Thomas Saunders, parliamentarian officer, served in the civil war as an officer in Thomas Thornhagh's horse regiment, succeeding him as its commander in 1648 upon Thornhagh's death at Preston. He and his regiment served in England in the early 1650s and campaigned in Scotland in 1652–1654. He became disillusioned with the Protectorate, subscribed to the critical colonels' petition of 1654 drafted by Okey and others, and was dismissed from the army. He, too, was reappointed on the fall of the Protectorate.

[177] 28 April.

the lord Howard's, major Packer and captain Gladman[178] to bee alsoe reinvested in their former commands. Major generall Overton and collonel Rich are likewise under debate to bee readmitted. That day at the councell of warre the lord Ingoldsbye's captain-lieutenant[179] and major Babington's[180] captain[181] were (at a councell of warre) adjudged to loose there commissions. Some citizens have lately lent a monthe's pay to the forces here and 6 weekes' more they expect suddenly. Our fleete is in the Sound; the Dutch fleete is not yet come thither. The peace betweene France and Spaine are not yet fully concluded, though the articles for that purpose are here printed. The councell of the officers have likewise ordered that love and union bee preserved in the army, that such as have disobeyed the lord Fleetwood's orders bee tryed by a court martiall and disbanded, that such as have beene displact by the late lord Protector bee restored as oportunity serves, that the lord Fleetwood shall have power to restore to place till further order, that letters bee written to the lord lieutenant of Ireland, generall Moncke and all the militia forces for a faire correspondency. Yesterday major Babington was secured for refuseing to appeare upon the somons of a court martiall. This day some eminent members of the Long Parlament were consulted with by severall officers (according to order) concerning the calling of the Long Parlament. A letter was agreed upon and ordered to bee sent to every regiment to give them satisfaction in their proceedings. I humbly subscribe myselfe, my lord,

Your excellencie's most humble and most obedient servant,

G Mabbott

[178] John Gladman, parliamentarian officer, served in Sir Thomas Fairfax's New Model horse regiment in the 1640s, going with that regiment, now Oliver Cromwell's, to Scotland in the early 1650s. However, he was one of a clutch of officers in that regiment who, perhaps influenced by the disaffection of Major Packer, in effect commander of the regiment in the mid- and later 1650s, became dissatisfied with the Protectorate and were dismissed by the Protector in February 1658. Again, he was one of the anti-Protectorate officers reappointed in the spring of 1659.

[179] Parry (his forename not recorded), parliamentarian officer, was one of a clutch of officers in Richard Ingoldsby's horse regiment who followed their colonel in briefly and ineffectively obeying the Protector's rather than Fleetwood's commands and who promptly lost their commands once the Protectorate had fallen.

[180] Thomas Babbington, parliamentarian officer, was, by the early 1650s, an officer in Nathaniel Rich's New Model horse regiment serving in Scotland and campaigned there until the mid-1650s. He remained in the regiment after Rich's dismissal in 1654, serving first under Charles Howard and then under Richard Ingoldsby, being promoted to major sometime in the late 1650s. As one of Ingoldsby's officers who rallied to the Protector in April 1659, he was promptly arrested and purged after the Protectorate's fall.

[181] Identity not known, although clearly another parliamentarian officer in Ingoldsby's regiment quickly purged for displaying loyalty and obedience to the Protector.

515. From William Petty, Neston, 5 May 1659, 823, fos 310–311.

May it please your excellency,

Sir Jerome, beeing now a very great man and one of the committee of safety,[182] did in a manner command mee to stay here, declaring his pleasure to have mee presented another way etc. Neverthelesse, when nothing else hindred, I came from London without his leave. Your excellency will have fresher newes by the post than any I can write. Wee overtooke a troop sent into Wales, for what new purpose I know not. Sir Henry Pierce[183] and leiutenant colonel Stephens are here at Neston; major Aston[184] upon the way. People take the late transactions very patiently. I hope I shall be permitted to proceed with my vindication at Dublin, if this bee a time for any particular busines lesse then the preservation of the whole. I remayne, may it please your excellency,

Your excellency's most obedient and faithfull servant,

Wm Petty

Sir Anthony Morgan thinks of retiring to Tame Parke this summer, but is at present at Chelsey.

516. From Gilbert Mabbott, 10 May 1659, 823, fos 312–313.[185]

May it please your excellencie,

The last weeke the councell of officers at Wallingford Howse agreed upon severall desires to bee presented to the parlament, vizt that £20,000 per annum bee settled upon his Highnes for life, £10,000 per annum upon his posterity for ever, £8,000 per annum upon her Highnes dowager, and a howse to bee appointed for their habitation; that the goverment bee settled in a commonwealth without king, kingship or howse of lords; the militia to bee settled in safe hands; lord Fleetwood bee made commander in cheife of all the forces of this commonwealth; liberty of conscience provided for; the time for sitting this parlament assertained; maintenance for a pious ministry; the schooles of learning countinanced; the lawes regulated. Tomorrow a generall councell meetes finally to conclude these particulers. Upon invitation

[182] Sankey was, in fact, a member of the council of officers, rather than the slightly later committee of safety.

[183] Parliamentarian politician and MP for Counties Westmeath, Longford, and King's in Richard Cromwell's Protectorate parliament.

[184] Another returning Irish MP, William Aston had sat in Richard Cromwell's Protectorate parliament for Counties Meath and Louth.

[185] Another version of part of this newsletter, with some variations in the text, is found in a newsletter by Mabbott, dated 5 May, which survives amongst the Clarke Papers at Worcester College, Oxford, and which is printed in *Clarke Papers*, IV, pp. 6–7.

of the inclosed the speaker Lenthall[186] and such members as were qualified sat in parlament (Saterday last).[187] The rest were kept out. Their nomber were 50, about 80 more are capable of sitting.[188] It's expected they will speedily joine with them. The parlament (that day) past the inclosed declaration, appointed for 7 dayes a committee of safety, vizt: lord Fleetwood, lord John Jones, Sidenham, Salway,[189] Vane, Haselrig and Ludlow. Yesterday Mr Prinne,[190] whoe was secluded this parlament, came into the howse before the sitting thereof and contrary to the declarations of the parlament and army. The howse sat not till one of clocke and then by a guard he was kept out. The judges mett but sat not. The howse added lord Lambert, major generall Berry, Mr Scotts and major generall Disbrowe to the committee of the safety. They voted that none but such as are of a pious life, capacitated for their imployments, shall subscribe to the government as it is already declared and have given testimony of their affections to the good old[191] shall bee capable of serving this commonwealth, either in a civill or military capacity, and for this purpose a list of all their names is to bee

[186]William Lenthall, parliamentarian politician, speaker of the House of Commons of the Long Parliament, had acquiesced in Pride's Purge and, while not actively supporting the regicide, continued to sit as speaker of the Rump and nominally, therefore, head of the new republican state. Although disturbed by the ejection of the Rump, he was loyal to the Protectorate, continuing to hold office as master of the rolls and was returned to both of Oliver Cromwell's Protectorate parliaments, serving again as speaker in the first. In the autumn of 1657, he was made a member of the new nominated parliamentary chamber.

[187]7 May.

[188]That is, the surviving members of the remnant of the Long Parliament who had not been purged by the army in December 1648 and who were qualified to sit in the Rump.

[189]Richard Salwey, parliamentarian politician, was elected to the Long Parliament in 1645 and, while he held aloof from the regicide, he took his seat in the Rump in the spring of 1649. In 1650, he was appointed one of the parliamentary commissioners for the civil government of Ireland, but he resigned that office within weeks. He opposed Oliver Cromwell's ejection of the Rump and, while he did accept the post of ambassador to Constantinople in 1654, he declined other offices after 1653, refusing to sit in the Nominated Assembly and not being returned to any of the Protectorate parliaments. Although, therefore, not one of the most strident republicans, he did return to the fore after the fall of the Protectorate and with the recall of the Rump.

[190]William Prynne, politician, lawyer, and propagandist, suffered during the Personal Rule and strongly supported the parliamentary cause during the early and mid-1640s, serving on various commissions. However, by the time of his election to the Long Parliament in November 1648, he was becoming disillusioned with the drift of events, he strongly opposed Pride's Purge and the regicide, and then spent several years in prison as an enemy of the new republican regime. The attempts by Prynne and several other MPs excluded after Pride's Purge to retake their seats in the spring of 1659 were thwarted and he did not return to favour and office until the Restoration.

[191]Word apparently omitted – almost certainly 'cause', since the phrase 'the good old cause' was much used in the spring of 1659.

prepared. They ordered the lord Fairefax[192] to sitt, he being chosen in the Long Parlament but because of his publique imploy could not then serve personally. They voted the lord Whitelocke, collonel Sidenham, collonel White, Sir James Harrington,[193] collonel Downes,[194] collonel Thompson[195] and Mr Holland[196] a committee to inspect the treasury. A bill was read for continueing the sitting of this terme but the draught thereof was not well presented. This day the howse ordered that blancke commissions for judges should bee drawne against Friday next, that the excise, customes and other assessments bee collected as formerly and no money payd out till further order, that a bill bee brought in to impower the justices and other civill officers to act till

[192] Sir Thomas Fairfax, third Lord Fairfax, parliamentarian officer and politician, was one of the leading parliamentary generals in northern England in 1643–1644 and, in the spring of 1645, became parliamentary lord general and commander of the New Model Army. Despite his military leadership and success, he was increasingly out of his depth with, and disillusioned by, army politics, opposing the regicide and then resigning his commission in the summer of 1650. Thereafter, he spent most of the 1650s living in semi-retirement on his Yorkshire estates, occasionally under suspicion of royalist leanings. He was elected to, but probably played little or no part in, the first Protectorate parliament; he was returned for his native Yorkshire to Richard Cromwell's Protectorate parliament and then played a rather more active role. He was also elected to the new council of state established by the Rump in May 1659 but he declined to serve.

[193] James Harrington, parliamentarian officer and politician, campaigned for parliament in and around London during the early years of the civil war and was returned to the Long Parliament in 1646. He attended some meetings of the high court trying the king but did not sign the death warrant, although he clearly supported the republic and was active in the Rump. He largely withdrew from public life after the ejection of the Rump and spent the Protectorate in semi-retirement.

[194] John Downes, parliamentarian politician and a regicide, was elected to the Long Parliament in 1641, tending to ally with the Independents and the army in the later 1640s and, although he expressed some disquiet at proceedings, he attended the king's trial and signed the death warrant; he was active and prominent in the Rump. He largely withdrew from public life after the ejection of the Rump and spent the Protectorate in semi-retirement.

[195] Probably George Thompson, parliamentarian officer and politician, who campaigned for parliament in the south-east during the civil war, rising to command a regiment of horse in London and fighting at the battle of Cheriton, where he lost a leg. He was returned to the Long Parliament in 1645 and, while he played no part in the regicide, he was prominent in the Rump, being very active in naval, colonial, and mercantile affairs, reflecting his background as a colonial merchant. He opposed the ejection of the Rump and was out of office and under suspicion during the Protectorate, but quickly returned to office and prominence in the spring of 1659 upon the recall of the Rump.

[196] Cornelius Holland, parliamentarian politician and deemed to be a regicide, was prominent in the Long Parliament as a radical and a strong critic of Charles I, whose trial he attended regularly, up to and including the day of sentence, although he did not actually sign the death warrant. He was prominent in the Rump but slipped into inactivity after its ejection and played little role in public life during the Protectorate, returning to the fore only after the fall of that regime and the return of the Rump.

further order. France and Spaine have agreed upon a cessation for 2 moneths. I humbly subscribe myselfe, my lord,

Your excellencie's most humble and most obedient servant,

Gilb Mabbott

517. From Anthony Morgan, London, 10 May 1659, 823, fos 314–315.

May it please your excellency,

I write because I would not seem to neglect rather then that I hope to give you any information more then everybody in the streets there may have. I now mett my lord Whitlock and lord Lisle; they named only 3 things that the old-new parliament have done: 1 is the enclosed declaration; 2 making a committee of safety to nominate military and civill officers; 3 a declaration to continue all justices of peace and to enable them to act. They sayd they had alsoe a great debate about the judges but resolved nothing. I can not say here is a generall satisfaction, but all men seem so or att least strangely indifferent who governs. I have not received any commands from your lordship since this great revolution, but I am told that you have sent a prudent and sober letter. I hope to goe this week to Tham Parke and as soon as I can conveniently fitt myselfe, returne to waite upon your lordship in Ireland. I am,

Your lordship's most obedient and most humble servant,

Ant Morgan

518. From Thomas Stanley,[197] Clonmel, 11 May 1659, 823, fos 316–317.

May it please your excellency,

Although I wayted on his Highnesse since my lord of Broghall left London and did receave his commands to give your excellency his kynde respects, with such an accompte of affaires at London as I was able to take notice of, yeett knowinge that yow doe receave the same more fully from my lord of Broghall's better hand, which is herewith sent, I doe forbeare to interrupt yow with further trouble then to lett your lordship know that as I am safely arived here through the providence of God, soe I shall endeavour by His blessinge faithfully to dischardge my trust on this place and therein that duty by which I am,

Your oblidged, faithfull and humble servant,

Tho Stanley

[197] Parliamentarian administrator and politician, sometime governor of Clonmel and knighted by Henry Cromwell in January 1659, he had newly returned to Ireland after representing Tipperary and Waterford in Richard Cromwell's Protectorate parliament.

519. From Richard Cromwell, *c.*12 May 1659, 823, fos 371–372.[198]

I shall not say in how sad a condittion I and owre famuly, nay the nations are in, for it is better for me to throwe my selfe in the dust and crye before the Lord, my sins hath brought what is come to pase upon us. But truly it is as low as men can make it and the flourishing bough of it (at spring) is weathered. I shal let my deportement be made knowne by my Broghill and Petty, the first beinge a spectator to my carriadge. Al the time the parliament sat I can assure you I stoode not so highe as my father did, yet I thought it was fitting I sohuld[199] keep the grounde of a good conscience, which I have done hetherto, though it be for my present ruen and famuly, for I could not have beleved that religion, relation and selfe interest wold have deceved me. Sense Petty' departure, whoe was fuly instructed the same for Scotland at the same time being sent for youre better correspondancy, the Rumpe of th[200] parliament hath met,[201] whoe are about sixty and are very violent upon him that is gone as wel flyinge high upon those that are living. There is a commite of safty apointed, who sits at Wallingford Howse, the names of them are Fleetwood, Desborough, Vane, Hasselrige, Ludlow, Lambert and others. They are propounding to the parliament five generals that shal have equal powres,[202] whoe are not to act a part in the government of the army. Though youre provocation is very greate and you have a greate sense of the honor of my deceassed father and the perishing condition of the famuly, yet youe wil be wary what you doe for youre owne sake and the sake of those that shal have an affection with you. Noting[203] giveth hopes but a

[198]This and the following letter (no. 520) were transcribed and printed with commentary and annotations by R.C.H. Catterall in 'Two letters of Richard Cromwell, 1659', *American Historical Review*, 8 (1902–1903), pp. 86–89. This is the first of two letters in this collection by Richard Cromwell (nos 519 and 520), both of May 1659, which he has written largely in code. The code is broadly similar to others in use at the time, with each number standing for an individual letter, plus occasional letters of the alphabet standing for a person or group of people. The two encoded letters have been almost completely decoded by their recipient – the letters and words have been entered above the numbers in a seventeenth-century hand – and those decoded sections provide the key to the occasional words and phrases that have not been decoded in the original, as well as correcting some minor slips in the original decoding. Accordingly, the decoded texts have been reproduced here.

[199]Code slightly garbled – clearly 'should' is the intended word.

[200]Code slightly garbled and word incomplete – clearly 'the' is the intended word.

[201]On 7 May.

[202]This proposal to create five powerful army commissioners was made in parliament on 11 May, so this letter can be no earlier than that date. However, Richard Cromwell makes no mention here of discussions in the Rump on 12 May about appointing a council of state, nor the fact that, on 13 May, seven rather than five senior officers were named as army commissioners. Thus, as Catterall concluded, this undated letter was almost certainly written on 12 May.

[203]Code slightly garbled – clearly 'nothing' is the intended word.

cleare understanding and good corespondancy with general Moncke, whoe hath written a letter which is very favorable, but I hope it is only to hold himselfe in a good opinion with them at Westminster until a faire opertunity. I beleive they here indends to be very vygorous and briske if not timely prevented, which cannot be but by a diversion from the forces <and garrisons> at the distant places. I knowe noe hope but some such way and that must be also assisted by frinds and strong places here, which if there be any hopes with you, there being none left here, it wil be necessary that we should keepe boeth often and close correspondancy. I am now in daly exspectation what course they wil take with me. My confidence is in God and to Him wil I put my cause. I have heard nothing from Scotland, nor Dunckerque, nor fleete. This nation is ful of raige and unquietnes, 500 horse would have turned al. But my <[. . .]>[204] Broghill was a spectator how corporals lead troops from there captaines and captaines from thore colonels. I beleive Fleetwood and Desborough are not longe lived if it wold please God to let them see there dainger, yet theings might be retreived but oure hopes are lowe. I knowe not whether a liberty or a prisson. The Lord be with you and for me pray doe nothing that may be for your ruen, but lay youre bussines with united strength and then leave the succese to God. I could wish you could have correspondancy by some ship from Ireland to general Mountague. I rest, deare brother, youres most affectionatly.

520. From Richard Cromwell, 17 May 1659, 823, fo. 370.

I am not able to advise, my freinds, my councel and my relations having all forsaken me. I am now attending the greate God, whoe is only my hope. I wish He had been more when in prosprity, but as to the ey of men I was not wanton. They have nothing to say, though I am in the duste with my mouth as to God. I shall now direct you to your owne counceles, being only able to offer you matter of fact which would be too tedious and suspitious to relate it in paper, and therefore I have as farre as I can instructed Doctor King,[205] whoe hath seen things and understood more by his generall convers then my selfe. Pray have a care whoe you trust, the world is false. And for my selfe, those that were my father's freinds, pretended ones only, were myne. It required time to acquaint my selfe with them, and they tripped up my heeles before I knew them, for though they were relations yet they forsooke me. I knowe Fleetwood and Desboroough regaurds not ruen soe that they may have there ends, they are pittiful creatures. God will

[204] Coded word or words heavily deleted and illegible.
[205] Ralph King.

avenge inocency. I have acquainted this bearer with Mounke's letter[206] in answer to what I sent him, which was the same I sent to you; it is a poore one; and withoute Broghill can retrive and the fleete stand stenche there is noe hopes as to my bussines. Greate severities are put upon me and I exspect the greatest. This afternoone I looke for comittee to come unto me with yesterday's votes.[207] This bearer shal alsoe be acquainted with them. Thes men intend nothing lese then ruen to us boeth. Yet let me not provocke agnse[208] youre judgement. I know not more to say but to let you know the great men doe not agre and that the army is in greate disorder, the horse and foote, the one for his penny a day, the other for his thrippence a day, besides honest men throwne out only because they were Protectorians. David's case was very heard, let us rely upon the God of oure father, and it will be as much our honour to know how to. I shall desire the Lord to be your helpe in all your straight and difficultyes, with myne and my wyfe's true resspects I rest.

I would faine knowe what Broghill sayes in this oure case. Pray have a familiar kindenes to him.

[206]Monck wrote on 12 May on behalf of the officers and army in Scotland, recognizing and accepting the new regime. The letter was formally reported to the Rump on 18 May.

[207]On 16 May, a committee of MPs was set up to consider Richard Cromwell's position and condition, thus providing a firm date for this undated letter.

[208]Code garbled – apparently 'against' is the intended word.

UNDATED LETTERS THAT CANNOT RELIABLY BE ASSIGNED A NARROW DATE (arranged in alphabetical order of the writer)

521. From Richard Beake, 823, fos 189–190.

May it please your excellencie,

The respect and honour I bare your excellencie will not suffer mee willingly to offer the least injury to your patience, and if I did not thinke it a duty incumbent uppon mee, I should choose much rather to be silent then give your excellencie this trouble and it is not without much feare least likewise the occation should not be pleaseing to you, but I beg your excellencie's beleife that I am cautious of doing the one or the other. What I have to write is to acquaint your excellencie that there is a treaty of marriage betweene my lady Reynolds[1] and myselfe, which I suppose is already knowen to your excellencie, for I must confesse I know not how to owne it, considering the relation shee stands in to your excellencie, but desired my lord Russell to intimate and excuse it for mee, whose intercession, I hope, hath in some measure procured my pardon. I have nothinge to say but that as I was induced to it out of a true and reall affection to my lady, soe twas without any presumption towards your excellencie and I am sure my discouragements were not a few, least it should be thought soe, but if your excellencie did but knowe the sinceritie and candidnesse of my heart in this thinge, you would rather pardon then condem mee. I trust I have learnt not to aime at greate thinges, but that wherein I may have comfort and satisfaction soe farre as this world can afford, which I doubt not but I shall in this, if I may obtaine your excellencie's favour, and I shall desire it noe longer then I shall approve myselfe, may it please your excellencie,

Your excellencie's most faythfull and most humble servant,

Ri Beke

I doe beg the tender of my most humble service to my lady, whose pardon and favour I earnestly entreate.

[1] Probably Sarah, daughter of Sir Francis Russell and widow of Sir John Reynolds. The letter is addressed to Henry Cromwell as lord lieutenant, so it probably dates from the closing weeks of 1658, since Fleetwood noted in early January 1659 that the marriage was off (*TSP*, VII, p. 589).

522. From Joseph Binks,[2] 823, fos 318–319.

Letter of religious exhortation, calling upon Henry Cromwell to work with God and to do His will; adds a religious poem, the opening letter of each line spelling out 'Oliver Cromwell'.

523. From Elizabeth Butler, Viscountess Thurles,[3] 823, fos 193–194.

Letter of request, asking Henry Cromwell to confirm the legal opinion she had had from others that she did not fall within the act of attainder; pointing out that she was English and that, because of her age, she had little time left to enjoy what she still possessed.

524. From Elizabeth Cromwell, 28 September, 823, fos 326–327.

My dearst,

Just now Mrs Harison came hom, how gives me lettell hopes of seing you ntill[4] the latter end of the weeke, wich inded I ded a lettell fere my slefe that it would be so long by your riting, but I desire to be contented and submet to the will of God in all things, knowing it is that work Hee has called you to and rejoyce to here you injoy your helth wich is a great mercy. My deare, the messenger is in such hast to be gon that I have not time to say that as I would, but the substanc of all that I am able to say is that you shall ever find me a loveing, constant wife.

My deare, beleve thes that coms from thy affictiton wife,

E Cromwell

Betty is well.

[2] Minister in Ireland, he was salaried minister at Tirawley, County Mayo, in 1656.

[3] The daughter of a Gloucestershire landowner, she was the widow of Thomas Butler, Viscount Thurles, son of the eleventh Earl of Ormond, and then of George Matthews, both of whom had died before the Irish rebellion and the civil wars. As an Irish-based Catholic with a questionable record of allegiance during the 1640s, she had lost her 4,000-acre estate at Thurles, County Tipperary, in the early 1650s and was in real danger of enforced transplantation to Connaught (Dunlop, pp. 606–607; *CSPI*, p. 475); although not made explicit in this letter, the fear of transplantation seems to have been her main concern. She did not die until 1673, aged 85. This letter is addressed to Henry Cromwell as lord lieutenant and so dates from the period November 1658 to spring 1659.

[4] Word amended – apparently originally written 'while' – and poorly formed.

525. From Bridget Fleetwood, 823, fos 341–342.[5]

Deare brother,

I am very unfitt and unaept to wright and yeet I woeld not alltegether nedleckt to ster up that afeckshoen which ought to be beetwexd soe ner relachoens and is very aept to dekae. I blaem non but mysellf. I desiar raether soe to doe than toe lae it upon oethers oor bee a judger of oethers. I coelld wish thaer haed not bin soe muech occation of the contraere wherin my corruept haert haeth taeken advaentaeg. I desiaer to be huembelld for it and not toe gove wae what ever oethers unkiendnessis mae be to weeken that love and afecksheon which oeght to be and is the desiaer of my soul toe fiend and nourish in me touerds yoursellf, though it mae be not muech kaerd foer. Yeet houe ever I shall laeboer to be fouend in my duety, which is to bee,

Your dear and very afecksheonit sister and saervaent,

B Fleetwood

526. From Charles Fleetwood, London, 5 August, 823, fos 349–350.

Letter of recommendation on behalf of the bearer, Mr Hutchinson,[6] *a godly and gracious minister and chaplain; asks that he be settled at Nenagh*[7] *with a salary of at least £150 per year.*

527. From Nicholas Lockyer, 5 March, 823, fos 361–362.[8]

Letter of courtesy, thanking Henry Cromwell for his letter and sending him religious exhortation in return, noting that he had few friends and many enemies in doing God's work, and reporting that he hoped to visit Henry Cromwell and his wife in Ireland; also of request, seeking Henry Cromwell's help in securing him land in Ireland where it was first allotted him rather than the poor ground he had been allocated by reallotment.[9]

[5] This letter is addressed to Henry Cromwell as lord deputy, so it must date from the period November 1657 to November 1658.

[6] Two salaried ministers with this surname served in Ireland in the 1650s: Alexander Hutchinson as Presbyterian minister at Tonachnimon, County Donegal; and – perhaps more likely – Edward Hutchinson, who in the early 1650s was chaplain with Abbott's regiment in Ireland.

[7] In County Tipperary.

[8] This letter is addressed to Henry Cromwell as 'Lord Henry Cromwell', so it may date from after his appointment to the new, nominated parliamentary chamber in the autumn of 1657; however, letters sent to him in Ireland were frequently addressed to 'Lord Henry Cromwell' from 1655 onwards, so this form of address may not, in fact, help narrow down the date.

[9] He was allocated land in County Limerick.

528. From Henry O'Brien, Earl of Thomond,[10] 823, fos 191–192.[11]

Letter of courtesy, recording his debt of obligation to Henry Cromwell, and noting that he had just attended Lady Waller's[12] *funeral.*

529. From Hugh Peters, Whitehall, 24 August, 823, fos 364–365.

My lord,

These are to returne you my harty acknowledgments of your care of young Mr Weld[13] and men of his constitution. I hope your lordshipp shall have no cause to repent you of any requests made by mee and answerd by you, for truly therin I shall bee tender, because I tender you as myne owne hart and doe after[14] please myselfe with my thoughts about you and the presence of the Lord with you in your worke. How well doe matters goe on when wee measure them by the other world where eternity dwells and where our works must bee weighd own[15] agayne. The blood of Christ mingled with them will give them their true alloy. Oh (my lord) labor after that meate which will never perish, that joy where no mixtures have accesse. You have knowne in your few dayes much vanity written upon most creatures, and you may see an end of all perfections, but the law is exceeding broad. Go on and prosper in the name and power of the Lord. You hear by others how it is here. I am very much taken of by age and other wayes from busy busines and would fayne see Jesus. None can more love you, I thinke, then your lordshipp's,

HP

Pray salue my lady, to them ever all with you.
Zack 8, 16, 17 et 19[16]

[10] In the autumn of 1657, he succeeded his father, who had come out in support of parliament in the mid-1640s and lived in London thereafter.

[11] The letter is addressed to Henry Cromwell as lord deputy and is endorsed '58', so it probably dates from the period January or March to October 1658.

[12] Probably the wife of Sir Hardress Waller, although, as her death is not recorded, this does not help to narrow down the date of this letter.

[13] Possibly Edmund Wells, though the identification is uncertain.

[14] Poorly formed word, which could alternatively be read as 'often'.

[15] Apparently a slip for 'over'.

[16] Biblical verses from Zechariah, stressing the need to be truthful to one another, to administer good justice, to love truth and peace, and to avoid doing evil or perjuring one another.

530. Draft of a letter [from William Petty to Charles Fleetwood, probably spring or summer 1656],[17] 823, fos 373–374.

My lord,

I had rather venture to trouble your lordship sometimes by an impertinent line then <to neglect after> <sometimes> not now and then to make <sometimes> some tender of my duty in what I am capable. <And although my presence in England could little emprove the advice your lordship hath concerning your health, yett it would bee a great satisfaction to mee but to see the best.> And now I wish that I could say anything to your lordship concerning your health which might bee of advantage unto it, but since I can not doe that in particular I shall onely humbly mind your lordship in generall to consider whether the change of aire doth not contribute to the encrease and frequency of your <lordship's> distempers. In as much as by enquirys I <heretofore> have formerly found that your lordship was more healthfull in Ireland then befor, and <I also> likewise to my greife I understand that your indisposition are greater now also in England then they were in Ireland.

Not to trouble your lordship with any accompt of the surveys (as they are my owne concernes) hath ever beene my care since your lordship's first trouble to passes the contract concerning them, although the great streights I have beene in have often urged mee to fly to my <best [...]>[18] greatest helps. Neverthelesse as they concerne the publiq (the care wherefore is committed to your lordship), I <take> humbly take leave to acquaint you<r lordship> that all the surveyes for the standing armie's satisfaction are not onely ready for their use but almost all of them drawne faire. And of all the rest of the whole undertaking, there is nothing undone (except a few church lands in Londonderry and what hath beene voluntarily neglected as <superfluous> unnecessary). And herein I much rejoice and blesse the Lord, as for other reasons, so for that your lordship's good opinion of mee as to this <service> undertaking will in some measure bee vindicated. And although the envy of many doth make mee say with David, how are my foes encreased and those that trouble mee without a

[17] This lightly corrected draft is unsigned and bears no address, though the endorsement describes it as 'to lord deputy concerning the survey'. The contents suggest that it concerns the survey of Irish lands that Petty contracted to undertake in December 1654, with the surveying itself to take place between February 1655 and March 1656. The work overran slightly, but was largely complete in the spring or early summer of 1656, thus providing an approximate date for this letter; if correct, that in turn indicates that the intended recipient was Fleetwood, since he was lord deputy at that time. The comment that the recipient was now living in England after a period in Ireland is consistent with this identification.

[18] Second deleted word not now legible.

cause <and>. Moreover, <al>though I doe expect but bare measure from some as to my reward, yet the <blessing> mercy which the Lord hath vouchsafd mee in this successe doth support mee against any the hard usages which I may find from the hands of men. My enemies have not <beene> yet beene able to convict mee of any miscarriage in this whole worke, although <many> complaints of all kinds have beene daily exhibited to that purpose. Your lordship might now expect an accompt whether the lands will hold out to a full satisfaction, but this can not bee <done> given untill <some other things> the debt and the accompt of the two last disbandings bee stated by the commissioners for accompts and the surveyor generall, which as I conceive will not bee done this month. I should not trouble your lordship with these matters had I any other occasion whereby to expresse myselfe,

Your.

531. From Edmund Temple, London, 1 January, 823, fos 366–367.

Letter of thanks to Henry Cromwell for giving him command of a troop in his regiment, even though he had failed to get a letter of recommendation for military promotion from the Protector and, despite Fleetwood's courtesy, had met with delays and obstructions in London; asks Henry Cromwell to inform the Protector and Fleetwood of his promotion; hopes soon to get permission to leave London and return to Ireland to serve Henry Cromwell there.

532. From John Ufflett, 6 June, 823, fos 368–369.

Letter of courtesy, presenting his duty to Henry Cromwell and offering his services running errands to Chippenham or elsewhere; and of request, seeking Henry Cromwell's help in securing arrears due to him from his work on the committee of accounts, thereby helping a withered and decayed family.

OTHER MISCELLANEOUS ITEMS

533. Draft of a loyal address from the officers in Ireland to Lord Protector Oliver Cromwell, [spring or summer 1657?],[1] 823, fos 375–376.

Address of loyalty to, and warm affection for, Oliver Cromwell as Lord Protector, who was empowered by the Lord and was working with the Lord to safeguard the state; expresses support for the existing constitutional arrangement of government resting with a single person and a parliament, together with other provisions ensuring liberty of conscience, guarding against a perpetual parliament, and so forth, though notes that if specific amendments were necessary the army would not interfere; pledges continuing support for the Protector and invites him, in turn, to depend upon the army.

534. A loyal address from George Monck's regiment to Lord Protector Oliver Cromwell, [spring 1658],[2] 823, fo. 363.

Address of loyalty to, and warm affection for, Oliver Cromwell as Lord Protector and his government.

535. A loyal address from the officers in Ireland to Lord Protector Oliver Cromwell, [spring 1658], 823, fos 377–380.

Address of loyalty to, and warm affection for, Oliver Cromwell as Lord Protector and his government.[3]

[1] The address alludes to parliament's recent or current activities reviewing and revising the constitution and, although there is no specific and explicit reference in the text to the offer of the crown or to the Protector's possible or actual response to that offer, this document is probably best seen as one of several petitions and addresses circulating in army circles in the spring or early summer of 1657, at the time that the second Protectorate parliament was revising the instrument of government and replacing it with the humble petition and advice, initially containing the offer of the crown.

[2] One of a stream of regimental addresses assuring the Protector of continuing loyalty in the wake both of the divisive second session of the second Protectorate parliament and its abrupt dissolution and of the outburst of military unrest that followed, focussed on Packer and a small group of officers.

[3] The address was drawn up in Ireland in March and early April 1658 and then carried to London during April by a small group of officers (*TSP*, VII, pp. 21, 49, 71–73, 114–115, 142). A version of it was published in the newspapers in mid-June.

536. Draft of a code to be used in correspondence between Henry Cromwell and Lord Broghill,[4] 823, fos 339–340.

Key for a code, parts of which have been deleted and replaced by a slightly revised scheme.[5]

[4] The draft is apparently in Henry Cromwell's hand and is endorsed 'for my lord Broghill'.

[5] The code itself is broadly similar to, but slightly more complex than, codes employed in some of the letters in this collection. It is mainly a numbered code, with the numerals 1–12 usually (but not always) standing for vowels and frequently used consonants; 31–45 for prominent individuals (the Protector, Richard Cromwell, Henry Cromwell, Fleetwood, Desborough, Lambert, Broghill, Thurloe, and others); 52–55 as well as selected upper case letters of the alphabet for common prepositions and conjunctions; and 46–51 and 56–64 for a mixture of institutions (parliament, the other house, the council, the church, the army, etc.), religious groups (ministers, Presbyterians, Independents, Anabaptists, and Fifth Monarchists), and countries (England, Scotland, and Ireland).

INDEX

This is a cumulative index, covering people, places, topics, and events. All entries refer to page numbers, not letter/item numbers. Numbers in **bold** indicate authors and (on those few occasions when Henry Cromwell was not the intended recipient) addressees of the letters. Numbers in *italics* point to footnotes giving significant (generally biographical) information.

Peers are indexed under their title, not their family name. Women are indexed under the surname they held at their first appearance in this collection. Thus Oliver Cromwell's daughters Bridget and Elizabeth are consistently shown as 'Fleetwood, Bridget, née Cromwell' and 'Claypole, Elizabeth, née Cromwell' respectively, as they were married from the outset. However, Oliver Cromwell's other two daughters, Frances and Mary, are consistently indexed under 'Cromwell', as they were both single in 1655–1656 when first mentioned here, even though in 1657, midway through this correspondence, both married and so took new surnames.

People with identical or very similar surnames, but mentioned in different letters and with insufficient supporting information to be sure they are the same person, have been indexed separately. Thus, for example, the Mr Alden mentioned on page 483 may be one and the same as the Mr Allden mentioned on page 350, but, with little further available information about their identity/identities, this remains unproven, and so they have been indexed separately here.